"Crawford has done a tremendous service to the scholarly community and the public alike by sifting through an extremely rich and complex body of literature and presenting her analysis lucidly and succinctly. In this sense, the book serves as an up-to-date and accessible introduction to the field. Simultaneously, however, it is also a work of immense scholarship, representing the culmination of years of study by one of the field's seasoned academics, and thus the book will surely and deservedly occupy a prominent place in future discussions and debates. . . . Through this book, Crawford has cemented her place as an authoritative voice in the Qumran debate."

—*Journal of the American Oriental Society*

"This book is the mature synthesis of the debates of the last generation that the field of Qumran studies has been waiting for. Sidnie White Crawford has eruditely assembled a very wide range of evidence from the caves, the Qumran site, and the manuscript finds, together with relevant comparative materials. She weighs that evidence judiciously, challenging, correcting, or endorsing a wide range of opinion. Overall, she courageously argues in a nuanced manner that the manuscript deposits in the eleven Qumran caves represent a single literary collection and that Qumran itself was established as a scribal center and library for the Essenes. The book will become a standard resource and reference point for the next generation."

—**George J. Brooke**, University of Manchester

"This volume, by a leading Dead Sea Scrolls scholar, looks at the Dead Sea Scrolls and the site of Qumran from the perspective of the study of ancient books and libraries, an approach that results in important new proposals regarding the function of the site, the various caves, and the history of the collection. This novel approach will make this a must-read for anyone interested in the scrolls and their importance for the history of Judaism and the background of Christianity."

—**Lawrence H. Schiffman**, New York University

"It is a pleasure to offer strong praise for Sidnie White Crawford's *Scribes and Scrolls at Qumran*. In it she offers a compelling case that Qumran and the nearby caves served as the scribal center and central library for the Essene 'wing' of Judaism. She supports her thesis with thorough, up-to-date studies of scribes and libraries, the scrolls, their owners, and the archaeological evidence. The result is a comprehensive and appealing theory advanced by a scholar of unquestioned expertise in the field."

—**James C. Vand**

"This is an insightful, well-researched, contextual study that reaches broadly to archaeology and the salient evidence to understand the nature of the Dead Sea Scrolls and the reasons why they were placed in caves around Qumran. Crawford presents a much-needed holistic and synthetic view. This accessible and lively study is expertly crafted, judicious, and well-argued and will be essential reading for anyone studying the scrolls."

—**Joan Taylor**, King's College London

"Crawford proposes that Qumran functioned as an Essene library and scribal center, based on a comprehensive and balanced analysis of the Dead Sea Scrolls and the archaeological remains. Her highly readable and up-to-date overview will serve as a basic resource for scholars as well as an excellent introduction to the field for nonspecialists."

—**Jodi Magness**, University of North Carolina at Chapel Hill

"Drawing on many decades of intense research, Sidnie White Crawford, a leading international expert on the Dead Sea Scrolls, has produced an impressively wide-ranging study on the state of play of research on the library and scribal profile of the texts and people reflected in the Dead Sea Scrolls, as well as offering her own comprehensive assessment of Qumran as home to the central library of the Essenes. This authoritative and admirably lucid and accessible volume makes an invaluable contribution to scholarship but will also serve excellently as a textbook for advanced students of the scrolls and is set to become a standard resource in the field."

—**Charlotte Hempel**, University of Birmingham

"More than seventy years after the discovery of Cave 1, Sidnie White Crawford has offered a new synthesis of the archaeological and textual finds from Qumran. She writes as one who knows intimately both the archaeology of Qumran and the manuscripts from the caves. By placing the Qumran collection in the wider context of scribes and libraries of the ancient world, this study sheds important new light on the finds. Crawford masterfully details the richness of the library, from its content to the physical features of the manuscripts. At times her investigation reads like a mystery novel that the reader will find hard to put down. Piece by piece, Crawford assembles a compelling case for understanding the settlement at Qumran as a scribal center of the Essenes and the collection of texts as their central library. All future scholarly reconstructions of the Qumran sect will have to reckon with this study. This volume is a must-read for students and scholars of early Judaism alike."

—**Cecilia Wassén**, Uppsala University

Scribes and Scrolls at Qumran

Sidnie White Crawford

WILLIAM B. EERDMANS PUBLISHING COMPANY
GRAND RAPIDS, MICHIGAN

Wm. B. Eerdmans Publishing Co.
2006 44th Street SE, Grand Rapids, MI 49508
www.eerdmans.com

© 2019 Sidnie White Crawford
All rights reserved

Hardcover edition 2019
Paperback edition 2025

Printed in the United States of America

31 30 29 28 27 26 25   1 2 3 4 5 6 7

ISBN 978-0-8028-8491-6

Library of Congress Cataloging-in-Publication Data

Names: Crawford, Sidnie White, author.
Title: Scribes and scrolls at Qumran / Sidnie White Crawford.
Description: Grand Rapids, Michigan : William B. Eerdmans Publishing Company,
    2019. | Includes bibliographical references and index.
Identifiers: LCCN 2018060808 | ISBN 9780802884916 (pbk. : alk. paper)
Subjects: LCSH: Qumran community. | Essenes. | Scribes, Jewish. | Qumran Site
    (West Bank) | Dead Sea scrolls—History.
Classification: LCC BM175.Q6 C655 2019 | DDC 296.8/15—dc23
    LC record available at https://lccn.loc.gov/2018060808

Unless otherwise indicated, all translated passages are from the following sources:
    Bible: The New Revised Standard Version
    Dead Sea Scrolls: *The Dead Sea Scrolls Reader*, 2 vols. Second Edition, Revised and
        Expanded, ed. by Donald W. Parry and Emanuel Tov (Leiden: Brill, 2014).

In Memoriam

Frank Moore Cross
(1921–2012)

John Strugnell
(1930–2007)

Contents

List of Figures	ix
Acknowledgments	xi
List of Abbreviations	xv
1. Introduction	1

PART I. SCRIBES AND LIBRARIES IN THE ANCIENT NEAR EASTERN AND MEDITERRANEAN WORLDS

2. Scribes and Libraries in the Ancient Near Eastern and Mediterranean Worlds	21
3. Scribes and Libraries in Ancient Israel	49

PART II. THE QUMRAN EVIDENCE

4. Caves and Scrolls: The Archaeology of the Caves and the Texts Found in Them	115
5. The Archaeology of Qumran	166
6. The Qumran Scrolls Collection: A Scribal Library with a Sectarian Component	217

CONTENTS

Part III. Conclusions

7. Who Owned the Scrolls?
The Qumran-Essene Hypothesis Revisited — 269

8. Scribes and Scrolls at Qumran: A New Synthesis — 309

Bibliography — 321

Index of Authors — 367

Index of Subjects — 373

Index of Scripture and Other Ancient Texts — 387

viii

Figures

(Following page 216)

Fig. 1 Cave 1
© Courtesy of Manchester Museum, The University of Manchester.

Fig. 2 Scroll jars
Qumranarchive Alexander Schick. © www.bibelausstellung.de. Used with permission.

Fig. 3 Wadi Qumran
© Dr. Avishai Teicher (Wikimedia Commons, CCA 2.5).

Fig. 4 Cave locations
Qumranarchive Alexander Schick. © www.bibelausstellung.de. Used with permission.

Fig. 5 Cave 4 interior
Qumranarchive Alexander Schick. © www.bibelausstellung.de. Used with permission.

Fig. 6 Qumran site plan
© École biblique. Used with permission.

Fig. 7 Aerial image
© Courtesy of Manchester Museum, The University of Manchester.

Fig. 8 Plan IB
© École biblique. Used with permission.

ix

FIGURES

Fig. 9 Plan II
© École biblique. Used with permission.

Fig. 10 Loci 2–4
Qumranarchive Alexander Schick. © www.bibelausstellung.de. Used with permission.

Fig. 11 Locus 4
Qumranarchive Alexander Schick. © www.bibelausstellung.de. Used with permission.

Fig. 12 Locus 30
Qumranarchive Alexander Schick. © www.bibelausstellung.de. Used with permission.

Fig. 13 Plastered tables
Qumranarchive Alexander Schick. © www.bibelausstellung.de. Used with permission.

Fig. 14 Inkwells
© Courtesy of Manchester Museum, The University of Manchester.

Acknowledgments

This volume has been many years in the making, and thus I have many institutions and people to thank. It is my pleasure to do so here. My editors at Wm. B. Eerdmans, Michael Thomson and Andrew Knapp, waited long past the original deadline for the manuscript. I thank them for their patience and their expert editing.

The University of Nebraska–Lincoln supported my research with both grants and in-kind support, in particular the Classics and Religious Studies Department, the Harris Center for Judaic Studies, and the Research Council. I spent a most pleasant semester at the Oxford Centre for Hebrew and Jewish Studies taking advantage of the superb research collection of the Bodleian Library. During the final stages of writing, the Institute for Research in the Humanities at the University of Wisconsin–Madison provided me with every scholar's dream: a private office, an excellent library, and time to write with no distractions. I am deeply grateful to all of these institutions.

Many of the ideas in this book were first presented at various scholarly venues. The members of the Biblical Colloquium and the Colloquium for Biblical Research heard several chapters and always made pertinent critiques and suggestions for improvement. My membership in these organizations, besides being a pleasure, has deepened my scholarship in many ways, and I am appreciative to all the members. I also presented papers at the Society of Biblical Literature, the International Society of Biblical Literature, and the American Schools of Oriental Research Annual Meetings, where I received constructive feedback. In addition, I was invited to lecture on this topic at the Anglo-Israel Archaeological Society, Brigham Young University, Edinburgh University, King's College London, the Oriental Institute of Oxford University, the University of Birmingham, the University of California at Davis, the University of Helsinki, and the

ACKNOWLEDGMENTS

University of Manchester. I thank all of these institutions for their gracious hospitality.

Many colleagues contributed in large ways to the research on this volume, patiently answering questions, reading drafts, and serving as sounding boards for my ideas. I would like in particular to thank Jodi Magness, Dennis Mizzi, and Joan Taylor for help with all archaeological questions. I also owe thanks to Walter Aufrecht, Andrea Berlin, Marc Brettler, Marcello Fidanzio, Vanessa Gorman, Charlotte Hempel, Jutta Jokiranta, Timothy Lim, Sarianna Metso, Steven Ortiz, Patricia Patton, Marjorie (Beth) Plummer, Christopher Rollston, Seth Sanders, Alexander Schick, Mark S. Smith, Ryan Stokes, Eibert Tigchelaar, David Vanderhooft, Robert Wilson, and Benjamin G. Wright III. George Brooke, Devorah Dimant, Lawrence Schiffman, Emanuel Tov, and Eugene Ulrich have been my conversation partners for all things Qumran since we were fellows at the Annenberg Institute for Jewish Studies in 1992–1993. I am indebted to all of these scholars; any errors, of course, remain my own.

Cecilia Wassén read drafts of several chapters and commented extensively on them. I owe her particular thanks for help with New Testament matters. My "dear readers," Dan D. Crawford and John Spencer, read every word of each chapter, and their comments improved every single chapter. Dan Crawford was always available as a conversation partner and sharpened my thinking as only a philosopher can do, and in the last stretch of preparation made room in our home life so that I was able to complete the manuscript. Lucas Schulte served as my able research assistant, preparing the bibliography and indices and copyediting the manuscript.

I would like to thank E. J. Brill for allowing me to utilize substantial sections of the following articles:

"The Inscriptional Evidence from Qumran and Its Relationship to the Cave 4Q Documents." In *The Caves of Qumran: Proceedings of the International Conference, Lugano 2014*, edited by Marcello Fidanzio, 213–20. STDJ 118. Leiden: Brill, 2017.
"Qumran Cave 4: Its Archaeology and Its Manuscript Collection." In *Is There a Text in This Cave? Studies in the Textuality of the Dead Sea Scrolls in Honour of George J. Brooke*, edited by Ariel Feldman, Maria Cioata, and Charlotte Hempel, 105–22. STDJ 119. Leiden: Brill, 2017.
"The Qumran Collection as a Scribal Library." In *The Dead Sea Scrolls and the Concept of a Library*, edited by Sidnie White Crawford and Cecilia Wassén, 109–31. STDJ 116. Leiden: Brill, 2016.

xii

Acknowledgments

This book is dedicated to the memory of my *Doktorvater* Frank Moore Cross and my teacher John Strugnell, who first engaged me in their research on the Dead Sea Scrolls and taught me how to read manuscript fragments. It is to them that I owe my largest debt of gratitude, a debt that cannot be repaid. They may not have agreed with all the conclusions I reach in this volume, but I hope they would have been proud to have been my teachers.

SIDNIE WHITE CRAWFORD
Lincoln, Nebraska

Abbreviations

AASOR	Annual of the American Schools of Oriental Research
AB	Anchor Bible
ABD	*Anchor Bible Dictionary*. Edited by D. N. Freedman. 6 vols. New York: Doubleday, 1992
ABS	Archaeology and Biblical Studies
AGJU	Arbeiten zur Geschichte des antiken Judentums und des Urchristentums
AnOr	Analecta Orientalia
ANYAS	Annual of the New York Academy of Sciences
AOAT	Alter Orient und Altes Testament
BA	*Biblical Archaeologist*
BAIAS	*Bulletin of Anglo-Israel Archeological Society*
BAR	*Biblical Archaeology Review*
BARIS	BAR (British Archaeological Reports) International Series
BASOR	*Bulletin of the American Schools of Oriental Research*
BETL	Bibliotheca Ephemeridum Theologicarum Lovaniensium
BibSem	Biblical Seminar
BJSUCSD	Biblical and Judaic Studies from the University of California, San Diego
BZNW	Beihefte zur Zeitschrift für die neutestamentliche Wissenschaft
CANE	*Civilizations of the Ancient Near East*. Edited by Jack M. Sasson. 4 vols. New York: Scribner, 1995
CBET	Contributions to Biblical Exegesis and Theology
CBQMS	Catholic Biblical Quarterly Monograph Series
CHANE	Culture and History of the Ancient Near East
DJD	Discoveries in the Judaean Desert
DMOA	Documenta et Monumenta Orientis Antiqui
DSD	*Dead Sea Discoveries*

ABBREVIATIONS

DSSR	*Dead Sea Scrolls Reader.* Edited by Donald W. Parry and Emanuel Tov. 2nd ed. 2 vols. Leiden: Brill, 2014
EA	Tell el-Amarna tablets
EDEJ	*Eerdmans Dictionary of Early Judaism.* Edited by John J. Collins and Daniel C. Harlow. Grand Rapids: Eerdmans, 2010
EDSS	*Encyclopedia of the Dead Sea Scrolls.* Edited by Lawrence H. Schiffman and James C. VanderKam. 2 vols. New York: Oxford University Press, 2000
EJL	Early Judaism and Its Literature
EncJud	*Encyclopedia Judaica.* Edited by Fred Skolnik and Michael Berenbaum. 2nd ed. 22 vols. Detroit: Macmillan Reference USA, 2007
ErIsr	*Eretz-Israel*
ExpTim	*Expository Times*
FAT	Forschungen zum Alten Testament
HSS	Harvard Semitic Studies
HTR	*Harvard Theological Review*
IEJ	*Israel Exploration Journal*
ISACR	Interdisciplinary Studies in Ancient Culture and Religion
JAJ	*Journal of Ancient Judaism*
JANESCU	*Journal of the Ancient Near Eastern Society of Columbia University*
JAOS	*Journal of the American Oriental Society*
JBL	*Journal of Biblical Literature*
JEA	*Journal of Egyptian Archaeology*
JJS	*Journal of Jewish Studies*
JNES	*Journal of Near Eastern Studies*
JQR	*Jewish Quarterly Review*
JRA	*Journal of Roman Archaeology*
JRASup	Journal of Roman Archaeology Supplement
JSJ	*Journal for the Study of Judaism*
JSJSup	Journal for the Study of Judaism Supplement
JSNTSup	Journal for the Study of the New Testament Supplement
JSOTSup	Journal for the Study of the Old Testament Supplement
LCL	Loeb Classical Library
LHBOTS	Library of Hebrew Bible/Old Testament Studies
LSTS	Library of Second Temple Studies
LXX	Septuagint
MT	Masoretic Text

Abbreviations

NCBC	New Century Bible Commentary
NEA	*Near Eastern Archaeology*
NETS	*A New English Translation of the Septuagint.* Edited by Albert Pietersma and Benjamin G. Wright. New York: Oxford University Press, 2007
NRSV	New Revised Standard Version
NTOA.SA	Novum Testamentum et Orbis Antiquus, Series Archaeologica
OBO	Orbis Biblicus et Orientalis
OHDSS	*Oxford Handbook of the Dead Sea Scrolls.* Edited by Timothy H. Lim and John J. Collins. Oxford: Oxford University Press, 2010
OLA	Orientalia Lovaniensia Analecta
OTL	Old Testament Library
OTP	*Old Testament Pseudepigrapha.* Edited by James H. Charlesworth. 2 vols. New York: Doubleday, 1983, 1985
PEQ	*Palestine Exploration Quarterly*
PTSDSSP	Princeton Theological Seminary Dead Sea Scrolls Project
RB	*Revue biblique*
ResOr	Res Orientales
RevQ	*Revue de Qumran*
RS	Ras Shamra
SAOC	Studies in Ancient Oriental Civilizations
SBLEJL	Society of Biblical Literature Early Judaism and Its Literature
SBT	Studies in Biblical Theology
SCS	Septuagint and Cognate Studies
SFSHJ	South Florida Studies in the History of Judaism
SJLA	Studies in Judaism in Late Antiquity
STDJ	Studies on the Texts of the Desert of Judah
SVTP	Studia in Veteris Testamenti Pseudepigraphica
SWBA	Social World of Biblical Antiquity
SymS	Symposium Series
TAD	*Textbook of Aramaic Documents from Ancient Egypt,* by Bezalel Porten and Ada Yardeni. 4 vols. Winona Lake, IN: Eisenbrauns, 1986–1993
TSAJ	Texte und Studien zum antiken Judentum
TUGAL	Texte und Untersuchungen zur Geschichte der altchristlichen Literatur
UF	*Ugarit-Forschungen*
VT	*Vetus Testamentum*

ABBREVIATIONS

VTSup   Supplements to Vetus Testamentum
WBC   Word Biblical Commentary
WDSP   Wadi Daliyeh Samaria Papyri
WUNT   Wissenschaftliche Untersuchungen zum Neuen Testament

CHAPTER 1

Introduction

Two bedouin, a goat, and a rock. Thus begins the saga of the Dead Sea Scrolls, one of the most important archaeological discoveries in the eastern Mediterranean world in the twentieth century.[1] Since their discovery in the winter of 1946/47, the Dead Sea Scrolls, especially the subset of the scrolls found in the eleven caves in the vicinity of Khirbet Qumran, have been the subject of enormous scholarly erudition and have revolutionized the study of the Hebrew Bible, ancient Judaism, and early Christianity. The discovery of the Dead Sea Scrolls has had wide ramifications in the fields of textual criticism, the history of the biblical text, the history and literature of Second Temple Judaism, and the development and thought of the early Christian community. However, the central mystery of the Qumran scrolls—how they were deposited in the caves and the nature of the relationship between the scroll caves and the settlement at Khirbet Qumran—has never been satisfactorily resolved. My purpose in this volume is to take the insights of the first generation of scrolls scholars that have withstood the test of time, combine them with new insights from scholars since the complete publication of the scrolls corpus and the much more complete archaeological picture that we now have of Khirbet Qumran, and create a new synthesis of text and archaeology that will yield a convincing history of and purpose for the Qumran settlement and its associated caves. My proposal is that Qumran served as the central library and scribal center for the Essene movement of Judaism, that it was established to serve that purpose in the first quarter of the first century BCE, and that it continued in that function without interruption until its destruction by a Roman legion during the First Jewish Revolt against Rome in 68 CE.[2]

1. For a complete account of the discovery of the Dead Sea Scrolls, see W. Fields, *The Dead Sea Scrolls: A Full History*, vol. 1: *1947–1960* (Leiden: Brill, 2009), 23–90.

2. The suggestion that Qumran served as the central library for the Essenes was first

1

INTRODUCTION

A word should be said about what I am *not* attempting to do in this volume. First, I am not trying to write the history of the Essene movement, beginning with its origins down to its disappearance. The Essene movement emerged in Judaism at least a generation before the settlement at Qumran was established, and therefore its origin falls outside the parameters of this volume. This is likewise the case for its disappearance. While the settlement at Qumran was destroyed by the Romans in 68 CE, there is no reason to suppose that the movement represented at Qumran died with the settlement. It could well have continued in the post-Qumran period, but that too lies outside the purview of this volume. Second, since my study is synchronic, being concerned only with the period during which Qumran was inhabited, rather than diachronic, I am not concerned with the sources, early stages, or literary development of the Qumran texts. There is no question that, like many of the works from what became the biblical literature (e.g., the Pentateuch, Isaiah, Jeremiah, Psalms), the sectarian and nonsectarian texts found at Qumran had sources and went through various redactional stages.[3] However, my focus is not on the prehistory of the Qumran texts, but on their presence in the Qumran library and in the Qumran caves. Questions of sources and redaction, therefore, are engaged only as they relate to those central questions. Finally, I do not attempt to trace the nuances of the Essene movement in all of its settlements in Judea. Thus I do not discuss the relationship(s) of the different communities represented by the major rule texts from Qumran (i.e., the manuscripts of the Serek Hayaḥad or Rule of the Community [S] and the Damascus Document [D]), or whether the rules found in S or D were followed in any settlement in Judea other than Qumran itself.[4] Rather, the

---

made, as far as I can ascertain, by D. C. Peck: "Qumran may have served as something of a central research library for Essenes throughout the country" ("The Qumran Library and Its Patrons," *Journal of Library History* 12 [1977]: 11).

3. I.e., the Serek Hayaḥad, the Damascus Document, and the Temple Scroll. See chs. 6 and 7.

4. Much excellent recent scholarship has been devoted to these questions, and the conclusions I have reached in this volume have been informed by all of them. See esp. J. Collins, *Beyond the Qumran Community: The Sectarian Movement of the Dead Sea Scrolls* (Grand Rapids: Eerdmans, 2010); J. Collins, *Scriptures and Sectarianism*, WUNT 332 (Tübingen: Mohr Siebeck, 2014); J. Collins, "Sectarian Communities in the Dead Sea Scrolls," *OHDSS* 151–72; T. Elgvin, "The *Yaḥad* Is More Than Qumran," in *Enoch and Qumran Origins: New Light on a Forgotten Connection*, ed. G. Boccaccini (Grand Rapids: Eerdmans, 2005), 273–79; C. Hempel, *The Qumran Rule Texts in Context: Collected Studies*, TSAJ 154 (Tübingen: Mohr Siebeck, 2013), and the literature cited there; S. Metso, "In Search of the *Sitz im Leben* of

Introduction

focus of this study is on Qumran, its library, and the activities taking place there during the Second Temple period.

The Classic Qumran-Essene Hypothesis

Early Qumran scholarship produced a narrative of the history of the Qumran sect that intertwined the contents of the sectarian texts—in particular the Serek Hayaḥad, the Damascus Document, the pesharim, and the Hodayot (Thanksgiving Hymns)—with the archaeology of the site of Qumran that held sway until the 1980s.[5] This narrative stated that Qumran was the main (if not the only) Essene settlement, founded about 150–135 BCE because of Essene opposition, led by their founder the Teacher of Righteousness, to the Hasmonean takeover of the Jerusalem high priesthood in the mid-second century BCE. Although attempts were made to identify the mysterious Teacher of Righteousness, who appears in the Damascus Document and some of the pesharim,[6] he remained elusive; however, the

---

the *Community Rule*," in *The Provo International Conference on the Dead Sea Scrolls: Technological Innovations, New Texts, and Reformulated Issues*, ed. D. Parry and E. Ulrich, STDJ 30 (Leiden: Brill, 1999), 306–15; S. Metso, "The Relationship between the Damascus Document and the Community Rule," in *The Damascus Document: A Centennial of Discovery*, ed. J. Baumgarten et al., STDJ 34 (Leiden: Brill, 2000), 85–93; and A. Schofield, *From Qumran to the Yaḥad: A New Paradigm of Textual Development for the Community Rule*, STDJ 77 (Leiden: Brill, 2009).

5. J. T. Milik, *Ten Years of Discovery in the Wilderness of Judaea*, trans. J. Strugnell, SBT 1/26 (Naperville, IL: Allenson, 1959); F. M. Cross, *The Ancient Library of Qumran*, 3rd ed., BibSem 30 (Sheffield: Sheffield Academic Press, 1995); G. Vermes, *The Dead Sea Scrolls: Qumran in Perspective* (London: Collins, 1977); and R. de Vaux, *Archaeology and the Dead Sea Scrolls: The Schweich Lectures of the British Academy 1959* (London: Oxford University Press, 1973). For a popular treatment of this narrative that was very influential, see E. Wilson, *The Scrolls from the Dead Sea* (New York: Oxford University Press, 1955). See also related articles in D. Dimant, ed., *The Dead Sea Scrolls in Scholarly Perspective: A History of Research*, STDJ 99 (Leiden: Brill, 2012); esp. S. W. Crawford, "The Identification and History of the Qumran Community in American Scholarship," 13–30; and D. Dimant, "Israeli Scholarship on the Qumran Community," 237–80.

6. H. Stegemann in particular argued that the Teacher of Righteousness served as the high priest during the intersacerdotal period (159–152 BCE) between Alcimus and Jonathan. See "The Qumran Essenes: Local Members of the Main Jewish Union in Late Second Temple Times," in *The Madrid Qumran Congress: Proceedings of the International Congress on the Dead Sea Scrolls Madrid 18–21 March 1991*, ed. J. Trebolle Barrera and L. Vegas Montaner, 2 vols., STDJ 11 (Leiden: Brill, 1992), 1:83–166.

INTRODUCTION

Wicked Priest was identified with Jonathan, the first Hasmonean high priest.[7] Because of the antagonism between the Teacher of Righteousness and the Wicked Priest, the Essenes left Jerusalem (or were driven out) and established Qumran as their desert retreat center and main (if not only) settlement. Except for a period of abandonment following a major earthquake in 31 BCE, the Essenes continued to reside at Qumran, following the rule of the Serek Hayaḥad, until Qumran was threatened with attack by the Romans during the Jewish Revolt against Rome (66–73 CE). The Essenes then deposited their library in the caves surrounding the site and fled, never to return. The site was burned by the Romans in 68.[8] This was the reigning hypothesis in Qumran scholarship until the 1980s when, under a barrage of new evidence and new hypotheses, it began to break down.

Critiques of the Qumran-Essene Hypothesis

As new studies of the Qumran scrolls took place, especially after the publication of the Cave 4Q corpus was completed in 2001,[9] the master narrative of the Qumran-Essene hypothesis began to be critiqued as presenting a too simplistic reading of both the contents of the scrolls and the archaeological evidence. In particular, it was noted that the sectarian texts had been read as if they were historical narratives, presenting a straightforward picture of the sect's origins, rather than texts replete with metaphor and symbolism, saturated with the language of the classical scriptural texts of Israel, which made them ideological constructions instead of literal historical accounts. For example, in the sentence "in a time of wrath three hundred and ninety years when He put them into the power of Nebuchadnezzar, king of Babylon he took care of them and caused to grow from Israel and from Aaron a root of planting to inherit His land" in the Admonition to the Damascus

---

7. Cross argued for the identification of Simon as the Wicked Priest, but this position did not gain support (*Ancient Library of Qumran*, 106–17).

8. For a recent defense of this narrative in its exact parameters, see É. Puech, "The Essenes and Qumran, the Teacher of Righteousness and the Wicked Priest, the Origins," in *Enoch and Qumran Origins*, ed. Boccaccini, 298–302.

9. E. Tov, "The *Discoveries in the Judaean Desert* Series: History and System of Presentation," in *The Texts from the Judaean Desert: Indices and an Introduction to the Discoveries in the Judaean Desert Series*, ed. E. Tov, DJD 39 (Oxford: Clarendon, 2002), 1–26. The exception was the 4QSamuel fragments, which were not published until 2005. See F. M. Cross et al., *Qumran Cave 4.XII: 1–2 Samuel*, DJD 17 (Oxford: Clarendon, 2005).

4

Introduction

Document (CD 1:5-8), the figure 390 years was taken literally, and a date of 175 BCE posited for the emergence of the sect.[10]

The archaeological evidence had been interpreted by Roland de Vaux, professor of archaeology at the École Biblique et Archéologique Française in Jerusalem and the chief excavator of Qumran, in light of the sectarian texts emerging from the caves. While it was methodologically appropriate to take the scrolls as one piece of the archaeological evidence of the site, the flaw came when de Vaux stretched the archaeological evidence to fit the emerging historical narrative.[11] For example, despite extremely meager evidence, de Vaux pushed the foundation of the settlement at Qumran (his Period IA) back into the last half of the second century BCE so that it fit into the supposed timetable of CD 1:5-8.

These methodological missteps have led in the last three decades to various reevaluations of both the textual and the archaeological evidence from Qumran. Jodi Magness's redating of the founding of the site of Qumran to the first quarter of the first century BCE has been decisive in this regard. If the site was founded not at the start of the Hasmonean dynasty but in its middle, during the reign of Alexander Jannaeus (103-76 BCE), then the chronology of the origins of the sect as coterminous with the building of the settlement needs to be drastically revised or abandoned. Further, newer interpretations of the archaeological evidence called into question de Vaux's understanding of Qumran as an Essene settlement.

Beginning with Henri del Medico and Karl Rengstorf in the late 1950s, and continuing in the 1990s with the work of Norman Golb, attempts were made to disassociate the scrolls from the site, leading to proposals that Qumran was a military fortress, some kind of rural estate, a pottery manufacturing center, or a seasonal industrial complex tied to Jericho.[12] That

---

10. An incisive critique of this approach was given by Maxine Grossman in *Reading for History in the Damascus Document: A Methodological Study*, STDJ 45 (Leiden: Brill, 2002). For a broader discussion of the pitfalls of reading for history in the scrolls, see J. Collins, "Reading for History in the Scrolls," in *Scriptures and Sectarianism*, 133-49.

11. J. Magness, *The Archaeology of Qumran and the Dead Sea Scrolls* (Grand Rapids: Eerdmans, 2002), 65.

12. H. del Medico, *The Riddle of the Scrolls*, trans. H. Garner (London: Burke, 1958); K. H. Rengstorf, *Hirbet Qumrân und die Bibliothek vom Toten Meer* (Stuttgart: Kohlhammer, 1960); N. Golb, *Who Wrote the Dead Sea Scrolls? The Search for the Secret of Qumran* (New York: Scribner, 1995); R. Donceel and P. Donceel-Voûte, "The Archaeology of Khirbet Qumran," in *Methods of Investigation of the Dead Sea Scrolls and the Khirbet Qumran Site: Present Realities and Future Prospects*, ed. M. Wise et al., ANYAS 722 (New York: New York Academy of Sciences, 1994), 1-38; Y. Hirschfeld, *Qumran in Context: Reassessing the*

5

INTRODUCTION

none of these proposals has won wide adherence points to their methodological weakness: the scrolls in the caves are an integral part of the archaeology of the site and must form a central piece of its interpretation.[13]

On the textual side, more sophisticated literary methodologies have been applied to the manuscripts, leading to convincing arguments for a more complex literary history for the Serek Hayaḥad, the Damascus Document, and the Temple Scroll (among others), including earlier sources within the received version(s) of the texts.[14] The full publication of the Cave 4Q corpus has led to the recognition of the varied nature of the Qumran collection; it is not limited to "biblical" or "sectarian" texts, but takes in a complete spectrum of Jewish literature from the Second Temple period.[15] Investigations of various pieces of the corpus have taken place, with the rule texts, the Aramaic texts, the liturgical texts, and the wisdom literature receiving particular attention.[16]

At the same time, a revolution was taking place in the recognition of the importance of the correct interpretation of the laws of the Torah in the self-identification of the sect. This revised understanding began in

---

Archaeological Evidence (Peabody, MA: Hendrickson, 2004); Y. Magen and Y. Peleg, "Back to Qumran: Ten Years of Excavation and Research, 1993–2004," in *Qumran, the Site of the Dead Sea Scrolls: Archaeological Interpretations and Debates,* ed. K. Galor et al., STDJ 57 (Leiden: Brill, 2006), 55–113; D. Stacey, "A Reassessment of the Stratigraphy of Qumran," in *Qumran Revisited: A Reassessment of the Archaeology of the Site and Its Texts,* ed. D. Stacey and G. Doudna, BARIS 2520 (London: Archeopress, 2013), 7–74.

13. As D. Mizzi states, "hypotheses that divorce the scrolls from the built settlement create more problems than they solve" ("Qumran at Seventy: Reflections on Seventy Years of Scholarship on the Archaeology of Qumran and the Dead Sea Scrolls," *Strata: Bulletin of the Anglo-Israel Archaeological Society* 35 [2017]: 25).

14. For early studies of these documents that posited sources and stages of composition, see S. Metso, *The Textual Development of the Qumran Community Rule,* STDJ 21 (Leiden: Brill, 1997); P. Davies, *The Damascus Covenant: An Interpretation of the "Damascus Document,"* JSOTSup 25 (Sheffield: JSOT Press, 1983); J. Murphy-O'Connor, "An Essene Missionary Document? CD II, 14–VI, 1," *RB* 77 (1970): 201–29; J. Murphy-O'Connor, "A Literary Analysis of Damascus Document VI, 2–VIII, 3," *RB* 78 (1971): 210–32; J. Murphy-O'Connor, "A Literary Analysis of Damascus Document XIX, 33–XX, 34," *RB* 79 (1972): 544–64; A. Wilson and L. Wills, "Literary Sources of the Temple Scroll," *HTR* 75 (1982): 275–88; and M. O. Wise, *A Critical Study of the Temple Scroll from Qumran Cave 11,* SAOC 49 (Chicago: University of Chicago Press, 1990).

15. The earliest study of the entire corpus was that of D. Dimant, "The Qumran Manuscripts: Contents and Significance," originally published in 1995, reprinted in *History, Ideology and Bible Interpretation in the Dead Sea Scrolls: Collected Studies,* FAT 90 (Tübingen: Mohr Siebeck, 2014), 27–56.

16. See the bibliographic references in ch. 6.

Introduction

the mid-1980s when the existence of 4QMiqṣat Maʿaśê ha-Torah (MMT) was first revealed publicly, and the fragmentary copies of the Damascus Document, as well as the smaller legal texts, began to be published.[17] It is now clear that what separated the sect from the rest of Judaism were primarily differences in legal practices, in particular the practice of purity regulations associated with food and drink, sexuality, and the temple cult.

All of these new studies and approaches are vital for our understanding of the Qumran library, the site of Qumran, and the people who lived there. However, the result has often been a fragmentation in the field; while the old synthesis had broken down, no new synthesis had emerged. That new synthesis, based on the latest archaeological data and the most recent textual scholarship, is what I wish to accomplish in these pages.

---

17. The bibliography is voluminous. For 4QMMT, see E. Qimron and J. Strugnell, "An Unpublished Halakhic Letter from Qumran," in *Biblical Archaeology Today: Proceedings of the International Congress on Biblical Archaeology, Jerusalem, April 1984*, ed. J. Amitai (Jerusalem: Israel Exploration Society, 1985), 400–407; E. Qimron and J. Strugnell, *Qumran Cave 4.V: Miqṣat Maʿaśe ha-Torah*, DJD 10 (Oxford: Clarendon, 1994); and J. Kampen and M. Bernstein, eds., *Reading 4QMMT: New Perspectives on Qumran Law and History*, SymS 2 (Atlanta: Scholars Press, 1996). For the Damascus Document, see J. M. Baumgarten, *Qumran Cave 4.XIII: The Damascus Document (4Q266–273)*, DJD 18 (Oxford: Clarendon, 1996); J. Charlesworth, ed., *The Dead Sea Scrolls: Hebrew, Aramaic, and Greek Texts with English Translations*, vol. 2: *Damascus Document, War Scroll, and Related Documents*, PTSDSSP (Tübingen: Mohr Siebeck; Louisville: Westminster John Knox, 1995); and J. Charlesworth, ed., *The Dead Sea Scrolls: Hebrew, Aramaic, and Greek Texts with English Translations*, vol. 3: *Damascus Document II, Some Works of the Torah, and Related Documents*, PTSDSSP (Tübingen: Mohr Siebeck; Louisville: Westminster John Knox, 2006). For the legal texts, see J. Baumgarten et al., *Qumran Cave 4.XXV: Halakhic Texts*, DJD 35 (Oxford: Clarendon, 1999); M. Bernstein et al., eds., *Legal Texts and Legal Issues: Proceedings of the Second Meeting of the International Organization for Qumran Studies Published in Honour of Joseph M. Baumgarten*, STDJ 23 (Leiden: Brill, 1997); the various studies of J. Baumgarten, some of which are collected in *Studies in Qumran Law*, SJLA 24 (Leiden: Brill, 1977); the many studies of L. H. Schiffman, some found conveniently in *The Halakah at Qumran* (Leiden: Brill, 1975) and *Qumran and Jerusalem: Studies in the Dead Sea Scrolls and the History of Judaism* (Grand Rapids: Eerdmans, 2010); and A. Shemesh, "Halakhah between the Dead Sea Scrolls and Rabbinic Literature," *OHDSS* 595–616. See most recently A. Amihay, *Theory and Practice in Essene Law* (New York: Oxford University Press, 2017).

INTRODUCTION

Definitions

A study of the complete corpus of the Qumran scrolls reveals it to be one collection that may be characterized as a library with both scribal and sectarian components. A "library," according to the *Oxford English Dictionary*, is "a place set apart to contain books for reading, study, or reference."[18] Thus its primary meaning is as an architectural element, that is, a building, a room, or a set of rooms to hold books. As we shall see, the "library" according to this definition did exist in the ancient Near East and Mediterranean world. The secondary meaning of "library," however, is the books contained in a library, and it is that secondary usage that I employ most frequently in this study. Of course, in the ancient world the "book," in the sense of a codex, did not exist, so ancient libraries contained tablets, papyrus rolls, or parchment rolls; at Qumran, the library consisted of papyrus and parchment rolls.[19] The differences between ancient libraries and ancient archives are important as well when considering the definition of the Qumran collection. A vast literature exists on the differences between archives and libraries in the ancient Near East. The essential difference is that an archive consists of business and political documents kept as records, while libraries contained literary and religious texts. However, a study of the various tablet and book collections from the ancient Near East and the Greco-Roman world demonstrates that, except for very large tablet or book roll collections, literary and documentary texts tended to be mixed together, so that very few collections were purely an archive or a library. In the case of the Qumran collection, the literary and religious texts dominate, making the designation "library" for the collection a valid one. [20]

18. *Oxford English Dictionary*, accessed on-line through Oxford University Press On-Line, February 23, 2018.

19. The lone exception is the Copper Scroll, which is inscribed on thin sheets of copper. However, I do not consider the Copper Scroll to be part of the Qumran library, but a separate deposit. See ch. 4.

20. See J. Black and W. J. Tait, "Archives and Libraries in the Ancient Near East," *CANE* 4:2197–2210; J. du Toit, *Textual Memory: Ancient Archives, Libraries and the Hebrew Bible* (Sheffield: Sheffield Phoenix, 2011); A. Lange, "The Qumran Dead Sea Scrolls—Library or Manuscript Corpus?," in *From 4QMMT to Resurrection: Mélanges qumraniens en hommage à Émile Puech*, ed. F. García Martínez et al., STDJ 61 (Leiden: Brill, 2006), 177–93; O. Pedersén, *Archives and Libraries in the Ancient Near East 1500–300 B.C.* (Bethesda, MD: CDL, 1998); and E. Posner, *Archives in the Ancient World* (Cambridge: Harvard University Press, 1972).

Introduction

By "scribal component" I am referring to the learned nature of the scrolls; scribes, in particular elite scholar-scribes,[21] were the literati of the ancient world. Trained in reading and writing, often in several languages and scripts, elite scholar-scribes were responsible for preserving and handing on their cultural traditions.[22] They did this not by merely copying earlier works, although this was an important activity, but also by expanding, updating, and interpreting them for their own times. They used earlier works, whether written or oral, as sources to create new compositions. They incorporated the knowledge of nearby cultures into their own cultural framework. In the context of Judea, scholar-scribes passed on the classical literature of ancient Israel (the biblical books) in multiple forms, as well as composing new works that became part of the literature of Second Temple Judaism. Jonathan Z. Smith defines the roles of scholar-scribes in the ancient world particularly well:

> The scribes were an elite group of learned, literate men, an intellectual aristocracy which played an invaluable role in the administration of their people in both religious and political affairs. They were dedicated to a variety of roles: guardians of their cultural heritage, intellectual innovators, world travelers ... lawyers, doctors, astrologers, diviners, magicians, scientists, court functionaries, linguists, exegetes, etc. Their greatest love was the story of themselves and they guarded and transmitted their teaching. ... They speculated about hidden heavenly tablets ... about the beginning and end and thereby claimed to possess the secrets of creation. Above all, they talked, they memorized and remembered, they wrote.[23]

---

21. The Talmud makes the distinction between a סופר ("scribe") and a חכם ("sage"), and that terminology is sometimes imported into modern scholarship on scribes in the ancient world. However, the term חכם does not appear in precisely that usage in texts earlier than the Talmud, but rather refers to one who is wise in a variety of pursuits. Therefore, I will avoid the term *sage*, preferring instead *scribe* or *scholar-scribe*.

22. Scribes had other functions in the ancient world, for example, as record keepers in government bureaucracies or as local functionaries writing up bills of sale, contracts, marriage documents, and the like. These lower-level scribes were not the "culture keepers" of their communities, but the "worker bees" of advanced agrarian societies. See most recently S. Adams, "The Social Location of the Scribe in the Second Temple Period," in *Sibyls, Scriptures, and Scrolls: John Collins at Seventy*, ed. J. Baden et al., 2 vols., JSJSup 175 (Leiden: Brill, 2017), 1:22–37.

23. J. Z. Smith, *Map Is Not Territory: Studies in the History of Religion* (Leiden: Brill, 1978), 70.

9

INTRODUCTION

The interests and activities of scholar-scribes are particularly apparent in the Qumran library, a quarter of which consists of the classical literature of ancient Israel (i.e., the "biblical" texts), which were their cultural heritage, along with new works that built on that cultural heritage, as well as esoteric texts concerning astronomy and astrology, calendar calculations, and other scholarly ephemera.

The phrase "sectarian component" incorporates the term *sect*, a common shorthand used to describe the particular wing of Judaism,[24] a part of which resided at Qumran, that I identify as the Essenes. The word *sect* is a sociological term that can be defined in several ways, some of them more strict than others.[25] The definition under which I will proceed is that a sect is a voluntary association within a larger social group (in this case Judaism) that exists in some degree of tension with the larger society,[26] establishes clear boundary markers between itself and outsiders, has rules of conduct for its members, and follows defined procedures for entrance into and expulsion from the sect.[27] The adjectival form *sectarian* applies both to the movement to which the Qumran settlement belonged and

24. I first heard the term *wing* used in this sense by Michael Stone. It is an apt term, since a "wing" in an architectural sense refers to a section of a building that is an identifiable feature but still part of the building, while a "wing" on a bird is an identifiable feature of the bird but still part of the whole. Likewise, a "wing" in Judaism has identifiable features that mark it as distinguishable within Judaism but is still part of the whole.

25. There is a growing literature on the permissibility of defining the Qumran group as a sect. See A. Baumgarten, *The Flourishing of Jewish Sects in the Maccabean Era: An Interpretation*, JSJSup 55 (Leiden: Brill, 1997); the essays in D. Chalcraft, ed., *Sectarianism in Early Judaism: Sociological Advances* (London: Equinox, 2007); P. Davies, *Sects and Scrolls: Essays on Qumran and Related Topics*, SFSHJ 134 (Atlanta: Scholars Press, 1996); J. Jokiranta, *Social Identity and Sectarianism in the Qumran Movement*, STDJ 105 (Leiden: Brill, 2013); J. Jokiranta, "Sociological Approaches to Qumran Sectarianism," *OHDSS* 200–231; C. Newsom, "'Sectually Explicit' Literature from Qumran," in *The Hebrew Bible and Its Interpreters*, ed. W. Propp et al. (Winona Lake, IN: Eisenbrauns, 1990), 167–87; C. Newsom, *The Self as Symbolic Space: Constructing Identity and Community at Qumran*, STDJ 52 (Atlanta: Society of Biblical Literature, 2004); and E. Regev, *Sectarianism in Qumran: A Cross-Cultural Perspective* (Berlin: de Gruyter, 2007).

26. I am adopting the term *tension* from C. Wassén and J. Jokiranta, "Groups in Tension: Sectarianism in the *Damascus Document* and the *Community Rule*," in Chalcraft, *Sectarianism in Early Judaism*, 205–45.

27. Note A. Baumgarten's definition of a sect as "a voluntary association of protest, which utilizes boundary marking mechanism—the social means of differentiating between insiders and outsiders—to distinguish between its own members and those otherwise normally regarded as belonging to the same national or religious entity" (*Flourishing of Jewish Sects*, 7).

10

Introduction

to the literature produced by that movement. This literature makes up approximately 25 percent of the Qumran corpus.

Throughout the volume I use four categories to divide the scroll collection found in the Qumran caves: the classical literature of ancient Israel; the nonsectarian works composed in the Hellenistic-Roman period; the affiliated texts; and the sectarian texts. The expression "classical literature of ancient Israel" refers to material that was composed by the early Hellenistic period (late fourth–early third centuries BCE).[28] From the perspective of the time period of the Qumran settlement (c. 100 BCE to 68 CE), this literature comprises the traditions handed down from the distant past, which carried a high status not only for the wing of Judaism represented in the scroll collection but for all Judaism. This category includes most of the later canon of Jewish Scripture (i.e., Torah, Prophets, and most of the Writings), but not, based on their dates of composition, Daniel or some of the psalms.

The second category, "nonsectarian texts composed in the Hellenistic-Roman period," comprises those Jewish literary texts that do not fall into any of the other three categories. Although this definition is rather vague, it is apt, since these texts are not classical, nor do they carry any sectarian or affiliated literary markers. As we shall see in ch. 6, a wide variety of literature is found in this category, which includes wisdom texts such as the book of the Wisdom of Jesus ben Sira (Sirach), hymns and prayers, previously unknown Aramaic works, and other wisdom texts. Many of these manuscripts are also extremely fragmentary, making them difficult to categorize in any meaningful sense.

The term "affiliated texts" designates those works that do not contain clear sectarian markers but that do contain ideas or concepts that were

---

28. Other terms that are frequently used to describe this literature are *biblical, scriptural,* or *authoritative literature.* The term *biblical,* referring to those books now in the Jewish canon of Scripture, is anachronistic, since "the Bible" did not exist in the Second Temple period. I have used the word *scriptural* in the past (e.g., in *Rewriting Scripture in Second Temple Times,* Studies in the Dead Sea Scrolls and Related Literature [Grand Rapids: Eerdmans, 2007]), but that term carries connotations of sacredness that do not necessarily apply to all the literature in this category. The same is true for the term *authoritative;* we do not know whether all of the literature in this category was considered authoritative either by all Jews or only the Essene movement. For definitions of the terms *authoritative work* and *scripture,* see E. Ulrich, "The Notion and Definition of Canon," in *The Canon Debate,* ed. L. McDonald and J. Sanders (Peabody, MA: Hendrickson, 2002), 29. I have chosen *classical* as a more neutral term, simply indicating the age of the literature and its status in the Second Temple period as the literary inheritance of ancient Israel.

INTRODUCTION

congenial to the sect. These are works that fall into the gray area between sectarian and nonsectarian.[29] For example, the Temple Scroll was assumed to be sectarian by Yadin, classified as an intermediary text by Dimant, and termed nonsectarian by Stegemann.[30] The Hebrew texts that fall into this gray area, along with many of the Aramaic texts, form a constellation of texts with affinities to the Qumran movement, although they are not sectarian. Some of these works were known prior to the discovery of the Qumran scrolls (e.g., the books of Enoch and Jubilees); others surfaced for the first time in the caves (e.g., the Aramaic Levi Document and the Temple Scroll). The calendar texts are a special group; it is clear that the sect had a strong interest in observing the correct dates for the festivals, and a strong preference for the 364-day calendar based on the solar year. However, interest in proper calendar observance was not limited to the sect, since the proper calculation of the festivals was a concern for all Jews;[31] also, the calendar texts do not contain sectarian vocabulary or other markers. Thus I place them in the affiliated category.[32] Nevertheless, it is likely that the calendar texts found in the Qumran caves were the product of the sect, demonstrating that one major interest of their scholar-scribes was calendar calculation.

The most difficult term to define is the *sectarian texts*, so I will spend more time on that definition. The sectarian texts belonged to the members of that wing of Judaism that collected the Qumran library. Upon examination, approximately 25 percent of the manuscripts discovered in the Qumran caves contain rhetoric and/or vocabulary that establish them as belonging to a sect, according to the definition given above.

29. Dimant has chosen to classify these texts as "intermediate," that is, "without sectarian terminology and style but with affinity to sectarian ideas" ("Qumran Manuscripts," 32).

30. Y. Yadin, *The Temple Scroll*, rev. ed., 3 vols. and supplement (Jerusalem: Israel Exploration Society, 1983); Y. Yadin, "Is the Temple Scroll a Sectarian Document?," in *Humanizing America's Iconic Book: Society of Biblical Literature Centennial Addresses 1980*, ed. G. Tucker and D. Knight (Chico, CA: Scholars Press, 1982), 153–69; Dimant, "Qumran Manuscripts," 51; H. Stegemann, "The Origins of the Temple Scroll," *VT* 40 (1988): 235–56; H. Stegemann, "Is the Temple Scroll a Sixth Book of the Torah—Lost for 2500 Years?" in *Understanding the Dead Sea Scrolls*, ed. H. Shanks (New York: Random House, 1992), 126–36. Other texts in this gray area include wisdom texts such as 4QInstruction.

31. See J. VanderKam, *Calendars in the Dead Sea Scrolls: Measuring Time* (New York: Routledge, 1998), especially part I.

32. Dimant, "Qumran Manuscripts," 46–47, places the calendar and *mishmarot* manuscripts in her sectarian classification.

Introduction

As Carol Newsom has stated, there are three possible uses of the term *sectarian* in regard to a body of literature: (1) a "sectarian text" is a text written by a member of the sect; (2) "sectarian" refers to the way a text is read by a particular community; or (3) the content and/or rhetorical stance of a particular composition identifies it as sectarian.[33] The first two uses are not particularly helpful when examining the Qumran collection of scrolls. Since none of the manuscripts preserves any indication of authorship (except for pseudonymous attribution) we do not know who is responsible for the final form of the text in question. In fact, several of the major Qumran texts labeled "sectarian" exist in multiple forms (e.g., the Serek Hayaḥad). Thus, while we may assume that the sectarian texts were penned by members of the sect, that assumption does not help us to identify which texts are sectarian.

The second criterion is likewise unhelpful. Since all the manuscripts in the Qumran caves were collected, preserved, and presumably at some point read by members of the sectarian group, in that sense all the manuscripts are sectarian. Common sense, however, rebels against that conclusion. Pesher Habakkuk, for example, demonstrates a sectarian reading of the book of Habakkuk, but the book of Habakkuk itself belongs to the classical literature of ancient Israel and thus to Judaism generally.[34] Thus the second criterion breaks down for the Qumran collection.

Only the third criterion is truly useful, because we do have the contents of the manuscripts, however fragmentary some of them may be, and we can examine their rhetorical stance and content. There is general consensus that a certain core group of texts from the Qumran collection are sectarian: the Serek Hayaḥad (S), the Damascus Document (D), the Serek Ha'edah (or Rule of the Congregation; Sa), the Rule of Blessings (Sb), the Hodayot (H), the War Scroll (1QM) and related texts, the Miqṣat Ma'aśê ha-Torah (MMT), and the pesharim.[35] All of these texts can be identified

33. Newsom, "'Sectually' Explicit Literature," 173.

34. See Newsom, "'Sectually' Explicit Literature," 173.

35. See Dimant, "The Vocabulary of the Qumran Sectarian Texts," in *History, Ideology and Bible Interpretation in the Dead Sea Scrolls*, FAT 90 (Tübingen: Mohr Siebeck, 2014), 64, who does not include MMT. Hempel, who confines her remarks to the rule texts, identifies her core texts as S, Sa, D, and 4Q265, on the basis of admission procedures, community organization, leadership, discipline, and shared histories (*Qumran Rule Texts*, 2). F. García Martínez has suggested abandoning the idea of a core of sectarian texts, preferring to speak of "clusters" of texts ("¿Sectario, no-sectario, o qué? Problemas de una taxonomía correcta de los textos qumránicos," *RevQ* 23 [2008]: 383–94).

INTRODUCTION

as sectarian by their rhetorical stance according to the definition of *sect* given above.

All of the rule texts (i.e., S, D, and Sa or the Rule of the Congregation) make clear by using the language of "joining" that this is a voluntary association. Almost all of the core texts have a strong emphasis on boundaries between the members, who have joined the sect voluntarily, and outsiders (see, e.g., S, D, the Hodayot, and the pesharim). While MMT does not demonstrate the same strict sense of separation between insiders and outsiders, by using the terms "we," "you," and "them" it does differentiate between its interpretation of certain Mosaic laws and the interpretation of others, thus demonstrating a sense of group identity over against other Jews of the period. The Hodayot and the pesharim evince a sense of persecution by outsiders (whether or not such persecution actually took place), while the War Scroll describes an eschatological conflict between a sect and the rest of humanity.

S, D, and Sa also contain procedures for joining the sect, rules of conduct and punishment inside it, and expulsion from it. The sect as described in S, D, and Sa was highly organized and hierarchical. The main organizing principle is that of the wilderness camp as laid out in Num 1–2, and the groupings of thousands, hundreds, fifties, and tens found in the Pentateuch. According to both S and Sa, each member is enrolled in a specific rank, and is expected to be obedient to those above him (e.g., 1QS 5:23; 1QSa 1:23–25).

Once this core group of documents is delimited from the rest of the collection because they reflect the definition of "sect" given above, it is possible to isolate vocabulary peculiar to these documents, and then to determine if that vocabulary appears in other more fragmentary manuscripts. This procedure enables us to identify more compositions outside the core group as sectarian. The first group of terms are epithets for the sect:[36]

1. עדה: "congregation, community." Used with the definite article or a pronominal suffix, or in construct, this word for the sect appears in Sa, Sb, D, 1QM, Pesher Habbakuk, Pesher Micah, and Pesher Psalms.

2. יחד: "community." In the sectarian texts this word is used with the definite article as a noun, a usage peculiar to these texts.[37] It appears in S, D, Sa, Pesher Habbakuk, Pesher Micah, and Pesher Psalms.

---

36. Dimant, "Vocabulary of the Qumran Texts," 68–69.

37. In Biblical Hebrew the root appears as a verb, an adjective, and an adverb, but not as a noun.

Introduction

3. עצת היחד: "council of the community." This phrase appears in S, Sa, Pesher Habbakuk, Pesher Micah, Pesher Isaiah, and Pesher Psalms.

4. Other terms: אנשי היחד ("men of the community"), אנשי תמים קודש ("men of perfect holiness"). These terms appear in S, D, and the pesharim.

Another set of terms involves leadership groups and leadership roles. Sometimes the duties or positions associated with these terms overlap with one another or are unclear.[38] Leadership groups include the רבים (S, D), the sons of Aaron (S, Sa, War Rules), and the sons of Zadok (S, D). Leadership roles belong to the Instructor/Sage or Maskil (משכיל; S, D, H), the Overseer/Guardian or Mebaqqer (מבקר; S, D), and "the one appointed" or Paqid (פקיד; S). Qualifications for these roles, based on birth, age, or standing in the sect, are mentioned in passing in various texts.

Other special vocabulary in the sectarian texts includes the word סרך (S, D, Sa, 1QM) in the sense of "rule" or "order"; this term is unknown in all other Hebrew sources of the period.[39] The word פשר, "interpretation," occurs frequently in the special interpretive works known as the *pesharim*, but also in the Damascus Document, Commentary on Genesis A, Florilegium, and Catena A. Epithets or sobriquets for historical figures also figure prominently in the sectarian texts: מורה הצדק ("Teacher of Righteousness") for the sect's founder and leader (D, Pesher Habbakuk, Pesher Micah, Pesher Isaiah, Pesher Psalms); הכוהן הרשע ("the Wicked Priest") for a political opponent of the sect (Pesher Habakkuk, Pesher Isaiah, Pesher Psalms); מטיף הכזב ("the Spreader [or: Spouter, or: Dripper] of Lies") // איש הכזב ("Man of the Lie") for the Teacher's chief ideological rival (D, Pesher Habakkuk, Pesher Micah, Pesher Psalms); and דורשי חלקות ("Seekers-after-Smooth-Things") for the sect's main rivals (D, H, Pesher Nahum, Pesher Isaiah; for their identity see ch. 7). Finding one or more of these terms in a manuscript can be taken as a marker of sectarian origin.

Thus we find evidence in the core group of texts from the Qumran caves for a voluntary association of Jews within the wider Jewish community, with special entrance requirements and a hierarchy beyond the usual divisions of priests, Levites, and Israel. It uses a distinct vocabulary that is not found in the other literature of the period. Having established

---

38. Hempel, *Qumran Rule Texts*, esp. 195–230.

39. Dimant, "Vocabulary of the Qumran Texts," 72. Dimant notes that the term does appear in Aramaic Enoch and the Aramaic Levi Document.

INTRODUCTION

a core group of sectarian texts, we may then relate other texts to them on the basis of content, vocabulary, and rhetorical stance.

Organization of the Volume

This book is divided into three parts; part I contains a general overview of scribes and libraries in the ancient world; part II describes the archaeological and textual evidence from Qumran; and part III draws conclusions concerning the function of the settlement at Qumran, the identity of its inhabitants, and the history of the settlement in the Second Temple period.

Part I: Scribes and Libraries in the Ancient Near Eastern and Mediterranean Worlds

Chapters 2 and 3 set the stage for an investigation of the Qumran scrolls and the settlement at Qumran by taking a broad overview of the role of scribes and the evidence for libraries in the ancient Near East and Greco-Roman world. In ch. 2 I survey evidence for scribes and libraries in Mesopotamia, Egypt, Persia, the Hellenistic world and the Roman world from the Bronze Age through the first century CE. In ch. 3 I narrow the focus to ancient Israel for the same period, excluding the evidence from Qumran. Seeing the comparative evidence as a whole will later make it abundantly clear why we are justified in identifying the Qumran collection as a sectarian library with a strong scribal component and arguing that the main purpose of the Qumran settlement was as an Essene scribal center and library.

Part II: The Qumran Evidence

In the next three chapters I present the archaeological and textual data from Qumran. In ch. 4 I investigate all of the scroll caves in the vicinity of the Qumran settlement, first examining the archaeological data from each cave and then describing the scroll collection found in that cave. This evidence demonstrates that the caves are related to one another by their pottery evidence, especially by the presence in large numbers of the hole-mouthed cylindrical jars with bowl-shaped lids, which are popularly

16

Introduction

known as "scroll jars." The scroll collections too are shown to be one large collection, as established by overlaps in content among all of the caves and in particular by overlaps with Cave 4Q, which contained the largest cache of manuscripts. However, there are also discernible differences among the caves, the most important being the differences between the natural caves located in the limestone cliffs at some distance from the settlement and the manmade marl terrace caves that are part of the built environment of the settlement. I suggest that the limestone cliff caves were used for some type of long-term or permanent storage, in particular for scrolls brought in from other Essene enclaves in Judea, while the marl terrace caves served the inhabitants of Qumran as "overflow storage" from their library complex in the buildings, or as workshops, or as temporary sleeping quarters.

In ch. 5 I present the archaeological evidence from the built environment of Qumran, with a focus on the Second Temple period settlement. I agree with the position that the Second Temple period settlement at Qumran was founded between 100 and 75 BCE, during the reign of Alexander Jannaeus,[40] and was continuously occupied without interruption until its destruction by the Romans in 68 CE.[41] I argue for the following crucial points: (1) The pottery evidence connects the caves and buildings, in particular the presence of the hole-mouthed cylindrical storage jars, which are unique to Qumran, in both locations. (2) There is evidence for the presence of scribes in the archaeological record at Qumran in the Second Temple period. (3) There is also evidence for a library complex and scribal workshop in the main building during the Second Temple period. (4) Last, the archaeological evidence from Qumran supports the hypothesis that the site was inhabited by a sectarian group of Jewish men, whom I identify with the Essenes.

In the last chapter in part II, ch. 6, I present a thorough overview of the manuscripts recovered from the Qumran caves. As explained above, I divide the manuscripts into four categories: the classical texts from ancient Israel, the sectarian literature, the affiliated literature, and general Hellenistic-Roman period literature. The classical literature makes up 25.7 percent of the collection, sectarian and affiliated texts together comprise 43.1 percent, while general Hellenistic-Roman literature accounts

---

40. Magness, *Archaeology of Qumran*, 63–67.

41. D. Mizzi and J. Magness, "Was Qumran Abandoned at the End of the First Century BCE?," *JBL* 135 (2016): 301–20.

INTRODUCTION

for 18.3 percent of the collection.[42] These percentages indicate a collection dominated by sectarian and affiliated literature, making the designation of the Qumran collection as a sectarian library appropriate.

In addition, in ch. 6 I investigate the evidence for scribal interests and activities throughout the collection. This evidence includes the presence of works in three languages (Hebrew, Aramaic, and Greek) and in different scripts, as well as texts reflecting particular scribal interests, including esoteric texts and calendar documents. The activity of scribes is demonstrated by the presence in the library of scribal exercises, lists, and excerpted texts used for study and worship. Taken together, the evidence from the Qumran scrolls decisively demonstrates that the collection is a sectarian library with a strong scribal component.

Part III: Conclusions and a New Synthesis

In ch. 7 I reinvestigate the Qumran-Essene hypothesis, reconsidering the evidence that led early scholars to identify the Qumran community with the Essenes as described by Josephus, Philo, and Pliny, and consider alternative identifications. I conclude that the best interpretation of our current textual and archaeological evidence still leads to the identification of the sect that inhabited Qumran with the Essenes.

Chapter 8 brings the volume to a conclusion. I argue that the archaeological and textual evidence from Qumran (both caves and buildings) leads inexorably to an interpretation of the Qumran scrolls collection as an Essene library and of the site of Qumran as an Essene scribal center and the movement's central library. The chapter includes a discussion of how the Essenes chose Qumran as the location of their central library and scribal center, who lived there and their daily activities, and how and why this large scroll collection was divided between long-term or permanent storage in the limestone cliff caves and the library facilities in the main building and the marl terrace caves. Finally, I paint the scenario of the last days of the Qumran Essene settlement before its destruction by the Romans in 68 CE, speculating on the sequence of events that led to the final hiding of their library in the Qumran caves.

---

42. Manuscripts that are too fragmentary to classify total 12.7 percent.

PART I

Scribes and Libraries
in the Ancient Near Eastern
and Mediterranean Worlds

CHAPTER 2

Scribes and Libraries in the Ancient Near Eastern and Mediterranean Worlds

> Be a scribe. It saves you from toil and protects you from all manner of work.
>
> Papyrus Anastasi II

To be a scribe in the ancient world was to be a practitioner of an elite profession, someone trained in the skills of writing, calculation, and administration. Scribes worked for powerful institutions, such as kings and their courts, temples and their priests, or for wealthy individuals. A scribe's training was arduous. In addition to the skills of writing and reading, scribes were often experts in law, business, math, science, and foreign languages. In other words, they were part of the learned elite in societies that had very low rates of literacy.[1]

Scribes with special aptitude received more specialized training, becoming masters of their religious and cultural traditions and holding important posts in their societies. They were also vital components of international diplomacy, since they spoke and wrote not only their own language(s), but other languages necessary for foreign correspondence.[2] It is to scribes, both named and anonymous, that we owe the legacy of the literature and culture of the ancient Near East. Philip Davies has put this point well: "Scribes, through their professional activities, both preserved

---

1. Estimates vary, but literacy rates in the ancient world hovered in the single digits, often as low as 1–3 percent. See W. Schniedewind, *How the Bible Became a Book: The Textualization of Ancient Israel* (Cambridge: Cambridge University Press, 2004), 25.

2. In Mesopotamia, scribes learned (at least) both Sumerian and Akkadian, and later Aramaic; in Egypt the language of international diplomacy was Akkadian, while Hittite was also necessary. Ugaritic scribes wrote in Akkadian, Hurrian, and Hittite. Less is known about Israelite scribes, but in the Persian period they at least knew Aramaic; in the Iron Age it is likely that they were trained in the languages of the surrounding kingdoms as well as Akkadian.

SCRIBES AND LIBRARIES

and controlled the cultural values of their societies. As archivists and historiographers, they controlled the narrative of the past; as writers of didactic literature, they maintained social values, and through predictive writing (manticism, prophecy), they even controlled the future."[3] In this chapter I investigate the scribal profession in Mesopotamia, Egypt, Ugarit, and the Hellenistic and Roman worlds, and then turn to the evidence for libraries and archives in those societies.

Scribes

Mesopotamia

Evidence for scribes first emerges in Mesopotamia in the third millennium BCE, when the Sumerian word *edubba*, "tablet house," Akkadian *bīt ṭuppi*, first appears.[4] A "scribe" was a person who could read and write in cuneiform; the word for the scribal profession in Akkadian is *ṭupšarrūtu*, whose primary meaning is "inscribing a tablet," although its meaning expands to connote all activities that involved writing. A scribe is a *ṭupšarru*, "one who inscribes a tablet."[5] All Mesopotamian scribes were educated in four major areas of instruction: language, literature, mathematics, and music; evidence for this basic curriculum exists from the third through the first millennium BCE. This curriculum emphasized memorization of cuneiform signs and words and the copying of uncomplicated texts. Apprentice scribes learned lexical lists of words and their spelling. The purposes of these lists were to train scribes in the cuneiform writing system and to function as vocabulary resources. They also studied geometry, land measuring, and legal terminology; and they copied model contracts, model letters, historical documents, and law codes. All scribes

---

3. P. Davies, *Scribes and Schools: The Canonization of the Hebrew Scriptures* (Louisville: Westminster John Knox, 1996), 74–75.

4. S. N. Kramer, "The Sage in Sumerian Literature: A Composite Portrait," in *The Sage in Israel and the Ancient Near East*, ed. J. Gammie and L. Perdue (Winona Lake, IN: Eisenbrauns, 1990), 31; L. Pearce, "The Scribes and Scholars of Ancient Mesopotamia," *CANE* 4:2270.

5. V. Hurowitz, "Tales of Two Sages—Towards an Image of the 'Wise Man' in Akkadian Writings," in *Scribes, Sages, and Seers: The Sage in the Eastern Mediterranean World*, ed. L. Perdue (Göttingen: Vandenhoeck & Ruprecht, 2008), 70n15; Pearce, "Scribes and Scholars," 2272.

were bilingual in Sumerian and Akkadian.[6] Scribes at this basic level of competence went on to staff the bureaucracies of palaces and temples.[7] Their duties included the writing and copying of routine administrative records, royal inscriptions, collections of laws, lists of year names, and king lists and chronicles. In the second millennium, scribes could work independently of palace or temple (for example, for wealthy landowners or businessmen); by the first millennium that type of independent work seems to have become rarer.[8]

Following their initial period of instruction, particularly able apprentices could go on to high-level specializations. The list of professions known as PROTO.LU includes eighteen varieties of scribes. Elite scribes, or scholar-scribes,[9] could specialize in astrology/astronomy, exorcism, medicine, divination, or lamentation singing.[10] Those who claimed a scholarly specialization in astronomy and astrology appear to be the largest group.[11] These scholar-scribes were employed by the palace (e.g., the "king's scribe," probably the private secretary to the king) or the temples.[12] Scholar-scribes belonged to the social elite of Mesopotamia and were responsible for the preservation and transmission of Sumerian and Akkadian culture.

6. Other languages could also be demanded of scribes, depending on their geographic location. For example, in the city of Emar, on the western periphery of Mesopotamia, Hittite was an important scribal language. See Y. Cohen, *The Scribes and Scholars of the City of Emar in the Late Bronze Age*, HSS 59 (Winona Lake, IN: Eisenbrauns, 2009). In the Persian period (c. 538–332 BCE) competence in both Akkadian and Aramaic was expected, although certain scribes, *sepiru*, specialized in Aramaic and the use of skin/parchment as the writing medium. See Pearce, "Scribes and Scholars," 2270–73; B. Alster, "Scribes and Wisdom in Ancient Mesopotamia," in Perdue, *Scribes, Sages, and Seers,* 50.

7. See R. F. G. Sweet, "The Sage in Mesopotamian Palaces and Royal Courts," in Gammie and Perdue, *Sage in Israel,* 103, who notes that the term "palace scribe" (Sum. *dub-sar-é-gal*; Akk. *ṭupšar ēkalli*) was already well established by the Ur III period.

8. Alster, "Scribes and Wisdom," 52. For an interesting description of the daily activities of a scribe in Old Babylonian Sippar, see M. Tanret, "The Works and the Days? On Scribal Activity in Old Babylonian Sippar-Amnānum," *Revue d'Assyriologie* 98 (2004): 33–62.

9. The term is Oppenheim's; see Sweet, "Sage in Mesopotamian Palaces," 105n18.

10. Pearce, "Scribes and Scholars," 2273; Hurowitz, "Tales of Two Sages," 67; Kramer, "Sage in Sumerian Literature," 106.

11. Pearce, "Scribes and Scholars," 2275.

12. Sweet, "Sage in Mesopotamian Palaces," 103; Pearce, "Scribes and Scholars," 2274–75. Pearce notes that these temple scribes were not officiants in the cult; the duties and responsibilities of scholar-scribes and priests were clearly differentiated. By the Hellenistic period, however, this distinction was breaking down.

SCRIBES AND LIBRARIES

This culture was handed down in the form of cuneiform tablets, incised and baked before being stored in libraries and archives throughout Mesopotamia. These clay tablets are virtually indestructible unless they are deliberately or accidentally shattered. Furthermore, they are cheap to manufacture and easy to obtain. Because of these factors, hundreds of thousands of these clay tablets have been unearthed in legal and illegal excavations throughout Mesopotamia, making our reconstruction of their scribal culture relatively straightforward in comparison with Egypt or Israel and Judah (see below and ch. 3).[13] These factors also had an important result for the ancient Mesopotamian scholar-scribes themselves: as Seth Sanders points out, the resilient nature of cuneiform tablets allowed expert scribes to handle and read thousand-year-old texts. The result was a scribal culture with multiple, extensive, physical connections with the remote past.[14] Thus scribes were fully aware of the past literary record and their place in that literary record going forward. This awareness is demonstrated by the use of colophons, which became a feature of many tablets in the first millennium BCE.[15] On the colophon, the scribe not only identified himself by name but often also recorded the source text he had used. For example, in a private house excavated in Uruk, which contained the libraries of two scribal families, 420 tablets were recovered. Of these, 112 had colophons; 50 of these state that the tablet is a copy of an earlier text.[16] Colophons usually had the following pattern:

1. Name of copyist
2. Lineage (optional)
3. Title (optional)

13. A second writing medium, the waxed writing tablet, was also widely used. These writing boards could be bound together to form polyptychs. Since these writing tablets were perishable, very few of them remain.

14. S. Sanders, *From Adapa to Enoch: Scribal Culture and Religious Vision in Judea and Babylon*, TSAJ 167 (Tübingen: Mohr Siebeck, 2017), 22. I would like to thank Professor Sanders for sharing his work with me prior to publication.

15. E. Robson, "The Production and Dissemination of Scholarly Knowledge," in *The Oxford Handbook of Cuneiform Culture,* ed. K. Radner and E. Robson (Oxford: Oxford University Press, 2011), 559.

16. Robson, "Production and Dissemination," 556. This house library dates from the second half of the first millennium BCE. The originals from which the tablets were copied were often identified as "old writing boards," which indicates that the texts were being copied on tablets to preserve them for posterity.

24

4. Status

5. Patron gods[17]

Although Mesopotamian scholar-scribes were aware of the past literary record since it was all around them on clay tablets, their literary culture was not static but characterized by scribal change. According to Kramer, the tablet house was not a place where texts were merely copied, but was a center of culture and learning, where literary works were studied and revised.[18] Sara Milstein argues that Mesopotamian literary texts underwent "extensive revision" in the process of transmission, the scribes using techniques such as updating grammar and vocabulary, conflation, harmonization and combination, and occasionally omission.[19] Major literary works such as Gilgamesh, the Epic of Anzu, Atrahasis, and Ishtar's Descent to the Underworld circulated in variant forms in the second and first millennia BCE.[20] Jeffrey Tigay's close study of the Gilgamesh Epic demonstrates this process at work, as he compares versions in Sumerian, Akkadian, and Hittite, and notes the changes that took place over several centuries of transmission.[21] "Scientific" works such as the astronomical treatise Enuma Anu Enlil also circulated in variant forms, and mathematical content was updated as knowledge advanced. Omen series were edited into new compositions. Finally, scholar-scribes also composed new works such as hymns, prayers, and royal inscriptions.[22] The scholar-scribes belonging to the tablet house and working in the palaces and temples, therefore, were the guides and transmitters of Mesopotamian cultural and intellectual life, the keepers of their tradition.

The scribal profession, while open to all who showed ability, was often handed down from father to son, in the familiar apprenticeship system of the ancient Near East. For example, the families of Sîn-leqe-unninni and Ekur-Zakir from Uruk seem to have been active in the scribal profession

---

17. Cohen, *Scribes and Scholars*, 61.

18. Kramer, "Sage in Sumerian Literature," 31–32.

19. S. Milstein, "Reworking Ancient Texts: Revision through Introduction in Biblical and Mesopotamian Literature" (PhD diss., New York University, 2010), 2. I would like to thank Seth Sanders for bringing this work to my attention.

20. Robson, "Production and Dissemination," 572.

21. J. Tigay, *The Evolution of the Gilgamesh Epic* (Philadelphia: University of Pennsylvania Press, 1982).

22. Robson, "Production and Dissemination," 569–71; Pearce, "Scribes and Scholars," 2275. See also Cohen, *Scribes and Scholars*, 2, 145, 222, 234, 237.

SCRIBES AND LIBRARIES

for centuries,[23] while from the city of Emar two prominent scribal families, those of Zu-Ba'la and Ba'al-barû, have been identified.[24]

Egypt

The first reference to a scribe in ancient Egypt is found in the Pyramid Texts, dating to the Old Kingdom (third millennium BCE).[25] During the Old Kingdom period a large body of educated scribes staffed the already burgeoning bureaucracy of centralized pharaonic Egypt. Those scribes identified by name were high officials in the kingdom, many of royal blood. The need for scribes only increased during the Middle (2040–1786 BCE) and New (1567–1085 BCE) Kingdom periods, as the bureaucracy expanded and the demands of the civil service increased.[26]

Scribal education during the Old Kingdom period seems to have been exclusively an apprenticeship system, which continued down through the New Kingdom. The word for "school" (*ansebe*) first appears in the 10th Dynasty; these schools were run by senior scribes.[27] Some of the works learned and copied by apprentice scribes include "In Praise of Learned Scribes" and "The Satire on the Trades," both of which extol the scribal profession as superior to all others.[28] During the New Kingdom period scribal schools proliferated and were located in both the palace and the temple. However, the scribal profession continued to be based on nepotism; father-son pairs of scribes recur throughout the literature.[29]

---

23. E. Lipiński, "Royal and State Scribes in Ancient Jerusalem," in *Congress Volume: Jerusalem, 1986*, ed. J. A. Emerton, VTSup 40 (Leiden: Brill, 1988), 163.

24. Cohen, *Scribes and Scholars*, 27.

25. Pyr. 954a–955a. See R. J. Williams, "Scribal Training in Ancient Egypt," *JAOS* 92 (1972): 214.

26. R. J. Williams, "The Sage in Egyptian Literature," in Gammie and Perdue, *Sage in Israel*, 19–22.

27. Williams, "Scribal Training in Ancient Egypt," 215; Williams, "Sage in Egyptian Literature," 22.

28. J. A. Wilson, "The Satire on the Trades," in *Ancient Near Eastern Texts Relating to the Old Testament*, ed. J. B. Pritchard, 3rd ed. (Princeton: Princeton University Press, 1969), 432–34.

29. In the 12th Dynasty the scribe named Khety puts his son Pepy in a scribal school. A 19th Dynasty tomb records a family of scribes, Amenwahsu and his sons Didia and Kha'emope. During the Ramesside period, a stele (Vienna 51) records the activities of Amenmose and his son Prenen. Diodorus Siculus (1.81.1–4) also mentions that priests train their sons

Scribal training in Egypt was arduous because of the difficulties of the languages and scripts involved. An apprentice scribe was first introduced to the hieratic script, then hieroglyphic; by the seventh century BCE demotic also appeared.[30] The elementary training period lasted four years and included, besides writing and reading, mathematics, geometry, natural phenomena, and administrative information.[31] Upon completing this curriculum most scribes disappeared into the lower levels of the pharaonic civil service. Those pupils with special aptitude, however, could be chosen to continue with higher levels of training, lasting as long as twelve years. Specialties included administration, the military, and the priesthood. Those studying administration or the military received further training in mathematics, accounting, geometry, surveying, and engineering. Further language study was also required; the language of international diplomacy was Akkadian, and scribes also studied Canaanite dialects, Hittite, and Minoan.[32] Those entering the priesthood studied medicine, astronomy, magic, dream interpretation, and the conduct of festivals.[33] Scholar-scribes of the priesthood could be priests themselves; by the Ptolemaic period this seems to have been the norm.[34] These scholar-scribes were the elites of their profession; they obtained high positions in the administration, the military, and the cult. As Herman te Velde puts it, these scholar-scribes "were the core and backbone of ancient Egyptian civilization. They were the elite."[35]

The ancient Egyptian scribal institution about which we know the most is the "House of Life." The House of Life, which became linked to the cult of Osiris, was usually located in proximity to a temple but was not itself a religious institution; rather, it was a workshop for scholar-scribes, what was called in the medieval period a scriptorium. It was a center for the composition, preservation, study, and copying of texts, most of which were religious in nature, as well as for the training of ap-

---

in the two kinds of writing. See Williams, "Scribal Training in Ancient Egypt," 214–15; and A. Gardiner, "The House of Life," *JEA* 24 (1938): 161, 164.

30. Williams, "Scribal Training in Ancient Egypt," 215; Williams, "Sage in Egyptian Literature," 23.

31. Williams, "Scribal Training in Ancient Egypt," 216, 218–19.

32. Williams, "Scribal Training in Ancient Egypt," 216, 219; E. Wente, "The Scribes of Ancient Egypt," *CANE* 4:2216–17.

33. Wente, "Scribes of Ancient Egypt," 2216; Gardiner, "House of Life," 176.

34. H. te Velde, "Scribes and Literacy in Ancient Egypt," in *Scripta Signa Vocis: Studies about Scripts, Scriptures, Scribes and Languages in the Near East*, ed. H. Vanstiphout et al. (Gröningen: Forsten, 1986), 216; Gardiner, "House of Life," 176.

35. Te Velde, "Scribes and Literacy," 253.

SCRIBES AND LIBRARIES

prentice scribes.[36] Many of the scholar-scribes who worked in a House of Life were priests as well; in trilingual inscriptions from the Ptolemaic period the word used for these scholar-scribes is ἱερογραμματεύς.[37] The texts produced in the Houses of Life were distributed around the country, mostly to temples, which had libraries of sacred texts (see below).[38]

The media on which Egyptian scholar-scribes produced their texts could not have been more different from those in Mesopotamia. Scribes worked on ostraca, wooden tablets, and papyrus.[39] Ostraca, broken potsherds that were reutilized as a writing surface, are extremely durable, but they seem to have been mostly used for school texts, as were wooden tablets. In contrast to the clay tablets of Mesopotamia, papyrus, the medium of choice for important documents, is quite fragile and easily destroyed by fire, flood, or simply the wear and tear of normal use. As a result, most of our knowledge of ancient Egyptian scribal activity until the later periods comes from tomb paintings and inscriptions, statuary, stelae, and ostraca. Very little papyrus survives from the earlier periods. The same problem would have faced the scholar-scribes working in the Houses of Life; they would have had much less physical access to ancient texts than their Mesopotamian counterparts. Their copy texts may have been two or three generations old, but no older. This lack of physical access to the remote past may have affected the way in which Egyptian scholar-scribes approached their texts. Anonymity was the rule, unless a pseudepigraphic name from antiquity was attached to the work.[40] However, scholar-scribes were not mere copyists of supposedly antique texts; at least the didactic works that were part of the school curriculum, which survive in multiple copies, show evidence of recensional or editorial activity.[41] Thus, as in Mesopotamia, Egyptian scholar-scribes were the preservers and transmitters of their literary tradition for later generations and did not hesitate to bring their immense learning to bear on their texts, updating and editing them in the process of handing them on.

---

36. Williams, "Sage in Egyptian Literature," 27; Gardiner, "House of Life," 175–76.

37. For discussion of ancient Egyptian scribal institutions, see Wente, "Scribes of Ancient Egypt," 2211–21; Gardiner, "House of Life," 170; te Velde, "Scribes and Literacy," 253–64; and Williams, "Sage in Egyptian Literature," 27.

38. Gardiner, "House of Life," 177.

39. Williams, "Scribal Training in Ancient Egypt," 216.

40. Williams, "Sage in Egyptian Literature," 24–25. Some of these pseudepigraphical names are Imhotep, Hardjedef, Neferti, and Khety, all from the Old Kingdom period.

41. Williams, "Sage in Egyptian Literature," 24.

Scribes and Libraries in the Ancient Near Eastern and Mediterranean Worlds

Ugarit

The site of Ras Shamra has revealed a Late Bronze Age Canaanite city-state, Ugarit, on the northwest coast of present-day Syria. Its language, Ugaritic, is assigned to the Northwest Semitic family of languages, and thus is closer to ancient Hebrew than either Akkadian (an East Semitic language) or Egyptian (a Hamitic language).

Ugarit yielded thousands of clay tablets, the vast majority dating from approximately 1400 BCE to the destruction of the city around 1180 BCE.[42] They testify to a highly educated scribal profession, although our knowledge of how scribes obtained that education is unfortunately very thin.

The Ugaritic tablets indicate scribes familiar with at least five languages and three or four scripts. Ugaritic was the everyday language of business and law, while Akkadian was the language of international diplomacy. Texts in Hurrian (possibly spoken by local elements of the population), Hittite (the language of the overlords of Ugarit during much of this period), and Egyptian also survive.[43] The scripts included an alphabetic cuneiform developed for Ugaritic, syllabic cuneiform for Akkadian, Egyptian hieroglyphic, and a Cypro-Minoan script. The Hurrian language was written in both alphabetic cuneiform and syllabic cuneiform, while Hittite was written in both syllabic cuneiform and hieroglyphic.[44]

Scribes at Ugarit signed their work with their names and profession, as in Mesopotamia.[45] As a result we know that the profession of scribe was familial; the colophons give evidence for several father-son pairs.[46] Scribes could reach high positions in the royal court, such as counselor (*sukallu*) of the king, or diplomat.[47] Šapšimalku, a notary of royal land-grant deeds,

42. D. Pardee and P. Bordreuil, "Ugarit: Texts and Literature," *ABD* 6:706.

43. See J. Healey and P. Craigie, "Languages: Ugaritic," *ABD* 4:227; and A. Rainey, "The Scribe at Ugarit: His Position and Influence," *Proceedings of the Israel Academy of Sciences and Humanities* 3 (1969): 129.

44. Pardee and Bordreuil, "Ugarit: Texts and Literature," 718.

45. W. H. van Soldt, "Ugarit: A Second-Millennium Kingdom on the Mediterranean Coast," *CANE* 4:1263. See also his list of all scribes' names found in the Ugaritic tablets: W. H. van Soldt, *Studies in the Akkadian of Ugarit: Dating and Grammar*, AOAT 40 (Kevelaer: Butzon & Bercker; Neukirchen-Vluyn: Neukirchener Verlag, 1991), 19–32.

46. See the list of scribes' names in L. Mack-Fisher, "The Scribe (and Sage) in the Royal Court at Ugarit," in Gammie and Perdue, *Sage in Israel*, 111–13. Some father-son pairs include Husanu and his son Yasiranu, Yarimmu and his son Murahimu, and the family of Nu'mî-Rašap, whose family extends at least three generations.

47. Mack-Fisher, "Scribe (and Sage)," 114; van Soldt, "Ugarit," 1263.

SCRIBES AND LIBRARIES

is titled (in Akkadian) *tupšarru emqu*, "wise [or: proficient] scribe."[48] The title *rb spr*, "chief scribe," appears in Ugaritic.[49]

Scribes were also associated with temples. Ilimilku, the scribe of the Baal, Kirta, and Aqhat epics, identifies himself as the "pupil" (*lmd*) of Attenu, a priest.[50] The mention of "pupil" leads to the question of where and how scribes in Ugarit were trained. No certain location for a school has emerged from the excavations.[51] However, texts containing school exercises and lexical lists, including quadrilingual vocabularies in Sumerian, Akkadian, Hurrian, and Ugaritic, were discovered in seven locations around the city; these indicate that scribes may have been trained as apprentices in family settings.[52] Juan-Pablo Vita shows that a study of the tablets and their epigraphy demonstrates that Ugarit had several well-established scribal traditions, and that each tradition or "family" was found concentrated in a single locus.[53]

As in Mesopotamia, the medium for writing at Ugarit was the extremely durable incised and baked clay tablet. However, the vast majority of documents from Ugarit are documentary/administrative, unlike those from Mesopotamia, where a larger percentage of the tablets are literary. Those written in Ugaritic deal with internal administration; those in Akkadian concern international diplomacy. Thus the primary function of the scribes seems to have been as record keepers for the palace and the temples. Literary and religious texts exist in far fewer copies. The famous literary myths from Ugarit copied by Ilimilku (Baal, Aqhat, and Kirta) are preserved in only one copy. More common are ritual texts dealing with

48. I. M. Rowe, "Scribes, Sages, and Seers in Ugarit," in Perdue, *Scribes, Sages, and Seers*, 103; Rainey, "Scribe at Ugarit," 128.

49. See C. Gordon, *Ugaritic Textbook*, AnOr 38 (Rome: Pontifical Biblical Institute, 1965), no. 73; Rainey, "Scribe at Ugarit," 128.

50. Rainey, "Scribe at Ugarit," 127-28; Rowe, "Scribes, Sages, and Seers," 102; A. Curtis, "Ilimilku of Ugarit: Copyist or Creator?" in *Writing the Bible: Scribes, Scribalism and Script*, ed. P. Davies and T. Römer (Durham: Acumen, 2013), 10-22.

51. M. Yon, "Ugarit: History and Archaeology," *ABD* 6:695-706. However, it has been suggested that the high priest's house, located between the temples of Baal and Dagan, where the epics inscribed by Ilimilku were discovered, may also have functioned as a scribal school. See Curtis, "Ilimilku of Ugarit," 10-12.

52. Rowe, "Scribes, Sages, and Seers," 106. Rainey, "Scribe at Ugarit," 127, suggests that the "library of the priest" (also called the House of the Hurrian Priest) may have been a training school for scribes.

53. J.-P. Vita, "Les scribes des textes rituels d'Ougarit," *UF* 39 (2007): 654. He further notes that at times a scribal hand is found in only a single area (655).

30

Scribes and Libraries in the Ancient Near Eastern and Mediterranean Worlds

lists of sacrifice or extispicy.[54] These ritual texts do preserve variation; for example, RS 1.003 and RS 18.056, texts containing rites to accomplish in the month of the grape harvest, are copied by the same scribe but with significant variants.[55] As for the paucity of literary texts, it is always possible that this is an accident of excavation, but the site has been extensively excavated over the course of several decades, so that seems unlikely. Late Bronze Age Ugarit, at least in the realm of religion, must have been a largely oral culture. Thus its scribes had a much smaller role in preserving their traditions for posterity; we may see the beginnings of such a move in the work of Ilimilku, but it had not had a chance to develop before the destruction of the city in the Late Bronze Age.

Thus far we have surveyed the evidence for the scribal profession in Mesopotamia, Egypt, and Ugarit; next we turn to the evidence for libraries and archives in those same societies.

Libraries and Archives in the Ancient Near East

Since the beginnings of excavations in Mesopotamia in the nineteenth century, in which hundreds of thousands of clay tablets have come to light, scholars have tended to draw a hard-and-fast line between an archive, which comprises administrative documents of a legal, political, or historical nature put into long-term storage, and a library, which includes literary, historical, religious, and scientific documents for the purpose of study.[56] In reality, however, that absolute distinction is difficult to maintain, since the vast majority of text collections unearthed in the ancient Near East contain both literary and documentary materials. As Jeremy Black and William Tait state: "In practice the distinction between archive and library is often impossible to make, since administrative, legal, and business records may

---

54. Pardee and Bordrieu, "Ugarit: Texts and Literature," 708–10.

55. Vita, "Scribes des textes rituels," 647.

56. See E. Posner, *Archives in the Ancient World* (Cambridge: Harvard University Press, 1972), 3–4; and J. du Toit, *Textual Memory: Ancient Archives, Libraries and the Hebrew Bible* (Sheffield: Sheffield Phoenix Press, 2011), 22–23. E. Robson points out that the closest word in Akkadian to our meaning of "library" is *gerginakku* (or *gerkinakku*), which means a room, usually in a temple, in which scholarly tablets were deposited, and the contents of that collection. The usage seems to indicate a differentiation from our "archive" ("Reading the Libraries of Assyria and Babylonia," in *Ancient Libraries*, ed. J. König et al. [Cambridge: Cambridge University Press, 2013], 41).

31

be stored in the same room as traditional or scientific texts used for scribal training, and priests or scholars kept their family records at home with their private libraries."[57]

Thus almost all libraries in the ancient Near East also had an archival function, and archives contained literary texts. In other words, the semantic distinction often made by modern librarians would have been meaningless to the owners of these collections.[58]

Mesopotamia

Two types of libraries and/or archives seem to have existed in ancient Mesopotamia: a large, at least somewhat organized state-sponsored collection, often housed in or near a royal palace or temple; and smaller private collections found in private homes.[59] The better known state-sponsored collections include the Ebla corpus (third millennium BCE), the library of Assurbanipal (seventh century BCE), and the library from the Shamash temple in Sippar, for which the latest datable tablet is from the reign of Cambyses II (529–522 BCE).[60] All of these collections contain both literary and documentary texts, in varying proportions.

The Ebla collection was unearthed at Tell Mardikh in northwest Syria. Ebla was a major Syrian city in the third millennium BCE. The tablet collection numbers approximately seven thousand complete or partial tablets, 80 percent of which are administrative. The tablets were discovered in Room L of Palace G; the tablets were originally arranged on wooden shelves along the walls of Room L 2769, which was only accessible through Room L 2875, a "typical scriptorium" with low benches along the walls.[61] The shelves collapsed at the time of the fire that destroyed the city. The tablets are written in Eblaite, a Semitic language, using the cuneiform writing system of Sumer.[62]

---

57. J. A. Black and W. J. Tait, "Archives and Libraries in the Ancient Near East," *CANE* 4:2197. See also M. Haran, "Archives, Libraries and the Order of the Biblical Books," *JANESCU* 22 (1993): 51–59.

58. Haran, "Archives, Libraries," 52.

59. See O. Pedersén, *Archives and Libraries in the Ancient Near East 1500–300 B.C.* (Bethesda, MD: CDL, 1998), for a catalog of these collections up until 1998.

60. Pedersén, *Archives and Libraries*, 194.

61. K. R. Veenhof, "Libraries and Archives," *The Oxford Encyclopedia of Archaeology in the Near East*, ed. E. M. Meyers, 5 vols. (New York: Oxford University Press, 1997), 3:352.

62. R. D. Bigg, "Ebla: Texts," *ABD* 2:263–70.

Scribes and Libraries in the Ancient Near Eastern and Mediterranean Worlds

The administrative texts document such activities as gathering food supplies for the palace, transactions in precious metals, and regulating the local textile industry. The archive also contained letters and diplomatic texts. Lexical lists known from elsewhere in Mesopotamia, including lists of geographical names, professions, birds, fishes, and practical vocabularies, were also discovered there. The small number of literary texts are primarily incantations.[63]

The most famous library collection to be excavated in the ancient Near East is the library of the Assyrian king Assurbanipal (c. 668–627 BCE), unearthed in Nineveh. This library was systematically collected by Assurbanipal; the king, who was not expected to ascend to the throne, was educated to be a priest and was proud of his scribal accomplishments: "I am versed in the craft of the sage Adapa; I studied the secret lore of the entire scribal craft, I know the celestial and terrestrial portents."[64] The king seems to have overseen the collecting process himself, and there was an organized, large-scale tablet production operation within the royal palace.[65] These tablets, very finely produced, all have colophons with Assurbanipal's name.

Assurbanipal also collected materials from around his empire, and, especially after the conquest of Babylonia in 648 BCE, from Babylon.[66] He seems to have been ruthless in his collecting policy. In a letter to his agents in Babylon he writes: "every last tablet in their establishments and all the tablets which are in Ezida. Gather together the entirety of . . . (a long list of text types) and send them to me. If you see any tablet which I have not mentioned and it is appropriate for my palace . . . send it to me!"[67] As a result, the library was huge; approximately five thousand tablets have been recovered, and it may be assumed that it contained an equal number of waxed writing board polyptychs, which have subsequently perished.

---

63. L. Casson, *Libraries in the Ancient World* (New Haven: Yale University Press, 2001), 3.

64. As quoted in Pearce, "Scribes and Scholars," 2277.

65. S. Parpola, "Assyrian Library Records," *JNES* 42 (1983): 10.

66. Parpola, "Assyrian Library Records," 4.

67. Quoted in A. K. Grayson, "Mesopotamia, History of: History and Culture of Assyria," *ABD* 4:749. This practice of raiding texts after a conquest still goes on in modern times; after the 1967 Six-Day War against Jordan, victorious Israeli general Yigael Yadin sent a deputy to Bethlehem, to the house of Dead Sea Scrolls dealer Kando, to retrieve the Temple Scroll, which Kando had hidden under the floorboards of his house. Kando, after a short stint in jail, very wisely handed it over.

SCRIBES AND LIBRARIES

The library itself took up several rooms in the royal palace complex, in the southwestern palace, the north palace, and the temple of Nabu.[68] Its contents are worth noting; while we might expect, given our own literary interests, that a large percentage of the collection would be copies of the myths and epics of Mesopotamia, they constitute only a small fraction of the whole. Instead, three-fifths of the identified works concern divination, while another quarter are hymns, incantations, rituals, and medical recipes.[69] In other words, the majority of what Assurbanipal collected was the professional literature of experts in Mesopotamian scientific and religious lore.

The library in the Shamash temple at Sippar, northwest of Babylon, is the oldest library in history that has been found essentially intact on its original shelves. It was excavated in 1985–1986; its approximately eight hundred clay tablets were discovered in Room 355 on shelves in pigeonhole wall niches on three sides of the room.[70] Room 356, next to the library room, may have served as a scriptorium and reading room.

The temple library contained a mixture of literary and documentary texts, either in Akkadian or bilingual Sumerian-Akkadian. The literary texts include omens of the traditional series, incantations, prayers, hymns, lamentations, scholarly lists, and mathematical and astronomical texts. Copies of the myths of Atrahasis, Enuma Elish, and Lugale were discovered. The documentary texts included economic documents, letters, and copies of royal inscriptions.[71] This eclectic collection, found in situ and perhaps intact, presents a good picture of a large palace/temple library from the ancient Near East.

The other type of library found in Mesopotamia is the small private library or archive found in homes; such small collections are found in practically every excavation.[72] These small collections contained both documentary texts belonging to the family and literary texts of particular interest to the collector, who was often a professional scribe who had become an expert diviner, lamentation singer, astronomer, medical professional, exorcist, and so on.[73] School texts, indicating scribal training exercises,

68. Nabu was the Mesopotamian patron deity of scribes.

69. Robson, "Reading the Libraries," 43.

70. Pedersén, *Archives and Libraries*, 193–94. There were fourteen tiers of niches, six on the back wall and four each on the two side walls.

71. Pedesén, *Archives and Libraries*, 194.

72. See Pedersén, *Archives and Libraries*, 198–212, for a listing.

73. See the various examples in the articles collected in Radner and Robson, *Oxford Handbook of Cuneiform Culture*.

often predominate. These small, private collections were usually stored in a jar or a basket.

To give just one example, excavations in Uruk uncovered a house occupied in the fifth-fourth centuries BCE by two families of scribes.[74] The first family, that of Anu-iksur and his father Shamash-idinna, belonged to the *šangû Ninurta*, who specialized in exorcism. Their library (from the fifth century BCE) contained texts concerned with exorcism, such as incantations and medical texts, as well as lexical lists, omens, astronomical and astrological texts, hymns, and myths. There were also documentary texts belonging to the family. In the next century, the second family, that of Iqisa, who was also an exorcist but belonged to a different family, the family of Ikur-zakir, occupied the same house. The texts from Iqisa's family collection included the same variety of texts: incantations, medical texts, lexical lists, omens, astronomical and astrological texts, myths, hymns, and a small number of documentary texts. These smaller collections, owned by professional scribes, document the working interests of scribes in the ancient Near East.

Egypt

Given the ephemeral nature of the main writing material used in ancient Egypt, papyrus, we have much less evidence for ancient Egyptian libraries than we do for Mesopotamia. Most of our knowledge comes from tomb paintings and inscriptions, statuary, stelae, and ostraca; only later in the long history of Egypt do we find papyrus remains. However, from all this information we can reconstruct the institutions in which the scholar-scribes of ancient Egypt worked.

The existence of a vast state bureaucracy throughout the entire recorded history of ancient Egypt led to a much sharper distinction between archives and libraries than we found in Mesopotamia.[75] The state archives were repositories of the documents recording the business of the royal administrative machinery. A well-known example is the archive found at Tell el-Amarna, the capital of Egypt under Akhenaten (c. 1350–1334 BCE);

---

74. Pedersén, *Archives and Libraries*, 211. For a discussion, see H. Drawnel, *The Aramaic Astronomical Book (4Q208–4Q211) from Qumran: Text, Translation, and Commentary* (Oxford: Oxford University Press, 2011), 55–56.

75. Posner, *Archives in the Ancient World*, 71–90.

SCRIBES AND LIBRARIES

the archive, found in the "office-house of the letters of Pharaoh," consists of cuneiform tablets, the majority of which were letters between the Egyptian court and foreign rulers, including the vassal kings of Canaan.[76]

Egyptian literary texts, by contrast, were the concern of the scholar-scribes working in the Houses of Life. The written works produced in the Houses of Life were stored in a "House of Books," the library of a temple, which was simply a room or rooms within the temple complex, accessible only to the priests. The earliest reference to a library in ancient Egypt is dated to about 2250 BCE, in a text listing officials associated with buildings storing sacred writings.[77]

Temple libraries contained works concerning cultic matters, medicine, magic, dream interpretation, astronomy, myths, and rituals. The largest and best-preserved papyrus collection in a temple library comes from the Tebtunis temple.[78] Tebtunis was the southernmost settlement in the Faiyum oasis in Egypt during the Greco-Roman period. Its temple was dedicated to the crocodile god Sobek. The archaeological context is unclear; according to the Italian excavators, at least one lot of papyri was found in two adjoining cellars inside the temenos wall. The very fragmentary remains date from the first to the third centuries CE; 60 percent of the texts are cultic, 20 percent are scientific, and 20 percent are literary. Four different scripts are represented: hieroglyphic, hieratic, demotic, and Greek. The cultic material includes a large number of manuals, often in multiple copies, concerning the ideal temple and its priesthood, the gods and their mythology, the characteristics of each geographical division in Egypt, and astronomy. Twenty copies of the Book of the Temple, for example, were discovered. Kim Ryholt suggests that a similar compendium of reference works would have been present in every temple library for the benefit of the priests who worked there.[79]

Private libraries belonging to scribes have also been recovered from Egypt. Twenty-three papyri from the first half of the second millennium

---

76. The letters of Abdi-Heba, the ruler of Jerusalem, contain the Akkadian title for a royal scribe, *ṭupšar šarri* (EA 286:61; 287:64; 288:62; and 289:47). See N. Fox, *In the Service of the King: Officialdom in Ancient Israel and Judah* (Cincinnati: Hebrew Union College Press, 2000), 101n82. The Amarna archive also contained a few lexical and literary texts, including the Myth of Adapa and the Myth of Nergal and Ereshkigal. There was also an Egyptian-Akkadian word list, presumably an aid in the foreign correspondence. See W. Moran, *The Amarna Letters* (Baltimore: Johns Hopkins University Press, 1992).

77. K. Ryholt, "Libraries in Ancient Egypt," in König et al., *Ancient Libraries*, 25.

78. See Ryholt, "Libraries in Ancient Egypt," 26–31.

79. Ryholt, "Libraries in Ancient Egypt," 31.

36

Scribes and Libraries in the Ancient Near Eastern and Mediterranean Worlds

BCE make up the earliest collection discovered; it was stored in a box in a tomb in Thebes and appears to have been the private professional library of the deceased. It consists of medical-magical and magical texts but also has copies of the Tale of Sinuhe and the Tale of the Eloquent Peasant.[80] A private collection of a thirteenth-century Egyptian lector-priest is likewise eclectic; it contained literary narratives, military dispatches, onomastica, medical remedies, magical spells, a hymn to Sobek, and fragments of a dramatic or ritual composition.[81]

Ugarit

At Ugarit collections of tablets were found at several locations around the city.[82] Most of these tablet collections may be classified as archives, that is, collections of administrative documents. These archival collections were found in the Royal Palace, the House of Yabninu (the southern mansion), and the House of Rašap-'abu. In the Royal Palace five separate archives were discovered. Each archive was part of a complex of rooms; the rooms on the ground floor were where the scribes themselves worked and the most recent tablets were kept, while older tablets were stored in the rooms above. The Western Archive consisted of mostly economic and administrative texts in Ugaritic, with a few letters; the Eastern Archive contained foreign correspondence and economic and administrative texts; the Southern Archive stored texts concerned with relations with foreign powers, notably Hatti; and the Southwestern Archive contained economic-administrative and Hurrian cultic texts.

The fifth archive in the Palace, the Central Archive, was by far the largest; it consisted of three wings organized around a central courtyard. The tablets found in this archive were well preserved; most of them had been baked before storage, indicating a desire for long-term preservation. A clear differentiation could be made archaeologically between old texts, which were stored on the top floors, and later texts, which had been left

80. Ryholt, "Libraries in Ancient Egypt," 26.

81. See A. Lange, "The Qumran Dead Sea Scrolls—Library or Manuscript Corpus?," in *From 4QMMT to Resurrection: Mélanges qumraniens en hommage à Émile Puech*, ed. F. García Martínez et al., STDJ 61 (Leiden: Brill, 2006), 180.

82. For an exhaustive survey, see van Soldt, *Studies*, 47–232. Most of the following information is taken from this source, unless otherwise noted. See also, more conveniently, Yon, "Ugarit: History and Archaeology," 702–10.

on the ground floors. The northern wing of the Central Archive contained legal texts dealing with domestic affairs, especially land transfers; the eastern and southern wings housed economic texts. In these Royal Palace archives, found in situ, there is clear evidence of principles of classifying the documents by subject and language.

Private houses usually contained smaller, more mixed collections. The archives in the Houses of Yabninu and Rašap-'abu consisted of economic, administrative, and legal texts relating to the business interests of their owners. Other collections, however, contained a greater percentage of literary/religious works. The House of the Literary Texts, which was a two-story building with tablets stored on both levels, contained sixty-four school texts (i.e., lexical lists and alphabetic exercises), five omen and incantation texts, three pieces of wisdom literature, a hymn to the sun god, a medical text, and a fragment of the Babylonian flood story copied by the scribe Nuʿmî-Rašap. In addition, this building contained some documents of state, including international correspondence and business documents.[83]

The House of Literary Texts seems to have belonged to the scribal family of Nuʿmî-Rašap, since his name appears on the colophon of the Babylonian flood fragment, and the names of his sons and grandson appear on other colophons.[84] The house must have been used as a scribal school for the family, given the number of school exercises found there. It also housed an active olive oil mill, indicating that scribes participated in industries separate from the scribal profession.[85]

The tablet collections discovered at other residences also demonstrate specialized interests. The House of the Hurrian (or the Magician) Priest had two separate collections; the first contained religious and magical texts written in Ugaritic or alphabetic Hurrian, while the second, in another location, had lexical texts and a compilation of Lamashtu incantations, all in syllabic cuneiform. Once again we see an organizing principle, by subject and language, at work.

The House of the High Priest, located between the temples of Baal and Dagan on the acropolis, contained only religious and literary texts, most

---

83. C. Roche-Hawley, "Scribes, Houses and Neighborhoods at Ugarit," *UF* 44 (2013): 414–22.

84. Roche-Hawley, "Scribes, Houses and Neighborhoods," 421.

85. Roche-Hawley notes that scribes were particularly active in the oil industry at Ugarit ("Scribes, Houses and Neighborhoods," 425–26).

Scribes and Libraries in the Ancient Near Eastern and Mediterranean Worlds

famously the epics of Baal, Kirta, and Aqhat, copied by the scribe Ilimilku. This collection also had a high proportion of alphabetic Hurrian religious texts, testifying to the Hurrian religious influence at Ugarit.[86]

Therefore, at Ugarit, where, it should be emphasized, all the tablet collections were found in situ, in every building where tablets were found we find evidence for deliberate planning for archival storage, with segregation of texts by genre, script, and language. This is especially evident in the larger collections. The presence of a high proportion of lexical and literary texts in a collection probably indicates a place where scribes were trained. Private collections mixed together documentary and literary texts; the only collections that contained exclusively literary texts were in houses where it is thought priests resided, in keeping with their specialized interests.

Throughout the ancient Near East we have evidence both for large, state-supported libraries (e.g., Assurbanipal's), and smaller libraries associated with institutions like temples (the Sippar temple, the Tebtunis temple) and individual families (the *šangû Ninurta* family in Uruk). The archaeological context of these collections is important; none of these collections was housed in a separate monumental public building. This includes even the library of Assurbanipal, a deliberate collection made by a king to enhance his prestige. There is also no indication that any of these libraries were public; they were private, intended for the use of the people who worked in the temple or school in which they were located, or, in Assurbanipal's case, for the king himself and those with whom he chose to share it. This tradition of the private library (whether of an individual or state-sponsored) continues in the Hellenistic period; it is not until the Roman Empire that we encounter truly public libraries.

Scribes and Libraries in the Hellenistic and Roman Worlds

Scribes

In the Hellenistic and Roman worlds, scribes had a very different social position than scribes of the ancient Near East. In fifth- and fourth-century BCE Athens, from which our best evidence comes, scribes were relegated to the status of mere secretaries, subordinate to the magistrates and legisla-

---

86. Van Soldt, *Studies*, 213–18.

39

SCRIBES AND LIBRARIES

tors of Athenian democracy.[87] Citizens of Athens did not work as scribes; indeed, clerks and scribes were often slaves. For example, the central archive of Athens, the *Metroon*, established in the fifth century BCE, was staffed by public slaves trained as scribes.[88] However, in order to function as citizens Athenian men had to have at least a minimal level of literacy. The higher offices would have required correspondingly higher levels of literacy. This requirement contributed to a more widespread system of education that continued throughout the Greco-Roman world. The elite class, of course, enjoyed an extensive literary education.[89]

The Greek world also had a much more robust idea of authorship than in the ancient Near East.[90] While much of the literature from Mesopotamia, Egypt, Ugarit, and (as we shall see in ch. 3) ancient Israel, was anonymous and the product of centuries of shaping by scribes, Greek literature carried the authority of a known author, and scribes were expected to produce accurate copies of that author's work. Professional scribes were hired by book collectors to copy manuscripts from a master copy; while annotations such as glosses, exegetical notes, and variant readings could be included, they were made clearly separate from the author's text.[91] Even for the epics of Homer, now understood to be the product of oral tradition, the concept of authorship drove the scholars of the Museion to seek to establish an authoritative text for the *Iliad* and the *Odyssey*.[92] These factors (i.e., the concept of the author, the growth of citizen literacy, and the use of slaves as scribes) functioned to diminish the scribal profession in the Greek world, including the Hellenistic and Roman empires.

The Hellenistic empires, both the Ptolemies in Egypt and the Seleucids in Mesopotamia and Syria, inherited the scribal bureaucracies of their

---

87. D. Jaillard, "Memory, Writing and Authority," in *Writing the Bible: Scribalism and Script*, ed. P. Davies and T. Römer (London: Routledge, 2016), 23–24.

88. R. Thomas, "Writing, Reading, Public and Private 'Literacies,'" in König et al., *Ancient Libraries*, 38–39. See also her *Literacy and Orality in Ancient Greece* (New York: Cambridge University Press, 1992). The practice of training slaves as scribes continued into the Roman Empire; see G. Houston, *Inside Roman Libraries: Book Collections and Their Management in Antiquity* (Chapel Hill: University of North Carolina Press, 2014), 14.

89. Thomas, "Writing, Reading," 16.

90. Casson, *Libraries of the Ancient World*, 27.

91. G. Houston, "Papyrological Evidence for Book Collections and Libraries in the Roman Empire," in *Ancient Literacies: The Culture of Reading in Greece and Rome*, ed. W. Johnson and H. Parker (Oxford: Oxford University Press, 2009), 255.

92. L. Reynolds and N. Wilson, *Scribes and Scholars: A Guide to the Transmission of Greek and Latin Literature*, 4th ed. (Oxford: Oxford University Press, 2013), 8.

Scribes and Libraries in the Ancient Near Eastern and Mediterranean Worlds

predecessors, and added to them (more) scribes trained in Greek. The primary writing materials for Greek (and Latin) were wooden boards (*pinakes*), whitened boards (*leukomata*), ostraca, and papyrus, with some parchment. Evidence for scribal activity in the form of preserved collections such as the Elephantine papyri and the Oxyrhyncus papyri, the majority of which were penned by professional scribes, abounds in the Hellenistic world.[93] Most of these scribes, unfortunately, are anonymous. Even when a papyrus roll contains identifying material, at its end or less commonly at its beginning, the scribe's name is absent. As George Houston notes, identifying material typically contained the title of the book and the name of the author, but not the name of the scribe, the place and date of copying, or the name of the person who commissioned the copy.[94] This contrasts with the practice in Mesopotamia and Ugarit, where the scribe included that information in a colophon. For the most part, scribes in the Hellenistic world were anonymous, and their identities are lost to history.[95]

Libraries

Between the fifth and fourth centuries BCE Greek culture underwent a massive shift, from a primarily oral culture to a book-centered one.[96] Ex-

93. Elephantine is an island in the Nile opposite Aswan, just north of the first cataract, where collections of papyri in Egyptian (demotic and hieratic), Aramaic, Greek, Coptic, Arabic, and Latin were discovered. For the complete catalog, see B. Porten, *The Elephantine Papyri in English: Three Millennia of Cross-Cultural Continuity and Change*, DMOA 22 (Leiden: Brill, 1996). The Oxyrhyncus papyri were discovered in rubbish dumps outside the nome capital of Oxyrhyncus, about five days (by boat) south of Memphis. The papyrus fragments range in date from the first to the sixth century CE. About 70 percent of known literary papyri comes from Oxyrhyncus, so their importance cannot be overestimated. See http://www.papyrology.ox.ac.uk/POxy/.

94. Houston, *Inside Roman Libraries*, 7–8, 116.

95. A famous example of a high-ranking scribe whose name is known to us comes from the Zenon papyri, from the third century BCE, discovered at ancient Philadelphia in the Faiyum region of Egypt. Zenon was the secretary to one Apollonius, an official of Ptolemy II. The papyri record details of Zenon's work on behalf of Apollonius, including trade, legal proceedings, travel, and the running of an extensive Ptolemaic estate. See P. W. Pestman, *A Guide to the Zenon Archive* (Leiden: Brill, 1981). The papyri also mention other scribes: in Papyrus 59006 a scribe (γραμματεύς) near Gaza receives pickled fish, and P.Lond. 7.1930 mentions "scribes" as an occupation.

96. P. M. Pinto, "Men and Books in Fourth-Century BC Athens," in König et al., *Ancient Libraries*, 85.

SCRIBES AND LIBRARIES

tensive literary references to libraries come down to us in the classical literature beginning in the late fifth century BCE. The Greek word normally translated as "library," βιβλιοθήκη, can refer to a physical object used to hold papyrus rolls (such as a box, a basket, or a bucket), their storage place, the book collection itself, or the institution that preserves them.[97] Libraries began as private institutions, whether for individuals or groups. For example, Aristotle collected a large private library for the use of his school, the *Peripatos* (Strabo, *Geogr.* 13.1.54).[98] Since the library belonged personally to Aristotle, he left it to his successor, Theophrastus, who in turn left it to his pupil Neleus.[99] Aristotle's library was extensive enough to require a system of classification developed by Aristotle himself; this may have been the system of classification eventually used by the library of Alexandria.[100]

The library of Alexandria stands as the most famous library in the ancient world. It was most likely the creation of Ptolemy I Soter (303–282 BCE) and was expanded by his son and grandson, Ptolemy II Philadelphos (282–246 BCE) and Ptolemy III Euergetes (246–221 BCE).[101] The Alexan-

97. Posner, *Archives in the Ancient World*, 141.

98. Also Athenaeus, *Deipn.* 1.3a. Athenaeus also lists Polycrates of Samos, Pisistratus of Athens, Euclides of Athens, Nicorrates of Samos, and Euripides as owning private libraries.

99. Neleus, however, did not become the next head of the *Peripatos*, and took the library back to his hometown, Scepsis. According to Strabo, his heirs stored and then buried the books until they sold them to Apellicon of Teos, who had (imperfect) copies made. Apellicon's library was eventually seized by Sulla (first century BCE) and brought to Rome (Strabo, *Geogr.* 13.1.54). On the other hand, Athenaeus, *Deipn.* 1.3a, claims that Ptolemy II Philadelphos purchased Aristotle's library from Neleus for the Museion. See R. Blum, *Kallimachos: The Alexandrian Library and the Origins of Bibliography* (Madison: University of Wisconsin Press, 1991), 52–58.

100. M. Berti, "Greek and Roman Libraries in the Hellenistic Age," in *The Dead Sea Scrolls and the Concept of a Library*, ed. S. W. Crawford and C. Wassén, STDJ 116 (Leiden: Brill, 2016), 36. Demetrius of Phalerum, a pupil of Aristotle, is associated with the Alexandrian library under Ptolemy II in the oldest extant mention of the library, *Let. Aris.* 9. However, Diogenes Laertius, *Lives of the Philosophers* 5.78, indicates that Demetrius was an adviser to Ptolemy I (and was out of favor with Ptolemy II). Nina Collins claims that *Let. Aris.* 9 is correct, and that Demetrius was active in the reigns of both Ptolemies (*The Library in Alexandria and the Bible in Greek*, VTSup 82 [Leiden: Brill, 2000], 58). B. G. Wright III, however, argues that the Letter to Aristeas is not historically trustworthy, but rather legendary, and that Demetrius's activity was limited to the reign of Ptolemy I (*The Letter of Aristeas: "Aristeas to Philocrates" or "On the Translation of the Law of the Jews,"* CEJL [Berlin: de Gruyter, 2015], 111–17). Regardless of when he was active, Demetrius, as a pupil of Aristotle, would have been familiar with his library and its classification system.

101. Berti, "Greek and Roman Libraries," 35.

42

drian library was not created for its own sake; it was set up for the use of the scholars of the Museion, the scholarly institution founded by Ptolemy I, most likely on the advice of Demetrius of Phalerum. The Museion was a gathering of scholars (both of literature and of science) from all over the classical world, supported financially by the Ptolemies and later the Caesars. According to Strabo,

> The Museum [Museion] is part of the palaces. It has a public walk and a place furnished with seats, and a large hall, in which the men of learning, who belong to the Museum, take their common meal. This community possesses also property in common; and a priest, formerly appointed by the kings, but at present by Caesar, presides over the Museum. (*Geogr.* 17.1.8)[102]

The purpose of the Museion was scholarly research,[103] which helped the Ptolemies establish Alexandria as the foremost city of the Hellenistic world, the heir to Athens.

The library itself was housed in several rooms in the Museion complex, rooms that have never been certainly identified.[104] It had a "sister" collection located downtown in the Temple of Serapis. Estimates of the number of volumes in the library collection vary, from a low of 40,000 (Seneca, *Tranq.* 9.5) to a high of 700,000 (Aulus Gellius, *Noct. att.* 7.17.3; Ammianus Marcellinus, *Hist.* 22.16.13). Under Ptolemy II especially book collecting was wide-ranging and sometimes ruthless: Let. Aris. 9 indicates that the king desired to collect "all the books in the world" (a collection policy very similar to Assurbanipal's!) while Galen records that ships putting into the harbor at Alexandria were subject to mandatory book searches (Galen, *In Hippocratis librum iii epidemiarum commentarii* 3.17a.605–606). The Athenians also learned to their detriment the extent to which Ptolemy II would go to obtain books for his Museion's library. Athens had kept master

---

102. As quoted by Werrett, "Is Qumran a Library?," in Crawford and Wassén, *Concept of a Library*, 85.

103. Casson, *Libraries of the Ancient World*, 33, calls it the "ancient version of a think tank."

104. Casson, *Libraries of the Ancient World*, 34. See also C. Jacob, "Fragments of a History of Ancient Libraries," in König et al., *Ancient Libraries*, 64. I. Werrett notes the difficulty of identifying the architectural features of a Hellenistic library, which usually consisted of simple rooms with shelves (or baskets or buckets) for papyrus rolls ("Is Qumran a Library?," 79).

43

SCRIBES AND LIBRARIES

copies of the tragedies of Aeschylus, Sophocles, and Euripides from at least the fourth century BCE. Ptolemy II asked the Athenians to lend him the masters so that he could have copies made for his library; they did so for a guarantee of fifteen talents, an enormous sum at that time. Ptolemy paid the guarantee, kept the originals, and sent copies back to Athens (Galen, *In Hippocratis librum iii epidemiarum commentarii* 3.17a.607–608).

The extensive library of the Museion demanded a system of classification, for record keeping and ease of retrieval. Papyrus rolls were commonly stored with a tab (a *sillybon*) attached to one end with the author's name and ethnic.[105] Zenodotus, the librarian of the Museion under Ptolemy II, is credited with first arranging the authors (and partially their works) in alphabetical order.[106] Callimachus, a grammarian of the Museion in the time of Ptolemy II, made what is evidently a classification of the entire collection in his famous *Pinakes*, "Tables of those who distinguished themselves in all branches of learning and their writings." The *Pinakes* was 120 books long, of which only a few fragments survive.[107] Callimachus divided Greek authors into classes and subclasses; within the classes and subclasses the authors were arranged alphabetically; brief biographical data was entered; the author's works were arranged alphabetically by title; and the first words of a work and its number of lines were listed. The *Pinakes* is a key marker of the importance of book culture in the Hellenistic world; knowledge was now transmitted via the written word, and the possession of book rolls (and an orderly record of them) was an indication of high culture.

Although the Museion of Alexandria and its library had no real rivals in the Hellenistic world, it did spark imitation in the various Hellenistic kingdoms. Antiochus III (242–187 BCE) established a library at Antioch-on-the-Orontes; all that is known of it is that its first librarian was Euphorion of Chalcis.[108] The library at Pergamum, founded by Eumenes II of the Attalid dynasty in the mid-second century BCE (Strabo, *Geogr.* 13.1.54), contained approximately two hundred thousand rolls. As at Alexandria, it has been difficult to identify the actual library rooms at Pergamum; the excavators tentatively identified four adjacent rooms in the Athena sanc-

---

105. Given the duplication of names in the ancient world, to distinguish between authors it was essential to use the designation "of [geographic name]." At least ten of these *sillyba* survive on literary works. See Houston, *Inside Roman Libraries*, 10n39.

106. Berti, "Greek and Roman Libraries," 41.

107. Berti, "Greek and Roman Libraries," 39–41. Berti notes that nowhere is it claimed that the *Pinakes* was a catalog of the Alexandrian library.

108. Casson, *Libraries of the Ancient World*, 48.

tuary as the reading room and storage sections of the library, based on the presence of sockets in the walls used for supporting bookshelves, and a podium around the walls in the main room.[109] However, that identification has been challenged on several fronts in recent years, so that the location of the Pergamum library remains uncertain.[110] That the actual physical location in the building ruins of the two most famous libraries of antiquity, Alexandria and Pergamum, remains undiscovered demonstrates the difficulty of identifying Hellenistic libraries by their architectural features, a fact that is important when it comes to identifying a library complex in the ruins of Qumran.

The Romans inherited and expanded the book culture of the Greeks. In the second and first centuries BCE Roman elites such as Scipio, Cicero, the elder and younger Lucullus, Varro, and Atticus collected fine libraries, often so large that they required a staff (of slaves) to manage.[111] This staff took care of copying, shelving, reshelving, repairing, and cataloging the book rolls in the library.[112]

At Herculaneum, a private library from the first century CE was discovered in situ, in the so-called Villa of the Papyri. Book rolls from this library were discovered in four different rooms. The main library room was a small room in the center of the villa (room V), which had wooden shelves lining the walls and a double-sided wooden *armaria*, or cupboard.[113] The other three rooms had papyrus rolls in portable wooden cases or simply in piles on the floor. So far, 1,850 separate items have been identified, ranging in date from the early third century BCE to the first century CE. The collection consisted of Greek philosophical works and Roman (Latin) literature, with an emphasis on the works of Epicurus and the Epicurean philosopher Philodemus of Gadara.[114] The dates of the Herculaneum papyri give important information about the useful life of a papyrus roll; they could evidently remain in use for two centuries or more.[115]

---

109. G. Coqueugniot, "Where Was the Royal Library of Pergamum? An Institution Found and Lost Again," in König et al., *Ancient Libraries*, 110–16.

110. Coqueugniot, "Where Was the Royal Library," 118–23.

111. Casson, *Libraries of the Ancient World*, 66–70.

112. Houston, *Inside Roman Libraries*, 217–30, and references there. Houston supplies the titles of these staff members, such as the *glutinatores*, who repaired papyrus rolls.

113. Casson, *Libraries of the Ancient World*, 74; Werrett, "Is Qumran a Library?," 97.

114. G. Houston, "The Non-Philodemus Book Collection in the Villa of the Papyri," in König et al., *Ancient Libraries*, 183–208; Houston, *Inside Roman Libraries*, 88–92.

115. Houston, "Papyrological Evidence," 250; Houston, *Inside Roman Libraries*, 121, 175.

SCRIBES AND LIBRARIES

The Romans are credited with launching the first truly public libraries in the ancient world. Asinius Pollio established the first public library in Rome, followed by Augustus, who founded a library on the Palatine hill. Others followed, notably Vespasian, who built a library as part of the Temple of Peace at the end of the First Jewish War (66–73 CE). Houston notes that Titus, Vespasian's son and the general victorious over the Jews, seized the Jerusalem temple library as part of the spoils of victory (Josephus, *J.W.* 7.150, 162), and suggests that those scrolls may have been stored in the Temple of Peace.[116] Trajan included a library in his bath complex in his new forum.[117] Outside Rome, four libraries have been identified by their dedicatory inscriptions: the library of Celsus in Ephesus, the forum library in Philippi, the library of Pantainos at Athens, and the library of Rogantinius at Timgad in modern Algeria.[118]

Because of their public nature, these libraries are monumental buildings built for the express purpose of reading and storing book rolls, in contrast to the anonymous rooms of the Hellenistic libraries. Therefore, the architectural features of libraries from the Roman period can be identified with greater ease. Roman libraries had two separate sections (sometimes, in larger libraries, separate rooms), one for Greek and one for Latin book rolls. Niches in the walls contained movable *armaria* (sometimes highly decorated) for book roll storage. The wall niches could be on two levels (e.g., Trajan's library, the library of Celsus), or one (e.g., the Rogantinius library). A podium ran in front of the niches, on which one stood to retrieve book rolls. The niches also housed statues of deities or of the human patrons of the library. The most important feature for the identification of library rooms in the Roman period is the presence of wall niches.[119]

What of the content of these libraries? For the most part (with the exception of a discovery like the Villa of the Papyri) we are reliant on chance literary references, such as Cicero's in *Fin.* 3.2.7–10, in which Cicero, visiting the library of his friend the young Lucullus, mentions that he came to borrow some commentaries by Aristotle (*commentarios Aristotelios*), and discovered there his friend Marcus Cato, surrounded by piles of books on Stoicism (*multis circumfusum Stoicorum libris*). Thus we

116. Houston, *Inside Roman Libraries*, 37n114.

117. Casson, *Libraries of the Ancient World*, 80–88; L. L. Johnson, *The Hellenistic and Roman Library* (PhD diss.; Ann Arbor, MI: University Microfilms International, 1984), 84–85.

118. Johnson, *Hellenistic and Roman Library*, 11–43; Werrett, "Is Qumran a Library?," 81.

119. Werrett, "Is Qumran a Library?," 94; Johnson, *Hellenistic and Roman Library*, 153–60.

46

Scribes and Libraries in the Ancient Near Eastern and Mediterranean Worlds

know that Lucullus's library contained works of Aristotle and the Stoics. Recently George Houston has made a study of book lists from, and smaller collections within, the vast corpus of the Oxyrhyncus papyri, from which he extracts evidence for personal book collections in Egypt from the first-fourth centuries CE.[120] Houston's study shows that collectors had a clear preference for classical authors rather than contemporary ones. Collections could be general or more specialized, the most specialized being a small collection of astrological texts, evidently for professional use.[121] They range in number from five to well over a thousand papyrus rolls. The following authors appear again and again:

> Poets: Homer, Hesiod, Pindar, Callimachus
> Tragedians: Aeschylus, Sophocles, Euripides
> Writers of Comedies: Aristophanes, Menander
> Philosophers: Plato, Aristotle, and their disciples
> Historians: Herodotus, Thucydides, Xenophon
> Orators: Demosthenes[122]

A picture thus emerges of a fairly uniform core of elite literature in the Greco-Roman period, at least in the Greek-speaking east.

Conclusions

From the survey presented in this chapter, it is evident that to be a scribe was to belong to a profession that operated at all levels of society and was integral to the functioning of that society in all its aspects: government, commerce, diplomacy, and cult. Scribes with the highest level of training became part of the elite and, particularly in Mesopotamia, Egypt, and Ugarit, worked with the priests (and, in some cases, *were* the priests) to ensure the smooth operation of the cult.[123] Elite scribes were multilingual; they could read and write in several languages, depending upon their location and professional expertise. Finally, there is clear evidence that part

---

120. Houston, "Papyrological Evidence."
121. Houston, *Inside Roman Libraries*, 171–73.
122. Houston, "Papyrological Evidence," 238–39.
123. This was not the case in the Greco-Roman world, where scribes were not part of the elite governing class, although scribes such as Zenon could be highly regarded professionals.

SCRIBES AND LIBRARIES

of a scholar-scribe's work in the ancient Near East was the transmission of the literary texts of their society, often with revision and updating.

Scribal education took place in both familial and school settings, with an apprenticeship component. Scribes often belonged to one family, at least in Mesopotamia, Egypt, and Ugarit, where father-son (and even grandson) pairs of scribes recur. In Mesopotamia and Ugarit, scribes signed their work in colophons, while in Egypt and the Greco-Roman world scribes usually remained anonymous.

The appearance of the library, in the sense of a book collection consisting primarily of literary works, occurred relatively late in the history of the ancient Near East; most early tablet collections are primarily archival, with a few literary texts included. The earliest true library would seem to be Assurbanipal's. The Houses of Life in Egypt produced collections of sacred texts for the use of the temples throughout Egypt. Private individuals also could possess small collections of literary works. It was not until the Hellenistic and Roman periods that a surge in book collecting, and thus in libraries, occurs.

Until the Roman period it is difficult to identify a library room or rooms in the archaeological remains, unless the tablets or book rolls were found in situ. Library rooms were simple and unmarked; they may have had shelves along the walls to store tablets or rolls, and sometimes a low bench for reading or copying. Larger libraries could consist of several rooms, with one serving as a scriptorium and the others for storage. However, in small private libraries tablets or book rolls were simply stored in baskets or buckets in the living quarters. In larger libraries, systems of classification become evident; the best evidence for a classification system comes from Alexandria, where Zenodotus used an alphabetic system. Callimachus's *Pinakes* may demonstrate an even more elaborate classification system.

In the Roman period the architectural features of libraries become easier to distinguish. Roman libraries were built with wall niches, into which shelving or *armaria* were fitted for book roll storage. Usually a podium ran around the room in front of the niches, to allow access to the higher shelves. A library could also contain statues of gods or patrons, and a dedicatory inscription.

With that overview in mind, the next chapter turns to the evidence for scribes and libraries in Israel and Judah from the Iron Age through the Second Temple period.

CHAPTER 3

Scribes and Libraries in Ancient Israel

The wisdom of the scribe depends on the opportunity of leisure; only the one who has little business can become wise.

Ben Sira 38:24

In the previous chapter I surveyed evidence for scribes and libraries in the ancient Near East and in the Hellenistic and Roman worlds. In this chapter I narrow the focus to biblical Israel, beginning with the Iron Age kingdoms of Israel and Judah until the Babylonian destruction in 587 BCE, continuing through the Persian and early Hellenistic periods, and concluding with the Second Jewish Revolt against Rome (135 BCE). I exclude the Qumran evidence (with the exception of a few pertinent texts), which I deal with in ch. 4. In the first section of the chapter I survey the epigraphic and literary evidence for scribes and writing, while in the second section I look at the archaeological evidence for book collections, archives, and libraries.

Scribes and Writing in Iron Age Israel and Judah

The societies of Mesopotamia and Egypt were ancient and well established, with many large population centers, capital cities, and major temples where scribes could ply their trade. Even Ugarit was a bustling palace and port city, with an estimated population of six to eight thousand.[1] The Iron Age kingdoms of Israel and Judah, even at their peaks, were comparatively smaller and poorer. Our evidence for the role of scribes in those kingdoms is correspondingly less.[2]

---

1. M. Yon, "Ugarit, History and Archaeology," *ABD* 4:705.

2. D. Jamieson-Drake, *Scribes and Schools in Monarchic Judah: A Socio-Archeological Approach,* SWBA 9 (Sheffield: JSOT Press, 1991), 153, emphasizes this point, noting that

SCRIBES AND LIBRARIES

Although we know very little concerning the training of scribes in ancient Israel or Judah,[3] we can surmise, from the comparative data surveyed in ch. 2, that Israelite or Judahite scribes would have received the same type of training, in school or family settings, as Mesopotamian or Egyptian scribes.[4] Those who went beyond mastery of the basics of the scribal craft would likewise have specialized in the religious/cultural traditions of their society and would have received advanced training in foreign languages and diplomacy.[5] We do know that professional scribes were active in ancient Israel and Judah from both epigraphic evidence and biblical references.[6]

The epigraphic or inscriptional evidence from ancient Israel is slim compared to that of Mesopotamia or Egypt. However, we do have some remains of monumental inscriptions, inscribed ostraca, seals and bullae, graffiti, inscribed jar handles, and other ephemera, all of which point to the activity of scribes in the kingdoms of Israel and Judah. The script in use in that time period was the ancient Israelite script, also known as Old Hebrew or Paleo-Hebrew.[7]

there were ten times as many urban sites in Mesopotamia as in Judah, the public works for Egypt and Mesopotamia were hugely disparate from those of Judah, and Jerusalem at its height was only 15 percent of the size of central cities in Mesopotamia.

3. Note the subtitle of J. L. Crenshaw's *Education in Ancient Israel: Across the Deadening Silence* (New York: Doubleday, 1998). On p. 4 Crenshaw states, "What do we know about education in ancient Israel? Not very much." On the other hand, A. Lemaire has argued for widespread schools and literacy in Iron Age Israel and Judah on the basis of the epigraphic evidence (*Les écoles et la formation de la Bible dans l'ancien Israël*, OBO 39 [Fribourg: Editions Universitaires; Göttingen: Vandenhoeck & Ruprecht, 1981]). Lemaire places particular weight on the discoveries of abecedaries in several remote locations in ancient Israel and Judah (7). See, however, the counterarguments to this proposal in Crenshaw, *Education in Ancient Israel*, 100–108; and Susan Niditch, *Oral World and Written Word: Ancient Israelite Literature* (Louisville: Westminster John Knox, 1996), 45.

4. See C. Rollston, "Scribal Education in Ancient Israel: The Old Hebrew Epigraphic Evidence," *BASOR* 344 (2006): 47–74, who calls attention to the evidence for scribal training in the paleography and orthography of the Iron Age Hebrew inscriptions.

5. David Carr has called this training "an oral-written process of enculturation that helped socialize and set apart . . . a scribal elite" (*Writing on the Tablet of the Heart: Origins of Scripture and Literature* [New York: Oxford University Press, 2005], 131).

6. For surveys of the epigraphical evidence see C. Rollston, *Writing and Literacy in the World of Ancient Israel: Epigraphic Evidence from the Iron Age*, ABS 11 (Atlanta: Society of Biblical Literature, 2010); and S. Ahituv, *Echoes from the Past: Hebrew and Cognate Inscriptions from the Biblical Period* (Jerusalem: Carta, 2008).

7. See the various studies by F. M. Cross on ancient Israelite paleography collected in *Leaves from an Epigrapher's Notebook: Collected Papers in Hebrew and West Semitic Palaeogra-*

50

Scribes and Libraries in Ancient Israel

Very little epigraphic evidence remains from the tenth through the early eighth century BCE. What little there is includes the Gezer Calendar, a harvest calendar whose script can be dated to the tenth century BCE, and the Kuntillet 'Ajrud graffiti from the early eighth century BCE. Most of our evidence comes from later in the Iron Age. The Siloam Tunnel inscription, carved on a wall slab found in situ in the tunnel itself, describes the engineering process that created it (cf. 2 Chr 32:30). It dates to the late eighth century BCE. Collections of ostraca were found in the Israelite capital city of Samaria and the Judean fortresses of Arad and Lachish. The Samaria ostraca, dated to the mid-eighth century BCE, are administrative documents recording the delivery of wine and oil to the city. The Arad ostraca, dating from the tenth to the sixth century BCE, are very fragmentary, but also appear to be administrative documents as well as letters; the largest single group comes from one room and belonged to the recipient of the letters, Eliashib ben Ishiyahu.[8] The Lachish ostraca are letters and administrative documents from the late eighth century BCE, the most important of which are military communications regarding the state of various Judean cities during the invasion of Sennacherib in the reign of Hezekiah (2 Kgs 18:13 // Isa 36:1). The word ספר appears on Lachish ostracon 3 (lines 9, 11), where it indicates either the title "scribe"[9] or the word "letter, document."[10]

Bullae and seals are important artifacts attesting to the presence of scribes in Iron Age Israel. When a contract such as a deed, a will, or a marriage arrangement was composed, it was written out by a scribe on papyrus or skin,[11] rolled up and tied with a cord, and then sealed by pressing the owner's stamp seal into a lump of wet clay fitted over the cord. This process is described succinctly in Jer 32:10-11, in which Jeremiah purchases a field from his cousin Hanamel. The impression left in the clay is called a "bulla," and it survives even after the organic material of the written document

---

phy and Epigraphy, HSS 51 (Winona Lake, IN: Eisenbrauns, 2003); and A. Yardeni, *The Book of Hebrew Script: History, Palaeography, Script Styles, Calligraphy and Design* (Jerusalem: Carta, 2002). "Paleo-Hebrew" better refers to the developed form of the ancient Israelite script in use in the Second Temple period, after it had been replaced with the Aramaic (Assyrian) square script, and became a script used for religious and/or nationalistic purposes.

8. Ahituv, *Echoes from the Past*, 92.

9. Preferred by F. M. Cross, "A Literate Soldier: Lachish Letter III," in *Leaves from an Epigrapher's Notebook*, 129-32.

10. N. H. Tur-Sinai, *The Lachish Ostraca* (Jerusalem: Bialik Institute, 1987), 53-55.

11. Papyrus seems to have been the most common formal writing material in ancient Israel and Judah, although skin (treated animal hide) was also used. See Rollston, *Writing and Literacy*, 74-79.

SCRIBES AND LIBRARIES

perishes. One important collection of bullae was discovered by Yigal Shiloh in the city of David excavations in Jerusalem.[12] These bullae date to the late seventh and early sixth centuries BCE (right before the destruction of the city in 587 BCE by the Babylonians), and most likely were part of an archive. One bulla in particular, no. 2, deserves mention: it preserves the name of Gemaryahu son of Shaphan, a man identified as a scribe, from a scribal family, in Jer 36:10.[13]

Since almost no papyrus or skin inscribed material has survived from the Iron Age, a papyrus fragment dating to the first half of the seventh century BCE found in the caves of Wadi Murabba'at is an important exception. The papyrus is a palimpsest, a papyrus sheet that has been reused by overwriting: a first text was written, then scraped off the papyrus and replaced with a second text. In the case of the Murabba'at palimpsest the first text does not survive; the second text consists of a list of names.[14] This reuse indicates that papyrus was an expensive commodity in Iron Age Judah.

Finally, a number of abecedaries (texts containing the letters of the Hebrew alphabet) have been discovered throughout the region, at Lachish, Kadesh-barnea, Khirbet el-Qom, Aroer, Kuntillet 'Ajrud, 'Izbet Ṣarṭah, Arad, Shiqmona, and Tel Zayit.[15] These abecedaries point to at least a rudimentary ability to write, diffused across a fairly wide area. However, they are not indicative of a high level of education throughout the population and the existence of a large network of schools, as Lemaire has suggested.[16]

---

12. Y. Shoham, "A Group of Hebrew Bullae from Yigal Shiloh's Excavations in the City of David," in *Ancient Jerusalem Revealed*, ed. H. Geva (Jerusalem: Israel Exploration Society, 1994), 55–61.

13. Shoham, "Group of Hebrew Bullae," 57.

14. J. T. Milik, "Palimpseste," in *Les grottes de Murabba'ât*, by M. Baillet et al., 2 vols., DJD 2 (Oxford: Clarendon, 1961), 1:93–100; 2: pl. 28. In October 2016 the Israel Antiquities Authority revealed a papyrus fragment claimed to have been looted from a Judean Desert cave. The fragment, written in an ancient Israelite script dating to the seventh century BCE, records the sending of wineskins from the country to Jerusalem (?). If authentic, this papyrus fragment would be more evidence for writing and literacy in ancient Judah. See antiquities.org.il // Press Releases.

15. M. Haran, "On the Diffusion of Literacy and Schools in Ancient Israel," in *Congress Volume: Jerusalem, 1986*, ed. J. A. Emerton, VTSup 40 (Leiden: Brill, 1988), 86. For the Tel Zayit abecedary, see R. Tappy et al., "An Abecedary of the Mid-Tenth Century B.C.E. from the Judaean Shephelah," *BASOR* 344 (2006): 5–46.

16. Lemaire, *Écoles*. For a critique of Lemaire's thesis, see Haran, "On the Diffusion of Literacy," 85–91, who has argued that there is no necessary connection between many of the abecedaries and schools.

Rather, some of these abecedaries may have had apotropaic or magical functions, as Niditch suggested.[17] The stone on which the Tel Zayit abecedary was inscribed was (secondarily?) used in the construction of a wall, possibly of a pillared house, making it unlikely that it was the remnant of a school at the site.[18]

Writing did have magical or apotropaic significance in Iron Age Israel and Judah, as is demonstrated by the function of the oldest inscribed biblical text now known, the Ketef Hinnom silver amulets.[19] The amulets are inscribed silver plaques, rolled into tight cylinders, and discovered inside a burial chamber on the outskirts of Jerusalem. Their paleography dates to the second half of the seventh century BCE. The first amulet does not contain an exact biblical quotation, but uses language similar to phrases in Exodus and Deuteronomy. The second amulet contains a quotation of the Aaronic Blessing found in Num 6:24-26:

> Yahweh bless you and keep you; Yahweh make his face to shine upon you and be gracious to you; Yahweh lift up his countenance upon you, and give you peace. (my trans.)

The texts of the amulets invoke divine protection and serve an apotropaic purpose. They were not meant to be read; they were meant to be worn to ward off evil for the wearer. The amulets do give us solid evidence that texts later deemed "biblical" already existed in some form in the late Iron Age and were imbued with religious significance.

The inscriptional material from Iron Age Israel and Judah indicates that the kingdoms had an active scribal presence. Some scribes worked as lower-level bureaucrats (the Samaria ostraca), while some were employed by the military for their communications (the Lachish ostraca). Still others were high-level craftsmen who worked for the wealthy who could afford their services (the Ketef Hinnom amulets). Next we turn to the biblical literature that has a literary setting in the preexilic period to see if we can supplement the epigraphic evidence for scribal activity in the kingdoms of Israel and Judah.[20]

17. Niditch, *Oral World and Written Word*, 45, who draws a parallel with Aramaic incantation bowls and Greek magical papyri.

18. Tappy et al., "Abecedary of the Mid-Tenth Century B.C.E.," 6, 22.

19. G. Barkay et al., "The Amulets from Ketef Hinnom: A New Edition and Evaluation," *BASOR* 334 (2004): 41-71.

20. By emphasizing the preexilic *setting* of this literature I am trying to separate the

SCRIBES AND LIBRARIES

The biblical references to "scribe" point to the royal court and the temple as the primary loci for scribal activity. The word ספר/סופר occurs numerous times in the HB, usually describing a particular person as an officer in the royal court and/or the temple, which were closely allied throughout this period.

The passages are as follows:

2 Sam 8:17: In a list of David's officials, Seraiah is listed as "scribe."

2 Sam 20:25: In another list of David's officials, following the rebellion of Absalom, Sheva is listed as "scribe."

1 Kgs 4:3: In a list of Solomon's officials, Elihoreph and Ahijah are listed as "scribes."

2 Kgs 12:11: During the reign of Jehoash, repairs to the temple are funded by donations; these donations are collected by the "king's scribe" (ספר המלך) and the high priest. This is the only time the exact phrase ספר המלך occurs in the Hebrew Bible.[21]

2 Kgs 18:18, 37; 19:2 // Isa 36:3, 22; 37:2: In the reign of Hezekiah, during the negotiations with the Assyrian officials besieging Jerusalem, Shebna the scribe is one of the king's officials sent to negotiate. The passage indicates that Shebna, along with the other officials, understands and speaks Aramaic as well as Hebrew (2 Kgs 18:26 // Isa 36:11).

2 Kgs 22:3, 8, 9, 10, 12: In the reign of Josiah, Josiah sends Shaphan the scribe to the temple, where he is told about the "book of the law" that has been discovered. Shaphan is subsequently among those who are sent to the prophet Huldah to authenticate the book.

2 Kgs 25:19 // Jer 52:25: Among those put to death by the Babylonians in 587 BCE is a figure described as "the scribe, commander of the army, who mustered the people of the land."

Ps 45:2(1): The psalmist describes his tongue as like "a skilled pen of a scribe."

---

setting from the date of composition. All of the biblical literature underwent a long period of composition and redaction, and most books did not reach their final form until the Persian period, if not later. The books of Chronicles, of course, are Persian period compositions; their evidence will appear in the next section on the Persian and early Hellenistic periods. However, many of the biblical books reflect what at least was historical memory of what the kingdoms of Israel and Judah were like in the preexilic period, and thus may cautiously be used as a supplement to the epigraphic evidence.

21. N. Fox, *In the Service of the King: Officialdom in Ancient Israel and Judah* (Cincinnati: Hebrew Union College Press, 2000), 97.

Isa 33:18: In an oracle predicting a golden future for Jerusalem, the prophet asks, "Where is a (foreign) scribe, one who weighs the tribute?" (my trans.).

Jer 8:8: In this important passage, Jeremiah inveighs against "the false pen of the scribes," who have turned the Torah of Yahweh into falsehood.[22]

Jer 36:10: In the story of the scroll read in the temple, Baruch reads the scroll containing Jeremiah's words in the temple complex, in the office (לשכה) of Gemariah the son of Shaphan, who is identified as a scribe. This facet of the scribal role, reading aloud what has been written down, will also be seen later in the figure of Ezra, who reads to the people from the law of Moses.

Jer 36:12, 20, 21: After hearing Baruch, Micaiah son of Gemariah son of Shaphan goes to the king's palace with the scroll, to the "לשכה of the scribe" (NRSV: secretary's chamber), who is identified as Elishama. The scroll is left in Elishama's office until the king sends for it.

Jer 36:26, 32: In these verses, Baruch is first identified as a scribe. Although Baruch was not identified earlier as a scribe, he acted as one, taking down Jeremiah's words at dictation and then reading them aloud in the temple.[23]

Jer 37:15, 20: Jeremiah is imprisoned in the house of Jonathan the scribe, which has become a prison during the siege of Jerusalem.

Nah 3:17: In an oracle against Assyria, the prophet describes Assyria's scribes as swarms of locusts, pointing to their numbers but also to their ephemerality.

Another reference that should be taken into account is in Prov 25:1, where "the men of Hezekiah" are credited with copying a collection of Solomon's proverbs. These must be scribes associated with Hezekiah's court.

---

22. Many scholars understand this passage to refer to the book of Deuteronomy; see K. van der Toorn, *Scribal Culture and the Making of the Hebrew Bible* (Cambridge: Harvard University Press, 2007), 35. W. Schniedewind, *How the Bible Became a Book: The Textualization of Ancient Israel* (Cambridge: Cambridge University Press, 2004), 115, however, argues that Jeremiah is making a critique of any written text that claims authority over against the oral word of the prophets.

23. D. Orton, *The Understanding Scribe: Matthew and the Apocalyptic Ideal*, JSNTSup 25 (Sheffield: JSOT Press, 1989), 45 and 190n19, suggests that Seraiah, Baruch's brother, was also a scribe, since Jeremiah instructs him to take one of his scrolls to Babylon and there read it aloud. He argues that it is "very likely" that the family of Neraiah was a scribal family.

SCRIBES AND LIBRARIES

A second term to take into consideration is שׁטֵר, usually translated as "official." These figures have varying functions; in Exod 5 the word refers to the Egyptian overseers of the Israelites; in Deuteronomy it refers to the minor tribal officials (e.g., Deut 1:15; 29:9; 31:28), while in the historical books the term often has a military function (e.g., Josh 1:10; 3:2). It is likely that some of these individuals performed scribal functions as well.[24]

What can we gather from this list of references? First, scribes are most often associated with the royal court (i.e., David, Solomon, Hezekiah, Josiah, Jehoiakim, and Zedekiah); in Jeremiah scribes are located in both the court (the לשׁכה of Elishama is located in the royal palace) and the temple (the לשׁכה of Gemariah is located in the temple complex). The scribes of the court were probably in charge of the bureaucracy of government, while the temple scribes assisted the priests and Levites with the administration of the temple cult. The two groups of scribes do not appear to be discrete; Gemariah's לשׁכה is in the temple, but he is in the palace when Jeremiah's words are reported to him (Jer 36:10, 12).

It is also evident that the scribal profession was often found in families, as was the case in Mesopotamia, Egypt, and Ugarit. This is illustrated by the Shaphan family, appearing in both 2 Kings and Jeremiah, whose activity extends from the reign of Josiah through that of Zedekiah.[25] Shaphan is first introduced with his patrimony in 2 Kgs 22:3; and in 2 Kgs 22:12, "Ahikam the son of Shaphan" appears.[26] Ahikam reappears in Jer 26:24 as a protector of Jeremiah. In Jer 36:10, Gemariah the scribe is identified as the son of Shaphan; the son is working for Jehoiakim, as Shaphan worked for Jehoiakim's father Josiah. Jeremiah 29:3 mentions another son of Shaphan, Elasah, who is sent by Zedekiah as an emissary to King Nebuchadnezzar.

In the third generation of the Shaphan family, Gedaliah son of Ahikam son of Shaphan is appointed as the governor of conquered Judah by the Babylonians, indicating the high status of the Shaphan family (2 Kgs 25:22; Jer 40:5). Finally, in Jer 36:11, Micaiah (who, however, is not identified as a

---

24. Carr argues that this was the case, interpreting the term as "literate officials" (*Writing on the Tablet,* 118). A. Demsky, "Scribe," *EncJud* 18:212, suggests the translation "recorder." The word שׁטֵר is commonly translated in the LXX as γραμματεύς, and in the Peshitta as ספרא, also indicating a scribal meaning in the root. Further, the Akkadian and Aramaic cognates mean "to write."

25. J. A. Dearman, "My Servants the Scribes: Composition and Context in Jeremiah 36," *JBL* 109 (1990): 403–21.

26. As Dearman notes, the father of Ahikam might be a different Shaphan, but it is more parsimonious to assume it is one family ("My Servants the Scribes," 406n8).

56

Scribes and Libraries in Ancient Israel

scribe) the son of Gemariah son of Shaphan hears Jeremiah's words being read by Baruch in the temple complex in his father's לשכה, and reports them to his father Gemariah and the other officials who are then in the palace. Thus we find three generations of one scribal family, in the employ of palace and temple.[27]

What the biblical references do not tell us is where the literary activity (as opposed to the daily activities associated with the government and cult) of Iron Age Israel was taking place.[28] We receive two hints in the verses listed above. First, in Jer 8:8, the prophet rails against "the false pen of the scribes" who turn the Torah of Yahweh into falsehood. This implies scribal activity in the transmission of a written law code, something of which Jeremiah disapproves. If, as some have suggested, this written law code was a form of Deuteronomy, then the fact that the "book of the law" that was "discovered" in the temple in Josiah's reign (2 Kgs 22) was probably some form of Deuteronomy is an important datum. This location in the temple would imply literary activity taking place there as early as the reign of Josiah. Second, the Prov 25:1 reference to Hezekiah's men copying Solomon's proverbs suggests literary activity centered in the royal court.[29] Thus we have two probable locations for literary activity, the temple and court, which coincides with what we know from Mesopotamia, Egypt, and Ugarit. But there may have been others; our evidence is too sparse to be certain.[30]

27. We also have bullae associated with this family in the Shiloh collection from sixth-century BCE Jerusalem. Bulla no. 2 belongs to Gemaryahu son of Shaphan, while bulla no. 32 belongs to Azriqam (son of) Mikhayahu. It is possible that this Mikhayahu (מכיהו) is the Micaiah (מכיהו) of Jer 36:11. See Shoham, "Group of Hebrew Bullae," 57–58.

28. There are differing opinions on when the literary traditions that eventually became the books of the HB began to be written. P. Davies takes a minimalist position, arguing that there is no solid evidence for any literary activity in Israel or Judah before the Persian period (*Scribes and Schools: The Canonization of the Hebrew Scriptures* [Louisville: Westminster John Knox, 1998], 61–63). Schniedewind takes a maximalist view, positing a move in the late eighth century BCE sponsored by Hezekiah to collect the literary traditions of Israel and Judah (*How the Bible Became a Book,* 68). Niditch emphasizes the orality of preexilic Israelite and Judean culture and how literacy was mixed with orality rather than supplanting it (*Oral World and Written Word*).

29. Schniedewind, *How the Bible Became a Book,* 75.

30. R. Wilson rightly queries those like Schniedewind or van der Toorn who would place all scribal activity in the royal court or the temple: Why would the government or the temple have been interested in preserving oracles that were hostile to them? He suggests that there must have been other venues (circles of disciples?) where the recording and shaping of prophetic traditions was taking place. See R. Wilson, "Orality and Writing in the Creation of

SCRIBES AND LIBRARIES

Following the destruction of the kingdom of Judah by the Babylonians in 587 BCE, Israel and Judah lost even their quasi-independent status and became parts of the empires that controlled their territories, that is, the Neo-Babylonian, the Persian, and the Hellenistic kingdoms. Since evidence for the activity of scribes in the (short-lived) Neo-Babylonian period is nonexistent, we next turn to the Persian period.

Scribes and Writing in the Persian Period (539–332 BCE)

The Persian Empire at its height stretched from the borders of India to Egypt.[31] The territories of the kingdoms of Israel and Judah were now part of its Transeuphrates satrapy (*ebir Nâri*); Samaria and later Yehud were provinces (*medinah*) within the satrapy, with their own governors.[32] The language of government, commerce, and diplomacy in the western parts of the empire was Aramaic, while local languages such as Hebrew continued in use within their respective ethnic communities. The common writing media were the more perishable skin, papyrus, and waxed wooden writing boards, rather than the indestructible tablet.[33] Because of the fragile nature of these writing materials, we have only a few archaeological discoveries of archives from this period, although several caches of seals and bullae, the remains of archives, have been recovered.

Exilic Prophetic Literature," in *Worship, Women and War: Essays in Honor of Susan Niditch*, ed. J. Collins et al. (Providence: Society of Biblical Literature, 2015), 91. I would like to thank Professor Wilson for sharing his article with me prior to publication.

31. The bureaucracy of this huge empire required the employment of innumerable scribes at all levels of government. The book of Esther, set in the Persian capital of Susa, mentions scribes copying letters and sending them throughout the empire (3:12; 8:9).

32. P. Briant, *From Cyrus to Alexander: A History of the Persian Empire*, trans. P. Daniels (Winona Lake, IN: Eisenbrauns, 2002), 487–88. In recent years the explosion in Samaritan studies has shown that Samaria and Yehud, far from being culturally distinct and politically estranged from each other, shared a common culture, which is demonstrated by material remains, languages, scripts, and onomastica, and that they maintained diplomatic ties with each other, as is shown by, e.g., the Elephantine documents. See G. Knoppers, *Jews and Samaritans: The Origins and History of Their Early Relations* (New York: Oxford University Press, 2013); and M. Kartveit, *The Origins of the Samaritans* (Leiden: Brill, 2009). Thus it is not only reasonable but necessary to consider Samaria when reconstructing the wider milieu from which the Qumran settlement emerged in the late second century BCE.

33. E. Posner, *Archives in the Ancient World* (Cambridge: Harvard University Press, 1972), 119.

Samaria

Samaria, the Persian province that occupied the heart of the old northern kingdom of Israel, had as its capital the city of Samaria, which was the seat of the Persian governor of the province. Its major shrine was the Yahwistic sanctuary on Mount Gerizim, which was first established in the mid-fifth century BCE.[34] In terms of evidence for writing and languages, coins[35] and ostraca in Hebrew and Aramaic have been discovered, along with two major corpora of epigraphic finds, the Mount Gerizim inscriptions and the Wadi ed-Daliyeh papyri.

The Mount Gerizim Inscriptions

The sacred precinct on Mount Gerizim was first constructed in the mid- to late fifth century BCE.[36] It was massively rebuilt in the late third–early second century BCE under Antiochus III; most of the architectural remains date from that rebuilding. The sanctuary was destroyed by John Hyrcanus around 110 BCE and never rebuilt.

Approximately four hundred inscriptions have been uncovered in and around the sacred precinct, although because of destruction and reuse only one was found in situ.[37] The majority are dedicatory and votive inscriptions. Three hundred eighty-one were written in Aramaic script and language, seven are in Paleo-Hebrew script and the Hebrew language, and several are in mixed script and language. There are also four medieval

34. Y. Magen et al., *Mount Gerizim Excavations,* vol. 1: *The Aramaic, Hebrew and Samaritan Inscriptions,* Judea and Samaria Publications 2 (Jerusalem: Israel Antiquities Authority, 2004), 1.

35. In general terms, the majority of coins from Persian period Samaria had Aramaic legends; some few were in Paleo-Hebrew (the successor to the ancient Israelite script) or had mixed scripts. All are marked with the name *šmryn*. See P. Machinist, "The First Coins of Judah and Samaria: Numismatics and History in the Achaemenid and Early Hellenistic Periods," in *Continuity and Change,* ed. H. Sancisi-Weerdenburg et al., Achaemenid History 8 (Leiden: Nederlands Instituut voor het Nabije Oosten, 1994), 366–72; Knoppers, *Jews and Samaritans,* 111.

36. Magen et al., *Mount Gerizim Excavations,* 1. J. Dušek dates the founding of the precinct to the reign of Darius II (424–405 BCE) (*Aramaic and Hebrew Inscriptions from Mount Gerizim and Samaria between Antiochus III and Antiochus IV Epiphanes,* CHANE 54 [Leiden: Brill, 2012], 3).

37. Magen et al., *Mount Gerizim Excavations,* 13.

SCRIBES AND LIBRARIES

Samaritan Hebrew inscriptions, and "some" Greek inscriptions from the Hellenistic period.[38] The inscriptions are the work of skilled craftsmen, most likely made under the supervision of the temple personnel. The vast majority belong to the Hellenistic era, although it is possible that a few come from the Persian period.[39]

A good example of the type of inscription found at the sanctuary is no. 147 (K28409), written in cursive Aramaic:

די הקרב דליה בר שמעון עלוהי ועל בנוהי אבנא [דה ל]דכרן טב קדם
אלהא באתרא דנה

"Delayah son of Shim'on offered [this] stone for himself and his sons [for] good remembrance before God in this place."[40]

The Mount Gerizim inscriptions give evidence for the robust religious life at the sanctuary until its destruction in 110 BCE, and point to the presence of scribes there, working for the sanctuary personnel, throughout its existence.

The Wadi ed-Daliyeh Papyri

The Wadi ed-Daliyeh papyri were discovered by Ta'amireh bedouin in 1962 in a cave, the Mugharet Abu Shinjeh, located halfway between Samaria and Jericho. The cave yielded fragmentary papyri, seals, and coins. The cave evidently served as a refuge for leading Samarian families fleeing the Macedonian army after their rebellion against the conquest of Alexander the Great in 332 BCE, since between thirty and fifty skeletons were uncovered in the cave. The hideout was evidently discovered by Alexander's

---

38. Magen et al., *Mount Gerizim Excavations*, 13; and Dušek, *Aramaic and Hebrew Inscriptions*, 5. I was unable to locate a catalog of the Greek inscriptions. The *editio princeps* uses idiosyncratic designations for the scripts in use on Mount Gerizim: "neo-Hebrew" for the more commonly used "Paleo-Hebrew" to signify the continuation of the ancient Israelite script, and "proto-Jewish" for what F. M. Cross and J. Naveh termed "proto-Hasmonean." A more appropriate name for the latter script, found in both Samaritan and Jewish contexts, is "cursive Aramaic." Following Dušek I will use the terms "Paleo-Hebrew" and "cursive Aramaic." See also Knoppers, *Jews and Samaritans*, 111n14.

39. Dušek, *Aramaic and Hebrew Inscriptions*, 5.

40. Magen et al., *Mount Gerizim Excavations*, 137.

60

Scribes and Libraries in Ancient Israel

troops, who built a fire at the entrance to the cave that smothered those inside. The written remains are their personal documents; no literary texts were discovered among them.

Twenty-seven separate papyrus documents have been published, along with fifteen groups of miscellaneous fragments.[41] Some of the documents were found still rolled and sealed (WDSP 1 had seven intact seals). All of the papyri are legal documents, including deeds of slave sales (seventeen), other deeds of conveyance, and loan settlements. The place where the documents were drafted is given in the first or last line; in the eleven instances where this is preserved the place name is "Samaria." The documents are dated by the regnal year of the Persian king, also given in the first or last line. They range in date from 375 to 335 BCE, from the reign of Artaxerxes II Memnon to Darius III. They are written in cursive Aramaic, in a conservative version of "Official Aramaic," the standard language of the Persian Empire, and their language is virtually identical to that of the earlier Elephantine papyri (see below).[42] The sale formulae found in the papyri are, according to Gropp, adaptations of Neo-Babylonian documents by Palestinian Aramaic scribes working in Samaria.[43]

In addition to the fragmentary papyri and their seals, approximately one hundred clay bullae, the remnants of sealed documents, were discovered.[44] Although the majority of these bullae are pictographic, with Greek and Persian motifs, two seals are inscribed. Both are in Paleo-Hebrew; the seal affixed to WDSP 5 reads: "[Belonging to Yesha]yahu, son of [San]ballat, governor of Samaria."[45]

The Wadi ed-Daliyeh papyri thus testify to the presence of professional scribes drafting legal documents in the provincial capital in the late Persian period.

41. D. M. Gropp, "The Samaria Papyri from Wadi Daliyeh," in *Wadi Daliyeh II: The Samaria Papyri from Wadi Daliyeh*; and *Qumran Cave 4: XXVIII: Miscellanea, Part 2*, by M. Bernstein et al., DJD 28 (Oxford: Clarendon, 2001), 3–116. The papyri have proved to be extraordinarily important for the study of late Persian period Samaria, since the names of several governors, most from the Sanballatid family, are preserved. See F. M. Cross, "The Papyri and Their Historical Implications," in *Discoveries in the Wâdi ed-Dâliyeh*, ed. P. W. Lapp and N. Lapp, AASOR 41 (Cambridge: American Schools of Oriental Research, 1974), 17–29.

42. Found among the Aramaic papyri were small scraps of papyrus on which a few Greek letters are legible, indicating some knowledge of Greek in late Persian period Samaria. See Gropp, *Wadi Daliyeh II*, pl. 39.

43. Gropp, *Wadi Daliyeh II*, 19–32.

44. M. J. W. Leith, *Wadi Daliyeh I: The Seal Impressions*, DJD 24 (Oxford: Clarendon, 1997).

45. Cross, "Papyri and Their Historical Implications," 18.

SCRIBES AND LIBRARIES

The Elephantine Papyri

Before turning to the epigraphic evidence for the presence of scribes in the province of Yehud, we will investigate one archive belonging to Jews found outside the lands of biblical Israel, the Elephantine papyri.

Elephantine is an island in the Nile opposite Aswan, just north of the first cataract, where collections of papyri in Egyptian (demotic and hieratic), Aramaic, Greek, Coptic, Arabic, and Latin were discovered.[46] The fifty-two Aramaic texts, belonging to several different persons, come from the Persian period; most belonged to a Jewish garrison stationed on Elephantine. The Jedaniah communal archive, discovered in House M, consists of eleven documents, dated from 419 to 407 BCE, belonging to Jedaniah son of Gemariah, a leader of the Jewish garrison.[47] The Mibtaiah family archive, belonging to Mibtaiah, an aunt of Jedaniah, consists of eleven documents dated from 471 to 410 BCE. The Ananiah family archive contained thirty legal documents that date between 457 and 402 BCE. All of these documents were written by professional scribes, resident at Elephantine or its vicinity. These collections consist of letters, marriage documents, deeds of sale or conveyance, and other legal matters. However, two literary texts, an Aramaic translation of Darius I's Behistun in-

46. For the complete catalog, see B. Porten, *The Elephantine Papyri in English: Three Millennia of Cross-Cultural Continuity and Change*, DMOA 22 (Leiden: Brill, 1996). For the Aramaic texts that are of interest here, see B. Porten and A. Yardeni, *Textbook of Aramaic Documents from Ancient Egypt*, 4 vols. (Winona Lake, IN: Eisenbrauns, 1986–93), hereinafter abbreviated as *TAD*.

47. Porten, *Elephantine Papyri in English*, 74–81. The Jedaniah communal archive is particularly important for what it reveals concerning relationships between various Yahwistic communities in the late Persian period. The Jewish garrison on Elephantine followed Yahwistic religious practices and maintained a Yahweh temple on the island. The earliest document in the archive (*TAD* A4.1) is a letter from a Hananiah reporting a missing directive from Darius II to the satrap Arsames instructing the Jewish troops to observe Passover correctly. The archive also contains two drafts of a petition from 407 BCE (*TAD* A4.7–8) addressed to Bagavahyu, the governor of Judah, for assistance in obtaining permission to reconstruct the garrison's temple after it was destroyed by the Egyptian Khum priests. The petition reports that they made the same request to Delaiah and Shelemaiah, the sons of Sanballat the governor of Samaria. This document indicates that, at least in the mind of Jedaniah and his colleagues, there was little difference between the Yahwistic communities in Yehud and Samaria. *TAD* A4.9 records a memorandum reporting that Delaiah and Bagavahyu supported the request to rebuild the temple on Elephantine for incense and grain offerings (animal sacrifice goes unmentioned). The document thus demonstrates cooperation, at least at the governmental level, between Samaria and Jerusalem in the late fifth century BCE.

62

Scribes and Libraries in Ancient Israel

scription (*TAD* C2.1) and a copy of the Aramaic Tale of Ahiqar (*TAD* C1.1), were also discovered.[48]

The Elephantine archives, along with the Wadi ed-Daliyeh papyri and the various coins and inscriptions discovered in Persian period Samaria, indicate the presence of scribes associated with the Persian appointed governor and the Samarian elites (coins and the Wadi ed-Daliyeh papyri), the Samaritan sanctuary (the Mount Gerizim inscriptions), and a Yahwistic military colony in Egypt that identified with both Samaria and Yehud.

Yehud

Epigraphic Evidence

Yehud, the Persian province located in the land of the former kingdom of Judah, was much smaller and poorer than Samaria throughout the Persian period. Judah had been devastated by the Babylonian destruction in the sixth century BCE, and would not really recover until the Hellenistic takeover in the third century. Excavations reveal a sharp decrease in the total number and size of settlements from the late Iron Age. The settlement pattern is mainly rural, with some larger administrative and military sites. The most thickly settled region was the hill country of Benjamin.[49] Jerusalem was much reduced in size; estimates of its population in the fifth century BCE range from a low of about four hundred to a more reasonable fifteen hundred.[50] The epigraphic evidence is correspondingly meager; there is almost none from

---

48. The Tale of Ahiqar is the story of a scribe named Ahiqar, who served Sennacherib (or Esarhaddon, according to the book of Tobit, which preserves a slightly different version of the tale), and trained his adopted son, his nephew Nadin, to succeed him. Owing to Nadin's machinations, Ahiqar fell from favor, but was later restored, in a typical royal courtier tale plot. Ahiqar is called a ספר חכים ומהיר ("a wise and skillful scribe") in the introduction to his story. The Tale of Ahiqar is further evidence of the high position scribes could attain in ancient Near Eastern society, as well as the familial aspect to the scribal profession.

49. O. Lipschits and O. Tal, "The Settlement Archaeology of the Province of Judah: A Case Study," in *Judah and the Judeans in the Fourth Century B.C.E.*, ed. O. Lipschits et al. (Winona Lake, IN: Eisenbrauns, 2007), 25–34.

50. E. Meyers and M. Chancey, *Archaeology of the Land of the Bible*, vol. 3: *Alexander to Constantine* (New Haven: Yale University Press, 2012), 2; O. Lipschits, "Achaemenid Imperial Policy, Settlement Processes in Palestine, and the Status of Jerusalem in the Middle of the Fifth Century B.C.E.," in *Judah and the Judeans in the Persian Period*, ed. O. Lipschits and M. Oeming (Winona Lake, IN: Eisenbrauns, 2006), 32.

SCRIBES AND LIBRARIES

the fifth century, but the evidence expands (along with the population) in the fourth century. The pattern of languages and scripts parallels that of Samaria.

Coins from the area contain Paleo-Hebrew legends, usually with the name of the governor, but in one case with the name of a (high) priest, Yohanan.[51] A collection of seals and bullae, written in Aramaic script but in the Hebrew language and dated to the sixth century BCE, have been published by N. Avigad.[52] A group of ten bear an identical inscription, לירמי הספר, "belonging to Jeremai the scribe." Avigad suggested that this scribe was working in an administrative context in Persian period Yehud.

Aramaic stamp impressions with the name of the province Yehud are numerous, especially at the administrative center of Ramat Raḥel.[53] Aramaic seals and bullae have also been discovered there, containing either the word "governor" or a personal name, along with the province name.[54] Administrative ostraca in Aramaic also turn up in excavations; a collection of eighty-five ostraca from the Persian period was discovered at Arad.[55]

Finally, fragments of papyrus documents have been unearthed from a group of caves in Ketef Yericho. These documents, written in Aramaic and Greek on papyrus, date from the fourth century BCE.[56] The largest, Jericho papList of Loans ar, which was discovered partially rolled up, was written on both sides in a fourth-century BCE formal Aramaic script. It contains lists of names with sums of money in shekels noted beside each name, and appears to be a record of loans and repayments.[57]

---

51. Meyers and Chancey, *Alexander to Constantine*, 5; A. Lemaire, "Administration in Fourth Century BCE Judah in Light of Epigraphy and Numismatics," in Lipschits et al., *Judeans in the Fourth Century*, 54; Machinist, "First Coins of Judah," 366–67.

52. N. Avigad, *Bullae and Seals from a Post-Exilic Judean Archive*, Qedem 4 (Jerusalem: Institute of Archaeology, Hebrew University of Jerusalem, 1976). These bullae and seals are unprovenanced and therefore caution is in order. Avigad states, "Unfortunately, we have been informed of nothing concerning the site of discovery and its circumstances, but only that the bullae were found 'in the Jerusalem region', hidden in a pottery vessel" (1).

53. O. Lipschits and D. Vanderhooft, "Yehud Stamp Impressions in the Fourth Century B.C.E.: A Time of Administrative Consolidation?" in Lipschits et al., *Judeans in the Fourth Century*, 75; Meyers and Chancey, *Alexander to Constantine*, 7.

54. Meyers and Chancey, *Alexander to Constantine*, 6.

55. O. Pedersén, *Archives and Libraries in the Ancient Near East 1500–300 B.C.* (Bethesda, MD: CDL, 1998), 231.

56. See H. Eshel et al., "Ketef Jericho 1–7," in *Miscellaneous Texts from the Judaean Desert*, by J. Charlesworth et al., DJD 38 (Oxford: Clarendon, 2000), 21–62.

57. H. Eshel and H. Misgav, "A Fourth Century B.C.E. Document from Ketef Yeriho," *IEJ* 38 (1988): 161–67.

All of this evidence taken together allows us to say that scribes were working in Persian period Yehud, especially in the administrative sector, but not much more. For more information we must turn to the literary evidence in Chronicles and Ezra-Nehemiah.

Chronicles and Ezra-Nehemiah

The books of Chronicles are a postexilic rewriting of Samuel-Kings, with a specific interest in the temple, its cult, and the institutions surrounding it. A range of dates has been proposed for its composition, from the mid-fifth to the mid-third century BCE, a two-hundred-year span. The majority of commentators now date Chronicles to the fourth century BCE; thus its picture of the temple and its personnel reflects the reality of the late Persian–early Hellenistic period.[58]

Chronicles mentions scribes in a number of passages. Several of these simply parallel their source in Samuel-Kings, and thus do not add to our knowledge concerning scribes in the late Persian period: 1 Chr 18:16 // 2 Sam 20:25; 2 Chr 24:11 // 2 Kgs 12:10; and 2 Chr 34:15–20 // 2 Kgs 22:8–14. However, Chronicles contains several unique references to scribes, which do reveal something about the role and status of elite scribes in postmonarchic Judah at a time when Judahite society was subject to a foreign power and dominated locally by the temple and its staff.

Part of the opening genealogical material in Chronicles, 1 Chr 2:55, contains the phrase ומשפחות ספרים ישבו יעבץ, "and families of the ספרים that lived at Jabez." The word ספרים is pointed as "scribes," and most commentators understand it that way.[59] The names of these scribal families at Jabez, the Tirathites, the Shimeathites, and the Sucathites, are then listed. If this understanding is correct, then the Chronicler is indicating that families of scribes were active in postexilic Yehud, as was the case for

---

58. G. Knoppers, *1 Chronicles 1–9: A New Translation with Introduction and Commentary*, AB 12 (New York: Doubleday, 2004), 111; R. Klein, *1 Chronicles: A Commentary*, Hermeneia (Minneapolis: Fortress, 2006), 14.

59. Knoppers, *1 Chronicles 1–9*, 295; Fox, *In the Service*, 79; and C. Schams, *Jewish Scribes in the Second Temple Period*, LHBOTS 291 (Sheffield: Sheffield Academic Press, 1998), 70. The LXX translates as γραμματέων, "scribes." However, H. G. M. Williamson and R. Klein argue that the Hebrew should be understood as "Siphrites," which refers to a clan of the Kenites, along with the other clans who settled at Jabez. See H. G. M. Williamson, *1 and 2 Chronicles*, NCBC (Grand Rapids: Eerdmans, 1982), 55; Klein, *1 Chronicles*, 83.

SCRIBES AND LIBRARIES

the Shaphan family in preexilic Jerusalem, and that one particular location, Jabez, was the ancestral home of families of scribes.

In 1 Chr 24:6 the scribe Shemaiah, a Levite, is credited with recording the organization of the priestly courses by David. This is the first mention of a *Levitical* scribe; the presence of scribes among the priests and the Levites is a key to understanding the transmission of the classical literature of ancient Israel, which most likely took place in temple circles during the Persian period.[60]

The list of David's counselors in 1 Chr 27:32–34 includes Jonathan, David's uncle, who is described as "a man of understanding and a scribe." This Jonathan is otherwise unknown.

Jeiel the scribe (הסופר) appears along with Maaseiah the officer (השוטר) in 2 Chr 26:11, in charge of the muster of King Uzziah's army. Here a scribe is portrayed in the employ of the armed services, a part of the government bureaucracy.

Finally, 2 Chr 34:13 contains a passing reference concerning the roles of the Levites: "And some of the Levites were scribes [סופרים], and officials [שוטרים], and gatekeepers." This significant reference indicates that Levites regularly served as scribes; to be a Levite was to be a member of the sacerdotal tribe, but to be a scribe was to pursue a particular professional role within one's sacerdotal duties. Again, this points to a central role for Levitical scribes in the passing down of Israel's sacred literature.

Ezra-Nehemiah is the second bloc of literature set in the Persian period from which we can garner information about the role and status of scribes. Although a range of dates has been proposed for these books, from the late fifth to the mid-second century BCE, a date around 300 BCE seems most reasonable.[61]

The first type of scribe encountered in Ezra-Nehemiah is in the employ of the local government. These scribes served the interests of the governors who reported to the Persian overlords. "Shimshai the scribe [Aram. ספרא]," one of the "officials" who wrote against Zerubbabel and Joshua in Ezra 4:8, 9, 17, 23, is an example of a highly placed government scribe employed at the provincial capital of Samaria. Another scribe of this type is Zadok (Neh 13:13), who is appointed by Nehemiah in his role as governor as one of the overseers of the storehouses for the priestly tithe in Jerusalem.

60. See Klein, *1 Chronicles*, 467.
61. H. G. M. Williamson, *Ezra, Nehemiah*, WBC 16 (Waco, TX: Word, 1985), xxxv; J. Blenkinsopp, *Ezra-Nehemiah: A Commentary*, OTL (Philadelphia: Westminster, 1988).

66

Scribes and Libraries in Ancient Israel

A second sphere of scribal activity in Ezra-Nehemiah was, as we have seen in the Chronicler, the temple in Jerusalem, in which scribes are associated with the priests and the Levites. The most important figure in this regard is Ezra, who, although historically obscure,[62] gives us an idealized portrait of the scribe as a scholar of the classical literature of Israel, particularly the law of Moses. Ezra is introduced as ספר מהיר בתורת משה, a "scribe skilled in the law of Moses," as well as a priest with full genealogy (Ezra 7:1–6).[63] Later in the chapter, when the narrative switches to Aramaic, Ezra is given the title כהנא ספר דתא די אלה שמיא, "the priest, the scribe of the law of the God of heaven" (7:12, 21), indicating that the Persian court understood his role as involving Jewish religious matters.[64] His role as a scribe, that is, as a person with expertise in "the words of the commandments of Yahweh and his statutes" (my trans.), is emphasized in 7:11, 12, 21, 25, as well as Neh 8:1, 4, 9, 13.[65] In these passages Ezra is also consistently labeled a priest.[66] In Neh 8 Ezra is supported by the Levites, who "caused the people to understand [מבנים] the law" (8:7, 12), "with interpretation," or "interpreting" (מפרש) it (8:8). This teaching role for

---

62. Doubts have been raised about Ezra's very existence. Ezra is not a popular figure in Second Temple Jewish literature written in Palestine after his eponymous book; for example, he is not named in Ben Sira's Hymn to Famous Men, which does mention Zerubbabel, Joshua, and Nehemiah (49:11–13). On the other hand, Ezra is the main figure in 1 Esdras (second century BCE), where he is even called the high priest (9:40, 49). Ezra rises to prominence in the first century CE, where he is the hero of 4 Ezra (2 Esd 3–14), and in rabbinic tradition is credited with being the first chair of the Great Assembly. See R. Kratz, "Ezra—Priest and Scribe," in *Scribes, Sages, and Seers: The Sage in the Eastern Mediterranean World*, ed. L. Perdue (Göttingen: Vandenhoeck & Ruprecht, 2008), 164.

63. This title, "skilled scribe," also occurs in the Aramaic Ahiqar tale, where Ahiqar is described as ספר חכים ומהיר, "a wise and skillful scribe."

64. An intriguing parallel to the role of Ezra is that of Udjahorresnet, an Egyptian scribe working in Susa who was sent by Darius I back to Egypt to reestablish the Houses of Life connected to the temple at Sais. This was part of Darius's reorganization of the Egyptian satrapy, including the institutions of the scribes and their religious learning. Udjahorresnet tells his own story in an autobiographical inscription written on a basalt statue of himself inscribed in 518 BCE. Like Udjahorresnet, Ezra, according to his book, was being sent on an official mission from the Persian court, to reestablish Judean institutions. See J. Blenkinsopp, "The Mission of Udjahorresnet and Those of Ezra and Nehemiah," *JBL* 106 (1987): 409–21.

65. Kratz, "Ezra—Priest and Scribe," 180–82. H. H. Schaeder, *Esra der Schreiber* (Tübingen: Mohr, Nendeln, 1930), termed Ezra a *Schriftgelehrte* to differentiate his role from that of someone like Shimshai, who was (merely) a *Schreiber*. However, the distinction of the two roles is not entirely clear.

66. Only at Ezra 10:10, 16, where Ezra is dissolving the mixed marriages, is the title "scribe" omitted. See Kratz, "Ezra—Priest and Scribe," 181.

SCRIBES AND LIBRARIES

the Levites may be part of their scribal function (cf. 2 Chr 34:13).[67] It is in these Ezra passages that a connection between scribes and priests and Levites in postexilic Judah is most firmly established.

Thus in the Persian period the scribe continues to play important roles in Judean and Samarian society. The epigraphic evidence shows scribes active in commerce, government administration, and legal affairs. The textual evidence corroborates this picture, but adds to it scribes connected to the temple and the Levites, and, in the person of Ezra, a scribe on a royal mission, charged with the propagation of the law of God as the law of the land.

The Literature Produced by the Scribes of the Persian Period

At this point it is appropriate to devote space to the literature produced and handed on by those scribes active in ancient Israel and Judah in the preexilic and exilic periods, and especially in the Persian period. These scribes are, as far as we know, anonymous, but their learning is evident in the works that they produced.

During the Persian period the literature I am referring to as the "classical" literature of Judaism took shape at the hands of the scribes. The term *classical* denotes literature that became the basis for the self-understanding and religious practice of the Jews in the Greco-Roman period.

First and foremost, the five books of the Torah or Pentateuch reached their recognizable shape[68] and became normative for religious practice in

---

67. Van der Toorn, *Scribal Culture*, 89–90.

68. By "recognizable shape" I am referring to the arc of the book, its beginning, middle, and end. Often this arc follows a narrative structure. Thus "Genesis" begins with the Priestly creation account followed by the Primeval History, moves through the patriarchal narratives, and finishes with Joseph and the Israelites in Egypt. That is the "recognizable shape" of the book of Genesis. Within that recognizable shape, however, the text was still fluid and subject to change. A good example of this textual fluidity within a more or less fixed shape is the book of Exodus. The shape of the book of Exodus begins with the infancy narrative of Moses, and moves through the exodus narrative to the sojourn at Sinai. The book ends with the instructions for the tabernacle in Exod 35–40. However, the text of Exod 35–40 is very different in the MT/ SP and the LXX, in regard to the internal order of the chapters. In other words, Exod 35–40 existed in two different literary forms after the book of Exodus reached its recognizable shape. Further, at some other point in its transmission the text of the book of Exodus was subjected to fairly substantial content editing, the result of which was a third literary form, of which the SP Exodus is an example. On the literary editions of Exodus, see E. Ulrich, *The Dead Sea Scrolls and the Developmental Composition of the Bible*, VTSup 169 (Leiden: Brill, 2015), 207–8.

68

Scribes and Libraries in Ancient Israel

the Persian period. Although the text of the pentateuchal books remained fluid until the end of the Second Temple period, the Torah as the law of Moses was accepted by the Jewish and Samaritan communities as the basis for their religious and communal life.[69] Some of the oldest manuscripts (mid-late third century BCE) in the Qumran collection are manuscripts of the books of the Pentateuch (i.e., 4QExod-Lev^f, 4QExod^d, 4Qpaleo-Deut^s), and the books of the Pentateuch were translated into Greek in the mid-third century BCE, thus indicating their centrality in Judaism by that time. Thus we can safely say that the books of the Pentateuch must have been in circulation in their recognizable shape by the end of the fourth century BCE.

Books from other parts of what became the Jewish canon were also in circulation by the end of the fourth century BCE, and many had gained some kind of authoritative status. From the prophetic books (Nevi'im) Isaiah, Jeremiah (in at least the shorter form preserved in the LXX and 4QJer$^{b, d}$), Ezekiel, and the Book of the Twelve were extant, as well as the historical books Samuel-Kings.

From the division later known as the Writings (Ketuvim) the picture becomes less clear. Chronicles, using Samuel-Kings as a source, and Ezra-Nehemiah were also composed in this period, although they may have had a limited circulation. The psalms were being collected during the Persian period, although the evidence from Qumran indicates that the book of Psalms did not reach its final edited form until the first century CE. The same scenario holds true for the book of Proverbs. As for the remaining books of the Ketuvim, their literary history is later and much disputed, although some of them should probably be dated to the Persian period. All of them, with the exception of Esther, appear in fragmentary form in the Qumran collection.

Other books that did not become part of the Jewish canon of Scripture also were composed during the late Persian period. A major example is the book of Tobit, which eventually became part of the Christian Apocrypha. Tobit was composed in Aramaic in the fourth century BCE, and is found at Qumran in five copies.

Thus in the Persian period we have good literary evidence for the work of scribes beyond their functions in governmental bureaucracy, which was all we could be certain of in preexilic Israel and Judah. We may assume, given the archaeological realities of the Persian period, in which major ur-

---

69. Knoppers, *Jews and Samaritans*, 178–94.

SCRIBES AND LIBRARIES

ban areas were few,[70] that much of this literary activity was connected with the scribes associated with the temple in Jerusalem and the sanctuary on Mount Gerizim. As the region began to grow physically and economically during the early Hellenistic period, literary production also increased. The classical literature of the previous period continued to be circulated and reworked by scribes, while new literary works were created.

Scribes and Writing in the Hellenistic and Roman Periods (300 BCE–135 CE)

In this section I collect references to scribes and their activities from literature that dates to the Hellenistic and Roman periods (ending with literature composed before the Great Jewish Revolt against Rome in 66 CE) and either was not found or was not found exclusively in the Qumran corpus. The literary references begin with short passages concerning scribes and end with longer treatments; at the end of the chapter there is an appendix on the Synoptic Gospels.

First Esdras is a Greek rendering of the story of Judah from the time of Josiah's Passover to Ezra's reforms, and probably dates to the mid- to late second century BCE.[71] The book's hero, Ezra, is introduced in 8:3 as a γραμματεύς, "scribe," the usual LXX translation of the Heb. סופר. However, in the next description of Ezra at 8:8, the word ἀναγνώστης is used instead (so also 8:9; 9:39, 42, and 49). This unusual word, which appears only here in the LXX, has as its primary meaning "reader," as in "one who reads a text aloud," while a secondary meaning is "secretary." The NETS of 1 Esdras here is "Ezra the priest and reader of the law."[72] The choice of ἀναγνώστης by the Greek translator of 1 Esdras puts emphasis on Ezra's public reading of the law.[73] This choice contrasts with the use of the word γραμματεύς for Shimshai the scribe in 2:15, 16, 21, and 25. In the eyes of the author of 1 Esdras, Shimshai is merely a high official in the Samarian government who produces documents, while Ezra has an important role in the oral propagation of the religious law of the Jews.

---

70. See, e.g., Lipschits and Tal, "Settlement Archaeology," 33–52.

71. J. M. Myers, *I and II Esdras: Introduction, Translation and Commentary*, AB 42 (Garden City, NY: Doubleday, 1974), 8–14.

72. R. G. Wooden, "1 Esdras," *NETS* 401.

73. Schams, *Jewish Scribes*, 109.

70

Scribes and Libraries in Ancient Israel

First Maccabees was written in a Semitic language (probably Hebrew) and later translated into Greek; it dates to the last quarter of the second century BCE.[74] Second Maccabees is an abridgement of a much longer work by Jason of Cyrene (2 Macc 2:23) and was written in Greek. A variety of dates have been proposed for 2 Maccabees, ranging from the 140s BCE (Schwartz) to slightly before 63 BCE (Goldstein).[75]

First Maccabees has two references to scribes. At 5:42 scribes are mentioned as army commanders, a strange reference given what we know about the role of scribes, who may be associated with armies in an administrative capacity, but not as commanders. Commentators have correctly suggested that γραμματεῖς here is a translation of שֹׁטְרִים, "officers," rather than סֹפְרִים.[76]

In 7:12 "a group [or: company] of scribes," συναγωγὴ γραμματέων, seeks to make peace with the newly appointed high priest Alcimus. It is probable that these scribes, community leaders of some kind, came from Jerusalem to seek out Alcimus. Some commentators have sought to equate these scribes with the Hasidim (Ασιδαίων, "pious ones"), who in 7:13 (also) make peace with Alcimus and Bacchides, but the equation is not certain.[77] As we have already seen with the Levites in Chronicles, scribes could be part of various other groups within Judaism, and scribes are found at all levels and in all factions of society.

Second Maccabees contains one reference to a scribe (6:18), where the martyr Eleazar is described as "one of the scribes in high position."[78]

---

74. J. A. Goldstein, *1 Maccabees: A New Translation and Commentary*, AB 41 (Garden City, NY: Doubleday, 1976), 63–64.

75. D. Schwartz, *2 Maccabees*, CEJL (Berlin: de Gruyter, 2008), 14; and J. A. Goldstein, *2 Maccabees: A New Translation with Introduction and Commentary*, AB 41A (Garden City, NY: Doubleday, 1983), 83.

76. F.-M. Abel and J. Starcky, *Les Livres des Maccabées*, 3rd ed., Sainte Bible (Paris: Cerf, 1961), 140; Goldstein, *1 Maccabees*, 305; J. Kampen, *The Hasideans and the Origin of Pharisaism: A Study in 1 and 2 Maccabees*, SCS 24 (Atlanta: Scholars Press, 1988), 118; Schams, *Jewish Scribes*, 114.

77. This view was championed by V. Tcherikover, *Hellenistic Civilization and the Jews* (New York: Atheneum, 1970), 198. See also Goldstein, *1 Maccabees*, 331–32; Kampen, *Hasideans*, 115–22. The Hasidim also appear in 1 Macc 2:42 as "mighty warriors of Israel" (Kampen suggests the alternative translation "leading citizens"; *Hasideans*, 107) and in 2 Macc 14:6, where they are associated with Judas Maccabeus. The equation "scribes = Hasidim" is rejected by W. Dommershausen, *1 Makkabäer, 2 Makkabäer* (Würzburg: Echter, 1985), 54. Schams, *Jewish Scribes*, 118, argues that the text is open to the interpretation that the two groups are identical.

78. Note that in 4 Macc 5:4 this same Eleazar is described as a learned priest, thus emphasizing the connection between priests and scribes in this period.

SCRIBES AND LIBRARIES

This is probably an oblique reference to Eleazar's expertise in the law of Moses, which he is willing to die to defend, and testifies to the esteem in which scribes could be held in Judean society.

The Seleucid Charter (Ant. 12.138–144)

A non-Jewish document preserved by the first-century Jewish historian Josephus, the Seleucid Charter of Antiochus III (r. 222–187 BCE), demonstrates that scribes worked in the Jerusalem temple in the early second century BCE (*Ant.* 12.138–144).[79] Antiochus, who has just conquered Judah from the Ptolemies (c. 200 BCE), writes,

> Inasmuch as the Jews, from the very moment when we entered their country, showed their eagerness to serve us . . . we have seen fit on our part to requite them for these acts and to restore their city which has been destroyed by the hazards of war. . . . we have decided, on account of their piety, to furnish them for their sacrifices an allowance of sacrificial animals, wine, oil and frankincense to the value of twenty thousand pieces of silver. . . . And it is my will that these things be made over to them as I have ordered, and the work on the temple be completed, including the porticoes and any other part that it may be necessary to build. . . . And all the members of the nation shall have a form of government in accordance with the laws of their country, and the senate, the priests, the scribes of the temple [οἱ γραμματεῖς τοῦ ἱεροῦ] and the temple-singers shall be relieved from the poll-tax and the crown-tax and the salt-tax which they pay. (*Ant.* 12.138–142 [LCL])[80]

In the charter, Antiochus III gives the people the right to be governed by their "ancestral laws," and relieves the priests, the scribes of the temple (οἱ γραμματεῖς τοῦ ἱεροῦ), and the singers from paying taxes. He also gives

79. Josephus uses the term γραμματεύς 29 times, in the majority of which he is simply following the LXX rendering. He also uses the term ἱερογραμματεύς (*Ant.* 2) in speaking of the Egyptian divines who oppose Moses by their magical arts. Philo, the Alexandrian contemporary of Josephus, uses γραμματεύς only once (*Flacc.* 1.4), referring to a political adviser.

80. For discussion, see E. J. Bickerman, "The Seleucid Charter for Jerusalem," and "A Seleucid Proclamation Concerning the Temple in Jerusalem," in *Studies in Jewish and Christian History: A New Edition in English Including The God of the Maccabees*, 2 vols., AGJU 68 (Leiden: Brill, 2007), 1:315–56, 357–75.

Scribes and Libraries in Ancient Israel

permission for work on the temple to be completed, and gives funds to supply sacrificial material for the temple.[81] This brief passage indicates that a recognizable body of scribes was associated with the temple, and that they were closely associated with, but not identical to, the priests.

The Wisdom of Jesus ben Sira

The Wisdom of Jesus ben Sira is one of the few Second Temple period compositions for which the scribal author's name is known: Jesus son of Eleazar son of Sira (Sir 50:27). Ben Sira was active in Jerusalem in the first quarter of the second century BCE, when he wrote his Hebrew book; his grandson translated it into Greek in Egypt after 117 BCE.[82] Although the book is available in its entirety only in Greek, five partial medieval Hebrew manuscripts from the Cairo Genizah survive, as well as one copy from Masada and two small fragments (2Q18) from Qumran.[83]

Ben Sira's portrait of the role of the scribe is much more extensive and detailed than anything we have seen until now. As Patrick Skehan and Alexander Di Lella put it, Ben Sira was "first and foremost, a professional scribe," in which the word סופר, "scribe," becomes the equivalent of חכם, "wise man."[84] According to the information we can glean from his book, Ben Sira likely served in the bureaucracy that supported the priests and the temple, and trained young men for similar careers.[85] Whether or not he himself was a priest is less clear, but he was certainly a supporter of the contemporary temple priests (see his encomium on the high priest Simeon II in 50:1–21).

In his book, Ben Sira constructs a portrait of the ideal scribe, the exemplar of a professional scribe, to which he desires his students to aspire.[86]

---

81. Note that Sir 50:1–3 gives Simeon II, the high priest at the time, credit for rebuilding the temple.

82. P. W. Skehan and A. Di Lella, *The Wisdom of Ben Sira: A New Translation with Notes, Introduction and Commentary*, AB 39 (New York: Doubleday, 1987), 8–9.

83. See Skehan and Di Lella, *Wisdom of Ben Sira*, 51–52, for publication information. Columns 21–22 of 11QPsalms[a] also preserve Sir 51.

84. Skehan and Di Lella, *Wisdom of Ben Sira*, 10.

85. B. G. Wright III, "The Master-Disciple Relationship in the Book of Ben Sira," paper presented at Oxford University, Oxford, UK, 25 May 2016. I would like to thank Professor Wright for sharing this article with me prior to publication.

86. B. G. Wright III, "Ben Sira on the Sage as Exemplar," in *Praise Israel for Wisdom*

73

SCRIBES AND LIBRARIES

In 38:34–39:11 Ben Sira makes his longest statement about the qualities of the ideal scribe:

> [34]How different the one who devotes himself
> to the study of the law of the Most High!
> [1]He seeks out the wisdom of all the ancients,
> and is concerned with prophecies;
> [2]he preserves the sayings of the famous
> and penetrates the subtleties of parables;
> [3]he seeks out the hidden meanings of proverbs
> and is at home with the obscurities of parables.
> [4]He serves among the great
> and appears before rulers;
> he travels in foreign lands
> and learns what is good and evil in the human lot.
> [5]He sets his heart to rise early
> to seek the Lord who made him,
> and to petition the Most High;
> he opens his mouth in prayer
> and asks pardon for his sins.
> [6]If the great Lord is willing,
> he will be filled with the spirit of understanding;
> he will pour forth words of wisdom of his own
> and give thanks to the Lord in prayer.
> [7]The Lord will direct his counsel and knowledge,
> as he meditates on his mysteries.
> [8]He will show the wisdom of what he has learned,
> and will glory in the law of the Lord's covenant.
> [9]Many will praise his understanding;
> it will never be blotted out.
> His memory will not disappear,
> and his name will live through all generations.
> [10]Nations will speak of his wisdom,
> and the congregation will proclaim his praise.
> [11]If he lives long, he will leave a name greater than a thousand,
> and if he goes to rest, it is enough for him.

---

and Instruction: Essays on Ben Sira and Wisdom, the Letter of Aristeas and the Septuagint (Leiden: Brill, 2008), 165–82.

Scribes and Libraries in Ancient Israel

According to Ben Sira, the scribal profession had four basic components: (1) to study "the law of the Most High" as well as wisdom, prophecies, and parables (38:34–39:3); (2) to serve rulers in political and diplomatic roles (39:4); (3) to seek the Lord in prayer and meditation (39:5); and (4) to teach (39:6–8).[87]

The second component, serving rulers in political and diplomatic roles, has been seen throughout our study of scribes (see esp. ch. 2). The first and fourth components, study and teaching, have grown as we have moved forward in time, being especially prominent in the portrait of Ezra (see also Eleazar in 2 Macc 6:18). The third component, prayer and meditation, is new, and indicates that for Ben Sira the scribe's role had acquired a strong religious component (again, like Ezra). Since in Ben Sira's time Judah was a temple-state ruled by the high priest under the Ptolemies and the early Seleucids, this fusion of the religious and political is not surprising.

It is with the first component of the scribal role that Ben Sira gives insight into what constituted the religio-cultural repertoire of Judean scribes in the early second century BCE. "The law [תורת] of the Most High" comes first. Although we cannot be certain of the boundaries that Ben Sira attaches to this term, it appears that it is a written source(s); in his Wisdom poem in 24:1–29, he identifies the figure of Wisdom with "the book of the covenant [βίβλος διαθήκης] of the Most High God, the law [νόμον] that Moses commands us" (24:23). Since we have fragments of Pentateuchal books from this period in the Qumran corpus (4QExod^d, 4QExod-Lev^f, 4QDeut^a, and 4QpaleoDeut^s), we can be practically certain that Ben Sira had written sources at his disposal as well as traditional teaching for his study of the law.

The ideal scribe also works with "the wisdom [σοφία] of all [πάντων] the ancients." This "wisdom" must have included Israelite wisdom such as Proverbs,[88] but may also have included Greek literature, which would have been available to upper-class Jerusalemites at the time.[89] The scholar-scribe also is "concerned with prophecies [προφητείας]" and "parables"

---

87. P. Tiller, "The Sociological Settings of the Components of 1 Enoch," in *The Early Enoch Literature*, ed. G. Boccaccini and J. J. Collins, JSJSup 121 (Leiden: Brill, 2007), 244–45. The word "teach" does not appear in this passage, although it appears as a descriptor of the scribal role elsewhere: 22:7; 24:33; 30:3; and 37:19.

88. See Skehan and Di Lella, *Wisdom of Ben Sira*, 40–45, for Ben Sira's use of Proverbs.

89. J. Gammie, "The Sage in Sirach," in *The Sage in Israel and the Ancient Near East*, ed. J. Gammie and L. Perdue (Winona Lake, IN: Eisenbrauns, 1990), 369; and Skehan and Di Lella, *Wisdom of Ben Sira*, 46–51.

75

SCRIBES AND LIBRARIES

(παραβολῶν), part of the particularly Judean cultural repertoire that the scribes had to master.

Benjamin G. Wright III points out that the emphasis on "the law of the Most High," along with other literature, indicates a particular "Torah piety" that transformed scribal teaching in the second century BCE.[90] Ben Sira now conceives of his teaching as rooted in the study and interpretation of the traditional sources. As Wright notes, study and interpretation words abound in 38:34–39:3: "devotes himself to the study," "seeks out," "is concerned," "preserves," "penetrates the subtleties," "seeks out the hidden meanings," and "is at home with obscurities."[91] In other words, part of the learned scribe's role is the interpretation of the classical sources of ancient Israel.[92] What is more, since the interpretive act is grounded in prayer and meditation, his teaching is both revealed and inspired: "The Lord will direct his counsel and knowledge, as he meditates on his mysteries" (39:7). Thus the scribe-teacher claims his own authority within the learned tradition, and now considers himself on a par with prophets and priests.[93] Ben Sira claims for himself this divinely given interpretive authority at 24:32–34:

> I will again make instruction shine forth like the dawn,
> and I will make it clear from far away.
> I will again pour out teaching like prophecy,
> and leave it to all future generations.
> Observe that I have not labored for myself alone,
> but for all who seek wisdom.

Here Ben Sira's instruction shines forth like the dawn (compare Dan 12:3 below, concerning the משכילים), and his teaching is likened to prophecy. Finally, in his colophon, Ben Sira again points to his claim that his teaching is inspired:

---

90. B. G. Wright III, "Conflicted Boundaries: Ben Sira, Sage and Seer," in *Praise Israel for Wisdom and Instruction*, 229–39. His examples include Ben Sira, 4QInstruction, and Jubilees.

91. Wright, "Conflicted Boundaries," 237.

92. As D. A. Teeter states, "In Ben Sira, if there are boundaries between sage, scholar, and scribe, they are difficult to discern" ("Scribes and Scribalism," *EDEJ* 1203).

93. R. A. Horsley, "The Politics of Cultural Production in Second Temple Judea: Historical Context and Political-Religious Relations of the Scribes Who Produced 1 Enoch, Sirach, and Daniel," in *Conflicted Boundaries in Wisdom and Apocalypticism*, ed. B. G. Wright III and L. M. Wills, SymS 35 (Leiden: Brill, 2006), 127.

Scribes and Libraries in Ancient Israel

Instruction in understanding and knowledge
I have written in this book,
Jesus son of Eleazar son of Sirach of Jerusalem,
whose mind poured forth wisdom. (50:27)

Ben Sira gives us a greatly expanded idea of the role and characteristics of an elite scholar-scribe in Hellenistic Jerusalem in the second century BCE, but he still maintains certain boundaries, especially in terms of esoteric or mantic wisdom, which he rejects (3:21–22; 34:1–8). For an acceptance of that mantle, we must turn to the figure of Enoch and the literature related to him.

The Books of Enoch, Jubilees, the Aramaic Levi Document, Daniel, and Related Literature

The books of Enoch, Jubilees, the Aramaic Levi Document, and related texts present a much expanded view of the role of the scribe over anything we have seen previously, although they also build on older notions of the scribal office. We begin with the books of Enoch, the oldest of this set of texts, and the one that sets out the new parameters of the scribal role.

The Books of Enoch

The books of Enoch (= 1 Enoch) comprise an extensive elaboration on the enigmatic figure of Enoch in Gen 5:21–24:[94]

When Enoch had lived sixty-five years, he became the father of Methuselah. Enoch walked with God after the birth of Methuselah three hundred years, and had other sons and daughters. Thus all the days of Enoch were three hundred sixty-five years. Enoch walked with God; then he was no more, because God took him.

---

94. This is the standard scholarly position on the priority of the Genesis pericope to the Enoch books. However, see now I. Fröhlich, "Origins of Evil and the Apocalyptic Tradition in 1 Enoch," in *Apocalyptic Thinking in Early Judaism: Engaging with John Collins' The Apocalyptic Imagination*, ed. S. W. Crawford and C. Wassén, JSJSup 182 (Leiden: Brill, 2018), 141–59, in which she argues that the short notice in Genesis is dependent on the Enoch literature.

SCRIBES AND LIBRARIES

First Enoch is now extant in its entirety only in Geʿez, the ancient language of the Abyssinian Orthodox Church. However, since 1 Enoch's introduction into Western scholarship in the nineteenth century, it was postulated that its original language was Hebrew or Aramaic.[95] When Aramaic copies of sections of 1 Enoch surfaced in the Qumran caves, it became evident that, at least for those sections of the book witnessed in the Qumran fragments, Aramaic was the language of composition.[96] In its present form 1 Enoch falls into five sections with an appendix; the oldest sections of 1 Enoch, the Book of the Watchers (chs. 1–36) and the Astronomical Book (chs. 72–82) date to the third century BCE.[97] The book of Dream Visions (chs. 83–90) dates to the second century BCE.[98] The Epistle of Enoch (chs. 92–105), according to Nickelsburg, was composed after the first third of the second century BCE,[99] while he dates its appendix,

95. G. W. Nickelsburg, *1 Enoch 1: A Commentary on the Book of 1 Enoch, Chapters 1–36; 81–108*, Hermeneia (Minneapolis: Fortress, 2001), 9, referencing the work of R. H. Charles.

96. Seven manuscripts preserve parts of chs. 1–36, 85–90, and 91–107: 4QEnᵃ (4Q201), 4QEnᵇ (4Q202), 4QEnᶜ (4Q204), 4QEnᵈ (4Q205), 4QEnᵉ (4Q206), 4QEnᶠ (4Q207), and 4QEnᵍ (4Q212). Four manuscripts preserve parts of the Astronomical Book: 4QEnastrᵃ (4Q208), 4QEnastrᵇ (4Q209), 4QEnastrᶜ (4Q210), and 4QEnastrᵈ (4Q211). Most of these manuscripts were originally published by J. T. Milik, *The Books of Enoch: Aramaic Fragments of Qumrân Cave 4* (Oxford: Clarendon, 1976). See now also L. Stuckenbruck et al., in *Qumran Cave 4.XXVI: Cryptic Texts,* by S. Pfann; and *Miscellanea, Part 1,* by P. Alexander et al., DJD 36 (Oxford: Clarendon, 2000), 3–171. In addition to the Aramaic fragments, several of the Greek fragments from Cave 7Q have been tentatively identified as parts of Enoch: 7Q 4 1 = 103:3–4; 7Q2 = 98:11 or 105:1; 7Q8 = 103:7–8; 7Q11 = 100:12; 7Q12 = 103:4; and 7Q13 = 103:15. See E. Puech, "Sept Fragments de la Lettre d'Hénoch (1 Hén 100, 103 et 105) dans la grotte 7 de Qumrân (=7QHén gr)," *RevQ* 19 (1997–1998): 313–23. See also P. Flint, "The Greek Fragments of Enoch from Qumran Cave 7," in *Enoch and Qumran Origins: New Light on a Forgotten Connection,* ed. G. Boccaccini (Grand Rapids: Eerdmans, 2005), 224–33. Nickelsburg, however, disagrees: G. W. E. Nickelsburg, "The Greek Fragments of 1 Enoch from Qumran Cave 7: An Unproven Identification," *RevQ* 22 (2004): 631–34.

97. Nickelsburg, *1 Enoch 1,* 7; G. W. Nickelsburg and J. VanderKam, *1 Enoch 2: A Commentary on the Book of 1 Enoch, Chapters 37–82,* Hermeneia (Minneapolis: Fortress, 2012), 339–45; J. VanderKam, *Enoch: A Man for All Generations,* Studies on the Personalities of the Old Testament (Columbia: University of South Carolina Press, 1995), 18, 26; and L. Stuckenbruck, *1 Enoch 91–108,* CEJL (Berlin: de Gruyter, 2007), 9. The Astronomical Book as found at Qumran is longer than the Ethiopic version, which contains an abbreviated form of the Aramaic Astronomical Book. See Milik, *Books of Enoch,* 273–75; H. Drawnel, *The Aramaic Astronomical Book (4Q208–4Q211) from Qumran: Text, Translation, and Commentary* (Oxford: Oxford University Press, 2011), 39–46.

98. Nickelsburg, *1 Enoch 1,* 347, 360–61; VanderKam, *Enoch,* 62.

99. Nickelsburg, *1 Enoch 1,* 427.

the Birth of Noah (chs. 106–107), to the last half of the second century BCE.[100] The Book of Parables (or Similitudes; chs. 37–71), of which no fragments were discovered at Qumran, is dated by a majority of scholars to the second half of the first century BCE.[101] Finally, a set of manuscripts from Qumran, the Book of Giants,[102] is not part of 1 Enoch but is clearly related to it by subject and themes.[103] On the basis of its earliest manuscript copy, the composition was in existence in the second century BCE. That these various parts of the Enoch corpus developed over a century or more indicates a degree of continuity in the scribal circles that produced them. As Richard Horsley states, "There was apparently some sort of circle of 'Enoch' scribes who cultivated and developed a succession of interrelated texts of 'Enochic' wisdom over a period of a century or more."[104]

The first introduction of Enoch in his eponymous book occurs in 12:3–4, where he is introduced as "Enoch the scribe" and addressed as "Enoch, righteous scribe" (ὁ γραμματεὺς τῆς δικαιοσύνης).[105] That the first descriptor used for Enoch is "scribe" indicates the importance of that

---

100. Nickelsburg, *1 Enoch 1*, 542. Stuckenbruck sees chs. 91–108 not as a unity but as five independent literary units (the Apocalypse of Weeks, Exhortation, Epistle, Birth of Noah, and Eschatological Admonition), and accordingly dates each one separately. His dates fall into the early second–early first centuries BCE (*1 Enoch 91–108*, 5–13).

101. Nickelsburg and VanderKam, *1 Enoch 2*, 58–65.

102. These nine manuscripts were originally published by Milik, *Books of Enoch*, 298–339. According to Stuckenbruck ("The Early Traditions Related to 1 Enoch from the Dead Sea Scrolls: An Overview and Assessment," in Boccaccini and Collins, *Early Enoch Literature*, 60–61), the certain Book of Giants manuscripts are 1QEnGiants[a] (1Q23), 2QEnGiants (2Q26), 4QEnGiants[a] (4Q203), 4QEnGiants[f] (4Q206a), 4QEnGiants[b] (4Q530), 4QEnGiants[c] (4Q531), 4QEnGiants[d] (4Q532), 4QEnGiants[e] (4Q533), and 6QpapGiants (6Q8). See E. Puech, *Qumrân Grotte 4.XXII: Textes araméens, première partie: 4Q529–549*, DJD 31 (Oxford: Clarendon, 2001), 9–116. See also L. Stuckenbruck, *The Book of Giants from Qumran: Texts, Translation, and Commentary*, TSAJ 63 (Tübingen: Mohr Siebeck, 1997).

103. Milik, *Books of Enoch*, 58, argued that the Book of Giants was the fifth book of an "Enochic Pentateuch" at Qumran, and was eventually replaced by the Book of Parables, but neither the manuscript evidence nor the texts support such a claim. See Nickelsburg, *1 Enoch 1*, 173, who notes that the Book of Giants is not an Enochic pseudepigraphon; and Stuckenbruck, *1 Enoch 91–108*, 12–13.

104. R. Horsley, *Scribes, Visionaries and the Politics of Second Temple Judea* (Louisville: Westminster John Knox, 2007), 155. Whether this "circle of 'Enoch' scribes" can be extended into a wing of Judaism known as "Enochic Judaism," as argued by Boccaccini, is less clear and beyond the scope of this book. See G. Boccaccini, *Beyond the Essene Hypothesis: The Parting of the Ways between Qumran and Enochic Judaism* (Grand Rapids: Eerdmans, 1998).

105. All translations of 1 Enoch are taken from Nickelsburg, *1 Enoch 1*; and Nickelsburg and VanderKam, *1 Enoch 2*.

SCRIBES AND LIBRARIES

role, both for the understanding of the figure of Enoch and for scribes generally in the third century BCE.[106] Since Enoch is called a scribe, we would expect that his first duty is to write. However, he is ordered to go and *speak* to the watchers, the angels who have sinned by consorting with human women, and condemn them for their deeds on earth. This is a prophetic action rather than a scribal one; the scribal circle that produced the Enoch books is attempting to establish itself as heir to the prophetic task.[107]

Enoch is soon writing, however. In 13:3–7 the watchers request that he draw up a petition to God on their behalf and recite it in the divine presence. This is a typical scribal act, drawing up a (quasi-legal) document and delivering it to the recipient. In 14:4 Enoch declares that he did draw up the petition, but the answer was negative. The whole answer to the petition is couched in 14:1 as "the book of the words of truth and the reprimand of the watchers who were from eternity," and 14:7 recapitulates the written form of the message with the phrase "the writing that I have written."

Enoch next appears as a scribe in 15:1, where he is delivering the watchers' petition to God in the heavenly throne room. Here he is called "Enoch, righteous man and scribe of truth" (γραμματεὺς τῆς ἀληθείας). Again, he is instructed, not to write, but to proclaim God's judgment to the watchers.

In 92:1, however, Enoch, who is identified again as a scribe, has written his epistle for his sons and for the last generations. The Epistle, which is identified as "wisdom," contains teaching, exhortation, and eschatological vision, specifically the Apocalypse of Weeks. In 93:2, in the introduction to the Apocalypse, Enoch states that his revelation comes from what he read in the heavenly tablets, a written form of revelation.[108] The introduc-

---

106. Scholars have called attention to the similarity of the figure of Enoch to that of Enmeduranki in Mesopotamian culture. Enmeduranki was listed as the seventh antediluvian king and king of the city of Sippar, the patron deity of which was Shamash, the sun god. Enoch is in the seventh generation of humans, according to the genealogy in Gen 5. Enoch lives only 365 years, the length of a solar year, before he is "taken by God" (Gen 5:23–24). Enmeduranki was the founder of the *baru* guild, scribes who specialized in the interpretation of dreams and omens. As we shall see, Enoch is a visionary who sees through dreams. See Horsley, *Scribes, Visionaries*, 154; and J. J. Collins, "The Sage in the Apocalyptic and Pseudepigraphic Literature," in *The Sage in Israel and the Ancient Near East*, ed. J. Gammie and L. Perdue (Winona Lake, IN: Eisenbrauns, 1990), 345–47.

107. Orton, *Understanding Scribe*, 81.

108. The heavenly tablets figure prominently in both Enoch (81:1, 2; 93:2; 103:2; 106:19) and Jubilees (28 times). The heavenly tablets are engraved with unchanging truths, which in Enoch are the actions and fate of humanity, past and present. In Jubi-

80

tion of these heavenly tablets in the Enoch literature indicates that revelation has moved from being primarily oral to primarily written. Therefore, the scribe, who can read and write, becomes the conduit for heavenly revelation.

However, in the Epistle it is clear that written revelation can mislead as much as oral revelation. In a series of woes, Enoch states, "Woe to those who write lying words and words of error; they write and lead many astray with their lies when they hear them" (98:15). In 104:10–13, Enoch predicts that his books will be given "to the righteous and pious and wise" (104:12), but other books will be written by sinners, which will "pervert many" (104:10; see also 99:10). These verses may point to other scribal groups that the Enoch circle opposed.[109] In the Similitudes 69:8–10 (not recovered at Qumran), writing is also viewed with deep suspicion, since it was taught to humanity by one of the fallen angels:

> And the name of the fourth is Penemue. This one showed the sons of men the bitter and the sweet and showed them all the secrets of their wisdom. He gave humans knowledge about writing with ink and papyrus, and therefore many went astray from old and forever and until this day. For humans were not born for this purpose, to confirm their trustworthiness through pen and ink.

Finally, Enoch is also termed a scribe in the Book of Giants. In 4QEnGiants[a] (4Q203), frag. 8 3–14, a letter is described as "A copy of the s[ec]ond tablet of the le[tter] in a do[cu]ment (written by) the hand of Enoch, the

---

lees the law is added, especially concerning the correct calendar and feasts. See, e.g., M. Segal, *The Book of Jubilees: Rewritten Bible, Redaction, Ideology and Theology*, JSJSup 117 (Leiden: Brill, 2007), 313–16. Enoch is only one of two humans privileged to read from (all of) the heavenly tablets; in Jubilees the Angel of the Presence reads from them to Moses, although in Jub. 23 Jacob is able to read from seven tablets. In 4QInstruction (4Q417 1 1:14–17), the "enlightened one" reads in the "(book of) remembrance," in which "the decree is engraved," and punishment is "inscribed." See F. García Martínez, "The Heavenly Tablets in the Book of Jubilees," in *Studies in the Book of Jubilees*, ed. M. Albani et al., TSAJ 65 (Tübingen: Mohr Siebeck, 1997), 243–60; Nickelsburg, *1 Enoch 1*, 59; and J. VanderKam, *Jubilees: A Commentary*, Hermeneia (Minneapolis: Fortress, 2018), 1:68–71. I would like to thank Professor VanderKam for sharing his manuscript with me prior to publication.

109. Nickelsburg, *1 Enoch 1*, 533–34, suggests that this passage refers to the rewriting of the Torah as found in, e.g., Jubilees and the Temple Scroll. Horsley suggests that it, along with 98:15, refers to opposing scribal circles ("Politics of Cultural Production," 139).

SCRIBES AND LIBRARIES

scribe of interpretation [בכ]ת[ב יד חנוך ספר פרשא]."[110] Enoch is evidently the scribe of a message of condemnation from God to "Šemîḥazah and all [his] co[mpanions]." In 4QEnGiants[b] (4Q530) frag. 2 14, Enoch is named a ספר פרשא, "the noted scribe" (lit. "the scribe of interpretation").[111] In this fragment, however, the giants who are speaking do not want Enoch to write, but to interpret (פרש) their troubling dream.

This last instance demonstrates the change in the role of the scribe that begins to be documented in the third century and continues into the second century BCE. Enoch is indeed a scribe in the way we have seen thus far in ancient Israel and Judah: he writes, drawing up documents on request and writing his own testimony; and he reads, most especially from the heavenly tablets (for the emphasis on writing, see 13:3–7; 81:1–2; 82:1; 89:61, 68, 76–77; 93:2). Also, like the "men of Hezekiah" who collected proverbs, and in the tradition of books like Proverbs and Sirach, he gives ethical exhortations to his children and the following generations (82:1–3; 91:1–4). But his role is much expanded. He proclaims the judgment of God to the watchers, like a prophet; he interprets dreams, like Joseph and Daniel; and he receives visions, again like a prophet but also like Daniel. (It is telling that Enoch received his first vision when he was learning to write, that is, as an apprentice scribe: "Two visions I saw before I took a wife, and the one was unlike the other. The first (was) when I was learning to write, and the second, before I took your mother" [83:2].) In Enoch we find the fusion of sapiential and prophetic traditions in the person of the scribe.[112]

These added functions would be enough to indicate that the role of the scribe has grown in importance by the third century BCE in Judah, at least in some circles. But Enoch the righteous scribe does still more. In the Astronomical Book (chs. 72–82), Enoch is the recipient of specialized knowledge of the heavens. This specialized knowledge connects the Astronomical Book, and the figure of Enoch, to the scribal communities of Mesopotamia, especially Babylon.

The Aramaic astronomical fragments from Qumran (4QEnAstr[a–d]; 4Q208–211), which were eventually distilled into the Astronomical Book found in 1 En. 72–82, testify to knowledge in Judean Aramaic scribal circles of Babylonian astronomy (i.e., the texts Enuma Anu Enlil and

---

110. The English translation is taken from L. Stuckenbruck, *The Book of Giants from Qumran: Texts, Translation, and Commentary*, TSAJ 63 (Tübingen: Mohr Siebeck, 1997), 91.
111. Milik, *Books of Enoch*, 305. Milik translates the phrase as "distinguished scribe."
112. Nickelsburg, *1 Enoch 1*, 59.

MUL.APIN).[113] No earlier Jewish text, Hebrew or Aramaic, exhibits this type of knowledge;[114] Seth Sanders ascribes it to a new "cosmopolitanism" in Judean scribal culture, and notes that it is telling that the Enoch astronomical manuscripts are written in Aramaic, the language of general scribal knowledge and communication from at least the Persian period.[115] Thus, in addition to the typical scribal proficiencies of writing and reading, and the new prophetic, visionary, and dream interpretation functions added to the portrait of Enoch the scribe, we can adduce a detailed knowledge of astronomy and cosmogony, such as we found in specialized groups of Mesopotamian scribes (see ch. 2). This astronomical knowledge, which is revealed to Enoch by the angels in the course of his heavenly journey, will take the form of written knowledge in books, to be passed down through the generations:

> Now my son Methuselah, I am telling you all these things and am writing (them) down. I have revealed all of them to you and have given you the books about all these things. My son, keep the book written by your father so that you may give (it) to the generations of the world. Wisdom I have given to you and to your children and to those who will be

113. M. Popović, "Networks of Scholars: The Transmission of Astronomical and Astrological Learning between Babylonians, Greeks and Jews," in *Ancient Jewish Sciences and the History of Knowledge in Second Temple Literature,* ed. J. Ben-Dov and S. Sanders (New York: New York University and the Institute for the Study of the Ancient World, 2014), 153–94. For two extremely detailed discussions of the astronomical and calendrical data found in the Astronomical Book and other Qumran calendrical texts, see J. Ben-Dov, *Head of All Years: Astronomy and Calendars at Qumran in Their Ancient Context,* STDJ 78 (Leiden: Brill, 2008); and Drawnel, *Aramaic Astronomical Book.*

114. We can assume that calendrical calculations took place in ancient Judah and Israel, but we have no direct knowledge of how this was done. As M. E. Stone puts it, "We know virtually nothing about astronomical views in the period of the First Temple while the details for the calendar are equally obscure" ("Enoch, Aramaic Levi and Sectarian Origins," *JSJ* 19 [1987]: 161).

115. S. Sanders, *From Adapa to Enoch: Scribal Culture and Religious Vision in Judea and Babylon,* TSAJ 167 (Tübingen: Mohr Siebeck, 2017), e.g., 369: "To be educated meant to know a Babylonian-based Aramaic scribal culture." Stone, "Enoch, Aramaic Levi and Sectarian Origins," 164–66, also notes the Mesopotamian character of the astronomical wisdom in the Astronomical Book, but makes the important point that by the time our earliest manuscript was copied, the information in it was outdated. Yet it continued to be copied. Also, there is no indication that the scribal circles that wrote and preserved the Enoch literature were interested in updating their literature with Greek science, which presumably would have been available to them at that time.

83

SCRIBES AND LIBRARIES

your children so that they may give this wisdom which is beyond their thought to their children for the generations. Those who understand will not sleep and will listen with their ear to learn this wisdom. It will be more pleasing to them than fine food to those who eat. (82:1-3)

These added functions, prophecy, visions, dream interpretation, and astronomical knowledge, all of which are some form of revealed wisdom, fall under the rubric of "mantic wisdom," a term evidently first coined by H.-P. Müller in 1971.[116] "Mantic wisdom" is meant as a description of a scribal category that includes both divination and wisdom literature. Since in Israel most forms of divination (such as extispicy) were categorically rejected (e.g., Lev 19:26; Deut 18:10-11), a better term for this phenomenon as found in Judean texts beginning with the books of Enoch is "esoteric wisdom." This esoteric wisdom includes cosmological and astronomical knowledge and its spinoffs, calendar calculations and astrological speculations, as well as dreams and visions and their correct interpretation. It is *revealed* wisdom; it is not accessible through empirical investigation.[117] The first place we see all of the characteristics listed above come together is in the portrayal of Enoch the scribe in his eponymous books.[118]

Finally, the books of Enoch indicate priestly concerns. Enoch's ascent to the heavenly throne room is modeled on Ezek 40-44, and in 1 En. 13:4-6 Enoch is found in an intercessory role. Further, Enoch's visions contain critiques of the contemporary sanctuary and its clergy: in the Book of the Watchers the archangel Michael is commissioned to cleanse the earth from impurity, and to initiate correct worship (10:20-22); 89:73-74 (from the Animal Apocalypse) argues that the sacrifices in the Second Temple were defiled from the beginning: "And they began again to place a table before the tower, but all the bread on it was polluted and not pure"; and the Apocalypse of Weeks omits any mention of the Second Temple,

---

116. As noted by J. Collins, "Sage," 347n17.

117. Nickelsburg and VanderKam, *1 Enoch 2*, 348.

118. Sanders, *From Adapa to Enoch*, 367, calls Enoch "the patron saint of scribes" in the Second Temple period. See also the discussion in Orton, *Understanding Scribe*, 79. Enoch continues to be lauded as the ideal scribe in literature later than the existence of the Qumran collection. In T. Ab. B 11:3-10 Enoch is identified as "scribe of righteousness." In 2 En. 23 Enoch is given a special pen for swift writing. Targum Pseudo-Jonathan on Gen 5:25 states, "he ascended to the firmament at the command of the Lord, and he was called Metatron, the Great Scribe." See VanderKam, *Enoch*, 157-67. In addition, 1QapGen ar 19:25-26 cites "the [Book] of the Words of Enoch," which may be a reference to the Book of the Watchers.

84

signaling disapproval.[119] These passages indicate that the scribes responsible for the production of the Enoch books may have been priests, or at least have had priestly connections.

This portrait of Enoch is deepened in the book of Jubilees. Jubilees, which used at least some of the books of Enoch as sources, portrays Enoch as the first scribe, and endows other patriarchs with scribal characteristics.[120]

Jubilees

The book of Jubilees, written in Hebrew (although now fully preserved only in Ge'ez) in the second century BCE,[121] was found at Qumran in fourteen certain and one probable copy, in Caves 1, 2, 3, 4, and 11.[122] In addition, three manuscripts, 4Q225–227, are designated "Pseudo-Jubilees" because they contain material characteristic of Jubilees but with no actual overlaps with the present book of Jubilees.[123]

Jubilees opens with Moses acting as a scribe, both for God and for the Angel of the Presence:[124]

> He [God] said to him [Moses]: "Pay attention to all the words that I tell you on this mountain. Write them in a book so that their generations may know that I have not abandoned them because of all the evil they

119. Nickelsburg, *1 Enoch 1*, 54–55, 67.

120. In what follows I am particularly indebted to VanderKam, *Jubilees*. All translations of Jubilees are taken from this commentary.

121. Dates for the composition of Jubilees vary widely, from the fifth-fourth centuries BCE to the first century CE. The majority of scholars favor a date in the second century BCE. VanderKam (*Jubilees*, 1:25–38, favors a date in the middle third of the second century BCE. Segal, following Kister, would date the (final redaction) of the book to the last third of the second century BCE (*Jubilees*, 322).

122. The certain copies are: 1Q17, 1Q18, 2Q19, 2Q20, 3Q5 3:1, 4Q176 19–21, 4Q216, 4Q218, 4Q219, 4Q220, 4Q221, 4Q222, 4Q223–224, and 11Q12. The probable copy is 4Q217. See D. Barthélemy and J. T. Milik, "17-18. Livre des Jubilés," in *Qumran Cave I*, DJD 1 (Oxford: Clarendon, 1955), 82–83; M. Baillet, *Les "petites grottes" de Qumrân*, by M. Baillet et al., 2 vols., DJD 3 (Oxford: Clarendon, 1962), 1:77–78, 96–97; J. VanderKam and J. T. Milik, "Jubilees," in *Qumran Cave 4.VIII: Parabiblical Texts, Part 1*, by H. Attridge et al., DJD 13 (Oxford: Clarendon, 1994), 1–140; and F. García Martínez et al., *Qumran Cave 11.II: 11Q2–18, 11Q20–31*, DJD 23 (Oxford: Clarendon, 1998), 207–20.

123. J. VanderKam and J. T. Milik, "4Qpseudo-Jubilees^a-c," in DJD 13, 141–76.

124. Moses is taught writing, according to Jubilees, by his father, Amram (47:9). This passing of the scribal art from father to son is important in Jubilees, as we will see below.

85

SCRIBES AND LIBRARIES

> have done in breaking the covenant between me and your children that
> I am making today on Mt. Sinai for their offspring." (1:5)

> "Now you write this entire message that I am telling you today, because
> I know their defiance and their stubbornness (even) before I bring them
> into the land that I promised by oath to their ancestors Abraham, Isaac,
> and Jacob: 'To your posterity I will give the land that flows with milk
> and honey.'" (1:7)

> "Now you write all these words that I tell you on this mountain: what
> is first and what is last and what is to come during all the divisions of
> the times that are for the law and for the testimony and for the weeks of
> their jubilees until eternity—until the time when I descend and live with
> them throughout all the ages of eternity." Then he told the Angel of the
> Presence to dictate to Moses (starting) from the beginning of creation
> until the time when "my temple is built among them throughout the
> ages of eternity." (1:26–27)

The purpose of Moses's writing is to bear witness against Israel in the future, when they will transgress the covenant (1:5). Thus Moses as scribe is drawing up a legal document, as scribes do; this document, however, is a legal document not between two human parties, but between God and Israel.[125] In v. 27, the Angel of the Presence is commanded to dictate to Moses.[126] The angel is to take his information from "the tablets (that told) of the divisions of the years from the time the law and the testimony were created" (1:29). Although the adjective is not used, these must be the *heavenly* tablets we have already encountered in the books of Enoch. Thus the writing that Moses will create is based on what is divine and permanent.[127]

125. J. Kugel suggests that Moses is told to write "in a book" (cf. Exod 34:27, where Moses is only told to write) "to stress that only *books* (like *Jubilees* itself) can be relied on (as opposed to the oral traditions espoused by his halakhic opponents)" (*A Walk through Jubilees: Studies in the Book of Jubilees and the World of Its Creation*, JSJSup 156 [Leiden: Brill, 2012], 21).

126. The Ethiopic here is *ṣaḥaf*, an imperative of the verb "to write," which seems to indicate that it is the Angel of the Presence who will do the writing. However, 4Q216 iv 6 preserves להכתיב, a hiphil, indicating that the angel is to dictate. See VanderKam and Milik, "Jubilees," 11–12.

127. In Jubilees the contents of the heavenly tablets are greatly expanded; everything concerning the creation and humanity is written therein. Examples include the parturient commandment in response to Eve's childbirth (3:10), the prohibition of beating someone

Scribes and Libraries in Ancient Israel

The next scribal figure encountered in Jubilees is Enoch himself. Enoch is, according to Jubilees, the very first scribe:

> He [Enoch] was the first of mankind who were born on the earth who learned (the art of) writing, instruction, and wisdom and who wrote down in a book the signs of the sky in accord with the fixed patterns of their months so that mankind would know the seasons of the years according to the fixed patterns of each of their months. He was the first to write a testimony. He testified to mankind in the generations of the earth. The weeks of the jubilees he related, and made known the days of the years; the months he arranged, and related the sabbaths of the years, as we had told him. While he slept he saw in a vision what has happened and what will occur—how things will happen for mankind during their history until the day of judgment. He saw everything and understood. He wrote a testimony for himself and placed it upon the earth against all mankind and for their history. (4:17–19)

Enoch is portrayed as a scribe, a sage, and a visionary. He is the first human to learn "(the art of) writing, instruction, and wisdom," the hallmarks of the scribal art.[128] Further, he wrote a book containing the signs of the heavens (most likely some form of the Astronomical Book is meant), and he organized the schematic calendar on which Jubilees is based (his "testimony"). He received visions and wrote them as a testimony (either the Book of Dreams or the Epistle). In 4:21 Enoch dwells with the angels for six jubilees, and he writes down everything they show him.

Thus far all of these characteristics are easily inferable from the Enoch books. However, the portrait in Jubilees goes further. Enoch, when he is removed from human society (cf. Gen 5:24), is placed in the garden of Eden, where he still resides, recording human sinfulness and its judgment: "He was taken from human society, and we led him into the Garden of Eden for (his) greatness and honor. Now he is there writing down the

---

to death, in response to Cain's murder of Abel (4:5), the commandments concerning the Festival of Weeks (6:17), the divisions of time (6:35), circumcision on the eighth day (15:25), Isaac's name (16:30), and the eradication of the Philistines (24:33).

128. H. Drawnel, *An Aramaic Wisdom Text from Qumran: A New Interpretation of the Levi Document* (Leiden: Brill, 2004), 81, 329, notes that the phrase "writing, instruction, and wisdom" is paralleled in Aramaic Levi Document 8:8: "writing [ספר], instruction, wisdom." Drawnel understands the term to encompass everything "linked to, and dependent upon, the knowledge of writing," including astronomical calculations. See further below.

SCRIBES AND LIBRARIES

judgment and condemnation of the world and all the wickedness of mankind" (4:23).[129] In Eden, Enoch serves as a priest, burning the evening incense offering (cf. Exod 30:7–8; he echoes Adam's action in Jub. 3:27).[130] Thus in Jubilees, Enoch is the master scribe, the model for all scribes in his practical and esoteric wisdom; his priestly character is emphasized; and he becomes the recorder of sin and judgment for all humanity.

The next patriarch associated with writing is Enoch's great-grandson Noah. In 7:20–26 Noah testifies (like Enoch) to his sons and grandsons, although writing is not mentioned in the passage. In 8:11 he consults a book, whose origin is not given, that gives the geographical division of the earth allotted to his three sons.[131] In 10:10–13 Noah writes in a book all that he has been taught about medicine by the angels (a necessary exercise to counteract the malevolent actions of the demons). Finally, just before his death he gives all his books to his oldest son Shem, the distant ancestor of Israel. Noah also acts as a priest. Upon exiting the ark he builds an altar and offers an atonement sacrifice (6:1–3); he establishes four memorial days (6:23–31) and celebrates at least one (7:3–5); and he celebrates the Festival of Weeks (6:17–18). Thus in Noah we again see the offices of scribe and priest combined in one person.

So far, scribal art in the hands of Enoch and Noah has been for the good of humanity. However, in the midst of the Noah story, the ability to read and write involves someone in sin. Kainan, the son of Arpachshad and thus Noah's great-grandson, is taught writing by his father (8:2). Here for the first time in Jubilees we see the scribal art being passed from father to son. Kainan, however, abuses his new-found ability. He discovers a prediluvian inscription from the watchers (8:3–4) that contains teaching about omens of the heavenly bodies—in other words, astrology and divination, which, according to Jubilees, is a cause of sin.[132] Kainan copies

---

129. T. Ab. B 11:3 also places Enoch in the garden of Eden, as the recording scribe at the trial of human souls.

130. Segal, *Jubilees*, 10–11, notes that portraying the patriarchs behaving like priests is part of the "priestly outlook" of the book. Orton, *Understanding Scribe*, 80, notes that Enoch's priestly role is a trait held in common with other eminent scribes, e.g., Ezra.

131. J. Van Ruiten notes that in 8:10 an Angel of the Presence is staying with Noah; thus the origin of the book may be divine (*Primaeval History Interpreted: The Rewriting of Genesis 1–11 in the Book of Jubilees*, JSJSup 66 [Leiden: Brill, 2000], 320–21). However, it may just as easily have been written by Noah, as suggested by Kugel, *Walk through Jubilees*, 77.

132. In Jub. 11:8, Nahor, the grandfather of Abram, is taught by his father "the studies of the Chaldeans: to practice divination and to augur by the signs of the sky." Here again, this kind of heavenly knowledge is negative and associated with idol worship. In 12:16–18, Abram observes

88

Scribes and Libraries in Ancient Israel

the inscription but keeps it secret, knowing it would anger Noah, another indication that this kind of divination, even though it can be part of the scribal art, is forbidden knowledge to Noah's righteous descendants.[133]

Chapter 11 begins the next major section in Jubilees, the story of the immediate ancestors of Israel, Abra(ha)m, Isaac, and Jacob. Once again, this section emphasizes scribal and priestly characteristics in those ancestors.

Our first introduction to Abram comes in 11:16, where he becomes aware of sin and his father teaches him writing. He then separates from his father to avoid idol worship. In this verse Abram's scribal ability is clearly tied, at least chronologically, to his budding righteousness. Abram, however, does not yet have the knowledge that will allow him to realize fully that righteousness. In 12:25–27 the Angel of the Presence teaches him Hebrew, which is identified as the language of creation that had fallen into disuse, presumably after the incident of the tower of Babel (Gen 11:1–9). Abram is now able to copy and study his ancestors' books. Jubilees thus establishes a chain of written tradition that begins with Enoch, goes through Noah, and continues with Abram.[134] Abra(ha)m also carries out priestly functions, adding more to those of Enoch and Noah (13:4, 9, 16; 14:11–12, 19; 15:2; 16:20–24; 18:5–8, 12). In this capacity he instructs Isaac on proper sacrifices, and says concerning them: "I found (it) written in the book of my ancestors, in the words of Enoch and the words of Noah" (21:10).

We are not told when or if Isaac learns to write, but since he learns proper sacrifices from Abraham, which are found in his book, it is safe to assume that he can. Jacob certainly does read and write, since it is one of the things that sets him apart favorably from Esau: "When the boys grew up, Jacob learned (the art of) writing, but Esau did not learn (it) because he was a rustic man and a hunter" (19:14). Because of this, Abraham realizes Jacob's superiority; writing is an essential virtue in the line of the patriarchs, beginning with Enoch: Enoch, Noah and Shem, Terah and Abram, and now Jacob.

Jacob is also the only human being in Jubilees to read from the heavenly tablets (not even Enoch has that privilege). It occurs in a night vision

---

the stars to predict the weather for the coming year. However, Abram realizes his mistake: "All the signs of the stars and the signs of the moon and the sun—all are under the Lord's control. Why should I be investigating (them)? If he wishes he will make it rain in the morning and evening; and if he wishes, he will not make it fall. Everything is under his control."

133. Van Ruiten, *Primaeval History*, 318. Josephus (*Ant.* 1.69–71) also has a story about prediluvian teachings from the Sethite line surviving the flood because they were inscribed on a stone pillar, but the story does not involve the watchers.

134. See van Ruiten, *Primaeval History*, 316.

SCRIBES AND LIBRARIES

at Bethel (32:21–26). Jacob is shown his own and his offspring's future and is commanded to write it all down, which he does in v. 26. Finally, Jacob too functions as a priest (31:3, 26; 32:4–6, 27; 44:1). He is particularly associated with the tithe; at Bethel he tithes all his goods (32:30), and then celebrates the Festival of Tabernacles (32:4–6). Jubilees uses the occasion of Jacob's tithe to move to the story of Levi, the final figure in the ancestral line of scribes and priests.

Jacob's tithe includes not only his goods but his son Levi: "At that time Rachel was pregnant with her son Benjamin. Jacob counted his sons from him. He went up (the list), and it came down on Levi in the Lord's share. His father put priestly clothes on him and ordained him" (32:3). Isaac has previously, in his deathbed blessing, declared Levi and his descendants to be priests (31:14–17), and in 32:1 Levi dreams that he has been appointed to the priesthood. Levi is thus set apart as priest, and to him will fall the scribal functions we have already seen in the ancestral figures beginning with Enoch. It is Levi who receives Jacob's books, including his ancestors' books, on his deathbed (45:15). Thus the scribal art in support of the priesthood is firmly lodged in the Levitical line.

Jubilees has continued the portrait of the ideal scribe that we encountered in the books of Enoch. Not only can the ideal scribe read and write, but he is a visionary, versed in astronomy and thus the calculations of the correct sacred calendar, and he functions as a priest. This portrait is also found in the Aramaic Levi Document, to be considered next.

The Aramaic Levi Document

The Aramaic Levi Document (ALD) was first identified among the Cairo Genizah documents by H. L. Pass and J. Arendzen, and its two fragments were published by R. H. Charles and A. Cowley in 1907. Pass also identified a section of a Greek Mount Athos Testament of Levi manuscript as containing a direct translation of a portion of the ALD.[135] Subsequently seven copies were identified in the Qumran corpus: 1QLevi (1Q21), 4QLevi[a] (4Q213), 4QLevi[b] (4Q213a), 4QLevi[c] (4Q213b), 4QLevi[d] (4Q214),

---

135. H. L. Pass and J. Arendzen, "Fragment of an Aramaic Text of the Testament of Levi," *JQR* 12 (1900): 651–61; R. H. Charles and A. Cowley, "An Early Source of the Testaments of the Patriarchs," *JQR* 19 (1907): 566–83.

90

Scribes and Libraries in Ancient Israel

4QLevi[e] (4Q214a), and 4QLevi[f] (4Q214b).[136] In 2004 Jonas C. Greenfield, Michael E. Stone, and Esther Eshel published a complete reconstruction and commentary, based on all the manuscript evidence.[137]

By common consensus, the ALD was written sometime in the third century BCE and served as a source for Jubilees.[138] The ALD, like Enoch and Jubilees, employs a solar calendar, although unlike Jubilees it is not polemical about it.[139] The purpose of the ALD is to demonstrate Levi's unique suitability for the priestly office and the characteristics required in an ideal priest. These characteristics include a rigorous purity, endogamy, and, most importantly for our purposes, a combination of the role of scholar-scribe with the priesthood.[140]

In the ALD emphasis is placed on the chain of transmission of written priestly lore that reaches back to Noah and his book (10:10), through Abraham (7:4), to Isaac, who teaches it to Levi (5:8). The importance of the scribal component in this priestly lore comes to the fore in the wisdom poem that contains Levi's teaching in ch. 13. In 13:4 Levi instructs his sons: "And now, my sons, <teach> reading and writing and teaching <of> wisdom to your children and may wisdom be eternal glory for you." The teaching that follows is typically sapiential. For example, compare 13:5 to Prov 3:35 and Sir 11:1:

For he who learns wisdom will (attain) glory through it, but he who despises wisdom will become an object of disdain and scorn. (ALD 13:5)

The wise will inherit honor, but stubborn fools, disgrace. (Prov 3:35)

The wisdom of the humble lifts their heads high, and seats them among the great. (Sir 11:1)

136. Published by J. T. Milik, "'Dires de Moïse,'" in *Qumran Cave I*, by D. Barthélemy and J. T. Milik, DJD 1 (Oxford: Clarendon, 1955), 87–90; and by M. E. Stone and J. C. Greenfield, "Aramaic Levi Document," in *Qumran Cave 4.XVII: Parabiblical Texts, Part 3*, by G. Brooke et al., DJD 22 (Oxford: Clarendon, 1996), 1–72.

137. J. C. Greenfield et al., *The Aramaic Levi Document: Edition, Translation, Commentary*, SVTP 19 (Leiden: Brill, 2004). All translations are taken from this volume. Drawnel published an alternative textual reconstruction with commentary in *Aramaic Wisdom Text*, esp. 54–55.

138. Greenfield et al., *Aramaic Levi Document*, 19. Drawnel, *Aramaic Wisdom Text*, 71, would date it as early as the end of the fourth century BCE. The ALD was also a source for the Levi booklet in the Testament of the Twelve Patriarchs, now found only in a later Christian redaction.

139. Greenfield et al., *Aramaic Levi Document*, 20.

140. See R. Kugler, *From Patriarch to Priest: The Levi-Priestly Tradition from Aramaic Levi to Testament of Levi*, EJL 9 (Atlanta: Scholars Press, 1996).

SCRIBES AND LIBRARIES

In 13:6, Joseph, a quintessential wisdom figure, is portrayed as an example; he also "taught reading and writing and the teaching of wisdom." It is the combination of this sapiential teaching with the disquisition on proper sacrifices in chs. 6–10, that is, linking the roles of scribe/sage with priest, that is unique to the ALD.[141]

According to the ALD, one of the most important functions of the scribe-priest is to teach, at least to their descendants, thereby indicating that the wisdom of which it speaks is not esoteric or hidden. The author of the ALD evinces little interest in the mysteries of astronomy or calendar calculation[142] or even in future prediction, although Levi does have a vision in 4:5–13 that predicts the exaltation of the priesthood and future strife in "the kingdom of the sword" in vague terms. Thus in the ALD the figure of Levi combines the office of priest with that of scribe; to be a scribe for the author includes teaching but also the ability to have and understand visions/dreams. In this the ALD is like Enoch and especially Jubilees.

Daniel

The last major text in this section to be considered is the book of Daniel.[143] Daniel is dated by common consensus between 168 and 164 BCE; the oldest manuscripts of Daniel found at Qumran, 4Q114 and 4Q116,

---

141. Drawnel, *Aramaic Wisdom Text*, 3. Kugler, *From Patriarch to Priest*, 109, notes that the priestly teaching "lacks substantial connection with known Pentateuchal laws," which indicates that at least in some third-century priestly circles sacrificial practice went beyond Torah legislation.

142. Drawnel, *Aramaic Wisdom Text*, 3, argues that the calculation of the meal offering in 9:9–13 "constitutes a metrological exercise according to the Babylonian sexigesimal system," but the text does not draw attention to it.

143. Eight copies of Daniel were recovered from the Qumran caves: 1QDan^a (1Q71), 1QDan^b (1Q72), 4QDan^a (4Q112), 4QDan^b (4Q113), 4QDan^c (4Q114), 4QDan^d (4Q115), 4QDan^e (4Q116), and 6QDan (6Q7), as well as several small fragments now in private collections. See D. Barthélemy, "Daniel (premier exemplaire)," in *Qumran Cave I*, by D. Barthélemy and J. T. Milik, DJD 1 (Oxford: Clarendon, 1955), 150–51 (republished in T. Elgvin, *Gleanings from the Caves: Dead Sea Scrolls and Artefacts from the Schøyen Collection* [London: Bloomsbury T&T Clark, 2016], 247–70); E. Ulrich, "Daniel," in *Qumran Cave 4.XI: Psalms to Chronicles*, by E. Ulrich et al., DJD 16 (Oxford: Clarendon, 2000), 239–90; M. Baillet, "Daniel," in *Les "petites grottes" de Qumrân*, by M. Baillet et al., 2 vols., DJD 3 (Oxford: Clarendon, 1961), 1:114–16. A small fragment of Daniel belongs to the Green Collection: R. Duke et al., "Daniel 10:18–20," in E. Tov et al., *Dead Sea Scrolls Fragments in the Museum Collection* (Leiden: Brill, 2016), 200–209. In addition, two small papyrus fragments of Daniel have been

Scribes and Libraries in Ancient Israel

dating to the late second or early first centuries BCE, are thus only about fifty years removed from the final form of the book.[144]

Strangely enough, the title "scribe" never appears in Daniel, although it is quite clear that the heroes of the book, Daniel and his companions, are portrayed as learned scribes and counselors, "wise men," in the court of the emperor(s).[145] In ch. 1 Daniel and his companions are described as "versed in every branch of wisdom, endowed with knowledge and insight, and competent to serve in the king's palace" (1:4); further, they are taught "the literature and language of the Chaldeans" (1:4; ספר ולשון כשדים). In the apocalyptic chapters (7–12), the depiction of Daniel as a scribe continues: Daniel writes down his dream (7:1), he consults the prophecy of Jeremiah (9:2), and he is instructed to keep a sealed book (12:4).[146]

In addition to the usual scribal talents of writing and reading, Daniel adds the esoteric abilities to interpret dreams (chs. 2, 4) and cryptic writing (ch. 5). In the apocalyptic chapters Daniel becomes a visionary; his visions are interpreted for him by an angelic mediator. As in Enoch and

---

purchased by Southwestern Baptist Theological Seminary; their designation is DSS F.Dan2 and DSS F.Dan3.

Further, seven sets of fragments related to Daniel were found in Cave 4: Prayer of Nabonidus (4Q242), 4QpsDan[a] (4Q243), 4QpsDan[b] (4Q244), 4QpsDan[c] (4Q245), an Aramaic Apocalypse (4Q246), Daniel–Susanna (4Q551), and Four Kingdoms[a, b] (4Q552–553). See J. Collins, "242. 4QPrayer of Nabonidus ar," 83–93; J. Collins and P. Flint, "243–245. 4Qpseudo-Daniel[a–c] ar," 95–164; and E. Puech, "246. 4QApocryphe de Daniel ar," 165–84, all in *Qumran Cave 4. XVII: Parabiblical Texts, Part 3*, by G. Brooke et al., DJD 22 (Oxford: Clarendon, 1996); E. Puech, *Qumran Cave 4. XXVII: Textes araméens, deuxième partie: 4Q550–575, 580–582*, DJD 37 (Oxford: Clarendon, 2009), 47–90. These texts contain scattered references to books and writing: in Prayer of Nabonidus 3:5, someone is commanded to write down the story; in 4Q243 5 2, a book is mentioned; and in 4Q245 1, Daniel reads in a book that contains a list of high priests and kings.

144. C. Newsom, *Daniel*, OTL (Louisville: Westminster John Knox, 2014), 11; J. J. Collins, *Daniel*, Hermeneia (Minneapolis: Fortress, 1993), 26. Daniel, like the book of Ezra, is written in both Hebrew and Aramaic. Chs. 1 and 8–12 are in Hebrew, while chs. 2–7 are in Aramaic. J. Collins, *Daniel*, 24, plausibly suggests that chs. 1–7 were originally in Aramaic, but chap. 1 was later translated into Hebrew by the redactor of the final form of the book in order to make an introduction to the book as a whole. The importance of Aramaic as a language of scribal learning will be discussed below.

145. Newsom, *Daniel*, 21. For a discussion of Dan 1–6 as royal courtier tales, see L. Wills, *The Jew in the Court of the Foreign King: Ancient Jewish Court Legends* (Minneapolis: Fortress, 1990).

146. Newsom, *Daniel*, 22, notes: "Scribal self-consciousness is even more marked in the apocalypses than in the narratives, with repeated references to books and writing."

93

SCRIBES AND LIBRARIES

Jubilees, Daniel refers to heavenly books (although not the heavenly tablets): in his vision of the heavenly court, books (ספרין) are opened (7:10); a book of truth (כתב אמת) is mentioned in 10:21; and in 12:1 a book (ספר) records those who are to be delivered from persecution.

Rather than ספרים ("scribes"), the title the final redactors of Daniel prefer is משכילים (*maskilim*), the "wise," who are teachers of the people (11:33).[147] These *maskilim* have a sense of their own authority, separate from their sponsors (who are unnamed), since they take it upon themselves to teach the עם (lit. "people") and the רבים ("the many").[148] The *maskilim* will eventually be vindicated; they will "shine like the brightness of the sky . . . like the stars" (12:3). These *maskilim* cannot be identified with any certainty.[149] The most that can be said is that they represent a circle of scholar-scribes opposed to the events leading up to the Antiochene crisis, and they opposed the pro-Hellenistic party by their teaching.

The books of Enoch, Jubilees, and the ALD constitute a constellation of texts that draw portraits of the ancestors of Israel as scribes and priests. The book of Daniel also belongs in this group, although it is not concerned with the ancestors. Scribes are not merely experts in writing and reading, but they also teach, and they may function as prophets and/or visionaries. There are several smaller texts within the Qumran corpus in which hints of this same portrait are present.

Related Texts

The Testament of Qahat (4Q542) and the Visions of Amram (4Q543–549) were recognized by Milik as related to the ALD as three documents that recounted the first generations of the priesthood: Levi > Qahat (Kohath)

---

147. J. Collins, *Daniel*, 385, states, "There can be little doubt that the author of Daniel belonged to this circle."

148. Horsley, *Scribes, Visionaries,* 174. The term משכיל figures prominently in some Qumran sectarian texts as a leadership designation, while the term רבים denotes the sectarian community. This similarity in vocabulary and the number of copies of Daniel and Pseudo-Daniel literature in the Qumran collection indicates the importance of the Daniel literature to the wing of Judaism that collected the Qumran scrolls.

149. Attempts have been made to identify them with the Hasidim of 1 Maccabees (see above), but that identity is uncertain at best. Horsley, *Scribes, Visionaries,* 191, points out that the *maskilim* do not take up arms in Daniel, unlike the Hasidim.

Scribes and Libraries in Ancient Israel

> Amram > Aaron.[150] Both texts are concerned with the role of the priesthood, although the Testament of Qahat contains a direct reference to the books of the priestly line that is absent from the Visions of Amram. In 4QTQahat 1 ii 9–13 we find:

> Now, to you my son Amram I command [. . .] and to your chil[dren], and to their descendants I command [. . .] and gave to my father Levi, and that my father Levi [gave] to me. [. . .] all my writings as a testimony, that you should take warning from them [. . .] great merit for you in them when you carry them along with you *va* [*cat . . .*

While the Visions of Amram does not contain any mention of the priests as scribes, it does contain, as its name suggests, visions by Amram concerning the battle between light and darkness on the earth. Here Amram, like his priestly ancestors, is shown as a visionary.

In 4Qpseudo-Jub[c] 2 1–6 (4Q227), Enoch appears; he is taught by the Angels of the Presence, and writes everything down, as he does in Jubilees. These small references strengthen the portrait of the scribe created by Enoch, Jubilees, and the ALD.

Finally, a small Aramaic text, 4Q550, is related to the Aramaic court tales found in Daniel. It was first published by J. T. Milik in 1992 under the title "4Qproto-Esther Aramaic."[151] Milik claimed that these fragments were the "models" or "sources" for the extant witnesses to the book of Esther (of which, famously, no fragments were recovered from the Qumran caves). Subsequent studies demonstrated that the connection to Esther was simply that of genre; the fragments contain the story of a Jew in the court of a foreign king (Xerxes), who, after misadventures, rises to prominence.[152] The genre of these fragments, then, is the royal courtier tale, like the book of Daniel.

---

150. J. T. Milik, "Écrits préessénniens de Qumrân: d'Hènoch à Amram," in *Qumrân: Sa piété, sa théologie, et son milieu*, ed. M. Delcor, BETL 46 (Paris: Duculot; Leuven: Leuven University Press, 1978), 91–106.

151. J. T. Milik, "Les modèles araméens du livre d'Esther dans la grotte 4 de Qumrân," *RevQ* 15 (1992): 321–99.

152. See S. W. Crawford, "Has *Esther* Been Found at Qumran? *4Qproto-Esther* and the *Esther* Corpus," *RevQ* 17 (1996): 307–25; and J. J. Collins and D. Green, "The Tales from the Persian Court (4Q550[a-c])," in *Antikes Judentum und frühes Christentum: Festschrift für Hartmut Stegemann*, ed. B. Kollmann et al., BZNW 97 (Berlin: de Gruyter, 1998), 39–50.

SCRIBES AND LIBRARIES

In these fragments the word "scribe" (ספרא) appears several times (frags. 2, 5, and 6). Bagasraw, a Jew, is described as a "good scribe" (ספרא טבא), and, in an enigmatic passage, "the fear of the house of the scribe [בית ספרא] fell on him."[153] Thus, as in Daniel, we have a Jew in a foreign court functioning as a scribe, some kind of court official; however, unlike in Daniel, the term ספרא is actually used.

That the majority of the texts discussed in this section are in Aramaic brings us to the importance of Aramaic as the language of scribal learning in the Persian and into the Hellenistic periods. As noted in ch. 2, scribes in Mesopotamia began to specialize in Aramaic beginning at least in the Assyrian period; known as *sepiru* (in which we recognize the root ספר), they specialized in writing on skin/parchment with ink. As recent studies have shown, the mechanism by which Mesopotamian learning reached Judaism was through Aramaic, and Jewish scholar-scribes would have been trained in Aramaic as well as Hebrew.[154] Scribes transmitted texts in Aramaic and Hebrew with equal skill and using the same set of techniques.[155]

The scribes in the Aramaic texts we have outlined above are the "founders" and "keepers" of the scribal art in Judaism, Enoch and Levi in particular. To this group we may add Ezra, part of whose eponymous book is preserved in Aramaic. Thus the presence of these Aramaic texts in the Qumran collection, with their emphasis on scribal knowledge, testifies to the importance of Mesopotamian (as opposed to Hellenistic) culture as the more cosmopolitan background to the Judean scribal repertoire in the Second Temple period. The presence of copies of the books of Enoch, Jubilees, the Aramaic Levi Document and its related texts, and Daniel in large numbers in the Qumran collection shows the centrality of those books to the wing of Judaism of which Qumran was a part, and points to the importance of the scribal art in that movement.

---

153. Milik understood ספרא as a proper name, Saphra.

154. Sanders, *From Adapa to Enoch*, 240, goes so far as to say that the dominant form of scribal training would have been Aramaic.

155. D. Machiela, in a study of the Aramaic texts from Qumran, notes that "there are no stark discrepancies between the Aramaic and Hebrew texts from the caves regarding . . . material features, such as the ink used, stitching, or other technologies" ("The Aramaic Dead Sea Scrolls: Coherence and Context in the Library of Qumran," in *The Dead Sea Scrolls at Qumran and the Concept of a Library*, ed. S. W. Crawford and C. Wassén, STDJ 116 [Leiden: Brill, 2014], 248).

96

Libraries and Archives in Israel and Judah: The Archaeological Evidence

Israel and Judah in the Iron Age

When we turn to ancient Israel and Judah for evidence of libraries and/ or archives, we are met with almost complete silence. The archaeological evidence is extremely sparse, and the textual evidence is nonexistent.[156] The Samaria ostraca seem to have come from a minor administrative archive, while the city of David bullae are probably the remnants of a private archive of some sort. One group of the Arad ostraca seems to have constituted a private archive. Otherwise, no archives or libraries, whether state-sponsored or private, have come to light in Iron Age Israel or Judah.[157]

The biblical record makes no mention of archives or libraries either. It is reasonable to postulate that archives were kept in the royal palaces; the presence of scribes in the palace in Jerusalem, mentioned above, suggests this. The references to (evidently) written sources like "The Chronicles of the Kings of Israel/Judah"[158] also is suggestive of a royal archive. However, this is only informed guesswork. Likewise, it is usually assumed that the royal sanctuaries at Bethel, Dan, and Jerusalem would have had archives or libraries, as did temples elsewhere in the ancient Near East. But again, this is in the realm of speculation. However, even exercising all caution, it is reasonable to state that the most likely places for the existence of state-sponsored archives or libraries would have been the royal capitals of Samaria and Jerusalem, and for temple libraries the royal sanctuaries of Dan, Bethel, and Jerusalem.

---

156. Niditch, *Oral World and Written Word*, 61–64.

157. Part of the explanation for this dearth of evidence is the fact that the Temple Mount in Jerusalem, the traditional site of Solomon's temple, has never been professionally excavated. Another probable explanation is that written records would have been on papyrus or skin, which is highly perishable.

158. 1 Kgs 14:19, 29; 15:7, 23, 31; 16:5, 14, 20, 27; 22:39, 45; 2 Kgs 1:18; 8:23; 10:34; 12:19; 13:8, 12; 14:15, 18, 28; 15:6, 11, 15, 21, 26, 31, 36; 16:19; 20:20; 21:17, 25; 23:28; 24:5.

SCRIBES AND LIBRARIES

The Postexilic Period

A Temple Library in Jerusalem?

Although we have no concrete material evidence for the temple of the postexilic period and its compound, there is some written evidence in later literature for the presence of a library and/or archive in the temple in Jerusalem. The Seleucid Charter, discussed above, demonstrates that scribes worked in the Jerusalem temple in the early second century BCE, which would indicate the presence of at least a working archive.

According to 2 Macc 2:13–15, Nehemiah founded a library in the Jerusalem temple that was restocked by Judas Maccabeus after the Antiochean crisis.[159] In the passage, Nehemiah is credited with founding a library, a βιβλιοθήκη, in Jerusalem, and collecting τὰ περὶ τῶν βασιλέων βιβλία καὶ προφητῶν καὶ τὰ τοῦ Δαυιδ καὶ ἐπιστολὰς βασιλέων περὶ ἀναθεμάτων—"books about the kings and prophets, and the writings of David, and letters of kings about votive offerings."[160] Further, after the war against Antiochus IV Epiphanes, Judas Maccabeus refounded this library, and τὰ διαπεπτωκότα διὰ τὸν γεγονότα πόλεμον ἡμῖν ἐπισυνήγαγεν πάντα, "collected all the books that had been lost on account of the war" (2:14 NETS). While we have no evidence (other than this passage) that Nehemiah founded a library,[161] this letter in 2 Maccabees enables us to

---

159. This passage is part of the second letter appended to the epitome of Jason of Cyrene that makes up the bulk of 2 Maccabees. Its date is disputed. T. Bergren, "Nehemiah in 2 Maccabees 1:10–2:18," *JSJ* 28 (1997): 249, gives a date range between 130 and 63 BCE. R. Doran, *Temple Propaganda: The Purpose and Character of 2 Maccabees*, CBQMS 12 (Washington, DC: Catholic Biblical Association of America, 1981), 113, prefers not to date the letter itself, but says it was linked to the epitome after 124 BCE. Schwartz, *2 Maccabees*, 11, prefers a much earlier date for the letter, arguing for 143/142 BCE. Goldstein, *II Maccabees*, 162–63, argues for a date of 103/102 BCE.

160. Trans. J. Schaper, *NETS*, 506.

161. It is not mentioned in his eponymous book, although he does produce a memoir, which may be referred to in 2 Macc 2:13: "in the records and the memoirs of Nehemiah concerning these things." Later references to Nehemiah likewise do not mention a library. For example, Sir 49:13 credits Nehemiah with rebuilding the wall of Jerusalem, setting up its gates, and rebuilding houses, but makes no mention of a library. Josephus, in *Ant.* 11.165, has Nehemiah request permission to build Jerusalem's wall and to finish the building of the temple. But Josephus here may be dependent on 2 Maccabees, which is our earliest attestation of this tradition. The point in 2 Maccabees seems to be to equate Judas with Nehemiah: both are military leaders, both defended Jerusalem and the temple, and both were zealous defenders of the Torah.

Scribes and Libraries in Ancient Israel

assume that there was a library in the Jerusalem temple, associated with the Hasmonean dynasty.[162]

Josephus is also a personal witness to a temple library, relating in *Antiquities* the deposit of sacred texts in the temple (5.51; 10.57–58) and in *Jewish War* the theft of Torah scrolls from the temple in 70 to be part of Vespasian's triumph in Rome (7.150, 162). A scroll is in fact pictured on the Arch of Titus in Rome among the spoils from the Jewish temple.[163] Josephus further claims to have sacred books from Jerusalem as a gift from Titus (*Life* 75). He also discusses archives (τῶν ἀρχείων) in which the genealogies of the priests were scrupulously kept (*Ag. Ap.* 1.30–35). These archives were destroyed by fire in 67 and 70 (*J.W.* 2.428; 6.354). Finally, he mentions the keeping of records (τὰς ἀναγραφὰς) assigned to the chief priests and prophets (*Ag. Ap.* 1.28–29).

Rabbinic sources also claim that the temple complex housed "biblical" scrolls, particularly Torah scrolls (e.g., m. Moʿed Qaṭ. 3:4; m. Kelim 15:6; y. Sanh. 2:6; y. Šeqal. 4:2). According to the rabbis, three Torah scrolls were kept in the temple court, which were used to compare readings (y. Taʿan. 4:2; ʾAbot R. Nat. 46; Sipre Deut 356; and Sop. 4.4).[164] While these traditions are late, it is likely that they maintain a historical memory of scrolls kept in the temple complex, even though their details may not be trustworthy.

Thus it is safe to say that there was a library and archive in the temple in Jerusalem, overseen by the priests, and staffed by scribes, at least some

---

162. One of the debates concerning this passage is whether it is an indication of an early notion of a Jewish canon. See, e.g., S. Z. Leiman, *The Canonization of Scripture: The Talmudic and Midrashic Evidence* (Hamden, CT: Archon, 1981), 28–29. Leiman suggests that it was Judas's collecting activity that closed the canon of Scripture, but this is putting much too much weight on the vague categories in this passage. A. van der Kooij, "The Canonization of Ancient Books Kept in the Temple in Jerusalem," in *Canonization and Decanonization*, ed. A. van der Kooij and K. van der Toorn (Leiden: Brill, 1998), 30, 32, believes that the passage indicates a tripartite canon, but not one that is necessarily closed or complete. Schwartz, *2 Maccabees*, 166, does not push the evidence so far, but does suggest "at least a whiff of a tripartite division." However, a rather important element of that tripartite division is missing, i.e., the Torah. See also the discussion in T. Lim, "A Theory of the Majority Canon," *ExpTim* 124 (2013): 368, who argues that Judas did not establish a library, but "gathered books in a general sense." See also now T. Lim, *The Formation of the Jewish Canon*, AYBRL (New Haven: Yale University Press, 2013), 94, 116–17.

163. A. F. J. Klijn, "A Library of Scriptures in Jerusalem?," TUGAL 124 (1977): 269.

164. M. Haran, "Archives, Libraries, and the Order of the Biblical Books," *JANESCU* 22 (1993): 56; Klijn, "Library of Scriptures in Jerusalem?," 270–71; S. Talmon, "The Three Scrolls of the Law That Were Found in the Temple Court," *Textus* 2 (1962): 14–27.

99

SCRIBES AND LIBRARIES

of whom were most likely also priests and Levites. This library housed sacred scrolls, definitely Torah scrolls but undoubtedly also the other books that became part of the later Jewish canon, as well as archival material. We cannot be certain what other types of literature may have been stored in the temple library (e.g., books of the later Apocrypha, or other Jewish literary works). The library may have been located in the outbuildings of the temple compound, where Josephus says that treasuries were located (*J.W.* 6.277).

A Library at Masada?

The desert fortress of Masada, at the southwest shore of the Dead Sea, was excavated by Yigael Yadin from 1963 to 1965.[165] The northern palace at Masada, built by Herod the Great, is a spectacular example of Herod's architecture. The palace was constructed in three levels; the middle level, in which our interest lies, contains the remains of a circular structure in front of a wall containing five large niches built against the cliff wall. These wall niches were interpreted by the excavators as being a purely constructive element built to support the ceiling (Yadin) or as having a cultic role (Avi Yonah). Recently, Hanan Eshel has suggested that the wall niches contained shelves (see below) that were used to hold food and drink for palace guests and thus were part of a refectory.[166]

However, as first recognized by Volker Strocka, these wall niches most closely resemble the type of niches found in Roman library construction.[167] The first three niches contain two pairs of parallel grooves for the insertion of book shelves, with a vertical space between the grooves of 0.9 centimeters. Debris found on the floor beneath the niches contained numerous pieces of charred wood (the remains of shelves), and ash with organic materials (the remains of book rolls?). Hirschfeld estimates that these three niches could have contained between 250 and 470 book rolls.[168]

The rest of the terrace contained storage rooms, a reading room attached to the niches, and the circular structure, which was a colonnade.

165. For the following, see Y. Hirschfeld, "The Library of King Herod in the Northern Palace of Masada," *Scripta classica Israelica* 23 (2004): 69-80.

166. H. Eshel, *Masada: An Epic Story* (Jerusalem: Carta, 2009), 119-20. I would like to thank Jodi Magness for this reference.

167. V. Strocka, "Römische Bibliotheken," in *Gymnasium Heidelberg: Zeitschrift für Kultur der Antike und humanistische Bildung* 88 (1981): 308n27.

168. Hirschfeld, "Library of King Herod," 74.

100

Scribes and Libraries in Ancient Israel

The walls were decorated with frescoes. Hirschfeld suggests the circular structure was used for reading in the open light.[169] Taken together, all these elements suggest that the identification of this middle terrace as a library in the Roman style is certainly possible, and thus gives us the only tentatively identified library complex in ancient Palestine.[170]

The Judean Desert Text Collections from Sites Other Than Qumran

Finally, we will explore the manuscript collections found at sites in the Judean Desert other than Qumran, which present us with primary evidence for collections of written texts in the late Second Temple period. A comparison of these collections with the Qumran scrolls corpus demonstrates how dissimilar the Qumran scrolls are from these other Judean collections, which are private and primarily documentary. What follows is a survey of the non-Qumran Judean Desert text collections from the late Second Temple period: those from Wadi Murabbaʿat, Nahal Hever, and Masada, before we turn to the Qumran collection in ch. 4.

Wadi Murabbaʿat

The caves of the Wadi Murabbaʿat, situated 18 kilometers south of Qumran and 25 kilometers southeast of Jerusalem, were first discovered by bedouin in 1952.[171] They served as refuge caves in both the Great Jewish Revolt against Rome (66–73 CE) and the Bar Kokhba revolt (132–135 CE). Over 150 manuscripts were discovered in the caves, although many are unclassified. The texts, all of which date to the first and second centuries CE, are both skin and papyri, and are written in Hebrew, Ara-

---

169. Hirschfeld, "Library of King Herod," 76–77.

170. J. Patrich, "The Warehouse Complex and Governor's Palace (Areas KK, CC, and NN, May 1993–December 1995)," in *Caesarea Papers 2: Herod's Temple, the Provincial Governor's Praetorium and Granaries, the Later Harbor, a Gold Coin Hoard, and Other Studies*, ed. K. G. Holum et al. (Portsmouth, RI: Journal of Roman Archaeology, 1999), 104, suggests that the rectangular building in stratum VII or VI in Area CC, identified as part of the governor's palace complex, may have been an archive or a library on the basis of the horizontal wall niches found there. To my knowledge, no other library or archive room has been identified in excavations in Greco-Roman Palestine.

171. H. Eshel, "Murabbaʿat, Wadi: Written Material," *EDSS* 1:583–86.

SCRIBES AND LIBRARIES

maic, and Greek. Several religious texts were discovered there, including one copy of Deuteronomy, one copy of Isaiah, a scroll containing the Minor Prophets, and a scroll containing parts of Genesis, Exodus, and Numbers, which may have been an entire Torah scroll when whole. In addition, there were phylacteries, a mezuzah, and a prayer. These religious texts were the personal property of those who found refuge in the caves. The vast majority of texts, however, are fiscal and administrative documents (e.g., contracts, deeds, and accounts) written on papyri in Aramaic and Greek, including a cache of letters from Simeon ben Kosiba, that is, Bar Kokhba, himself.[172]

Naḥal Ḥever

The caves of Naḥal Ḥever, located south of Wadi Murabbaʿat and north of Masada, were first explored in 1953 by Yohanan Aharoni. The caves served as hiding places for refugees fleeing the Romans during the Bar Kokhba revolt. Written materials were found in two caves, the Cave of Letters (Cave 5/6) and the Cave of Horrors (Cave 8). In addition, groups of unprovenanced fragments sold to the Palestine Archaeological Museum by the bedouin (who claimed they came from Wadi Seiyal) are thought to come from Naḥal Ḥever.[173] Over seventy texts were found in controlled excavations, while over fifty are unprovenanced. The Cave of Letters yielded three scriptural texts: a manuscript of Numbers, one of Deuteronomy, and one of Psalms. There were also a phylactery and a hymn text. All the other manuscripts are documentary texts from the last decade of the first century CE through the year 135 CE, in Hebrew, Aramaic, Nabatean, and Greek. They include letters from Bar Kokhba and the personal archives of the women Babatha and Salome Komaïse. The Cave of Horrors revealed a Greek Minor Prophets scroll, a prayer, and a letter (?) in Greek.[174] The vast majority of the manuscript finds from

172. For the publication see Benoit et al., DJD 2.
173. See P. Flint, "Biblical Scrolls from Naḥal Ḥever and 'Wadi Seiyal': Introduction," in *Miscellaneous Texts from the Judaean Desert*, by James Charlesworth et al., DJD 38 (Oxford: Clarendon, 2000), 133; and H. M. Cotton and A. Yardeni, "General Introduction," *Aramaic, Hebrew and Greek Documentary Texts from Naḥal Ḥever and Other Sites*, DJD 27 (Oxford: Clarendon, 1997), 1–6.
174. H. Cotton, "Ḥever, Naḥal: Written Material," *EDSS* 1:359–61; E. Tov, *The Greek Minor Prophets Scrolls from Naḥal Ḥever (8ḤevXIIgr)*, DJD 8 (Oxford: Clarendon, 1990).

102

the two caves combined are documentary, that is, legal or administrative texts, in which are mixed a few literary texts, which apparently belonged to the people who took refuge in the caves.

Masada

Fifteen documents belonging to the Jewish rebels who held the fortress against the Roman legion were discovered at Masada.[175] The Jewish Masada scrolls are all religious texts, written in Hebrew on parchment, with the exception of one Greek letter written on papyrus.[176] Most of the documents were brought from Jerusalem by the rebels, and at least two (MasDeut, MasEzek) were used in the temporary synagogue they constructed in the fortress.[177] The documents include one manuscript of Genesis, two manuscripts of Leviticus, one of Deuteronomy, two of Psalms, and one of Ezekiel, as well as one apocryphal Genesis work, a copy of Sirach, a Joshua Apocryphon, a copy of the Songs of the Sabbath Sacrifice, a work similar to Jubilees, and a liturgical composition that has been identified as Samaritan.[178] What is striking about the Masada collection is the much higher proportion of literary/religious texts to documentary texts than in the other two collections. The lack of personal archives, such as we saw in the Wadi Murabbaʿat and Naḥal Ḥever collections, is especially notable, indicating that those who fled south from the siege of Jerusalem chose not to bring their personal documents with them.

The presence of a copy of the Songs of the Sabbath Sacrifice, found in nine copies in the Qumran caves, as well as a Joshua Apocryphon, may

175. Latin and Greek papyri belonging to the Roman occupants of the site after its fall in 73 were also discovered. These are all documentary texts, with the exception of a copy of Virgil and an unidentified poetic text. See A. Lange with U. Mittmann-Richert, "Annotated List of the Texts from the Judaean Desert Classified by Content and Genre," in *The Texts from the Judaean Desert: Indices and an Introduction to the Discoveries in the Judaean Desert Series,* ed. E. Tov, DJD 39 (Oxford: Clarendon, 2002), 162–64.

176. In addition to the Greek letter, three letters on ostraca were found, as well as two ostraca with writing exercises.

177. Most of the fragments were found scattered in various locations around the site. The Deuteronomy and the Ezekiel scrolls were buried under the floor of the synagogue. See E. Tov, "A Qumran Origin for the Masada Non-Biblical Texts?," *DSD* 7 (2000): 58–60.

178. S. Talmon, "Masada: Written Material," *EDSS* 1:521–25. See also Tov, "Categorized List of the 'Biblical Texts,'" in DJD 39, 179–82; and Lange and Mittmann-Richert, "Annotated Lists," 162.

SCRIBES AND LIBRARIES

indicate the presence of Qumran inhabitants among the refugees on Masada.[179] This scenario is quite plausible; Qumran was destroyed in 68 CE, and some of its inhabitants may have fled southward, eventually taking refuge at rebel-held Masada. They could well have carried their precious scrolls with them.[180]

Thus the collections from Wadi Murabb'at and Naḥal Ḥever, both of which served as refugee caves in times of conflict, contained primarily or even exclusively documentary texts, written on papyrus. The few literary texts recovered seem to have been the personal property of a refugee(s). The Masada corpus is different; although the scrolls found there were the property of the rebels who fled there from Jerusalem, religious texts, written on skin, dominate. They were likely used by the rebels and their families for study and worship. They even built a synagogue on the mountain for that purpose.

Conclusion

Our survey of the role of the scribe in ancient Israel and Judah, while limited in the earlier periods because of a paucity of evidence, leads to the conclusion that the scribe filled many of the same functions that were described in ch. 2 and was trained in similar ways. Scribes served in the royal court and the temple, supporting the king and the cultic personnel, and could reach positions of influence and authority (witness the Shaphan family). However, we could not ascertain with any degree of assurance where literary production in ancient Israel and Judah occurred, although some must have been done under the auspices of temple and court.

The role of the scribe expanded during the Persian period. The figure of Ezra, an emissary of the Persian overlord, is described as an expert in the law of Moses (תורת משה), a written source of some kind. Now that the classical literature of ancient Israel begins to reach written form, the scribe

179. A. Yardeni claims that the scribe of the Joshua Apocryphon also penned at least fifty of the Qumran manuscripts; if she is correct (her identification of this hand is supported by Puech), then it would be practically certain that the Joshua Apocryphon was brought south to Masada by a refugee after the destruction of Qumran ("A Note on a Qumran Scribe," in *New Seals and Inscriptions, Hebrew, Idumean, and Cuneiform*, ed. M. Lubetski, Hebrew Bible Monographs 8 [Sheffield: Sheffield Phoenix Press, 2007], 287).

180. See also Tov, "Qumran Origin."

Scribes and Libraries in Ancient Israel

is no longer just a bureaucratic arm of king or priest; he is carving out his own independent status as an expert in his people's religio-cultural repertoire. According to the Chronicler, the Levites become active in the scribal profession in this period, doubtless in support of the priesthood and the cult. Finally, more emphasis is placed on the scribe's role as a teacher, passing on his expertise not only to other scribes but to the people in general. The culmination of this idea of the scribe is found in the Wisdom of ben Sira, where Ben Sira draws a portrait of the exemplary scribe that contains all of these characteristics, including a major emphasis on the scribe as the interpreter of the classical literature of ancient Israel. In this way the scribe begins to supersede the prophet in the triad king-priest-prophet, since the scribe controls these written sources (cf. Jer 8:8).

Another literary corpus from the late Persian/early Hellenistic period, however, adds even more to this scribal portrait, under the influence of Mesopotamian culture found mainly in Aramaic literary texts. Enoch and his heirs (both literally and figuratively) are not only scribes in Ben Sira's sense, but add to that role expertise in astronomy and astrology (including calendar calculations) and in the interpretation of dreams and visions. These scribal figures are often also portrayed as priests, thus melding the two roles, although it is important to note that the identity of scribe is the primary one. Thus the elite scholar-scribe in Hellenistic period Judah has become a fully independent figure, often associated with the priesthood and its cult (not a surprise in theocratic Judah), but having their own expertise and place in society.

Unfortunately, the evidence for libraries and book collections, aside from Qumran, is incredibly sparse. We are reduced almost entirely to speculation about the nature or even existence of a library or archive in the royal court or the First or Second Temple, and the scroll collections that have surfaced in the Judean Desert are small, personal archives. The only major text collection from ancient Judea was found in the Qumran caves; it is to that collection that we turn in the next chapter.

Appendix: Scribes in the Synoptic Gospels

Scribes are frequently mentioned in the NT, particularly in the Synoptic Gospels; indeed, there are more references to scribes in the three Gospels of Matthew, Mark, and Luke than in the rest of the literature we have surveyed in this chapter put together. Unfortunately, since the Gospels are the

SCRIBES AND LIBRARIES

product of the late first century CE[181] and are strongly biased in favor of Jesus and his movement, their references to scribes and their roles in the lifetime of Jesus must be approached with a certain degree of skepticism.[182] Indeed, in the vast majority of cases, scribes are listed as a group (although the nature of this group is never explained) among the opponents of Jesus, along with the Pharisees, the Sadducees,[183] the chief priests, and the elders, thus creating a bifurcated narrative of "us versus them" that is unlikely to reflect historical reality. However, with due caution the Gospel accounts may be used to confirm our picture of the characteristics and roles of scribes in late Second Temple Judaism.[184]

Mark has twenty-one verses in nineteen pericopes that refer to scribes (γραμματεύς or forms thereof): 1:22; 2:6, 16; 3:22; 7:1, 5; 8:31; 9:11, 14; 10:33; 11:18, 27; 12:28, 32, 35, 38; 14:1, 43, 53; 15:1, and 31. In Mark, scribes have teaching authority, high status in society, and are associated with other powerful groups (e.g., the chief priests and the elders in Jerusalem).

The first reference to scribes occurs in Mark 1:21–22: "They went to Capernaum; and when the sabbath came, he [Jesus] entered the synagogue and taught. They were astounded at his teaching, for he taught them as one having authority, and not as the scribes." Here we find a contrast between the teaching of the scribes and that of Jesus; Jesus teaches "with authority." While the meaning of the phrase "with authority" in regard to Jesus's teaching is not entirely clear (although it is certainly positive),[185]

181. I will not tackle here the evidence for the dating of the Synoptic Gospels. The literature is vast, and it is sufficient to note that a basic consensus has emerged to date all three Gospels to the last third of the first century CE. Likewise, I will assume Markan priority, with Matthew and Luke using Mark as their primary source, in addition to a common source (usually referred to as "Q"), and their own distinctive traditions. The reader is referred to the commentaries and dictionary articles on the subjects.

182. As A. Saldarini notes, none of the Gospel writers is a firsthand witness to the life of Jesus, and they "have woven Jesus' opponents into a dramatic narrative which is controlled by their purposes" (*Pharisees, Scribes and Sadducees in Palestinian Society: A Sociological Approach* [Wilmington, DE: Glazier, 1988], 144). I will not be concerned with the historicity of the individual episodes in the Gospels, but rather with the overall picture they create of life in first-century CE Galilee and Judea.

183. The scribes and the Sadducees are never coupled together in any of the Gospels.

184. Other passages in the NT that mention scribes are John 8:3, in the passage concerning the woman taken in adultery, which is not considered a genuine Johannine passage since it does not appear in the earliest manuscripts; Acts 4:5; 6:12; 19:35; 23:9; and 1 Cor 1:20.

185. According to J. Marcus, *Mark 1–8: A New Translation with Introduction and Commentary*, AB 27 (New York: Doubleday, 2000), 191, the word translated "authority," ἐξουσία,

106

Scribes and Libraries in Ancient Israel

what we can extrapolate from the passage is that scribes had a recognized teaching role in Jewish society as custodians of the traditional interpretation of Scripture, which is contrasted with Jesus's new (and divinely authorized, according to Mark) understanding. Other passages that emphasize the teaching role of scribes include 9:11 (in a question from the disciples about the traditional Jewish expectation, based on Mal 4:5–6 [MT 3:23–24], that Elijah would prepare the way for the expected messiah), 12:35 (in a saying of Jesus), and 12:28, 32. In the last passage, Jesus has a positive interaction with a scribe (for the only time in the Gospel) who questions him concerning the greatest commandment, and responds, "You are right, Teacher; you have truly said that 'he is one, and besides him there is no other'; and 'to love him with all the heart, and with all the understanding, and with all the strength,' and 'to love one's neighbor as oneself,'—this is much more important than all whole burnt offerings and sacrifices" (12:32–33).[186]

However, scribes as a group are usually the subject of Jesus's invective in Mark: "Beware of the scribes, who like to walk around in long robes,[187] and to be greeted with respect in the marketplaces, and to have the best seats in the synagogues and places of honor at banquets! They devour widows' houses and for the sake of appearance say long prayers. They will receive the greater condemnation" (12:38–40). Here scribes qua scribes are clearly leaders in the society, respected by the people for their piety and social standing and given marks of honor (but condemned by Jesus).

Scribes in Mark are often associated with (other) leadership groups in Jewish society: the Pharisees, the elders, and especially the chief priests. Scribes are associated with the Pharisees in Mark 2:16 ("the scribes of the Pharisees"), 7:1 ("the Pharisees and some of the scribes who had come from Jerusalem"), and 7:5 ("the Pharisees and the scribes"), where they question Jesus's food purity practices. Once Jesus reaches Jerusalem and

---

denotes divine authority and refers to Jesus's eschatological divine power. Jesus's authority to teach is also questioned in 11:28 by the chief priests, the scribes, and the elders.

186. Note that the parallel passages in Matthew and Luke (Matt 22:34–40; Luke 10:25–28) recast the interaction as hostile; the scribe (called a νομικός, "lawyer," in both Gospels) is "testing" Jesus.

187. The word στολή is used in the LXX to refer to the garments of priests (especially the high priest; see, e.g., Exod 28:2; 29:21; 31:10). The use of this term here indicates that at least some of the scribes were priests and Levites. See J. Marcus, *Mark 8–16: A New Translation with Introduction and Commentary*, AB 27A (New Haven: Yale University Press, 2009), 852.

begins to teach in the temple, his primary opponents become the chief priests and the scribes, and the Pharisees disappear. This is particularly clear in the passion narrative, where the chief priests, the scribes, and the elders are the main accusers of Jesus (11:27; 14:43, 53; 15:1; in 14:1 the elders are omitted).[188] The chief priests, of course, are associated with the temple; we can assume that the scribes in these passages are part of the temple staff as well, as we saw in the decree of Antiochus III. Thus we can conclude that scribes were among the leadership elite in Jerusalem by virtue of their learning, as well as being closely associated with the priestly caste.[189]

The way in which Mark (followed by Matthew and Luke) usually refers to "the scribes," connected to other groups with the conjunction καὶ (e.g., Mark 7:5: οἱ φαρισαῖοι καὶ γραμματεῖς), might leave the impression that scribes are a discrete group within Judaism, completely separate from other, equally discrete groups.[190] If this picture were correct, it would signal a change from what we have observed thus far: that the role of the scribe is a professional one, and that scribes, while often identified by their professional role, belonged to other groups in society at the same time. Ezra, of course, was both a scribe and a priest (one a professional, the other a genealogical identity), and some of the Levites also seem to have been trained as scribes. However, Mark occasionally demonstrates that scribes were not actually a discrete group, but were found within other groups. Mark 2:16 refers to "the scribes *of* the Pharisees" (οἱ γραμματεῖς τῶν φαρισαίων), while Luke, in the parallel passage 5:30, refers to "the Pharisees and their scribes" (οἱ φαρισαῖοι καὶ οἱ γραμματεῖς αὐτῶν).[191] Thus it is probable that scribes, while recognizable separately for their learning and their teaching function in society, could be members of various other groups, such as the priests, the elders, and the Pharisees, or simply be professionals with no other affiliation.

188. Marcus, *Mark 8–16*, 101, refers to the "typical Markan triumvirate of chief priests, elders, and scribes."

189. Note that Mark 3:22 has scribes "coming down from Jerusalem" to observe Jesus. Saldarini, *Pharisees, Scribes and Sadducees*, 155, emphasizes the place of scribes as members of the "retainer class," but acknowledges that some of them had a certain degree of political power.

190. Saladarini, *Pharisees, Scribes and Sadducees*, 241, notes that scribes are presented as a coherent social group only in the Synoptic Gospels. See also Teeter, "Scribes and Scribalism," 1203: "it appears historically unlikely that scribes formed a unified faction or political party."

191. Acts 23:9 also refers to "some of the scribes of the Pharisees' party" (τινὲς τῶν γραμματέων τοῦ μέρους τῶν φαρισαίων).

Scribes and Libraries in Ancient Israel

Matthew and Luke, through their common source and individually, add to this picture. Matthew mentions scribes twenty-two times, once more than Mark.[192] In six instances (7:29; 9:3; 15:1; 16:21; 17:10; 20:18) he simply repeats Mark. In the other thirteen passages that he has in common with Mark, he changes his Markan source in some way: he omits any mention of scribes in 9:11, 34; 12:24; 17:14; 21:23; 26:3–4, 47; and 27:1. In 22:35 he changes the Markan γραμματεύς to νομικός ("lawyer," i.e., one who is trained in the law of Moses), and makes him a Pharisee. In 22:41–43 he takes what had been a question by Jesus, "How can the scribes say that the Christ is the son of David?" (Mark 12:35), and turns it into a debate between Jesus and the Pharisees, omitting any mention of scribes. In the passion narrative, Matthew often leaves out the scribes among the opponents of Jesus (26:3–4, 47; 27:1). Matthew's handling of his Markan material has two effects: there is a sharper polemic against the Pharisees, and consequently a more positive picture of the scribes.[193]

Luke also differs from his Markan source. In six instances (four in the passion narrative) he simply repeats Mark (5:30; 9:22; 20:1, 46; 22:2, 66), but he more often changes Mark. He omits Mark 3:22 and 9:11 altogether. He omits scribes at 4:32, 9:37, and 20:41; reads "the scribes and Pharisees" at 5:21;[194] and adds "the leaders of the people" at 19:47. Most significantly, he changes "scribe(s)" in Mark to something else in five instances: 10:25 (νομικός, "lawyer"),[195] 11:37–38 (a Pharisee), 18:32 (Gentiles), 22:47 (a crowd), and 23:35 (the rulers). The changes in the passion narrative at 18:32, 22:47, and 23:35 have the effect of making Jesus's opponents vaguer than in Mark or Matthew; in Luke the passion is portrayed as Jesus (and his disciples) against the world. Only once does Luke add "scribes" to a Markan passage, at 23:10 (where it has been transferred into the unique Lukan pericope of the trial before Herod).

Matthew and Luke's common source has one major pericope that concerns scribes: the so-called woe passages in Matt 23:23–36 and Luke 11:42–

---

192. Schams, *Jewish Scribes*, 180.

193. Orton, *Understanding Scribe*, 25.

194. They are referred to as νομοδιδάσκαλοι, "teachers of the law," in 5:17, a term that occurs only here in Luke's Gospel; in Acts 5:34 it is used of Gamaliel. According to J. Fitzmyer, "they are probably to be understood as a specific group within the Pharisees" (*The Gospel according to Luke [I–IX]: Introduction, Translation, and Notes*, AB 28 [Garden City, NY: Doubleday, 1981], 581).

195. Luke prefers the term "lawyer" as a substitute for "scribe," emphasizing their legal expertise. See Schams, *Jewish Scribes*, 170; Saldarini, *Pharisees, Scribes and Sadducees*, 183.

SCRIBES AND LIBRARIES

54. These woes are aimed at the scribes and the Pharisees in Matthew, and scribes, Pharisees, and lawyers (νομοκοί) in Luke,[196] and emphasize in a critical way their insistence on correct observance:

> Woe to you, scribes and Pharisees, hypocrites! For you tithe mint, dill, and cummin, and have neglected the weightier matters of the law: justice and mercy and faith. It is these you ought to have practiced without neglecting the others. You blind guides! You strain out a gnat but swallow a camel!
>
> Woe to you, scribes and Pharisees, hypocrites! For you clean the outside of the cup and of the plate, but inside they are full of greed and self-indulgence. You blind Pharisee! First clean the inside of the cup, so that the outside also may become clean. (Matt 23:23–26)

Leaving aside the harsh polemic,[197] these "woes" portray the scribes (and the Pharisees) as concerned with proper legal observance, and therefore the correct interpretation of Scripture. They also receive the social position promised to the learned scribe in Sir 38: "Then Jesus said to the crowds and to his disciples, 'The scribes and the Pharisees sit on Moses' seat; therefore, do whatever they teach you and follow it; but do not do as they do, for they do not practice what they teach'" (Matt 23:1–3).[198]

Three passages found only in Matthew should be highlighted in regard to the portrait of scribes. In Matt 2:1–4, when the magi arrive in Jerusalem seeking the infant Jesus, a concerned Herod consults "the chief priests and scribes of the people [γραμματεῖς τοῦ λαοῦ]." They respond to his question with Scripture quotations from Mic 5:2 and 2 Sam 5:2, fulfilling the typical scribal task at this time of Scripture interpretation. It is worth noting that the eastern (i.e., Babylonian) magi are following a star, an astronomical sign associated with esoteric wisdom, as we have seen especially in Enoch.[199]

---

196. Luke makes the woe passage into two sets of three woes: vv. 42–44 are aimed at the Pharisees, while vv. 46–52 are against the lawyers. See J. Fitzmyer, *The Gospel according to Luke (X–XXIV): Introduction, Translation, and Notes*, AB 28A (Garden City, NY: Doubleday, 1985), 943.

197. Orton notes that Matthew uses the hendiadys "scribes and Pharisees" in contexts of acute controversy (*Understanding Scribe*, 29).

198. C. Keith, *Jesus against the Scribal Elite: The Origins of the Conflict* (Grand Rapids: Baker Academic, 2014), 32.

199. Schams, *Jewish Scribes*, 193.

110

Scribes and Libraries in Ancient Israel

Matthew 13:52 contains a unique saying of Jesus: "And he said to them, 'Therefore every scribe who has been trained for the kingdom of heaven is like the master of a household who brings out of his treasure what is new and what is old.'" The word translated as "trained" in the NRSV is μαθητεύω, "to make a disciple of, teach." While Matthew probably has in mind early Christian scribes who understand the correct interpretation of Scripture (the "treasure") vis-à-vis Jesus,[200] it is important to notice that he understands that scribes are taught their art and have special expertise in Scripture interpretation, as we have seen previously, especially in Sirach.[201]

In Matt 23:34, in the midst of the "woe" passages, Jesus says: "Therefore I send you prophets, sages, and scribes [προφήτας καὶ σοφοὺς καὶ γραμματεῖς], some of whom you will kill and crucify, and some you will flog in your synagogues and pursue from town to town." Most NT scholars understand this verse as a reference to offices within the early Christian community.[202] That may well be the case, but we should note the continuity with Sirach and 1 Enoch, where the role of the scribe/sage is associated with that of the prophet.

Thus in the Synoptic Gospels "the social positions and functions assigned to the scribes . . . are sociologically probable and fit first century Jewish society as we know it."[203] Scribes are teachers, interpreters of Scripture, and experts in the law of Moses; they may be members of religious parties such as the Pharisees, and they can be associated with powerful leadership groups in Roman Judea, for example, the chief priests and the elders. This NT picture of scribes adds another layer of evidence to what we have constructed concerning the roles and functions of scribes from Second Temple Jewish literature.

---

200. Saldarini, *Pharisees, Scribes and Sadducees*, 159.

201. Orton, *Understanding Scribe*, 139–42.

202. Schams, *Jewish Scribes*, 192; and Saldarini, *Pharisees, Scribes and Sadducees*, 159–60, and references.

203. Saldarini, *Pharisees, Scribes and Sadducees*, 172.

PART II

The Qumran Evidence

CHAPTER 4

Caves and Scrolls: The Archaeology of the Caves and the Texts Found in Them

> We have learnt from trustworthy Jews . . . that some books were found
> ten years ago in a rock-dwelling near Jericho.
> Patriarch Timotheus of Seleucia to Sergius of Elam

In part I, I surveyed the evidence for the work of scribes and the existence of libraries and archives in the ancient Near East and Mediterranean worlds, with particular focus on Israel and Judah from the Iron Age through the Greco-Roman period. As we observed, by the Greco-Roman period elite scholar-scribes had reached positions of influence and importance in Jewish society. They were associated with the temple and priesthood (especially those scribes who were also Levites), and were responsible for preserving and interpreting the classical literature of ancient Israel, as well as curating and extending its religio-cultural tradition. In part II, I take a deep dive into the archaeological and textual evidence associated with the caves surrounding Khirbet Qumran and the ruins of its building. The purpose of this deep dive is to determine whether the corpus of the Qumran scrolls,[1] the largest collection of written material ever discovered in the territory of Roman Judea, constituted a library; and, if so, what type of library. In addition, I ask whether the archaeological evidence from the caves and the ruins support an active scribal presence with a library at Qumran during the late Second Temple period.

I begin with an exploration, from an archaeological point of view, of the Qumran scrolls by considering the scrolls themselves, both their content and their physical characteristics, along with the archaeology of the caves in which they were discovered. In this chapter I demonstrate that

---

1. "The Qumran scrolls" refers to the manuscripts found in the eleven caves within a three-kilometer radius of the site of Khirbet Qumran, located on the northwest shore of the Dead Sea south of Jericho.

115

THE QUMRAN EVIDENCE

the Qumran scrolls corpus is one large collection of scrolls, tied together by the archaeological evidence of the caves and the contents of the manuscripts. The archaeology of the site of Qumran, and its relationship to the scroll caves, I discuss in ch. 5.

This investigation starts with a profile of each of the manuscript caves, its archaeology, and the number of scrolls found in it. The scrolls are sorted according to the categories described in the introduction: the classical literature of ancient Israel, the literature of the Hellenistic-Roman period, and the sectarian and affiliated literature. This is followed by a synthesis of the cave archaeology and a profile of the scroll collection as a whole.

Although the Qumran caves are traditionally numbered in the order in which they were found, I will deal with them in two geological groups: the limestone cliff caves (1Q–3Q, 6Q, 11Q, and 53),[2] and the marl terrace caves (4Qa-b, 5Q, and 7Q–9Q).[3]

---

2. Information concerning Cave 53 is taken from O. Gutfeld and R. Price, "The Discovery of a New Dead Sea Scrolls Cave at Qumran" (paper presented at the Annual Meeting of the SBL, Boston, 19 November 2017). I would like to thank Dr. Price for sharing this paper and other results of his research with me prior to publication. In early media reports this cave was referred to as "a twelfth Dead Sea Scrolls cave" or as "Cave 12." However, according to the Israel Antiquities Authority's numeration of caves in the area, the cave being excavated by Gutfeld and Price is correctly referred to as Cave 53.

3. De Vaux's numbering system for these caves differs, depending on whether he was discussing the archaeology of the caves or the manuscripts found in them. In his field notes and notebooks, he numbers the limestone cliff caves according to the geographical order of the caves in the cliffs. In 1952, he and his team surveyed over 250 caves in the cliffs, all of which are enumerated in his field notes. Forty of them contained evidence of human tenancy; twenty-six of these are from the second century BCE to the first century CE. See also the map in R. de Vaux, "Archéologie," in Les "petites grottes" de Qumrân, by M. Baillet et al., 2 vols., DJD 3 (Oxford: Clarendon, 1962), 1:5. In de Vaux's numbering system, manuscript Cave 1Q = GrQ 14; Cave 2Q = GrQ19; Cave 3Q = GrQ8; and 6Q = GrQ26. In the marl terrace, the caves were numbered in the order of their discovery, which is the order with which most scholars are familiar. See M. Bélis, "Révision commentée des différent systems de numérotation," in Khirbet Qumrân et 'Aïn Feshkha, vol. 2: Études d'anthropologie, de physique et de chimie, ed. J.-B. Humbert and J. Gunneweg, NTOA.SA 3 (Göttingen: Vandenhoeck & Ruprecht, 2003), 409–15; and M. Fidanzio and J.-B. Humbert, "Finds from the Qumran Caves: Roland de Vaux's Inventory of the Excavations (1949–1956)," in The Caves of Qumran: Proceedings of the International Conference, Lugano 2014, ed. M. Fidanzio, STDJ 118 (Leiden: Brill, 2017), 270. Although in the present chapter I discuss only the caves in which manuscript remains were found, it is important to recognize that more than fifty caves with archaeological remains have been discovered and excavated in the vicinity of Qumran. The material evidence from the manuscript caves is not qualitatively different from the remains of nonmanuscript caves; the ceramic repertoire in particular is extremely uniform.

Caves and Scrolls: The Archaeology of the Caves and the Texts Found in Them

The Limestone Cliff Caves

Archaeology

The limestone cliff caves are found in the rocky cliffs that rise above the Dead Sea and its plateau on the western side of the Jordan Valley.[4] According to G. Lankester Harding, the head of the Jordanian Department of Antiquities in the 1940s when the discoveries began, the region was "very barren and desolate . . . and the cliffs are pierced with hundreds of natural caves of all sizes and shapes."[5] The caves in which fragmentary scrolls were found are all in the neighborhood of the ruins of Khirbet Qumran; Cave 3Q, the farthest away, is approximately two kilometers north of Qumran, while Cave 6Q, the closest, is located at the mouth of the Wadi Qumran within sight of the building ruins. All of the limestone cliff caves are natural caves, with difficult entrances, low ceilings, and uneven, rocky floors; they are poorly lit and badly ventilated. It is unlikely that they could have been used for long-term habitation (any more than a few days or weeks) by humans.[6]

---

4. The final archaeological report on all the excavations at Qumran and its vicinity is not yet completed, although good progress has been made in that direction. Until the publication is completed, the best sources for information about the excavations are first and foremost those by Roland de Vaux: his series of articles in *Revue biblique* from 1949 to 1959; *Archaeology and the Dead Sea Scrolls* (London: Oxford University Press, 1973); "La Poterie," in *Qumran Cave I*, by D. Barthélemy and J. T. Milik, DJD 1 (Oxford: Clarendon, 1955), 8–17; "Archéologie," in DJD 3, 3–44; and "Archéologie," in *Qumrân grotte 4.II: Part I: Archéologie*, by R. de Vaux; and *Part II: Tefillin, Mezuzot et Targums (4Q128–4Q157)*, by J. T. Milik, DJD 6 (Oxford: Clarendon, 1977), 3–32. In addition, three volumes have now been released by the École Biblique et Archéologique Française, edited by J.-B. Humbert, who is responsible for the final publication of de Vaux's excavations: *Fouilles de Khirbet Qumran et de 'Aïn Feshkha,* vol. 1: *Album de photographies; Répertoire du fonds photographique; Synthèse des notes de chantier du Père Roland de Vaux OP,* ed. J.-B. Humbert and A. Chambon, NTOA.SA 1 (Göttingen: Vandenhoeck & Ruprecht, 1994); *The Excavations of Khirbet Qumran and 'Ain Feshkha,* vol. 1B: *Synthesis of Roland de Vaux's Field Notes, English Edition,* ed. J.-B. Humbert and A. Chambon, trans. S. Pfann, NTOA.SA 1B (Göttingen: Vandenhoeck & Ruprecht, 2003); *Khirbet Qumrân et 'Aïn Feshkha,* vol. 2: and *Khirbet Qumrân et 'Aïn Feshkha,* vol. 3A: *Fouilles du P. Roland de Vaux,* ed. J.-B. Humbert, NTOA.SA 5 (Göttingen: Vandenhoeck & Ruprecht, 2016). Finally, the recent volume by Fidanzio, *Caves of Qumran,* contains invaluable syntheses and studies by leading scholars.

5. G. L. Harding, "Introductory, the Discovery, the Excavation, Minor Finds," in DJD 1, 6.

6. See also J.-B. Humbert, "Cacher et se cacher à Qumrân: Grottes et refuges. Mor-

THE QUMRAN EVIDENCE

Cave 1Q was, famously, accidentally discovered in 1947 by Ta'amireh bedouin shepherds, who removed seven scrolls from the cave: the Serek Hayaḥad (1QS), Pesher Habakkuk (1QpHab), the Great Isaiah Scroll (1QIsa[a]), the Genesis Apocryphon (1QapGen ar), 1QIsaiah[b], the Hodayot scroll (1QH), and the War Scroll (1QM).[7] By 1949, pressure to find the cave where these scrolls had been discovered was growing; and it was located by Captain Akkash el Zebn of the Arab Legion in January 1949, and subsequently excavated by the Jordanian Department of Antiquities under the direction of Harding and de Vaux. The cave, approximately one and a half kilometers northwest of Qumran, is a natural crevice in the cliff face, originally entered through a small hole (subsequently enlarged by the bedouin diggers). The chamber is about eight meters long and two meters wide. The floor of the cave is uneven; it is poorly lit and ventilated, and was difficult to access.[8]

According to the bedouin, they found two of the scrolls that they removed from the cave, the Serek Hayaḥad and Pesher Habakkuk, wrapped in linen and stored in a jar. Another, the Great Isaiah Scroll (1QIsa[a]), was found in the same jar without wrappings. It is not clear whether the other four scrolls retrieved by the bedouin (the Genesis Apocryphon, 1QIsaiah[b], the Hodayot, and the War Scroll) were either stored in jars or wrapped in linen, although their relatively intact condition would suggest that they were at least stored in jars. The type of jar in which the scrolls were found is a tall storage jar, hole-mouthed, with a cylindrical body, a well-marked (carinated) shoulder, a short neck, and a flat, ring-shaped base. It often lacks handles, but some examples have ledge handles high on the shoulder. It is associated with a bowl-shaped lid, which has a carinated shoulder and a ring-shaped knob as a handle.[9] Since scrolls were found stored inside, this

---

phologie, fonctions, anthropologie," in Fidanzio, *Caves of Qumran*, 36, 42, who emphasizes the inaccessibility of the cliff caves and their lack of water.

7. See W. Fields, *Dead Sea Scrolls: A Full History*, vol. 1: *1947–1960* (Leiden: Brill, 2009), 23–90, for a recent narration of the discovery of Cave 1Q and the subsequent history of its manuscripts.

8. See the recent article by J. Taylor, D. Mizzi, and M. Fidanzio, who note that the upper entrance was only high enough to pass a jar through on its side, and the lower entrance involved crawling in on all fours ("Revisiting Qumran Cave 1Q and Its Archaeological Assemblage," *PEQ* 149 [2017]: 297).

9. See also the description of J. Magness, "The Community of Qumran in Light of Its Pottery," in *Debating Qumran: Collected Essays on Its Archaeology*, ISACR 4 (Leuven: Peeters, 2004), 3.

Caves and Scrolls: The Archaeology of the Caves and the Texts Found in Them

type of jar has become known as a "scroll jar" (see fig. 2).[10] De Vaux and his team also found one congealed scroll, still in its wrapping, adhering to the mouth of its broken jar.[11] Other seemingly empty whole jars of the same type were also found by the bedouin, lined up in a row against the wall of the cave. As we shall see in ch. 5, this cylindrical jar type is also found in large numbers in the ruins of Qumran, and is a strong link between the natural limestone cliff caves and the settlement at Khirbet Qumran.

During the excavation of the cave, fragments of 72 scrolls were found (outside jars), thus bringing the total of Cave 1Q manuscripts to 79.[12] Sherds from at least fifty cylindrical jars and their bowl-shaped lids were recovered. Given the floor space available in Cave 1Q, when those fifty jars were whole they would have packed the cave, leaving no available space for anything else.[13] The other material finds were meager: six phylactery cases,[14] three bowls, a pot, a juglet, a plate, two Hellenistic period lamps, and two Roman period lamps.[15] In addition, the cave yielded one wooden comb, small and large pieces of wood, date and olive pits, pieces of linen, and palm fibers.

Cave 2Q, a natural cave 100 meters south of Cave 1Q, was found by the bedouin in 1952. It consisted of two levels of chambers, and yielded two whole jars and one lid, remains of six other jars, and thirty-three fragmentary manuscripts.[16] The lack of material remains other than remains of

10. Not all of the jars correspond with the above description. One variation has an "ovoid" body, sometimes with an outturned rim to its opening, and two ring handles on its shoulder. Some are "bag-shaped," i.e., wider at the base and tapering to the neck. The "bag-shaped" or "ovoid" variations are more common throughout the region. See J. Magness, *The Archaeology of Qumran and the Dead Sea Scrolls* (Grand Rapids: Eerdmans, 2002), 80–81.

11. Barthélemy and Milik, DJD 1, pls. 1, 8–10.

12. The number of manuscripts found in each cave is taken from E. Tov, *Revised Lists of the Texts from the Judaean Desert* (Leiden: Brill, 2010). These numbers are only approximate, since the fragmentary texts are scholarly reconstructions and their actual extent in antiquity is not ascertainable.

13. Taylor et al., "Revisiting Qumran Cave 1Q," 319.

14. This is the figure given by Harding in DJD 1, 7. See also the survey by Y. Adler, "The Distribution of Tefillin Finds," in Fidanzio, *Caves of Qumran*, 161–73. According to Adler (162), only four cases were found in Cave 1Q.

15. The information on the excavated finds in the caves is taken from DJD 1, DJD 3, and DJD 6; from D. Mizzi, "Miscellaneous Artefacts from the Qumran Caves: An Exploration of Their Significance," in Fidanzio, *Caves of Qumran*, 137–60; and from Fidanzio and Humbert, "Finds from the Qumran Caves." For Cave 1Q Mizzi lists only three lamps.

16. In *Archaeology*, 50, de Vaux lists six jars and three bowls. De Vaux's inventory (Fidanzio and Humbert, "Finds from the Qumran Caves," 278) also lists two arrowheads and

THE QUMRAN EVIDENCE

scroll jars and manuscript fragments in Cave 2Q indicates that it was never used as a dwelling place.

The discovery of Cave 2Q prompted the professional archaeologists to undertake a survey of the caves in the limestone cliffs overlooking Qumran. In a race with the bedouin, the archaeologists discovered Cave 3Q to the north of Cave 1Q. Cave 3Q's ceiling had collapsed in antiquity, making it very difficult to excavate.[17] The cave yielded fragments of fourteen manuscripts, sherds of thirty-five cylindrical jars, twenty-one bowl-shaped lids, two jugs, a lamp, and a spindle whorl.[18] The scrolls and jars were placed behind the rock wall formed by the collapsed ceiling, the height of which was so low that the jars, when whole, would have touched the ceiling.[19] The Copper Scroll was also found in Cave 3Q, deposited not in the back of the collapsed cave with the other finds, but set against the north wall at the front of the cave, concealed by a boulder.[20] The lack of material remains in Cave 3Q leads to the conclusion that it was not a dwelling cave.

The bedouin discovered Cave 6Q, which is located at the foot of the limestone cliff above the plateaus to the west of the Dead Sea, below the aqueduct leading into Qumran, within sight of Caves 4Q and 5Q. It is thus within the archaeological landscape of Qumran. It contained leather and papyrus fragments of thirty-one manuscripts, one jar, a bowl, and an inscribed sherd. Its lack of material remains aside from manuscripts indicates that Cave 6Q was never used for habitation. It is significant that the remains of only one scroll jar were found in 6Q; as we shall see, this makes 6Q more like the marl terrace caves than the limestone cliff caves.

Finally, in 1956, the bedouin discovered Cave 11Q, which is located just south of Cave 3Q. Cave 11Q is the largest of the limestone cliff caves

---

two *feuilles de cuivre* ("thin copper sheets"). The last two items are on different types of inventory cards, and are not referred to by de Vaux in the DJD volumes. This may be a mistake for Cave 3Q (GrQ 8).

17. De Vaux suggested that it collapsed after the scrolls were deposited in the cave; but J. Patrich, in a second excavation, removed the ceiling collapse and found only Chalcolithic sherds, indicating that the ceiling had collapsed before the Second Temple period scrolls were deposited there ("Khirbet Qumran in Light of New Archaeological Explorations in the Qumran Caves," in *Methods of Investigation of the Dead Sea Scrolls and the Khirbet Qumran Site: Present Realities and Future Prospects*, ed. M. Wise et al., ANYAS 722 [New York: New York Academy of Sciences, 1994], 77).

18. De Vaux's inventory lists only five jars.

19. Humbert, "Cacher et se cacher," 46.

20. De Vaux, DJD 3, 7, who states: "Juste à l'angle nord de la chamber, deux rouleaux de cuivre étaient déposés." See DJD 3, pl. III.2, for a photograph of the Copper Scroll in situ.

Caves and Scrolls: The Archaeology of the Caves and the Texts Found in Them

in which manuscripts were discovered; it is easy to access (unlike Caves 1Q, 2Q, and 3Q), but its entrance was sealed with stones in antiquity. The cave contained thirty manuscripts or fragments of manuscripts, including the Temple Scroll (11QT[a]), which was found, according to its discoverers, wrapped in linen in a scroll jar.[21] Cave 11Q was the richest cave in terms of material finds; in addition to one bowl-shaped lid and a juglet, de Vaux and his team uncovered one iron blade, one iron chisel or file, one iron pickaxe, one iron rod, one iron key, one copper buckle, one bead of uncertain date, fragments of leather, many pieces of cloth, and fragments of basketry and rope, all dating to the first century BCE–first century CE.[22] The recent publication of the artifacts in the Schøyen Collection adds a linen scroll wrapper and cord (purportedly used to wrap the Temple Scroll), and a palm fiber tool that may have been used for mixing ink.[23]

The context of the limestone cliff caves in which manuscripts were discovered must be kept in mind when considering how and when the manuscripts were placed in these caves. When de Vaux decided in 1952 to make a survey of the caves in the limestone cliffs in the vicinity of the ruins of Qumran, he and his team made soundings in 270 caves in a section of the cliffs eight kilometers long, with Khirbet Qumran approximately in the middle. They found nothing in 230 of the caves, but 40 contained pottery and other objects. Some were as old as the Chalcolithic period, some as late as the modern period, but 26 contained remains from the Greco-Roman period similar to the finds from Caves 1Q, 2Q, 3Q, 6Q, and 11Q. De Vaux gives a complete list of these finds in DJD 3.[24] The list includes, again and

---

21. S. W. Crawford, *The Temple Scroll and Related Texts*, Companion to the Qumran Scrolls 2 (Sheffield: Sheffield Academic Press, 2000), 12. The Temple Scroll jar is still in the possession of the Kando family (Fields, *Full History*, photograph on 301).

22. Cave 11Q was the only cave in which the excavators were able to determine any sort of strata, which went down to the Chalcolithic period before hitting bedrock. A small jar from the Chalcolithic period was discovered, as well as two lamps, one juglet, and one jar from the Iron Age.

23. See especially the articles by T. Elgvin (323–36), I. Rabin (327–38), N. Sukenik (339–50), J. Taylor and J. van der Plicht (351–56), and I. Rabin (357–60) in *Gleanings from the Caves: Dead Sea Scrolls and Artefacts from the Schøyen Collection*, ed. T. Elgvin et al., LSTS 71 (New York: Bloomsbury T&T Clark, 2016). Two other "palm fibre tools" have been located in the area of Qumran; the first appears in a photograph in DJD 3, vol. 2, pl. VII; the second was purchased by Southwestern Baptist Theological Seminary from the Kando family. According to Steven Ortiz (personal communication), the second palm fiber tool is not a pen, but may have been used to stir ink.

24. Baillet et al., DJD 3, 6–13. Humbert, "Cacher et se cacher," 42, lists GrQ1–3, GrQ7,

THE QUMRAN EVIDENCE

again, storage jars (cylindrical and ovoid), bowl-shaped lids, lamps, juglets, and bowls. In other words, the same limited repertoire of pottery types occurs in nonmanuscript caves as were found in the manuscript caves.[25] Pieces of linen, which are most likely the remains of scroll wrappers, were also found.[26] The ancient accounts of scroll discoveries in jars in the Dead Sea region should be recalled here; some of the caves explored by de Vaux's team were disturbed centuries before their (re)discovery by the bedouin explorers and the archaeologists. De Vaux further notes that the density of usage increases as one gets closer to Qumran.[27]

Other discoveries and later surveys underscore de Vaux's findings. During the 1952 survey, J. T. Milik discovered a cave, GrQ29 (subsequently called "Timothy's Cave" after Patriarch Timothy's eighth-century account of the discovery of a cave with scrolls), in which Milik found unbroken but empty scroll jars. According to his testimony, the jars had been emptied and the lids set to one side.[28] It is probable that this cave was a scroll cave in antiquity. Joseph Patrich conducted surveys in the limestone cliffs in the 1980s, during which he basically confirmed de Vaux's conclusions.[29] In the 1990s, Magen Broshi and Hanan Eshel excavated two caves (C and F) 200 meters north of Qumran, and discovered pottery sherds from the first century BCE and the first century CE.[30]

In January 2017 a limestone cliff cave located 500 meters *south* of Qumran,[31] labeled Cave 53, was excavated by Oren Gutfeld and Randall Price

---

GrQ12, GrQ15, GrQ17, GrQ19, GrQ21–22, GrQ28–29, GrQ31–32, and GrQ39 as caves that may have been used for scroll storage in antiquity, given the presence of cylindrical jars and bowl-shaped lids.

25. See Mizzi, "Miscellaneous Artefacts," 137, 139–40, for a discussion.

26. W. Reed, "The Qumran Caves Expedition of March 1952," *BASOR* 135 (1954): 13; J. Taylor, "Buried Manuscripts and Empty Tombs: The Qumran *Genizah* Theory Revisited," in *"Go Out and Study the Land" (Judges 18:2): Archaeological, Historical and Textual Studies in Honor of Hanan Eshel*, ed. A. Maeir et al., JSJSup 148 (Leiden: Brill, 2012), 277.

27. The earliest reference to manuscript finds in the Judean Desert comes from Origen, who states that he used a Greek translation that was discovered "together with other Hebrew and Greek books in a jar near Jericho" (Eusebius, *Eccl. Hist.* 6.16.1). In about 800 CE the Nestorian patriarch of Seleucia, Timotheus I, mentioned in a letter manuscripts found in a cave near Jericho.

28. F. Mébarki and C. Grenache, "Józef Tadeusz Milik: Memories of Fieldwork," *NEA* 63 (2000): 132; and Fields, *Full History*, 137.

29. Patrich, "Khirbet Qumran," 73–96. This survey was done in the winter of 1984/85; only fifteen caves yielded further remains.

30. M. Broshi and H. Eshel, "Residential Caves at Qumran," *DSD* 6 (1999): 328.

31. Caves 1Q–3Q, 6Q, and 11Q are located to the north and west of Qumran.

on behalf of the Israel Antiquities Authority.[32] The cave consists of a main chamber and a twelve-meter tunnel at the back. While the cave is a natural cave, it contains worked (manmade) elements, including two pillars, at least six niches or shelves along the wall of the cave, and an enclosure wall in front of one of the niches. These niches contained jar fragments that have been preliminarily dated to the second-first centuries BCE. The jars had been smashed in situ from earthquake debris, but found among the debris were leather and papyrus fragments, as well as fragments of linen textiles and rope. One rolled-up fragment of parchment or papyrus (the report is not clear) was found in the remains of a large jar.[33] Since this cave has been entirely professionally excavated, using the most up-to-date equipment and methodology, it is profoundly important for understanding the function of the limestone cliff caves related to Khirbet Qumran. That its material assemblage closely resembles that of the other limestone cliff caves indicates use by the same group of people at the same period of time, and indicates that scroll storage in jars in those caves had been taking place since at least the beginning of the first century BCE (the period of the establishment of the Qumran settlement; see ch. 5).

What we have in the limestone cliff caves is a homogenous assemblage of material artifacts, especially the pottery. These caves saw human activity at the same time that Khirbet Qumran was inhabited (first quarter of the first century BCE through the First Jewish Revolt; see ch. 5), and the same pottery types (especially hole-mouthed cylindrical jars) were in use in both places, indicating that there is a connection between the ruins and the caves. There is also more concrete archaeological evidence for that claim. A main path from Qumran led north to caves 1Q–3Q and 11Q, connecting those caves with the settlement.[34] Only five of the caves out of the 270 surveyed in 1952, and now Cave 53, contained manuscript remains (although the evidence indicates that GrQ29 also contained manuscripts in antiquity). Because the debris from the other caves that de Vaux surveyed was not retained, it is impossible now to know whether the other caves he surveyed contained minute manuscript remains. Because it is unlikely that

32. The following information is taken from O. Gutfeld and R. Price, "The Discovery of a New Dead Sea Scrolls Cave at Qumran" (paper presented at the Annual Meeting of the SBL, Boston, 19 November 2017).

33. Other artifacts included two iron pickaxes tentatively dated to the Second Temple period (possibly used by the workers who created the niches and stored the jars in the cave), woven mats, and other organic material (olive pits, date pits). No coins were discovered.

34. Broshi and Eshel, "Residential Caves at Qumran," 339–40.

THE QUMRAN EVIDENCE

these caves in the limestone cliffs were used for long-term occupancy, since they are all small, not well ventilated, or well lit, and with uneven floors and ceilings,[35] some kind of long-term or permanent storage of scrolls is the best explanation for their purpose.

Scrolls

Cave 1Q

The seven documents originally removed from Cave 1Q by the bedouin are extremely well known, and their early discovery and publication in some ways colored subsequent understandings of the Qumran scrolls collection.[36] This is because four of those documents are part of the sectarian literature found in the overall collection: the Serek Hayaḥad (1QS), Pesher Habbakuk (1QpHab), the Hodayot (1QH), and the War Scroll (1QM). The scroll that contained the Serek Hayaḥad included two other separate sectarian compositions, the Serek Ha'edah and the Rule of the Blessings.[37] Two copies of Isaiah were also removed from the cave, as well as a previ-

35. Mizzi ("Miscellaneous Artefacts," 152–53) suggests that Caves 1Q and 11Q, which had a relatively richer repertoire of material finds, may have been used as very short term shelters by refugees c. 70 CE. Two nonscroll caves from the area of Qumran, GrQ37 and P24, may also have been used as refuge caves following the First Jewish Revolt; Mizzi does not believe, based on the material finds, that these caves were associated with Qumran (151–52).

36. In his aptly named article, S. Pfann notes, "For scholars, Cave 1Q was the prototype. It became the cave against which every subsequently discovered cave was to be compared." "But what if that stone had landed elsewhere? What if it had landed, for example, in Cave 11Q?" ("The Ancient 'Library' or 'Libraries' of Qumran: The Specter of Cave 1Q," in *The Dead Sea Scrolls at Qumran and the Concept of a Library,* ed. S. W. Crawford and C. Wassén, STDJ 116 [Leiden: Brill, 2016], 169, 168). While I sympathize with Pfann's questions, I disagree with his conclusions.

37. According to J. Trever's initial report, these three documents belong to one scroll. However, no pictures of the three documents sewn together were ever published, leading to uncertainty. It may be the case that the three documents were separate but were rolled together and stored in the same jar. They were all copied by the same scribe. See F. M. Cross, *Scrolls from Qumrân Cave I: The Great Isaiah Scroll, The Order of the Community, The Pesher to Habakkuk* (Jerusalem: Albright Institute of Archaeological Research and the Shrine of the Book, 1974), 4; and J. T. Milik, "28. Annexes à la Règle de la Communauté," in *Qumran Cave I,* by D. Barthélemy and J. T. Milik, DJD 1 (Oxford: Clarendon, 1955), 107–32. Milik (107) states that "c'est probable" that the three compositions were part of one scroll.

Caves and Scrolls: The Archaeology of the Caves and the Texts Found in Them

ously unknown interpretive work entitled by its editor the Genesis Apocryphon, which, as its name implies, is based on the book of Genesis along with elements of Enoch and Jubilees. Because the sectarian scrolls (along with the nonsectarian but affiliated Genesis Apocryphon) far outweighed the classical literature in this small sample of the Cave 1Q collection, it led early scholars to place more emphasis on the sectarian elements in the collection than was perhaps warranted.

A survey of the entire Cave 1Q corpus reveals a different proportion between the classical literature, Hellenistic-Roman literature, and sectarian and affiliated literature than was originally thought. Of the fragments that have been identified as separate compositions,[38] thirteen belong to the classical literature of ancient Israel, twelve are sectarian compositions, ten are affiliated works, and thirty-one are part of the Hellenistic-Roman literature collected and studied by the wing of Judaism to which the Cave 1Q corpus belonged. These proportions are more in keeping with those of the other caves, as we shall see below; in fact, the proportion of nonsectarian literature from the Hellenistic-Roman period is larger than that found in the Qumran corpus as a whole.

The Cave 1Q collection is notable because it contained complete or nearly complete scrolls, and those scrolls are easier to decipher and make sense of. This phenomenon, however, is an accident of preservation, since the complete scrolls were recovered from unbroken cylindrical jars that had protected them from predators and the elements; thus they should not be allowed to color our perception of the collection as a whole.

Caves 2Q, 3Q, and 6Q

The number of documents retrieved from Caves 2Q, 3Q, and 6Q is much smaller than the number from Caves 1Q and 11Q. Cave 2Q contained seventeen works from the classical literature and nine works from the Hellenistic-Roman period, including the only copy of the book of the Wisdom of Ben Sira found in the Qumran caves. Seven groups of fragments are unidentified. While Cave 2Q held no works classified as sectarian, it did contain two copies of Jubilees and one of the Book of Giants from the Enoch books, both of which are affiliated texts, extensively studied and used by the sectarian community.

38. Fragments 1Q41–1Q70bis are labeled "unclassified" in Tov, *Revised Lists*, 19–20.

THE QUMRAN EVIDENCE

The Cave 3Q fragments that have been identified include three scrolls from the classical literature, three from the Hellenistic-Roman period, two sectarian works, including a pesher on Isaiah, and a copy of the affiliated work Jubilees. The Copper Scroll, found in a separate location in Cave 3Q, is most likely a later deposit and should not be considered part of the Qumran collection.

EXCURSUS ON THE COPPER SCROLL

The Copper Scroll is anomalous in several ways.[39] As its name implies, it is engraved on thin copper sheets, the only composition from antiquity on copper. Its language is an early form of Mishnaic Hebrew, not the (archaizing) Biblical Hebrew of the rest of the Qumran scrolls.[40] It is not in any sense a literary composition, but is a listing of treasure deposits and their hiding places. Whether these treasures (which were enormous) were real is the subject of great controversy.[41] Given the Copper Scroll's unique characteristics, and the fact that it was deposited in another area of Cave 3Q, away from the main deposit, I believe that the Copper Scroll was deposited in Cave 3Q separately,[42] by a different group or individual (possibly from the Jerusalem temple) than the rest of the Qumran scrolls.[43]

---

39. For the *editio princeps* see J. T. Milik, "Le rouleau de cuivre provenant de la grotte 3 (3Q15)," in DJD 3, 201–99; and most recently E. Puech, *The Copper Scroll Revisited*, trans. D. Orton, STDJ 112 (Leiden: Brill, 2015).

40. Puech, *Copper Scroll Revisited*, 6.

41. Milik argued that they were imaginary (DJD 3, 211–302). John Allegro, on the other hand, believed that they were real, and mounted an expedition to find them (*The Treasure of the Copper* Scroll [London: Routledge, 1960]).

42. Milik, DJD 3, 277 (who also thinks the Copper Scroll was deposited separately from the other Cave 3Q artifacts), puts its deposition in the cave c. 100 CE.

43. See A. Wolters, "Copper Scroll," *EDSS* 1:144–48; and Hershel Shanks, *The Copper Scroll and the Search for the Temple Treasure* (Washington, DC: Biblical Archaeology Society, 2007). J. Lefkovits, *The Copper Scroll—3Q15: A Reevaluation*, STDJ 25 (Leiden: Brill, 1999), argues that it belonged to the Jerusalem temple. Puech, *Copper Scroll Revisited*, 16–17, believes the scroll belonged to the same group that deposited the other scrolls in Cave 3Q, a position with which F. García Martínez, "The Contents of the Manuscripts from the Caves of Qumran," in Fidanzio, *Caves of Qumran*, 74, agrees.

Caves and Scrolls: The Archaeology of the Caves and the Texts Found in Them

Cave 6Q, another small corpus, contained eight works from the classical literature, twelve works from the Hellenistic-Roman period, and two sectarian works, including a copy of the Damascus Document. In addition, there is one account or contract (6Q26). Eleven sets of fragments are unclassified. The Cave 6Q corpus is distinguished by a higher proportion of papyrus fragments; nineteen out of thirty-one sets of fragments were copied on papyrus.

Cave 11Q

Cave 11Q is famous as the cave in which the Temple Scroll, an almost complete scroll, was discovered. Of its identified manuscripts, ten belong to the classical literature, including a targum of Job; two are from the Hellenistic-Roman period; six are affiliated literature (including three copies of the Temple Scroll, a copy of Jubilees, and the Melchizedek scroll); and four are sectarian. Eight groups of fragments are unidentified. Again, the proportions are what we would expect in a Qumran cave, although there is a slightly higher percentage of classical literature manuscripts. It is noteworthy that five copies of what eventually coalesced into the biblical book of Psalms and three copies of the Temple Scroll were located in 11Q; this may be an indication that they were kept together elsewhere before being removed to the cave.

Reasons for Deposition

Now that we have surveyed the contents of the limestone cliff manuscript caves, the question must be asked as to *why* scrolls were stored, some of them in jars, in these remote, relatively inaccessible caves. We have seen in chs. 2 and 3 that it was common in the Hellenistic and Roman periods to keep small collections of book rolls in baskets or jars, in addition to placing them on shelves or in cupboards in ordinary rooms within palaces, temples, or houses. However, this type of storage in jars was for scrolls that belonged to the inhabitants of the building in which they were found.[44]

---

44. M. and K. Lönnquist observed that papyrus rolls have been found stored in jars in Egypt; at Elephantine twenty-four Greek and demotic papyri were found in oval and elongated jars. At the site of Deir el-Medina, two jars closed and sealed with ropes were

THE QUMRAN EVIDENCE

On the other hand, collections of manuscripts were found in the caves of Wadi ed-Daliyeh, Wadi Murabbaʻat, and Nahal Hever, but these manuscripts were the personal possessions of refugees fleeing from conflict and war, who brought their precious documents with them to their hideout. In contrast, the scrolls found in the jars in Caves 1Q, 11Q, and 53 (as well as the other manuscript fragments found scattered in the debris of 1Q, 2Q, 3Q, 6Q, and 11Q) had evidently been deliberately hidden there, not for easy access but for some type of permanent storage. When we look to the literature of the period, there is not much evidence attesting to such a practice. In Jer 32:6–15, when Jeremiah buys the field at Anathoth from his cousin Hanamel, he orders Baruch to put the deed in an earthenware jar as a sign-act:

> In their presence I charged Baruch, saying, Thus says the LORD of hosts, the God of Israel: Take these deeds, both this sealed deed of purchase and this open deed, and put them in an earthenware jar, in order that they may last for a long time. For thus says the LORD of hosts, the God of Israel: Houses and fields and vineyards shall again be bought in this land. (Jer 32:13–15)

Here the purpose of storing the document in a jar is long-term preservation.

In an intriguing parallel to the cave discoveries, the late Second Temple work the Assumption (or Testament) of Moses contains a passage in which Moses is speaking to Joshua:

> But (you) take this writing so that later you will remember how to preserve the books which I shall entrust to you. You shall arrange them, anoint them with cedar, and deposit them in earthenware jars. (1:16–17)[45]

Unfortunately, we cannot make any direct connection between this text and the act of storing the scrolls in jars in the limestone cliff caves, since no fragments of the Assumption of Moses were recovered from the Qumran

---

excavated from a house. The jars contained a family archive of thirty-three Greek and Demotic papyri, dating between 188 and 101 BCE. The Lönnquists suggest that jars may have served as "portable archives" ("Parallels to Be Seen: Manuscripts in Jars from Qumran and Egypt," in *The Dead Sea Scrolls in Context: Integrating the Dead Sea Scrolls in the Study of Ancient Texts, Languages, and Cultures*, ed. A. Lange et al., 2 vols., VTSup 140 [Leiden: Brill, 2011], 2:471–88).

45. Translation of J. Priest, *OTP* 1:927.

Caves and Scrolls: The Archaeology of the Caves and the Texts Found in Them

caves. However, both the Jeremiah and the Assumption of Moses passages indicate that there was some kind of tradition of using jars for long-term storage of documents. Joan Taylor has suggested that the natural limestone caves were used for the *burial* of scrolls that were no longer in use; the jars, the linen wrappers, and the bitumen associated with some of the linen all were part of this burial procedure.[46] Her suggestion, as it relates to the limestone cliff caves, may be helpful in explaining why these remote caves were used to deposit some manuscripts stored in jars. However, it is unclear that those manuscripts stored in jars and deposited in the caves were old, worn, or beyond use; neither 1QIsa[a] nor 11QTemple[a], the best-preserved manuscripts discovered in the caves, seems to have been beyond use when stored in their jars. Further, far older manuscripts than either of these were discovered in Cave 4Q (see below); why were these not prepared for burial in jars, but instead were found among the tattered remains of Cave 4Q?[47] Finally, at least some of the manuscripts discovered in the limestone cliff caves were not found in jars or among jar fragments, although we cannot be certain whether they were originally associated with jars or jar fragments, given that they were (with the exception of Cave 3Q) looted by the bedouin or disturbed in antiquity.[48] Cave 6Q, from which thirty-one manuscripts were recovered, contained fragments of only one cylindrical jar, indicating that not all of its manuscripts were stored in jars. Therefore, it cannot be argued that *all* of the manuscripts found in the limestone cliff caves were placed there for "burial" in scroll jars. The most we can say at this point is that the limestone cliff caves were being utilized for long-term or permanent storage of scrolls in scroll jars and that this activity was occurring during the entire life of the settlement at Qumran, from the first century BCE to its destruction in 68 CE.

---

46. Taylor, "Buried Manuscripts," 280–88. She notes a parallel with the Nag Hammadi codices, which were buried in a jar that was closed with a bowl-shaped lid and sealed with bitumen.

47. Taylor suggests, in response to this question, that cave 4Q was a temporary storage cave in which manuscripts were housed before being prepared for burial in jars in the limestone cliff caves. "Buried Manuscripts," 295.

48. In the case of 3Q, which was entirely excavated by de Vaux and his team, de Vaux recovered a large quantity of broken cylindrical jars and their covers; however, he does not mention recovering manuscript fragments from among the jar fragments. He states that many of the fragments were found among rats' nests, indicating that they had been carried away from their original position in the cave by rodents. De Vaux, DJD 3, 5–6.

THE QUMRAN EVIDENCE

The Marl Terrace Caves

Archaeology

The context of the second group of caves to be discovered, the marl terrace caves, is very different from that of the limestone cliff caves. In 1952, the bedouin discovered what is the most famous of the Qumran caves, Cave 4Q. Cave 4Q is actually two caves adjacent to one another, 4a and 4b, hollowed out by human hands from the marl plateau situated to the north of the Wadi Qumran, on the southwest spur of the same plateau on which the building remains of Qumran are located. After the clandestine diggers were dislodged from Cave 4Q and their place taken by de Vaux's team, the discovery of Caves 5Q, 7Q–9Q, and 10Q, all by the archaeologists, followed.[49] Caves 5Q, 7Q–9Q, and 10Q are also all manmade caves dug into the soft limestone of the plateaus on which Qumran is situated. Caves 5Q and 10Q are located in the southwest spur near 4Q; Caves 7Q–9Q are on the southern spur, on the same terrace of the plateau on which the buildings sit (see fig. 4).[50] In addition to these manuscript caves, Broshi and Eshel discovered Caves A and F to the north of the site and Cave H to the east of Cave 9Q during their excavations at Qumran in the 1990s. These caves had been occupied in antiquity, as well as several more collapsed artificial caves in the marl terrace. Broshi and Eshel estimate that there may have been between twenty and forty artificial caves dug into the plateau surrounding Qumran at the time of its Second Temple period occupation.[51] All of these caves located on the marl terrace plateau are part of the "built" environment of Qumran; that is, they are as much a part of the architecture of the site as the buildings of the settlement.

The quarrying out of these caves on the marl terrace would have been an enormous undertaking, requiring much manpower and time. It is impossible to determine when the caves were actually excavated; the date

49. According to Fields, *Full History*, Milik discovered 5Q in 1952 while 4Q was being excavated (142), and 7Q–10Q were excavated by de Vaux in 1955 during his fourth campaign at Qumran (252).

50. Humbert, "Cacher et se cacher," 48, makes the point that they are found inside the "long wall" that runs along the east edge of the settlement.

51. M. Broshi and H. Eshel, "Three Seasons of Excavations at Qumran," *JRA* 17 (2004): 325; Broshi and Eshel, "Residential Caves at Qumran," 328–35. This was already suggested by de Vaux in DJD 3, 27, in view of the evidence of collapsed caves and the pottery he collected in the vicinity of Caves 4Q, 5Q, and 10Q.

130

Caves and Scrolls: The Archaeology of the Caves and the Texts Found in Them

of the pottery finds and the paleographic dates of the manuscripts point to the late Second Temple period, when the settlement at Qumran was constructed.[52] David Stacey has suggested that the marl caves were dug to supply clay to make the mud bricks that were used to construct the buildings.[53] The caves may not have been dug specifically for that purpose, but the leftover clay would have been a handy source of construction material for the buildings. As we will see below, the marl terrace caves were not used for permanent, full-time habitation, although they seem to have been used as temporary sleeping quarters or work spaces.

After Cave 4Q was opened by the bedouin in 1952, they began to bring their manuscript finds to the Palestine Archaeological Museum (PAM) for sale.[54] De Vaux and Harding then discovered the location of the cave and removed the illicit diggers. De Vaux undertook the excavation of the cave in September 1952. A preliminary report of the findings, written by de Vaux, was published posthumously in DJD 6. According to de Vaux's report, the archaeologists explored for themselves the lower layers of the cave and one small concealed chamber (probably de Vaux's "obscure nook"; see below), as well as discovering the original entrance (the bedouin had dug their own entrance). Although by the time the archaeologists entered the cave the bedouin had already removed at least a meter of debris containing manuscript fragments, de Vaux and his workers collected nearly a thousand fragments from perhaps a hundred manuscripts.[55]

---

52. F. M. Cross suggested in an interview in the 1990s that the marl caves, including Cave 4Q, were originally constructed as Iron Age tombs. See H. Shanks, *Frank Moore Cross: Conversations with a Bible Scholar* (Washington, DC: Biblical Archaeology Society, 1994), 114. Humbert, "Cacher et se cacher," 48, 55, 58, suggests that the marl caves were older than the settlement, but believes they were constructed as emergency storage or hiding places.

53. D. Stacey, "A Reassessment of the Stratigraphy of Qumran," in *Qumran Revisited: A Reassessment of the Archaeology of the Site and Its Texts*, ed. D. Stacey and G. Doudna, BARIS 2520 (London: Archeopress, 2013), 37.

54. Because the bedouin did not distinguish fragments from 4a and 4b, but instead mixed them together, the two caves were collectively designated "Cave 4Q." The bedouin who removed fragments from these caves claimed that most of them originated in 4a, with almost none from 4b; these claims were borne out by the fragments found by the archaeologists, most of which also came from 4a. Thus de Vaux deemed 4a the more important of the two.

55. This information, and all of the following information, unless noted, is taken from de Vaux, DJD 6, 3–22. See also J. T. Milik, *Ten Years of Discovery in the Wilderness of Judaea*, trans. J. Strugnell, SBT 1/26 (Naperville, IL: Allenson, 1959); and F. M. Cross, *The Ancient Library of Qumran*, 3rd ed., BibSem 30 (Sheffield: Sheffield Academic Press, 1995). Milik was present at the excavation of Cave 4Q, and Cross was the first to examine its excavated fragments.

THE QUMRAN EVIDENCE

Altogether, fragments of 550–600 manuscripts have been identified as coming from Cave 4Q.

Cave 4Qa consisted of multiple chambers.[56] Its principal chamber (Chamber 1) had an east-west orientation, and was open to the east (toward the settlement) by a "window" that overlooks the ravine that separates Caves 4Q–5Q and 10Q from the south end of the marl plateau on which the ruins of Qumran sit.[57] In front of this "window" an oblong one-meter-long trench was dug. Chamber 1 also had small niches hollowed out of its walls above floor height. According to de Vaux, "almost all" of the recovered documents and pottery came from this chamber.[58]

In the center of the south wall of Chamber 1, a second chamber (Chamber 2) was dug toward the south. It sits at a higher level than Chamber 1. A third chamber was dug at a southwest angle from the main chamber, at a lower level. Between Chambers 2 and 3 an "obscure nook"[59] was dug out from the south wall, which was accessed by an irregular descent cut into the floor of Chamber 1. It was sunk 1.3 meters below the floor, and was 1.45 meters in height. According to de Vaux, it contained a lot of debris that had slid down from Chamber 1, in addition to a small jug.

The original entrance to Cave 4Qa was constructed to the north; it consisted of a circular opening with a sunken passage that slopes gently down several meters, finishing in several steps that issue out in the north wall of Chamber 1. In the passage de Vaux discovered a lamp, which dates to the first quarter of the second century CE.[60] Finally, a small trench between Caves 4Qa and 4Qb had been formed by erosion; some fragments, pottery, and phylactery cases had drifted into it, evidently from Chamber 1.[61]

---

56. For a detailed description of Caves 4Qa and b, see S. W. Crawford, "Qumran Cave 4: Its Archaeology and Its Manuscript Collection," in *Is There a Text in This Cave? Studies in the Textuality of the Dead Sea Scrolls in Honour of George J. Brooke*, ed. A. Feldman et al., STDJ 119 (Leiden: Brill, 2017), 105–22.

57. Humbert, "Cacher et se cacher," 55, plausibly suggests that this opening was not actually a window, but a hole left when another chamber of the cave collapsed into the wadi.

58. De Vaux, DJD 6, 9.

59. "Un réduit obscur" (de Vaux, DJD 6, 9).

60. See J. Mlynarczyk, "Terracotta Oil Lamps," in Fidanzio, *Caves of Qumran*, 109. She plausibly suggests that this lamp, which was found at the entrance to the cave, was "left there by a Roman soldier searching the caves" (117).

61. Although de Vaux believed that this trench was formed by erosion, Humbert has argued that it was made as a deliberate connection between Caves 4Qa and 4Qb ("Cacher et se cacher," 52, 55).

Caves and Scrolls: The Archaeology of the Caves and the Texts Found in Them

As the photograph in fig. 5 shows, a series of small niches appear in the walls of the principal chamber. The purpose of these niches is unclear. Many interpret them as niches for lamps, but no remains of lamps were found in the niches, and there is no soot from burning oil to be seen in them. It has been suggested that the niches were used to support wooden shelves on which the scrolls were placed. For example, Lawrence Schiffman argues:

> it seems most likely that this entire cave was constructed to serve as a library for the inhabitants of the nearby building complex. . . .
> On the sides of the cave's main chamber—at specified intervals and at a uniform height—are holes clearly intended to hold wooden supports to accommodate the scrolls. When the cave . . . was abandoned, the wooden planks rotted, spilling the entire collection onto the floor.[62]

Three details help to support this theory. First, from an interview with the bedouin diggers, Weston Fields states that they found pieces of wood in the cave that they threw into the wadi as worthless.[63] This is a great loss, since the evidence of those pieces of wood might reveal a great deal about the purpose and function of the Cave 4Q complex. Second, according to Daniel Stökl Ben Ezra's statistical analysis, the Cave 4Q fragments are *as a whole* older than those from the other marl terrace caves.[64] Thus it is reasonable to argue that Cave 4Q was used as a storage cave for older manuscripts prior to the site's destruction in 68 CE. Third, according to de Vaux and Cross, the manuscripts were found on the floor of the cave in great disorder, leaving open the possibility that the collapse of shelves led to the disarray on the floor. However, it is also the case that de Vaux, Milik, and Cross described the manuscripts as lying in compact layers on the floor. This may indicate that the scrolls were laid on the floor itself in layers, rather than falling from collapsed shelves.

To summarize, Cave 4Qa was intentionally dug into the marl terrace that lies to the west of the buildings of Qumran; it was visible and easily accessible from the settlement. Entrance was made from above, coming

62. L. Schiffman. *Reclaiming the Dead Sea Scrolls: The History of Judaism, the Background of Christianity, the Lost Library of Qumran* (Philadelphia: Jewish Publication Society, 1994), 56.

63. Fields, *Full History*, 150.

64. D. Stökl Ben Ezra, "Old Caves and Young Caves: A Statistical Reevaluation of a Qumran Consensus," *DSD* 14 (2007): 313-33.

THE QUMRAN EVIDENCE

south on the ridge of the marl plateau, and consisted of an opening, ramp, and stairs. The cave consisted of one principal chamber (Chamber 1), with two smaller chambers dug off it (Chambers 2 and 3). All three chambers were high enough for an adult male to stand in. Chamber 1 contained a niche dug into the floor below its "window," as well as a small space accessed from its floor. Cave 4Qa may have contained wooden shelves in antiquity, although this is uncertain.

Cave 4Qb is situated immediately to the west of 4Qa. Although a trench formed by erosion now connects the two caves (see above), according to de Vaux they were not connected in antiquity.[65] Cave 4Qb consists of one chamber, oriented east-west. Originally it had a second chamber on its east, which has been carried away by erosion. On the west, Cave 4Qb had a large open "window" in the cliff face, overlooking Wadi Qumran. The cave's entrance was an opening in its north wall, with a steep passage now almost entirely eroded, which stopped on a platform from which one jumped down into the cave.

Humbert has recently argued that Caves 4Qa-b are the remains of a series of interconnected caves (a-l), most of which have collapsed into the wadi.[66] The "windows" in Cave 4Qa and b, according to Humbert, were not deliberately constructed as windows, but are holes created when parts of the cave complex collapsed. This proposal is very plausible, since it makes little sense to suppose manuscripts would have been stored or hidden in caves open to the elements.

Pottery and other debris (in addition to manuscript fragments) were recovered from both caves (although de Vaux described Cave 4Qb as "very nearly sterile" by the time the excavators reached it).[67] Both de Vaux and Dennis Mizzi have commented on the overall dearth of small finds coming out of the two caves.[68] According to de Vaux, almost all of the pottery, which was very broken, came from Cave 4Qa. His inventory consists of eleven cylindrical or ovoid jars,[69] one bag-shaped jar, three bowl-shaped lids, one "casserole," five bowls, three plates, two jugs, one juglet, and

65. But see Humbert, "Cacher et se cacher," 52, 55.

66. Humbert, "Cacher et se cacher," 52–56; see esp. fig. 2.22b. Some of the spaces that de Vaux labeled "chambers" off of Cave 4Qa Humbert labels as separate caves.

67. De Vaux, DJD 6, 13.

68. De Vaux, DJD 6, 52; Mizzi, "Miscellaneous Artefacts," 139–44.

69. Elsewhere de Vaux lists only five "scroll jars." J. Taylor gives the number twelve ("The Qumran Caves in Their Regional Context: A Chronological Review with a Focus on Bar Kokhba Assemblages," in Fidanzio, Caves of Qumran, 13).

134

Caves and Scrolls: The Archaeology of the Caves and the Texts Found in Them

the early-second-century CE lamp discussed above.[70] All of the recovered pottery (with the exception of the lamp) dates from the first century BCE to the first century CE, thus matching the dates of the pottery recovered from the buildings of Qumran, as we shall see.

Other small finds included fourteen phylactery cases, some textiles that may be the remains of scroll wrappers, scroll tags and ties, pieces of wood, and blank pieces of treated leather. In her 2003 inventory, Mireille Bélis also lists a fragment of linen with a border, and a leather thong.[71] The textiles, tags and ties, and the blank pieces of leather all support the contention that scribal activity, including scroll preparation and repair, was occurring in the vicinity.

The floor of Cave 4Qb was covered in palm branches, spread to a thickness of 0.25 meters. Underneath the palm branches was a powdery layer mixed with ash, then a layer of brown dust.[72] The palm branch floor indicates human use.

Cave 5Q is located to the north of Cave 4Q, separated from it by a small ravine. It consists of a single chamber with a domed ceiling. Part of the ceiling and the front wall has collapsed into the wadi. Humbert suggests that Cave 5Q was also part of a larger complex, possibly that of Cave 4Q.[73] According to de Vaux's report, most of the fragments were recovered from a layer of thick debris from the collapse, but at the bottom of the layer he recovered a "small heap" of fragments, evidently in situ. This indicates that when the scrolls were deposited in the cave they were simply stacked on the floor. Cave 5Q yielded approximately twenty-five manuscripts, as well as a single sherd and some animal bones. On the basis of the material finds it is unlikely that Cave 5Q was used as a residential cave. It is plausible to argue that Caves 4Q and 5Q, at a short remove from the settlement, are the remnants of a larger complex of manmade caves that were used primarily for the storage of manuscripts belonging to the inhabitants of the settlement.

Cave 10Q is located between Caves 4Q and 5Q, high on the slope of the wadi's ravine. It is almost entirely collapsed; nothing was recovered from it except an inscribed potsherd, fragments of a woven mat, and some date

70. De Vaux, DJD 6, 15–20; Mizzi, "Miscellaneous Artefacts," 155–57, table 9.1.

71. De Vaux, DJD 6, 15; M. Bélis, "Des textiles, catalogues et commentaires," in Humbert and Gunneweg, *Khirbet Qumrân et 'Ain Feshkha*, 2:207–76 at tableau 1.

72. De Vaux, DJD 6, 13.

73. Humbert, "Cacher et se cacher," 55.

THE QUMRAN EVIDENCE

pits. These finds point to human occupation rather than scroll storage, although Cave 10Q was probably part of the Caves 4Q–5Q complex in antiquity.

Caves 7Q–9Q are all located at the end of the marl terrace that extends to the south of the visible ruins of Qumran. They were reached by stairs cut into the side of the terrace, and joined by paths; Humbert suggests they were all part of one complex prior to collapse.[74] Cave 7Q consisted of one chamber, mostly eroded away. The written fragments, all in Greek and on papyrus, were recovered from the lower part of the steps leading to the cave.[75] Fragments of approximately nineteen manuscripts were recovered, as well as three cylindrical jars, one bowl-shaped lid, two bowls, one inscribed jar fragment, and one inscribed ostracon.

Lying to the southeast of Cave 7Q is Cave 8Q, of which only one chamber, partly collapsed, remains. Fragments of only three manuscripts, one inscription, and three phylactery cases were recovered. However, the small finds were relatively extensive: one jar, four bowl-shaped lids, one plate, and one lamp; in addition, leather thongs and ties used to tie manuscripts were retrieved, as well as a leather sandal sole and date and olive pits. This cave, therefore, yields evidence of human activity rather than scroll storage.

Cave 9Q was found a little to the north of Cave 8Q; it was connected by steps to another cave that was completely collapsed. Cave 9Q itself consisted of one small room, two-thirds of which was eroded away. Only one unidentified papyrus fragment was recovered, along with an inscribed ostracon, date and olive pits, and fragments of rope and cord.[76] Again, the material evidence points to human activity.

Beginning with de Vaux, the marl terrace caves were thought to be dwelling caves for the community that resided at Qumran: "All the chambers hollowed out in the marl terrace give the impression of having been designed as dwelling-places, and the objects found in them, vases for domestic use, date-stones, scraps of leather, rags, ropes, and a mat, prove that they were in fact inhabited."[77] In an earlier publication I also espoused

---

74. Humbert, "Cacher et se cacher," 57–58.

75. De Vaux, DJD 3, 27.

76. According to Humbert, "Cacher et se cacher," 58, de Vaux also retrieved an Iron Age sherd.

77. De Vaux, *Archaeology,* 56. This position was affirmed by M. Broshi and H. Eshel in, e.g., "How and Where Did the Qumranites Live?," in *The Provo International Conference*

Caves and Scrolls: The Archaeology of the Caves and the Texts Found in Them

this position,[78] but I am now convinced by Mizzi's analysis that these caves were not "habitation caves" on any long-term basis. Mizzi states, "the Qumran caves simply lack clear evidence reflecting the carrying out of daily activities within them, or evidence for their intensive use over a prolonged period of time."[79] For example, there are no remains of hearths, which would be indicative of cooking. However, it remains possible that Caves 7Q–9Q, accessed only through the buildings of the settlement, as well as Cave 10Q, could have been used as occasional sleeping quarters. Cave 8Q, with its collection of scroll tabs and ties, may have been a workshop of some kind. Caves 4Q and 5Q, however, seem only to have been used for scroll storage.[80]

The Scrolls

Cave 4Q: The Hub of the Collection

Since the publication of the Qumran scrolls was completed in the 1990s, Cave 4Q has been acknowledged as the hub of the collection.[81] It contained examples from all languages and scripts found in the Qumran caves (Hebrew, Aramaic, Greek; Aramaic square script, Paleo-Hebrew, Greek, and cryptic scripts) as well as all four categories of texts that we have established (classical, sectarian, affiliated, and general Hellenistic-Roman liter-

---

on the Dead Sea Scrolls: Technological Innovations, New Texts, and Reformulated Issues, ed. D. W. Parry and E. Ulrich, STDJ 30 (Leiden: Brill, 1999), 266–73.

78. S. W. Crawford, "Qumran: Caves, Scrolls, and Buildings," in *A Teacher for All Generations: Essays in Honor of James C. VanderKam*, ed. E. F. Mason, 2 vols., JSJSup 153 (Leiden: Brill, 2012), 1:253–74.

79. Mizzi, "Miscellaneous Artefacts," 147.

80. Taylor suggests that the marl terrace caves served as temporary resting places (genizot) for scrolls awaiting burial either in the limestone cliff caves or in the cemetery. She further suggests that Caves 7Q–9Q were workshops where the work of processing the scrolls for preservation burial took place ("Buried Manuscripts," 292–95). However, as we shall see in ch. 6, the contents of Cave 4Q make it unlikely that its manuscripts were awaiting burial of some kind. Rather, Cave 4Q seems to have contained at least in part a working collection of manuscripts.

81. See ch. 6, and also D. Dimant, "The Qumran Mauscripts: Contents and Significance," in *History, Ideology and Bible Interpretation in the Dead Sea Scrolls: Collected Studies*, FAT 90 (Tübingen: Mohr Siebeck, 2014), 36; and C. Hempel, *The Qumran Rule Texts in Context: Collected Studies*, TSAJ 154 (Tübingen: Mohr Siebeck, 2013), 306–12.

THE QUMRAN EVIDENCE

ature). It preserved the oldest manuscripts by paleographic date (c. 250 BCE) and the latest (c. 50–75 CE).[82] All of these characteristics demonstrate without doubt the centrality of Cave 4Q to any understanding of the Qumran collection as a whole.

A quick scan of the Cave 4Q collection demonstrates how diverse and broad it was. It contained multiple copies of the classical literature of ancient Judaism, most of which were included in the Jewish canon of Scripture at a later date. It contained a cross-section of later Second Temple literature (with some notable exceptions, which we explore in ch. 6), including previously unknown works.[83] Cave 4Q also contained a large proportion of what has been identified as sectarian literature, such as the Damascus Document and the Community Rule. Finally, it contains several idiosyncratic elements that are important for understanding the character of its manuscript collection.

Since the archaeologists interrupted the bedouin in their clandestine digging of Cave 4Q, only about 25 percent of the manuscripts fragments from the cave were properly excavated. De Vaux and Milik provide eyewitness accounts of what they encountered in Cave 4Q when they first entered. According to de Vaux,

> The many fragments recovered by us from Cave 4 went right down to the original floor of the cave and were coated with a marl sediment which had accumulated and solidified over a long period.
>
> Fragments from the same manuscripts had been scattered about [the cave].[84]

---

82. According to B. Webster's index, there are five manuscripts, all from Cave 4Q, whose dates range from the mid- to late third century BCE: 4QExod-Lev[f], 4QSam[b], 4QpaleoDeut[s], 4QJer[a] and 4QEnastr[a] ar ("Chronological Index of the Texts from the Judaean Desert," in DJD 39, 378). Stökl Ben Ezra has demonstrated statistically that the Cave 4Q manuscript collection as a whole is older (along with Cave 1Q) than those of the other Qumran manuscript caves. He suggests on that basis that there were two subcollections in Cave 4Q, the first deposited prior to a fire in 9–8 BCE, and the second at the time of the Roman attack in 68 CE. See Stökl Ben Ezra, "Old Caves and Young Caves," 316. But it seems more likely that manuscripts were deposited in Cave 4Q continuously over the length of its usage.

83. This includes books that date from the third century BCE onward, such as the Enoch literature and Jubilees. The exceptions are works from other cultures or those supportive of the Hasmonean regime. See S. W. Crawford, "The Qumran Collection as a Scribal Library," in Crawford and Wassén, Concept of a Library, 120–22.

84. De Vaux, Archaeology, 100n3.

138

Caves and Scrolls: The Archaeology of the Caves and the Texts Found in Them

In DJD 6, de Vaux observes that almost all the excavated fragments were also represented among the purchased fragments.[85]

Milik recalls the following account from the bedouin when they first entered Cave 4Q: "They [the bedouin] had already turned over several cubic metres of earth when, suddenly, their hands came upon a compact layer of thousands of manuscript fragments."[86] Of his own experience inside the cave, Milik states,

> The cave was accessible through a kind of tube. It was full of dust and dried mud that formed little mounds here and there where they had encircled the scrolls. From one of these mounds I extracted the Book of Enoch, like a cork is extracted with a corkscrew. I understood immediately what we had here. The passage I had before me was from approximately Chapter XX. The cave was cleaned right down to the ground.[87]

Unfortunately, de Vaux made no differentiation between the fragments obtained from the bedouin and those that he himself excavated; the only eyewitness testimony is that of F. M. Cross, who was the first to examine the excavated fragments in 1953: "I was struck with the fact that the relatively small quantity of fragments from the deepest levels of the cave nevertheless represented a fair cross section of the whole deposit in the cave, which suggests . . . that the manuscripts may have been in great disorder when originally abandoned in the cave."[88] In another publication he states,

> I had a cross section of Cave 4 manuscripts, eloquent evidence of the chaotic mix of fragments surviving in the cave. I remember coming on the calendrical documents, *Mišmarot* I called them, a designation which has stuck, and working for the first time in my life on technicalities of calendar. I identified and deciphered a papyrus copy of the *Serek Hay-Yahad*, the Order of the Community, written in an extreme cursive script. There were fragments inscribed in a minuscule Palaeo-Hebrew script, and an odd document written in what I called at that time a proto-Mishnaic dialect [4QMMT].[89]

85. De Vaux, DJD 6, 4.

86. Milik, *Ten Years of Discovery*, 17.

87. Mébarki and Grenache, "Józef Tadeusz Milik," 132.

88. Cross, *Ancient Library of Qumran*, 34n1. Cross also mentions there were "good finds in the remaining untouched levels" (33).

89. F. M. Cross, "Reminiscences of the Early Days in the Discovery and Study of the

THE QUMRAN EVIDENCE

According to Cross, fragments of one hundred or more manuscripts were *excavated* from Cave 4Q, but there was no discernible order even in these excavated fragments.[90]

Certain plates of the PAM photograph series, E (for excavation) series 40.962–40.985, were taken in 1954. These fragments are unidentified on the plates, but Tigchelaar has identified some fragments as belonging to the following manuscripts: 4Q94 (Ps^m), 4Q149 (Mez A), 4Q179 (apocrLam A), 4Q258 (S^d), 4Q261 (S^g), 4Q276 (Tohorot B^a), 4Q289 (Ber^d), 4Q334 (Ordo), 4Q381(Non-Canonical Psalms B), 4Q387 (apocrJer C), 4Q401 (ShirShabb^b), 4Q418c (Instruction^f?), 4Q419 (Instruction-like Composition), 4Q423 (Instruction^g), 4Q432 (papH^f), and 4Q521 (Messianic Apocalypse).[91] In addition, H. Cotton and E. Larson have identified two fragments of 4Q460 (Narrative Work and Prayer) on PAM 40.978 and 40.979.[92] Even this partial identification of excavated fragments indicates that there seems to have been no discernible principle of organization at work in the storage of manuscripts in Cave 4Q. Further, none of the fragments identified are from the oldest manuscripts by paleographical date from Cave 4Q, demonstrating that the fragments found in the lower levels of the cave (i.e., those levels that were excavated) were not necessarily the oldest, which would have been expected if the manuscripts had been placed on the floor of the cave in layers and left undisturbed.

Cave 4Q contained manuscripts from all four of the categories we have established, including copies of every classical work that eventually became part of the Jewish canon of Scripture with the exception of Esther; known and previously unknown works from the Hellenistic-Roman period; and every type of sectarian document, including rule texts (e.g.,

---

Dead Sea Scrolls," in *The Dead Sea Scrolls Fifty Years after Their Discovery: Proceedings of the Jerusalem Congress, July 20–25, 1997*, ed. L. H. Schiffman et al. (Jerusalem: Israel Exploration Society, 2000), 935.

90. Cross, *Ancient Library of Qumran*, 33 (originally written in 1959). In a later interview he puts the number of excavated manuscripts at only twenty-five (Shanks, *Conversations with a Bible Scholar*, 115). S. Pfann puts the count at seventy-two ("Towards an English Edition of de Vaux's Notes: Progress Update from Stephen Pfann," as quoted by S. Reed, "Find-Sites of the Dead Sea Scrolls," *DSD* 14 [2007]: 206). I would like to thank Eibert Tigchelaar for bringing this article, and the existence of the PAM plates, to my attention.

91. E. Tigchelaar in a private communication, February 2017.

92. H. Cotton and E. Larson, "4Q460/4Q350 and Tampering with Qumran Texts in Antiquity?," in *Emanuel: Studies in Hebrew Bible, Septuagint and Dead Sea Scrolls in Honor of Emanuel Tov*, ed. S. M. Paul et al., VTSup 94 (Leiden: Brill, 2003), 119.

Caves and Scrolls: The Archaeology of the Caves and the Texts Found in Them

the Serek Hayaḥad and the Damascus Document), pesharim, and liturgical compositions (e.g., the Hodayot and the Songs of the Sabbath Sacrifice).

I would like to highlight three elements of the Cave 4Q corpus: (1) the oldest manuscripts in the collection; (2) the number of single-copy works; and (3) "working" texts, such as student exercises and brief lists. Some of the items to be discussed fall into more than one category.[93]

The Oldest Manuscripts in the Collection

As noted above, Cave 4Q contained an unusually high proportion of paleographically older manuscripts, certainly older than the site of Qumran itself.[94] Accepting the date of the first quarter of the first century BCE for the founding of the settlement, at least seventy-nine manuscripts in the Aramaic square script, five Paleo-Hebrew manuscripts, and one Greek manuscript can be dated to before the settlement began.[95] That means that at least eighty-five manuscripts (about one-fifth of the Cave 4Q collection) are older than the settlement and were brought from elsewhere to the region of Qumran. Many of these manuscripts (thirty-seven) are from the classical literature of ancient Israel. However, the rest are either from the categories sectarian literature (ten), affiliated literature (twenty-two), or Hellenistic-Roman literature (sixteen). These paleographic dates indicate that the wing of Judaism that composed, collected, and copied these sectarian texts was already in existence prior to the founding of Qumran; thus the scroll collection cannot be tied solely to the settlement, even though Cave 4Q is firmly within the archaeological parameters of the settlement. That is, because these scrolls were brought from outside and are older than the settlement, we must assume that the group who owned them is older than the settlement, and that Qumran is only one of the places where they were located.

93. It is important to remember that, as we catalog works by various means, we do not have the entire collection as it existed in antiquity. There is good evidence that Cave 4Q was disturbed between the time of the final deposit of manuscripts and its discovery in 1952. See Taylor, "Buried Manuscripts," 299.

94. The general consensus among archaeologists now is that the Second Temple settlement at Qumran began c. 100–75 BCE. See Magness, *Archaeology of Qumran*, 68–69; and ch. 5 below.

95. According to the lists of Webster, "Chronological Index," 378–90. I have not included the Cryptic A manuscripts or the phylactery texts, whose paleographical dating is much less certain, in this count.

141

THE QUMRAN EVIDENCE

Further, according to the testimony of de Vaux, Milik, and Cross, the Cave 4Q scrolls were found not in layers according to age (with the most recent manuscripts on top and the older ones underneath) but mixed together. Thus we cannot determine if the older scrolls were placed in the cave earlier, or separately. It is possible that this was the case, but unfortunately it is not provable now.

Single-Copy Works

Cave 4Q had a large number of single-copy works from all parts of its collection.[96] From the classical literature are single copies of Kings (4Q54), Lamentations (4Q111), Ezra-Nehemiah (4Q117), and Chronicles (4Q118).

From the literature (including affiliated texts) of the Hellenistic-Roman period we find single copies of many different genres of texts. The following list is by no means complete, but includes targums to Leviticus and Job (4Q157, 158), various types of parabiblical literature such as the Vision of Samuel (4Q160) or the Admonition on the Flood (4Q370), and liturgical texts such as the Personal Prayer (4Q443) or the Purification Liturgy (4Q284). There are also texts that have been identified as wisdom texts, including the Wiles of the Wicked Woman (4Q184). A number of single-copy works may be termed esoteric, that is, requiring specialized knowledge or interest, such as Zodiology and Brontology ar (4Q318) and Physiognomy/Horoscope (4Q561). Another group are single-copy Aramaic texts, for example, the Testament of Qahat (or: Qohath; 4Q542), the Prayer of Nabonidus (4Q242), and Jews at the Persian Court (4Q550).

Many single-copy works have been identified as sectarian, including the pesharim on Micah, Nahum, and Zephaniah (4Q168–170). There are also several single-copy anthologies like the Florilegium (4Q174) and the

---

96. Although I am emphasizing here works that occur in single copies, the presence of works that occur in multiple copies is equally important, indicating as it does the desire of the collectors to preserve as many examples as possible of what must have been important texts in their worldview. As examples from all parts of the collection, Cave 4Q contained at least twenty-three copies of Deuteronomy, twelve copies of various books of Enoch, nine copies of Jubilees, ten copies of the Serek Hayaḥad, and eight copies of the Damascus Document. See also C. Hempel, "'Haskalah' at Qumran: The Eclectic Character of Qumran Cave 4," in *Qumran Rule Texts*, 329–31. It is also important to reemphasize that we do not have the entire scroll collection as it existed in antiquity; works that exist in only single copies now may have existed in multiple copies in Cave 4Q in antiquity.

142

Caves and Scrolls: The Archaeology of the Caves and the Texts Found in Them

Testimonia (4Q175), and single-copy collections of laws and rules, such as Miscellaneous Rules (4Q265).

The presence of all these single-copy works points to the Cave 4Q collection as retaining a large portion of the scrolls that were kept in the buildings of Qumran, which were brought to Cave 4Q in anticipation of the Roman attack in 68 CE. The number of single-copy works in Cave 4Q also implies an interest in collecting as much Jewish literature as possible, perhaps simply for its own sake to preserve it, or perhaps for completeness in a "research" library.[97] This points to the scholarly-scribal character of the Cave 4Q collection, and may indicate that at least some of the manuscripts from Cave 4Q were in regular use at some time during the life of the Qumran settlement before being stored in the nearby cave.[98]

"Working" Texts

Some of the single-copy manuscripts found in Cave 4Q, such as 4QTestimonia, had a draft-like quality, which may indicate that they were working notes of some kind. We can add to the list of draft-like documents, beginning with the three scribal exercises found there: 4Q234, 4Q341, and 4Q360.[99] These three documents were penned by apprentice scribes; 4Q234 contains short words evidently coming from Gen 27:19-21 written in three different directions; 4Q341 preserves a series of letters and names;[100] and 4Q360 is again written in different directions and repeats the name Menahem three times.

---

97. In much the same way Ptolemy Philadelphus collected books rolls for the library in Alexandria and Assurbanipal collected copies of texts for his library. See also M. Popović, "Qumran as Scroll Storehouse in Times of Crisis? A Comparative Perspective on Judaean Desert Manuscript Collections," *JSJ* 43 (2012): 554, who notes the "scholarly, school-like collection of predominately literary texts."

98. The Testimonia is penned by the same scribe who copied 1QS. This scribe was active c. 100–75 BCE, which means that even if he were resident at Qumran at the beginning of the settlement, he would have been long dead by the time the settlement was destroyed in 68 CE. Therefore, the Testimonia could have been placed in Cave 4Q at any time during the life of the settlement.

99. See A. Yardeni, "234. 4QExercitium Calami A," 185–86; J. Naveh, "341. 4QExercitium Calami C," 291–93; and Yardeni, "360. 4QExercitium Calami B," 297—all in DJD 36.

100. In a recent careful study of 4Q341, J. Taylor concludes that this exercise was written by an accomplished scribe for the purpose of testing a writing instrument and its ink flow ("4Q341: A Writing Exercise Remembered," in Feldman et al., *Is There a Text in This Cave?*, 150–51).

THE QUMRAN EVIDENCE

Other "working" documents include the List of Netinim (4Q340), the List of False Prophets (4Q339), and Rebukes Reported by the Overseer (4Q477). The presence of these scribbled exercises and notes in Cave 4Q indicates the local nature of the collection; that is, it is highly unlikely that such draft-like documents would have been transported to Qumran from Jerusalem or elsewhere. Their place of origin must have been Qumran.[101]

Another indication of the "working" quality of Cave 4Q is the presence of a large number of papyrus texts, palimpsests, and opisthographs.[102] Cave 4Q contained eighty-six papyrus manuscripts, the largest number for any cave.[103] Papyrus, a less expensive material that was easy to erase, was commonly used for documents, letters, and literary texts in this time period.[104] At the other Judean Desert find sites, the vast majority of the papyrus manuscripts are documentary texts.[105] Qumran is exceptional, since the majority of its papyrus manuscripts are literary. The Cave 4Q papyrus manuscripts include both documentary and literary texts; the literary texts fall mainly into the sectarian and affiliated categories, with a large proportion of cryptic manuscripts. George Brooke has made the intriguing suggestion that when we find one or two copies of a work on papyrus when the majority of the copies are on skin, there might have been a deliberate decision to preserve at least one copy on papyrus, perhaps for archival purposes.[106]

Other types of "working" manuscripts are the palimpsest and the opisthograph. There are very few palimpsests (manuscripts on which an older text has been erased and replaced by a later text) in the Qumran library, and all are from Cave 4Q. They include Midrash Sefer Moshe (4Q249), 4QRenewed Earth (4Q475), 4Q457a and b, and 4Q468e (His-

---

101. Crawford, "Qumran Collection as a Scribal Library," 129.

102. Hempel, *Qumran Rule Texts*, 336, makes a similar point regarding the papyrus manuscripts.

103. However, Cave 6Q, with twenty-one papyrus manuscripts, and Cave 7Q, with nineteen, had higher percentages of papyrus, 67 percent and 100 percent, respectively.

104. C. Hezser, *Jewish Literacy in Roman Palestine*, TSAJ 81 (Tübingen: Mohr Siebeck, 2001), 131, 139. Although the later rabbis frowned on the use of papyrus for copying sacred texts (y. Meg. 1:11, 71), 4QpapGen°, 4QpapIsa^p, 6QpapDeut, 6QpapKings, and 6QpapPsalms were all copied on papyrus.

105. E. Tov, *Scribal Practices and Approaches Reflected in the Texts Found in the Judean Desert*, STDJ 54 (Leiden: Brill, 2004), 44.

106. G. Brooke, "Choosing Between Papyrus and Skin: Cultural Complexity and Multiple Identities in the Qumran Library," in *Jewish Cultural Encounters in the Ancient Mediterranean and Near Eastern World*, ed. M. Popović et al. (Leiden: Brill, 2017), 127.

144

Caves and Scrolls: The Archaeology of the Caves and the Texts Found in Them

torical Text F). Twenty-one opisthographs (manuscripts that are inscribed on both sides of the material) have been discovered in the Qumran caves, twenty of them from Cave 4Q.[107] Eight of these are papyrus Cryptic A manuscripts, mostly unidentified. Two of them are documentary texts (4Q342 and 343), which are often opisthographs. However, six have two different literary texts on the verso (first use) and recto (second use), while two (4Q324/355 and 4Q460 frag. 9/4Q350) have a literary text on the verso and a documentary text on the recto. Literary opisthographs are often casual reuses by scribes of older, possibly worn-out manuscripts; this is probably the case for the Cave 4Q opisthographs.[108] While we cannot know for sure if the reuse of a particular text happened at Qumran, it is reasonable to suggest that it did.[109]

By examining the collection through the lens of the three categories above, the breadth of the Cave 4Q corpus becomes clear. Given the age of a portion of the manuscripts, one can argue that this collection was the product of a long-term collection process, which stretched from at least the beginning of the first century BCE, when the oldest manuscripts began to be assembled (according to the archaeology of both Cave 4Q and the settlement at Qumran), through the late first century BCE. Because we do not know the place of origin of the pre–100 BCE manuscripts, we cannot

---

107. One opisthograph was recovered from Cave 1Q, 1Q70; it is papyrus, and its contents are unclassified. For a discussion of the opisthographs from Qumran, see Tov, *Scribal Practices*, 68–73 and appendix 3.

108. Note esp. 4Q324/355, which has a *mishmarot* text on the recto and an account on the verso.

109. 4Q460 frag. 9 and 4Q350 are a special case where we can be practically certain that the reuse occurred locally. The recto has a Narrative Work and Prayer in Hebrew, which contains the divine name; the verso is a list or receipt of cereals in Greek. See H. Cotton, "350. 4QAccount Gr," in DJD 36, 294–95; E. Larson, "460. 4QNarrative Work and Prayer," in DJD 36, 369–86. Cotton and Larson have suggested that it was reused as a scrap by Roman soldiers who had entered Cave 4Q, basing their argument on the fact that 4Q460 contains the Tetragrammaton. They argue that the Qumran sect would never have reused a scroll containing the divine name, and that therefore the reuse must have been by Roman soldiers. There are, however, several difficulties with this scenario. First, there is no other evidence for Roman tampering in Cave 4Q. A Roman-period lamp was discovered in the passageway leading into the cave, suggesting that Roman soldiers stuck their heads into the cave, but there is no other evidence of Roman reuse of any manuscripts. Second, why would a Roman remove a manuscript from Cave 4Q, use it to record cereal shipments, and then put it back into the cave? That scenario seems rather implausible. Thus it seems more probable the reuse was made by a member of the sect that resided at Qumran, indicating that Greek was in some use as an everyday language. 4Q350 remains, however, the only Greek documentary manuscript found in the caves.

145

THE QUMRAN EVIDENCE

say with certainty where this collection process began, but it certainly continued at Qumran.

The large number of single-copy works, some of which are what I have termed "working" texts, points to the active quality of the Cave 4Q collection. That is, this collection was not a frozen relic of a collection brought from elsewhere to be hidden in the caves as several have suggested,[110] but was a living collection, being used and added to up until its final deposit in the caves. The presence of these "working" manuscripts in Cave 4Q strengthens the argument that the built area of Qumran (which includes Cave 4Q) had an active scribal contingent living there during the first century BCE through its destruction in 68 CE.

Caves 5Q, 7Q–9Q

The number of scrolls retrieved from the remaining marl terrace caves is much smaller, since these caves collapsed in antiquity and their contents have been mostly lost. Thus the collections from these caves are only a fraction of what they originally contained.

Since Cave 5Q is located next to Caves 4Qa-b, and may have been part of its larger cave complex, it is likely that Cave 5Q's scrolls were part of the Cave 4Q collection. At the time of its discovery, Cave 5Q contained two works from the classical literature, three from the Hellenistic-Roman period, and four sectarian texts. Ten groups of fragments remain unidentified.

Cave 7Q contained one or two classical works in Greek translation, one or two texts from the Hellenistic-Roman period, also in Greek, and no sectarian texts. All of the Cave 7Q fragments are papyrus, making its collection unique among the manuscript caves. Most of the Cave 7Q fragments remain unidentified. Cave 8Q contained two classical text fragments along with a phylactery and a mezuzah. Cave 9Q contained only one unidentified fragment. The very small corpora in Caves 8Q and 9Q suggest that they were not used for scroll storage, but for other purposes such as workrooms or temporary sleeping quarters.

---

110. For various scenarios, see, e.g., N. Golb, "Khirbet Qumran and the Manuscript Finds of the Judaean Wilderness," in Wise et al., *Methods of Investigation,* 51–72; Y. Magen and Y. Peleg, "Back to Qumran: Ten Years of Excavation and Research, 1993–2004," in *Qumran, the Site of the Dead Sea Scrolls: Archaeological Interpretations and Debates,* ed. K. Galor et al., STDJ 57 (Leiden: Brill, 2006), 55–116; and Stacey, "Reassessment of the Stratigraphy," 63.

146

Caves and Scrolls: The Archaeology of the Caves and the Texts Found in Them

The Cave 7Q corpus is unique in containing only Greek fragments on papyrus. Two explanations for this phenomenon are possible: either this was a private collection belonging to the inhabitant of the cave who read Greek, or the scrolls came from the Greek section of the originating library. It should be remembered in this context that Roman libraries shelved their Greek and Latin collections separately; on this basis we may suggest that the original Qumran library had separate sections for Hebrew/Aramaic and Greek. Since the Cave 4Q collection also contained Greek manuscripts, the second explanation may be more likely.

The Inscriptions

Among the miscellaneous finds in the caves were eight inscriptions, found on both whole vessels and sherds.

TABLE 1

DE VAUX'S NUMERATION	LANGUAGE	MANUSCRIPT CAVE	OTHER
Gr4Q1	Heb/ar	4Q	Fragment of an ovoid jar
6Q1	Heb/ar	South of Cave 6Q	Whole jar; letters and figures
6Q2	Heb/ar	South of Cave 6Q	
Gr7Q1		7Q	
Gr7Q6	Heb/ar	7Q	Whole jar
Gr7Q7	Greek	7Q	
Gr8Q10	Heb	3Q	Whole jar
Gr10Q1	Heb/ar	10Q	

No inscriptions were found in Caves 1Q–2Q, 5Q–6Q, 8Q–9Q, and 11Q. Milik purchased two jars with Hebrew/Aramaic inscriptions on the antiquities market in 1952, whose purported provenance was 100 meters south of Cave 6Q.[111]

111. See J. T. Milik, "Appendice: Deux jarres inscrites provenant d'une grotte de Qumrân," in DJD 3, 37–42. In "The Inscriptional Evidence from Qumran and Its Relationship to

THE QUMRAN EVIDENCE

The readable inscriptions are as follows:

Gr4Q1: לאפך יאיר ם[ ]לֹ. Lemaire suggests that the word לאפך is an aramaizing form of Heb. הפך, "to return or exchange," and may indicate trade of some kind.[112] יאיר is a well-attested male Jewish name of the period.

6Q1: II II III לג II ס. The inscription on this whole round jar indicates a measurement or quantity. A לג is a liquid measure; ס is probably an abbreviation for סאה, a measurement for dry goods such as grain or flour.

6Q2 has either the Greek letter μ or the Roman numeral M.

7Q6 (Kh.Q681/691?) רומא (inscribed twice; Ruma? Roma?). De Vaux (followed by Lemaire and Eshel) suggested that this was a proper name, "Ruma," common in Nabatean and also found in Palmyrene, but unattested in contemporary Jewish contexts.[113]

Gr8Q10 (= 3Q)[114] has the letter ט inscribed twice; once on the neck and once on the shoulder of the jar. This ט may stand for טחור, "pure."[115]

---

the Cave 4Q Documents," in Fidanzio, *Caves of Qumran*, 213, I mistakenly listed these jars as coming *from* Cave 6Q.

112. A. Lemaire, "Inscriptions du khirbeh, des grottes et de 'Aïn Feshkha," in Humbert and Gunneweg, *Khirbet Qumrân et 'Aïn Feshkha*, 2:373. According to M. Jastrow, *A Dictionary of the Targumim, the Talmud Babli and Yerushalmi, and the Midrashic Literature*, 2 vols. (repr., Brooklyn: Shalom, 1967), 1:105, the verb אפך can mean "to turn, turn around, to reverse"; "to overturn, destroy"; "to have to do with, care for"; and "to move about, travel, traffic." M. Sokoloff, *A Dictionary of Jewish Babylonian Aramaic of the Talmudic and Geonic Periods* (Ramat-Gan: Bar Ilan University Press, 2002), 156, gives a definition of "to move around," with a citation referring to wine barrels (b. 'Abod. Zar. 31b).

113. De Vaux further suggested that "Ruma" might also be related to רמי at Elephantine. He also noted that the Greek name Ῥούμας, frequent at Dura Europos, is a transcription from the Aramaic. See R. de Vaux, "Archéologie," in DJD 3, 30. D. Mizzi, "'Rome' at Qumran—What If? Some Remarks on the So-Called Roma Jar from Qumran Cave 7Q," in *The Lure of the Antique: Essays on Malta and Mediterranean Archaeology in Honour of Anthony Bonanno*, ed. N. C. Vella et al., ANESSup 54 (Leuven: Peeters, 2018), 351–74, very hesitantly suggests reasons why the inscription might actually refer to Rome, but this does not seem likely. I would like to thank Professor Mizzi for sharing this article with me prior to publication.

114. Lemaire, "Inscriptions du khirbeh," 376–77, mistakenly identifies this inscription as coming from marl terrace Cave 8Q. Gr8Q10 is correctly identified as from Cave 3Q in G. W. Nebe, "Inscriptions," *EDSS* 1:376.

115. Lemaire, "Inscriptions du khirbeh," 376–77. Lemaire gives an alternative interpretation of the letter, טבל, indicating a product that was not subject to the priestly tithe.

Caves and Scrolls: The Archaeology of the Caves and the Texts Found in Them

Very little information can be gleaned from these inscriptions, apart from the fact that they are Jewish, given the language and the name Yair; there may have been some concern with storing pure goods (Gr8Q10); finally, trade outside the settlement was occurring.

The Scrolls from the Qumran Caves as One Collection

Now that we have surveyed each cave separately, what general observations can we make concerning the caves and their contents? We begin with the geographical location of the caves, continue with a discussion of the nonmanuscript remains, and conclude with an examination of the caches of manuscripts. It will become clear that the caves are connected to one another in several different ways, and it is not only legitimate but necessary to consider them as one group, and the manuscripts found in them as one collection.

Geographical Location

The eleven caves we have surveyed are all located within an easy walk of the ruins of Khirbet Qumran, and Qumran is the closest archaeological site in the vicinity. The farthest caves, 1Q, 2Q, 3Q, and 11Q, are essentially located in a line north of Qumran,[116] while Caves 4Q–10Q are located within sight of the buildings. Caves 7Q–9Q cannot be accessed without walking through the buildings to the end of the plateau. Thus, from the point of view of landscape archaeology, the caves must be included in any discussion of the purpose and function of the ruins of Qumran, and vice versa. However, it should be emphasized that the caves are of two different types, and therefore of two different functions. The limestone cliff caves, being unsuitable for habitation, must have been used primarily for storage, even hiding.[117] The marl caves, on the other hand, may have been used for a variety of purposes, such as workshops, storage, or temporary shelter, since they are manmade, regular in shape, and relatively light and airy.

116. Cave 53 lies south of Qumran.

117. See also Humbert, "Cacher et se cacher," 42, who states that the cliff caves are ideal for secret storage.

149

THE QUMRAN EVIDENCE

The Nonmanuscript Remains

The Pottery

In his Schweich lectures, de Vaux stated concerning the pottery, "The pottery from the caves is identical with that of the khirbeh. The same pastes have been used and the same forms recur here, particularly in the case of the many cylindrical jars."[118] Since the time of de Vaux's statement, the Judean Desert region has been extensively excavated, and much more comparative material is available. Jodi Magness has done a thorough study of the pottery remains from Qumran, both from the caves and the site.[119] Rachel Bar-Nathan has made an extensive survey of pottery types in the Jericho region, which includes Qumran.[120] She notes that the pottery types found at Qumran are also found throughout the region, most notably the pottery from the palaces at Jericho.[121] Therefore, according to Bar-Nathan, the pottery at Qumran is not unique, but part of the larger regional repertoire of the period. Magness agrees with this conclusion, but argues that the "peculiarities" of the Qumran assemblage have to be taken into account in any interpretation.[122] The most important peculiarity for our purposes is the ubiquity of the hole-mouthed cylindrical storage jars at the site of Qumran and in the Qumran caves.

We have already noted the unusual number of cylindrical jars, their fragments, and their bowl-shaped lids that were found in the caves, particularly the natural caves in the limestone cliffs.[123] Only two manuscript caves, 5Q and 9Q, did not contain either cylindrical jars or bowl-shaped

118. De Vaux, *Archaeology*, 54.

119. Magness, *Archaeology of Qumran*, 73–89; see also her "Community of Qumran," 1–15; and, most recently, "The Connection between the Site of Qumran and the Scroll Caves in Light of the Ceramic Evidence," in Fidanzio, *Caves of Qumran*, 184–93.

120. R. Bar-Nathan, "Qumran and the Hasmonaean and Herodian Winter Palaces of Jericho: The Implication of the Pottery Finds for the Interpretation of the Settlement at Qumran," in Galor et al., *Qumran*, 263–80.

121. Bar-Nathan, "Qumran," 263–64.

122. Magness, *Archaeology of Qumran*, 75–77.

123. In a recent article, Magness gives the following inventory of cylindrical or ovoid jars (either whole or in pieces) from the caves: 1Q: 50; 3Q: 6; 4Q: 12 "more or less complete jars, most . . . ovoid"; 6Q: 1; 7Q: 3 ovoid jars; 8Q: fragments of four cylindrical jars; 11Q: de Vaux does not mention cylindrical jars, but according to the bedouin testimony the Temple Scroll was found in one. See Magness, "Connection," 186. Now the cylindrical jar fragments found in Cave 53 must be added to the count.

150

Caves and Scrolls: The Archaeology of the Caves and the Texts Found in Them

lids, and these caves were mostly eroded and their contents washed away. The jars are, therefore, an important material connection among the caves. Now, it is the case that storage jars (especially the ovoid and bag-shaped types) appear in other sites in Judea in the same period. But the *cylindrical* jars are almost entirely absent from other sites.[124] Why were these hole-mouthed cylindrical jars found in such large quantities in the Qumran caves?

Bar-Nathan has connected the function of the jars to the scrolls. She claims that most of the cave pottery comes only from the first century CE (contra de Vaux), and that the cylindrical jar only appears (at all sites) in the late first century BCE. She argues that the cylindrical jar was created in this period to hold scrolls, and that the cave jars should be narrowly dated to the Great Jewish Revolt against Rome, when they were manufactured to hide scrolls in caves. According to Bar-Nathan, they are "archival" jars, and they do not point to any necessary connection between the caves and the site of Qumran. Their presence in both locations is just evidence of the broad regional repertoire of which Qumran is a part.[125]

This argument contains several weaknesses. First, as Bar-Nathan herself admits, this type of jar is so far absent from other sites, in particular Jerusalem, which might be expected to house several archives. Second, while the jars in the limestone cliff caves were definitely used to store scrolls, it may be the case that not all of the scrolls in those caves were placed in jars before storage. This seems to have been particularly the case for Cave 6Q, where the remains of only one scroll jar were found. Finally, several of these cylindrical jars were found sunk into the floor at Qumran, which is certainly not optimal for scroll storage. The cylindrical jars may have had other uses besides scroll storage.[126]

---

124. Magness, *Archaeology of Qumran*, 81, lists some examples from Herodian Jericho and possible single examples from Quailba, Masada, 'Ain Feshkha, 'Ein ez-Zara, and 'Ein-Boqeq. Mizzi notes that only caves in the region of Qumran have yielded cylindrical and/or ovoid jars, and states, "these jars remain characteristic of and synonymous with Qumran" ("Miscellaneous Artefacts," 149n77).

125. Bar-Nathan, "Qumran," 275, 277. The Lönnquists have suggested that this type of jar stored "portable archives"; see n44 above.

126. Magness has suggested that these cylindrical jars (and the ovoid jars, of the same type) were used primarily for storage of the ritually pure food and drink of the Qumran community at the settlement. This suggestion would explain why several jars were sunk in to the floor; it would have been easier to dip out their contents. She further suggests that the inhabitants were storing supplies of pure food and drink *in the caves* ("Why Scroll Jars?," in *Debating Qumran*, 163). The inscription GrQ10 (which was found in manuscript Cave 3Q) contains the letter ט

THE QUMRAN EVIDENCE

The Miscellaneous Finds

Two important observations can be made about the miscellaneous finds from the manuscript caves. First, as we saw above, the number of objects coming from these caves is remarkably small, and second, it is quite limited in repertoire. Date and olive stones, palm fibers, rope and cords, phylactery cases (some with slips, some without), leather thongs and tabs used for fastening scrolls, and linen textiles occur again and again in the inventory. The only cave with a larger and more varied repertoire is Cave 11Q, which Mizzi suggests may have been inhabited for a short period of time during the First Revolt by refugees from Qumran or elsewhere.[127]

The linen textiles merit special mention. Textiles were found in Caves 1Q, 3Q, 8Q, and 11Q;[128] all the recovered textiles are of linen; that no wool textiles were recovered is unusual in ancient Judea.[129] All the textiles, with one exception,[130] are undyed; some of the scroll wrappers have a decorative border of blue thread. None of them in their present state is large enough to be used as a garment, although they were probably originally

---

written twice and may offer support for her thesis, since the ט may stand for טהור, "pure," indicating the contents. However, it is a strange scenario that full jars of foodstuffs and liquid would have been hauled up to remote caves like 1Q, 2Q, and 3Q. Also, as far as I am aware, no tests have been conducted on the excavated jars to learn if the organic matter found in them was indeed the remains of foodstuffs. However, it is entirely possible that the cylindrical jars were being used to store pure foodstuffs (or foodstuffs generally) in the settlement. See P. Patton, "Pottery and Purpose: Using GIS to Evaluate the 'Scroll Jars' at Qumran," MA thesis, University of Nebraska–Lincoln, 2018. I would like to thank Ms. Patton for sharing her research with me.

127. Mizzi, "Miscellaneous Artefacts," 153.

128. M. Bélis, "The Unpublished Textiles from the Qumran Caves," in Fidanzio, *Caves of Qumran*, 123; and O. Shamir and N. Sukenik, "Qumran Textiles and Garments of Qumran's Inhabitants," *DSD* 18 (2011): 208–9. In addition to the textiles found in the caves, three small linen remnants were found in Tomb 1 in the Southern Cemetery, and some carbonized linen textiles were located in L96 in the khirbeh. Linen textiles have also recently been excavated from Cave 53.

129. N. Sukenik, "The *Temple Scroll* Wrapper from Cave 11: MS 5095/2, MS 5095/4, MS 5095/1," in Elgvin et al., *Gleanings from the Caves*, 346, notes the "rich quantity of wool found in other excavations in the area." She goes on to say, "In most of the sites from this period, with the exception of cemeteries, where linen burial shrouds were found, the use of linen is less than 35 percent." A comparison of the textiles found in the Christmas cave, a refugee cave from the Bar Kokhba period, forms a telling comparison: of the 184 Roman period textiles found there, 113 were of wool, 63 of linen, and 8 of goat hair. Most were dyed or decorated, some with bright colors. See Shamir and Sukenik, "Qumran Textiles," 211.

130. The exception is a piece of linen that comes from Cave 8Q, which was dyed in a violet-purple. See Bélis, "Unpublished Textiles," 133.

Caves and Scrolls: The Archaeology of the Caves and the Texts Found in Them

garments that were reused.[131] An analysis of the linen cloths from Cave 1Q was done by Grace Crowfoot, who states that some of these cloths "were certainly scroll wrappers," but some were "covers once tied over the jar tops," and some may have been used as packing material in the jars.[132] The same types of textiles were found in the other caves; Bélis comments that all the textiles follow "a basic and unique pattern, which can be described as 'sober.'"[133] Given the absence of spindle whorls and loom weights at Qumran, it is likely that the linens were manufactured in a workshop and purchased.[134] Sukenik, who studied the scroll wrapper alleged to have been used for the Temple Scroll, states concerning the origin of the fabric,

> A comparison of this scroll wrapper with other textiles that were found in Qumran reveals the following similarities: the method of spinning, the manner of weaving, the decorations, the method of making the borders, the varying thickness of the thread, and even the similarity in the simplicity of the textiles, from which the colourful decorations characteristic of the Roman period are absent. All these features suggest that the textiles were made in the same workshop.[135]

131. Shamir and Sukenik, "Qumran Textiles," 218, state: "Most of the textile remains found at Qumran, except for the blue decorated scroll wrappers, were not originally produced for the purpose of covering jars or protecting scrolls, but were cut from larger pieces of textile which were originally intended as apparel."

132. G. Crowfoot, "The Linen Textiles," in DJD 1, 19, 20. Bélis has recently published an analysis of a jar stuffed with textiles that was deposited in the Amman museum by G. Lankester Harding, Jar GrQ39-2. It is a typical cylindrical scroll jar, filled at least three-quarters full of pieces of white linen with blue decoration similar to that found at Qumran. Although it is clear from de Vaux's notes that the jar was discovered in a cliff cave in the vicinity of Qumran, its exact provenance is uncertain (Bélis, "Unpublished Textiles," 126–30).

133. Bélis, "Unpublished Textiles," 134.

134. Shamir and Sukenik, "Qumran Textiles," 220–21.

135. Sukenik, "*Temple Scroll* Wrapper," 347. In the same volume, J. Taylor and J. van der Plicht present the results of the carbon-14 dating of the scroll wrapper. It was dated between 30 and 215 CE with an 88.5 percent confidence for an actual date between 50 and 180 CE (353). Although Taylor and van der Plicht note that this is later than the usual parameters of carbon-14 dating from Qumran, it still lies within the boundary set by the destruction of the settlement, 68 CE. They ask (354) if the scroll could have been deposited later than 68 CE. Given the carbon-14 date, this is of course possible, but seems unlikely given the other material remains in the cave. If the Temple Scroll was deposited in the cave after the destruction of the Qumran settlement, I would suggest that it was stored there in its jar by refugees from Qumran itself. See J. Taylor and J. van der Plicht, "Radiocarbon Dating of the *Temple Scroll* Wrapper and Cave 11Q," in Elgvin et al., *Gleanings from the Caves*, 351–56.

THE QUMRAN EVIDENCE

Thus once again a subset of the archaeological evidence of the caves points to the caves being used by a specific group over a limited time frame in the late Second Temple period.

Another question raised by the miscellaneous finds is whether there is any evidence for the presence of women in the caves. The short answer is no. "Feminine-gendered" objects from this time period include jewelry, mirrors, cosmetic articles, spindle whorls, needles, and combs.[136] Cave 1Q contained the remains of a comb, which could have been used by either a man or a woman; Cave 3Q yielded one spindle whorl of uncertain date; and one bead was found in Cave 11Q, which also cannot be dated with any certainty.[137] This dearth of evidence is, as we shall see, similar to the dearth of evidence from the settlement at Qumran, and argues against the presence of women there in any number or for any length of time.

Could the Qumran Caves Have Been Refugee Caves?

Various scholars have raised the possibility that the Qumran caves and their scrolls were not related to the site of Qumran, but were used by refugees fleeing from the two Jewish revolts against Rome in 66–73 and 132–135 CE. The dearth of miscellaneous artifacts from these caves (both the marl terrace and limestone cliff caves) argues against this conclusion. A comparison of the artifacts found in the caves of Wadi Murabba'at and Naḥal Ḥever with the Qumran caves is instructive. The excavations at Wadi Murabba'at yielded a rich and varied repertoire of material:

> ropes and cables, a stone cup, "Herodian" lamps, storage jars, cups and bowls, arrow heads, rings from armour, wooden plates, nails, a hook, knives, medical items, a die, wooden spoons, combs and earrings, woollen textiles, basketry, leather (including sandals with hobnails, but also two children's sandals), a hairnet, hair needles, spindle whorls, cosmetic equipment, military equipment, a key, and tools.[138]

---

136. J. Taylor, "The Cemeteries of Khirbet Qumran and Women's Presence at the Site," *DSD* 6 (1999): 318.

137. Mizzi, "Miscellaneous Artefacts," 154.

138. Taylor, "Qumran Caves," 11. De Vaux's report on the archaeology of the Murabba'at caves is found in "Archéologie," in DJD 2, 3–66.

Caves and Scrolls: The Archaeology of the Caves and the Texts Found in Them

Note especially the implements associated with women and children (combs and earrings, hairnet, hair needles, spindle whorls, cosmetic equipment, and children's sandals), which are completely lacking in the Qumran caves. The textiles also are different; some are woolen rather than linen, and Taylor notes, "The textiles are particularly beautiful, including a piece of blue linen with a tapestry band ... and another piece of linen with silk."[139] These artifacts indicate that men and women, with their children, had come to Murabba'at for refuge, bringing with them whatever they could carry.

The same is true for the caves in Naḥal Ḥever. In the "Cave of Letters" and the "Cave of Horror," archaeologists discovered jars, pithoi, cooking pots, casseroles, jugs, lamps, glass vessels, wooden vessels, metal vessels, a pyxis, a comb, two mirrors, a spindle, two spindle whorls, several beads, hairnets, a key, pieces of furniture, awls, needles, one handle, knives, sickles, an axe, arrowheads, coins, pieces of leather, shoes, sandals, colored textiles, baskets, ropes, unspun wool and skeins of wool, a net, and gaming counters. They also found the skeletal remains of over fifty men, women, and children.[140] Again, we note the presence of women and children, and a rich repertoire of household goods.

The second-century CE remains from Cave 2 in Wadi ed-Daliyeh paint the same picture. That cave yielded storage jars, cooking pots, jugs, bowls, lamps, glass vessels, wooden bowls, a bronze jug handle, combs, a kohl stick, a pin, ninety stone beads, a key, an iron blade, an iron pike, a bronze coin, and linen.[141] Once again, the material finds point to the use of the cave by families of refugees.

The picture is utterly different for the Qumran caves. The meager artifacts listed above demonstrate that the caves were not used for habitation for any period of time, either short- or long-term. The only cave that might have been used for very short-term habitation by fleeing refugees on the basis of its material goods is Cave 11Q. What did find refuge in the Qumran caves is manuscripts, and to those we now turn.

The Manuscripts

The most important archaeological find from the caves surrounding Qumran is, of course, the scrolls themselves. Do these manuscripts, in some

139. Taylor, "Qumran Caves," 11.
140. Mizzi, "Miscellaneous Artefacts," 142nn26–27.
141. Mizzi, "Miscellaneous Artefacts," 140n15.

155

THE QUMRAN EVIDENCE

cases in extremely fragmentary condition, demonstrate that they were one collection, owned by one group of people, or are they several collections, deposited in the caves at different times and by different groups of people? As I will make clear, I believe the evidence of the manuscripts points overwhelmingly to the former conclusion, that the manuscripts from the eleven caves were one collection, owned by one group of people.[142] In support of this claim, we will investigate the location for the preparation of the skins used for the scrolls, the composition of their ink, their scripts, their scribal hands, and their general contents. The scrolls' relationship to the site of Qumran and the identity of the group of people who owned them are discussed in chs. 5–7.

The manufacture of the scrolls does not stand out in any way as unusual for Jewish religious texts in the late Second Temple period (although it must be remembered that this is the only major collection that we have, so a collection of the same size is not available for comparison).[143] The scrolls are made from papyrus, imported from Egypt, or from treated animal skin, presumably manufactured locally in Judea. The skins were mostly sheep, goats, and bovine; for example, the Temple Scroll (11QTemple[a]) was manufactured from domestic goatskin, and the thread used to stitch its sheets together was also from the goat.[144] The composition of the black inks used to copy the scrolls is carbon (soot) mixed with water and some type of stabilizer; no metal inks were used. Thus far this does not tell us anything about the place of manufacture. However, recent chemical tests carried out on certain scroll fragments to see if the leather or the ink could have

142. D. Dimant, surveying the manuscripts from a purely literary standpoint, agrees: "all the manuscript caves (perhaps with the exception of caves 7–10, due to the paucity of the findings) housed segments of one and the same collection. This conclusion is also corroborated by the fundamental homogeneity of all the manuscript caves (caves 1–6, 11) both in their contents and generic configuration" ("The Qumran Manuscripts: Contents and Significance," in *History, Ideology and Bible Interpretation in the Dead Sea Scrolls: Collected Studies*, FAT 90 [Tübingen: Mohr Siebeck, 2014], 35).

143. The much smaller Masada collection exhibits the same materials (skin, papyrus) and the same technical aspects (guide dots and ruling, number of columns per sheet, etc.) as the Qumran collection, which indicates that these were common scribal practices in Judea in the Second Temple period. See E. Tov, "A Qumran Origin for the Masada Non-Biblical Texts?," *DSD* 7 (2000): 72n27.

144. E. Tov, "The Sciences and the Reconstruction of the Ancient Scrolls: Possibilities and Impossibilities," in *The Dead Sea Scrolls in Context: Integrating the Dead Sea Scrolls in the Study of Ancient Texts, Languages, and Cultures*, ed. A. Lange et al., 2 vols., VTSup 140 (Leiden: Brill, 2011), 1:13n43.

156

Caves and Scrolls: The Archaeology of the Caves and the Texts Found in Them

been prepared using water from the Dead Sea region (which has a distinct chemical fingerprint) indicate that some leather was produced in the Dead Sea region, and that the ink used to copy 1QH[a] was mixed from water in the Dead Sea region.[145] While this does not prove that scrolls were copied at Qumran itself, it at least makes it possible (if not likely) that some scrolls were copied there, since Qumran is the nearest settlement to the caves in the Dead Sea region. However, it is equally clear from the chemical tests that other scrolls (e.g., the Temple Scroll) were brought from elsewhere in Judea (that is, the chemical composition of their leather does not indicate manufacture in the Dead Sea region). This accords with the evidence from the paleographical dates of the manuscripts, the main parameters of which were determined before these chemical tests were conducted. These dates indicated that at least 25 percent of the manuscripts from the caves are older than the site of Qumran itself, which was established around 100–75 BCE. Thus those manuscripts with paleographical dates before approximately 100 BCE must have been brought to the settlement from outside. The Temple Scroll, while copied during the settlement period at Qumran (late first century BCE), also was brought in from the outside, and we may assume many other scrolls were as well. In any case, the material from which the scrolls were constructed does not help us answer the question of whether they were one collection, although it does determine that some of the scrolls were made and copied in the Dead Sea region.

However, the contents of the manuscripts do indicate that they were one collection. Any consideration of this statement must begin with Cave 4Q, which contained the largest cache of manuscripts, with approximately six hundred identified.[146] Cave 4Q may have been used as a storage cave during the period in which Qumran was inhabited, since a larger percentage of its manuscripts are older than the general collection, indicating that it was most likely used for storing manuscripts while the settlement was occupied.[147] It is the hub of the collection as well, with the other caves acting like spokes on a wheel. Almost every manuscript found in Caves

---

145. I. Rabin, "Archaeometry of the Dead Sea Scrolls," *DSD* 20 (2013): 124–42; T. Wolff et al., "Provenance Studies on Dead Sea Scrolls Parchment by Means of Quantitative Micro-XRF," *Analytical and Bioanalytical Chemistry* 402 (2012): 1493–1503; I. Rabin et al., "On the Origin of the Ink of the Thanksgiving Scroll (1QHodayot[a])," *DSD* 16 (2009): 97–106. It must be kept in mind that the tests conducted so far on manuscripts do not yield a sufficient sample from which to draw any certain conclusions.

146. Tov, *Revised Lists*, 22–62.

147. Stökl Ben Ezra, "Old Caves and Young Caves," 317.

THE QUMRAN EVIDENCE

1Q–3Q and 5Q–11Q is also found in Cave 4Q, sometimes in multiple copies. Using the four categories of literature described in the introduction (the classical literature of ancient Israel, literature of the Hellenistic and Roman periods, sectarian literature, and affiliated literature), we can enumerate manuscripts from Cave 4Q that also surfaced in other caves, thus tying all the caves together through their commonalities with Cave 4Q.

TABLE 2. Classical Literature

BOOK	4Q	1Q	2Q	3Q	5Q	6Q	7Q	8Q	11Q
Genesis	16	1	1			1		1	
Exodus	14	1	3				1		
Leviticus	14	1	1			1			2
Numbers	4	1	4						
Deuteronomy	26	2	3		1	1	1(?)[1]		1
Judges	3	1							
Samuel	3	1							
Kings	1			1	1				
Isaiah	18	2			1				
Jeremiah	5		1						
Ezekiel	3			1					1
The Twelve	7				1				
Psalms	23	3	1	1	1	1			5
Job (including Aramaic)	4		1						11
Ruth	2		2						
Canticles	3					1			
Lamentations	2			1	2				

Note: For the classical literature I have counted those scrolls identified as copies of a specific book, whether or not they were complete copies in antiquity. I have also counted scrolls containing more than one book under each separate book, e.g., 4QExod-Lev^f has been counted under both Exodus and Leviticus. All the manuscript counts are taken from Tov, *Revised Lists.* I have not included scroll fragments of uncertain provenance.

1 Puech has reconstructed a Greek Deuteronomy manuscript from Cave 7Q ("Les fragments de papyrus 7Q6 1–2, 7Q9 et 7Q7 = pap7QLXXDt," *RevQ* 29 [2017]: 119–28).

158

Caves and Scrolls: The Archaeology of the Caves and the Texts Found in Them

TABLE 3. Affiliated Works from the Hellenistic-Roman Period (selected)

WORK	4Q	1Q	2Q	3Q	5Q	6Q	7Q	11Q
Daniel	5	2				1		
Enoch (including the Book of Giants)	17	2	1			1	1 (Greek)	
Jubilees	13	2	2	1				1
New Jerusalem	13	1	1		1			1
Temple Scroll	1							3
Aramaic Levi Document	6	1						

TABLE 4. Sectarian Literature (selected)

WORK	4Q	1Q	2Q	3Q	5Q	6Q	7Q	8Q	11Q
Serek Hayaḥad	10	1		1					
Damascus Document	8			1	1				
War Rules[1]	6	1							1
Serek Ha'edah	8 or 9 (cryptic script)[2]	1							
Songs of the Sabbath Sacrifice	8								1[3]
Pesharim[4]	12	4		1 (?)					
Hodayot	6	2							
Instruction	5	1[5]							

1 The War Rules are not all copies of the same work, but are all concerned with the final eschatological war.

2 This is according to the identifications made by S. Pfann, "Cryptic Texts," in *Qumran Cave 4.XXVI: Cryptic Texts*; and *Miscellanea, Part 1*, by P. Alexander et al., DJD 36 (Oxford: Clarendon, 2000), 515–702. Pfann made his separation of the cryptic script fragments into separate manuscripts on the basis of paleographic considerations and the writing materials, especially the physical characteristics of the papyrus (517–18). However, more recent studies have questioned some of his decisions. See now A. Gayer et al., "A New Join of Two Fragments of 4QcryptA Serekh haEdah and Its Implications," *DSD* 23 (2016): 139–54; and J. Ben-Dov et al., "Reconstruction of a Single Copy of the Qumran Cave 4 Cryptic-Script Serekh haEdah," *RevQ* 29 (2017): 21–77, who argue that the fragments assigned by Pfann to

THE QUMRAN EVIDENCE

eight or nine copies represent a single cryptic copy of Serek Ha'edah. The important point for my argument is that the Serek Ha'edah does appear in Cave 4Q.

3 One copy of the Songs of the Sabbath Sacrifice was discovered at Masada. While its editor, Carol Newsom, believes that the location of one copy outside of the Qumran caves indicates that the Songs are not sectarian in origin, the one copy could have been carried to Masada by a refugee fleeing from Qumran after its destruction in 68.

4 This category includes any manuscript identified as a pesher by its editors.

5 Cave 4Q contained many compositions, including single-copy works, not found in the other caves. This is not surprising given the size of the Cave 4Q corpus in comparison with that of the other caves. It must always be kept in mind, however, that an unknown percentage of the collection has been lost since antiquity, especially from the collapsed marl terrace caves. Other cave collections also included single-copy works; for example, Cave 1Q contained Pesher Habakkuk and the Genesis Apocryphon, Cave 2Q contained a copy of Sirach, Cave 3Q had a copy of a Testament of Judah, Cave 7Q had a copy of the Epistle of Jeremiah, and Cave 11Q contained the Melchizedek scroll.

These tables demonstrate the overlaps among the different cave corpora. While copies of Israel's classical literature certainly dominate, and thus could give rise to the argument that this is simply a Jewish collection from the period with no defining characteristics, the affiliated literature from the Hellenistic-Roman period that is represented in more than one cave includes those works that we isolated in ch. 3 as having a specific set of interests: an expanded understanding of the role of the scribe, combined with such esoteric interests as astronomical knowledge (along with calendar calculations and a preference for a calendar based on the solar year) and dreams and visions and their correct interpretation (for more discussion see ch. 6). The works represented are the books of Enoch (Caves 1Q, 2Q, 4Q, 6Q, and 7Q), Daniel (Caves 1Q, 4Q, and 6Q), Jubilees (Caves 1Q, 2Q, 3Q, 4Q, and 11Q), the Temple Scroll (Caves 4Q and 11Q), and the Aramaic Levi Document (Caves 1Q and 4Q); these works have special affinities with the wing of Judaism represented in the sectarian texts.

Most importantly, the sectarian literature is spread throughout the caves. It is these sectarian compositions especially that mark the collection as a particular one, belonging to a specific group of Jews in the late Second Temple period. Caves 1Q, 3Q, 4Q, 5Q, 6Q, and 11Q all contain sectarian texts; thus the only cave with a manuscript collection of any size (the textual material found in Caves 7Q–10Q being negligible) that is lacking sectarian texts is Cave 2Q. However, Cave 2Q contained manuscripts of Enoch, the New Jerusalem, and Jubilees, works held in esteem by the members of the group to which the sectarian texts belonged. Thus I be-

160

Caves and Scrolls: The Archaeology of the Caves and the Texts Found in Them

lieve we can safely claim that on the basis of their contents Caves 1Q–11Q represent one collection.[148]

Scripts also show that the Qumran manuscript caves constitute one collection. First, scribal hands recur throughout the caves. It is true that there are many different scribal hands found on the Qumran manuscripts, as is indicated by the paleographical dates of the manuscripts (ranging from the third century BCE to the first century CE), the different styles of writing (formal, semiformal, semicursive, cursive), and the different scripts (Aramaic square script, Paleo-Hebrew, cryptic, Greek).[149] This diversity of scribal hands, and in particular those paleographical dates that indicate copying before the settlement of Qumran came into existence, demonstrates that perhaps the majority of the Qumran scrolls were brought to Qumran and its caves from elsewhere in Judea. However, it is also the case that individual scribes, recognized by their distinctive handwriting, copied more than one manuscript in the Qumran corpus. The best-known case is the scribe of the Cave 1 scroll that contains the Serek Hayaḥad, the Serek Ha'edah, and the Rule of the Blessings (1QSb). This scribe also copied 4QSam[c], 4QTestimonia (4Q175), and 4QNarrative G (4Q481b); was the second hand in 1QpHab; and made corrections to 1QIsaiah[a] (the Great Isaiah Scroll). In addition, John Strugnell ascribed 4QTestament of Qahat, 4QIndividual Thanksgiving A (4Q441), 4QPersonal Prayer (4Q443), and 4QEschatological Hymn (4Q457b) to that scribe.[150] This scribe worked in the first half of the first century BCE, around 100–75 BCE, the period at which the Qumran settlement was founded. Other proposals of recurring scribal hands have been made over the years. J. T. Milik suggested that

148. C. Newsom makes the same argument: the pattern of multiple copies "suggests that the scrolls do not simply represent a random collection of texts" ("'Sectually Explicit' Literature from Qumran," in *The Hebrew Bible and Its Interpreters*, ed. W. H. Propp et al., [Winona Lake, IN: Eisenbrauns, 1990], 171).

149. See F. M. Cross, "The Development of the Jewish Scripts," in *Leaves from an Epigrapher's Notebook: Collected Papers in Hebrew and West Semitic Palaeography and Epigraphy*, HSS 51 (Cambridge: Harvard University Press, 2003), 3–43; A. Yardeni, *The Book of Hebrew Script: History, Palaeography, Script Styles, Calligraphy and Design*, 3rd ed. (Jerusalem: Carta, 2010), 47–66; Tov, *Scribal Practices*, 20–24; and E. Puech, "La paléographie des manuscrits de la Mer Morte," in Fidanzio, *Caves of Qumran*, 96–105, who remarks "L'analyse paléographique ci-dessus a révélé une grande diversité de mains des scribes sur plusieurs siècles" (103).

150. All this information is taken from Tov, *Scribal Practices*, 23–24, who also includes a full bibliography. See also E. Tigchelaar, "In Search of the Scribe of 1QS," in Paul et al., *Emanuel*, 439–52.

161

THE QUMRAN EVIDENCE

4QEnoch[f] ar (4Q207) and 4QLevi[d] ar (4Q214) were written by the same scribe. Milik also suggested that one scribe penned 4QCurses (4Q280), 5QSerek Hayaḥad (5Q11), and 5QRule (5Q13).[151] J. P. M. van der Ploeg identified the same scribal hand in 11QTemple[b] (11Q20) and the first hand of 1QpHab. Eugene Ulrich has identified 4QIsa[c], 1QPs[b], and 11QM as having been copied by the same scribe.[152]

By far the most sweeping claim comes from Ada Yardeni, who has identified one scribal hand in at least 54 manuscripts; Émile Puech agrees with her identification of this scribe.[153] These manuscripts come from Caves 1Q, 2Q, 3Q, 4Q, 6Q, and 11Q, and one is from Masada (a Joshua Apocryphon).[154] They comprise classical literature manuscripts (e.g., 4QNum[b], 4QDeut[k1, k2]), Jewish works from the Hellenistic-Roman period (e.g., 4QText Concerning Rachel and Joseph), and sectarian compositions (e.g., 4QD[b, d], 4QMMT[d]). Yardeni dates this scribal hand to the late first century BCE, the floruit of the Qumran community.[155] Concerning this scribe she writes, "The general appearance of his handwriting is orderly, spacious and elegant, indicating a skilled, professional and trained hand, easily recognizable thanks to its peculiar *lamed*, with the 'pressed' and curved lower part."[156]

That manuscripts penned by the same scribe turned up in different caves makes it difficult to argue that the caves are not connected to one another. The three major examples I have given of scribal identification demonstrate this. The first common scribe to be identified, of 1QS, 4QSam[c], and 4QTestimonia (as well as others), has manuscripts found in Cave 1Q, a limestone cliff cave, and Cave 4Q, a marl terrace cave. Ulrich's scribe's manuscripts were found in Caves 1Q and 4Q, as well as 11Q.

---

151. J. T. Milik, "Milkî-ṣedeq et Milkî-reša' dans les anciens écrits juifs et chrétiens," *JJS* 23 (1972): 129.

152. E. Ulrich, "Identification of a Scribe Active at Qumran: 1QPs[b]-4QIsa[c]-11QM," in *Meghillot: Studies in the Dead Sea Scrolls* 5–6 (2007): *201–*10. Ulrich has informed me (private communication) that this same scribe also penned 4QDan[b]. Ulrich describes this scribe as displaying "an elegant, careful, distinctive hand" that is immediately recognizable. The scribe uses Paleo-Hebrew for the Tetragrammaton in his biblical manuscripts.

153. A. Yardeni, "A Note on a Qumran Scribe," in *New Seals and Inscriptions: Hebrew, Idumean, and Cuneiform*, ed. M. Lubetski (Sheffield: Sheffield Phoenix Press, 2007), 286–98; Puech, "Paléographie," 104–5.

154. Like the copy of the Songs of the Sabbath Sacrifice mentioned in Table 4, note 3, this manuscript may have been carried to Masada by a refugee fleeing the destruction of Qumran.

155. Yardeni, "Note on a Qumran Scribe," 288.

156. Yardeni, "Note on a Qumran Scribe," 288.

Caves and Scrolls: The Archaeology of the Caves and the Texts Found in Them

Yardeni's scribe has the widest distribution, with Caves 1Q, 4Q, and 11Q, but also 2Q, 3Q, and 6Q. It becomes very difficult to argue that the caves are not connected if manuscripts from the same scribal hand are found across them.

While manuscripts written in the Aramaic square script predominate throughout the caves, other scripts are also found and occur in more than one cave. Paleo-Hebrew manuscripts were found in Caves 1Q, 4Q, and 11Q. Manuscripts in the cryptic script were also found in more than one cave. All but one of the cryptic manuscripts come from Cave 4Q, but a manuscript in the Cryptic A script also appears in 11Q, tying together these two caves, one a marl terrace cave and one a limestone cliff cave.

Finally, while Hebrew is the dominant language in the collection, Aramaic and Greek texts were also found, and in more than one cave. Greek manuscripts were recovered from Caves 4Q and 7Q, while Caves 1Q, 2Q, 3Q, 4Q, 5Q, 6Q, and 11Q all contained Aramaic texts.

All of the elements listed above concerning the manuscripts—the overlaps in contents among the caves (especially the sectarian texts), the fact that individual scribal hands are found in more than one cave, the presence of Paleo-Hebrew and cryptic scripts in more than one cave, and the presence of the three languages across the caves—indicate that the manuscripts should be considered one collection, belonging to a specific wing of Judaism in the Second Temple period. It is true that different caves among the ten manuscript caves have distinct profiles. Only Greek manuscripts were found in 7Q. Cave 6Q contained a greater proportion (more than 50 percent) of papyrus manuscripts than any other cave. The manuscripts of Caves 1Q and 4Q are statistically older than those of the other caves, while those of 11Q are statistically younger. Cave 2Q did not contain any sectarian manuscripts. Those differences, however, are not enough to suggest that the manuscripts found in each cave belonged to different groups and were deposited at different times.[157] Rather, the commonalities among the cave

---

157. The most detailed argument for this position is found in S. Pfann, "Reassessing the Judean Desert Caves: Libraries, Archives, Genizas and Hiding Places," *Bulletin of the Anglo-Israel Archaeological Society* 25 (2007): 147–69. Pfann distinguishes between caves that contain "manuscripts providing typical *Yahad* doctrine" (1Q, 4Q, 5Q, 6Q), and those that do not (2Q, 3Q, and 11Q) (156). He suggests that Caves 4Q and 5Q were genizot for an institutional library from Jerusalem, and that Caves 3Q and 11Q contained manuscripts that belonged to the Zealots associated with Yehuda ben Yair, who deposited them there at the end of the First Revolt (he includes Cave 2Q in this group as well, although he associates its collection with Simon bar Giora; 159–62). While Pfann makes some good points, the main

THE QUMRAN EVIDENCE

collections demonstrate convincingly that they are the remnants of the literary collection of a distinct wing within Judaism during the Second Temple period.[158]

The difference that is evident between the limestone cliff caves and the marl terrace caves is one of function, not of content. Caves 1Q, 2Q, 3Q, 11Q, GrQ29, and Cave 53 all appear to have been used almost exclusively for the long-term or permanent storage of scrolls in jars.[159] The fifty jars from Cave 1Q would have taken up all the available floor space in the cave. The jars in Cave 3Q were hidden behind a rock wall, positioned so that the tops of the jars would have reached the roof of the cave. Cave 53 had manmade niches into which jars were deliberately placed. All of the limestone cliff caves were difficult to access, and it is probable that once a cave received its quota of jars it was sealed (or at least the entrance was concealed) and was not visited again. Since the pottery from these caves dates from the first century BCE on, this process was going on during the life of the settlement. While the purpose of this long-term storage may have been, as Joan Taylor has suggested, scroll "burial," her evidence is not conclusive; and at the present time the more neutral scenario of long-term or permanent storage is preferable.

The marl terrace caves are quite different in their archaeological profile. These caves are manmade, part of the built environment of Qumran, and were most likely used on a daily basis by the inhabitants. They fall into

---

weakness of his theory lies precisely in the overlaps among the caves that we have presented above. For example, a copy of a pesher on Isaiah comes from Cave 3Q, and the Songs of the Sabbath Sacrifice and a War Rule occur in Cave 11Q. The sectarian literature is not limited to Serek Hayaḥad, the Damascus Document, and Serek Ha'edah, important as those texts are. Further, we know nothing about Zealot literature, or even if such a thing existed. Finally, while the Temple Scroll (11QT^a) is not sectarian, it contains themes (the solar calendar) and legal rulings (the prohibition of uncle-niece marriage) that are congenial to the wing of Judaism represented by the sectarian texts. For my argument concerning the differences among the cave collections and what they may signify, see ch. 8.

158. F. García Martínez reaches the same conclusion: "My review of the contents of all the caves leads me more in the direction of the traditional opinion, a single collection and a single deposit" ("The Contents of the Manuscripts from the Caves of Qumran," in Fidanzio, *Caves of Qumran*, 79).

159. The archaeological evidence from Cave 6Q is different from that of the other limestone cliff caves. Fragments of only one scroll jar were recovered there, indicating that its manuscripts were not all placed in jars before being deposited in the cave. Also, its location at the base of the aqueduct of the water system of Qumran puts it within the built environment of the settlement. These two factors suggest that it was more like Caves 4Q and 5Q in its function than the other limestone cliff caves.

164

Caves and Scrolls: The Archaeology of the Caves and the Texts Found in Them

two groups, Caves 4Q–5Q and 7Q–9Q.[160] Caves 4Q and 5Q are the remains of what I would argue was the "remote storage facility" for the library of the Qumran settlement.[161] As we have observed, Cave 4Q may have had wooden shelves in antiquity for the placement of and easy access to scrolls. These two caves are within walking distance of the compound but outside it, making a short-term storage function likely.

Caves 7Q–9Q, on the other hand, are within the compound itself at the end of the plateau. Stairs from the plateau led into them, indicating regular traffic. Cave 8Q, with its collection of scroll ties and tabs, may have been a workshop of some kind.[162] At the time the settlement was abandoned, Greek manuscripts were left in Cave 7Q, possibly from the library complex in the buildings. As a group, the marl terrace caves are intimately connected with the buildings at Qumran and the activities taking place there. In the next chapter I explore the archaeological evidence from Qumran for its daily life, in particular the evidence for the presence of scribes and a library there.

160. Cave 10Q probably belonged to the same cave complex as Caves 4Q–5Q, but its archaeological remains are so sparse that little can be said about it.

161. For the evidence for a library complex in the Qumran buildings, see ch. 5.

162. See R. de Vaux, *Qumrân Grotte 4.II: Part I: Archéologie*; and *Part II: Tefillin, Mezuzot et Targums (4Q128–4Q157)*, by J. T. Milik, DJD 6 (Oxford: Clarendon, 1977), pl. 5, for photographs of the tabs and ties.

CHAPTER 5

The Archaeology of Qumran

> Khirbet Qumran is not a village or a group of houses; it is the establishment of a community.
>
> Roland de Vaux, *Archaeology and the Dead Sea Scrolls*

Khirbet Qumran is one of the most thoroughly excavated sites in the Middle East. Although the ruins of Qumran were visited in the nineteenth century by de Saulcy, Condor and Tyrwhitt-Drake, and Clermont-Ganneau,[1] it was not until the discovery of Cave 1Q in its vicinity that a systematic excavation of the site was undertaken by Roland de Vaux of the École Biblique et Archéologique Française (EBAF) between 1951 and 1956. Since de Vaux's excavations, the site of Qumran has been interpreted as a community settlement of the sect of the Essenes, a fortress, a rural villa, a pottery production center, and a seasonal industrial site, among other suggestions. My contention is that Qumran was built to function as a scribal center and library for the Essenes in Judea. In this chapter I explore whether or not the archaeology of Qumran can support this hypothesis.

De Vaux, the site's chief excavator and first interpreter, understood the site of Qumran to be a community settlement belonging to the Essenes, one of the three Jewish sects identified by Josephus that emerged in the second century BCE, the other two being the Sadducees and the Pharisees (*Ant.* 13.171–172). The scholars who had first seen the Cave 1Q scrolls had already suggested that the nonbiblical scrolls from Cave 1Q were Essene, on the basis of parallels between those scrolls and the descriptions of the Essenes in Josephus and Philo.[2] De Vaux accepted this identification. For

---

1. G. Lankester Harding, "Khirbet Qumran and Wady Murabba'at: Fresh Light on the Dead Sea Scrolls and New Manuscript Discoveries in Jordan," *PEQ* 84 (1952): 104.

2. Among them were Eleazar Sukenik, John Trever, and Millar Burrows. See J. Taylor, *The Essenes, the Scrolls, and the Dead Sea* (Oxford: Oxford University Press, 2012), 11–12,

The Archaeology of Qumran

de Vaux, however, it was Pliny's testimony concerning the location of the Essene settlement that was decisive for his assertion that Qumran was Essene. Pliny states,

> To the west [of the Dead Sea] the Essenes have put the necessary distance between themselves and the insalubrious shore. They are a people unique of its kind and admirable beyond all others in the whole world, without women and renouncing love entirely, without money, and having for company only the palm trees. . . . Below [*infra hos*] the Essenes was the town of Engada [Engedi], which yielded only to Jerusalem [*sic*; Jericho] in fertility and palm-groves but is today become another ash-heap. From there, one comes to the fortress of Masada, situated on a rock, and itself near the lake of asphalt. (*Nat. Hist.* 5.73)[3]

On the basis of Pliny's statement, de Vaux concludes,

> if the writings of Qumran exhibit certain points of resemblance to what is known from other sources about the Essenes, and if the ruins of Qumran correspond to what Pliny tells us about the dwelling-place of the Essenes, his evidence can be accepted as true. And this evidence serves to confirm that the community was Essene in character. This is no vicious circle, but rather an argument by convergence, culminating in that kind of certitude with which the historian of ancient times often has to content himself.[4]

De Vaux's interpretation of the site of Qumran was therefore guided by his understanding of Qumran as an Essene settlement. This interpretation became known as "the Qumran-Essene hypothesis."

The understanding of Qumran as an Essene settlement held almost unquestioned sway in the field until the 1990s.[5] At that time, a new gener-

---

for a discussion. See also the pertinent articles in D. Dimant, ed., *The Dead Sea Scrolls in Scholarly Perspective: A History of Research*, STDJ 99 (Leiden: Brill, 2012).

3. Translation according to G. Vermes and M. Goodman, *The Essenes according to the Classical Sources* (Sheffield: JSOT Press, 1989), 32. All translations of the classical sources in this book are taken from Vermes and Goodman unless otherwise noted.

4. De Vaux, *Archaeology and the Dead Sea Scrolls: The Schweich Lectures of the British Academy 1959*, rev. ed. (London: Oxford University Press, 1973), 137.

5. The classic English language handbooks, i.e., F. M. Cross, *The Ancient Library of Qumran*, 3rd ed., BibSem 30 (Sheffield: Sheffield Academic Press, 1995); and G. Vermes,

ation of archaeologists looked at the evidence with fresh eyes, a process greatly aided by the publication of de Vaux's field notes in 1994. None of these new analyses accepted all of de Vaux's conclusions, but they fell into essentially two camps. The first camp accepted the Qumran-Essene hypothesis with revisions; today it includes Magen Broshi, the late Hanan Eshel, Jodi Magness, Eric Meyers,[6] and Dennis Mizzi, all of whom accept the Second Temple period site as Essene from its inception. Jean-Baptiste Humbert, de Vaux's successor at EBAF and the person responsible for the final publication of the excavations, offers a modification of de Vaux's theory. He argues for three levels of occupancy in the Second Temple period, beginning with Level (*niveau*) 2, which was a Hasmonean seasonal villa (first half of the first century BCE). Level 3, which began in the second half of the first century BCE and ended in 68 CE, was "a religious center for a Jewish sect living around the Dead Sea."[7] Level 4 was a post–68 reoccupation of the site, first by Roman soldiers, then by Jewish refugees.[8] Joan Taylor similarly divides the site into a Hasmonean fortified settlement (c. 80–37 BCE); a Herodian/Essene settlement (c. 37 BCE–68 CE), during which time she believes Qumran was used by the Essenes as a scroll burial site; and a temporary Roman auxiliary post followed by a reinstated Essene settlement (68–115 CE).[9]

The second position is not so much a position as an antiposition, arguing against the Qumran-Essene hypothesis. Those who hold this position

---

The Dead Sea Scrolls: Qumran in Perspective (London: Collins, 1977), were firm supporters of the Qumran-Essene hypothesis. Early voices of opposition included Solomon Zeitlin and G. R. Driver. In a series of articles Zeitlin argued that the scrolls were either medieval manuscripts or forgeries ("A Commentary on the Book of Habakkuk: Important Discovery or Hoax?," *JQR* 39 [1949]: 235–47; "Scholarship and the Hoax of the Recent Discoveries," *JQR* 39 [1949]: 337–63; "The Alleged Antiquity of the Scrolls," *JQR* 40 [1949]: 57–78). Driver argued that the Qumran sect should be identified with the Zealots (*The Judaean Scrolls: The Problem and a Solution* [Oxford: Blackwell, 1965]).

6. E. M. Meyers, "Khirbet Qumran and Its Environs," *OHDSS* 21–45.

7. J.-B. Humbert, "Some Remarks on the Archaeology of Qumran," in *Qumran, the Site of the Dead Sea Scrolls: Archaeological Interpretations and Debates*, ed. K. Galor et al., STDJ 57 (Leiden: Brill, 2006), 37.

8. J.-B. Humbert, "Les moyens de la chronographie," in *Khirbet Qumrân et 'Aïn Feshkha: Fouilles du P. Roland de Vaux*, vol. 3A: *L'archéologie de Qumrân; Reconsidération de l'interprétation; Les installations périphériques de Khirbet Qumrân*, ed. J.-B. Humbert et al., NTOA.SA 5A (Göttingen: Vandenhoeck & Ruprecht, 2016), 119.

9. J. Taylor, *The Essenes, the Scrolls, and the Dead Sea* (Oxford: Oxford University Press, 2012), 261–65.

The Archaeology of Qumran

do not agree on the particulars, but do agree that Qumran was not a Jewish sectarian settlement and that the manuscripts found in the caves are not related to the site of Qumran. The better-known proponents of this position are Robert Donceel and Pauline Donceel-Voûte, Norman Golb, the late Yizhar Hirschfeld, Yitzhak Magen and Yuval Peleg, and David Stacey. The Donceels argued that Qumran was a "villa rustica," with wealthy inhabitants.[10] Golb insisted that Qumran was a Hasmonean/Herodian fortress, and that the scrolls were part of library holdings from Jerusalem, hidden in the caves before the siege and destruction of the temple in 70 CE.[11] Hirschfeld held that Qumran was a rural estate complex and that the scrolls were brought for concealment in the caves from some public library, probably in Jerusalem.[12] Magen and Peleg contended that Qumran was at first a fortified Hasmonean outpost and then became an "important pottery production center." The scrolls, meanwhile, were hidden by fleeing refugees during the Great Jewish Revolt.[13] Finally, Stacey understood Qumran to have been a satellite colony of the royal estate in Jericho, used for seasonal industrial activities such as leather production, wool preparation, and pottery production. Stacey suggested that the scrolls were brought to the caves from Jericho and deposited there in genizot.[14] That these various interpretations differ so widely and have not won widespread

10. R. Donceel and P. Donceel-Voûte, "The Archaeology of Khirbet Qumran," in *Methods of Investigation of the Dead Sea Scrolls and the Khirbet Qumran Site: Present Realities and Future Prospects*, ed. M. Wise et al., ANYAS 722 (New York: New York Academy of Sciences, 1994), 1–38.

11. N. Golb, *Who Wrote the Dead Sea Scrolls? The Search for the Secret of Qumran* (New York: Scribner, 1995).

12. Y. Hirschfeld, "Qumran in the Second Temple Period," in Galor et al., *Qumran*, 223–40; and Y. Hirschfeld, *Qumran in Context: Reassessing the Archaeological Evidence* (Peabody, MA: Hendrickson, 2004). One difficulty with the scenario of Golb and Hirschfeld is that the area of Jerusalem is riddled with natural caves, as observed by D. Mizzi, "Qumran at Seventy: Reflections on Seventy Years of Scholarship on the Archaeology of Qumran and the Dead Sea Scrolls," *Strata: Bulletin of the Anglo-Israel Archaeological Society* 35 (2017): 25. Why bring the contents of Jerusalem libraries to the Qumran caves for hiding when perfectly good caves were available nearby?

13. Y. Magen and Y. Peleg, "Back to Qumran: Ten Years of Excavation and Research, 1993–2004," in Galor et al., *Qumran*, 55–113; and Magen and Peleg, *The Qumran Excavation 1993–2004: Preliminary Report*, Judea and Samaria Publications 6 (Jerusalem: Israel Antiquities Authority, 2007).

14. D. Stacey, "A Reassessment of the Stratigraphy of Qumran," in *Qumran Revisited: A Reassessment of the Archaeology of the Site and Its Texts*, ed. D. Stacey and G. Doudna, BARIS 2520 (London: Archeopress, 2013), 7–74, esp. 63.

THE QUMRAN EVIDENCE

acceptance indicates the difficulty of understanding the site of Qumran, and demonstrates that, if the scrolls are excluded from the interpretation, the site remains an enigma.

What can be characterized as the "anti-de Vaux" interpretations are united by the way that they each reinterpret only the archaeological data from the ruins of the buildings of Khirbet Qumran. What they do not do, or at best do only superficially, is to take into account the archaeological data from the caves, which of course includes the manuscript remains found in those caves. However, as we have seen in ch. 4, the caves and the scrolls are an integral part of the broad parameters of the archaeological site of Qumran, and must be considered in any understanding of the activities going on at the site.

Methodologically, the correct way to proceed is to present the archaeological data as neutrally as possible, and then determine if that data can support any particular hypothesis concerning the identity of the inhabitants. Archaeology alone will not solve the puzzle of the identity of the inhabitants of Qumran or its purpose, since archaeology can answer only certain questions, such as how the structures were used, what types of ceramic vessels were in use at a particular site, or (perhaps) whether the inhabitants were Jewish. As Taylor has stated regarding the Qumran-Essene hypothesis, archaeology can "establish that certain sites such as Qumran . . . were Jewish, with additional features very appropriate to Essene occupation."[15] Therefore, in this chapter I first present the archaeological data, and then ask if that data can lend support to my thesis that Qumran was a scribal center with a library complex, staffed by Essene scribes.[16]

---

15. Taylor, *Essenes*, 258.

16. I will not be considering the small agricultural satellite of 'Ain Feshkha, which lies 3 km. to the south of Qumran at a naturally occurring spring. 'Ain Feshkha was inhabited at the same time and most likely by the same group that inhabited Qumran, and served mainly for agricultural activities such as date harvesting and animal husbandry. The most interesting installation at 'Ain Feshkha for our purposes is a small industrial area to the north of the main building, which contains a system of basins and water channels. De Vaux, *Archaeology*, 79, suggested that this was a tannery, but acknowledged problems with this interpretation, especially the absence of traces of tannin. F. E. Zeuner, "Notes on Qumran," *PEQ* 92 (1960): 36, suggested instead that these were pools for raising fish. Other suggestions have included flax retting or date wine pressing, but no evidence exists for either explanation. Stacey, "Reassessment of the Stratigraphic Evidence," 53-55, has argued that one of the seasonal activities that took place at Qumran was leather tanning, but the only evidence he provides is the water installations, from which, to my knowledge, no evidence of tanning has been recovered.

170

A History of the Excavations

In 1949 de Vaux and G. Lankester Harding of the Jordanian Department of Antiquities surveyed the site and dug up two (empty) tombs in its adjoining cemetery (Tombs 1 and 2) in conjunction with their excavation of Cave 1Q, but they initially discounted any relationship between the cave and the site.[17] However, they returned to the site in 1951 and did some preliminary clearing in what became known as the "main building."[18] In Locus (L) 2 they discovered a cylindrical jar identical to those from Cave 1Q sunk into the floor.[19] This, along with other pottery and coin evidence, was sufficient to bring de Vaux back for another four seasons of excavations (1952–1956). De Vaux published his conclusions in preliminary form in a series of articles in *Revue biblique*, as well as in the Schweich Lectures delivered in 1959 and published posthumously in English in 1973.[20]

Since de Vaux's excavations, other smaller-scale explorations have occurred. In 1966 Solomon Steckoll excavated ten graves in the cemetery.[21] Following a hiatus after the 1967 Six-Day War, when control of the site shifted from Jordan to Israel, new investigations were undertaken in the 1990s: Yitzhak Magen and Yuval Peleg, 1993–2004; Magen Broshi and Hanan Eshel in 1993–1994 on the north end of the marl terrace on which the buildings sit; the late James F. Strange of the University of South Florida in 1996; and in 2002 Eshel, Broshi, Richard Freund, and Brian Schulz

---

17. De Vaux, *Archaeology*, vii: "it [the Khirbet Qumran ruins] had not seemed to have any evident connection with the discoveries in the cave."

18. De Vaux: "Le bâtiment principal" ("Fouilles au Khirbet Qumrân: Rapport préliminaire," *RB* 60 [1953]: 89).

19. Harding: "Sunk into the floor of one of the rooms was a jar identical with most of those found in the Scrolls cave: the jar was covered by a small flagstone but was empty" ("Khirbet Qumran and Wady Murabbaʿat," 105).

20. See the bibliographic references in ch. 4. EBAF is now publishing, under the direction of Humbert, a series of volumes with the final reports of de Vaux's excavations. De Vaux's field notes and excavation photographs are available in J.-B. Humbert and A. Chambon, eds., *Fouilles de Khirbet Qumrân et de Aïn Feshkha,* vol. 1: *Album de photographies; Répertoire du fonds photographique; Synthèse des notes de chantier du Père Roland de Vaux OP*, NTOA.SA 1 (Fribourg: Éditions Universitaires; Göttingen: Vandenhoeck & Ruprecht, 1994). For the English translation, see Humbert and Chambon, eds., *The Excavations of Khirbet Qumran and Ain Feshkha*, vol. 1B: *Synthesis of Roland de Vaux's Field Notes, English Edition*, trans. S. Pfann, NTOA.SA 1B (Fribourg: Éditions Universitaires; Göttingen: Vandenhoeck & Ruprecht, 2003).

21. S. Steckoll, "Preliminary Excavation Report in the Qumran Cemetery," *RevQ* 6 (1968): 323–36.

THE QUMRAN EVIDENCE

in the cemetery. In 2015 a salvage excavation was undertaken in the north cemetery by the Israeli Antiquities Authority.[22] In what follows I take into account the results of all of these explorations.

The Site of Qumran: Its Archaeological Phases and Its Buildings

The Archaeological Phases of Khirbet Qumran

Before beginning a survey of the architectural remains of the khirbeh, a word must be said on the problem of the archaeological phases of the site. De Vaux discerned three main phases at Qumran:[23] an Iron II phase from the eighth-seventh centuries BCE; a reoccupation, after a centuries-long break, in the second century BCE that lasted until 68 CE, and a post-destruction phase that trickled out in the second century CE. After that, Qumran remained uninhabited until it was excavated in the twentieth century.

De Vaux subdivided the Second Temple period settlement into two occupation phases: Period I, 130–31 BCE; and Period II, 4 BCE–68 CE. He further divided Period I into two subphases: Ia, 130–100 BCE; and Ib,

---

22. Magen and Peleg, "Back to Qumran"; Magen and Peleg, *Qumran Excavation*; Broshi and Eshel, "Three Seasons of Excavations at Qumran," *JRA* 17 (2004): 321–32; J. Strange, "The 1996 Excavations at Qumran and the Context of the New Hebrew Ostracon," in *Qumran, the Site of the Dead Sea Scrolls*, 41–54; H. Eshel et al., "New Data on the Cemetery East of Khirbet Qumran," *DSD* 9 (2002): 135–54. See also H. Eshel, "Excavations in the Judean Desert and at Qumran under Israeli Jurisdiction," in *The Dead Sea Scrolls in Scholarly Perspective: A History of Research*, ed. D. Dimant, STDJ 99 (Leiden: Brill, 2012), 381–400, esp. 387–97. The 2015 excavation was reported by Y. Nagar et al., "The People of Qumran—New Discoveries and Paleo-demographic Interpretations" (paper presented at the Annual Meeting of the American Schools of Oriental Research, Boston, 16 November 2017).

23. De Vaux did not follow what has now become customary stratigraphic rules in his field notes. He assigned each architectural element (e.g., a room, a cistern, a courtyard) a separate locus number, but he did not necessarily renumber a locus when a new floor was revealed. He did change the locus number when the architectural configuration of that element changed (e.g., when a wall or partition was added). The result is a certain confusion as to which element belonged to which phase, or whether a small find was associated with one phase or another. Humbert comments, "De Vaux failed to establish a stratigraphy, because he never encountered a clear stratification" (J.-B. Humbert, "Reconsideration of the Archaeological Interpretation," in *Khirbet Qumrân et 'Aïn Feshkha*, vol. 2: *Études d'anthropologie, de physique et de chimie*, ed. J.-B. Humbert and J. Gunneweg, NTOA.SA 3 [Göttingen: Vandenhoeck & Ruprecht, 2003], 422). See also Hirschfeld, *Qumran in Context*, 49–50.

172

The Archaeology of Qumran

100–31 BCE. He argued that the end of Period I was caused by an earthquake, which left discernible damage to some of the buildings and the water system.[24] This damage, according to de Vaux, caused the inhabitants to abandon the site for a relatively lengthy period of time. The same group of inhabitants returned to Qumran in 4 BCE, reopened the buildings, and remained until the site was destroyed by the Roman *Legio X Fretensis* (Tenth Roman Legion) in 68 CE. The site was then occupied by a garrison of Roman soldiers for several years, followed by refugees during the Bar Kokhba revolt (132–135 CE).[25] De Vaux relied mainly on the coin evidence to establish his phases of occupation.

There are several difficulties with de Vaux's reconstruction of the occupational phases of the site. First, architectural evidence for Period Ia is almost nonexistent; what de Vaux saw as a distinct subphase seems to be instead the earliest structures built as the site took on its definitive form. There is also very little coin evidence for Period Ia.[26] Second, a twenty-seven-year period of abandonment, followed by a reoccupation by the very same group, is inexplicable. Where did they go, and why did they return?[27] Third, the return date of 4 BCE is arbitrary; de Vaux associated the return with the troubles surrounding the death of Herod the Great,[28] but there is no clear archaeological evidence supporting that hypothesis.

Concerning the end of the settlement, however, it is quite clear that it suffered a massive, violent destruction toward the end of the first century CE. De Vaux states:

> The end of Period II is marked by a violent destruction . . . all the rooms of the south-west and north-west were filled with debris from the collapse of the ceilings and superstructures to a height which varies between 1.10 m. and 1.50 m. In the centre and south-east, where the courtyard is situated and certain lighter structures had been put up, the damage was less considerable, but the destruction extended throughout

---

24. De Vaux dates the earthquake so precisely by relying on the testimony of Josephus, who reports a major earthquake in the area in 31 BCE (*Ant.* 15.121–147; *J.W.* 1.370–380).

25. De Vaux, *Archaeology*, 3–48.

26. J. Magness, *The Archaeology of Qumran and the Dead Sea Scrolls* (Grand Rapids: Eerdmans, 2002), 63–67, was the first to call into question de Vaux's dates and to propose a revised chronology for the site.

27. Earlier scholars, accepting de Vaux's period of abandonment, proposed various theories to account for it: e.g., a return to Jerusalem or an exile to Damascus.

28. De Vaux, *Archaeology*, 33–36.

173

THE QUMRAN EVIDENCE

the entire building. Iron arrow-heads have been recovered, and almost everywhere a layer of a powdery black substance gives evidence of the burning of the roofs. The buildings, therefore, were reduced to ruins by a military action.[29]

The evidence for the end of the settlement is conclusive. Qumran was destroyed by a Roman army action during the First Jewish Revolt against Rome (66–73 CE). Since the latest coins from the site belong to the second or third years of the revolt (67–68 CE), and the city of Jericho was destroyed by the *Legio X Fretensis* in 68,[30] it is reasonable to assume that Qumran met the same fate at approximately the same time.[31] The questions regarding the beginning of the site and the existence of subphases, however, still remain.

In her 2002 book Magness proposed the following revision of de Vaux's chronology: she did away completely with Period Ia, and lowered the date of occupation to the first half of the first century BCE (i.e., 100–50 BCE). She retained Period II but suggests a much shorter period of abandonment, not caused by an earthquake in 31 BCE but by a fire in 9/8 BCE. According to Magness, Period II began about 4 BCE and ended in 68 CE.[32] This revision was generally accepted, but the problem of the lack of distinction between Periods I and II, and the lack of an explanation for the abandonment and reoccupation, remained.

More recently, Magness and Dennis Mizzi have proposed doing away with Periods I and II entirely.[33] The basis for this more radical reconsider-

---

29. De Vaux, *Archaeology*, 36. The iron arrowheads have three barbed wingtips and a long tang, the characteristic type used by the Romans in the first century CE. See Magness, *Archaeology of Qumran*, 61.

30. Josephus, *J.W.* 4.486–490.

31. It is noteworthy that no skeletal remains or other signs of resistance were discovered in the buildings. Whether the inhabitants put up any show of resistance or simply fled in advance of the Roman legion is not ascertainable.

32. Magness, *Archaeology of Qumran*, 68.

33. D. Mizzi and J. Magness, "Was Qumran Abandoned at the End of the First Century BCE?," *JBL* 135 (2016): 301–20: "we propose collapsing Periods I and II into one long phase of occupation with various architectural subphases" (301). This idea was first proposed by Humbert in 2003: "It would be better to accept the idea of a continuous occupation" ("Chronology during the First Century B.C.: De Vaux and His Method: A Debate," in Humbert and Gunneweg, *Khirbet Qumrân et 'Aïn Feshkha*, 2:437). Humbert, however, dates the settlement to 40/39 BCE. Mizzi also hints at the idea of a continuous occupation in "Qumran Period I Reconsidered: An Evaluation of Several Competing Theories," *DSD* 22 (2014): 1–42, esp. 21, 30, but does not make an outright statement.

174

ation is, first, a revision of the date of the deposit of the silver coin hoard found buried in L120 beneath the Period II floor, but above the Period I floor. Magness, on the basis of the reported dates of the coins, suggested that the hoard was abandoned in 9/8 BCE, and the Period II floor was eventually built over it.[34] However, it now appears that coins from the first century CE were part of the hoard, and the deposition of the hoard is undatable, except that it must have occurred before the destruction of the site in 68. Therefore, it cannot be used as proof for an abandonment of the site between Periods I and II.[35]

Second, the floor levels de Vaux marked in various loci do not correspond to his three main chronological periods. For example, the lowest floor in L1 and L2 in the main building was still in use at the beginning of Period II, and a new floor was laid only in the mid-first century CE. Thus it is more likely that the buildings were changed in a more organic and continuous fashion than in two distinct phases.[36]

Third, there is no conflagration or destruction layer in the late first century BCE in the main building. Only a limited number of loci outside the main building were affected by a fire, which could have had any number of causes. Again, there is no evidence for a full-scale abandonment of the site. Magness and Mizzi therefore conclude that Periods I and II are artificial constructs that distinguish between the Hasmonean and Herodian chronological periods and that Qumran had one long, continuous occupation from the early first century BCE (c. 100–75 BCE) to 68 CE.[37] Mizzi also has determined that, regarding the material goods found at the site (i.e., pottery, glass, stone vessels, small finds, metal objects, and coins), the same repertoire of objects continues without great change, indicating again a long period of habitation by the same group.[38]

The revision proposed by Mizzi and Magness seems to make the best sense of the evidence, and to solve the problems of the confusion of the phases and the inexplicable abandonment of the site in the first century BCE. This is the chronological scheme I follow below, where I outline the growth of the settlement and the final configuration of the site. I use de Vaux's terminology of Periods I (Hasmonean period), II (Herodian/

34. Magness, *Archaeology of Qumran*, 67–68.
35. Mizzi and Magness, "Was Qumran Abandoned," 304–9.
36. Mizzi and Magness, "Was Qumran Abandoned," 314–17.
37. Mizzi and Magness, "Was Qumran Abandoned," 319–20.
38. D. Mizzi, "The Archaeology of Khirbet Qumran: A Comparative Approach" (DPhil. thesis, University of Oxford, 2009), as quoted by Taylor, *Essenes,* 260.

THE QUMRAN EVIDENCE

Roman period), and III (post–68 phase) for the sake of clarity when necessary.

The Architecture of Qumran

The buildings of Khirbet Qumran sit on a marl plateau to the west of the Dead Sea; the (usually dry) Wadi Qumran runs along its south side. According to the survey of Taylor and Gibson,[39] the site was connected by "rough paths" to Jericho to the north, 'Ein-Gedi to the south, and the Buqeia to the west.[40] These paths were first constructed in the Iron II period and reused in the late Second Temple period. These rough paths indicate that Qumran was moderately connected locally to 'Ein-Gedi and Jericho, but compared to those towns was somewhat isolated. This relative isolation is an important point in determining the purpose and function of the settlement.

The Iron II Site

Very little was recovered of the Iron Age remains, which date from the late eighth to the sixth century BCE. De Vaux identified some foundations of walls, from which he reconstructed a large building, consisting of a courtyard with rooms along at least its eastern wall. The large round cistern (L110) also comes from this period,[41] as do the foundations of the long wall that ran along the eastern side of the esplanade to the Wadi Qumran.[42] In addition, sherds from the Iron Age were recovered, as well as two inscriptions, including a *lmlk* stamp seal.[43] Magen and Peleg uncovered further

39. J. Taylor and S. Gibson, "Qumran Connected: The Qumran Pass and Paths of the North-Western Dead Sea," in *Qumran und die Archäologie: Texte und Kontexte*, ed. J. Frey et al., WUNT 278 (Tübingen: Mohr Siebeck, 2011), 163–210.

40. A "rough path" is a small, private thoroughfare, wide enough to allow one man leading a loaded pack mule to pass. See Taylor and Gibson, "Qumran Connected," 165.

41. Magen and Peleg, "Back to Qumran," 79, reject this claim, dating the cistern to the Hasmonean period. However, K. Galor, "Plastered Pools: A New Perspective," in Humbert and Gunneweg, *Khirbet Qumrân et 'Aïn Feshkha*, 2:308, points out that all the other water installations from the Second Temple period occupation are of a completely different type, making more plausible the claim that the circular pool in L110 is a reuse from the Iron Age.

42. De Vaux, *Archaeology*, 1–3.

43. The Paleo-Hebrew inscriptions discovered by de Vaux are KhQ 1235 (a *lmlk* stamp

176

The Archaeology of Qumran

Iron Age remains: a plastered floor in L77, three silos in the center of the southern plateau, and a north-south wall inside L 51 and 53 that continued east of L48.[44] They also found more Iron Age pottery and evidence of a conflagration that destroyed the site in the early sixth century BCE (during the Babylonian conquest).

The Second Temple Period Site

This is the period of the site that coincides with the archaeological finds from the Qumran caves, and thus is most important for our discussion.[45] In the first century BCE a traveler would have approached Qumran from the northwest, the direction of Jericho. What the traveler would have seen upon approach were two main groups of buildings, the eastern sector and the western sector (for the plan of Qumran with loci numbers see figs. 8 and 9). The main entrance to the complex was through a gate in an enclosure wall (south of L141). Immediately to the left, on the northwest corner of the eastern sector, stood a two-story watchtower. The ground floor rooms of this tower, which had no windows or ground floor entrances, were used for storage. The second floor was accessed by a wooden gangway. The watchtower anchored the main building of the eastern sector, a square building consisting of one and two floors with rooms surrounding an open-air courtyard. These rooms had a variety of purposes; L1–2 and 4 may have been a library complex, which we investigate further below; L30 was labeled by de Vaux as a "scriptorium"[46] (also discussed below); L38–41 contained a kitchen, identified by the presence of ovens and hearths; and L51 contained a toilet, which went out of use later in the site's history.

Attached to this main building to the south and east were additions, again with a variety of functions. L77, a long rectangular room built to the south of the main building, was identified by de Vaux as a "refectory";[47]

---

seal) and KhQ 1236. See Lemaire, "Inscriptions du khirbeh, des grottes et de ʿAïn Feshkha," in Humbert and Gunneweg, *Khirbet Qumrân et ʿAïn Feshkha*, 2:353. A second *lmlk* stamp seal was discovered by Magen and Peleg on the southeast side of the site ("Back to Qumran," 76).

44. Magen and Peleg, "Back to Qumran," 76.

45. In what follows I have freely utilized the descriptions found in de Vaux, *Archaeology*, 1–48; Magness, *Archaeology of Qumran*, 47–72; and C. M. Murphy, *Wealth in the Dead Sea Scrolls and in the Qumran Community*, STDJ 40 (Leiden: Brill, 2002), 296–305.

46. De Vaux, *Archaeology*, 30.

47. De Vaux, *Archaeology*, 11. Hirschfeld, *Qumran in Context*, 104, agrees that it was an

THE QUMRAN EVIDENCE

next to it was a small room (L86–89) with dining utensils (cups, plates, bowls) stacked in rows. L77 could have been used as a communal dining facility; the dining utensils in its annex would argue in favor of this interpretation. But the room may have had other functions as well.[48]

A triangular enclosure beginning at the corner of L51 to the east of the main building housed a water installation that de Vaux identified as a laundry (L52),[49] as well as a potter's workshop with a kiln (L64 and 84). A date-press (L75) was also built in this area.[50] A long wall, which began at the corner of L51, continued south to Wadi Qumran and enclosed the esplanade to the south of the buildings, where Caves 7Q, 8Q, and 9Q are located.

The western sector, built around the large round cistern (L110), has a more industrial or working flavor than the main building. The rooms or structures included elements identified as a stable (L97), a mill (L100), four ovens found in L101, 105, and 109, storerooms equipped with silos (L115–116), and various workshops (L125–127).

The most striking feature of Qumran is its hydraulic or water system, consisting of aqueducts, cisterns, and stepped pools (the purpose of which is discussed below). Qumran has no naturally occurring fresh water spring (the closest is at 'Ain Feshkha), so in order for the site to be inhabited, water had to be captured from the flash floods occurring in the limestone

---

eating facility, but for the use of laborers at the villa. Magen and Peleg, *Qumran Excavations*, 64, argue that L77 was used for the display of pottery for sale.

48. Humbert demonstrates, on the basis of the excavation photographs, that the elements that de Vaux identified as "pillars" supporting the roof of L77 could not have had that function. He argues that these elements were in fact tables ("les présentoirs") for offerings presented for the Shavuot celebration (*Khirbet Qumrân et Aïn Feshkha,* 3A:71–75). Both the interpretation of Magen and Peleg—that the "tables" were used to display pottery—and Humbert's interpretation are unsupported by the archaeological evidence; rather, they depend on their own idiosyncratic understandings of the site. The function of the square stone installations in L77 is at present unresolved.

49. Magen and Peleg, "Back to Qumran," 65, dispute this identification, claiming that it is a "sophisticated industrial installation," possibly for the production of perfume.

50. The function of this installation has been disputed. De Vaux, *Archaeology and the Dead Sea Scrolls,* 16, thought it was used to prepare clay for the potter's workshop. Humbert, *Khirbet Qumrân et Aïn Feshkha,* 3A:267–69, identifies it as a winepress. S. Pfann also identified it as a winepress ("The Winepress [and Miqveh] at Khirbet Qumran [loc. 75 and 69]," *RB* 101 [1994]: 212–14). Magen and Peleg ("Back to Qumran," 59; and *Qumran Excavations,* 1) argue that it is a date-press, given the large quantity of date pits and burnt dates found in the area. The presence of the date pits argues for L75 being a date-press.

The Archaeology of Qumran

cliffs in the winter, and stored to last through the hot, dry summer.[51] The water system begins at the waterfall at the head of Wadi Qumran; the pool at the foot of the waterfall was dammed and the water channeled into an aqueduct that ran along the northern bank of the wadi to the buildings. The aqueduct was cut into the limestone or marl, coated with thick layers of plaster, and roofed with stone slabs. It entered the settlement at its northwest corner, where it wound through the western and eastern sectors and supplied all the cisterns and stepped pools. The cisterns and stepped pools were plastered and either roofed over or covered with branches to prevent evaporation. According to Catherine Murphy, the water system could have contained up to 1,300 cubic meters of water when full.[52] However, as Taylor observes, the system was probably very rarely full; by the time the water traveled to the southeast corner of the site that cistern (L71) may have been no more than half-full most of the time.[53] Magen and Peleg suggest, on the basis of gutters that they discovered on the eastern wall of L91, that the aqueduct system was supplemented by collecting rainwater from the roofs.[54] In other words, the system was built to utilize every drop of this precious resource.

When the architecture of the buildings is examined, it is striking how uniformly plain and simple it is. The outer walls are made of rough uncut fieldstones with mud mortar; dressed (cut) stones were used only at the corners of buildings and the areas around the windows and doors.[55] The interior partition walls were made of mud brick (which may have been harvested from the marl terrace caves), and some of the interior walls were

51. Although reliance on flash floods for a sufficient water supply seems somewhat precarious, R. Reich, "Some Notes on the Miqva'ot and Cisterns at Qumran," in *Viewing Ancient Jewish Art and Archaeology: VeHinnei Rachel—Essays in Honor of Rachel Hachlili*, ed. A. Killebrew and G. Faßbeck, JSJSup 72 (Leiden: Brill, 2015), 418, notes that one flash flood in the Wadi Qumran would be sufficient to fill all the water installations at Qumran. The water system reached its definitive form in de Vaux's Period Ib. Galor, "Plastered Pools," 292, states that it is almost impossible to reconstruct the different stages preceding the water system's final form.

52. Murphy, *Wealth*, 299. She contrasts this with Masada, whose cisterns could hold 40,000 cubic meters of water.

53. Taylor, *Essenes*, 253.

54. Magen and Peleg, *Qumran Excavations*, 19, 40.

55. Note Harding's remark concerning the initial excavation in 1951: "The quality of the work is very poor, and in no way resembles that of a Roman fort which we first took it to be. Inner walls are of equally poor workmanship, being mostly rubble and mud" ("Khirbet Qumran and Wady Murabba'at," 104).

179

coated with mud plaster. There are no remains of frescoes, and very few other decorative elements. The floors were made of packed earth; some were plastered or cobbled (for example, L1 and 2 had cobblestone floors). No mosaic floors have been found. There is some evidence for windows and built-in wall niches or cupboards (L1–2, 61). The remains of staircases indicate a second story on parts of the main building and some other rooms (e.g., L77). The roofs, which were flat, were beamed with palm trunks and covered with a thatch made of dried palm leaves and mud. All in all, the buildings were undecorated and utilitarian, which argues against its having been any type of villa for a wealthy inhabitant.[56]

The description above gives the main parameters of the site in the Second Temple period. The buildings, however, were not static; a process of change and rebuilding went on throughout the life of the site. The main building was probably the first structure to be built, along with the beginnings of the water system, with the other structures added according to the needs of the group who lived there. For example, the toilet in L51 seems to be an original part of the main building; however, in de Vaux's Period II it went out of use and became part of an open-air courtyard.[57] Other examples of change or reconstruction include a glacis being added to the base of the watchtower in the late first century BCE. L86, the pantry, began as one large room, but was damaged (possibly by a minor earthquake); the stacked dining utensils, which had been shattered, were walled off by a partition, the space divided into three loci (L86, 87, 89; L89 was where the pottery was found), and the exterior walls were buttressed by stone retaining walls to prevent further collapse.[58] The large stepped pool (L58) located between the main building and L77 was divided into two pools (L56 and 58). Various reasons are proposed for these changes, but regardless of the reasons they are part of the natural growth and evolution of the site.

---

56. See also Murphy, *Wealth*, 304, who notes the lack of mosaics, frescoes, hot and cold baths, pools, or gardens. She states, "in general the complex lacks evidence of architectural craftsmanship and luxurious appointments."

57. Magness, *Archaeology of Qumran*, 51.

58. In a recent article, B. Wagemakers and J. Taylor discuss the different phases in L86 on the basis of newly discovered photographs. Although the details of their findings are too extensive to be covered here, their article illustrates the importance of considering the phases of each locus separately. They state, "The chronology of L86 as a whole then would indicate not necessarily a template for the periods of the whole site but a partially localized chronology relevant to the clearly attested instability of this room, so that within Periods Ib and II . . . there are idiosyncratic subdivisions" ("New Photographs of the Qumran Excavations from 1954 and Interpretations of L. 77 and L. 86," *PEQ* 143 [2011]: 154).

180

The Archaeology of Qumran

As stated above, the end of the Second Temple period settlement was brought about by a violent destruction by fire. Damage is evident throughout the entire site; rooms were filled with the debris of collapsed roofs (made from palm beams and thatch) and walls. All organic material at the site was reduced to ash or carbonized. Iron arrowheads of the characteristic Roman type of the first century CE were found in the destruction layer, indicating that a Roman army unit was responsible for the end of the settlement. Most of these arrowheads were found in loci in the main building (L4, L19, L30, L33, and L41), indicating that the attack came from the northwest, in the direction of Jericho, where the *Legio X Fretensis* was operating in 68 CE.[59] Most likely flaming arrowheads were shot at the rooftops and set fire to the site. Thus the Second Temple period settlement came to an end.

Population Estimates for the Second Temple Period Phase

Various estimates have been given for the population of Qumran during its Second Temple period occupation, from a high of approximately 150 (Broshi)[60] to a low of 10–15 (Humbert).[61] Joseph Patrich calculated that 50–70 people lived there, while Bryant Wood, on the basis of the water capacity of the site, suggested that 312 people could have lived there at once.[62] Hirschfeld, on the basis of a density formulation of 15 people per dunam, arrives at a figure of 72 permanent residents.[63] Magen and Peleg argue that, given the small number of baking ovens and cooking pots, 20–30 people

---

59. J. Taylor, "Khirbet Qumran in Period III," in Galor et al., *Qumran*, 133n4. Other Roman-type weapons were found in L45, 103, and 109. See also M. Popović, "Roman Book Destruction in Qumran Cave 4 and the Roman Destruction of Khirbet Qumran Revisited," in Frey et al., *Qumran und die Archäologie*, 252–55.

60. M. Broshi, "Qumran: Archaeology," *EDSS* 2:735, estimates a population of 120–150 on the basis of the seating capacity of L77, which he understands as a dining hall and/or worship center.

61. Humbert, "L'espace sacré à Qumrân: Propositions pour l'archéologie," *RB* 101 (1994): 175.

62. J. Patrich, "Khirbet Qumran in Light of New Archaeological Exploration," in *Methods of Investigation of the Dead Sea Scrolls: Present Realities and Future Prospects*, ed. M. Wise et al., ANYAS 722 (New York: New York Academy of Sciences, 1994), 95–96. B. Wood, "To Dip or to Sprinkle? The Qumran Cisterns in Perspective," *BASOR* 256 (1984): 58.

63. Hirschfeld, *Qumran in Context*, 90.

THE QUMRAN EVIDENCE

at most could have resided at Qumran.[64] A safe estimate would be that the site accommodated 25–75 inhabitants at any given time.

The Postdestruction Phase

Qumran's postdestruction phase began as a small Roman military outpost. The main building of the eastern sector was reused as the headquarters; the tower was fortified, the defenses strengthened, and a ditch was dug along the western wall. The water system was minimally cleared for limited use. The western sector was allowed to lie in ruins.[65] Material evidence for Roman presence is found in the large number of bronze and other metal items, especially twelve buckles associated with Roman armor, and some weaponry.[66] Other finds from the postdestruction phase indicate the presence of women at the site during this period. These include a green faience bead, the fragment of a bracelet, a needle, an alabaster spindle whorl, and a glass perfume phial.[67]

Following the Roman occupation, which lasted into the early part of the second century CE,[68] Qumran was briefly used as a refuge during the Bar Kokhba revolt (132–135 CE). After that the site was never inhabited again.

Was There a Library at Qumran in the Second Temple Period?

The question of greatest concern for the thesis of this book is, of course, whether a library room or rooms can be identified in the buildings of the khirbeh. Before tackling this question it would be well to recall what we know of physical libraries in the ancient Mediterranean world. It was not until the Roman period that separate structures meant to house book collections were constructed (e.g., the library of Celsus at Ephesus). These

64. Magen and Peleg, *Qumran Excavations*, 53.

65. De Vaux, *Archaeology*, 42–43.

66. Taylor, "Khirbet Qumran in Period III," 140. She also notes the presence of iron sandal nails on paths leading out of Qumran, which she associates with Roman military sandals. Here she disagrees with M. Broshi and H. Eshel, "Residential Caves at Qumran," *DSD* 6 (1999): 337, who associated the sandal nails with the earlier inhabitants.

67. Taylor, "Khirbet Qumran in Period III," 141.

68. Taylor, *Essenes*, 265.

The Archaeology of Qumran

libraries had clearly defined architectural features, such as niches built into the walls to house book cupboards (*amaria*) and a podium around the perimeter of the room. Prior to that period, however, libraries were simply housed in rooms in a building complex, whether a temple, palace or government building, or a private home. They had no features to identify them as libraries or archives, except for the tablets or book rolls found in them. In the case of book rolls, these were commonly laid on shelves (as at Herculaneum) or stored in baskets, boxes, or jars. It is important to remember that even in the case of the famous libraries at Alexandria and Pergamum, which we know contained well-organized libraries of book rolls, the actual library rooms have not been identified with any certainty.

Further, we have no comparable examples from ancient Judea. Only one room complex, in a royal palace at Masada, has been proposed as a library, and that identification is disputed (see ch. 3). Therefore, when we search in the building complex at Qumran for a library, the best we can do is to suggest rooms that *may* have housed the library that was eventually deposited in the caves. Absolute certainty is not possible.

The best place to begin the search would be the main building. It is the best-constructed building and was the first to be built. It is fortified by the tower in the northwest corner. It stands to reason that a precious library belonging to the inhabitants would be housed here. Are there any candidates?

We can rule out those rooms that we know served other functions, such as the tower, the kitchens, and the room with the toilet. The best candidate would seem to be the room complex in the southwest corner of the main building (L1, 2, 4, and 13; see figs. 10 and 11). This complex was identified early on as a possible library.[69]

L1 began as one large room; it was later divided into two smaller rooms (L1 and 2). In his field notes[70] de Vaux describes L1 as having a paved floor

---

69. See K. Greenleaf Pedley, *The Library at Qumran: A Librarian Looks at the Dead Sea Scrolls* (Berkeley: Peacock, 1964). Cross, *Ancient Library of Qumran*, 64, states "It is not unlikely, moreover, that the library of the community found in Cave IV nearby was normally housed in this quadrant of the main building." See also H. Stegemann, *The Library of Qumran: On the Essenes, Qumran, John the Baptist, and Jesus* (Grand Rapids: Eerdmans, 1998), 39–41. One does not have to agree with all of Stegemann's reconstruction to concur that the rooms in question may have housed the library. De Vaux, *Archaeology*, 29–32, thought that L4 was perhaps an assembly room, although he entertained the possibility that scrolls could have been piled into the three niches on the south wall.

70. The following information, except where noted, is taken from de Vaux's preliminary report in "Fouilles au Khirbet Qumran," 83–106; and Humbert and Chambon, eds., *Fouilles de Khirbet Qumrân,* vol. 1. The photographs referred to are found in this volume.

183

THE QUMRAN EVIDENCE

with well-plastered walls. After its division, there was a threshold between L1 and L2. L2 contained three "cupboards" or wall niches along its north wall. De Vaux acknowledges that these cupboards can be compared to cupboards for books in ancient private libraries.[71] In addition, L2 had a "high bench" that may have been a support for shelving or a podium. L2 also had an empty cylindrical jar covered with a tile fragment embedded in the floor.

A door led from L1 into L4; this door was blocked up and a new door was constructed between L2 and L4 when L1 was divided in half.[72] L4 also had a plastered floor. It contained two wall niches on its south wall, and one on its north. A low step, 10 centimeters high, ran around most of its four walls. De Vaux considered this a bench for sitting, but photographs 133 and 135 show that it is too low for seating. However, it could have been used as a podium for jars used for scroll storage.[73] An ovoid jar was embedded in the floor in the middle of the room. L4 contained a small water installation, a plastered basin that was fed by a small channel that went through the north wall. The function of this water installation is not clear; it may have been used for hand washing, although Katharine Greenleaf Pedley suggests that the water was necessary for the processes of mixing inks and pastes.[74] L4 had a wooden door (indicated by the presence of scattered nails and a lock on its threshold) that shut off L1, 2, and 4 from L13.

L13 was a courtyard-like structure leading off of corridor L12. De Vaux believed L13 was not roofed. It contained stairs that led to an upper story or terrace above L4. Against its common wall with L12 it had a low stone bench. Three cylindrical/ovoid jars were found embedded in the floor of a wall niche.

Could L1–2, 4, and 13 have served as a library complex? The answer is a cautious yes. The rooms contain wall niches, which could have contained shelves or cupboards for scroll storage. Jars of the type used to store scrolls in Caves 1Q and 11Q were embedded in the floors. Very little pottery, aside from these jars, was discovered, indicating the rooms were not used for everyday living.[75] A wooden door with a lock closed off L1, 2, and 4 from the rest of the main building, indicating a need or desire to protect the

---

71. De Vaux, *Archaeology*, 32–33n2.

72. De Vaux, *Archaeology*, 21.

73. In fact, according to de Vaux's notes, some pottery was found lying on the bench. Hirschfeld, *Qumran in Context*, 100, argues from this that L4 was a storeroom for storage jars.

74. Pedley, *Library at Qumran*, 18.

75. The pottery includes the usual repertoire of plates, cups, and bowls, but not in sufficient quantities to indicate pantry-type storage. See P. Patton, "Pottery and Purpose: Using GIS to Evaluate the 'Scroll' Jars at Qumran," MA Thesis, University of Nebraska–Lincoln.

The Archaeology of Qumran

contents. All of these features allow us to tentatively identify these rooms as the library complex at Qumran.

The function of L30, located immediately to the east of this room complex, also enters into the discussion. This is the locus that de Vaux famously identified as the "scriptorium." He made this identification on the basis of the "plastered elements" that had crashed from the second floor of L30, which he identified as benches and tables used for writing, and the recovery of two inkwells in the locus (see figs. 13 and 14). Is de Vaux correct in his identification of the function of L30?

Constructed to the east of L1, 2, 4, and 13, L30 abuts the east wall of L1–2 and 4. It is a long room, the second largest roofed space in the buildings, and was originally two stories in height. It had a door with a lock leading in from the courtyard L13, but at no time was it directly connected to the rooms in L1–2 and 4. According to Humbert, L30 was added to the original footprint of the main building (which included L1 and 4) and was carefully constructed.[76]

The main feature of L30 of interest to the question of the presence of a library complex at Qumran is the discovery in its debris of what de Vaux described as:

> fragments of structures made of mud-brick covered with carefully smoothed plaster. These . . . fragments were collected and taken to Jerusalem where they were painstakingly re-assembled . . . [into a] table . . . a little more than 5 m. in length, 40 cm. in breadth, and only 50 cm. in height. There were also . . . fragments from two smaller tables. These tables had certainly fallen from the upper floor where the long table had been set up parallel to the eastern wall; they had been used there in association with a low bench fixed to this wall.[77]

76. J.-B. Humbert, "Un bain à la grecque," in Humbert and Gunneweg, *Khirbet Qumrân et Aïn Feshkha*, 3A:103. At the lowest level of L30 de Vaux exposed the remains of an oven, with ashes continuing underneath the wall. There was also a collection of cooking pots, plates, and bowls. Mizzi (as quoted by Magness) proposes that the oven was a cooking facility in the open-air courtyard prior to the construction of L30. Magness argues on the basis of the excavation photographs that at least the east wall of L30 was constructed before the oven was built. See J. Magness, "Was Qumran a Fort in the Hasmonean Period?," *JSJ* 64 (2013): 234–37. It makes more sense to have an oven in an open-air courtyard where ventilation would not be a problem. De Vaux does not mention the oven in later descriptions of L30.

77. De Vaux, *Archaeology*, 29. R. Reich, "A Note on the Function of Room 30 (the 'Scriptorium') at Khirbet Qumran," *JJS* 46 (1995): 158, puts the original height of the plastered tables at about 70 cm. K. Clark, "The Posture of the Ancient Scribe," *BA* 26 (1963): 64, puts the original height much lower, at 44 cm.

185

THE QUMRAN EVIDENCE

De Vaux also discovered two inkwells in the debris, one bronze and the other ceramic. Finally, de Vaux unearthed "a low platform which will have rested against the north wall of the same room.... This too is made of plaster. It has a surrounding rim and is divided into two hollowed out compartments, each with a shallow cup-shaped cavity," evidently for holding water.[78] These finds led him to identify the upper floor of L30 as a room where scrolls were copied: "Is it not reasonable to regard these tables and inkwells as the furniture of a room where writing was carried on, a *scriptorium* in the sense in which this term later came to be applied to similar rooms in monasteries of the Middle Ages?"[79]

Various objections have been raised against this identification. The most compelling objection is that ancient representations of scribes indicate that they did not use a table to copy, but sat on the ground or on a bench, with the scroll on their knees. Bruce Metzger, noting this problem, proposed that the "tables" were actually benches for the scribe, and that the "benches" were footrests.[80] Thus the scribe still wrote on his lap. This position, however, seems very awkward, especially as the tables/benches taper toward the bottom; hence Kenneth Clark proposed that the scribe sat on the bench, copied on his lap, and used the table for implements.[81] This reconstruction is possible but not provable.

Therefore, other interpretations of the plastered furniture have been proposed. A popular alternative explanation is that the tables were actually the reclining couches from a triclinium, a Roman style dining room found in upper-class villas. According to this theory, the upper story of L30 was a dining room. This idea was evidently first proposed by Henri del Med-

78. De Vaux, *Archaeology*, 31. De Vaux interpreted this feature as a handwashing facility for use when copying or handling sacred scrolls, which the inhabitants considered defiling. This appears to be a case of overinterpretation on de Vaux's part; we do not know whether or not the inhabitants of Qumran considered handling sacred scrolls defiling. According to rabbinic testimony, the Pharisees ruled that touching sacred scrolls defiled the hands, while the Sadducees evidently disagreed. See the passages collected by S. Z. Leiman, *The Canonization of Hebrew Scripture: The Talmudic and Midrashic Evidence*, Transactions of the Connecticut Academy of Arts and Sciences 47 (Hamden, CT: Archon, 1976), 102–20. See also the discussion in J. Magness, "Scrolls and Hand Impurity," in *The Dead Sea Scrolls: Texts and Contexts*, ed. C. Hempel, STDJ 90 (Leiden: Brill, 2010), 89–97. A more mundane explanation for this basin installation, such as holding water for mixing ink, would be preferable.

79. De Vaux, *Archaeology*, 30.

80. B. M. Metzger, "The Furniture of the Scriptorium at Qumran," *RevQ* 1 (1959): 509–15.

81. Clark, "Posture of the Ancient Scribe," 68–69.

The Archaeology of Qumran

ico, and championed in the 1990s by Pauline Donceel-Voûte.[82] However, the tables cannot be the dining couches from a triclinium; they are too high and narrow,[83] they taper down to a narrow base (as narrow as about 14 cm.), and they were evidently attached to the wall of the upper story, unlike a freestanding dining couch. Further, L30 does not conform to the profile of a triclinium, which is a large room with windows open to a view, often with elaborate interior decoration. In addition, no collection of dining ware, most especially fine dining ware, was found in L30. Therefore, the identification of L30 as a triclinium must be rejected.

Could the functions of the tables and benches be tied in some way to the production, including the copying, of scrolls? Pedley suggested that the tables in L30 were used to spread out the prepared skins, cut them in sheets, and sew them together.[84] The discovery of a bronze needle in L30, which could also have been used for repair work on scrolls, lends support to this theory. She also notes that water is necessary for the mixing of ink and the preparation of paste, thus explaining the water installation.[85] Stacey, who otherwise completely rejects the theory of a community settlement at Qumran, supports this interpretation, since it fits with his claim that one of the seasonal industries carried on at Qumran was leather production.[86] Other aspects of the furnishings of the upper floor of L30 may reinforce this idea; the "bench" along the east wall may actually have been a podium, which would have held blank parchment and other scroll production accoutrements.

Some of the scrolls recovered from the caves indicate repair work. 4QSam[a] had two leather patches, and the back of the scroll seems to have been reinforced with papyrus.[87] 1QIsa[a] col. 12 was repaired with sewing after the sheet was torn or split.[88] 1QS had leather strips glued on the back

82. H. E. del Medico, *The Riddle of the Scrolls*, trans. H. Garner (London: Burke, 1958). The fullest explication by Donceel-Voûte is found in her "'Coenaculum'—la salle à l'étage du *locus* 30 à Khirbet Qumran sur la Mer Morte," in *Banquets d'Orient*, ed. R. Gyselen, ResOr 4 (Leuven: Peeters, 1992), 61–84. Hirschfeld, *Qumran in Context*, 96, supports this interpretation.

83. Reich, "Note," 158.

84. Pedley, *Library at Qumran*, 15.

85. Pedley, *Library at Qumran,* 18.

86. Stacey, "Reassessment of the Stratigraphy," 53–55, 66.

87. F. M. Cross et al., "51. 4QSam[a]," in *Qumran Cave 4.XII: 1–2 Samuel*, by F. M. Cross et al., DJD 17 (Oxford: Clarendon, 2005), 3.

88. E. Ulrich and P. W. Flint, *Qumran Cave 1.II: The Isaiah Scrolls; Part 1: Plates and Transcriptions*, DJD 32 (Oxford: Clarendon, 2010), pl. XII.

THE QUMRAN EVIDENCE

of some columns for reinforcement.[89] Other manuscripts that were repaired before deposit in the caves include 4QGen[g], 4QLev[c], 4QJer[c], 4QPs[k], 4QCant[b], 4QD[a], and 4Q242.[90] While we cannot be certain where these repairs took place, it is at least reasonable to suggest that some of them took place at Qumran itself.

Therefore, the best identification for the function of L30 is as a type of "scroll workshop," where copying, correction, and repair of scrolls took place. Its proximity to the tentatively identified library complex strengthens this suggestion.

The final verdict on the architectural evidence is as follows. The suite of rooms in the southwest corner of the main building, L1–2, 4, and 30, which are all accessed by courtyard L13, fit what we know concerning library complexes in the ancient Mediterranean world (excluding the monumental buildings built by the Romans). L1–2 and 4 had wall cupboards that could have been used for scroll storage; L4 had a kind of podium around its walls that could have held jars or baskets used to store scrolls; L1–2 and 4, and L30, were shut off from the rest of the main building by locked doors; and some of the implements used for scroll preparation and copying (i.e., inkwells and a needle) were found in L30. Further, the water installations and the plastered tables and benches could be associated with work on scrolls. This room complex most closely resembles the libraries in the Shamash temple in Sippar, the Tebtunis temple, the House of the Literary Texts at Ugarit, the tentatively identified library rooms at Pergamon, and the Villa of the Papyri at Herculaneum (see ch. 2). Thus we can affirm that this room complex is the most likely candidate for a library complex at Qumran.

Inscriptions and Other Evidence for Writing from the Khirbeh

In this section I describe in broad strokes the inscriptional evidence from Qumran as well as other archaeological evidence for writing from the settlement itself.

---

89. J. C. Trever, "Preliminary Observations on the Jerusalem Scrolls," *BASOR* 111 (1948): 5.

90. E. Tov, *Scribal Practices and Approaches Reflected in the Texts Found in the Judean Desert*, STDJ 54 (Leiden: Brill, 2004), 123.

Inscriptions

The corpus of inscriptions found in the ruins of the buildings at Qumran was either inked or inscribed on ceramic remains, both on intact vessels and on pieces of vessels (ostraca), or found on stone seals or weights.[91] The inscriptions on the ceramics were either incised into the clay before firing, or scratched, written, or painted on after firing. If the inscription was written or painted on after firing, it was done either with black carbon ink or red ochre.[92] The stone seals and weights were incised.

The inscriptions are written in Hebrew/Aramaic (often it is difficult to determine if the language is Hebrew or Aramaic), Greek, and one possible Latin inscription in the form of Roman numerals. Forty-nine Hebrew/ Aramaic inscriptions were discovered by de Vaux (thirteen are marked by Lemaire as questionable), seven in Greek (one marked as questionable), one in Latin (questionable), two with Hebrew/Aramaic letters and Roman numerals, and four in which the language is unidentified. Finally, there were six graffiti that contained only line figures.

Later excavations at Qumran also uncovered inscriptions. James Strange discovered two inscribed sherds (KhQ Ostracon 1 and KhQ Ostracon 2) in 1996 along the base of the eastern wall.[93] Magen and Peleg found ten ostraca, "most" in the eastern dump, others in the northern dump. Their languages are also Hebrew, Aramaic, and Greek.[94]

---

91. The majority of the inscriptions have been published by A. Lemaire, "Inscriptions du khirbeh, des grottes et de 'Ain Feshkha," in *Khirbet Qumrân et 'Aïn Feshkha*, vol. 2: *Études d'anthropologie, de physique et de chimie*, ed. J.-B. Humbert and J. Gunneweg, NTOA.SA 3 (Göttingen: Vandenhoeck & Ruprecht, 2003), 341–88.

92. J. Gunneweg and M. Balla note that red ochre was found in L2 in the main building, indicating that it is possible that the red painted inscriptions were made at Qumran ("Possible Connection between the Inscriptions on Pottery, the Ostraca and Scrolls Found in the Caves," in Humbert and Gunneweg, *Khirbet Qumrân et 'Aïn Feshkha*, 2:391). De Vaux's notes (Humbert and Chambon, *Excavations of Khirbet Qumran*, 12) mention a sample of red ochre (object no. 46).

93. Strange, "1996 Excavations at Qumran," 41–54. These ostraca were published by F. M. Cross and E. Eshel, "Ostraca from Khirbet Qumran," in *Qumran Cave 4.XXVI: Cryptic Texts*, by S. Pfann; and *Miscellanea, Part 1*, by P. Alexander et al., DJD 36 (Oxford: Clarendon, 2000), 497–508. See also F. M. Cross and E. Eshel, "Ostraca from Khirbet Qumrân," *IEJ* 47 (1997): 17–28. In ch. 7 we will discuss the reading יחד proposed by Cross and Eshel on KhQ1.

94. One of these inscriptions has been published. The language is Aramaic, and the script appears to be from the first century CE. Its three lines read אלעזר בר ישוע הבורית, "Eleazar son of Yeshua the Borite." See Magen and Peleg, "Back to Qumran," 72–73, fig. 3.21.

THE QUMRAN EVIDENCE

The location of the inscriptions (the find sites) may give some clues as to the distributions of writing at the site.[95] It is important to remember that by their very nature ostraca are "temporary" documents; they were the scratch pads of the ancient world. Therefore, unless an inscription is found in situ on an intact vessel, it is often difficult to determine anything certain about it, other than its language and its contents. This is especially the case for those ostraca found in dumps or fills (often of water installations), where they were discarded or drifted in antiquity.[96] When studying the locus numbers associated with the inscriptions, it is evident that inscriptions were found scattered in every area of the site, including the main building, the southeast annex, and the western industrial complex. At least one inscription was found in the following loci: Trench A, "Tranche Voie" (the "Railroad Trench"),[97] 4, 8, 10A, 15, 23, 27, 28, 29, 30, 34, 35, 38, 39, 54, 59, 61, 63, 73, 78, 84, east of 84, 89, 110, 111, 116, 121, 124, 125, 129, 130, 135, and 143. In most of these loci only one inscription was found. In some loci, however, more than one inscription was found, which is of interest because it may indicate a concentration of writing activity in those areas. These loci fall into three groups.

In the main building, more than one inscription was found in L30, 34, 35, and 39. L30, the room identified above as a scroll workroom, yielded two Second Temple period inscriptions. Two inscriptions were found in L34, a "small room" in the southeast corner of the main building in the Second Temple period settlement. L35, also with two inscriptions, is a room next to L34 in the southeast quadrant. L39, where two inscriptions were found, is a square room in the northeast quadrant of the main building. Thus no real pattern emerges for the inscriptions found in the main building, since no more than two inscriptions were found in any one room.

The loci of the southeastern annex where more than one inscription was found are L61 (three inscriptions), L84 (two, including the inscription found to the east), and L143 (two). L61 and 84 are workrooms associated with the pottery kilns, while L143 is a small shelter at the furthest southern end of the

95. See table 1 for a chart detailing the object number, language, locus, and de Vaux's stratigraphy for each inscription.

96. The following loci at Qumran that contained inscriptions and were dumps or fills are Trench 1, "Tranche Voie," L54, L110, and L124.

97. This trench was opened in the corridor between the main building and the western sector. It was dug in order to install a rail track to remove debris. However, de Vaux apparently discovered evidence of an ancient trench dug by the Roman garrison in the post–68 phase (*Archaeology*, 42–43). I would like to thank Dennis Mizzi for his help with this information.

The Archaeology of Qumran

southeast annex. The association with the pottery kilns is natural, since there presumably would have been more available sherds there than elsewhere in the settlement; thus no significance should be attached to these find sites.

The western industrial complex had five loci where more than one inscription was found: L110 (the large round cistern; four inscriptions), L111 (three inscriptions), L124 (which de Vaux described as "a solid mass of masonry to support the building of the storeroom to the west of the western outbuilding"; seven or eight inscriptions),[98] L129 (two), and L130 (two). A total of nineteen or twenty inscriptions were found in this area. This may seem at first glance to be an important indicator of writing activity in the western industrial complex, but it must be noted that for the two loci where the most inscriptions were found, L110 (four) and L124 (eight), the pottery sherds were either fill that had fallen into the round cistern (L110) or were deliberately used to reinforce a wall (L124). Thus these sherds could have come from anywhere around the site and give no information about writing activity in that particular area.[99] Taken together, then, the find sites of the inscriptions give no indication of a concentration of writing anywhere in the ruins.[100]

The contents of the inscriptions include male Jewish names, some indications of trade, two abecedaries (KhQ161[= KhQ Ostracon 3][101] and KhQ2289), and one student exercise (KhQ2207).[102] The main language is Hebrew/Aramaic, with some Greek and (perhaps) Latin.[103] The pres-

---

98. Humbert and Chambon, *Excavations of Khirbet Qumran*, 6.

99. Contra Gunneweg and Balla, "Possible Connection," 393, who argue that it is unlikely that this is a dump. However, de Vaux does not describe L124 as a dump; his notes read, "Massif de fondation pour soutenir les magasins à l'ouest des dépendances, construits au bord abrupt du wadi" (*Fouilles de Khirbet Qumrân*, 1:14).

100. Contra the assertion of Gunneweg and Balla, "Possible Connection," 393, who claim on the basis of the number of inscriptions found there that L30, 124, and 61 were the centers of scribal activity at Qumran. See also J. Saukkonen, "A Few Inkwells, Many Hands: Were There Scribes at Qumran?," in *Houses Full of All Good Things: Essays in Memory of Timo Veijola*, ed. J. Pakkala and M. Nissinen (Helsinki: Finnish Exegetical Society; Göttingen: Vandenhoeck & Ruprecht, 2008), 542n6.

101. E. Eshel, "3. Khirbet Qumran Ostracon," in DJD 36, 511–12.

102. E. Puech in a private communication has informed me that this inscription is a student exercise with practice sentences. I would like to thank Professor Puech for sharing this information with me prior to publication.

103. Since the stratigraphy of the inscriptions is quite uncertain, it may be that those inscriptions identified as Latin belong to the post-68 occupation phase, when a Roman garrison was quartered at Qumran.

191

THE QUMRAN EVIDENCE

ence of the abecedaries and the student exercise lend support to the argument that scribes were present and active at Qumran, while the other inscriptions indicate that the inhabitants engaged in commerce (importing goods) in at least a small way outside the settlement.

TABLE 5[1]

KhQ Number	Language[2]	Locus	Stratigraphy[3]	Other
161 (= KhQ Ostracon 3)	Heb/ar	Trench A	Disordered/ Level 1	abecedary
192	Greek	L8	Period 2 or 3	incised
386		L23	Period 2	graffito (lines)
387	Greek[4]	L27	Period 2	incised
425	Heb/ar?	L10A	Period 2	
426	Heb/ar	L30	Period 3?	
427	Heb/ar?	L28	Period 1?	
439	Greek	L30	Period 3?	inscribed seal
461	Heb/ar	L29	Disordered	
498	Heb/ar	L30	Period 2	
498bis	Heb/ar?	L30	Period 2	
572	Heb/ar?	L9A	Disordered	
621	Aramaic	L34	Period 1	Whole jar
635	Greek	L35	Period 2	Incised
680		Tranche voie		graffito; incised
681	Heb/ar?	L35	Surface	Join with 691
691	Heb/ar	L37	Surface	Join with 681
682	Heb/ar?	L34	Period 2	Incised
701		L39	Surface	
711	Heb/ar	L38	No stratigraphy	Incised
734	Heb/ar?[5]	L39	Period 2	
935	Heb/ar	L28	Period 2	Whole jar; incised
979	Greek	L54	Period 2	Incised
1095		L59	Period 2?	

192

The Archaeology of Qumran

KhQ Number	Language[2]	Locus	Stratigraphy[3]	Other
1110	Heb/ar?	L61	Period 2	Intact pierced bowl
1264	Heb/ar?	L63	No stratigraphy	
1313	Heb/ar?	L61	Period 2	
1401	Latin?	L84	End of Period 2	Whole jar[6]
1403	Heb/ar?	L61	Period 2	Whole jar; incised
1416	Heb/ar	East of L84	No stratigraphy	
1650	Heb/ar	L89	Period 2	Bowl fragment; incised
2088		L111	Period 3?	Seal decorated with a rosette
2108	Heb/ar	L110	Fill	
2109	Heb/ar	L110	Fill	
2215		L111	Period 2	Stone weight; graffito; incised
2124	Greek	L110	Fill	Stone weight; incised
2125	Heb/ar	L116	Period 2	
2136	Heb/ar?	L110	Fill	Stone vessel; incised
2145	Greek?	L121	Surface	Stone; incised
2176	Heb/ar	L125	Surface	
2207	Heb?	L129	Surface	Stone plaque; student exercise?
2289	Heb/ar	L135	Surface	Abecedary?
2416	Heb/ar	L130	Period 2	Broken jug
2417	Heb/ar	L130	Period 2	Broken jug
2507	Heb/ar	North of Cave 1		Base of a cylindrical jar
2538	Heb/ar	L124	Period 2? fill	
2539	Heb/ar	L124	Period 2? fill	
2553	Aramaic	L124	Period 2? fill	

THE QUMRAN EVIDENCE

KhQ Number	Language[2]	Locus	Stratigraphy[3]	Other
2554	Heb	L124	Period 2? fill	
2556	Heb?	L124	Period 2? fill	
2557	Heb/ar	L124	Period 2? fill	
2563	Heb/ar?	L143	Period 2?	Intact jar
2575		L30	Earlier than Period 2	Graffito
2587	Heb?	L143	Earlier than Period 2	Bowl; the same letters are inscribed twice on two sides of the bowl.
2609	Latin? Greek?	L78	Period 2	Incision
2661c	Heb	L124	Period 2? fill	
3759		L4		Graffito (lines); incision
4037	Greek?	L111	Period 2	
5167	Heb/ar	?		
Ostracon 1	Heb	Eastern side of the marl terrace wall	30–68 CE	
Ostracon 2	Heb	Eastern side of the marl terrace wall	30–68 CE	

1 This table includes only inscriptions from the Second Temple period and the post–68 phases; Iron Age inscriptions are excluded.

2 The language is documented according to Lemaire's publication.

3 The stratigraphy is according to de Vaux's field notes, unless otherwise indicated.

4 The identification of the language by Lemaire as Greek is uncertain; it could as easily be Hebrew/Aramaic.

5 Lemaire, "Inscriptions du khirbeh," 350, also suggests a possible Latin reading.

6 This jar type, ovoid with handles high on the shoulder, is common at Second Temple period Qumran. The Latin letters, if correctly identified, may indicate a reuse by the Roman garrison stationed there in the post–68 CE phase.

The Archaeology of Qumran

The Inkwells and Other Evidence

Inkwells are an obvious marker of writing activity at a site. At Qumran, de Vaux discovered three inkwells: one bronze and one ceramic inkwell in L30 (proposed as a scroll workroom associated with the library complex), and one in L31 (from the post–68 phase). Jan Gunneweg and Marta Balla recently identified the fragment of a fourth ceramic inkwell from L129 (QUM 221).[104] Steckoll discovered a fifth inkwell at Qumran, although its exact locus is unknown.[105] Magen and Peleg report finding one ceramic inkwell in their eastern dump.[106] Finally, a bronze inkwell reportedly sold by Kando to John Allegro is part of the Schøyen Collection and has been recently published by Torleif Elgvin.[107] Thus at least six and possibly eight inkwells have surfaced at Qumran in the Second Temple period, which is a large amount for a small first-century BCE–first-century CE site.[108] These inkwells present concrete evidence of writing activity at the site, and perhaps more than simple administrative sorts of writing.

Evidence from the marl terrace caves, previously discussed in ch. 4, should be considered here as well, since (as we continue to emphasize) the marl terrace caves are part of the archaeological site of Qumran. Caves 4Q and 8Q contained over a hundred leather thongs and ties used for fastening scrolls, indicating at least the repair of scrolls going on at the site (Cave 8Q contained 68 reinforcing tabs),[109] and Cave 4Q contained uninscribed pieces of leather. Finally, Stacey reports that leather in various stages of preparation was found in three caves near Qumran, including "thin pieces

---

104. Gunneweg and Balla, "Neutron Activation Analysis: Scroll Jars and Common Ware," in Humbert and Gunneweg, *Khirbet Qumrân et ʿAïn Feshkha*, 2:32. They also report another inkwell purportedly from Qumran, in the archaeological research collection of the University of Southern California, and a third now in Jordanian hands. According to S. Goranson, "Qumran—The Evidence of the Inkwells," *BAR* 19.6 (1993): 67, the inkwell now at USC was purchased from Kando, and he claimed that it came from Qumran.

105. S. H. Steckoll, "Marginal Notes on the Qumran Excavations," *RevQ* 7 (1969): 2. This inkwell is now in the collection of the Hecht Museum in Haifa.

106. Magen and Peleg, *Qumran Excavation*, 27.

107. T. Elgvin, "Bronze Inkwells from Naḥal Ḥever(?) and Nabataea: MS 1622/5 and 1987/15," in *Gleanings from the Caves: Dead Sea Scrolls and Artefacts from the Schøyen Collection*, ed. T. Elgvin et al., LSTS 71 (London: Bloomsbury T&T Clark, 2016), 451.

108. Mizzi, "Qumran at Seventy," 25.

109. J. Carswell, "Fastenings on the Qumrân Manuscripts," in *Qumran Grotte 4.II: Part I: Archéologie*, by R. de Vaux; and *Part II: Tefillin, Mezuzot et Targums (4Q128–4Q157)*, by J. T. Milik, DJD 6 (Oxford: Clarendon, 1977), 23–28.

THE QUMRAN EVIDENCE

to be used as parchment."[110] These remnants of scroll manufacture and repair are important pieces of evidence that some kind of work on scrolls was going on at Qumran in the Second Temple period.

Unusual Features of Khirbet Qumran

The Pottery

The pottery corpus from Khirbet Qumran is, to paraphrase de Vaux, monotonous, limited, and very repetitive.[111] It consists mainly of cups, plates, bowls, cooking pots, jars, jugs, juglets, flasks, lids, and lamps.[112] The majority of the types date to the first centuries BCE and CE. Magness offers the following generalized description: "The vessels tend to be made of smooth, well-levigated clay and have relatively thin, hard-fired walls. The clay is usually pink, red, or grey in color, and there is often a whitish slip covering the exterior."[113] Most of the pottery types found at Qumran are also found either throughout Judea or in the Dead Sea region during the late Second Temple period.

However, the Qumran pottery corpus has several unique characteristics that set it apart from other corpora of the region and period. First is the ubiquity of the cylindrical storage jars with their bowl-shaped lids, described in ch. 4. Dozens of specimens of these jars were discovered in the ruins, some embedded in the floors of various loci. Wasters of these jars were discovered in the eastern dump near the pottery workshop, indicating that they were being manufactured on site. Some specimens of the ovoid type of this jar have been found at other sites, such as 'Ein-Boqeq, 'Ein-Gedi, and Machaerus, but the absence of the cylindrical jar type at other places, and the plethora of them at Qumran, suggests that the cylindrical jar is a Qumran innovation that was manufactured there, and spread in small quantities from Qumran to other sites in the region.[114]

---

110. D. Stacey, "Seasonal Industries at Qumran," *BAIAS* 26 (2008): 14.

111. De Vaux, *Archaeology*, 17. See most recently Humbert and Gunneweg, *Khirbet Qumrân et Aïn Feshkha*, vol. 3A, which contains drawings and photographs of the pottery found in the various loci.

112. J. Magness, "The Community of Qumran in Light of Its Pottery," in *Debating Qumran: Collected Essays on Its Archaeology*, ISACR 4 (Leuven: Peeters, 2004), 3.

113. Magness, "Community of Qumran," 3.

114. D. Mizzi, "Miscellaneous Artefacts from the Qumran Caves: An Exploration of

The Archaeology of Qumran

Second, the majority of the Qumran pottery is undecorated; it is rarely even painted, merely covered with a whitish slip. Like Qumran's architecture, its pottery is plain and utilitarian. This is just as true for the dining utensils and the lamps as it is for such things as cooking pots (dining ware tends to be decorated, as do lamps, since they were used in more "public" spaces).[115] This lack of decoration on the majority of the pieces must have been a deliberate choice on the part of the inhabitants, perhaps for economic or ideological reasons.[116]

Third, the absence of certain types of pottery is equally significant. Various imported types of pottery, such as Western Sigillata and pseudo-Nabatean ware, are missing. These pottery types are present in palaces and some upper-class homes in Jerusalem, and would not be expected at a less opulent site such as Qumran. However, the type Eastern Sigillata A, which was produced in the eastern Mediterranean, is found in abundance in Jerusalem, Jericho, Herodium, and Machaerus. Only a few fragments (less than a dozen) were found at Qumran.[117] Other types of fine wares, such as Roman mold-made lamps, painted "Jerusalem" bowls, red-painted wares, and imported amphorae (for wine, oil, or fish sauce) are rare or completely missing at Qumran.[118]

In recent years pottery samples from Qumran have been subjected to both Instrumental Neutron Activation Analysis (INAA) and petrographic

---

Their Significance," in *The Caves of Qumran: Proceedings of the International Conference, Lugano 2014*, ed. M. Fidanzio, STDJ 118 (Leiden: Brill, 2017), 149n77. A. Berlin, "Jewish Life before the Revolt: The Archaeological Evidence," *JSJ* 36 (2005): 425–46, notes that the most common jar type in the late Second Temple period is the bag-shaped jar, which was used for Jewish-made olive oil and wine. Bag-shaped jars were also discovered at Qumran.

115. For the roughly two hundred (fragments of) lamps found at Qumran, see the catalog by J. Mlynarczyk, "Qumran Terracotta Oil Lamps," in Humbert and Gunneweg, *Khirbet Qumrân et Aïn Feshkha*, 3A:447–521. The photographs show mostly undecorated bodies and nozzles; a few mold-made lamps are the exception that proves the rule.

116. Berlin, "Jewish Life before the Revolt," 433–36, 442–48, notes that throughout Judea, apart from elite settings, a deliberately simple type of pottery is prevalent. Thus Qumran's pottery fits in with most village pottery in Judea, but not that from elite settings such as palaces, villas, or palatial homes.

117. Magness notes that Eastern Sigillata A is relatively rare in the Dead Sea region overall, and suggests that this may be due to the high costs of transport ("Community of Qumran," 7, 14).

118. Magness, "Community at Qumran," 13. Mlynarczyk lists one example of a Roman relief lamp, KhQ3136 ("Qumran Terracotta Oil Lamps," 515, pl. 113). Berlin, "Jewish Life before the Revolt," 441, also notes that no examples of Italian-style cooking pans (an import and imitation) were recovered.

THE QUMRAN EVIDENCE

analysis.[119] The results may be considered somewhat surprising in view of the claim made above that much of the Qumran pottery was made on site.

According to the INAA analysis of pottery samples from Qumran (both from the buildings and the caves) carried out by Gunneweg and Balla, five separate chemical groups are present.[120] Their Group I, which they identify as clay from a local source, includes kiln linings, oven covers, clay balls, Qumran puddle mud, stucco from the tables found in L30, and Dead Sea mud. The samples from the kiln linings, oven covers, puddle mud, and stucco are clearly local; that is, the inhabitants used local mud for their kilns and ovens, and to make their stucco. However, the *pottery* in this group is made from a different clay (even though Gunneweg and Balla place it in the same group), and a clay source in the region of Qumran suitable for making pottery has not been located.[121] The other four groups are not local, and at least one, Group II, is from the Motza clay formation near Jerusalem. This extensive clay deposit was the main source for clay for pottery manufacture in Judea in the Hasmonean and Herodian periods. Group IV, a tiny sample, contains clay that Gunneweg and Balla "cautiously" conclude comes from the region of Edom.[122] Thus the chemical analysis demonstrates that, although the presence of the potters' workshop indicates that the inhabitants were making at least some of their own pottery, a percentage of the Qumran pottery, or at least its clay, was imported from the Jerusalem region, from Edom, and elsewhere.

The petrographic analysis of scroll jar samples carried out by Jacek Michniewicz and Miroslaw Krzyško clarifies this somewhat surprising picture.[123] Their conclusions are:

1. The Qumran jars under investigation were made of a raw material which is not present in the vicinity of the Qumran site.

119. Magness gives the following helpful definitions: "Petrography is the study of thin sections of pottery or fired clay which compares visible mineralogical inclusions including temper"; INAA "is a nuclear method to determine the chemical composition of clay or pottery, with groupings based mainly on the trace elements present" ("The Connection between the Site of Qumran and the Scroll Caves in Light of the Ceramic Evidence," in Fidanzio, *Caves of Qumran*, 187).

120. Gunneweg and Balla, "Neutron Activation Analysis," 3–53.

121. Magness, "Connection," 189.

122. Gunneweg and Balla, "Neutron Activation Analysis," 23.

123. J. Michniewicz and M. Krzyško, "The Provenance of Scroll Jars in the Light of Archaeometric Investigations," in Humbert and Gunneweg, *Khirbet Qumrân et 'Ain Feshkha*, 2:59–99.

2. The Qumran jars under investigation were made by the same technique from similar but not homogenous raw materials. . . . Most jars were fired at the temperature of 650–750°C.

3. Most of the jars were probably made from the Moza Formation clays, known and widely utilized in Judaea.[124]

In other words, the raw material suitable for the production of kiln-fired pottery is not available in the vicinity of Qumran. Therefore, even for locally produced pottery, suitable clay (most likely from the Motza formation) was imported.[125] This argues against the identification of Qumran as a major pottery production center (contra Magen and Peleg). In order to manufacture pottery in quantity for sale to the public, four factors must be present: a main road access, a regular water supply, a good source of wood for fuel, and a local supply of good clay.[126] None of these features is present at Qumran.

In sum, Qumran's pottery consists of a limited repertoire of types, dating from the Hasmonean and Herodian periods. It is almost entirely plain, undecorated, and utilitarian in nature. While the majority of the pottery was manufactured on site from imported clay, a certain percentage was imported, most likely through local trade. The number of cylindrical and ovoid jars with bowl-shaped lids ("scroll jars") is unique to Qumran, indicating a definite preference (and, indeed, local development and manufacture).[127] Thus the pottery from Qumran, while at home in the region, presents a unique profile that must be considered when attempting to discern the nature and function of the site.

---

124. Michniewicz and Krzyško, "Provenance of Scroll Jars," 76. In a study in the same volume, K. Rasmussen concludes, "The firing temperatures in the local group are very confined and vary between 710 and 860 °C." ("On the Provenance and Firing Temperature of Pottery," in Humbert and Gunneweg, *Khirbet Qumrân et 'Aïn Feshkha*, 2:101–2).

125. See Magness, "Connection," 193.

126. Berlin, "Jewish Life," 422.

127. According to M. Burdajewicz, in the category "storage and transport jars" bag-shaped jars, the most common form in the late Second Temple period, predominate (61.8 percent), while cylindrical/ovoid jars comprise 37 percent of the total ("Typology of the Pottery from Khirbet Qumran [French Excavations 1953–1956]," *ASOR Newsletter* 51 [2001]: 14).

THE QUMRAN EVIDENCE

Other Artifacts from the Khirbeh

The remaining assemblage of material finds from the Second Temple period levels is heterogeneous and what one might expect from any settlement in the period. There are limestone vessels, which begin to appear in Judean sites in the late first century BCE and may indicate an increased concern with ritual purity.[128] Fragments of approximately 89 glass vessels were recovered; of these, only 23 can be securely dated to the pre–68 context, while 29 others fall within the range first century BCE to first century CE.[129] Mizzi describes the Qumran glassware as having no peculiar features, but as typical of the poorer glass assemblages found in Palestine in this period. Most of the glass is hand-blown and with natural colors; there are some fragments of sagged glass (made by "sagging" a disc of glass over a convex mold), but no examples of the finest glassware.[130]

Other artifacts include metal implements such as tools (e.g., a sickle in L52), nails, rings, hooks, keys, and locks.[131] As mentioned above, a bronze needle was found in L30. In L52 three groups of metal implements (iron and bronze) were found melted together, presumably from the heat of the fire that destroyed the settlement. These types of implements are typical for a nonroyal or non-upper-class settlement in late Second Temple Palestine and simply indicate the carrying on of everyday activities.

128. Stone does not convey or retain impurity. See J. Magness, *Stone and Dung, Oil and Spit: Jewish Daily Life in the Time of Jesus* (Grand Rapids: Eerdmans, 2011), 70–74. However, as Cecelia Wassén has pointed out to me in a private communication, the rise in the use of stone vessels in the late Second Temple period may also have to do with fashion, durability, and availability. See C. Wassén, "The Connection between Purity Practices and the Jerusalem Temple—the House of God—around the Turn of the Era," in *The House of God*, ed. C. Grappe (Tübingen: Mohr Siebeck, forthcoming). I would like to thank Professor Wassén for sharing this with me prior to publication. According to Mizzi, at Qumran there are a larger than usual number of stone kraters and stone stoppers/lids (as quoted by Taylor, *Essenes*, 260). Magen and Peleg, "Back to Qumran," 71, list measuring cups, bowls, and large jars. However, the general quantity of stone vessels is small compared to the quantity of ceramic vessels.

129. D. Mizzi, "The Glass from Khirbet Qumran: What Does It Tell Us about the Qumran Community?," in *The Dead Sea Scrolls: Texts and Context*, ed. C. Hempel, STDJ 90 (Leiden: Brill, 2010), 110.

130. Mizzi, "Glass from Khirbet Qumran," 109–17. Mizzi (119) emphasizes that a luxurious lifestyle at Qumran cannot be inferred on the basis of the glassware, contra R. Donceel and P. Donceel-Voûte ("The Archaeology of Khirbet Qumran," in *Methods of Investigation of the Dead Sea Scrolls and the Khirbet Qumran Site: Present Realities and Future Prospects*, ed. M. Wise et al., ANYAS 722 [New York: The New York Academy of Sciences, 1991], 7–9, 37).

131. Murphy, *Wealth*, 329.

200

The Archaeology of Qumran

Coins, like pottery, are ubiquitous at every archaeological site in this period, and are a useful tool for establishing the chronological parameters of any given place. De Vaux recovered 1,234 coins from Qumran, and several more have been recovered in subsequent excavations. Of de Vaux's coins 1,060 come from the Second Temple period settlement.[132] The coin evidence from the Second Temple period can be divided into two groups: (1) coins scattered throughout the site, and (2) the silver coin hoard found in three ceramic pots buried beneath the floor of L120. The coins scattered over the settlement are all bronze, dating from the Seleucid period to the second year of the First Jewish Revolt against Rome. Most plentiful are the coins of Alexander Jannaeus, during whose reign (103–76 BCE) the settlement was founded. Jannaeus minted a lot of coins, and they stayed in circulation for a long time, so this datum is not surprising and does not indicate anything about economic life at Qumran. The "loose coin" evidence does not give us much information beyond the dating parameters for the site; that they are all bronze and relatively few may indicate a poorer site.[133]

The silver coin hoard is more mysterious and hence more interesting. There were a total of 561 coins in the three pots: Pot A contained 153 coins, Pot B 185, and Pot C 223. Most of these are Tyrian shekels or half-shekels (which were used for the temple tax), minted between the late second and late first century BCE. The most recent coin may be dated as late as 65/66 CE.[134] The homogeneity of the hoard is unique; it contained only silver coins, and no bronze coins, jewelry, or other valuables. Mizzi and Magness characterize it as a "savings hoard,"[135] but its purpose remains unclear. Various suggestions have been made, such as a collection for the annual temple tax, taxes for the Romans,[136] or simply as the monetary wealth of the site's inhabitants.[137] If the latest coin is correctly dated, then one might surmise that the coins began to be collected in the first century BCE; the last deposit was made shortly before the Roman attack in 68 CE; and the pots were buried for safekeeping and later retrieval.[138] The most

132. Murphy, *Wealth*, 305, 309.

133. Murphy, *Wealth*, 308–9.

134. Mizzi and Magness, "Was Qumran Abandoned," 304–5, 309.

135. Mizzi and Magness, "Was Qumran Abandoned," 310.

136. Murphy, *Wealth*, 313.

137. Hirschfeld, *Qumran in Context*, 143.

138. The excavation at Ramat Raḥel uncovered a similar hoard of Tyrian coins from the first century BCE. The hoard contained fifteen Tyrian shekels found inside a small ceramic cooking pot that had been placed in one of the columbarium's compartments. The coins

THE QUMRAN EVIDENCE

that can be said on the basis of the archaeological evidence is that the hoard contained someone's wealth (an individual or a group of people) and that it was buried prior to the destruction of the site in 68.

The Absence of Evidence for the Presence of Women at Qumran

One remarkable feature of the material finds is the almost complete absence of gendered objects associated with women. As we noted in ch. 4, the presence of women at a particular site is indicated in the archaeological record by the discovery of jewelry, mirrors, cosmetic articles, spindle whorls, needles, and combs. According to de Vaux's field notes (in which it is sometimes difficult to ascertain the level with which the artifact is associated), in the Second Temple period settlement levels he uncovered one spindle whorl, but its context in L7 is uncertain. He also found only four beads in the entire settlement.[139] This dearth of female finds, stretched out over a 150-year period, is very striking, especially compared to the much shorter post–68 period, from which de Vaux recovered a green faience bead, the fragment of a bracelet, a needle, an alabaster spindle whorl, and a glass perfume phial. It is true that "the absence of evidence is not the evidence of absence," but the almost complete nonexistence of any material evidence for the presence of women at the site in the Second Temple period begs for an explanation.

The Stepped Pools

A unique feature of the Qumran water system is the presence of a majority of stepped pools, as opposed to unstepped cisterns (rectangular or round). The "stepped pools" at Qumran are characterized by a set of steps that

---

were considered a single collection, all minted in Tyre and dated from 38/37 BCE to 11/10 BCE. The excavators postulate that it was buried in haste sometime after 11 BCE, perhaps even after King Herod's death in 4 BCE. See O. Lipschits et al., *What Are the Stones Whispering? Ramat Raḥel: 3000 Years of Forgotten History* (Winona Lake, IN: Eisenbrauns, 2017), 126–28. I would like to thank Lucas Schulte for bringing this reference to my attention.

139. Magness, *Archaeology of Qumran*, 177–78. Magness compares the female-gendered finds from Qumran to those from Masada and the Bar Kokhba caves, both of which yielded a much greater percentage of female-gendered objects over a much shorter time frame. See also ch. 4.

202

The Archaeology of Qumran

run the width of the pool. In some of the pools the steps are divided by a low partition running down the middle of the steps. The steps in L48, 56, 71, 117–118, and 138 combine a broad tread sandwiched between steps with narrower treads; the broad tread may have served as a landing when descending into the pool.

Stepped pools themselves are not unique to Qumran; according to Galor: "stepped pools and . . . concentrations of stepped pools can be found in all geographical areas of Palestine inhabited by Jews prior to and after 70 A.D."[140] The question is, why there are so many of them at Qumran, and did they have a special function?

De Vaux refused to speculate on any special function for the stepped pools, simply dividing the water installations into cisterns (L48, 56, 58, 71, 91, and 110), decantation basins and settling pools (L69, 83, 119bis, 132, and 137), and baths (L68 and 138).[141] It was Robert North in 1962 who first suggested that the stepped pools at Qumran may have had a ritual purpose.[142] Bryant G. Wood expanded the arguments in 1984, emphasizing especially the capacity of the water system; he concluded that the stepped pools were used for immersion.[143] In his 1991 dissertation, Ronny Reich categorically identified the following ten water installments as mikvaoth: L48, 56, 68–69, 71, 83, 85, 117–118, and 138.[144] In this identification he is followed by Magness, who notes that certain of the stepped pools are located at strategic points throughout the site: L138 is near the northwest entrance; L56–58 are found at the entrance to L77 (the "dining room"), L117–118 are located to the east of a reconstructed dining room above L111 and 120–122, L48 and 49 are near the toilet in L51, and L71 is next to the east entrance from the cemetery and the pottery workshop.[145] She argues

140. Galor, "Plastered Pools," 310.

141. De Vaux, Archaeology, 7–10. Cross, Ancient Library of Qumran, 64, following de Vaux, likewise rejects any ritual function for the stepped pools. Humbert has recently argued that L34 contained a Greek-style bath, which would have been for regular washing, not for any ritual purpose ("Bain à la grecque," 103–14).

142. R. North, "The Qumran Reservoirs," in The Bible in Current Catholic Thought, ed. J. McKenzie (New York: Herder & Herder, 1962), 100–132.

143. Wood, "To Dip or to Sprinkle?"

144. R. Reich, "Miqwa'ot (Jewish Ritual Immersion Baths) in Eretz-Israel in the Second Temple and the Mishnah and Talmud Periods" [in Hebrew] (PhD diss., Hebrew University of Jerusalem, 1990). An updated version of the study has been published: Miqwa'ot (Jewish Ritual Baths) in the Second Temple, Mishnaic and Talmudic Periods [in Hebrew] (Jerusalem: Yad Yizhak Ben-Zvi and Israel Exploration Society, 2013).

145. Magness, Archaeology of Qumran, 124, 127, 138.

THE QUMRAN EVIDENCE

that these locations may indicate a concern for maintaining ritual purity in the site as a whole, but especially near foodstuffs, the making of pottery, and before entering the buildings from the cemetery. Magen and Peleg and Stacey, however, reject the identity of the majority of the stepped pools as mikvaoth, arguing that they are either for the mundane water needs of the inhabitants, or for industrial purposes.[146]

The two camps outlined above take diametrically opposed positions: either the stepped pools are mikvaoth or they are not. For Reich especially the presence or absence of steps in a water installation is the basic criterion for identifying a mikva.[147] However, perhaps a more moderate approach may be helpful in identifying the functions of the stepped pools. It is not clear that in the Second Temple period water installations that were used as mikvaoth could *only* be used as mikvaoth. The Torah legislation concerning what became known as ritual immersion calls for bathing the body in water, but does not specify anything about the water. For example, Lev 15 calls for washing in the case of several bodily impurities:

> When any man has a discharge from his member, his discharge makes him ceremonially impure. . . . Anyone who touches his bed shall wash his clothes, and bathe in water, and be impure until the evening. . . . Any earthen vessel that the one with the discharge touches shall be broken; and every vessel of wood shall be rinsed in water.
>
> If a man has an emission of semen, he shall bathe his whole body in water, and be impure until the evening.
>
> When a woman has a discharge of blood that is her regular discharge from her body, she shall be in her impurity for seven days. . . . Whoever touches her bed shall wash his clothes, and bathe in water, and be impure until the evening.
>
> If a woman has a discharge of blood for many days. . . . Whoever touches these things [bed, chairs] shall be impure, and shall wash his clothes, and bathe in water, and be impure until the evening. (Lev 15:2, 5, 12, 13, 19, 22, 25, 27)[148]

146. Stacey, "Reassessment of the Stratigraphy," 40–43, 52–53. Magen and Peleg ("Back to Qumran," 88; and *Qumran Excavations*, 43) identify only L138, 68, and 117 as mikvaoth. Hirschfeld, *Qumran in Context*, 79, 111, admits that some of the stepped pools may have been used by the inhabitants as mikvaoth.

147. Reich, "Some Notes," 143.

148. I have changed the NRSV's translation of טמא as "unclean" to the more correct "impure."

The Archaeology of Qumran

Note that it is not only the body and clothing that must be washed, but wooden vessels must be rinsed as well. The method of washing, and what type of water for washing is suitable, is not specified.[149]

In the rabbinic period, in contrast, an entire tractate of the Mishnah (Miqwa'ot) is devoted to the rules and practices of ritual immersion. According to the rabbis, the water must be "living," that is, not drawn by human effort. The stepped pools at Qumran would qualify, since they were filled with water coming from the flash floods in the cliffs. Any pool made for immersion (i.e., not a pond or spring) must hold at least 40 seahs (approximately a cubic meter) of ritually pure water.[150] Again, most of the stepped pools at Qumran qualify, and most of them hold far more water.[151] Thus far it appears that the stepped pools at Qumran meet the rabbinic criteria for mikvaoth. However, we do not know which Jews in the Second Temple period, if any, followed the prescriptions codified in the Mishnah.[152] While it is important to note the similarities between the stepped pools at Qumran and rabbinic prescriptions, those similarities do not mean that every stepped pool at Qumran was a mikva, or that the stepped pools were used exclusively as mikvaoth.[153] It is clear that Second Temple period Jews, especially those of the priestly caste, were practicing some form of ritual immersion because of the sudden appearance of stepped pools in the archaeological record, especially in Jerusalem. However, that does not mean that every stepped pool in Judea functioned exclusively as a mikva.

Therefore, the question we should ask is, Could the stepped pools at Qumran have been used as ritual immersion pools in addition to water storage units? The points in favor of an affirmative answer are: (1) The stepped pools would function well for ritual immersion: the steps facilitate going down and coming back up from the water; the broad treads serve as landings, so that the immersers only had to go down into the water as far as they could stand while achieving full immersion; at least two of the

---

149. As Wassén notes, the verb רחץ, "to wash," can have a variety of connotations: to wash, bathe, douse with water, rinse off. None of these implies full bodily immersion ("Connection").

150. B. R. McCane, "Miqva'ot," *EDEJ* 954–56.

151. Reich, "Some Notes," 420, suggests that the number and size of the stepped pools "enabled a group . . . to take a ritual immersion within a short period of time."

152. As noted by Y. Adler, "The Myth of the *'ôṣār* in Second Temple–Period Ritual Baths: An Anachronistic Interpretation of a Modern-Era Innovation," *JJS* 65 (2014): 263–83.

153. Galor, "Plastered Pools," 316, rightly criticizes Reich for his exclusive use of post–70 textual evidence.

THE QUMRAN EVIDENCE

proposed mikvaoth, L48/49 and 56/58, were located within roofed structures, which indicates a function beyond water storage; and the stepped pools are impractical for water storage and retrieval.[154] (2) The stepped pools at Qumran resemble other stepped water installations throughout Judea, and especially those in the priests' quarter in the Upper City of Jerusalem prior to the fall of the temple in 70, which have been identified as ritual immersion facilities.

There are three large water installations that have no steps and clearly functioned as cisterns, in which the water was most likely drawn up via a bucket and rope (L58, 91, and 110). Therefore, the inhabitants' preference for stepped pools must have another explanation besides architectural convention. The inhabitants built a large number of stepped pools deliberately.[155] The totality of the evidence indicates that the stepped pools could very well have functioned as ritual immersion pools, and thus we may extrapolate that the inhabitants were practicing ritual immersion in the stepped pools. However, the stepped pools (or some of them) may also have served other purposes connected to the water needs of the inhabitants.[156]

The Animal Bone Deposits

The animal bone deposits are a mysterious and unique feature of the archaeological record at Qumran. De Vaux first reported on them in 1956.[157] In the Schweich Lectures he described them as follows:

> In the free spaces between the buildings or round them the excavations have laid bare animal bones deposited between large sherds of pitchers

154. The steps displace up to 40 percent of the capacity of the pool, which seems foolish when trying to store the greatest amount of water to survive the dry summer season. Further, the steps make it physically much harder to draw water with a bucket. See Reich, "Some Notes," 420–21; Galor, "Plastered Pools," 304.

155. "The Qumran engineers put a great deal of thought and planning into their water system, so full-width steps were not merely an arbitrary addition on their part" (Wood, "To Dip or to Sprinkle?," 49).

156. See also Galor, "Plastered Pools," 316–17; and S. Miller, *At the Intersection of Texts and Material Finds: Stepped Pools, Stone Vessels, and Ritual Purity among the Jews of Roman Galilee* (Göttingen: Vandenhoeck & Ruprecht, 2015), 51.

157. R. de Vaux, "Fouilles de Khirbet Qumrân: Rapport préliminaire sur les 3ᵉ, 4ᵉ et 5ᵉ campagnes," *RB* 63 (1956): 533–77.

206

The Archaeology of Qumran

or pots . . . , or sometimes placed in jars left intact with their lids on. In one instance such bones have been found covered simply by a plate. In the majority of these cases the sherds come from several jars or pots to which fragments from one or more bowls, lids, or plates have been added. As a rule these deposits have hardly been covered with earth. They are flush with the level of the ground.[158]

Although de Vaux does not associate the bones with ash, the loci where they were found also contained a layer of ash. The pottery found with these bones dates from the first century BCE to the first century CE, that is, it is coterminous with the entire length of the Second Temple period settlement. The bones, analyzed by F. E. Zeuner, were mainly of sheep and goats, with some cattle; they had been cooked, in some cases charred, and had cut marks on them.[159] These depositions were clearly deliberate; that is, they were not random discards. As early as 1958, F. M. Cross thought that the bone deposits could be evidence for sacrifice occurring at Qumran, although de Vaux questioned this view and preferred to note simply their probable "religious significance."[160] The consensus view is that these bone deposits were the remains of ritual, but not sacrificial, meals. That is, the bones are the remains of group meals that had a religious significance or purpose, but are not the remains of actual sacrifices performed on an altar.[161]

The notion of the animal bone deposits as an indication of sacrifice occurring at Qumran has been opened again by Humbert, who argues that they are remnants of Passover sacrifices, and most recently by Magness.[162]

---

158. De Vaux, *Archaeology*, 12–13. Magen and Peleg, *Qumran Excavations*, 49, claim that these deposits were "buried at considerable depth," but this does not accord with de Vaux's account.

159. Zeuner, "Notes on Qumrân," 27–36.

160. Cross, *Ancient Library of Qumran*, 85–86; de Vaux, *Archaeology*, 14.

161. For example, see L. Schiffman, *Reclaiming the Dead Sea Scrolls* (Philadelphia: Jewish Publication Society, 1994), 45, 337–38. Stacey, on the other hand, considers the bones to be "the inevitable by-product of animal slaughter ("Reassessment of the Stratigraphy," 71). But everyday garbage is thrown away in dumps, not in all the open areas of a site, and bones from meals were usually not disposed of in whole pots with lids. Magen and Peleg, *Qumran Excavataions*, 50, also believe that the bones are simply refuse, but were buried to avoid attracting scavengers.

162. Humbert, "L'espace sacré"; and most recently in *Khirbet Qumrân et Aïn Feshkha*, 3A:59–64. J. Magness, "Were Sacrifices Offered at Qumran? The Animal Bone Deposits Reconsidered," *JAJ* 7 (2016): 5–34. Magness's views on the matter have evolved. In *Archaeology of Qumran*, 113–26, she accepted the deposits as evidence of communal meals. In *Stone and*

THE QUMRAN EVIDENCE

Noting that the majority of the animal bone deposits were found in open areas of the site, especially L130, 132, and 135 in the northwest, and south of L77 in the eastern sector,[163] Magness reanalyzed the composition and context of the deposits and concluded that the bones, mixed with potsherds and ash, most closely resemble the "sacrificial refuse and consumption debris" of ancient sanctuaries.[164] Magness's evidence that the bones, found in layers of ash and mixed with broken and unbroken pottery, present unambiguous parallels to other cultic sites in the Greco-Roman world is convincing.[165] In support of her claim that sacrifice was indeed taking place at Qumran, she posits an altar (in negative imprint) in L130, the locus in which the most bone debris was found. Humbert had earlier suggested the remains of an altar in L138.[166] However, neither of these suggestions is particularly strong, and the architectural plan of Qumran does not contain the footprint of anything that looks like a sanctuary.[167] Further, no sacrificial implements seem to have been recovered at the site (with the exception of knives, which would also be used for general food consumption). Thus, what Magness is proposing is a simple altar in an open-air courtyard, not a tent sanctuary as described in Exodus, and certainly not a temple building like the temple in Jerusalem. Magness has offered the most convincing explanation to date of the animal bone deposits; however, whatever type of sacrificial activity was taking place at the site, there is no indication that it was of the scope of the sacrificial cult of the Jerusalem temple.[168] Further,

---

Dung, she argued that the bones were remains of meals which *imitated* the sacrifices of the Jerusalem temple, but were not actually sacrificed ("we do not know how and where the animals consumed at Qumran were slaughtered" [51]).

163. For a convenient summary of the find sites from all excavations, see D. Mizzi, "The Animal Bone Deposits at Qumran: An Unsolvable Riddle?," *JAJ* 7 (2016): 53.

164. Magness, "Were Sacrifices Offered," 15. G. Ekroth agrees with her interpretation of the bones as consumption debris from sacrifices, but is more skeptical of her claim that the calcined bones are the remains of bones burned on an altar ("A View from the Greek Side: Interpretations of Animal Bones as Evidence for Sacrifice and Ritual Consumption," *JAJ* 7 [2016]: 40–41).

165. See also Mizzi, "Animal Bone Deposits," 52.

166. Magness, "Were Sacrifices Offered," 21–24; Humbert, "L'espace sacré," 184–91.

167. Mizzi, "Animal Bone Deposits," 60. Mizzi also notes (63) that no cultic inscriptions, such as were found on Mount Gerizim, have been uncovered at Qumran.

168. The sectarian texts found in the caves support this conclusion. They describe ritual meals (e.g., 1QS 6:4-5, 22 and 1QSa 2:11–22 [in an eschatological context]) while at the same time focusing on Jerusalem as the holy city and hence the proper place of sacrifice (see particularly MMT B 29–33). While the sectarian texts describe the contemporary temple

The Archaeology of Qumran

the presence of a sacrificial cult at Qumran does not obviate the identification of Qumran as a scribal center and library; libraries in the ancient Near East are often associated with temples (see especially the Egyptian evidence), and we have already argued that in the Second Temple period Levites could also function as scribes.

The Cemeteries

The cemeteries at Qumran are located on the marl terrace about 35 meters east of the "long wall," which extends to the southern end of the plateau and to the north and south of the buildings.[169] The cemeteries can be divided as follows. The Main Cemetery, located directly east of the settlement, is organized into three plots, separated by two paths, with orderly rows of graves. Extending from the Main Cemetery toward the east are three fingers or extensions: the North, Middle, and South Extensions. The North Cemetery is north of the North Extension, across the modern road. The Main Cemetery, with its extensions and the North Cemetery, can be considered a single cemetery. Another small, secondary cemetery was located to the north of the North Cemetery, Qumran North. This cemetery is now lost.[170] The South Cemetery is located away from the settlement on the southern side of the wadi.

There are about twelve hundred graves in the cemeteries; however, very few of these have been excavated.[171] In the nineteenth century both Henry Poole and Charles Clermont-Ganneau excavated one grave (locations unknown).[172] De Vaux excavated forty-three, including twenty-eight

---

cult as deeply flawed (CD 4:17–18, 6:11–20), they do not necessarily indicate a wholesale abandonment of the Jerusalem temple.

169. The most recent, thorough studies on the cemeteries have been undertaken by R. Hachlili, "The Qumran Cemetery Reassessed," *OHDSS* 46–78; J. Norton, "Reassessment of Controversial Studies on the Cemetery," in Humbert and Gunneweg, *Khirbet Qumrân et 'Aïn Feshkha*, 2:107–27; and H. Eshel et al., "New Data on the Cemetery East of Khirbet Qumran," *DSD* 9 (2002): 135–54. I have followed Norton's terminology for the various cemeteries.

170. According to Eshel et al., "New Data," 136n1, "As the result of military activity north of Khirbet Qumran, this cemetery was destroyed and is no longer identifiable."

171. Eshel et al., "New Data," 141, using modern mapping techniques and GPR radar, have located a total of 1,178 graves in the cemeteries.

172. H. Poole, "Report of a Journey in Palestine," *Journal of the Royal Geographical Society* 26 (1856): 69; C. Clermont-Ganneau, *Archaeological Researches in Palestine in the*

THE QUMRAN EVIDENCE

from the Main Cemetery, six from the Southern Extension, one from the Middle Extension, two from the North Cemetery, four from the South Cemetery, and two from Qumran North. Steckoll excavated eleven more graves in 1966–1967;[173] Eshel et al. excavated one grave in the small building at the end of the Middle Extension;[174] Magen and Peleg excavated nine from the southern extension;[175] and Yossi Nagar, Hanania Hizme, and Yevgeny Aharonovich excavated twenty-seven graves in the North Cemetery, for a total of ninety-three (about 8 percent of the total number of graves).[176]

The "classic form" of a Qumran grave has the following characteristics. It is oriented in a north-south direction, and marked on the surface by a pile of fieldstones. The grave itself is a shaft grave, 1.2–2 meters deep, with a loculus at the bottom, dug on the east side of the grave. The (single) body is placed in the loculus in a supine position, with the head oriented to the south, and with hands either crossed over the breast or stretched alongside the body. The single inhumation indicates that the deceased is not buried as part of a family group, which fits with the lack of family dwellings in the khirbeh. The loculus is often closed off with flat stones, limestone slabs, or crude bricks made on site. There were very few grave goods associated with these burials, at most some pottery vessels.[177] Several remains of wooden coffins, in T17–19, were found by de Vaux (there was also brown dust, perhaps the remains of a coffin, in T32–33), and a grave with

---

Years 1873–1874, vol. 2 (London: Palestine Exploration Fund, 1898), 15–16. The grave Poole excavated was empty.

173. For Steckoll's graves, see his "Preliminary Excavation Report." Steckoll did not give the exact location of the graves he excavated. However, in 2002 R. Donceel published a report in which he attempted to locate Steckoll's graves. He places those graves in the Main Cemetery and the Middle and Southern Extensions (*Synthèse des observations faites en fouillant les tombes des nécropoles de Khirbet Qumrân et des environs* [Cracow: Enigma, 2002], 103–7 and fig. 12).

174. Eshel et al., "New Data," 147–53. They consider this square building to be a "mourning enclosure," but this is speculative.

175. Magen and Peleg, "Back to Qumran," 98.

176. Y. Nagar et al., "The People of Qumran—New Discoveries and Paleo-demographic Interpretations" (paper presented at the Annual Meeting of the American Schools of Oriental Research, Boston, 16 November 2017).

177. Hachlili, "Qumran Cemetery Reassessed," 57–61. Small amounts of jewelry were found in T32 and 33 in the Southern Extension, and S1 in the South Cemetery. All these graves were oriented east-west, which may indicate a later intrusion. See C. Clamer, "Jewellery Finds from the Cemetery," in Humbert and Gunneweg, *Khirbet Qumrân et 'Aïn Feshkha*, 2:171–83.

The Archaeology of Qumran

a wooden coffin was excavated by Magen and Peleg.[178] In addition, Eshel et al. discovered the remains of a metal coffin lid, which they identified as zinc, in their tomb no. 978, in the Middle Extension.[179] Finally, Steckoll reported burnt wood in tombs G3–6, 9–11. The use of coffins may, but does not necessarily, point to reinhumation (i.e., that bodies were transported to Qumran from elsewhere for burial).[180]

Most of the tombs in the Main Cemetery, its Extensions, the North Cemetery, and Qumran North have these features. However, the graves in the South Cemetery were rudimentary, without consistent orientation, and with none of the features of the "classic form." This is enough to posit that there have been some intrusions into the cemetery over the years, probably from passing bedouin.[181] It is likely, then, that the South Cemetery is a "non-Qumran" cemetery. However, the majority of the excavated graves in the remaining cemeteries at Qumran are of the classic type, and date from the Second Temple period.[182]

Although at the time of de Vaux's excavations the "classic form" of the Qumran grave was otherwise unknown, leading to speculation that this was a particular type of sectarian burial, since then graves of this type have been located at other sites, notably at 'En el-Ghuweir, Hiam el-Sagha, and in Khirbet Qazone (a non-Jewish site) at the southeastern end of the Dead Sea.[183] This evidence indicates that the Qumran "classic form" burials are not sectarian, or even necessarily Jewish, but are found throughout the region, regardless of ethnicity. Taylor has suggested that this type of grave reflects burial customs among the poor, and that they were followed by the inhabitants of Qumran, regardless of their socioeconomic status.[184]

---

178. Magen and Peleg, *Qumran Excavations*, 51.

179. Eshel et al., "New Data," 143–47. Nagar et al., "People of Qumran," suggest that this grave is a later intrusion, not associated with the Second Temple period settlement.

180. Humbert, "Chronology," 430, points out that coffins would have to have been transported to Qumran by boat (the paths leading to Qumran could not accommodate a coffin loaded onto a wagon), while disarticulated bones could be transported overland.

181. Hachlili, "Qumran Cemetery Reassessed," 61. See also J. Zias, "The Cemeteries of Qumran and Celibacy: Confusion Laid to Rest?," *DSD* 7 (2000): 220–53.

182. Mizzi, "Qumran at Seventy," 17, suggests that some of the Second Temple graves may have been those of refugees during Period III. This suggestion might also account for some of the female burials.

183. Hachlili, "Qumran Cemetery Reassessed," 67–70. Berlin, "Jewish Life before the Revolt," 463, notes that Jewish sites which use this type of burial are concentrated in settlements at the northern end of the Dead Sea.

184. Taylor, *Essenes*, 258–59. Magen and Peleg, "Back to Qumran," 97, also note that

THE QUMRAN EVIDENCE

The question of the gender identity of the corpses is important for our understanding of the identity of the inhabitants of Qumran. The skeletons preserved from de Vaux's excavations are now housed in Munich, Paris, and Jerusalem. Olav Röhrer-Ertl, Ferdinand Rohrhirsch, and Diebert Hahn have identified the twenty-two skeletons in the Munich collection as consisting of nine males, eight females, and five children.[185] The remains of the Paris and Jerusalem collections (the "French Collection") have been identified by Sheridan, Ullinger, and Ramp as seventeen males, two unknown, and one female found in Tomb A.[186] Finally, the bones of the 2015 excavation were examined in situ before being reburied. In twenty-seven graves there were thirty-three individuals; the gender distribution consisted of thirty males and three unidentified skeletons—no females, and no infants or children. If we discount those from the South Cemetery (one female, four children) as a non-Qumran cemetery on the basis of the form of its burials, then there are fifty-six males, nine females, and one child in the cemeteries associated with the khirbeh.[187] As Norton has noted, the proportion of men to women and children is exceptionally high; it is more usual to find a greater proportion of women and children, owing to their higher mortality rates.[188] That a few women were buried at Qumran in the Second Temple period can enable the case that women did live at Qumran, which is contrary to the evidence from the caves and the khirbeh. However, given the new evidence from the 2015 salvage excavation, the gender evidence from the cemetery is more in accord with the evidence from the caves and the khirbeh than previously thought. It is very likely that the vast majority of Qumran burials from the Second Temple period were adult males, in keeping with the lack of evidence for women and children in the

---

this is a type of burial used by the poor. Berlin, "Jewish Life," 463, agrees, and suggests that this type of tomb is suitable for "Essene-type" burial.

185. O. Röhrer-Ertl et al., "Über die Graberfelder von Khirbet Qumran, insbesondere die Funde der Campagne 1956, I: Anthropologische Datenvorlage und Erstauswertung aufgrund der Collectio Kurth," *RevQ* 19 (1999): 3–46.

186. S. Sheridan et al., "Anthropological Analysis of the Human Remains: The French Collection," in Humbert and Gunneweg, *Khirbet Qumrân et 'Aïn Feshkha*, 2:143. This article gives much-needed detail about the history of the skeletal remains from the cemeteries and the difficulties entailed in analyzing them.

187. B. Schultz calculates that there were only five women and no children ("The Qumran Cemetery," *DSD* 13 [2006]: 219).

188. Norton, "Reassessment of Controversial Studies," 123. Since Norton's publication, the salvage excavation in the North Cemetery pushes the number of males relative to females even higher.

khirbeh and the caves. The female skeletons may be explained as secondary burials or post-68 CE inhumations.

The final phenomenon that I wish to discuss regarding the cemeteries is the presence of evidently empty graves (i.e., tombs in which human remains were not present). The first empty grave was excavated by Poole in 1856. One of Steckoll's eleven graves was empty.[189] Finally, four out of the nine graves dug by Magen and Peleg were empty. However, in two of these tombs fourteen jars sealed with lids were discovered, which evidently contained date honey. These jars date from the end of the second or beginning of the first century BCE. Magen and Peleg suggest that they were buried because the contents had become impure due to corpse contamination, but this is speculative.[190]

Several explanations have been offered for these empty tombs. One is that the contents were robbed in antiquity. This is always possible, but since most of the graves were undisturbed, it seems unlikely. Magen and Peleg suggest that they were "superfluous" graves, dug for those killed in war at the beginning of the Hasmonean period, but then unused.[191] Since there is no other evidence from the cemetery that the bodies were victims of military conflict (none of the skeletons carry wounds from armed conflict, and no military grave goods were associated with the bodies), this military explanation must be rejected. Taylor suggests that the graves were used to bury scrolls that were old, worn out, or perhaps rejected for their contents, and their organic remains have decayed beyond detection.[192] This theory is possible but unprovable for now, since the soil from the excavated graves was not retained. The reason for the empty graves remains uncertain.

Conclusions

What, then, does the archaeological evidence tell us about Khirbet Qumran in the Second Temple period? In some ways it is easier to determine

189. Steckoll, "Preliminary Excavation Report," 327–28.

190. Magen and Peleg, "Back to Qumran," 98.

191. Magen and Peleg, "Back to Qumran," 98.

192. J. Taylor, "Buried Manuscripts and Empty Tombs: The Qumran *Genizah* Theory Revisited," in *"Go Out and Study the Land" (Judges 18:2): Archaeological, Historical and Textual Studies in Honor of Hanan Eshel*, ed. A. M. Maeir et al., JSJSup 148 (Leiden: Brill, 2012), 288–90.

THE QUMRAN EVIDENCE

what Qumran was *not*, rather than what it was. It was not a fortress; the only part of the khirbeh that was fortified was the watchtower and the outer wall of the main building. Otherwise the buildings were unfortified and open to attack. Further, no concentrations of military gear or weapons were found.[193] It was not a village; there were no family dwellings, and the only evidence for the presence of women and children at the site, which should be there in abundance if Qumran were a village, is two female burials in the main cemeteries. It was not a pottery production center; while pottery was certainly made there, there is no clay source suitable for large-scale pottery production in the vicinity, and the type of pottery manufactured there was plain and utilitarian, with no "luxury" forms. Most tellingly, the hole-mouthed cylindrical jar form, which is found in quantity at the site and was made there, is glaringly absent elsewhere in Judea. If Qumran was a pottery manufacturing center, why would it not be exporting its major product around the region?

Qumran was also not a Hasmonean villa. Although its main building was built on the footprint of a Hasmonean villa, it has none of the other features of that type of villa, such as mosaic floors, frescoes, luxury water installations, or a triclinium. The few architectural and decorative elements that may have belonged to a villa were found only in secondary contexts, that is, as part of fills, incorporated into later walls, or reused in other ways.[194] In addition, there should be evidence for the presence of women at any kind of villa, evidence that Qumran sorely lacks. Thus the totality of the data argues against Qumran being a villa.

Stacey's thesis that Qumran was an annex of the royal estate at Jericho, established to undertake seasonal industries, at least has the merit of considering the generally poor construction of the buildings, the elaborate water system, and the absence of women from the site. However, this theory, like the others listed above, falters on the fact that it dismisses the caves and the scrolls found in them as at best secondary to other evidence. But as we have seen in ch. 4, the caves (especially the marl terrace caves) and their scrolls are an integral part of the archaeological evidence of the site and must be part of any interpretation concerning the purpose and function of Qumran. When the caves and the scrolls are added into the evidence, what can be said about Qumran on the basis of the archaeological data alone?

193. See also Magness, "Was Qumran a Fort?"
194. Mizzi, "Qumran Period I Reconsidered," 33.

The Archaeology of Qumran

First, Qumran is some kind of community settlement. There are no private dwellings; the inhabitants worked and ate together in the buildings, and slept in the second stories or in the marl terrace caves.[195] The inhabitants were men; if any women were present at all it was in incredibly small numbers or for short periods of time.

Second, Jewish names found on the inscriptions indicate that these were Jewish men (not surprising, given Qumran's location). The languages of the scrolls (majority Hebrew/Aramaic) and their contents also indicate a Jewish site. Further, the presence of large-capacity stepped pools that could have been used for ritual immersion indicates a concern with the Jewish laws of purity.

Third, various small-scale industrial and agricultural activities took place at Qumran.[196] There is evidence for animal husbandry, given the presence of stables. Date honey was apparently produced, perhaps in sufficient quantities for local trade or export. The making of pottery was an important activity, certainly for the needs of the community and possibly for local trade (although they evidently did not export their cylindrical jars). Finally, there is evidence for scroll manufacture, copying, and repair. In the caves, in addition to the scrolls themselves, blank pieces of parchment, leather thongs and tabs, and ink stirrers were discovered. Inkwells were found in the ruins, and the two abecedaries and the student exercise found among the inscriptions argue for the presence of apprentice scribes at the site. In addition, we have identified a possible library complex in the main building, alongside a scroll workshop. All of this evidence points to a population of scholar-scribes that resided at Qumran and worked with the scrolls that were found there.

Finally, the site of Qumran contains some interesting anomalies (not least of which are the scrolls found in the caves surrounding the site). The cemetery contains twelve hundred fairly uniform graves (excluding those graves that are late intrusions), which are characterized by a north-south orientation, lack of grave goods, very few women, and no children. The animal bone remains mixed with ash and pottery and found deposited in open areas around the buildings point to ritual meals, if not actual sacrifices. The presence of a large number of water installations suitable for use

195. It is possible that temporary tents or huts were used, but this would only be on "overflow" occasions.
196. This is especially true if 'Ain Feshkha is considered as part of the larger Qumran site.

215

THE QUMRAN EVIDENCE

as mikvaoth indicates a concern for ritual purity. All of these features point to a "religious sensibility" in the inhabitants.[197] The absence of women, and the generally "poor" construction of the buildings and the material remains (including the pottery), also must be accounted for in any final interpretation of the site.

Archaeology, however, does not tell us who dwelt there, or what exactly their relationship was to the scrolls in the caves. We cannot tell, from the archaeological evidence alone, whether the inhabitants were Essenes, Sadducees, Pharisees, or something else entirely. For that we must turn, in the next two chapters, to the evidence of the scrolls themselves and to the outside sources.

---

197. The phrase is Berlin's ("Jewish Life," 466).

Figure 1. Cave 1

Figure 2. Scroll jars

Figure 3. Wadi Qumran

Figure 4. Cave locations

Figure 5. Cave 4 interior

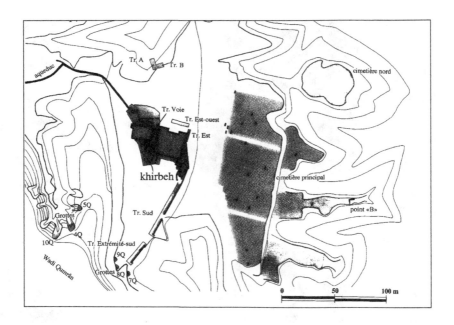

Figure 6. Qumran site plan

Figure 7. Aerial image

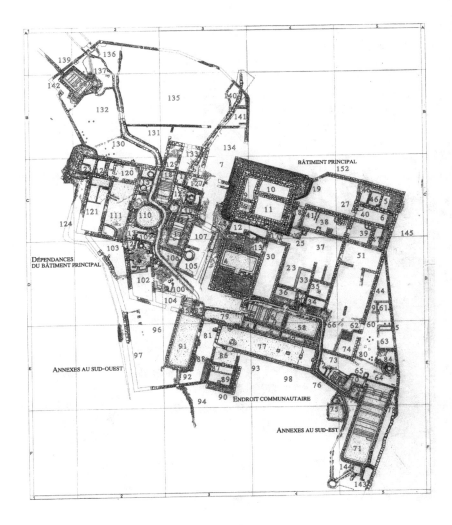

Figure 8. Plan IB

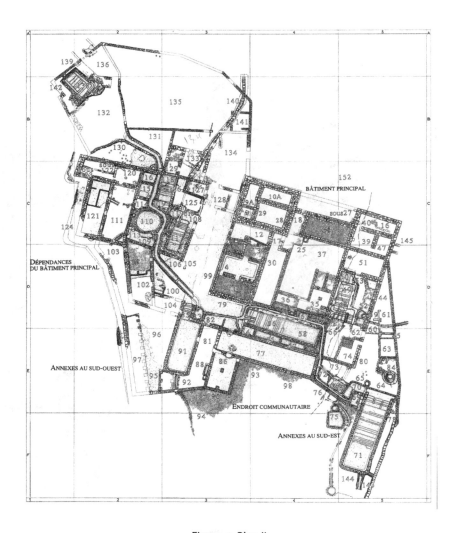

Figure 9. Plan II

Figure 10. Loci 2–4

Figure 11. Locus 4

Figure 12. Locus 30

Figure 13. Plastered tables

Figure 14. Inkwells

CHAPTER 6

The Qumran Scrolls Collection:
A Scribal Library with a Sectarian Component

> The general membership will be diligent together for the first third of every night of the year, reading aloud from the Book, interpreting Scripture and praying together.
>
> (1QS 6:7–8)

In ch. 4 I introduced the manuscripts of the Qumran library as part of the exploration of the archaeology of the caves, and I argued that similarities among the scrolls across the caves, both in content and materiality, bound them together as one collection. In this chapter I focus on the content of the scrolls and what those contents reveal about the group to which they belonged. Then I continue with a discussion of their material characteristics (i.e., paleographic dates, etc.).

The Contents of the Qumran Scroll Collection

The Qumran scroll collection can be characterized as a scribal collection, reflecting the concerns and interests of a community of scholar-scribes, especially as the role of scholar-scribes is laid out in the Second Temple period books encountered in ch. 3. Further, the contents of the scrolls demonstrate that the scribes who collected them belonged to a particular wing of Judaism; that is, the Qumran scrolls, while containing literature belonging to what may be termed general Judaism of the Second Temple period, also contain literature identified as the product of a self-differentiated wing within Second Temple Judaism, the Essenes (as I will demonstrate in ch. 7).

One can classify the contents of the Qumran library in several ways: by age, by language, by script, by contents, or by genre.[1] The last is always

---

1. For example, D. Dimant uses a division of five distinct groups for the scrolls: biblical

THE QUMRAN EVIDENCE

risky, since the idea of genre is relatively recent and foreign to ancient Judaism. Therefore, any attempt to separate the scrolls by genre or even the looser term *category* is open to criticism; on the other hand, it serves as an important heuristic device in any description of the scrolls collection. We will work within the four broad categories established in the introduction and used in ch. 4: the classical literature of ancient Judaism, composed before the third century BCE; the sectarian literature, that is, works reflecting the particular vocabulary, ideas, and beliefs of the wing of Judaism that collected the Qumran library; affiliated texts, that is, works bearing a special affinity for the sectarian community that collected them; and nonsectarian works composed in the Hellenistic-Roman period. What immediately becomes evident from surveying the collection according to these categories is that the library is dominated by the classical literature and the sectarian and affiliated texts. Working with the figure of 823 manuscripts that can be categorized,[2] the classical literature makes up 25.7 percent of the collection, sectarian manuscripts 25.5 percent, affiliated texts 17.6 percent, and finally nonsectarian Hellenistic-Roman literature 18.3 percent. Texts that are either too fragmentary to categorize or do not fall into any of the four categories (e.g., documentary texts) total 12.7 percent. Thus the classical texts and the sectarian and affiliated literature make up close to 70 percent of the Qumran library, indicating its nature as a deliberate collec-

---

manuscripts, sectarian literature, nonsectarian texts, intermediary texts, and Aramaic texts. This is a mixture of contents, language, and age ("The Qumran Manuscripts: Contents and Significance," in *History, Ideology and Bible Interpretation in the Dead Sea Scrolls: Collected Studies*, FAT 90 [Tübingen: Mohr Siebeck, 2014], 31). The main difficulty with her classification is that it makes the Aramaic texts a separate category. This separation by language blurs the fact that the Aramaic texts also belong, by content, in her other categories, with the exception of the sectarian literature. I do not separate the Aramaic texts from my other categories, since it is evident that Jewish literature in the Second Temple period was composed both in Hebrew and in Aramaic. I will discuss the Aramaic texts separately as important evidence for the scribal nature of the Qumran collection.

2. This figure comes from the tables in Dimant, "Qumran Manuscripts," 41–56. My percentages differ from Dimant's (56) because I categorize the texts differently. Since I eliminate the Aramaic texts as a separate category and place them in the other four categories, the result is a higher number of texts in three categories: classical texts (+ 7), nonsectarian texts (+ 7), and affiliated texts (+ 75). The last number is particularly striking, since that increase in the number of texts demonstrating affiliation with sectarian thought gives a more partisan picture to the library as a whole. In addition, I categorize some individual texts differently than does Dimant; a major example is the calendar and *mishmarot* texts, which I include under affiliated texts, given that they contain no sectarian language.

The Qumran Scrolls Collection: A Scribal Library with a Sectarian Component

tion reflecting the particular predilections of a specific wing of Judaism in the Second Temple period.

To reinforce this point, I begin with a description of the literature within each category. This description is followed by a discussion of particularly scribal concerns demonstrated in those texts. I end the chapter with physical evidence from the manuscripts that might aid in an identification of the inhabitants of Qumran and their activities there.

The Classical Literature

The classical literature of ancient Judaism makes up approximately 25 percent of the Qumran library.[3] At least one copy of every book that later became part of the Jewish canon, with the exception of Esther,[4] was found in Cave 4Q, and copies of at least some of the classical books were found in all the manuscript caves. Thus we can assume that the collection and preservation of this literature was deemed important by this particular wing of Second Temple Judaism. Further, certain books, by the number of their copies, must have been especially important, for example, the books of the Torah (96 in total), especially Deuteronomy (32 copies); Isaiah (21 copies); and Psalms (36 copies).[5] These books are also the most frequently

---

3. Dimant, "Qumran Manuscripts," 34. E. Tov, *Textual Criticism of the Hebrew Bible*, 3rd ed. (Minneapolis: Fortress, 2012), 95, gives the figure 22 percent. Most of the works in the category "classical literature" later became part of the Jewish canon of Scripture, although other early (pre-third-century BCE) works such as Tobit are also included in this category.

4. The status of Esther at Qumran is debated. Its absence may simply be a result of the vicissitudes of time: some percentage of the original collection has been lost owing to cave collapse, animal depredations, and looting in earlier centuries. S. Talmon argued on the basis of vocabulary in surviving scrolls that Esther was known to the owners of the Qumran collection ("Was the Book of Esther Known at Qumran?," *ErIsr* 25 [1996]: 377–82). However, it is the case that no mention of Purim is made in any of the calendar texts, indicating that Esther may have been unknown to or rejected by this particular wing of Judaism.

5. It is not always evident whether a manuscript containing material from a particular classical book comprised a complete copy of that book. For example, 4QDeut^a consists of one fragment containing Deut 23:26–24:8. It cannot be determined whether or not that fragment was part of a complete copy of Deuteronomy. On the other hand, 4QDeut^c consists of 66 fragments, containing passages beginning in Deut 3 and ending in Deut 32. It is practically certain that 4QDeut^c was a complete scroll of Deuteronomy. Barring other evidence, the original editorial team classified manuscript fragments containing material from classical books as single copies of that book. As we will discuss below, it was later determined that some of these manuscripts contained excerpts from the classical books but were not complete copies of those books.

219

THE QUMRAN EVIDENCE

quoted or alluded to in other works in the collection. Thus by sheer numbers alone it is evident that the classical literature of ancient Judaism was an important aspect of the collection.

These classical texts make up the oldest part of the collection as well, according to their paleographic dates. The manuscripts dated to the Archaic period, 250–150 BCE,[6] include 4QExod^d, 4QExod-Lev^f, 4QDeut^a, 4QpaleoDeut^s, 4QSam^b, 4QJer^a, 4QJer^d, 4QpaleoJob^c, 4QQoh^a, 4QLXX-Deut, 5QDeut, 6QpaleoGen, and 6QpaleoLev.[7] These manuscripts were copied before the settlement came into existence; whether they were brought by the original inhabitants or carried in later is not known. However, they were preserved for over two centuries and stored at some point in Cave 4Q, indicating their importance to the inhabitants of Qumran.[8]

The list of the oldest classical manuscripts also indicates that the owners of the collection were gathering manuscripts in different scripts, Paleo-Hebrew and Aramaic square script, and in different languages, the original Hebrew as well as Greek and Aramaic translations. The following classical books were found in both Paleo-Hebrew and Aramaic square script: Genesis, Exodus, Leviticus, Deuteronomy, and Job.[9] Books found in languages

6. As defined by B. Webster, "Chronological Index of the Texts from the Judaean Desert," in *The Texts from the Judaean Desert: Indices and an Introduction to the Discoveries in the Judaean Desert Series*, ed. E. Tov, DJD 39 (Oxford: Clarendon, 2002), 358.

7. Webster, "Chronological Index," 371.

8. D. Stökl Ben Ezra, "Old Caves and Young Caves: A Statistical Reevaluation of a Qumran Consensus," *DSD* 14 (2007): 327-28, posits that there were two main deposits in Cave 4Q, one prior to 9–8 BCE and the second when the settlement was destroyed in 68 CE. This scenario relies on the suggestion of a destruction and short period of abandonment at Qumran in 9–8 BCE, which has now been superseded by the argument that there was only one long period of uninterrupted occupation at Qumran in the Second Temple period (see ch. 5). Further, the archaeological evidence from Cave 4Q, in which manuscripts of different paleographic dates seem to have been found at all levels of the cave, does not support Stökl Ben Ezra's "two deposit" theory. According to J. Taylor, "Buried Manuscripts and Empty Tombs: The Qumran *Genizah* Theory Revisited," in *"Go Out and Study the Land" (Judges 18:2): Archaeological, Historical and Textual Studies in Honor of Hanan Eshel*, ed. A. M. Maeir et al., JSJSup 148 (Leiden: Brill, 2012), 293–95, Cave 4Q was used as a genizah for scrolls awaiting proper burial. However, some of the types of manuscripts found in Cave 4Q would not be the type of text needing burial, e.g., 4Q477, "Rebukes Reported by the Overseer"; 4Q318, "Zodiology and Brontology ar"; or 4Q341, the scribal exercise "Exercitium Calami C." The presence of these and similar manuscripts in Cave 4Q indicates that the cave was not a temporary genizah facility, but must have had some other function.

9. That the Torah and Job are found in Paleo-Hebrew may be significant, since both

220

The Qumran Scrolls Collection: A Scribal Library with a Sectarian Component

besides their original Hebrew are Leviticus, Numbers, and Deuteronomy in Greek, and Leviticus and Job in Aramaic. The book of Tobit was found both in its original Aramaic and in a Hebrew translation. This variety of scripts and languages points to scribal interests, since well-trained scribes were masters of various scripts and languages.

Finally, the texts of these classical manuscripts also disclose the textual preoccupations of scribes. The manuscripts of the classical literature demonstrate textual variety; that is, different editions or recensions of these books were found side-by-side in the Qumran caves.[10] Famous examples include manuscripts that reflect the later Samaritan recension of the Torah, without the final Samaritan editorial layer: 4QpaleoExod^m, 4QExod-

---

are ascribed to Moses. See E. Tov, *Scribal Practices and Approaches Reflected in the Texts Found in the Judean Desert*, STDJ 54 (Leiden: Brill, 2004), 247. However, a fragmentary manuscript not related to the Torah or Job, 4Qpaleo paraJosh (4Q123), has also been discovered, so we cannot be sure that Paleo-Hebrew was limited to those particular books. P. Alexander has suggested that all the Paleo-Hebrew manuscripts originated in Jerusalem, but this cannot be proved ("Literacy Among Jews in Second Temple Palestine: Reflections on the Evidence from Qumran," in *Hamlet on a Hill: Semitic and Greek Studies Presented to Professor T. Muraoka on the Occasion of His Sixty-Fifth Birthday*, ed. M. F. J. Baasten and W. Th. van Peursen, OLA 118 [Leuven: Peeters, 2003], 20). Paleo-Hebrew was also used to write the divine name and for scribal markings in manuscripts. Several sectarian texts, e.g., 1QH^a, 1QpHab, 4QpIsa^a and 4QpPs^a, used Paleo-Hebrew for the divine name. See Tov, *Scribal Practices*, 206–8, 238–46.

10. See E. Tov, "Textual History of the Pentateuch," in *The Hebrew Bible*, vol. 1B: *Pentateuch and Former and Latter Prophets*, ed. A. Lange and E. Tov, Textual History of the Bible (Leiden: Brill, 2017), 18; the various articles of E. Ulrich collected in both *The Dead Sea Scrolls and the Origins of the Bible* (Grand Rapids: Eerdmans, 1999) and *The Dead Sea Scrolls and the Developmental Composition of the Bible*, VTSup 169 (Leiden: Brill, 2015); and A. Lange, "The Textual Plurality of Jewish Scriptures in the Second Temple Period in Light of the Dead Sea Scrolls," in *Qumran and the Bible: Studying the Jewish and Christian Scriptures in Light of the Dead Sea Scrolls*, ed. N. Dávid and A. Lange, CBET 57 (Leuven: Peeters, 2010), 43–96. It should be emphasized that the complete exemplars of the text of the Hebrew Bible to which the fragments are compared are relatively late products in the stream of textual tradition. Thus, when the Qumran manuscripts are compared to the Masoretic Text, the Septuagint, and the Samaritan Pentateuch and labeled, e.g., "proto-MT," "an example of the Vorlage of the Septuagint," or "a pre-SP text," the text critic is in essence moving in the wrong direction. A manuscript such as 4QpaleoExod^m is not really a "pre-SP" manuscript; it is part of the same stream of transmission that produced the Samaritan Pentateuch. S. W. Crawford, "Interpreting the Pentateuch through Scribal Processes: The Evidence from the Qumran Manuscripts," in *Insights into Editing in the Hebrew Bible and the Ancient Near East*, ed. R. Müller and J. Pakkala, CBET 84 (Leuven: Peeters, 2017), 61.

THE QUMRAN EVIDENCE

Lev^f, 4QReworked Pentateuch B (4Q364), and 4QNum^b.[11] The Hebrew text behind the LXX translation is found in 4QExod^b, 4QDeut^j, 4QDeut^q, 4QSam^a, 4QJer^b, 4QJer^d, and Ps 151 in 11QPs^a.[12] The proto-rabbinic recension, which became the basis for the MT, is well represented among the books; examples include 4QGen^b, 4QGen-Exod^a, 4QpaleoGen-Exod^l, 4QExod^c, 4QDeut^g, 1QIsa^b, 4QJer^a, 4QJer^c, 11QEzek, 4QPs^d, 4QPs^h, and 4QEzra.[13] Finally, many or most of the classical manuscripts from Qumran do not reflect any specific recension; that is, they either reflect an older form of a text before it split into textual families (such as 4QSam^b),[14] or their variants do not align neatly with any of the later recensions, or not enough of the text remains to determine its textual affiliation. Many of the Qumran classical text manuscripts fall into this category, including twenty-nine Pentateuch manuscripts, 4QJosh^a, 4QJudg^a, 1QIsa^a, the majority of the manuscripts of the Twelve (Minor) Prophets, and the majority of the manuscripts of the Ketuvim.[15]

This textual variety indicates that, at least for the collectors of the Qumran scrolls, no one text edition was favored over another. Indeed,

---

11. S. W. Crawford, "Samaritan Pentateuch," in *The Hebrew Bible*, vol. 1A: *Overview Articles*, ed. A. Lange and E. Tov, Textual History of the Bible (Leiden: Brill, 2016), 171.

12. E. Tov, "Septuagint," in Lange and Tov, *Overview Articles*, 208.

13. Tov distinguishes between manuscripts whose texts are close to the Masoretic recension ("M-like"), and manuscripts whose texts are identical to the consonantal text of the Masoretic recension (*Textual Criticism*, 31; "Textual History of the Pentateuch," 16). According to Tov, in the Qumran collection the texts that are close to but not equivalent to the Masoretic recension predominate, while in the other Judean Desert find sites only manuscripts with texts equivalent to the consonantal text of MT were found. Tov attributes this distribution to the promulgation of the consonantal proto-MT recension by the temple authorities in the first century CE before the temple's destruction by the Romans; thus the rebels at Masada, having fled Jerusalem, only had proto-MT recension manuscripts, which had been copied from a "master copy" kept in the temple. The inhabitants at Qumran, having a more antagonistic relationship with the temple authorities, remained open to other text editions. See, e.g., E. Tov, "A Qumran Origin for the Masada Non-Biblical Texts?," *DSD* 7 (2000): 61, 70–74. This scenario is possible but assumes more about the temple library than we really know, since all the information on which Tov bases his account is from later rabbinic material.

14. According to its editors, F. M. Cross, D. W. Parry, and R. J. Saley, "the readings of 4QSam^b agree with the Old Greek when it is superior, but agree with the Masoretic tradition when it is superior. We must add in some fifteen unique readings that are superior to both the Old Greek and M. These are marks of a remarkably pristine textual witness" (*Qumran Cave 4.XII: 1–2 Samuel*, DJD 17 [Oxford: Clarendon, 2005], 223).

15. Tov, *Scribal Practices*, 332–35.

222

The Qumran Scrolls Collection: A Scribal Library with a Sectarian Component

texts that we would identify as coming from different editions or recensions were used simultaneously, with no distinction made between them. For example, 4QTestimonia, a single-sheet collection of messianic quotations, uses a pre-Samaritan text for its quotation of Exod 20:21, a version close to MT for Num 24:15–17, and a text for Deut 33:8–11 that is closest to the text of 4QDeut^h, an unaffiliated scroll.[16] The existence of textual variety does not seem to have been a negative in the eyes of the owners of the scrolls. This points to the collection of scrolls being a learned scribal collection; it was a working library where different forms of the classical text tradition were preserved and used by the scribes who studied them.

Sectarian and Affiliated Texts

It is important to recognize that these two categories are intimately related to each other, and that, taken together, they make up approximately 43 percent of the Qumran library. The affiliated texts, although they do not contain distinct sectarian markers, were clearly of great importance in forming the thought of the sect. This is especially true for the Aramaic affiliated texts, many of which appear in multiple copies and are alluded to in the sectarian texts. While the sectarian texts do not seem to have circulated very far beyond the wing of Judaism that composed them,[17] the affiliated texts were more widely known in Judaism and in early Christianity.

Sectarian Texts

A certain core group of compositions found in the Qumran library are commonly agreed to be sectarian (see ch. 1). These include the Serek

---

16. See Tov, "Textual History of the Pentateuch," 18. In addition, A. Lange has demonstrated that in the biblical quotations and allusions preserved in other Qumran scrolls no specific text or textual group is preferred (*Handbuch der Textfunde vom Toten Meer*, vol. 1: *Die Handschriften biblischer Bücher von Qumran und den anderen Fundorten* [Tübingen: Mohr Siebeck, 2009], 158–68).

17. The exception to this is the Damascus Document, which was first discovered in two copies in a Karaite synagogue in Old Cairo.

THE QUMRAN EVIDENCE

Hayaḥad (S; Community Rule),[18] the Damascus Document (D),[19] the Serek Ha'edah (Sa; Rule of the Congregation), Miqṣat Ma'aśê ha-Torah (MMT), the Hodayot (H; the Thanksgiving Hymns), and the pesharim. Other works that are included in this group are the War Scroll and other texts concerning the eschatological conflict, and liturgical texts such as the Songs of the Sabbath Sacrifice, the Berakhot texts (4Q286–290), and the Rule of Blessings (1QSb).[20]

By investigating these texts, we can ascertain what sets them apart as well as their shared characteristics. From there we may extrapolate the particular interests of the movement or sect to which they owe their existence. First, what makes them sectarian? Using the criteria in the definition established in the introduction, it is evident that the community envisioned in these texts, especially in S, D, and Sa, is a voluntary associa-

---

18. When speaking of the Serek Hayaḥad I mean the collective tradition preserved in the Serek manuscripts found in Caves 1Q, 4Q, and 5Q, although the reference numbers will usually be to the most complete copy of that work, 1QS (with parallels when appropriate). S. Metso has shown that the Serek underwent growth and change, which is reflected in the textual traditions preserved in the Qumran manuscripts (*The Textual Development of the Qumran Community Rule*, STDJ 21 [Leiden: Brill, 1997]). J. Jokiranta has recently emphasized that the designation "Serek Hayaḥad" or "S" is a modern construction, and that not one of the manuscripts labeled "S" is an exact copy of another. She suggests that we conceptualize S as "a *family resemblance* concept that marks these manuscripts as related" ("What Is 'Serekh ha-Yahad [S]'? Thinking about Ancient Manuscripts as Information Processing," in *Sibyls, Scriptures, and Scrolls: John Collins at Seventy*, ed. J. Baden et al., 2 vols., JSJSup 175 [Leiden: Brill, 2017], 1:611–12, 624, 631). A. Schofield has proposed that different Essene communities in Judea preserved different versions of the Serek, which were united when Qumran became a collecting point for Essene manuscripts (*From Qumran to the Yahad: A New Paradigm of Textual Development for the Community Rule*, STDJ 77 [Leiden: Brill, 2009]).

19. "D" also refers to a family of manuscripts, the most complete copy of which is the Cairo Damascus copy (CD). This is the copy to which I will usually refer (with parallels when appropriate). The manuscripts of D, however, are more homogenous than the manuscripts of S.

20. The liturgical texts are notoriously difficult to categorize. For example, the editor of the Songs of the Sabbath Sacrifice, C. Newsom, is not convinced that they were sectarian ("'Sectually Explicit' Literature from Qumran," in *The Hebrew Bible and Its Interpreters*, ed. W. H. Propp, B. Halpern, and D. N. Freedman [Winona Lake, IN: Eisenbrauns, 1990], 179–85). D. Falk, on the other hand, argues that they are sectarian (*Daily, Sabbath, and Festival Prayers in the Dead Sea Scrolls*, STDJ 27 [Leiden: Brill, 1998], 126–29). I have included the Sabbath Songs under the sectarian rubric on the basis of the heading למשכיל at the beginning of each composition, since the Maskil was a leadership figure in the sectarian community.

224

The Qumran Scrolls Collection: A Scribal Library with a Sectarian Component

tion, one that the members have chosen to join. S begins with instructions to the leader:

> He is to induct all who volunteer to live by the laws of God into the Covenant of Mercy, so as to be joined to God's society and walk fault-less before Him, according to all that has been revealed for the times appointed them. (1QS 1:7–9)

It continues with instructions for entry into the (community's) covenant:

> All who enter the *Yahad*'s Rule shall be initiated into the Covenant be-fore God, agreeing to act according to all that He has commanded and not to backslide because of any fear, terror, or persecution that may occur during the time of Belial's dominion. While the initiates are being inducted into the Covenant, the priests and the Levites shall continu-ously bless the God of deliverance and all His veritable deeds. All the initiates into the Covenant shall continuously respond "Amen, amen." (1QS 1:16–20)[21]

The Damascus Document refers to "those entering the new covenant in the land of Damascus" (CD 6:19), while the Serek Ha'edah (which prescribes the rule for the "last days") requires instruction for "all the newcomers" or "all those who are entering" (את כול הבאים): "They shall be indoctri-nated in all of their laws, for fear that otherwise they may sin accidentally" (1QSa 1:5).

All the sectarian texts place a strong emphasis on boundaries between the members and outsiders. For example, S admonishes its adherents to "love all the Children of Light—each commensurate with his rightful place in the council of God—and to hate all the Children of Darkness, each com-mensurate with his guilt and the vengeance due him from God" (1QS 1:9–11). D opens with a call to the "sons of light" to separate from transgressors and to walk in "the path of integrity" or "the perfect way" (4QD[a] frag. 1a–b, frag. 2 i 4). It goes on to admonish its members "to separate from corrupt people [lit. "the sons of the Pit"], and to avoid filthy wicked lucre" (CD 6:14–15). When describing its legal positions to an unknown recipient,

---

21. The Berakhot texts appear to contain liturgy for this ceremony of entry into the cov-enant; 4Q286 7a ii b–d 1–6 and 4Q287 6 1–4 contain the line: "of the council of the commu-nity, all of them will say together: 'Amen. Amen,'" followed by curses on Belial and his lot.

225

THE QUMRAN EVIDENCE

MMT uses the terms "we," "you," and "them," distinguishing the writer(s) of the document from both the recipient and his followers and those whose legal rulings the writer opposes.[22] In its epilogue, MMT states, "We have separated ourselves from the multitude of the people [and from all their impurity] and from being involved with these matters and from participating with [them] in these things" (MMT[c] 7–8).[23] The pesharim also display a strong sense of group identity, and an equally strong sense of the opponents of the group, especially through its use of such sobriquets as the Teacher of Righteousness, the Wicked Priest, the Scoffer, and so on.

Rules of conduct for members, above and beyond a strict adherence to the commands of the Torah, are emphasized. This is self-evident in the rule texts S and D, both of which contain columns of material (the penal codes) regulating the conduct of their members.[24] Other more fragmentary texts, such as 4Q265, also illustrate these rules of conduct. One short text, Rebukes Reported by the Overseer (4Q477), actually contains a list of members who have violated the rules of the sect: "And Hananiah Notos was rebuked because he[. . . to dis]turb the spirit of the *Yah*[*ad*" (4Q477 2 ii 5–6).

Finally, there are procedures for entry into and expulsion from the sect. S contains the most information about entrance procedures. It opens with several columns of instruction on entry into "the Covenant." The Instructor/Sage or Maskil oversees the entrance procedures. The ceremony for entering the covenant involves a confession of sin, blessings on those within the covenant and curses on those outside, and a binding oath on

---

22. Although in its *editio princeps* MMT is described as a letter from the Teacher of Righteousness to the Wicked Priest (E. Qimron and J. Strugnell, *Qumran Cave 4.V: Miqṣat Ma'aśe ha-Torah*, DJD 10 [Oxford: Clarendon, 1994], 1), that identification was almost immediately called into question (see Strugnell, "Additional Observations on 4QMMT," in DJD 10, 204–5). Instead, MMT appears to be a hortatory document modeled on Deuteronomy (J. Strugnell, "MMT: Second Thoughts on a Forthcoming Edition," in *The Community of the Renewed Covenant: The Notre Dame Symposium on the Dead Sea Scrolls*, ed. E. Ulrich and J. VanderKam [Notre Dame: University of Notre Dame Press, 1994], 62–63). S. Fraade suggests that the numbers of copies in Cave 4Q indicate that the document was used as a text for intramural sectarian instruction during the life of the Qumran settlement ("To Whom It May Concern: 4QMMT and Its Addressee[s]," *RevQ* 19 [2000]: 524).

23. Unless otherwise noted, the form of reference to MMT and all translations of it are from Qimron and Strugnell, DJD 10.

24. While some of these rules differ in detail, there is enough overlap to be certain that the same sectarian movement is in view. For the differences and what they may signify, see ch. 7.

226

The Qumran Scrolls Collection: A Scribal Library with a Sectarian Component

the part of the new member. This "covenant renewal" ceremony is to take place each year, with new members admitted at this time (1QS 5:20–23). For the new member, there then seems to be a probationary period of instruction by the Guardian or Overseer (מבקר); the initiate must wait a year, and be examined by the congregation, before he can touch the "pure meal" (and other pure items) of the sect. After that first year, his property and earnings are registered with the sect. After a second full year and another examination, he becomes a full-fledged member, able to touch the pure liquids of the sect, give counsel, and have his property merged with that of the sect (1QS 6:13–23).

S also outlines, in its list of punishments for violations of the sect's rules, conduct that can lead to expulsion:

> [An]yone who speaks aloud the M[ost] Holy Name of God, [whether in . . .] or in cursing or as a blurt in time of trial or for any other reason, or while he is reading a book or praying, is to be expelled, never again to return to the party of the *Yahad*. (1QS 6:27–7:2)

> But if a man gossips about the general membership, he is to be banished from them and may never return. (1QS 7:16–17)

> The man who murmurs against the secret teachings of the *Yahad* is to be banished, never to return. (1QS 7:17)

> Any man who, having been in the party of the *Yahad* for ten full years, backslides spiritually so that he forsakes the *Yahad* and leaves the general membership, walking in his willful heart, may never again return to the party of the *Yahad*. (1QS 7:22–25)

The Damascus Document also outlines an entrance procedure into the covenant.[25] Here the leadership figure who oversees the procedure is

---

25. This entrance procedure is less elaborate than that of S, leading to arguments that it reflects either a different community or a different phase in the history of the community. While the differences between S and D are evident, their significance for a reconstruction of the practices of the community who owned both the S and D scrolls or its history remains unresolved. That copies of both S and D were deposited in the Qumran caves and contain important overlaps with each other indicates that the same Jewish movement composed and preserved them. For recent discussions see C. Hempel, *The Qumran Rule Texts in Context: Collected Studies*, TSAJ 154 (Tübingen: Mohr Siebeck, 2013); S. Hultgren, *From the*

THE QUMRAN EVIDENCE

the Guardian already encountered in S; the entrant swears an oath: "On the day he speaks to the Overseer of the general membership, they shall register him by the oath of the covenant that Moses made with Israel" (CD 15:7-9). There is no probationary period mentioned; however, if the new member transgresses, the Guardian is responsible for a year of instruction before the member can be fully reinstated (4Q266 8 i 4-6; 4Q270 6 ii 6-7). D also mentions the entrance of children into the sect;[26] "any children who reach the age to be included in the registrants, they shall impose the covenant oath upon them" (CD 15:5-6).

D also mentions the possibility of expulsion from the sect: the fragmentary 4QD[a] states, "If he bears malice in a capital matter he [shall] return [no] more" (4Q266 10 ii 1-2). Likewise, 4QD[e] reads, "[one who slanders the Many is to be expelled] and return no mo[re]" (4Q270 7 i 7-8; also 7 i 11). Very interestingly, 4QD[e] mentions the violation of sexual purity as a reason for expulsion: "One who comes near to fornicate [לזנות] with his wife contrary to the law shall depart and return no more" (4Q270 7 i 12-13).[27] Finally, 4QD[a] seems to outline a procedure for expulsion:

> And anyone who rejects these regulations, (which are) in accordance with all the statutes found in the law of Moses, shall not be reckoned among all the sons of his truth; for his soul has despised righteous instruction. Being in rebellion let him be expelled from the presence of the Many. The priest appointed [ov]er the Many shall declare . . . the one being expelled shall depart. (4Q266 11 5-8, 14)

Damascus Covenant to the Covenant of the Community: Literary, Historical, and Theological Studies in the Dead Sea Scrolls, STDJ 66 (Leiden: Brill, 2007); and J. J. Collins, "Sectarian Communities in the Dead Sea Scrolls," *OHDSS* 151-72.

26. Both D and Sa take for granted the presence of women and children in the sectarian community, and contain rules that pertain to them in various ways. S, on the other hand, does not mention women or children at all. As we have seen in ch. 5, the archaeological evidence does not support the presence of women at Qumran. This contradictory evidence has led some scholars to argue for two separate communities, or a "parent" movement and a "sect." The overlaps in S and D make it probable that they are the product of the same overall movement. How the two rule texts related to each other remain a matter of unresolved discussion (see above, nn24, 25).

27. For a discussion about the meaning of illicit intercourse with one's wife, see C. Wassén, *Women in the Damascus Document,* Academia Biblica 21 (Atlanta: Society of Biblical Literature, 2005), 173-84. The possibilities include intercourse during menstruation or pregnancy and/or nonprocreative intercourse.

The Qumran Scrolls Collection: A Scribal Library with a Sectarian Component

The Serek Ha'edah contains rules of entry for those born within the sect:

> From [early ch]ildhood each boy [is to be in]structed in the Book of Meditation [ו/ההגי]. As he grows older, they shall teach him the statutes of the Covenant, and he [will receive in]struction in their laws. Starting at age ten he is to be considered a youth. Then, at a[ge] twenty, [he shall be enrolled in] the ranks and take his place among the men of his clan, thereby joining the holy congrega[tion]. (1QSa 1:6–9)

There is no extant material about departure or expulsion in Sa, most likely because Sa describes the community in the eschatological age when such a possiblity is not envisioned.

The sectarian texts also contain a distinctive vocabulary, including epithets for the sect (יחד, עדה, עצת היחד, רבים); words describing the sect's officials (משכיל, מבקר, פקיד); titles for the sect's putative founder, the Teacher of Righteousness (מורה הצדק), and its enemies (הכוהן הרשע, מטיף הכזב, דורשי חלקות); and other distinctive terms such as פשרו ("its interpretation is"). The presence of these vocabulary words helps to determine sectarian provenance in otherwise fragmentary texts, for example, 4Q510–511, the Songs of the Maskil (Sage/Instructor).

The sectarian category includes legal texts containing explications of Torah commandments, such as D, MMT, 4QHalakha A and B (4Q251, 4Q264a), and 4QTohorot A, B, and C (4Q274, 4Q276–277, 4Q278). The Damascus Document contains both explications of Torah commandments and rules of conduct for members. The sectarian category also includes liturgical texts,[28] eschatological texts,[29] sapiential texts,[30] and exegetical works.[31] Many of these works were found in multiple copies and in more than one cave. The Serek Hayahad was found in twelve copies from Caves 4Q, 1Q, and 11Q. The Damascus Document was recovered in ten copies, in caves 4Q, 5Q, and 6Q. The Hodayot were found in twelve copies in Caves 4Q and 1Q, while the Sabbath Songs were retrieved from Caves 4Q and 11Q in nine copies. Twenty-six pesharim on various prophetic books and

---

28. The Hodayot and related works, including the Self-Glorification Hymn (4Q471b), the Songs of the Sabbath Sacrifice, the Berakhot, the Songs of the Maskil, Purification Rituals (4Q414, 4Q512, 4Q284), Communal Confession (4Q393), and the Ritual of Marriage (4Q502).

29. The War Scroll (1QM) and related texts.

30. E.g., 4QWords of the Maśkîl to All the Sons of Dawn.

31. The pesharim and the Commentary on Genesis A, B, and C, as well as more fragmentary texts.

THE QUMRAN EVIDENCE

Psalms were discovered in Caves 4Q, 1Q, 3Q, 5Q, and 11Q. The War Scroll and texts related to it were found in Caves 4Q, 1Q, and 11Q.[32] Other sectarian texts were found in multiple copies in Cave 4Q: MMT (five copies), Berakhot (five copies), and Commentary on Genesis (four copies).

To summarize, sectarian texts were discovered in every major manuscript cave except 2Q, and once again we see the centrality of Cave 4Q to the entire collection. There were multiple attestations of many of the sectarian texts, testifying to the importance of these works to the sect that collected them. Finally, an analysis of the paleography of these manuscripts indicates that no certain sectarian writing has survived in a copy earlier than the last quarter of the second century BCE, indicating that these manuscripts, at least, do not predate the founding of the settlement at Qumran by more than fifty years.[33]

EXCURSUS: WOMEN IN THE SECTARIAN TEXTS

Between the 1950s and 1980s, guided by the statements in Josephus, Philo, and Pliny that the Essenes avoided marriage, and the complete absence of any mention of women in the Serek Hayaḥad, the scholarly literature was replete with statements emphasizing the "celibacy" of the sect (identified with the Essenes) that inhabited Qumran. A representative quotation is from Geza Vermes:

32. As D. Dimant and others have noted, none of the 4Q manuscripts is a precise copy of 1QM ("The Composite Character of the Qumran Sectarian Literature as an Indication of Its Date and Provenance," *RevQ* 22 [2006]: 181).

33. Webster, "Chronological Index," 371–72. Some of the Cryptic A manuscripts are dated to the mid-third to late second century BCE, i.e., Midrash Sefer Moshe (4Q249), the Serek Ha'edah fragments (4Q249^{a-i}), and some smaller fragmentary texts that are difficult to identify (the remainder of the numbers 4Q249 and 4Q250). 4Q249 is dated by the title on the back of the scroll, which is written in Aramaic square script; this manuscript was also subject to carbon-14 testing, which produced a date range of 191–90 BCE (S. Pfann, "249. 4Qpap cryptA Midrash Sefer Moshe," in *Qumran Cave 4.XXV: Halakhic Texts*, by J. Baumgarten et al., DJD 35 [Oxford: Clarendon, 1999], 1–5). Midrash Sefer Moshe has no clear sectarian markers, but it is extremely fragmentary, and it is at least an affiliated text. For the Serek Ha'edah manuscripts, the editor states: "it is likely that . . . the nine 4QSE manuscripts, should be confined to dates ranging from the early second century BCE . . . to the end of the second century" (S. Pfann, *Qumran Cave 4.XXVI: Cryptic Texts*; and P. Alexander et al., *Miscellanea, Part 1*, DJD 36 [Oxford: Clarendon, 2000], 525). If Pfann's dating is correct, then these Serek Ha'edah fragments would be the earliest sectarian texts in the library.

230

It has long been debated whether the Qumran sectaries were married or celibate. From the image of their life projected so far, few will probably disagree that the idea of the presence of women among them appears incongruous. The impression received is that of a wholly masculine society: indeed, they were actually enjoined "not to follow a sinful heart and lustful eyes, committing all manner of evil" (1QS 1:6). Moreover, in support of the argument for celibacy, the word *ishah*, woman, occurs nowhere in the Community Rule.[34]

However, the discovery of female skeletons in the cemetery at Qumran, and the mention of women and children in the Damascus Document and the Serek Ha'edah, raised doubts about this "celibate" picture.

The debate was reopened by Eileen Schuller in a seminal article in 1994.[35] She argued that, based on the material concerning women in the Damascus Document and the Serek Ha'edah, it was evident that women were full members of the sect. Since that time the literature concerning women in the Qumran scrolls has grown apace.[36] The consensus now holds that the Qumran scrolls provide ample evidence for women (and children) as part of the sectarian community. A representative quotation comes from Schuller and Wassén:

> Most of the documents found in the Qumran caves that are about how daily life is to be lived according to the true interpretation of the Law of Moses contain some passages that discuss women. . . . It is clear that women were part of the life of the community or various communities that produced these texts.[37]

The sectarian texts D, Sa, and 4Q265 legislate for communities made up of families, while MMT, 4QTohorot A, and 4QRitual of Marriage (4Q502)

---

34. G. Vermes, *The Dead Sea Scrolls: Qumran in Perspective* (London: Collins, 1977), 96–97.

35. "Women in the Dead Sea Scrolls," in *Methods of Investigation of the Dead Sea Scrolls and the Khirbet Qumran Site: Present Realities and Future Prospects*, ed. M. Wise et al., ANYAS 722 (New York: New York Academy of Sciences, 1994), 115–32.

36. A representative sample includes E. Schuller and C. Wassén, "Women," *EDSS* 2:981–84; Wassén, *Women in the Damascus Document*; S. W. Crawford, "Not According to Rule: Women, the Dead Sea Scrolls and Qumran," in *Emanuel: Studies in Hebrew Bible, Septuagint and Dead Sea Scrolls in Honor of Emanuel Tov*, ed. S. Paul et al., VTSup 94 (Leiden: Brill, 2003), 127–50; and T. Ilan, "Women in Qumran and the Dead Sea Scrolls," *OHDSS* 123–50.

37. Schuller and Wassén, "Women," 981.

THE QUMRAN EVIDENCE

all refer to women and/or marital life. S is the only sectarian rule text that does not contain legislation for women and family life. Therefore, the only reasonable conclusion to draw is that the wing of Judaism represented in the sectarian texts included the active and meaningful presence of women. However, this evidence has proved difficult to reconcile with the almost complete absence of evidence in the form of gendered female objects for the presence of women in the buildings of the Qumran settlement. That contradiction must be resolved before a complete picture of life at Qumran can be drawn. We return to this question in chs. 7 and 8.

Affiliated Works

This category of manuscripts is extremely important for understanding the nature of the Qumran library. These compositions share a certain constellation of traits: an interest in calendaric matters, in particular calendars based on the 364-day solar year and the proper dating of Israel's holy days; legal interpretation that resembles legal interpretation in the sectarian texts; revelation placed in the mouths of the remote ancestors of Israel (i.e., Enoch and his descendants and the patriarchs, in particular Levi), which is then passed on in *written* as opposed to oral form from father to son; and an eschatological, apocalyptic worldview that includes a much expanded angelology.[38] Many of these texts were written in Aramaic, the common scribal language of learning in the early Second Temple period. However, these texts lack the specific sectarian markers we have isolated in our definition of the sectarian literature. Nevertheless, some of the works in this category are among the most prominent in the library, as we outline below.

The books of Enoch, including the Book of the Giants, survived in twenty-one copies, more than many books of the classical literature, and were found in Caves 4Q and 7Q. The Astronomical Book (roughly equivalent to 1 En. 72–82) contains the oldest Jewish calendar calculations, and describes a 364-day solar calendar with lunar months, the basis for the

38. See B. Reynolds, "A Dwelling Place of Demons: Demonology and Apocalypticism in the Dead Sea Scrolls," in *Apocalyptic Thinking in Early Judaism*, ed. S. W. Crawford and C. Wassén, JSJSup 182 (Leiden: Brill, 2018), 23–54.

The Qumran Scrolls Collection: A Scribal Library with a Sectarian Component

calendar in several sectarian works. The other booklets (i.e., the Book of the Watchers, the Dream Visions, the Epistle of Enoch, and the Book of Giants) place revelation in the mouth of the remote ancestor Enoch, and describe him as a scribe (ספרא) with far-ranging functions. Thus it is not surprising that Enoch and his books would have a position of prominence in the collection of a community that had a strong scribal element. The books of Enoch are also alluded to in the sectarian texts; for example, the Damascus Document mentions the Watchers and their offspring (CD 2:18–19).

Eighteen manuscripts of the book of Jubilees and the related Pseudo-Jubilees were recovered from Caves 4Q, 1Q, 2Q, 3Q, and 11Q. Jubilees polemicizes in favor of a 364-day calendar, features special revelation to Israel's ancestors, and emphasizes the passing on of these revelations from father to son *in writing*, as in Enoch. Jubilees is referred to by name in the Damascus Document (CD 16:2–4),[39] and possibly in CD 10:7–10. The Commentary on Genesis A seems to know the chronology of the flood given in Jubilees (Jub 5:23–27), although it corrects it (4Q252 1, 2 i 4–12).

The Aramaic Levi Document (ALD), which also embraces a 364-day calendar, was found in seven copies in Caves 4Q and 1Q. It too is alluded to in the Damascus Document (CD 4:15). The ALD also emphasizes the transmission of revealed teaching in writing through the Levitical line. Along with the ALD, other fragmentary Aramaic texts discovered in Cave 4Q concern the line of Levi and its teachings: the Visions of Amram (seven copies; 4Q543–549), the Testament of Qahat (4Q542), and two copies of a Levi Apocryphon (4Q540–541).

The book of Daniel carries tremendous importance in the Qumran library. Fragments of eight copies of the canonical book were found in Caves 4Q, 1Q, and 6Q, along with four related texts from Cave 4Q: Pseudo-Daniel[a-c] (4Q243–245) and an Aramaic Apocalypse (the so-called Son of God text, 4Q246). The Prayer of Nabonidus (4Q242), while not naming Daniel explicitly, is widely understood as a source for Dan 4. Daniel's apocalyptic thought and angelology made a strong impact on the sectarian literature. The sectarians also seem to have adopted vocabulary found in

---

39. But see D. Dimant, "Two 'Scientific' Fictions: The So-Called Book of Noah and the Alleged Quotation of Jubilees in CD 16:3–4," in *Studies in the Hebrew Bible, Qumran, and the Septuagint: Essays Presented to Eugene Ulrich on the Occasion of His Sixty-Fifth Birthday*, ed. P. W. Flint et al., VTSup 101 (Leiden: Brill, 2006), 353–68.

233

THE QUMRAN EVIDENCE

Daniel and expanded it. The pesher form of interpretation, so widespread in the sectarian texts, is found in Dan 9:2, 24–27. The word רבים, a sectarian vocabulary word, is used in Daniel to describe the remnant who will receive Daniel's teaching at the end time (12:3). Most importantly, Daniel uses the term משכילים ("the wise"; 11:35; 12:3) for those who will teach wisdom at the end of days. The term משכיל functions as a substitute for סופר ("scribe") in Daniel (see 1:4; 12:3, 10), while it is used for the most important teaching official in the sectarian texts, which also avoid the term סופר (see 1QS 3:13; 9:12, 21; 1QSb 1:1; 3:22; 5:20; CD 12:12; 13:22; 1QH^a 5:12; 7:20, 21; and numerous other examples). The reason why the sectarians avoid the word סופר and preferred משכיל is uncertain; it may be that they wished to differentiate their own scholar-scribes from other scribes active in the Second Temple period.

Two previously unknown yet extensive wisdom texts, Instruction and Mysteries, also number among the affiliated texts. Although these two compositions are often placed among the sectarian texts,[40] they do not contain explicit sectarian markers and thus are best placed among the affiliated texts.[41]

Instruction was discovered in six fragmentary manuscripts from Caves 4Q and 1Q (1Q26, 4Q415–418, 4Q423), which date from the late first century BCE to the early first century CE. It consists of long admonitions interspersed with reflective passages addressed to a מבין, "understanding one."[42] Instruction combines an apocalyptic worldview with traditional wisdom topics. Much of the work is concerned with wisdom topics such as family relations, finances, social relations, and study and instruction. However, these topics are placed in a framework of heavenly revelation and eschatology reminiscent of the apocalyptic setting of the wisdom teachings in Enoch. This heavenly revelation is summed up in the phrase רז נהיה, "the mystery that is to be." This phrase, which occurs twenty times in the text, indicates the divine plan that gives order to the cosmos and to

---

40. E.g., D. Dimant, "The Vocabulary of the Qumran Sectarian Texts," in *History, Ideology and Bible Interpretation*, 91–93; D. Harrington, "Wisdom Texts," *EDSS* 2:977.

41. See also M. Goff, *Discerning Wisdom: The Sapiential Literature of the Dead Sea Scrolls*, VTSup 116 (Leiden: Brill, 2007), 62 and 65n218, who notes that there is no citation of Instruction in the sectarian literature; and A. Lange, "Wisdom Literature and Thought in the Dead Sea Scrolls," *OHDSS* 459.

42. מבין appears several times in the plural, indicating a group audience. Remarkably, 4Q415 2 ii is addressed to a woman, a unique occurrence in Jewish wisdom texts. See B. G. Wright III, "Wisdom and Women at Qumran," *DSD* 11 (2004): 252–53.

The Qumran Scrolls Collection: A Scribal Library with a Sectarian Component

history.[43] The רז נהיה can be learned through study and contemplation by the מבין himself.[44] This concept of the רז also appears in the books of Daniel and Enoch, and in the sectarian compositions Damascus Document, Serek Hayaḥad, Pesher Habakkuk, and the Hodayot, linking Instruction to these works.

The book of Mysteries is found in four manuscripts from Caves 4Q and 1Q (1Q27, 4Q299–301), all copied from the late first century BCE to the early first century CE. It combines sapiential thought with an apocalyptic worldview and an interest in priestly matters.[45] As Goff notes, Mysteries contains a deterministic theology that results in the ultimate obliteration of the wicked, a mind-set congenial to the sectarians.[46] Mysteries also refers to the רז נהיה, connecting it to Instruction and the sectarian texts mentioned above.

Many other works fall under the rubric "affiliated texts." The Temple Scroll (11QT^{a-c}, 4Q524) embraces a 364-day calendar, contains festivals evidently observed by the sectarians (e.g., the festivals of New Oil and New Wine), and agrees with sectarian legislation in many important points,[47] yet lacks specific sectarian markers. The New Jerusalem text (seven copies found in Caves 4Q, 1Q, 2Q, 5Q, and 11Q) is an Aramaic revelatory text in which an unknown visionary is taken on a tour through an ideal Jerusalem. The Genesis Apocryphon, an Aramaic text from Cave 1Q, combines material from Enoch and Jubilees to renarrate the events leading to Noah and the flood in its first half, and translates the story of Abraham from the original Hebrew in Genesis in its second half, with embellishments.[48]

This survey demonstrates the importance of the affiliated texts to the Qumran library as a whole. Most of these texts are found in multiple copies (e.g., Enoch, Jubilees, ALD, Daniel, Instruction), often in more copies

---

43. Goff, *Discerning Wisdom*, 10, 21.

44. Unlike in many apocalyptic compositions, no otherworldly mediator is necessary. See Goff, *Discerning Wisdom*, 22.

45. Lange, "Wisdom Literature and Thought," suggests that it was written in the Jerusalem temple, but this is highly speculative. Alternatively Goff, *Discerning Wisdom*, 99, places Mysteries in the sectarian category.

46. Goff, *Discerning Wisdom*, 69.

47. For example, the Temple Scroll legislation prohibits uncle-niece marriage (11QT^a 66:15–17); this practice becomes the subject of polemic in the Damascus Document (CD 5:7–11).

48. Other works in this category include the Apocryphon of Joshua (three copies; quoted in 4QTestimonia), the Apocryphon of Jeremiah C (seven copies), the Elect of God text (three copies), Four Kingdoms (two copies), and the Words of Michael (three copies).

THE QUMRAN EVIDENCE

than most of the books in the classical literature category. They are found in every major manuscript cave, 4Q, 1Q, 2Q, 3Q, 5Q, 6Q, and 11Q, as well as 7Q. Paleographically they date from the third century BCE (4Q208, a manuscript of the Astronomical Book) to the early first century CE. When combined with the sectarian texts, they make up almost half of the library, giving that library a unique coloring that indicates it is the possession of a particular wing of Judaism, a sect, that collected it at Qumran for reasons we delve into in part III.

Nonsectarian Compositions in the Hellenistic-Roman Period

This final category makes up approximately 18 percent of the library. A major group of texts in this category are parabiblical works in Hebrew; these texts use a biblical (classical) character or event as a jumping-off point for the composition. They include the Apocryphon of Moses and other apocryphal Moses texts (seven copies from Caves 4Q, 1Q, and 2Q); the pseudo-Ezekiel texts (six copies from Cave 4Q), 1QNoah (two copies from Cave 1Q), and the Apocryphal Jeremiah (two copies from Cave 4Q). A striking feature of this group is the number of single-copy works (all from Cave 4Q): Admonition on the Flood (4Q370), Text Mentioning the Flood (4Q577), Exposition on the Patriarchs (4Q464), Text concerning Rachel and Joseph (4Q474), Paraphrase of Genesis and Exodus (4Q422), Vision of Samuel (4Q160), Paraphrase of Kings (4Q382), Apocryphon of Elisha (4Q481a), and Text Mentioning Zedekiah (4Q470). There was an Apocryphal Samuel–Kings found in Cave 6Q (6Q9), and a copy of the Epistle of Jeremiah was found in Cave 7Q (7Q2). That all of these works were found only in single copies, most from Cave 4Q, points to the "collecting" aspect of the library; these works were collected by the group that owned the library, perhaps to ensure the completeness of the collection, or perhaps because the copy was brought in from outside and stored in the library.[49]

Another group in this category is the sapiential literature. One copy of Ben Sira was unearthed in Cave 2Q (2Q18). Other previously unknown sapiential texts, all single copies from Cave 4Q, include the Wiles of the Wicked Women (4Q184), Sapiential Work (4Q185), Instruction-Like Com-

---

49. A word of caution is in order here. Many of these manuscripts are so fragmentary that it is difficult to ascertain their subjects and contents. Therefore, when whole these compositions may have looked very different and belonged to different categories.

236

The Qumran Scrolls Collection: A Scribal Library with a Sectarian Component

position B (4Q424), the Two Ways (4Q473), and Beatitudes (4Q525). A small Aramaic wisdom text also belongs here (4Q563). Again, the existence of these single copies demonstrates the collecting aspect of the library.

There is an important group of single-copy Aramaic texts, which do not bear any indications of affinity to the sectarian texts, but demonstrate the learned scribal character of the library. Two literary texts, the Prayer of Nabonidus (4Q242, mentioned above) and 4QJews at the Persian Court (4Q550), are works from the royal courtier tale genre. The Prayer of Nabonidus was probably a source for Dan 4, while Jews at the Persian Court resembles the book of Esther in its setting. These two compositions indicate the rich nature of Jewish Aramaic narrative works of the period. A special subset of the nonsectarian Aramaic texts are the esoteric texts (4Q318, 560, and 561), discussed in more detail below.

Finally, many of the hymns, prayers, and liturgies discovered in the Qumran caves fall into the nonsectarian category. These include, to name only a few, the Non-Canonical Psalms (4Q88, 380–381), Festival Prayers (1Q34, 4Q505/509, 507, 508), Works of God (4Q392), and the Words of the Luminaries (4Q504, 506).[50] A subset of liturgical texts involves magic or divination: Apocryphal Psalms[a] (11Q11), 4QCurses (4Q280), 5QCurses (5Q14), 4QIncantation (4Q444), and two apotropaic hymn fragments (6Q18 and 8Q5).[51] However, two caveats are in order when discussing the liturgical texts. First, these texts are extremely difficult to categorize as sectarian or nonsectarian, and the status of several is disputed.[52] Second, regardless of whether a specific hymn or prayer was composed by a sectarian, their presence in the library, and especially in Cave 4Q, may indicate that they were adopted and used by the sectarians in their liturgical practices.[53]

---

50. See further the listing in *DSSR* 2:viii–ix: Fragmentary Poetic or Liturgical Texts.

51. E. Eshel, "Apotropaic Prayers in the Second Temple Period," in *Liturgical Perspectives: Prayer and Poetry in Light of the Dead Sea Scrolls; Proceedings of the Fifth International Symposium of the Orion Center for the Study of the Dead Sea Scrolls and Associated Literature, 19–23 January, 2000*, ed. E. Chazon, STDJ 48 (Leiden: Brill, 2003), 69–88.

52. E.g., the Songs of the Sabbath Sacrifice, Barkhi Nafshi, and Daily Prayers (4Q503). See Falk, *Daily, Sabbath, and Festival Prayers*, 21–22, 29, 126; E. Chazon, "Shifting Perspectives on Liturgy at Qumran and in Second Temple Judaism," in *The Dead Sea Scrolls in Context: Integrating the Dead Sea Scrolls in the Study of Ancient Texts, Languages, and Cultures*, ed. A. Lange et al., 2 vols., VTSup 140 (Leiden: Brill, 2011), 2:516; and E. Chazon, "Is *Divrei Ha-me'orot* a Sectarian Prayer?," in *The Dead Sea Scrolls: Forty Years of Research*, ed. D. Dimant and U. Rappaport (Leiden: Brill, 1992), 3–17.

53. E. Chazon, "Psalms, Hymn, and Prayers," *EDSS* 2:714.

THE QUMRAN EVIDENCE

This survey of the Qumran collection demonstrates the extraordinarily varied nature of the Qumran library, as well as its learned, elite quality. However, some Jewish works from the Second Temple period that might have been expected in such a collection are absent. With the exception of one copy of the Epistle of Jeremiah, found in Cave 7Q, there are no works of the Hellenistic diaspora found at Qumran (e.g., the Wisdom of Solomon). In addition, works primarily concerned with or supportive of the Maccabean/Hasmonean family, such as 1 and 2 Maccabees or Judith, are conspicuously absent, again with the possible exception of 4QPrayer for (or against) King Jonathan (4Q448). These absences point against the collection simply being scrolls brought down from several libraries in Jerusalem at the time of the First Jewish Revolt, or deposited in the caves by the temple authorities.[54] Further, the preponderance of sectarian and affiliated texts demonstrates that those who collected the library belonged to a particular wing of Judaism with very particular interests, interests reflected in the scrolls collected by them.

Texts That Indicate a Particular Scribal Interest

In this section I discuss different groups of texts that demonstrate a particularly scribal interest, as I have defined those interests in ch. 3. These groups of texts include excerpted texts, calendars and *mishmarot*, esoteric texts and lists, the Aramaic texts, texts written in a cryptic script, and scribal exercises. In some cases, we can witness scribal work on texts that help to demonstrate that the Qumran collection was a living collection, not simply a depository for collected texts or a genizah for manuscripts no longer in circulation.

Excerpted Texts

One subgroup of the classical manuscripts, the "excerpted" texts, demonstrates in a concrete way the activity of scribes. An "excerpted" text, as its

---

54. N. Golb, *Who Wrote the Dead Sea Scrolls? The Search for the Secret of Qumran* (New York: Scribner, 1995); and D. Stacey, "A Reassessment of the Stratigraphy of Qumran," in *Qumran Revisited: A Reassessment of the Archaeology of the Site and Its Texts*, ed. D. Stacey and G. Doudna, BARIS 2520 (London: Archeopress, 2013), 63.

The Qumran Scrolls Collection: A Scribal Library with a Sectarian Component

name suggests, contains one or more scriptural passages collected on a single manuscript.[55] Some of these manuscripts may be local to Qumran, which implies that the scribe who composed the manuscript resided there. Almost twenty excerpted (or abbreviated) classical text manuscripts have been identified. The most comprehensive list is given by Emanuel Tov:[56]

4QExod^d (4Q15)
4QExod^e (4Q16)
4QDeut^j (4Q37)
4QDeut^{k1} (4Q38)
4QDeut^n (4Q41)
4QDeut^q (4Q44)
4QPs^b (4Q84)[57]
4QPs^g (4Q89)
4QPs^h (4Q90)
4QIsa^d (4Q58)[58]

55. The identification of these excerpted texts in the Qumran collection was first suggested by H. Stegemann, who identified 2QExod^b and 4QDeut^n as excerpted manuscripts ("Weitere Stücke von 4QpPsalm 37, von 4Q Patriarchal Blessings und Hinweis auf eine unedierte Handschrift aus Höhle 4Q mit Exzerpten aus dem Deuteronomium," *RevQ* 6 [1967]: 193–227). I disagree with Stegemann's characterization of 2QExod^b as an excerpted text; it appears to be simply an extremely fragmentary manuscript of Exodus, which may insert a verse from chapter 19 (19:9b) before 34:10. I am not including in this discussion the tefillin and mezuzot slips found at Qumran, even though these are also excerpted texts. Their specialized use as prayer slips inserted into the capsules means that they were not meant to be read, only worn for prayer, and their tiny size and method of copying sets them apart from the excerpted texts.

56. E. Tov, "Excerpted and Abbreviated Biblical Texts from Qumran," in *Hebrew Bible, Greek Bible, and Qumran: Collected Essays,* TSAJ 121 (Tübingen: Mohr Siebeck, 2008), 4–13. Tov characterizes 4QCant^a and 4QCant^b as "abbreviated rather than excerpted texts," since the choice of passages in the manuscripts is "of an undetermined nature, probably reflecting the excerptors' literary taste" (8).

57. 4QPs^b contains parts of fifteen psalms, from Psalms 91–118. On the manuscript Psalm 112 directly follows Psalm 103; Psalms 104–111 are absent. This absence leads Tov to classify the manuscript as excerpted ("Excerpted and Abbreviated Texts," 36). However, we do not know if Psalms 104–111 were completely absent from this manuscript or were situated elsewhere; what the manuscript most likely represents is a variant text of the Psalter rather than an excerpted text. See P. Flint, *The Dead Sea Psalms Scrolls and the Book of Psalms,* STDJ 17 (Leiden: Brill, 1997), 141–46, who notes that, from Psalm 90 and beyond, the Qumran Psalms scrolls present several different arrangements, indicating that the order of the psalms had not yet stabilized.

58. 4QIsa^d contains portions of chapters 45–49, 52–54, and 58. It gives no particular

239

THE QUMRAN EVIDENCE

4QEzek[a] (4Q73; Tov lists it as "possible")[59]
4QCant[a] (4Q106)
4QCant[b] (4Q107)
5QDeut (5Q1)
5QPs (5Q5)

Tov also includes 4QTestimonia (4Q175), which contains passages from Exodus, Numbers, Deuteronomy, and the Apocryphon of Joshua. Although the Apocryphon of Joshua is an affiliated work rather than a classical text,[60] its use alongside excerpts from the Pentateuch indicates that it must have had some sort of authoritative standing, at least to the scribe who excerpted it.

While I remove 4QPs[b], 4QIsa[d], and 4QEzek[a] from Tov's list, I would add:[61]

4QReworked Pentateuch D (4Q366)
4QReworked Pentateuch E (4Q367)[62]

Note that all of these manuscripts come out of Cave 4Q or its sister Cave 5Q.

---

indication of being an excerpted text, although Lange has argued that its columns were too short to contain all of Isaiah and that therefore it may have contained only chapter 40 to the end (A. Lange, review of *Qumran Cave 4.X: The Prophets*, DSD 8 [2001]: 102.

59. 4QEzek[a] contains 10:6–11:1; 23:14–15, 17–18; 23:44–47; and 41:3–6. G. Brooke has suggested that the survival of these particular passages is not coincidental, but that the passages reflect a choice of topics of some special significance, since they occur in other Qumran texts ("Ezekiel in Some Qumran and New Testament Texts," in *The Madrid Qumran Congress: Proceedings of the International Congress on the Dead Sea Scrolls, Madrid 18-21 March 1991*, ed. J. Trebolle Barrera and L. Vegas Montaner, STDJ 11, 1 [Leiden: Brill; Madrid: Editorial Complutense, 1992), 319. However, these particular passages do not seem to have been especially significant in the sectarian literature. See A. Lange and M. Weigold, *Biblical Quotations and Allusions in Second Temple Jewish Literature*, JAJSup 5 (Göttingen: Vandenhoeck & Ruprecht, 2011), 147–52.

60. Although the Apocryphon of Joshua contains none of the characteristic sectarian vocabulary, it contains ideas shared by the sectarian literature. Therefore, it belongs to the category of texts with special affinity to the sectarian literature. See the detailed analysis of D. Dimant, "Between Sectarian and Nonsectarian: The Case of the *Apocryphon of Joshua*," in *History, Ideology and Bible Interpretation*, 113–33.

61. 4QReworked Pentateuch A (4Q158) contains excerpts from Genesis and Exodus, but with more overt exegesis than is found in the excerpted texts. See M. Zahn, "Building Textual Bridges: Towards an Understanding of 4Q158 (4QReworked Pentateuch A)," in *The Mermaid and the Partridge: Essays from the Copenhagen Conference on Revising Texts from Cave 4*, ed. G. Brooke and J. Høgenhaven, STDJ 96 (Leiden: Brill, 2011), 13–32.

62. Manuscripts such as 4QFlorilegium (4Q174) and 4QCatena A and B (4Q177, 182) are similar to the excerpted texts but differ in that they include commentary interlaced with the scriptural excerpts.

The Qumran Scrolls Collection: A Scribal Library with a Sectarian Component

These manuscripts can be characterized as follows:

1. They do not contain a running text from one book, but rather excerpts from one or more classical books. 4QDeut^q (Deut 32) and 4QPs^{g,h} and 5QPs (Ps 119) each contains only one specific chapter or psalm. In manuscripts that contain more than one excerpt, the passages are juxtaposed on the manuscript without explanation, but sometimes with paragraph markings or other scribal notations.[63] This can be clearly seen on 4QTestimonia, which excerpts Exod 20:21 (according to the pre-Samaritan version), Num 24:15–17, Deut 33:8–11, and the Apocryphon of Joshua (the excerpted passage is found in 4Q379). Each excerpt is followed by a blank space, with the next excerpt beginning on the following line. In addition, there is a hook-shaped marking between the excerpts. 4QDeutⁿ's first extant sheet contains Deut 8:5–11 followed by several blank lines, before continuing on the next sheet with Deut 5:1–6:1, where the text breaks off.[64] 4QReworked Pentateuch D (4Q366) frag. 2 preserves Lev 24:20–22 and 25:39–43, with a space between the passages, and frag. 4i contains Num 29:32–30:1, followed, after a *vacat*, by Deut 16:13–14.[65]

2. Many of these manuscripts are of small dimensions, such that it is evident that an entire book would not have fit on them (e.g., 4QExod^e, 4QDeut^j, 4QDeutⁿ, and 4QPs^g).

3. Many (but not all) of the passages chosen for excerpting are known for their liturgical/religious use, for example, Exod 12–13 (4QExod^d, 4QExod^e, and 4QDeut^j) and Deut 5, 8, 11, and 32 (see especially 4QDeut^j, 4QDeutⁿ, and 4QDeut^q). The excerpted Psalms manuscripts contain only Psalm 119.

It is probable that these excerpted manuscripts were created for particular uses, such as study or in worship settings.[66] These small manuscripts would have been much easier to handle and manipulate than a large, bulky

---

63. Tov, "Excerpted and Abbreviated Biblical Texts," 4.

64. We do not have the beginning of 4QDeutⁿ; there is sewing on the right-hand side of the sheet that contains 8:5–11, indicating that at least one sheet preceded it. See S. W. Crawford, "41. 4QDeutⁿ," in *Qumran Cave 4.IX: Deuteronomy, Joshua, Judges, Kings*, by E. Ulrich et al., DJD 14 (Oxford: Clarendon, 1995), 117–28.

65. See also 4QExod^d, 4QReworked Pentateuch E (4Q367) frags. 2a–b and 3, 4QCant^a, and 4QCant^b.

66. In NT studies, scholars beginning with Burkitt argued that the NT authors used collections of HB prooftexts ("Testimonia") when composing their works. See E. Mroczek, "Testimonia," in *T&T Clark Companion to the Dead Sea Scrolls*, ed. G. Brooke and C. Hempel (London: T&T Clark, 2018), 149–52.

THE QUMRAN EVIDENCE

scroll that contained an entire book, as witnessed by the size, weight, and length of 1QIsa[a], the only classical text preserved whole among the Qumran finds. For example, 4QDeut[n], of which at least six columns are preserved (the beginning and end of the manuscript did not survive), is only 7 centimeters in height, while a single column from 1QIsa[a] is approximately 25 centimeters in height. Further, scrolls at that time were not divided by chapter and verse, making individual passages more difficult to find in a whole scroll. The creation of these excerpted texts would have facilitated the study of important passages.

What we may have in at least some of these excerpted manuscripts is the visible work of a scholar-scribe, putting together (or "jotting down") individual passages that illustrated a particular theme on which he was working. 4QTestimonia is a good example of this; its four passages, from four different books, illustrate the theme of messianic expectations.[67] 4QDeut[n] may be another illustration of this phenomenon, being a juxtaposition of Deut 8:5-11, used for grace after meals, and the Decalogue.[68]

Two other manuscripts where we may see a scribe at work are 4Q366 and 4Q367. These manuscripts were originally classified by their editors, Emanuel Tov and myself, as Reworked Pentateuch manuscripts.[69] We made no remarks on the extent of either manuscript, although 4Q364 and 4Q365, published as part of the same group of manuscripts, were probably complete manuscripts of the Pentateuch when whole. 4Q366 and 4Q367 are different, however. 4Q366 contains the following passages: Exod 21:35-22:5 (frag. 1); Lev 24:20-22 and 25:38-43 (frag. 2); Num 29:14-[25] (frag. 3); Num 29:32-30:1 and Deut 16:13-14 (frag. 4i); and Deut 14:[13]-17 (frag. 5). All of these passages are legal in nature, although the reason they were gathered together in one manuscript is not transparent. Exodus

---

67. A. Steudel has suggested that 4Q175 is a "personal set of notes" ("einen privat ... 'Handzettel'") to be used for discussion (*Der Midrasch zur Eschatologie aus der Qumrangemeinde [4QMidrEschat[a, b]]: Materielle Rekonstruktion, Textbestand, Gattung, traditionsgeschichtliche Einordnung des durch 4Q174 ["Florilegium"] und 4Q177 ["Catena A"] repräsentierten Werkes aus den Qumran funden*, STDJ 13 [Leiden: Brill, 1994], 180). M. Popović, "Qumran as Scroll Storehouse in Times of Crisis? A Comparative Perspective on Judaean Desert Manuscript Collections," *JSJ* 43 (2012): 577, makes a similar suggestion for 4Q175, 4Q339, and 4Q340.

68. M. Weinfeld, "Grace after Meals in Qumran," in *Normative and Sectarian Judaism in the Second Temple Period*, LSTS 54 (London: T&T Clark, 2005), 112-21.

69. E. Tov and S. A. White, "4QReworked Pentateuch[d]," and "4QReworked Pentateuch[e]," in *Qumran Cave 4.VIII: Parabiblical Texts, Part I*, by H. Attridge et al., DJD 13 (Oxford: Clarendon, 1994), 335-44, 345-52.

242

The Qumran Scrolls Collection: A Scribal Library with a Sectarian Component

21:35–22:5 begins in the midst of a passage concerning ox goring, and ends with the setting of a fire in a field. Leviticus 24:20–22 is the *lex talionis*; it is followed by 25:39–43, the treatment of an Israelite debt slave. Numbers 29:14–[25], 29:32–30:1, and Deut 16:13–14 are all about the laws for the Festival of Sukkot. Deuteronomy 14:[13]–21 concerns the dietary laws. I believe that what we have in this manuscript are scribal notes; some scribe collected these passages for reasons that are not clear to us. Thus 4Q366, although it overlaps textually with 4Q158, is a single-copy work that was an excerpted text.[70]

4Q367 collects a selection of passages from Leviticus: 11:47–13:1 (frag. 1a–b); 15:14–15, 19:1–4, and 19:9–15 (frag. 2a–b); and 20:13 and 27:30–34, with four lines of unknown text at the beginning of the fragment (frag. 3). As was the case for 4Q366, the reason for the selection of these particular passages is difficult to understand, although again they are all legal. The last passage, 27:30–34, is also the end of Leviticus; we might have understood this manuscript simply as a copy of Leviticus, except for the sequence of passages on frgs. 2 and 3. Once again we seem to have a collection of passages on a single-copy work, copied by a scribe for purposes that are not now clear to us.

These small single-copy excerpted texts were for the most part quick copies, not the carefully prepared, elegant manuscripts that we have in some of the larger texts in the Qumran library.[71] Some of them were most likely copied locally in the Qumran settlement by the scribes who resided there, for their own use. For example, 4QDeut[n], which dates paleographically to the late first century BCE–early first century CE, could easily have been copied at Qumran.[72]

Another one of the excerpted texts, 4QTestimonia, was copied by the same scribe who copied the Cave 1Q copy of the Serek Hayaḥad (1QS).

---

70. 4Q366 overlaps with 4Q158 at Exod 22:2–4, where both have an expansion in agreement with the Greek and pre-Samaritan text traditions. Accordingly, Tov and White stated, 4Q366's "first allegiance . . . is with 4Q158" ("4Q366," in DJD 13, 190).

71. Tov, *Scribal Practices*, 125–29, terms these carefully prepared manuscripts "deluxe editions." He does classify 4QDeut[kl] as a deluxe manuscript on the basis of its margin size, but this classification is uncertain.

72. Other manuscripts that fall into the second half of the first century BCE through the first century CE are 4Q37, 4Q38, 4Q44, 4Q89, 4Q90, 4Q366, 4Q367, and 5Q5. See Webster, "Chronological Index," 372–75. Some of them, indeed, are quite late (30–68 CE), having been copied in the last days of the Qumran settlement (4Q37, 4Q89), suggesting that this excerpting activity was going on during the entire life of the settlement.

THE QUMRAN EVIDENCE

Since 1QS is a sectarian text and its scribe also copied an excerpted text, we can legitimately use that sectarian text to help determine what the purpose of these excerpted texts was. A well-known passage in 1QS reads:

> In any place where is gathered the ten-man quorum, someone must always be engaged in study of the Law, day and night, continually, each one taking his turn. The general membership will be diligent together for the first third of every night of the year, reading aloud from the Book, interpreting Scripture and praying together. (1QS 6:6–8)

If the adherents of this wing of Judaism were indeed following this dictum, these small scrolls with selected passages would have been ideal for study in small groups. I propose that this was one of their purposes; they were created for and used as study guides in the communities belonging to this wing of Judaism. Some of them were also used in the worship and prayer activities of the community. Since all but one of these excerpted texts were recovered from Cave 4Q, which as I argued in ch. 4 was one of the caves in which manuscripts local to Qumran were stored, these excerpted texts may have been used in the daily devotional life of the community that resided there.

Calendars and Mishmarot

The study of time and the seasons is a peculiarly scribal preoccupation, and the number of calendar texts found in the Qumran library demonstrates the learned nature of the group that collected it. Astronomical texts and calendar reckonings reached Judea from Mesopotamia; the Mesopotamian calendar was lunisolar.[73] After Alexander's conquest in the fourth century BCE, Macedonian and Babylonian calendars were correlated. The Julian calendar, with a 365-day year with leap years, was also available to Judean scholar-scribes in 47/46 BCE.[74] The calendars from Qumran, however, seem essentially to reflect the Babylonian tradition.

---

73. Represented by MUL.APIN and Enuma Anu Enlil. According to S. Sanders, the later Mesopotamian astronomical tradition of the "Lunar Three" appears in 4Q319, 320, 321, and 321a (*From Adapa to Enoch: Scribal Culture and Religious Vision in Judea and Babylon*, TSAJ 167 [Tübingen: Mohr Siebeck, 2017], 158).

74. Glessmer, "Calendars in the Dead Sea Scrolls," in *The Dead Sea Scrolls after Fifty Years: A Comprehensive Assessment*, ed. P. Flint and J. VanderKam, 2 vols. (Leiden: Brill, 1999), 2:214–18.

244

The Qumran Scrolls Collection: A Scribal Library with a Sectarian Component

Older works in the Qumran collection certainly reflect this Babylonian astronomical tradition. The Astronomical Book of Enoch, which is reflected in 1 En. 72–82 but was extant in a much longer form in the Qumran fragments, uses the 364-day calendar, synchronized with the lunar months. The 364-day (often referred to as the "solar") calendar is based on a calculation of fifty-two weeks of seven days, with four quarters of thirteen weeks. Each quarter contained three months of thirty, thirty, and thirty-one days, respectively. The extra four days from the thirty-one-day months are cardinal days. When this calendar is synchronized with the twelve-month lunar calendar of 354 days, an additional month is added at the end of every three years to bring the two calendars into synchronicity. While the Astronomical Book's calendar is a 364-day calendar synchronized with the lunar months, Jubilees uses the 364-day solar calendar exclusively, polemicizing in favor of a pure 364-day calendar. The Aramaic Levi Document mentions the cardinal days of the year, connecting it to the 364-day calendar tradition.[75]

According to the list found in DJD 39, thirty-three texts in one way or another concern calendar and/or *mishmarot*.[76] All of them, with the exception of one from Cave 6Q (6Q17), come from Cave 4Q, again emphasizing the scholarly, scribal nature of the 4Q collection. Of these, most involve the 364-day calendar, often synchronized with the lunar calendar. The 360-day ideal calendar is also represented.[77] Interestingly, none of the Qumran calendar texts, with the possible exception of 4Q319, has any evidence for a system of intercalation for the true solar year of 365.25 days, even though the true solar year was known in the first century BCE.[78] The

---

75. J. Ben-Dov, *Head of All Years: Astronomy and Calendars at Qumran in Their Ancient Context*, STDJ 78 (Leiden: Brill, 2008), 40.

76. The term *mishmarot* refers to the tables for the courses of the priests' service in the temple (1 Chr 24:7–19). The calendar/*mishmarot* texts are published in DJD 3, 21, and 28 (plates only). The following texts are listed as calendar/*mishmarot* manuscripts: 4Q317 (cryptic script), 4Q319, 4Q320–330, 4Q334, 4Q337, 4Q394 1–2, and 6Q17. Some of the numbered texts are divided up into discrete manuscripts. These manuscripts all date to the first century BCE or first century CE, suggesting that at least some of them may be local copies.

77. This calendar is based on the astronomical compendium MUL.APIN, in which one month = thirty days, and one year = twelve months = 360 days. See Glessmer, "Calendars in the Dead Sea Scrolls," 216.

78. J. VanderKam, *Calendars in the Dead Sea Scrolls: Measuring Time* (London: Routledge, 1998), 80–84, argues that 4Q319 does show evidence for solar intercalation; J. Ben-Dov, "319. 4QOtot," in *Qumran Cave 4.XVI: Calendrical Texts,* by S. Talmon et al., DJD 21

THE QUMRAN EVIDENCE

study of these various calendar texts has demonstrated that they do not all agree with one another in their details.[79] This has led some scholars to posit that different groups, each following a slightly different calendar, lay behind them.[80] While this is historically possible, it does not explain why this variety of calendars was found in Cave 4Q. It seems more probable that these variant calendars were being collected by scholar-scribes for study purposes.[81]

Some of these 364-day calendar texts are appended to other works, such as the calendar attached to the beginning of 4QMMT[a] (4Q394 1–2), and 4QOtot, which appears on the same manuscript as 4QS[e]. Since both MMT and 4QS[e] are sectarian texts, this demonstrates that this particular wing of Judaism favored the 364-day calendar, probably synchronized with the lunar calendar as in the Astronomical Book of Enoch. In addition, the 364-day calendar underlies the Temple Scroll, "David's Compositions" in 11QPs[a], 4QCommentary on Genesis A, the Songs of the Sabbath Sacrifice, and 1QMysteries. Further, both the Serek Hayaḥad and the Damascus Document demonstrate concern for the correct times for festivals (1QS 1:13–15; CD 3:14–15), while the Damascus Document seems to cite with approval the book of Jubilees (CD 16:2–4).

In sum, the Qumran collection expresses a clear preference for a 364-day calendar coordinated with lunar months, in which the solar element takes precedence. As is well known, the rabbis and later Judaism used (and continue to use) a lunar calendar coordinated with the solar year, in which the lunar element takes precedence. The correct calendar in the Second Temple period seems to have been a matter of dispute. In the mid-second century BCE Dan 7:25 says concerning the "little horn" (Antiochus IV Epiphanes): he "shall speak words against the Most High, shall wear out

---

(Oxford: Clarendon, 2001), 211, disagrees, arguing that there is no apparent awareness of the length of the true solar year at Qumran.

79. See VanderKam, *Calendars*; H. Jacobus, "Calendars in the Qumran Collection," in *The Dead Sea Scrolls and the Concept of a Library*, ed. S. W. Crawford and C. Wassén, STDJ 116 (Leiden: Brill, 2016), 217–43.

80. S. Pfann, "The Ancient 'Library' or 'Libraries' of Qumran: The Specter of Cave 1Q," in Crawford and Wassén, *Concept of a Library*, 168–216.

81. Jacobus, "Calendars in the Qumran Collection," 241, also argues that the differences among the calendars more likely stem from an interest in the preservation of historical knowledge. S. Stern suggests that the calendars found in the Qumran library were idealistic models for study, rather than practical documents for use in real life ("Qumran Calendars: Theory and Practice," in *The Dead Sea Scrolls in Their Historical Context*, ed. T. Lim [London: T&T Clark, 2000], 242).

The Qumran Scrolls Collection: A Scribal Library with a Sectarian Component

the holy ones of the Most High, and shall attempt to change the sacred seasons [literally, the times] and the law."[82] This vague reference may indicate that the Seleucid government attempted to change the Jewish sacred calendar. Although we have no direct evidence for which calendar was in use in the temple during this period, the fact that Qumran documents are so concerned with calculating the correct calendar may indicate that the sectarians were at odds with the temple authorities concerning the times of the sacred festivals. One intriguing piece of evidence in this regard comes from Pesher Habakkuk 11:2–8:

> "*Woe to the one who gets his friend drunk, pouring out his anger, making him drink, just to get a look at their holy days.*" (2:15) This refers to the Wicked Priest, who pursued the Teacher of Righteousness to destroy him in the heat of his anger at his place of exile. At the time set aside for the repose of the Day of Atonement he appeared to them to destroy them and to bring them to ruin on the fast-day, the Sabbath intended for their repose.

This passage has been understood as saying that the Wicked Priest, identified with a Hasmonean high priest, came to Qumran to confront the sectarian leader (the Teacher of Righteousness) on the Day of Atonement, which was being observed on a different day than the temple observed it. Therefore, the Qumran sectarians must have been following a different festival calendar than the temple (and thus the majority of Jews).[83] However, there are some difficulties with this interpretation. It rests on an understanding that the Wicked Priest was the reigning high priest, and therefore could not have left Jerusalem on the Day of Atonement, and that "his place of exile" refers to Qumran. It is not clear, however, that the Wicked Priest was the reigning high priest; another priest (certainly a "wicked" one) could have left the temple to attack the Teacher and his followers. Further, "his place of exile" does not necessarily refer to Qumran, but could be another place (possibly in Jerusalem) where the sectarians gathered. Regardless, this passage in Pesher Habakkuk does seem to indicate that the sectarians had a different Day of Atonement than the temple authorities, and thus were following a different sacred calendar than that of the temple.

---

82. VanderKam, *Calendars*, 114.

83. S. Talmon, *The World of Qumran from Within: Collected Studies* (Jerusalem: Magnes, 1989), 188–92.

247

THE QUMRAN EVIDENCE

Furthermore, the preponderance of the 364-day calendar, the subject of learned study and calculation in numerous manuscripts, argues in favor of a more than ideal interest in the workings of this calendar. In this regard, it is appropriate at this point to discuss the sundial found at Qumran. This object, KhQ1229, was first identified by Matthias Albani and Uwe Glessmer as a sundial.[84] It allows the user to determine the season and the hour of the day and could also identify the four cardinal days of the 364-day year. This is solid evidence that the residents at Qumran were calculating the solar year, certainly for scholarly purposes and probably also for practical use in determining their festival days. Thus, while there may not have been any kind of permanent schism over the correct calendar between the sect and its opponents,[85] it is abundantly clear that the sect favored, and perhaps followed, the 364-day calendar synchronized with the lunar year, as first laid out in the Astronomical Book of Enoch.

Esoteric Texts and Lists

We know from the study of Mesopotamian textual troves found in situ by excavators that scribes collected works pertaining to their specializations, including astronomical/calendrical lore and augury/divination. At a house in Uruk occupied by two families of scribes in the fifth-fourth centuries BCE, tablets were discovered containing incantations and medical texts. The library in the Shamash Temple in Sippar contained omens, incantations, and mathematical and astronomical texts. The presence of these same types of texts, which I am calling "esoteric" texts, in the Cave 4Q collection is striking. The term *esoteric texts* refers to works that are concerned with the scholarly ephemera of the Second Temple

---

84. M. Albani and U. Glessmer, "Un instrument de mésures astronomiques à Qumran," *RB* 104 (1997): 88–115. See also M. Albani and U. Glessmer, "An Astronomical Measuring Instrument from Qumran," in *The Provo International Conference on the Dead Sea Scrolls: Technological Innovations, New Texts, and Reformulated Issues*, ed. D. Parry and E. Ulrich, STDJ 30 (Leiden: Brill, 1999), 407–42; S. Pfann, "The Writings in Esoteric Script from Qumran," in *The Dead Sea Scrolls Fifty Years after Their Discovery*, ed. L. Schiffman et al. (Jerusalem: Israel Exploration Society, 2000), 188–90; G. Hollenback, "The Qumran Roundel: An Equatorial Sundial," *DSD* 7 (2000): 123–39; and G. Hollenback, "More on the Qumran Roundel as an Equatorial Sundial," *DSD* 11 (2004): 289–92.

85. Jacobus, "Calendars in the Qumran Collection," 241, notes that "there is no evidence from the manuscripts themselves . . . of any kind of calendrical polarization" or schism.

The Qumran Scrolls Collection: A Scribal Library with a Sectarian Component

period, matters of interest only to scholar-scribes trained in astrology, magic, and divination.

There are three manuscripts whose primary concern is astrological and/or physiognomic knowledge: 4Q186, first named 4QHoroscope but better described as Zodiacal Physiognomy;[86] 4Q318, Zodiology and Brontology ar;[87] and 4Q561, published as Horoscope ar but better described as 4QPhysiognomy ar.[88] There is also a single manuscript with the fragmentary remains of an Aramaic magical book: 4Q560, Magical Booklet ar.[89]

Interest in horoscopy was widespread in the Greco-Roman period. Cuneiform horoscopes from Mesopotamia are known from the fifth century BCE, and spread rapidly through the Hellenistic world after the conquests of Alexander.[90] Physiognomy, the art of judging a person's character by studying his bodily features, likewise was found both in Babylon and the Hellenistic world.[91] Two of the three Qumran texts are, unsurprisingly, in Aramaic, which was the language by which Mesopotamian scientific knowledge was transmitted in the Jewish world. 4Q318 contains a selendromion, which describes the course of the moon through the zodiacal signs within the framework of a 360-day ideal year, and a brontologion, a manual of divination based on thunder in a particular zodiacal house. 4Q561 preserves the remains of a physiognomic list, with predictions for each physiognomic type.

---

86. J. Allegro, "186. —," in *Qumrân Cave 4.I (4Q158–4Q186)*, DJD 5 (Oxford: Clarendon, 1968), 88–91; M. Popović, *Reading the Human Body: Physiognomics and Astrology in the Dead Sea Scrolls and Hellenistic–Early Roman Period Judaism*, STDJ 67 (Leiden: Brill, 2007), 1.

87. J. C. Greenfield and M. Sokoloff, "318. 4QZodiology and Brontology ar [Aramaic]," in *Qumran Cave 4.XXVI: Cryptic Texts,* by S. Pfann; and *Miscellanea, Part 1,* by P. Alexander et al., DJD 36 (Oxford: Clarendon, 2000), 259–74. 4Q318 dates paleographically from the late first century BCE to the early first century CE.

88. E. Puech, *Qumran Grotte 4.XXVII: Textes en Araméen, deuxième partie: 4Q550–575, 580–582,* DJD 37 (Oxford: Clarendon, 2009), 303–22; Popović, *Reading the Human Body,* 1. 4Q561 dates paleographically to the second quarter of the first century BCE.

89. Puech, DJD 37, 241–302. 4Q560 dates to the first half of the first century BCE.

90. M. Albani, "Horoscopes in the Dead Sea Scrolls," in *Dead Sea Scrolls after Fifty Years,* ed. Flint and VanderKam, 2:281.

91. M. Popović, "Reading the Human Body and Writing in Code: Physiognomic Divination and Astrology in the Dead Sea Scrolls," in *Flores Florentino: Dead Sea Scrolls and Other Early Jewish Studies in Honour of Florentino García Martínez,* ed. A. Hilhorst et al., JSJSup 122 (Leiden: Brill, 2007), 284, who cites the Babylonian physiognomic omen series *Alamdimmû* and the pseudo-Aristotelian work *Physiognomica.*

THE QUMRAN EVIDENCE

4Q186 is both the most extensively preserved and the most interesting of the three manuscripts. It contains the remains of a physiognomic list, along with astrological data and predictions. It is written in Hebrew, not Aramaic, indicating a Jewish copyist who drew on Aramaic sources.[92] However, the Hebrew text is not straightforward, but encoded. The script is inverted, reading from left to right instead of right to left, and the scribe used Paleo-Hebrew and Greek characters, and even in one case a cryptic letter.[93] 4Q186, therefore, demonstrates a high degree of scribal craft. The purpose of the encoding is not transparent; it certainly marks the text as containing some kind of secret knowledge, which was available only to those capable of deciphering the code, that is, other scholar-scribes. The inverted writing and use of different characters may also have been intended to have a magical effect.[94]

The presence of these three documents in the Qumran library indicates, as do the calendar texts, the "research" interests of scholar-scribes. Although it is debated whether the Qumran sect used astrology,[95] the presence of these manuscripts in their library indicated that their scholar-scribes at least studied it. Physiognomic descriptions do appear in other works from the collection, indicating a more widespread use of this "science": the Genesis Apocryphon contains a long description of Sarah's beauty, which begins with her head and ends with her feet, imitating the order of 4Q186 1 iii 2–5 and 2 i 1–5. First Enoch 106:1-2, which narrates the birth of Noah, describes the baby Noah as having unusual physical features; and 4Q534, The Elect of God text, includes a description of that figure's physical characteristics (1 i 1–3).

4Q560 is a different type of text: it contains the remains of a series of incantations against demons. The belief in the existence of demons, and the need to defend against them, is demonstrable from many compositions

---

92. The contents of 4Q561 and 4Q186 are very close to one another; Puech suggests that 4Q186 is a version or adaptation of an Aramaic composition like 4Q561 (DJD 37, 303).

93. The presence of that cryptic letter has been enough for some scholars to argue that 4Q186 is a sectarian text. However, we do not know enough about the Cryptic A script to argue that it was only used in sectarian contexts. 4Q186 has no other sectarian markers. See also Popović, *Reading the Human Body*, 10. Mixed script ostraca have also been found at Masada, indicating a more widespread use for the type of cryptic encoding found in 4Q186.

94. Popović, *Reading the Human Body*, 228.

95. 4QInstruction and 1Q/4QMysteries contain references to times of birth, the position of the stars, and horoscopes. However, the books of Enoch and Jubilees both polemicize against astrology.

250

The Qumran Scrolls Collection: A Scribal Library with a Sectarian Component

from the Hellenistic-Roman period.[96] For example, in Jub. 10:10–14 an angel instructs Noah in the arts of healing illnesses caused by demons; Noah writes down his knowledge in a book and passes it down to his son Shem. In 4Q560 the evil spirit is adjured (in the name of God?) to depart from the suffering person. Although the Aramaic 4Q560 is nonsectarian, other manuscripts from the Qumran library, some with sectarian markers, indicate that incantations and apotropaic prayers and hymns were used by the sectarians.[97] The presence of 4Q560, a sourcebook of incantations, shows that the sectarians were drawing on a wider body of knowledge concerning the defense against demons going back to at least the early Second Temple period.

The presence of these esoteric texts in the Qumran library demonstrates decisively that elite scholar-scribes were responsible for at least part of the collection. Their presence in Cave 4Q, which housed (at least in part) the "local" collection from Qumran, strengthens the immediate connection of scribes to the Qumran settlement.

Further evidence for the presence of scribes in the Qumran settlement comes from the lists found in Cave 4Q: 4Q339 (a list of false prophets in Aramaic), 4Q340 (a list of נתינים, "temple servants"), and 4Q477 (Rebukes Reported by the Overseer).[98] 4Q339 is a single sheet of leather, which Magen Broshi and Ada Yardeni describe as a "small square 'card'";[99] it seems to have been a personal document, a collection of notes on a topic, made by a scribe. 4Q340 is too fragmentary to gauge its extent. As we have seen, a common activity for scribes throughout the ancient Near East and Greco-Roman worlds was the compiling of lists of various types of scholarly knowledge (see chs. 2 and 3). These two lists are of the same

---

96. See Reynolds, "Dwelling Place of Demons," 23–54.

97. The list includes 4Q444 (Incantation), 4Q510–511 (Songs of the Maskil), 6Q18 (Hymn fragment), 8Q5 (Hymn), 11Q5 (Ps^a 27:2–11), and 11Q11 (Apocryphal Psalms^a). The last contains three songs against demons, the third a version of Ps 91, commonly used for defense against demons in late antique Judaism. See Eshel, "Apotropaic Prayers."

98. M. Broshi and A. Yardeni, "339. 4QList of False Prophets ar," and "340. List of Netinim," in *Qumran Cave 4.XIV: Parabiblical Texts, Part 2*, by M. Broshi et al., DJD 19 (Oxford: Clarendon, 1995), 77–84; E. Eshel, "477. 4QRebukes Reported by the Overseer," in DJD 36, 474–83. J. Milik early on suggested that 4Q338 (4QGenealogical List?) was a genealogical list of the patriarchs, written as a "school exercise" (*The Books of Enoch: Aramaic Fragments of Qumrân Cave 4* [Oxford: Clarendon, 1976], 139). The text is an opisthograph, written on the verso of 4Q201 (4QEn^a). According to its editor, the contents of 4Q338 have been obliterated. See E. Tov, "338. 4QGenealogical List?," in DJD 36, 290.

99. DJD 19, 77.

THE QUMRAN EVIDENCE

type: works of scholarship in which a scribe has collected the biblical data on a given topic.[100]

4Q477, Rebukes Reported by the Overseer, is a different type of list. It is, as its name suggests, a list of members of the community (frag. 2 ii 6) who are being rebuked after committing some sort of sin or offense. The word הרבים ("the *Rabbim*"; lit. "the many"), also a sectarian term, appears on frgs. 2 i 3 and 2 ii 3; the word [הי]ח[ד] (the *Yahad*) appears in a broken context on 2 ii 6, while the phrase אנשי ה]יחד ("the men of the [*Yahad*]") appears on frag. 2 i 1. Rebukes of members who have strayed are called for in both the Serek Hayahad (1QS 5:24–6:1) and the Damascus Document (CD 9:2–4). Esther Eshel dates 4Q477 to the first century CE, that is, the last half of the Qumran settlement.[101] This text, though tiny, is important since it demonstrates that the group who deposited the scrolls in Cave 4Q were following at least some of the prescriptions found in the rule texts. Accordingly, it appears that the inhabitants of Qumran were following some sort of sectarian rule, and that this list records the names of the local inhabitants who violated that rule.

The Aramaic Texts

The compositions in Aramaic, which are found in several of the categories listed above, make up an important subsection of the collection. These compositions are all literary (with the exception of a few documentary texts) and constitute approximately 15 percent of the entire collection.[102] Aramaic texts were found in Caves 1Q, 2Q, 3Q, 4Q, 5Q, 6Q, and 11Q, all of the main storage caves. Caves 4Q and 11Q contained the highest number of Aramaic texts, 93 and 13, respectively. The majority were copied on

---

100. S. Cohen, "Hellenism in Unexpected Places," in *Hellenism in the Land of Israel*, ed. J. Collins and G. Sterling, CJAS 13 (Notre Dame: University of Notre Dame Press, 2001), 220. I would like to thank Professor Benjamin G. Wright III for bringing this article to my attention.

101. E. Eshel, "477. 4QRebukes," in DJD 36, 474–76. The names on 4Q477 are as follows: Yohanan ben Ar[(frag. 2 ii 3), Hananiah Notos (frag. 2 ii 5), and Hananiah ben Shim[on] (frag. 2 ii 9).

102. D. Machiela, "The Aramaic Dead Sea Scrolls: Coherence and Context in the Library of Qumran," in Crawford and Wassén, *Concept of a Library*, 245. Many of the Aramaic fragments remain unidentified (1Q63–68, 3Q12–13, 4Q536–568, 570–575, 580, 582, 5Q24, 6Q23, and 11Q24–25). Additionally, several of these manuscripts are so fragmentary that very little can be said about them (e.g., 4Q488, Apocryphon, and 4Q489, Apocalypse).

252

The Qumran Scrolls Collection: A Scribal Library with a Sectarian Component

leather, though a small number were on papyrus. Although individual manuscripts have peculiar traits, by and large the method of manufacture and copying does not differ from the Hebrew manuscripts. Thus the Aramaic texts do not differ in archaeological context or materiality from the Hebrew scrolls.[103]

The Aramaic texts fall into two broad categories. The first is the "scientific" texts, which leave no indications that they are Jewish in any way. These non-Jewish Aramaic works consist of the Aramaic esoteric texts discussed above (4Q318, 560, and 561). The second category, into which the majority of the Aramaic texts fall, are compositions written in Aramaic but involving specifically Jewish figures and concerns. There are Aramaic translations of Leviticus (4Q156) and Job (4Q157 and 11Q10), but the majority are independent compositions, most often involving antediluvian figures (e.g., Enoch) and biblical patriarchs (e.g., Levi, Amram, Qahat). Most of them were written in the early Hellenistic period,[104] by what Daniel Machiela describes as "highly-educated, Jewish teaching scribes" connected with priestly circles.[105] They include, to cite only the major documents, the Aramaic portions of Daniel, the New Jerusalem, the Aramaic Levi Document, the Testament of Qahat, the Visions of Amram, the Genesis Apocryphon, and the books of Enoch (including the Book of Giants). As can be seen by their titles, the use of pseudepigraphy is a common literary device, setting the work in the distant past.

A variety of classifications has been proposed for the Jewish Aramaic texts, from Eibert Tigchelaar's minimalist "texts related or ascribed to pre-Mosaic figures," and "narratives that have an Eastern Diaspora setting," to Devorah Dimant's more complex six rubrics.[106] The difficulty with a more refined classification such as Dimant's is that several of the texts fall into more than one category; for example, the Genesis Apocryphon in its first

---

103. Machiela, "Aramaic Dead Sea Scrolls," 254.

104. Their paleographic dates range from the late third–early second century BCE to the first half of the first century CE. See E. J. C. Tigchelaar, "Aramaic Texts from Qumran and the Authoritativeness of Hebrew Scriptures: Preliminary Observations," in *Authoritative Scriptures in Ancient Judaism*, ed. M. Popović, JSJSup 141 (Leiden: Brill, 2010), 160.

105. Machiela, "Aramaic Dead Sea Scrolls," 250.

106. Tigchelaar, "Aramaic Texts from Qumran," 159; Dimant, "The Qumran Aramaic Texts and the Qumran Community," in Hilhorst et al., *Flores Florentino*, 197–206. Dimant's six rubrics are: (1) works concerning the period of the flood; (2) works dealing with the history of the patriarchs; (3) visionary compositions; (4) legendary narratives and court tales; (5) astronomy and magic; and (6) others, including targumim.

THE QUMRAN EVIDENCE

columns is concerned with the period of the flood and with the history of the patriarchs and contains visions, while its second half is a targum beginning in Genesis 11:27, with some additions. On the other hand, Tigchelaar's minimalist classification leaves out some compositions, for example, the New Jerusalem, which is neither concerned with a pre-Mosaic figure nor has an Eastern Diaspora setting. I propose dividing the texts into two distinct subgroups: (1) compositions containing apocalyptic elements, which often are set in the prediluvian period; and (2) legendary stories about Jewish courtiers and sages (which may also contain apocalyptic elements). All of the identified Aramaic literary texts can be placed into one of these two subgroups.[107]

The subgroup "compositions containing apocalyptic elements" includes the books of Enoch, the New Jerusalem, Four Kingdoms, Words of Michael, Visions of Amram, the Testament of Qahat, and the Birth of Noah. These works contain the revelation of secret/special knowledge from a divine mediator (a developed angelology is a hallmark of these texts), otherworldly journeys, dream visions, and eschatological predictions. Indeed, as Dimant has noted, the Aramaic texts contain the most apocalyptic elements in the Qumran library and serve as a main source for sectarian apocalyptic and dualistic doctrines.[108] It is also in these texts that scientific knowledge (which was in fact derived from Babylonian sources) is revealed to the protagonists. Enoch does not learn his astronomical and calendrical lore from studying the sun, moon, and stars or by reading Babylonian treatises; it is revealed to him by the angel Uriel (1 En. 72:1).[109] Thus in these Aramaic compositions all knowledge comes ultimately from God, and it is passed into Hebrew literature (e.g., Jubilees) as such.

The Jewish Aramaic texts that include legendary stories about Jewish courtiers and sages comprise the Aramaic portions of Daniel and the book of Tobit, as well as previously unknown works such as Jews at the Persian Court (4Q550), Prayer of Nabonidus (4Q242), and the Pseudo-Daniel literature (4Q243–245). The presence of these didactic works, adapted from Aramaic models such as Ahiqar, testifies to the rich literary tradition

107. The Aramaic documentary texts and the translations (targumim) of the classical books Leviticus and Job are not included in either subgroup, since they represent different genres of texts.

108. D. Dimant, "Apocrypha and Pseudepigrapha at Qumran," in *History, Ideology and Biblical Interpretation*, 168. See also Machiela, "Aramaic Dead Sea Scrolls," 256.

109. Sanders, *From Adapa to Enoch*, 129–32.

254

The Qumran Scrolls Collection: A Scribal Library with a Sectarian Component

available to scribes trained in Aramaic, as at least some of the scribes responsible for the Qumran library must have been.[110] However, these narratives have a transparent purpose: it is the Jewish heroes (e.g., Daniel, the unnamed seer in Prayer of Nabonidus, and Bagasraw in 4Q550) who prevail over obstacles because of the help of God.

The Jewish Aramaic texts, while testifying to the larger intellectual universe available to a learned scholar-scribe, are placed firmly in a Jewish milieu. Ultimate knowledge comes from God, and it is revealed to those figures from the remote past by God's agents. Protection from obstacles in a non-Jewish setting also comes from God. The Jewish scribes responsible for transmitting material derived from Mesopotamian sources took care to transform it into their own theological categories, and thus made it available and acceptable to Jewish intellectuals. This accounts for their presence in the Qumran library.

The Cryptic Script Manuscripts

Three cryptic scripts are recognized in the Qumran manuscripts: Cryptic A, Cryptic B (which has only been partially deciphered), and Cryptic C.[111] The majority of the manuscripts are in Cryptic A,[112] and all but one (11Q23) were found in Cave 4Q. They are written on both papyrus and skin, and Tov has noted that the materials are prepared and used in the same way as those with other scripts.[113] Stephen Pfann, the editor of the cryptic manuscripts, notes that these texts are penned by "numerous" scribes.[114]

110. As Sanders notes, well-trained scribes would have been fluent in both Aramaic and Hebrew, as the switching from Hebrew to Aramaic and back in the books of Daniel and Ezra testifies (*From Adapa to Enoch*, 151).

111. A "cryptic" script indicates a script that is not publicly known to anyone with training in reading and writing, such as the Aramaic square script or Paleo-Hebrew, but a "secret" or "hidden" script that is known and used only by those scribes who are specially trained to use it.

112. There are only two manuscripts in Cryptic B, 4Q362–363, and one in Cryptic C, 4Q363a.

113. Tov, *Scribal Practices*, 259.

114. Pfann, DJD 36, 524. Pfann has listed at least fifty separate cryptic manuscripts ("Writings in Esoteric Script," 178–80). That number is debatable, since for the papyrus fragments Pfann separated them into separate manuscripts on the basis of fiber patterns. More work is called for on these manuscripts, especially the papyrus ones (see n116).

THE QUMRAN EVIDENCE

Several of the texts preserved in cryptic script are sectarian: the Serek Ha'edah (4Q249[a–i]),[115] Midrash Sefer Moshe (4Q249), the Words of the Maskil to All Sons of Dawn (4Q298), and MMT (4Q313). In addition, several calendrical documents, 4Q317 (Phases of the Moon), 4Q313[c], and 4Q324[c–g], were recovered. Finally, several fragments containing quotations from Leviticus, the only classical text found in cryptic script, were identified (4Q249[j–l]).[116]

In addition to manuscripts written entirely in cryptic script, one manuscript, 4Q186 (Zodiacal Physiognomy), used cryptic script as part of its encoding. Other manuscripts have cryptic letters written in their margins, often in conjunction with Paleo-Hebrew letters.[117] While some of the manuscripts that contain these marginal cryptic letters are sectarian (e.g., 4QS[e] = 4Q249, 4QShir[b] = 4Q511, and 4Qpap pIsa[c] = 4Q163), several are from the affiliated category (e.g., 4QMyst[c] = 4Q301, 4QInstr[c] = 4Q417, and 4QDibHam[a] = 4Q504). Most interestingly, several classical manuscripts have marginal Cryptic A letters: 1QIsa[a], 4QpapTob[a] ar (4Q196), 4QCant[b], and possibly 4QExod[c]. The purpose of these single letters is not transparent, but Tov plausibly suggests that "these letters may well refer to a sectarian coded message."[118]

The presence of these cryptic script manuscripts in the Qumran library demonstrates scholar-scribes at work, using a cryptic script to conceal, or at least limit access to, the texts being copied. Further, scribes were annotating square script manuscripts with cryptic letters, presumably to alert readers to certain passages or perhaps themes.

J. T. Milik suggested early on that the cryptic script, or at least Cryptic A, was a script used by the Maskil,[119] a suggestion followed by Pfann and Hempel.[120] This suggestion is plausible as long as it is remembered that

---

115. Pfann identified nine manuscripts of Sa, 4Q249[a–i]. Recently, however, D. Stökl Ben Ezra, J. Ben-Dov, and A. Gayer have argued that those fragments should be reclassified as one manuscript ("Reconstruction of a Single Copy of the Qumran Cave 4 Cryptic-Script Serekh haEdah," *RevQ* 29 [2017]: 21–77).

116. Many of the cryptic fragments, including the specimen from Cave 11Q, remain unidentified.

117. Tov, *Scribal Practices*, 203, 206.

118. Tov, *Scribal Practices*, 204. Interestingly, cryptic script is never used to write the divine name in square script manuscripts. That practice is reserved for Paleo-Hebrew.

119. For the amusing story of when Milik deciphered Cryptic A, see F. M. Cross, *The Ancient Library of Qumran*, 3rd ed., BibSem 30 (Sheffield: Sheffield Academic Press, 1995), 45.

120. Pfann, "Writings in Esoteric Script," 178; Hempel, *Qumran Rule Texts*, 303, 314–16. Recently Pfann has published Cryptic A script on a stone cup found in first-century CE fill to

The Qumran Scrolls Collection: A Scribal Library with a Sectarian Component

משכילים is the preferred sectarian term for their scholar-scribes; thus the cryptic scripts were used by the משכילים in their work as scribes for their sect, whether in copying whole texts or annotating texts copied in square script. The cryptic scripts are further evidence for the work of scholar-scribes in the Qumran collection.

Scribal Exercises and Other Documentary Texts

Although 99 percent of the Qumran library can be classified as religious literary compositions, a small number are documents, that is, texts recording the details of everyday life.[121] Three small scribal exercises were found in Cave 4Q, as well as a small number of documentary texts. The presence of these small manuscripts, entirely from 4Q, points to the local nature of the 4Q collection.

Scribal exercises are clear evidence for local scribal presence. De Vaux early announced the discovery of an ostracon from the ruins inscribed with a complete alphabet, which he identified as the work of a "pupil-scribe."[122] This ostracon would appear to be KhQ161. KhQ2289 is also an abecedary. André Lemaire has suggested that KhQ2207, a stone plaque with five lines of writing of unknown content, was "probably an incomplete apprentice scribe's exercise."[123] 4Q234, 341, and 360 have all been identified as scribal exercises. 4Q234, Exercitium Calami A, written in a first-century BCE script and penned in various directions, may contain a quotation of Gen 27:19–21, but this identification is uncertain, since only two words are extant.[124]

---

the east of and outside the Zion Gate in Jerusalem. On the basis of this cup he now believes that these scripts were used within the Jewish priesthood of the period, and suggests that they be called "hieratic scripts." See S. Pfann, "The Mount Zion Inscribed Stone Cup: Preliminary Observations," *New Studies in the Archaeology of Jerusalem and Its Region* 4 (2010): *47.

121. This contrasts sharply with the Wadi Murabba'at and Nahal Hever collections, which are almost entirely documentary. See Crawford, "The Qumran Collection as a Scribal Library," in Crawford and Wassén, *Concept of a Library*, 117–20; and ch. 3 above.

122. De Vaux, *Archaeology and the Dead Sea Scrolls: The Schweich Lectures of the British Academy 1959*, rev. ed. (London: Oxford University Press, 1973), 103.

123. Lemaire, "Inscriptions du khirbeh, des grottes et de 'Ain Feshkha," in *Khirbet Qumrân et 'Aïn Feshkha*, vol. 2: *Études d'anthropologie, de physique et de chimie*, ed. J.-B. Humbert and J. Gunneweg, NTOA.SA 3 (Göttingen: Vandenhoeck & Ruprecht, 2003), 360. Émile Puech, who is working on an edition of KhQ2207, has informed me (email communication) that he too believes that this is a student exercise.

124. A. Yardeni, "234. 4QExercitium Calami A," in DJD 36, 185–86.

THE QUMRAN EVIDENCE

4Q360, Exercitium Calami B, in an early Herodian bookhand, is also penned in various directions. It contains the name Menahem, repeated three times.[125] Although this is in the realm of speculation, it seems possible that here we have the name of the scribe himself. 4Q341, Exercitium Calami C,[126] is also clearly a writing exercise. Joan Taylor notes that it was found almost whole, written on a purposely cut snippet of leather.[127] Lines 1–3 contain a series of letters, sometimes alphabetical. Lines 4–7 and 9 contain some personal names: Magnus, Malchiah, Mephiboshet, Gaddi, Dalluy, Hyrcanus, Vanni, and Zakariel. In addition, there is a name written in the right-hand margin, Omriel(?). The name Mephiboshet has an obvious biblical reference (2 Sam 9), and Hyrcanus could refer to the Hasmonean John Hyrcanus. However, the most likely explanation for the list of names is that they are the names of individuals known to the scribe, who practiced his craft by writing the names of his friends.

Why were these small, seeming worthless exercises placed in Cave 4Q? 4Q234 may contain a scriptural text, but otherwise these small scraps are not even literary. I would suggest that they are part of the material from the khirbeh that was thrust helter-skelter into Cave 4Q in anticipation of the Roman attack.

A small number of documentary texts (i.e., deeds, accounts, etc.) are also purported to come from Cave 4Q (4Q342–359). These manuscripts are more controversial than the scribal exercises, since, while the bedouin claimed they came from Cave 4Q, Yardeni has shown that at least one (4Q347) and possibly more actually came from Wadi Seiyal (Naḥal Ṣe'elim).[128] On the other hand, Armin Lange and Uwe Mittmann-Richert have argued on the basis of paleography that some of them did indeed come from Cave 4Q.[129] To err on the side of caution, I discuss only those

125. A. Yardeni, "360. 4QExercitium Calami B," in DJD 36, 297.

126. *Olim* 4QTherapeia, 4QList of Proper Names. See J. Naveh, "341. 4QExercitium Calami C," in DJD 36, 291–93.

127. J. Taylor, "4Q341: A Writing Exercise Remembered," in *Is There a Text in This Cave? Studies in the Textuality of the Dead Sea Scrolls in Honour of George J. Brooke*, ed. A. Feldman et al., STDJ 119 (Leiden: Brill, 2017), 135.

128. A. Yardeni, "Appendix: Documentary Texts Alleged to Be from Qumran Cave 4," in *Aramaic, Hebrew and Greek Documentary Texts from Naḥal Ḥever and Other Sites*, DJD 27 (Oxford: Clarendon, 1997), 284.

129. See A. Lange with U. Mittmann-Richert, "Annotated List of the Texts from the Judaean Desert Classified by Content and Genre," in DJD 39, 144. The documents they list as coming from Cave 4 are 4Q345, 4Q346, 4Q350, 4Q351, 4Q352, 4Q352a, 4Q353, 4Q354, 4Q355, 4Q356, 4Q357, and 4Q358.

258

The Qumran Scrolls Collection: A Scribal Library with a Sectarian Component

documents with paleographic and/or carbon-14 dates that fall within the first century BCE–first century CE. The chief interest in these documentary texts for our purposes lies in ascertaining whether any of the names found in them are also found in inscriptions from the Qumran settlement, which may point to an explicit connection between the settlement and Cave 4Q.[130] The repetition of the names in these documentary texts, Eleazar (4Q342, 348), Shimon (4Q343, 345, 346, 348), and Manasseh (4Q346, 348), suggests a personal archive of some kind, perhaps belonging to Shimon, whose name appears five or six times. Further, there are evident family relationships among the names: Shimon is listed as the father of Ishmael, Mattatyah, and Eleazar, which also suggests a personal archive. Some of these names also occur on inscriptions from the khirbeh: Honi/Honiah (KhQ Ostracon 1, KhQ1313), Eleazar (KhQ1650, KhQ Ostracon 1), Yehohanan/Yohanan (KhQ621), Yehosef/Yosef (4Q1), and Shimon (4Q1). Further, in 4Q348 Shimon is identified as the son of Honi (see KhQ Ostracon 1).

It is important to emphasize that none of these names necessarily refers to the same individual, especially since these are common Jewish names of the period. However, the last example, that of Shimon son of Honi (4Q348), gives the best possibility for a connection with an inscription, placing Shimon, the owner(?) of the personal archive found in Cave 4Q into a familial relationship with Honi, the giver of the gift in KhQ Ostracon 1. The ostracon and the deed date paleographically to the same period (1–68 CE), which strengthens the connection.[131]

---

130. 4Q342, an early-first-century CE Aramaic letter, contains the names Judah (line 3), Eleazar (line 3), and Elishua (line 4). 4Q343, a Nabatean letter from the mid-first century BCE, contains the name Shimon in line 13, and possibly an unknown proper name in line 14. 4Q345, an Aramaic or Hebrew deed of the middle-late first century BCE, contains the name Yeshua on the recto upper line 6, the name Hoshayah on verso line 20, and Ishmael son of Shimon on verso line 21 (note the appearance of the name Shimon in 4Q343). 4Q346, an Aramaic deed of sale from the late first century BCE, contains the name Shimon (again!) on line 3, and Manasseh on line 6. 4Q348, a Hebrew deed of the middle to late Herodian period, contains the following names: Menahem . . . son of Eleazar (upper, line 1); Shimon (upper, line 5); Yehohanan son of Yehosef (upper, line 9); Yehosef, Mattatyah son of Shimon, and Eleazar (lower, line 14); Hanan and Eleazar son of Shimon, son of Honi (lower, line 15); Manasseh (lower, line 17); and Shimon "from the Timber Market," a district in Jerusalem (lower, line 18).

131. The documentary corpus also contains two accounts that most likely were actually from the Qumran caves. The first is 4Q350, Account gr, which is an opisthograph of 4Q460, Narrative Work and Prayer. See H. Cotton and E. Larson, "4Q460/4Q350 and Tampering

THE QUMRAN EVIDENCE

The presence of these small scraps of exercises as well as a cache of personal documents with onomastic connections to inscriptions from the khirbeh points to the "working quality" of Cave 4Q, a subject I address in the next section.

The "Working Quality" of Cave 4Q

Another characteristic of the 4Q corpus is its "working" quality.[132] That is, the manuscripts found in it attest to the living quality of its collection. Cave 4Q did not merely contain whole scrolls of recognized books that may have been used for study and reference, although it certainly did contain such scrolls. It also encompassed small manuscripts bearing witness to the ongoing work of scholar-scribes as teachers, researchers, and functionaries within the sectarian community responsible for collecting the Qumran library.

Some of these "working" manuscripts have already been discussed above. The presence of scribal exercises points to scribal activity and training in the settlement. The excerpted classical texts such as 4QDeut[n] are also working texts, since these collections of scriptural passages were put together by scribes for study and/or liturgical use. To these excerpted texts may be added other manuscripts that demonstrate the scholarly activity of scribes collecting material together from earlier sources, that is, anthologies of passages around a particular theme, for example, Testimonia (4Q175), Tanḥumim (4Q176), Florilegium (4Q174); and lists of laws or rules, such as Ordinances[a] (4Q159) and Miscellaneous Rules (4Q265).[133]

The Qumran caves also contained palimpsests and opisthographs, all but one of which are from 4Q.[134] The presence of palimpsests and opistho-

---

with Qumran Texts in Antiquity?," in Paul et al., *Emanuel*, 113–25. The second, 4Q355, Account C ar or heb, is written on the verso of 4Q324, Mishmarot C. Its contents are illegible.

132. Hempel, *Qumran Rule Texts*, 332, uses the similar term "workaday quality" to describe the same phenomenon I am discussing in this section.

133. 4Q265 is especially important in this regard, since it contains many parallels with both S and D, suggesting that the scribe who compiled it had an intimate knowledge of both texts. See J. Baumgarten, "Miscellaneous Rules (4Q265)," in *The Dead Sea Scrolls: Hebrew, Aramaic, and Greek Texts with English Translations*, vol. 3: *Damascus Document II, Some Works of the Torah, and Related Documents*, ed. J. Charlesworth, PTSDSSP (Tübingen: Mohr Siebeck; Louisville: Westminster John Knox, 2006), 253–54.

134. Tov, *Scribal Practices*, 68–73; and DJD 39, 211–13. The lone exception is 1Q70, an unidentified papyrus manuscript.

260

The Qumran Scrolls Collection: A Scribal Library with a Sectarian Component

graphs in Cave 4Q is noteworthy less for its own sake than in comparison with their almost entire absence from the limestone cliff caves located the furthest from the settlement (i.e., 1Q, 2Q, 3Q, and 11Q). Only caves within the landscape of the settlement, mainly 4Q but also 6Q and 7Q, contained the sorts of "working" manuscripts outlined above. The ramifications of this statement are explored in greater depth in the conclusions to part II.

Paleography and Orthography

The study of the paleography of the manuscripts reveals important insights into the collection. The dates of the manuscripts are chronologically coherent; the earliest manuscripts date paleographically to the mid-third century BCE. Clusters of manuscripts' dates then slowly increase, reaching a peak in the first century BCE; the curve then dips and flattens in the first century CE, to end abruptly in the last quarter of the first century CE.[135] Further, while the manuscripts from Caves 1Q and 4Q are statistically older than those of the other caves, all the caves contained the same range of dated manuscripts. For example, while the majority of the earliest manuscripts come from Cave 4Q, Caves 5Q and 6Q also contained manuscripts dated between 250 and 150 BCE.[136] Cave 11Q, while statistically younger in manuscript dates than the other caves,[137] also contained a few early manuscripts.

Many scribal hands are represented in the manuscripts, and it is extremely probable that many, perhaps a plurality, of the scrolls were copied elsewhere and brought to Qumran. This is obvious for the manuscripts whose paleographic dates are older than the settlement at Qumran (approximately 25 percent), but it is most likely the case for many of the other manuscripts. However, as noted in ch. 4, scribal hands do recur among the manuscripts, and they recur across the caves. Most telling in this regard is Yardeni's contention (supported by Puech) that the same late-first-century BCE scribe copied some 54 manuscripts, spread over Caves 1Q, 2Q, 3Q, 4Q, 6Q, and 11Q (plus one from Masada, the Joshua Apocryphon, an "affiliated" text). Although we cannot be certain, it is not unreasonable to argue that this scribe could have been resident at Qumran itself, since Yardeni

---

135. Consult the tables in B. Webster, "Chronological Lists," in DJD 39, 371–75.
136. Webster, "Chronological Lists," 371.
137. Stökl Ben Ezra, "Old Caves, Young Caves," 328.

THE QUMRAN EVIDENCE

dates his hand to the late first century BCE.[138] Thus the paleographic evidence of the manuscripts argues in favor of the Qumran corpus being one collection, a library gathered at Qumran by the particular wing of Judaism evident in the sectarian texts.

The orthographic and morphological practices exhibited in the Qumran manuscripts range along a spectrum from "defective" to "full" to "super-full."[139] Based on statistical evidence, Tov has argued that there existed a "Qumran scribal practice," demonstrated by full orthography and a preference for long-form morphology, as well as certain scribal features such as the use of cancellation dots for mistakes in the manuscripts and the rendering of the divine name in Paleo-Hebrew letters.[140] Tov uses the term "Qumran scribal practice" to indicate scrolls copied by a sectarian group of scribes, although he acknowledges that those scrolls could have been penned anywhere in Judea.[141] Indeed, this must be the case, since some of the manuscripts that he identifies as using the "Qumran scribal practice" are older than the settlement. The question is whether Tov has successfully isolated a particular scribal practice peculiar to the sectarians, which would add some weight to our evidence that the Qumran scrolls collection was the possession of a particular sect. While it is the case that he has identified a cluster of texts, many of them sectarian, that contain one or more of the features he has correlated with the "Qumran scribal practice," it is also the case that not all sectarian manuscripts exhibit these features.[142] Further, it

138. A. Yardeni, "Notes on a Qumran Scribe," in *New Seals and Inscriptions, Hebrew, Idumean, and Cuneiform*, ed. M. Lubetski, Hebrew Monograph Series 8 (Sheffield: Sheffield Phoenix Press, 2007), 288.

139. The terminology is that of P. Alexander and G. Vermes, *Qumran Cave 4.XIX: Serekh ha-Yaḥad and Related Texts*, DJD 26 (Oxford: Clarendon, 1998), 8, referring to the use of *matres lectionis* to indicate vowels, even short /o/, /u/, and /i/. In morphology, the use of lengthened independent pronouns and lengthened pronominal suffixes, e.g., הואה, היאה, -המה, and -כמה, often appears in manuscripts with fuller orthography. See E. Tov, "Further Evidence for the Existence of a Qumran Scribal School," in Schiffman et al., *Dead Sea Scrolls Fifty Years after Their Discovery*, 212-13.

140. Tov has made his case in a series of articles, beginning with "The Orthography and Language of the Hebrew Scrolls Found at Qumran and the Origin of These Scrolls," *Textus* 13 (1986): 31-57. See also his "Further Evidence"; and *Scribal Practices*, 261-73.

141. Tov, *Scribal Practices*, 261.

142. Tov, *Scribal Practices*, appendix 9, lists 4QpIsa[b], 4QpNah, 4QS[d], 4QS[j], and 4QBarkhi Nafshi[a] as not possessing features of the "Qumran scribal practice." E. Tigchelaar, "Assessing Emanuel Tov's 'Qumran Scribal Practice,'" in *The Dead Sea Scrolls: Transmission of Traditions and Production of Texts*, ed. S. Metso et al., STDJ 92 (Leiden: Brill, 2010), 201, adds 4QD[e]. See also the discussion of Alexander and Vermes, DJD 26, 8.

262

is important to note that we have no control group with which to compare the Qumran corpus, since the only contemporary corpus, that of Masada, is too small to allow a statistically accurate comparison.[143] Therefore, while it would be helpful to our overall argument to claim that a particular sectarian scribal school can be discerned in the manuscripts and was operative at Qumran, the evidence is not sufficient to make such a claim. However, we can say that during the period of the Qumran settlement, spelling practices and scribal habits varied, perhaps depending on the type of text being copied or the scribe making the copy. Thus classical texts tended to be copied using a more defective orthography and short-form morphology, such as we see in the majority of the Qumran classical manuscripts. This would fit with the earlier dates of composition of these texts. Nevertheless, some classical texts, such as 4QQoh[a], exhibit fuller orthography and morphology, so the correlation is not strict. Later compositions tend to sit further along the spectrum, using fuller orthography and morphology. Finally, it seems clear that sectarian scribes did favor certain scribal conventions, such as writing the divine name in Paleo-Hebrew characters, the use of cancellation dots, and annotating manuscripts with cryptic or Paleo-Hebrew letters. It is unlikely, however, that all these conventions were limited to sectarian scribes, and it is evident that not all scribes copying sectarian manuscripts adhered to them.

Conclusions Based on Chapters 4, 5, and 6

In chs. 4, 5, and 6 we have studied the archaeology of the Qumran caves and their individual contents; the archaeology of Khirbet Qumran, its connections with the caves, and evidence for scribal activity in the settlement; and the manuscript collection itself, a sectarian scribal library. Based on all the evidence presented, we may draw the following conclusions:

1. The archaeology of the caves and of the settlement ties the two firmly together, demonstrating beyond doubt that the inhabitants of the settlement were the ones who deposited the scrolls in the caves.

---

143. Tov, "Further Evidence," 213–16, argues that the two types of tefillin found in the Qumran caves function as a control. "Rabbinic-type" tefillin are not written in "Qumran scribal practice," while "Qumran-type" tefillin are. This is accurate, but the art of copying tefillin scrolls has its own peculiarities, and it is hazardous to use this very limited corpus as a control group.

THE QUMRAN EVIDENCE

2. The scrolls found in the eleven caves are one collection, and that collection has a pronounced sectarian element. Further, the collection contains evidence for the particular interests of scribes, leading to the conclusion that the scrolls were not just the general collection of the sect (although it is that), but were the remains of the working library of a group of elite scholar-scribes residing at Qumran.

3. There is sufficient evidence to argue for scribal activity taking place at Khirbet Qumran. This is not to say that other activities, such as pottery manufacture or date farming, did not also take place,[144] but that the settlement housed a working group of scribes. Further, we have identified a possible library complex in the main building of the khirbeh, strengthening the argument for the presence of scholar-scribes.

4. The two groups of caves, the limestone cliff caves and the marl terrace caves, had different functions during the life of the settlement. The marl terrace caves were "working" caves. Caves 7Q, 8Q, and 9Q, part of a larger complex of caves carved out of the edge of the plateau on which the settlement sat, most likely served as workshops (e.g., Cave 8Q), or temporary sleeping quarters (e.g., Cave 9Q). Across the ravine on the southwest spur of the plateau, Caves 4Qa-b, 5Q, and 10Q are the remains of a larger cave complex that was used for the storage of scrolls during the life of the settlement. These marl terrace caves were the only caves that contained the "working quality" texts discussed earlier in the chapter. The size and mixed nature of the Cave 4Q collection indicate that it was being used for storage during the life of the settlement, and the same use may be extrapolated for Caves 5Q and (probably) 10Q, part of the same larger cave complex.

The limestone cliff caves (1Q, 2Q, 3Q, 6Q, 11Q, 53), all located at a further remove from the settlement, were used exclusively for storage. Some scrolls were found in situ by the bedouin and now by archaeologists sealed in hole-mouthed cylindrical jars in Caves 1Q, 11Q, and 53, while the presence of many sherds of hole-mouthed cylindrical jars in all of the limestone cliff caves (with the exception of 6Q, which may have functioned more like a marl terrace cave) suggests that all of the fragments from these caves were originally stored away sealed in jars. Thus the archaeological evidence suggests completely different functions for the limestone cliff caves and the marl terrace caves during the life of the Qumran settlement.

---

144. As D. Mizzi notes, "the sectarians had to earn a living"! ("Qumran at Seventy: Reflections on Seventy Years of Scholarship on the Archaeology of Qumran and the Dead Sea Scrolls," *Strata: Bulletin of the Anglo-Israel Archaeological Society* 35 [2017]: 29).

264

The Qumran Scrolls Collection: A Scribal Library with a Sectarian Component

Thus we can conclude that the Qumran scrolls constitute a scribal library with sectarian elements that was collected, copied, and annotated by a particular wing of Judaism. At least part of that library was permanently stored in the limestone cliff caves, while the majority of what survived from the library was hidden in the marl terrace caves. The identity of that particular wing of Judaism, why it had a settlement at Qumran, and why it stored its manuscripts in the fashion described above, I explore in part III.

PART III

Conclusions

CHAPTER 7

Who Owned the Scrolls?
The Qumran-Essene Hypothesis Revisited

> We know of no other sect arising in the second century B.C. which can
> be associated with the wilderness community. . . . I prefer to be reckless
> and flatly identify the men of Qumrân with their perennial houseguests,
> the Essenes.
>
> Frank Moore Cross, *Canaanite Myth and Hebrew Epic*

In part II I demonstrated that the scrolls collection found in the eleven
caves in the vicinity of Khirbet Qumran is one collection that can be described as a scribal library with a prominent sectarian component. The
scrolls caves are tied to the settlement at Qumran by virtue of geographic
proximity (including paths between the caves and the settlement) and material finds. The settlement was the residence of a Jewish, predominately
male community, with evidence of scribal activity and the plausible identification of a library complex in the main building. Finally, I described
the main characteristics of the sect that owned the library deposited in
the caves, noting the following features: an emphasis on maintaining ritual
purity, a distinct approach to legal interpretation; a clear preference for
the 364-day, solar-based calendar; a strict hierarchy with defined entrance
procedures; some degree of shared property; and a disdain for the contemporary temple in Jerusalem and its administration. My task in this chapter
is to determine whether we can identify this sect with any of the groups
known from other sources in Second Temple Judaism.

The consensus position concerning the identity of the inhabitants of
the site of Khirbet Qumran has been fixed since the 1950s when the first
generation of Dead Sea Scrolls scholars identified the Qumranites with the
Jewish sect of the Essenes as described by the classical authors Josephus,
Philo, and Pliny. Beginning in the 1980s, however, that identification was
increasingly called into question. In this chapter I reexplore the Qumran-
Essene hypothesis, beginning from the perspective of the Qumran scrolls,

269

CONCLUSIONS

followed by the archaeological evidence from the ruins of Qumran and its caves that may support an Essene identification, and ending with the testimony of the classical authors. Proceeding in this order allows us to test the premises of the hypothesis and reach a conclusion concerning its validity. I hope to show that identifying the inhabitants as part of the wing of Judaism known as the Essene movement is still the best conclusion based on the evidence we have to this point.

First, a brief historical overview of the Essene question is in order. Eleazar Sukenik was the first to propose, on the basis of three of the Cave 1Q scrolls, that the writers/owners of the scrolls were Essenes, one of the three Jewish αἱρέσεις or philosophies described by Josephus.[1] Sukenik's proposal was also adopted by de Vaux.[2] As we saw in ch. 5, de Vaux noted in particular that the site of Qumran fit the geographical description of the Essene settlement given by Pliny, in the northwest region of the Dead Sea below Jericho.[3] Further, the Serek Hayaḥad from Cave 1 (1QS) seemed to be the product of a closed Jewish community that had noticeable parallels with the Essenes as described by Josephus and Philo, including the absence of women, the community of goods, a doctrine of predeterminism, a belief in an afterlife, a common (pure) meal, complicated entrance procedures, a hierarchical community structure, the nonuse of oil, and a prohibition against spitting in meetings.[4]

1. E. Sukenik, *Hidden Scrolls from the Genizah Found in the Judaean Desert* [in Hebrew], vol. 1 (Jerusalem: Bialik Institute, 1948-1949). In the English-speaking world, in the first American news release of the discovery of the scrolls, dated April 11, 1948, the scrolls were tentatively identified with the Essenes. See J. Trever, *The Untold Story of Qumran* (Westwood, NJ: Revell, 1965), 89, 117. The word αἱρέσεις has as its root meaning "choice" (implying a voluntary association); a secondary meaning is "a philosophical school or sect." Josephus uses the word to describe the Pharisees, Sadducees, and Essenes (*J.W.* 2.119; *Life* 10). The book of Acts uses the same word to describe the Sadducees (5:17), the Pharisees (15:5; 26:5), and the early Christians (24:5, 14; 28:22). Josephus also uses the word φιλοσοφεῖται, "philosophical schools," to describe his three αἱρέσεις (*J.W.* 2.119).

2. R. De Vaux, *Archaeology and the Dead Sea Scrolls: The Schweich Lectures of the British Academy 1959*, rev. ed. (London: Oxford University Press, 1973), 126-38.

3. Pliny, *Nat. Hist.* 5.73: "Ab occidente litora Esseni fugiunt usque qua noscente" ("to the west [of the Dead Sea] the Essenes have put the necessary distance between themselves and the insalubrious shore").

4. For a slightly different version of this list, see J. VanderKam, *The Dead Sea Scrolls Today* (Grand Rapids: Eerdmans, 1994), 75-87: determinism, the afterlife, nonuse of oil, common property, the pure meal, bodily functions, and spitting. See also the list of H. Stegemann, "The Qumran Essenes—Local Members of the Main Jewish Union in Late Second Temple Times," in *The Madrid Qumran Congress: Proceedings of the International Congress*

270

Who Owned the Scrolls? The Qumran-Essene Hypothesis Revisited

This Essene identification was adopted and fleshed out by F. M. Cross, André Dupont-Sommer, J. T. Milik, and Geza Vermes into what came to be known as the Qumran-Essene hypothesis.[5] Stated briefly, the Qumran-Essene hypothesis says that Qumran was established by the Essenes in the second half of the second century BCE as a desert exile from Jerusalem and the temple controlled by the Hasmonean high priesthood, whom they opposed. According to this hypothesis, the Essenes were celibate males, led by Zadokite priests, who lived a simple lifestyle of study and prayer. They held all their property in common, kept to a stringent rule of life, and shunned outsiders. The scrolls found in the eleven caves in the vicinity of the settlement constituted the Essene library. This settlement was destroyed by the Romans in 68 CE during the Great Jewish Revolt. Prior to the Roman attack, the Qumran Essenes hid their scrolls in the nearby caves for safekeeping, and either unsuccessfully defended their community center or fled.

Almost every aspect of the Qumran-Essene hypothesis has been called into question since the 1980s. The objections raised are too numerous to list in their entirety, so I will simply highlight those that are most salient.

1. While Josephus, Philo, and Pliny all claim in one way or another that Essenes eschewed marriage or were celibate,[6] nothing in the scrolls themselves clearly forbids marriage or advocates for celibacy. Indeed, the opposite is true; many texts legislate for marriage or mention the presence of women and children. These include, most importantly, the Damascus Document and the Rule of the Congregation, as well as various collections of ordinances and purification rules. The Community Rule is silent on the subject of women and does not legislate for celibacy.

---

on the Dead Sea Scrolls Madrid 18–21 March 1991, ed. J. Trebolle Barrera and L. Vegas Montaner, 2 vols., STDJ 11 (Leiden: Brill, 1992), 1:108–14: common meals, purificatory baths, hierarchical structure, entrance procedures, and common property.

5. F. M. Cross, *The Ancient Library of Qumran*, 3rd ed., BibSem 30 (Sheffield: Sheffield Academic Press, 1995), 54–87; A. Dupont-Sommer, *The Essene Writings from Qumran*, trans. G. Vermes (Oxford: Blackwell, 1961); J. T. Milik, *Ten Years of Discovery in the Wilderness of Judaea*, trans. J. Strugnell, SBT 1/26 (Naperville, IL: Allenson, 1959), 56–98; and G. Vermes, *The Dead Sea Scrolls: Qumran in Perspective* (London: Collins, 1977), 116–30. For a recent defense of the classic Qumran-Essene hypothesis, see E. Puech, "The Essenes and Qumran, the Teacher and the Wicked Priest, the Origins," in *Enoch and Qumran Origins: New Light on a Forgotten Connection*, ed. G. Boccaccini (Grand Rapids: Eerdmans, 2005), 298–302.

6. The pertinent passages are Josephus, *J.W.* 2.120; *Ant.* 18.21; Philo, *Hyp.* 14-17; and Pliny, *Nat. Hist.* 5.73. It is important to note that Josephus discusses "another order" of Essenes who do marry, for the purposes of procreation (*J.W.* 2.160–161).

CONCLUSIONS

2. Some of the legal positions found in the scrolls, especially in MMT, are the same as those attributed to the Sadducees in rabbinic literature,[7] raising the question of whether the owners of the scrolls were related to the Sadducees rather than the Essenes. These include the ruling on the purity of liquid streams (MMT[b] 55–57) and the ruling on the purity of the priest who sprinkles the ashes of the red heifer (MMT[b] 13–17).

3. The name "Essene" (Gk. Ἐσσαῖοι, Ἐσσηνοί, Ὀσσαῖοι [Philo, *Prob.* 75; *Hypoth.* 1; Josephus, *J.W.* 1.78; 2.133; etc.]; Lat. *Esseni* [Pliny, *Nat. Hist.* 5.73]) never appears in the scrolls, and the word "Essene" does not appear in the NT or the rabbinic sources. This has led some scholars to question their very existence.[8]

4. The physical evidence of the scrolls indicates that many, if not most, of them were not produced locally, but came to the caves from elsewhere. This evidence includes the fact that at least a quarter of the scrolls were penned before the settlement was established; there are numerous scribal hands and different scribal styles represented in the scrolls; and chemical tests on the ink and the hides indicate that, while some of the scrolls may have been locally produced, many were not.[9] Thus, even if the Qumran scroll collection is an Essene library and Qumran is an Essene settlement, it cannot have been the only one.

Because of these objections, numerous modifications and nuances have been proposed to the Qumran-Essene hypothesis. One of the most influential modifications was proposed by Lawrence Schiffman, who suggested, based on the evidence of MMT, that the community at Qumran was composed of disaffected Sadducees who refused to accept the Hasmonean status quo in the temple and abandoned Jerusalem for

---

7. As noted in E. Qimron, "The Halakha," in *Qumran Cave 4.V: Miqṣat Maʿaśe ha-Torah*, by E. Qimron and J. Strugnell, DJD 10 (Oxford: Clarendon, 1994), 123–77. See also L. Schiffman, *Reclaiming the Dead Sea Scrolls: The History of Judaism, the Background of Christianity, the Lost Library of Qumran* (Philadelphia: Jewish Publication Society, 1994), 83–87.

8. R. Elior, *Memory and Oblivion: The Secret of the Dead Sea Scrolls* [in Hebrew] (Jerusalem: Van Leer Institute and Kibbutz haMeuchad, 2009).

9. For a thorough treatment of the scribal characteristics of the Qumran scrolls, see E. Tov, *Scribal Practices and Approaches Reflected in the Texts Found in the Judean Desert*, STDJ 54 (Leiden: Brill, 2004). On the chemical tests on the ink and hides see, e.g., T. Wolff et al., "Provenance Studies on Dead Sea Scrolls Parchment by Means of Quantitative Micro-XRF," *Analytical and Bioanalytical Chemistry* 402 (2012): 1493–1503. For the paleographic dates of the manuscripts, see B. Webster, "Chronological Index of the Texts from the Judaean Desert," in *The Texts from the Judaean Desert: Indices and an Introduction to the Discoveries in the Judaean Desert Series*, ed. E. Tov, DJD 39 (Oxford: Clarendon, 2002), 351–446.

272

Who Owned the Scrolls? The Qumran-Essene Hypothesis Revisited

Qumran.[10] Another alternative (embraced by much of the secondary literature) is to avoid the quest to identify the group living at Qumran at all, speaking rather of the "Qumran Community" or *Yahad*.[11] This brings us to this chapter, in which I hope to cast a fresh eye upon all the evidence.

Contents of the Sectarian Texts

It is appropriate to begin with the evidence of the Qumran library itself. Since in ch. 6 I have covered the physical and content evidence that identifies the Qumran collection as a scribal library with a prominent sectarian component, I concentrate here on the contents of the sectarian texts themselves, in order to isolate the characteristics of the sect that produced them.[12] These characteristics include their admission procedures, organization and leadership roles, legal interpretation, the sharing of property among members, their prayer and worship practices, their self-separation from the rest of Israel, and an eschatological and predeterministic outlook.

EXCURSUS: ON THE DIFFERENCES AMONG THE SECTARIAN TEXTS

In the following discussion I emphasize the similarities among the sectarian texts, which are numerous, but I am not unaware of the differences among them, which are also numerous. These differences include organizational structures (including the terminology used to refer to the sect and its leadership), varying procedures for joining the sect, differing punishments in the penal codes, the presence (or not) of women and children in the sect, the degree of private property, and possibly the attitude toward

---

10. Schiffman, *Reclaiming the Dead Sea Scrolls*, 87–89.

11. E.g., M. Goodman, who states, "it is more probable than not that the sectarian scrolls were produced by a group or groups of Jews unattested in any of these later sources, and that any and all similarities between groups are to be explained through their common origin in early forms of Judaism" ("Constructing Ancient Judaism from the Scrolls," *OHDSS* 84). One difficulty with the nomenclature "Qumran community" is that it exacerbates the tendency to identify the community that produced the scrolls solely with the site of Qumran.

12. See also S. W. Crawford, "The Qumran Collection as a Scribal Library," in *The Dead Sea Scrolls and the Concept of a Library*, ed. S. Crawford and C. Wassén, STDJ 116 (Leiden: Brill, 2016), 109–31.

CONCLUSIONS

the temple.[13] These differences have led some scholars to posit that different sects, or different movements within one sect, lie in the background of the documents.[14] Complicating the question is that the manuscript evidence of S indicates different recensions of the Serek Hayaḥad;[15] there is also evidence for interrelationship between S and D, and within both S and D older sources can be discerned.[16] The question is whether one is more

13. For an overview, see C. Hempel, "Community Structures and Organization," in *The Qumran Rule Texts in Context: Collected Studies*, TSAJ 154 (Tübingen: Mohr Siebeck, 2013), 25–46.

14. One influential theory has been the "Groningen Hypothesis" of F. García Martínez and A. van der Woude, who argue that the Qumran community was a "splinter movement" within the larger Essene movement. See F. García Martínez and A. van der Woude, "A 'Groningen' Hypothesis of Qumran Origins and Early History," *RevQ* 14 (1990): 521–42. See also F. García Martínez, "The Groningen Hypothesis Revisited," in *The Dead Sea Scrolls and Contemporary Culture: Proceedings of the International Conference Held at the Israel Museum, Jerusalem (July 6–8, 2008)*, ed. A. Roitman et al., STDJ 93 (Leiden: Brill, 2011), 17–29. For various critiques of the Groningen Hypothesis see the articles by C. Hempel, A. Baumgarten, M. Elliott, T. Elgvin, L. Grabbe, B. W. Wright III, and T. Lim in Boccaccini, *Enoch and Qumran Origins*. Boccaccini argued that the Qumran community was a splinter group of a wider movement he termed "Enochic Judaism." See his *Beyond the Essene Hypothesis: The Parting of the Ways between Qumran and Enochic Judaism* (Grand Rapids: Eerdmans, 1998). However, his view, that the Qumran collection represents a movement he terms "Enochic" Judaism as opposed to a more Torah-centered Judaism, is at odds with the textual reality in the Qumran collection; while it is true that the books of Enoch were accorded a high standing in the sect, the books of the Torah and other works associated with Moses (e.g., the Temple Scroll and Jubilees) form a far larger part of the collection. For a helpful synthesis of recent views of the emergence of the sect as well as her own assessment, see Hempel, "Part II: Beginnings," in *Qumran Rule Texts*, 65–105.

15. S. Metso suggests that the different recensions of S exist because S was not a rule book per se, but a "record of judicial decisions and an accurate report of oral traditions." The contradictions found in the regulations in S are of the same type as those found in the Torah, and do not point to different communities, but are the result of compilations of traditions, which could then have been applied to real-life circumstances. S. Metso, "In Search of the *Sitz im Leben* of the *Community Rule*," in *The Provo International Conference on the Dead Sea Scrolls: Technological Innovations, New Texts, and Reformulated Issues*, ed. D. Parry and E. Ulrich, STDJ 30 (Leiden: Brill, 1999), 314. See also S. Metso, *The Textual Development of the Qumran Community Rule*, STDJ 21 (Leiden: Brill, 1997). For a different approach to the textual development of S, see P. S. Alexander and G. Vermes, "4QSerekh ha-Yaḥad," in *Qumran Cave 4.XIX: Serekh ha-Yaḥad and Two Related Texts*, DJD 26 (Oxford: Clarendon, 1998), esp. 9–12, who argue for a chronological development of S based on the paleographic dates of the manuscripts.

16. All dates for sources and/or composition of S and D are considered to be *before* the founding of the Qumran settlement in the first half of the first century BCE. F. M. Cross dated the oldest copy of S (4QSᵃ) to the end of the second century BCE ("Paleographical Dates of the Manuscripts," in *The Dead Sea Scrolls: Hebrew, Aramaic, and Greek Texts with English Translations*, vol. 1: *Rule of the Community and Related Documents*, ed.

Who Owned the Scrolls? The Qumran-Essene Hypothesis Revisited

impressed with the similarities or the differences between the documents. To my mind, the similarities are pronounced enough to demonstrate that they all belong to one movement or sect, a distinct wing within the Judaism of the period.[17] In addition, the fact that S and D were found together in Cave 4Q, as well appearing across the other nine manuscript caves, indicates that they were collected and deposited by the same group, who must have considered them to be important documents belonging to their sect, whatever the reality of their relationship/interrelationship.

Could a version of one of the rule texts have been in force at the Qumran settlement? It must be recalled here what I emphasized in ch. 5, that the archaeological evidence from the settlement will at most indicate *compatibility* with a sectarian occupation following a rule text, rather than one-to-one correspondence with each regulation. Bearing that in mind, the rule text with which the archaeological evidence of the settlement is more compatible is S. S does not mention women and children as active participants in the sect, which fits with the lack of archaeological evidence for women and children at Qumran (D and Sa, on the contrary, presume the presence of women and children in the daily life of the sect). The presence of many vessels for eating and drinking (especially in L86, 87, 89), at least one room suitable for communal dining (L77) as well as a community

---

J. Charlesworth, PTSDSSP [Tübingen: Mohr Siebeck; Louisville: Westminster John Knox, 1994], 57). The oldest copy of D, 4Q266, dates to the first half of the first century BCE. J. M. Baumgarten, "266. 4QDamascus Document*," in *Qumran Cave 4:XIII: The Damascus Document (4Q266–273)*, DJD 18 (Oxford: Clarendon, 1996), 26. In addition, the radiocarbon date range of 4Q267 places the earliest date of its range in the second century BCE. See Webster, "Chronological Index," 366. The *composition* of these works must therefore be earlier, although there is disagreement as to how much earlier. For discussion, see C. Hempel, *The Damascus Texts*, Companion to the Qumran Scrolls 1 (Sheffield: Sheffield Academic Press, 2000), 54–70; and Hempel, *Qumran Rule Texts*, 65–108.

17. It is not my purpose to try to determine when or where any particular rule or form of a rule was in force among the sectarians in Judea during this period. J. J. Collins, "Sectarian Comunities in the Dead Sea Scrolls," *OHDSS* 151–52, argues that the significant variations in the S copies suggest that different recensions were in use in different communities. These variant recensions were brought to Qumran to be hidden away. A. Schofield, *From Qumran to the Yaḥad: A New Paradigm of Textual Development for the Community Rule*, STDJ 77 (Leiden: Brill, 2009), makes a similar suggestion, with the addition of a "radial-dialogic" model of development for the S rule. As I will argue below, if any rule was in force at Qumran, the most likely was some form of S. It is also not my purpose to determine whether the various rule texts and their sources indicate different stages in the history of the sect to which they belonged. My working assumption is that the sect had its origins at least a generation before the settlement at Qumran was established.

CONCLUSIONS

kitchen (L38–41), and the animal bone deposits found in the open areas and between the buildings also fits with the discussions of communal meals found in S and Sa (1QS 6:2–6; 1QSa 2:17–22). The number of mikvaoth at Qumran reflects a concern for maintaining ritual purity, found extensively in S, D, and MMT as well as in the smaller legal texts.[18] Finally, 1QS was carefully preserved in a scroll jar and stored away in a limestone cliff cave; this may indicate reverence for the manuscript and a desire to make sure that it survived. Therefore, if a particular rule was being followed in the Qumran settlement, that rule would most likely have been some form of S.[19]

Admission Procedures

The major rule texts—the Serek Hayahad and the Damascus Document (and, secondarily, the Rule of the Congregation, a rule for the coming eschaton)— make clear by using the language of "joining" that this is a voluntary association. All three contain procedures for joining the sect, a set of guidelines for conduct and punishment within the community, and a process for expulsion from the sect. The procedures for joining the sect, as outlined in the rule texts, will be crucial for determining its identity. The rule texts all discuss entrance requirements and procedures, but they differ in certain ways.

The Serek Hayahad (S), chiefly in its Cave 1Q recension, gives us the most information about entrance procedures. It opens with several columns of instruction on entry into "the Covenant," that is, the sect. The Maskil oversees the entrance procedures. The ceremony for entering the covenant involves a confession of sin, blessings on those within the covenant and curses on those outside, and a binding oath on the part of the new member. This "covenant renewal" ceremony is to take place each year, with new members admitted at this time (1QS 5:20–23). For the new member, there then seems to be a probationary period of instruction by the Mebaqqer

---

18. A difference in the recensions of S may indicate that it was the recension found in 1QS that was followed at the Qumran settlement. 1QS 5:13 reads אל יבוא במים לגעת בטהרת אנשי הקודש ("not to enter the waters to touch the purity of the men of holiness"). This seems to indicate ritual bathing before consuming the pure food (4QS[b, d] lack the reference to "the waters" טהרה). The number of mikvaoth at Qumran may point to ritual bathing before meals. See Metso, *Textual Development*, 81; and Hempel, "Community Structures," 41.

19. The evidence of 4Q477, discussed in ch. 6, also indicates that some sort of sectarian rule was being followed in the Qumran settlement.

276

Who Owned the Scrolls? The Qumran-Essene Hypothesis Revisited

("Guardian"/"Overseer"); the initiate must wait a year, and be examined by the congregation, before he can touch the "pure meal" (and other pure items) of the sect. After that first year, his property and earnings are registered with the sect. After a second full year and another examination, he becomes a full-fledged member, able to touch the pure liquids of the sect, give counsel, and have his property merged with that of the sect (1QS 6:13–23).[20]

S also outlines, in its list of punishments for violations of the sect's rules, conduct that can lead to expulsion:

[An]yone who speaks aloud the M[os]t Holy Name of God, [whether in . . .] or in cursing or as a blurt in time of trial or for any other reason, or while he is reading a book or praying, is to be expelled, never again to return to the party of the *Yahad*. (1QS 6:27–7:2)

But if a man gossips about the general membership, he is to be banished from them and may never return. (1QS 7:16–17)

The man who murmurs against the secret teaching of the *Yahad* is to be banished, never to return. (1QS 7:17)

Any man who, having been in the party of the *Yahad* { } for ten full years, backslides spiritually so that he forsakes the *Yahad* and leaves the general membership, walking in his willful heart, may never again return to the party of the *Yahad*. (1QS 7:22–24).

The Damascus Document (D) also sketches an entrance procedure into the Covenant (also called "the new covenant in the land of Damascus," CD 8:21). Here the leadership figure who oversees the procedure is the Mebaqqer (already encountered in S); the entrant swears an oath: "On the day he speaks to the Overseer [מבקר] of the general membership, they shall register him by the oath of the covenant that Moses made with Israel" (CD 15:7–9). There is no probationary period mentioned; however, if the new member transgresses, the Guardian is responsible for a year of instruction before the member can be fully reinstated. D also mentions the entrance of children into the sect: "any children who reach the age to

---

20. Most commentators see two source texts here, with two entrance procedures. The first, 5:20–23, is simpler and older, while the second, more elaborate procedure is later (6:13–23). See Metso, *Textual Development*, 115–17; Hempel, *Qumran Rule Texts*, 28–31.

277

CONCLUSIONS

be included in the registrants, they shall impose the covenant oath upon them" (CD 15:5–6).

D discusses the possibility of expulsion from the sect. 4Q266 10 ii 1–2 states, "If he bears malice in a capital matter he [shall] return [no] more." Likewise, 4Q270 7 i 6–7 reads "[one who slanders the Many is to be expelled] and shall return no mo[re]." 4Q267 9 vi 4–5 // 4Q270 7 i 12–13 mentions the violation of sexual purity as a reason for expulsion: "One who comes near to fornicate [לזנות] with his wife contrary to the law shall depart and return no more." Disrespect toward male elders in the sect warrants expulsion; disrespect toward female elders resulted only in a ten-day penalty: "[One who murmur]s against the fathers [shall be expelled] from the congregation and not return; [if] it is against the mothers, he shall be penalized for ten days" (4Q270 7 i 13–14).[21] Finally, 4Q266 outlines a procedure for expulsion:

> And anyone who rejects these regulations, (which are) in accordance with all the statutes found in the law of Moses, shall not be reckoned among all the sons of his truth; for his soul has despised righteous instruction. Being in rebellion let him be expelled from the presence of the Many. The priest appointed [ov]er the Many shall declare. . . . the one being expelled shall depart. (4Q266 11 5–8, 14)[22]

Organization and Leadership Roles

The sect itself was highly organized and hierarchical. The main organizing principle is that of the wilderness camp as laid out in Num 1–2, and the groupings of thousands, hundreds, fifties, and tens, which recur throughout the Pentateuch (e.g., Exod 18:21, 25; Deut 1:15). According to both S and Sa, each member is enrolled in a specific rank and is expected to be obedient to those above him (e.g., 1QS 5:23).

21. S. W. Crawford, "Mothers, Sisters, and Elders: Titles for Women in Second Temple Jewish and Early Christian Communities," in *The Dead Sea Scrolls as Background to Postbiblical Judaism and Early Christianity*, ed. J. Davila, STDJ 46 (Leiden: Brill, 2002), 178–80.

22. Uniquely, the Serek Ha'edah (Sa) contains rules of entry for those born within the sect (1QSa 1:6–9) and does not have any discussion about departure or expulsion from the sect. This is most likely because Sa is envisioning the eschatological future community, which is no longer a voluntary association but one in which all Israel participates. Thus the time for affirming one's membership would be when one reached adulthood, after being instructed in the correct conduct since childhood.

Who Owned the Scrolls? The Qumran-Essene Hypothesis Revisited

Regular meetings of the sectarians, with firm rules of conduct, are provided for:

> This is the rule for the session of the general membership, each man being in his proper place. The priests shall sit in the first row, the elders in the second, then the rest of the people, each in his proper place. In that order they shall be questioned about any judgement, deliberation or matter that may come before the general membership. (1QS 6:8–9)

> The rule for those who live in all the camps. All shall be mustered by their names: the priests first, the Levites second, the children of Israel third, the proselyte fourth. Then they shall be recorded by name, one after the other: the priests first, the Levites second, the children of Israel third, the proselyte fourth. In the same order they shall sit, and in the same order they will inquire of all. (CD 14:3–6)

The rules of conduct in these meetings were strict; violators were usually punished by reduced rations or exclusion from the pure food for a period of time:

> Anyone interrupting his companion while in session: ten days. Anyone who lies down and sleeps in a session of the general membership: thirty days. The same applies to the man who leaves a session of the general membership without permission and without a good excuse three times in a single session. Up to the third time he shall be punished by reduced rations only ten days. But if they have risen for prayer when he leaves, then he is to suffer thirty days reduced rations. (1QS 7:9–12)

> A man who spits into the midst of a session of the general membership is to be punished by reduced rations for thirty days. (1QS 7:13)[23]

Several leadership groups and/or roles are mentioned in the sectarian rule texts, although their various functions often overlap or are unclear.[24] These include the רבים ("the many"), the עדה (the "Congregation"), the sons of Aaron, the sons of Zadok, the Maskil, the Mebaqqer, and the Paqid.

---

23. This prohibition presents us with a minor but important parallel to Josephus's description of the Essenes in *J.W.* 2.147: "In addition they refrain from spitting in the middle of the company, or to the right."

24. Hempel, *Qumran Rule Texts*, 36–40.

279

CONCLUSIONS

Qualifications for these roles, based on birth, age, or standing in the sect, are mentioned in passing in various texts. For example, the Serek Ha'edah states:

> These are the men appointed to the party [or: congregation] of the *Yahad* [עצת היחד]: from the age of twe[nty] *vacat* all the [wis]e of the congregation, the understanding and knowledgeable—who are blameless in their behaviour and men of ability—together with the tri[bal officials,] all judges, magistrates, captains of thousands, [hundreds,] fifties and tens, and the Levites, each a full mem[ber of]his[div]ision of service. (1QSa 1:27–2:1)

Thus this voluntary association of Jews within the wider Jewish community had a hierarchy beyond the usual divisions of priests, Levites, and Israel, with special leadership roles (with titles) within the group.

Legal Interpretation

Joining oneself to the sect involved agreeing by oath to follow its particular legal rulings, that is, the sect's interpretation of the laws of the Torah. MMT is the best-known text that demonstrates the centrality of correct legal interpretation in the sect's ideology, but D also contains important examples of sectarian legal interpretation. Added to these texts are the more fragmentary legal texts; according to the reckoning in DJD 39 there are at least twelve others, including 4QTohorot A (4Q274), 4QOrdinances[a-c] (4Q159, 513–514), and 4QHalaka A (4Q251). In addition, the predominance of the books of the Torah among the classical literature preserved in the caves as well as the presence of the book of Jubilees and the Temple Scroll with their emphasis on correct legal procedures makes clear the importance of the Torah and its correct interpretation and practice to the sect.

The legal rulings of the sect may be characterized as strict.[25] As an example, the Damascus Document contains a long section on the proper

---

25. A. Amihay, *Theory and Practice in Essene Law* (New York: Oxford University Press, 2017), 8, makes the salient observation that "stringency" versus "leniency" categories reflect rabbinic concepts of approaches to legal interpretation that would not have been relevant categories for the Essenes. He notes that the Essenes (he equates the Qumran sect with the Essenes) regarded themselves not as "strict" but as "correct." His observation is likewise correct, but using the term *strict* is a useful heuristic device to distinguish between various stances to the laws of the Torah in the Second Temple period.

280

Who Owned the Scrolls? The Qumran-Essene Hypothesis Revisited

Sabbath observances (CD 10:14–11:18, with parallels in 4Q266, 267, 270, and 271), which regulates many activities and behaviors on the Sabbath.

> On the Sabbath day, one may not speak any coarse or empty word. One is not to seek repayment of any loan from his fellow. One may not go to court about property or wealth. One may not discuss business or work to be done the next day. (CD 10:17–19)

> Any living human who falls into {water} a body of water or a cistern shall not be helped out with ladder, rope, or instrument. (CD 11:16–17)[26]

Some of these regulations are in line with later rabbinic legislation, but some are more rigorous. For example, while the rabbis allowed travel up to 2,000 cubits on the Sabbath, the sectarians limit it to 1,000 cubits (CD 10:21).[27]

The purity regulations of the sect are also rigorous and careful to follow what the sect believed was the correct interpretation of the Torah law in question. D emphasizes the importance of knowing the difference between the pure and the impure: "to separate unclean from clean and to discriminate between holy and profane" (CD 12:19–20; cf. Lev 10:10).

Several of MMT's regulations concern proper observance of purity regulations, for example:

> And concerning the purity-regulations of the cow of the purification-offering [i.e., the red heifer]: he who slaughters it and he who burns it and he who gathers its ashes and he who sprinkles the [water of] purification—it is at sun[se]t that all these become pure so that the pure man may sprinkle upon the impure one. (MMT[b] 13–16)[28]

26. According to sectarian legal interpretation, it is permitted to save a human life on the Sabbath but it is forbidden to use an implement of any kind to do so, because it is forbidden to carry any implement on the Sabbath. 4Q265, a manuscript that contains material similar to both S and D, has a similar ruling: "And if it is a human being who falls in[to] the water [on] the Sabbath [day,] let him cast his garment to him to raise him up therewith, but an implement he may not carry [to raise him up on] the Sabbath [day]" (6 6–8). This text makes clear that it is the use of instruments that is prohibited, not saving a life on the Sabbath. See Schiffman, *Reclaiming the Dead Sea Scrolls*, 280–81.

27. L. H. Schiffman, "Sabbath," *EDSS* 2:805–7.

28. This ruling concerns the question of when the person who is impure and then immerses becomes pure and is able to sprinkle the ashes of the red heifer (Num 19:1–10). MMT states that the impure person who has immersed must wait until sundown to be

CONCLUSIONS

And concerning the hi[des and the bones of unclean animals: it is forbidden to make] handles of [vessels from their bones] and hides. [And concerning] the hide of the carcass of a clean [animal]: he who carries such a carcass [shall not] have access to the sacred food. (MMT[b] 21–23)

This concern for maintaining purity can also be demonstrated in the rulings concerning marriage and sexuality found in the sectarian texts.[29] Prohibitions in the sectarian literature strictly control acceptable marriage partners. D opposes uncle-niece marriage, considering it part of the "three nets of Belial":

Furthermore they marry each man the daughter of his brothers and the daughter of his sister, although Moses said, "*Unto the sister of your mother you shall not draw near; she is the flesh of your mother*" (cf. Lev 18:13). But the law of consanguinity is written for males and females alike, so if the brother's daughter uncovers the nakedness of the brother of her father, she is the flesh (of her father). (CD 5:7–11; see also 11QT[a] 66:15–17 and 4QHalaka A 12)

---

considered pure for carrying out the requirements of the law. See Qimron, DJD 10, 152–54. The Sadducees also maintained that the purified priest had to wait until after sunset to perform his task. The Pharisees held that immersion rendered the priest ritually pure, and therefore he did not have to wait until sunset to sprinkle the ashes. In m. Parah 3:7, the Pharisees deliberately rendered impure before sunset the priest who was to sprinkle the ashes, then promptly immersed him and allowed him to perform his task. See J. Klawans, *Impurity and Sin in Ancient Judaism* (New York: Oxford University Press, 2000), 73. This evident disagreement by the sect with the practice of the Pharisees has led some scholars to see in this text an anti-Pharisaic polemic. See J. Baumgarten, "The Pharisaic-Sadducean Controversies about Purity and the Qumran Texts," *JJS* 31 (1980): 163–64; and L. Schiffman, "The New Halakhic Letter (4QMMT) and the Origins of the Dead Sea Sect," *BA* 53 (1990): 64–73. M. Himmelfarb argues that MMT is not polemicizing against another practice, but engaging in careful exegesis to clarify when the person who sprinkled the water mixed with ashes is pure. I agree with her analysis, but the fact remains that the Pharisees followed a different practice, and the sect is carefully outlining their own practice, which implies that they are concerned that someone else is doing it incorrectly. This difference in practice demonstrates that the sect cannot be the Pharisees. See M. Himmelfarb, "The Polemic against the *Tevul Yom*: A Reexamination," in *New Perspectives on Old Texts: Proceedings of the Tenth International Symposium of the Orion Center for the Study of the Dead Sea Scrolls and Associated Literature*, ed. R. Clements and B. Halpern-Amaru (Leiden: Brill, 2010), 199–214.

29. For an overview, see W. Loader, *The Dead Sea Scrolls on Sexuality: Attitudes towards Sexuality in Sectarian and Related Literature at Qumran* (Grand Rapids: Eerdmans, 2009).

Who Owned the Scrolls? The Qumran-Essene Hypothesis Revisited

MMT[b] enjoins male Israelites to shun any "illegal marriage" or "forbidden unions," and also condemns marriage between the priestly and lay orders (referred to as "mating with another species" or "mixing," כלאים; MMT[b] 77, 80–82). D (4Q271 3 9–10) contains the statement that a woman's father "should not give her to one unfit for her," evidently referring to forbidden degrees of marriage.

The sectarian texts also exhibit a disapproving attitude toward polygamy, as opposed to the Torah, which allows it (Deut 21:15–17; 24:1–4). According to the Damascus Document, polygamy is a form of זנות ("fornication"):

> The "Shoddy-Wall-Builders" who went after "Precept" [צו]— Precept is a Raver of whom it says, *"they shall surely rave"* (Mic 2:6)— they are caught in two: fornication, by taking two wives in their lifetimes although the principle of creation is *"male and female He created them"* (Gen 1:27) and those who went into the ark *"went into the ark two by two"* (Gen 7:9). (CD 4:19–5:1)

The Temple Scroll (an affiliated text) also prohibits polygamy for the king (11QT[a] 57:17–18).

The sectarian scrolls even betray an austere attitude toward sexual activity within marriage, which seems to be driven by purity concerns. We have cited above D's statement that זנות within marriage is punishable by expulsion. D elsewhere specifically prohibits intercourse during pregnancy (4Q270 2 ii 15–16) and possibly on the Sabbath or perhaps during the daylight hours (4Q270 2 i 18–19).[30] D forbids sexual intercourse within the city of the temple for purity reasons (CD 12:1–2; paralleled in 11QT[a] 45:11–12). Thus the legal regulations of the sectarian scrolls (and texts with which the sect had a special affinity) place restrictions on sexual expression for both men and women that are more severe than those of the Torah.[31]

The purity or impurity of food and drink is, of course, of great importance in Jewish law, and the sectarian texts demonstrate a high level of concern for maintaining the purity of food and drink. We have already mentioned MMT's ruling on liquid streams, which states the sect's position:

---

30. C. Wassén, *Women in the Damascus Document* (Atlanta: Society of Biblical Literature, 2005), 109–11; Loader, *Dead Sea Scrolls on Sexuality*, 140–41.

31. This may have led to a lower rate of marriage within the sect. See S. W. Crawford, "Not According to Rule," in *Emanuel*, ed. S. Paul et al., VTSup 94 (Leiden: Brill, 2003), 135.

283

CONCLUSIONS

> And concerning liquid streams: we are of the opinion that they are
> not pure, and that these streams do not act as a separative between
> impure and pure (liquids). For the liquid of streams and (that) of
> (the vessel) which receives them are alike, (being) a single liquid.
> (MMT B 55–58)[32]

MMT contains other rulings concerning food impurity, such as prohibiting eating wheat purchased from gentiles or using it for a grain offering (4Q394 i 7–8; CD 12:8–11 forbids selling produce to gentiles). A concern with liquid impurity is demonstrated in 4QTohorot A 3 i 6–8: "[if] its juice [has not oozed out] he shall eat it in purity, but any (fruits) [whi]ch are crushed so that their juice has oozed out should not be eaten by anyone [if] an unclean person has [to]uched them."

Both S and D discuss the pure food and drink of the sect. In S's entrance procedure, the probationer is not allowed to touch the pure (non-liquid) items of the sect until one year has passed, and the pure liquids after two years. Several of the punishments in S's penal code involve exclusion for various periods of time from the pure food and drink; the infractions include defiance toward a fellow member or a priest, false accusations, gossip, and return after apostasy from the sect. D also mentions exclusion from the pure meal as a punishment for transgression, often in parallel with S.

Other legal rulings by the sect betray the same mind-set. We can therefore conclude that we are dealing with a sect that had its own system of legal interpretation, which it took very seriously. Disputes about legal rulings seem to have been a major part of the impetus that formed the sect, and separated those within the sect from those outside it.

---

32. This ruling concerns the purity or impurity of a liquid stream that is poured from a pure vessel into an impure one. The sect believes that impurity from the lower vessel travels up the liquid stream to contaminate the pure vessel. There is no biblical precedent for this ruling; however, in the Mishnah two passages are concerned with this case. M. Ṭehar. 8:9 lays out the position that an uninterrupted flow of liquid from a pure source to an impure one does not communicate or produce impurity. In m. Yad. 4:7 the Sadducees "protest" (קובלים) against the Pharisees for holding the position that an unbroken stream of liquid does not convey impurity. Since the sect holds the opposite position from the Pharisees, once again the sect cannot be the Pharisees. See Qimron, DJD 10, 161–62.

284

Who Owned the Scrolls? The Qumran-Essene Hypothesis Revisited

The Sharing of Property

An unusual feature of this sect is that they seem to share their property within the sect beyond the temple tithes and taxes prescribed for all Jews. The Damascus Document requires members to give at least two days' earnings from every month to the leaders of the sect for charitable purposes (CD 14:12–17). Another passage is concerned with one who lies about money to the community: "Whoever lie[s] knowingly in a matter of money shall be ex[pelled . . . and pun]ished six days" (CD 14:20–21), indicating some community control over the member's property.[33]

The Serek Hayaḥad envisions a more comprehensive community of goods. During the entry process outlined in 1QS, after the first year the probationer hands over his property to the Overseer or Bursar, who holds it but does not spend it. When the probationer becomes a full-fledged member, his property is merged with the sect's. It is not clear whether the property in question is everything that belongs to the member; there is some indication that it is not, since the penal code states,

> If money belonging to the *Yahad* is involved in a fraudulent scheme and lost, [ ] must repay the sum { } from his own funds. If he lacks sufficient resources to repay it, then he is to suffer reduced rations ^{for sixty days}. (1QS 7:6–8)

This regulation would suggest that at least some members of the sect continued to control some portion of their own wealth outside the sect.[34]

33. See C. M. Murphy, *Wealth in the Dead Sea Scrolls and in the Qumran Community*, STDJ 40 (Leiden: Brill, 2002), 52–53.

34. An ostracon found at the settlement may give further evidence that the sectarians shared their property. This ostracon, KhQ1, was discovered by James Strange in 1996 on the east side of the south wall that extends down the marl terrace. Cross and Eshel, the editors, date its script to 30–68 CE (the last years of the settlement). The ostracon is a draft of a deed of gift; one Ḥoni is turning property over to Elazar son of Naḥamani. In a broken context in line 8, Cross and Eshel read, "when he fulfills (his oath) to the community [ליחד]," and understand it to mean that Ḥoni is turning his wealth over to the sectarian community, in keeping with the S rule. If their reading is correct, this ostracon would be valuable evidence that the Qumran settlement was following the regulations of S and holding their property in common. The reading, however, has been contested by Yardeni, who reads line 8 as "and every other tree" (וכול אילנ אחנ[ר]), a simple continuation of the property Ḥoni is turning over to Elazar. If her reading is accepted, ליחד disappears, and the ostracon does not bear on the issue of common property at all. See J. Strange, "The 1996 Excavations at Qumran and the

285

CONCLUSIONS

Once again, this feature sets this group apart from the Judaism of the period, for whom individual property was the norm.

Prayer and Worship

All indications from the Qumran library are that the sect enjoyed a robust worship life. The sheer quantity of psalms, hymns, and prayers, especially previously unknown ones, demonstrates this. Many unfortunately exist only in single copies and/or are very fragmentary, but we may assume that many were copied in order to be remembered and reused (see ch. 6). Works that exist in multiple copies, such as the Hodayot and the Songs of the Sabbath Sacrifice, must have been central to the liturgical life of the sect. In addition, tefillin texts and capsules found in the caves indicate daily prayer by the inhabitants of Qumran.

The rule texts also illustrate the importance of worship and study in the life of the sect. S, 1QSa, and D all legislate for regular continuing prayer and study, as well as periodic ceremonies such as the covenant renewal ceremony outlined in S. Examples include:

> He [the Maskil] shall bless Him at the times ordained of God: when light begins its dominion—each time it returns—and when, as ordained, it is regathered into its dwelling place; when night begins its watches— as He opens His storehouse and spreads darkness over the earth—and when it cycles back, withdrawing before the light; when the luminaries show forth from their holy habitation, and when they are regathered into their glorious abode; when the times appointed for new moons arrive, and when, as their periods require, each gives way to the next. (1QS 9:26–10:4)

> to keep the sabbath day according to specification and the holidays and the fast day according to the commandments of those entering the new covenant in the land of Damascus. (CD 6:18–19)

Context of the New Hebrew Ostracon," in *Qumran, the Site of the Dead Sea Scrolls: Archaeological Interpretations and Debates; Proceedings of a Conference Held at Brown University, November 17–19, 2002*, ed. K. Galor et al., STDJ 57 (Leiden: Brill, 2006), 41–54; F. M. Cross and E. Eshel, "1. KhQOstracon," in *Qumran Cave 4.XXVI: Cryptic Texts*, by S. Pfann; and *Miscellanea Part 1*, by P. Alexander et al., DJD 36 (Oxford: Clarendon, 2000), 497–507; and A. Yardeni, "A Draft of a Deed on an Ostracon from Khirbet Qumran," *IEJ* 47 (1997): 233–37.

Who Owned the Scrolls? The Qumran-Essene Hypothesis Revisited

> [When they] gather [at the] communal [tab]le, [to drink w]ine so the communal table is set and [the] wine [poured] for drinking, [none may re]ach for the first portion of the bread or [the wine] before the Priest. For [he] shall [bl]ess the first portion of the bread and the win[e, reach]ing for the bread first. Afterw[ard] the Messiah of Israel [shall re]ach for the bread. [Finally,] ea[ch] member of the whole congregation of the *Yahad* [shall give a bl]essing, [in descending order of] rank. This procedure shall govern every me[al], provided at least ten me[n are ga]thered together. (1QSa 2:17–22)

These passages indicate that the sect's worship life revolved around the daily, seasonal, and festival ceremonies of Judaism, as well as a strictly controlled table fellowship.

Their worship life was also intrinsically entwined with the study of Scripture. The library itself gives evidence of the importance of Scripture study: 25 percent of the library consists of copies of the classical texts of Judaism, with a plurality of Torah manuscripts represented. In addition, the excerpted texts, the majority of which are Torah texts, were most likely used as personal or group study texts. When the scripturally based exegetical works such as Jubilees and the pesharim are included in this total, it is evident that a great deal of energy in sectarian life was devoted to Scripture study and its accompaniment, exegesis.[35]

Indeed, the rule texts enjoin constant Scripture study. As we have already noted, S states unequivocally:

> In any place where is gathered the ten-man quorum, someone must always be engaged in study of the Law, day and night, continually, each one taking his turn. The general membership will be diligent together for the first third of every night of the year, reading aloud from the Book, interpreting Scripture and praying together. (1QS 6:6–8)

A question that is persistently raised regarding the Qumran sect is whether it participated in the temple cult in Jerusalem. One point that is often mentioned in this regard is the evident preference for the 364-day solar calendar coordinated with the lunar months that we see in the Qum-

---

35. That several of the pesharim are single-copy manuscripts (e.g., 1QpHab, 4QpNah, 4QpMic) may indicate that they are not formal documents, but notes taken during study sessions of the sect and retained for future reference.

CONCLUSIONS

ran library. If the sectarians observed a different sacred calendar than the Jerusalem temple (at which the evidence suggests a lunar calendar was in force), it would have made the sectarians' participation in many of the ceremonies of the temple cult unlikely if not impossible, since the dates of their festivals would have differed from those of the temple.

Besides the question of differing calendars, there is other evidence from the texts that the sectarians thought that the temple cult was flawed. D states that one of the three "traps [or: nets] of Belial" in which sinful Israel is ensnared is profanation of the temple (CD 4:14–18), which has occurred because they neglect the laws of sexual purity as understood by the sect. It also warns its members: "None who have been brought into the covenant shall enter into the sanctuary to light up His altar in vain," quoting Mal 1:10 (CD 6:11–12). This admonition seems to be a veiled polemic against those (non–New Covenant) Jews who offer flawed sacrifices, presumably the priests in charge of the Jerusalem temple. MMT contains several rulings indicating the sect's disagreement with current temple practice, including the rites of the purification offering, the cereal offering, the ashes of the red heifer, and the extent of the sanctuary limits. The pesharim of Nahum, Habbakuk, and Psalms are concerned about corrupt priests, especially the activities of the Wicked Priest, one of the main opponents of the Teacher of Righteousness. Finally, in chap. 5 we accepted Magness's contention that the animal bone deposits indicate that sacrifice of some kind was taking place at Qumran. The cumulative force of this evidence suggests that although the sect may have continued in some ways to participate in the temple cult in Jerusalem, albeit grudgingly, they certainly considered it corrupted.[36]

Regardless of whether or not the sect continued to participate in some way in the Jerusalem temple cult, it considered its own worship to be a sacrificial act. For example, S states,

> When, united by all these precepts, such men as these come to be a community in Israel, they shall establish eternal truth guided by the instruction of His holy spirit. They shall atone for the guilt of transgres-

36. See Goodman, "Constructing Ancient Judaism," 82, who notes that "No text actually states that sectarians should avoid the temple altogether." H. Stegemann, *The Library of Qumran: On the Essenes, Qumran, John the Baptist, and Jesus* (Grand Rapids: Eerdmans, 1998), 176, suggested that the Essenes may have continued to offer sacrifices at the temple that were not tied to the festival calendar, such as Sabbath offerings. The sect could also have brought votive and thanksgiving offerings to the temple.

288

Who Owned the Scrolls? The Qumran-Essene Hypothesis Revisited

sion and the rebellion of sin, becoming an acceptable sacrifice for the land through the flesh of burnt offerings, the fat of sacrificial portions and *prayer* [lit. *offering of the lips*], becoming—as it were—justice itself, a sweet savour of righteousness and blameless behaviour, a pleasing free-will offering. (9:3–5; emphasis mine)[37]

In this text prayer takes its place alongside burnt offerings as an atoning sacrifice.

Finally, 4QFlorilegium (4Q174) implies that the eschatological temple will be not simply a place where cultic sacrifice is offered, but a place where the works of Torah are also considered proper offerings:

This is the house which [he will build] for [him] in the latter days, as it is written in the book of [Moses, "*The sanctuary,*] *O Yahweh, which your hands have fashioned. Yahweh will reign for ever and ever.*" (Exod 15:17–18) This (is) the house which these will not enter [for]ever, nor an Ammonite, a Moabite, a bastard, a foreigner, or a proselyte forever, for his holy ones (are) there. [His glory shall] be revealed for[ev]er; it shall appear over it perpetually. And strangers shall lay it waste no more, as they formerly laid waste the sanctuary of Israel because of their sin. And he has commanded that a sanctuary of human(s) [מקדש אדם] be built for him, so that they may offer incense in it to him, before him, works of Torah [מעשי תורה]. (4Q174 1–2, 21 i 3–7)

Separation from All Israel

One of the factors that mark the sectarian texts as sectarian rather than just part of general Jewish literature of the period is their consciousness of separateness and claims of persecution. Exhortations to separate themselves from fellow Jews permeates the sectarian literature. MMT, although irenic in tone, still separates itself as "we" against a "you" and a "them." In its opening exhortation giving the history of the sect, CD refers to it as "the remnant [שארית] of Israel." S famously calls the members of the sect the בני אור, "Children of Light," opposing the בני חושך, "Children of Darkness":

---

37. Note that the text of 4QS^d differs here slightly, removing the ambiguity of the מן particle; Vermes and Alexander, DJD 26, 110–11. I would like to thank Sarianna Metso for bringing this reference to my attention.

CONCLUSIONS

He [the Maskil] is to teach them both to love all the Children of Light—
each commensurate with his rightful place in the council of God—and
to hate all the Children of Darkness, each commensurate with his guilt
and the vengeance due him from God. (1QS 1:9–11)

The Hodayot and the pesharim illustrate not only a consciousness of
separateness from the rest of Judaism, but also a sense of persecution. In
the Hodayot, the poet claims:

f[or] ruthless people have sought my life when I held fast to your covenant. They are a council of deception and a congregation of Belial. They
do not know that my station comes from you and that by your kindness
you save my life, for from you come my steps. And because of you they
have threatened my life, so that you may be glorified in the judgement
of the wicked and manifest your strength through me before mortal
beings, for by your kindness do I stand. (1QH^a 10:23–27)

The pesharim contain many terms describing the opponents of the sect, individuals like the Wicked Priest, the Scoffer, and the Spreader (or: Spouter)
of Lies, and groups, most prominently the "Seekers-after-Smooth-Things,"
and claim to have been persecuted by these figures.[38]

Eschatology and Predeterminism

Hand in hand with the feelings of separateness and persecution goes a
strong eschatological mood. It is clear from the texts that the sectarians
believed they were living in the last days and that the grand denouement of
history, when they would be vindicated by God, was rapidly approaching.[39]
The phrase אחרית הימים, "the last days," occurs throughout the pesharim,
D, the Florilegium, 4QCatena A and B, and MMT.[40] Of course, the War
Rules are entirely concerned with the final eschatological battle between
good and evil, when the sect, fighting on the side of God's angels, would
prove victorious over their enemies:

---

38. See esp. 1QpMic, 4QpNah, and 1QpHab.
39. For an overview, consult J. Collins, *Apocalypticism in the Dead Sea Scrolls* (London:
Routledge, 1997).
40. A. Steudel, "אחרית הימים in the Texts from Qumran," *RevQ* 16 (1993): 225–46.

290

Who Owned the Scrolls? The Qumran-Essene Hypothesis Revisited

the priests shall continue sounding on the trumpets of the slain to direct the fighting, until the enemy is defeated and turns in retreat. The priests shall blow the alarm to direct the battle, and when they have been defeated before them, the priests shall blow the trumpets of assembly, and all the infantry shall go out to them from the midst of the front battle lines and stand. . . . All these shall pursue in order to destroy the enemy in God's battle; a total annihilation. (1QM 9:1–5)

Also strongly present in the sectarian texts is the theme of predestination or predeterminism, illustrated by terms such as "chose" and "chosen" (בחר) and "destined" and "destiny" (תעודה). The Serek Hayaḥad and the Hodayot in particular illustrate this concept, as we saw in the Hodayot passage quoted above. A famous passage from 1QS, the Doctrine of the Two Spirits (cols. 3–4), divides humanity into two lots, based on their "destiny" (פעולתם). These two theological concepts of predestination and eschatology are far more prominent in the sectarian literature (and its affiliated literature) than we find overall in Jewish literature of the period.

The characteristics and themes illustrated above demonstrate a strong sectarian consciousness in the literature found in the Qumran caves, and we have seen how this sectarian literature gives the scrolls collection its particular profile. Having examined what the sectarian texts reveal about the sect, the next step is to determine whether the archaeology of Qumran is compatible with habitation by this sect.

The Archaeological Evidence

Qumran's archaeology consists of a set of buildings with large communal rooms, without private dwellings or evidence for family life. This physical layout would not fit with the type of community envisaged by D or Sa, which legislate for marriage, family life, and some degree of private property. However, it does, as Roland de Vaux recognized in the 1950s, fit with the type of community envisioned by S, which makes no mention of marriage or family life and requires an (almost) absolute community of goods. Further, the remains of Qumran testify to a rather austere lifestyle. The walls are simply whitewashed, without any evidence of frescoes or other decoration. The floors are almost entirely packed earth; no mosaic floors were uncovered. Further, the pottery is mostly plain and undecorated, with the same few utilitarian forms repeating over and over.

CONCLUSIONS

Another peculiarity in the physical remains is the almost total lack of evidence for the presence of women and children. In the buildings themselves, in the predestruction phases, no female-gendered remains (such as spindle whorls or female jewelry) were found. The human remains from the small number of excavated graves in the main cemetery are almost entirely male; female remains are mostly found in the satellite cemeteries, and some of these may be later bedouin intrusions. The recent excavation of thirty-three graves in the North Cemetery, from which the skeletal remains whose gender could be determined were entirely male, reinforces this picture of male exclusivity.[41] This lack of female presence fits with S but not with D or Sa.

Elements of the architecture also evince a concern for ritual purity. There are ten mikvaoth, an unusually high number for a small complex. The cemetery is separated from the buildings by a low dividing wall, probably signaling a concern with corpse impurity.[42]

The remnants of linen from scroll wrappers and jar stoppers found in the caves adds to the impression of a sectarian consciousness in the archaeological remains. The linens are plain and undyed and almost entirely undecorated (except for some decorative borders of blue thread). This plainness contrasts sharply with fabric remains from other Second Temple period sites, and adds to the evidence for a sectarian community.

Finally, there are the enigmatic remains of animal bones (sheep, goat, and cow), found in several locations outside the buildings. These bones, as we saw in ch. 5, are most likely the consumption debris of sacrifices, indicating some sort of cultic practices separate from those of the temple. This again points to habitation by a sectarian group.

One element in the archaeological record does raise questions about whether Qumran was a sectarian settlement highly concerned with ritual purity, and that is the presence of the toilet in L51, in the middle of the buildings. The toilet went out of use and was not replaced at the time of the earthquake (probably in 31 BCE). Both the War Scroll and the Temple Scroll mandate the placement of toilet facilities outside an inhabited area, so the location of a toilet in the middle of the buildings at Qumran

41. Y. Nagar et al., "The People of Qumran—New Discoveries and Paleo-demographic Interpretations" (paper presented at the Annual Meeting of ASOR, Boston, 16 November 2017).

42. J.-B. Humbert, "L'espace sacré à Qumrân: Propositions pour l'archéologie," *RB* 101 (1994): 161–214; J. Branham, "Hedging the Holy at Qumran: Walls as Symbolic Devices," in Galor et al., *Qumran, Site of the Dead Sea Scrolls*, 117–32.

Who Owned the Scrolls? The Qumran-Essene Hypothesis Revisited

would seem to violate sectarian practice as mandated by these documents. However, the War Scroll is discussing toilet facilities to be used during the eschatological last battle:

> Any man who is not ritually clean in respect to his genitals shall not go down with them into battle, for holy angels are present with their army. There shall be a distance between all their camps and the latrine of about two thousand cubits, and no shameful nakedness shall be seen in the environs of all their camps. (1QM 7:6-7)

Similarly, the Temple Scroll is concerned with toilet facilities around the ideal temple city:

> And you shall make them a place for a "hand," outside the city, to which they shall go out, to the northwest of the city—roofed houses with pits within them, into which the excrement will descend, so that it will not be visible at any distance from the city, three thousand cubits. (11QT[a] 46:13-16)

Qumran is certainly not the ideal temple city envisioned in the Temple Scroll and also does not seem to have been considered any type of battle camp; therefore, the rules concerning toilet practices found in the War Rule and the Temple Scroll would probably not have been observed at Qumran, at least during the period the toilet was in use.[43] The rule texts for everyday life, S and D, make no mention of toilet habits and therefore are compatible with the archaeological remains.

Thus we can say that the archaeological remains at Qumran fit with (or at least do not contradict) the kind of life envisioned by the sectarian scrolls, especially S. Would it be possible to interpret the archaeological remains in other ways if the scrolls were set aside, as Golb, Hirschfeld, and others have attempted? Yes, perhaps; but as we have seen, the scrolls are part of the archaeological landscape of Qumran and cannot, on methodological grounds, be separated from them. Therefore, any attempt to separate scrolls and buildings is methodologically flawed from the outset.

Let us summarize the textual and archaeological evidence presented thus far. The sect that inhabited Qumran and whose library was deposited in the caves surrounding the site had the following characteristics: a

---

43. See also J. Collins, *Beyond the Qumran Community: The Sectarian Movement of the Dead Sea Scrolls* (Grand Rapids: Eerdmans, 2009), 205-6.

CONCLUSIONS

sense of separateness and even persecution from wider Judaism; entrance requirements and procedures that separated the members out from the wider Jewish community and enforced a hierarchical community structure; an emphasis on correct legal interpretation that tended toward strictness and emphasized a high degree of purity for its members; some degree of property sharing within the sect; a robust liturgical life, accompanied by a negative view of the current temple administration; and a theology that included eschatological beliefs and predeterminism. The site of Qumran can be construed as the living quarters of members of such a sect, especially as outlined in the Serek Hayaḥad, which does not mention women and children in its regulations. If we next turn to the outside sources that enumerate various Jewish movements in the first centuries BCE and CE, is it possible to make an identification between the sect and one of those movements?

The Classical Sources

The sources that discuss Jewish movements in the late Second Temple period are primarily the classical sources of Philo and Josephus, and other secondary sources such as Pliny, Dio of Prusa (also known as Dio Chrysostom), and Hippolytus, as well as brief notices in the later writers Hegesippus, Justin Martyr, Porphyry, and Epiphanius.[44] The evidence of the NT and the rabbinic material may also be cautiously used as a supplement, since it is for the most part later than Josephus and Philo.

Using the classical sources, written in Greek or Latin for a Greco-Roman audience, is methodologically fraught.[45] As Joan Taylor puts it,

> As every ancient historian well knows, the writing of current affairs or history in antiquity could be openly polemical, propagandistic, selective, or exaggerated, and not intended . . . to create a coherent identity for either an individual or a group.

44. For an extended study of all these sources, see the excellent treatment by J. Taylor in *The Essenes, the Scrolls, and the Dead Sea* (Oxford: Oxford University Press, 2012), 3–194. All quotations of these sources, unless otherwise noted, are taken from G. Vermes and M. Goodman, *The Essenes according to the Classical Sources* (Sheffield: JSOT Press, 1989).

45. S. Mason has emphasized this methodological issue in his many publications on Josephus., e.g., "Excursus 1: The Essenes of Josephus' *War*," in *Flavius Josephus: Translation and Commentary*, vol. 1B: *Judean War 2* (Leiden: Brill, 2008), 84–95.

294

Who Owned the Scrolls? The Qumran-Essene Hypothesis Revisited

She continues,

> The way forward for a historian or archaeologist when faced with literary rhetoricity is not a simple one of either simply accepting all that is written as being entirely the truth, or viewing everything as the writer's imagination or selective summarizing of rumour: factuality and exaggeration, history and hearsay, are woven together, and only careful understanding of the contexts of the work in question and the grand themes within a writer's surviving corpus can lead us towards intelligent understanding.[46]

Thus we must be aware of the purposes for which the classical sources are using their historical data, and try to separate out facts from rhetoric.

Our sources present us with several groups or movements in the Second Temple period with which the Qumran sect could be identified. The main groups are the Samaritans, the Pharisees, the Sadducees, and the Essenes; Josephus and the NT also mention the Herodians and the Zealots, while rabbinic literature refers to the Boethusians. Since the last three groups are all associated with the reign of Herod the Great and later events, and Qumran was settled in the first half of the first century BCE, these groups are too late to be identified with the Qumran sect and thus are not considered in detail here. However, it is possible that the sect or its members had connections with these later groups.[47]

The Samaritans, mentioned in Josephus, the NT, and rabbinic sources, identified themselves with the ancient Israelite northern kingdom. They were worshipers of Israel's God, and during most of the postexilic period their sanctuary was located on Mount Gerizim in the central hill country, around which their communities clustered. This sanctuary was destroyed by John Hyrcanus in 104–103 BCE, leading to an irreparable rupture between the Samaritans and the Judeans. The Samaritans accepted only the Torah as their Scripture. It is quite clear that the Qumran sect is not Samar-

---

46. Taylor, *Essenes*, 19–20.

47. Taylor, *Essenes*, 247, suggests that the Qumran sect, whom she identifies as the Essenes, should be equated with the Herodians mentioned in the NT (Mark 3:6; 12:13; Matt 22:16). Stegemann, "Qumran Essenes," 164, also identifies the Essenes and the Herodians. The Boethusians, who appear only in rabbinic sources, are part of the Sadducean priestly aristocracy. See E. Regev, "Boethusians," in *Encyclopedia of the Bible and Its Reception*, ed. H.-J. Klauck et al., 30 vols. (Berlin: de Gruyter, 2009–), 4:445–47; and G. Stemberger, "Sadducees," *EDEJ* 1180.

CONCLUSIONS

itan; Qumran is located within the wider geographical orbit of Jerusalem; the temple mentioned in the sectarian texts is clearly located in Jerusalem; and their classical texts include much more than the Torah. A few of the Torah manuscripts found in the caves share a base text with the Samaritan Pentateuch, but they contain no Samaritan ideological markers such as the building of the temple on Mount Gerizim, and their presence is explained by a shared textual history.[48] Therefore it is most improbable that the inhabitants of Qumran were Samaritans.

The Pharisees appear in Josephus, the NT, and the rabbinic sources.[49] According to Josephus, they are one of the three αἱρέσεις that arose in the second century BCE, and Josephus is the source for our most direct information about them. The Pharisees were a voluntary association within Judaism who followed the "tradition from the fathers" alongside the Mosaic law, emphasized ritual purity in everyday life (including table fellowship), and believed in fate, the afterlife, and rewards and punishments after death.[50] Some of these characteristics do agree with those of the Qumran sect, for example, the emphasis on ritual purity in everyday life and the belief in fate and the afterlife, which agreement led some early scholars to identify the sect with the Pharisees.[51] However, we know from the sectarian texts themselves that the sect is not the Pharisees. In MMT we saw that the sect disagreed with Pharisaic legal positions on some key rulings (e.g., the ruling on liquid streams and the status of the *ṭevul yom*; see n 28). The argument concerning the permissibility of uncle-niece marriage also indicates that the sect is not the Pharisees. Since the prohibition on

48. S. W. Crawford, "Samaritan Pentateuch," in *The Hebrew Bible*, vol. 1A: *Overview Articles*, ed. A. Lange and E. Tov, Textual History of the Bible (Leiden: Brill, 2016), 166–75. A small fragment from the Azusa Pacific Dead Sea Scroll collection, DSSF 154, contains Deut 27:4–6. It includes the reading בהרגריזימ, in agreement with the Samaritan Pentateuch. However, the authenticity of this fragment has been called into question, and it may be a modern forgery.

49. A. Saldarini, *Pharisees, Scribes and Sadducees in Palestinian Society* (Grand Rapids: Eerdmans, 2001), 277, gives a pertinent warning when discussing the Pharisees: "Data on the Pharisees is so sparse and difficult to evaluate that any historical reconstruction must remain incomplete and uncomfortably hypothetical." He also warns against equating the Pharisees and the rabbis.

50. S. Mason, *Flavius Josephus: Translation and Commentary*, vol. 9: *Life of Josephus* (Leiden: Brill, 2001), 16.

51. A prominent example is Louis Ginzberg, who identified the sectarians of the Damascus Document with the Pharisees (*An Unknown Jewish Sect* [New York: Jewish Theological Seminary, 1976]).

296

Who Owned the Scrolls? The Qumran-Essene Hypothesis Revisited

uncle-niece marriage is polemical in the Damascus Document (CD 5:7–11), where it is associated with the "three traps [or: nets] of Belial," we can be certain that uncle-niece marriage was practiced among some Jews in the Second Temple period. While the position of the Pharisees on uncle-niece marriage is never specifically articulated in rabbinic literature, we know that it was permitted by the rabbis, who often reflect Pharisaic legal positions. Thus it is likely that the Pharisees allowed marriages between uncles and nieces.[52]

Further, the epithet given to the main opposition group of the sect, the דורשי החלקות or "seekers of smooth things," is most likely a punning reference to the הלכות ("regulations"; literally "walking [in the Law]") to which the Pharisees adhered (see, e.g., CD 1:14–21; 1QH[a] 10:31–38; 12:5; 4QpIsa[c]; and Catena A 9 4–5). The דורשי החלקות are excoriated in the Damascus Document as followers of the "Man of Mockery" who lead Israel astray:

When the Man of Mockery [איש הלצון] appeared, who sprayed on Israel lying waters, *"he led them to wander in the trackless wasteland"* (Ps 107:40; Job 12:24). He brought down the lofty heights of old, turned aside from paths of righteousness, and shifted the boundary marks that the forefathers had set up to mark their inheritance, so that the curses of His covenant took hold on them. Because of this they were handed over *"to the sword that avenges the breach of His covenant"* (Lev 26:25). For they had *sought flattery* [or *smooth things*, דרשו בחלקות], choosing travesties of true religion; they looked for ways to break the law; they favoured the fine neck. They called the guilty innocent, and the innocent guilty. They overstepped covenant, violated law; and *"they conspired together to kill the innocent"* (Ps 94:21), for all those who lived pure lives they loathed from the bottom of their heart. (CD 1:14–21)

The "seekers of smooth things" are thus legal opponents of the sect.[53]

---

52. This understanding was first proposed by Ginzberg, *Unknown Jewish Sect*, 23–24. See also J. VanderKam, "The Pharisees and the Dead Sea Scrolls," in *In Quest for the Historical Pharisees*, ed. J. Neusner and B. Chilton (Waco, TX: Baylor University Press, 2007), 235; and J. VanderKam, "Those Who Look for Smooth Things, Pharisees, and Oral Law," in *Emanuel: Studies in Hebrew Bible, Septuagint and Dead Sea Scrolls in Honor of Emanuel Tov*, ed. S. Paul et al., VTSup 94 (Leiden: Brill, 2003), 467.

53. VanderKam, "Those Who Look for Smooth Things," 470–71, notes that the epithet accuses the opponents of misusing speech and relaxing legal requirements, as well as being "lying interpreters," מליצי כזב.

297

CONCLUSIONS

In Pesher Nahum 3–4 i 2–3 the דורשי החלקות are accused of counseling Demetrius of Greece (III Eukarios; ruled 95–88 BCE) to attack Jerusalem and King Alexander Jannaeus, who later "will hang people alive" (7). Josephus recounts the same episode in *J.W.* 1.4 and *Ant.* 13.376–380, where Jannaeus crucifies eight hundred of his opponents. While the Pharisees are not specifically named here in Josephus, Jannaeus later confesses that he had "badly treated" the Pharisees (*Ant.* 13.401–402). It seems safe, therefore, to identify those he crucified with the Pharisees.[54] This accumulation of evidence enables us to identify with confidence the דורשי החלקות with the Pharisees. Since the "seekers of smooth things" were the main opponents of the sect, the sect cannot be identified with the Pharisees.

This leaves the Sadducees and the Essenes as possibilities. The Sadducees, unfortunately, are the least known among the groups.[55] According to Josephus (*J.W.* 2. 164–165), the Sadducees are associated with the temple and the elite class in Jerusalem; they deny the afterlife and the role of fate, and they adhere only to the Mosaic law (this seems to be a deliberate contrast with the Pharisees on the part of Josephus; as Mason points out, the Sadducees must have had some kind of interpretive tradition).[56] This information is corroborated by the NT: in both the Synoptic Gospels and Acts, the Sadducees are located among the chief priests and temple officials in Jerusalem; and in Mark 12:18–27, in a dispute with Jesus, the Sadducees say there is no resurrection. In addition, Acts 23:8 states that the Sadducees do not believe in angels.

In the rabbinic literature, the צדוקים are identified as the descendants of Zadok the priest. They usually appear alongside the Boethusians, probably a subgroup of the Sadducees. According to the rabbis, the Sadducees reject resurrection, challenge the ritual and purity prescriptions of others, and use a different calendar for some festivals (m. Ḥag. 2:4; m. Menaḥ. 10:3).[57] While, as we have seen above, some of the Qumran sect's legal positions agree with those of the Sadducees, and the mention of the use of a different calendar for some festivals is suggestive, the Sadducean denial of the resurrection and the existence of angels and of the role of fate (predestination) would indicate that they are not coterminous with the sect of the Qumran scrolls. Their common legal positions may indicate that the

---

54. VanderKam, "Pharisees and the Dead Sea Scrolls," 226–30.
55. Saldarini, *Pharisees, Scribes and Sadducees*, 79–80.
56. Mason, *Life*, 16–17.
57. Mason, *Life*, 16–17.

298

Who Owned the Scrolls? The Qumran-Essene Hypothesis Revisited

Sadducees of Josephus's time and the Qumran sect had common roots in the earlier Second Temple period.[58]

Only the Essenes, therefore, remain as a possible identification. Notably, the classical sources give us far more information about the Essenes than about the other groups. Both Philo and Josephus devote a great deal of space to discussions of Essene beliefs and practices. Philo, who discusses the Essenes in *Prob.* 75–91 and *Apologia pro Iudaeis*,[59] presents them as examples of philosophical perfection within the Greek tradition. They love virtue, do not care about money or reputation, are "pious, ascetic, controlled, orderly, enduring, frugal, simple-living, content, humble, respectful of the law, steady, and humanity-loving."[60] Since these are all terms from the Greek and Roman philosophical traditions, they tell us very little about the actual Essenes, but more about the impression Philo wishes to make on his Greco-Roman audience. However, the particulars that Philo uses to back up his claims give us more concrete information.

In Philo's understanding the Essenes were a voluntary association that numbered over four thousand members, and lived in both towns and villages in Judea (*Hypoth.* 11.1; *Prob.* 76 claims that the Essenes spurned cities and lived only in villages). On the subject of property Philo claims that the Essenes deposited their money into a communal fund, owned houses but shared them, did not own slaves, and engaged in farming and simple crafts (*Prob.* 77–86). They did not have wives or even younger members, spurned animal sacrifice (considering prayer a substitute), and ate common meals. From this list of characteristics we see overlaps with the Qumran sect: communal property, a negative attitude toward the temple cult and the substitution of prayer for sacrifice, and common meals.

The major difference is the attitude toward marriage: Philo is unequivocal in his statement that the Essenes did not marry, saying, "On the other hand, shrewdly providing against the sole or principal obstacle threatening

---

58. See esp. L. Schiffman, *Qumran and Jerusalem: Studies in the Dead Sea Scrolls and the History of Judaism* (Grand Rapids: Eerdmans, 2010), 112–14; J. Baumgarten, "The Pharisaic-Sadducean Controversies about Purity and the Qumran Texts," *JJS* 31 (1980): 157–70; and D. Dimant, "Israeli Scholarship on the Qumran Community," in *The Dead Sea Scrolls in Scholarly Perspective: A History of Research*, ed. D. Dimant, STDJ 99 (Leiden: Brill, 2012), 260–65.

59. The *Apologia pro Iudaeis* should probably be identified with the *Hypothetica*; only fragments remain, which are quoted by Eusebius in *Praep. ev.* 8.6–7. See Vermes and Goodman, *Essenes*, 26.

60. Taylor, *Essenes*, 24.

CONCLUSIONS

to dissolve the bonds of communal life, they shun marriage at the same time as they ordered the practice of perfect continence" (*Hypoth.* 8.6–7). However, we saw that two of the sectarian rule texts (the Damascus Document and the Rule of the Congregation) contain rules for marriage and the raising of children, which would seem to indicate that Philo's Essenes and the sect reflected in the Qumran scrolls cannot be one and the same. However, as Taylor notes, Philo's discussion of the sexual continence of the Essenes is part of his presentation of them as a subgroup of all Israel who practice a life of ascetic philosophy. In such a life, marriage and family have no part.[61] Philo also emphasizes the age of the Essenes; they are τέλειοι ("mature"), and there are no young men or children among them. It is questionable, therefore, whether Philo's presentation of Essene celibacy, made in the interests of a philosophic ideal, equates with the actual practices of the Essenes. As we shall see below, Josephus's evidence on the question of Essene celibacy is ambiguous.

Josephus discusses the Essenes in three places (*J.W.* 2; *Ant.* 13 and 18). He also has scattered references to individual Essenes or the Essenes as a whole in both of these works as well as in *Life*. Josephus presents the Essenes as a tight-knit group that resembles the Pythagoreans (*Ant.* 15.37; he also compares the Essenes to the otherwise obscure Dacians, *Ant.* 18.22). He, like Philo, extols the Essenes as a Jewish example of Greco-Roman philosophical virtue. They renounce pleasure, embrace continence, despise riches and are extremely frugal,[62] practice a communal lifestyle, and are notably pious and just. As with Philo, it is in the details that Josephus provides that we may obtain a more realistic picture of the Essenes, while at the same time being aware that Josephus would omit features that did not fit the portrait he was attempting to convey.

Josephus claims that there were over four thousand Essenes who lived together in towns throughout Judea; he also locates some of them specifically in Jerusalem, mentioning the location of an Essene Gate in the city wall (*J.W.* 5.145). According to Josephus, the Essenes practiced community of goods, although some control of private property may have remained.[63] They organized themselves hierarchically, with elected overseers. Each member was

61. Taylor, *Essenes*, 42–45.

62. See the discussion of Josephus's rejection of τρυφή ("luxury") as corrupting in R. Gorman and V. Gorman, *Corrupting Luxury in Ancient Greek Literature* (Ann Arbor: University of Michigan Press, 2014), 401–7.

63. According to *J.W.* 2.134, the Essenes are allowed, on their own discretion, to help the poor and needy, which implies some degree of private finances.

300

Who Owned the Scrolls? The Qumran-Essene Hypothesis Revisited

expected to obey his superiors, and expulsion was possible. They observed a particular form of piety, rising every morning before sunrise to pray. Their Sabbath observance was notable for its rigor. They regarded oil as defiling and kept their skin clean. He especially remarks on their toilet habits: "they dig a hole one foot deep with their mattocks. . . . They squat there, covered by their mantles so as not to offend the rays of God. Then they push back the excavated soil into the hole. For this operation they choose the loneliest places" (*J.W.* 2.148–149). Regarding the Essene attitude toward the temple and its cult, Josephus states, "They send [votive] offerings to the Temple, but perform their sacrifices using different customary purifications. For this reason, they keep away[64] from entering into the common enclosure, but offer sacrifice among themselves" (*Ant.* 18.19).

In *J.W.* 2.120 Josephus writes that the Essenes "disdain marriage" but did not abolish it, while in *Ant.* 18.21 he states that they did not take wives. However, in *J.W.* 2.160–161 he notes,

> There exists another order [τάγμα] of Essenes who, although in agreement with the others on the way of life, usages, and customs, are separated from them on the subject of marriage. Indeed, they believe that people who do not marry cut off a very important part of life, namely, the propagation of the species; and all the more so that if everyone adopted the same opinion the race would very quickly disappear. Nevertheless, they observe their women for three years. When they [the women] have purified themselves three times and thus proved themselves capable of bearing children, they then marry them. And when they are pregnant they have no intercourse with them, thereby showing that they do not marry for pleasure but because it is necessary to have children. The women bathe wrapped in linen, whereas the men wear a loin-cloth. Such are the customs of this order.

64. Here I am following the translation of Taylor (*Essenes*, 187 and n143), who suggests reading εἰργόμενοι as a middle verb rather than a passive ("they are barred"). This translation implies that the Essenes *voluntarily* kept themselves away from the Court of the Gentiles and perhaps the Court of the Israelites for purity reasons, which also fits with the sectarian practice of voluntary separation from the rest of Israel. What the phrase "offer sacrifice among themselves" means is disputed. J. E. Taylor, "The Classical Sources on the Essenes," *OHDSS* 181, suggests that Josephus means that Essene priests engaged in sacrifices separately "to one side of the main altar." J. Magness, "Were Sacrifices Offered at Qumran? The Animal Bone Deposits Reconsidered," *JAJ* 7 (2016): 25, argues that it means that the Essenes sacrificed away from the temple in Jerusalem, at Qumran.

301

CONCLUSIONS

Josephus's two orders of Essenes appear to coincide with the differences in lifestyle we have noted between S and D (and Sa), in which women and children seem to have no place in the S community, whereas they are present in the D community. Thus Josephus's side remark on a second order of Essenes reflects the reality of the genuine Essene movement in Judea; some Essenes, perhaps the majority, practiced marriage and lived according to some form of the D rule, while some, who were perhaps older and chose not to remarry, lived a chaste, single lifestyle.

Josephus also outlines the procedure for entrance into the Essene community:

> Those desiring to enter the sect do not obtain immediate admittance. The postulant waits outside for one year; the same way of life is propounded to him and he is given a hatchet, the loin-cloth which I have mentioned, and a white garment. Having proved his continence during this time, he draws closer to the way of life and participates in the purificatory baths at a higher degree, but he is not yet admitted into intimacy. Indeed, after he has shown his constancy, his character is tested for another two years, and if he appears worthy he is received into the company permanently. But before touching the common food [τῆς κοινῆς] he makes solemn vows before his brethren. (*J.W.* 2.137–139)

Notice that the two-year probationary period, the examination, and the swearing of oaths in Josephus's description closely resemble 1QS 6:13–23.[65] Josephus also notes that Essenes can be expelled from the order for egregious transgressions (*J.W.* 2.143).

The purificatory baths and the common food of the Essenes are described by Josephus in another passage:

> Then, after working without interruption until the fifth hour, they reassemble in the same place and, girded with linen loin-cloths, bathe themselves in cold water. After this purification they assemble in a special building to which no one is admitted who is not of the same faith; they themselves only enter the refectory if they are pure, as though into a holy precinct. When they are quietly seated, the baker serves out the loaves of bread in order, and the cook serves only one bowlful of one dish to each man. Before the meal the priest says a prayer and no one is

---

65. See Metso, *Textual Development*, 129–33, for a thorough comparison.

302

Who Owned the Scrolls? The Qumran-Essene Hypothesis Revisited

permitted to taste the food before the prayer, and after they have eaten the meal he recites another prayer. (*J.W.* 2.129–131)

Finally, Josephus emphasizes several times (*J.W.* 2.154–158; *Ant.* 13.172; 18.18) that the Essenes believed in an afterlife (which Josephus paints in glowing Greek terms) and predeterminism: "The race of the Essenes, by contrast, makes Fate mistress of all and says that nothing comes to pass for humans unless Fate has so voted" (*Ant.* 13.172). He also emphasizes their study of holy books and gives three individual Essenes, Judas, Simon, and Menahem, credit for successful prophecies (*J.W.* 1.78; 2.113; *Ant.* 15.373).

The parallels with the Qumran sectarian literature, especially with S and D, are obvious and remarkable. Community of goods, entrance procedures, hierarchical organization, strict legal observance, concern for purity that included frequent immersion, a notable worship life with Torah study, and an ambivalent attitude toward the temple cult are all present in Josephus's description. Further, two minor parallels are remarkably accurate: the avoidance of oil as a source of defilement (*J.W.* 2.123; 4Q513 13 4; and CD 12:15–27), and the prohibition of spitting in the assembly (*J.W.* 2.147; 1QS 7:13). Another parallel comes from the archaeological evidence: the finds concerning the linen textiles (which are the remnants of garments reused as scroll wrappers and jar stoppers) agree with Josephus's statement that the Essenes always wore white (*J.W.* 2.122).[66] In some cases (such as the entrance procedures) the details do differ, but we must recall that Josephus was not an Essene and is describing the sect to an outside audience. Therefore we should accept the evidence of the sectarian texts as more accurate in detail and not require that they fit with Josephus's description at every point.[67]

Regarding the question of marriage versus celibacy, while Philo claimed the Essenes were (only) celibate,[68] Josephus is more ambiguous. First he says that the Essenes disdained marriage but did not abolish it, and later he says that one order of Essenes did marry, but observed very strict rules for sexual relations. I would argue that, while Josephus downplays the marrying Essenes for the purposes of his portrait of them as Greco-Roman

---

66. O. Shamir and N. Sukenik, "Qumran Textiles and Garments of Qumran's Inhabitants," *DSD* 18 (2011): 2.

67. A parallel case is the details of the life of Paul as found in his own letters versus the testimony of the book of Acts.

68. Pliny also claims that the Essenes lived "without women" (*Nat. Hist.* 5.73).

303

CONCLUSIONS

paragons of virtue, they were indeed the norm.[69] However, there may have been a higher proportion of unmarried members in the sect, since the rules for proper marriage and sexual conduct were so strict. It is also possible that certain members of the Essenes, perhaps older males, did not seek remarriage after widowhood. To outside observers such as Josephus and Philo, perhaps this looked like a deliberate practice of celibacy.[70]

A major theme in the sectarian literature that goes unmentioned in both Philo and Josephus is apocalyptic eschatology. This absence does not negate the Essene identification, since to a Greco-Roman audience Jewish apocalyptic eschatology would have been completely foreign and would have ruined the portrait of the Essenes as a perfect example of philosophical virtue; thus Josephus would not have included it. Further, writing in the aftermath of the Great Jewish Revolt against Rome, he may have preferred not to remind his Roman patrons of the consequences of Jewish apocalyptic thinking.

A second issue not found in Philo or Josephus, but evidently important to the sectarians, was the issue of the calendar.[71] As we have seen, the Qumran library contains many documents concerned with the calendar in one way or another, with a clear preference for a solar-based 364-day calendar. Its absence from Philo and Josephus, however, can be easily explained as an inner-Jewish concern that would not have been relevant to the Greek and Roman audiences they were addressing, and was therefore extraneous to their portrait of the Essenes.

On the question of whether the Essenes offered sacrifices in the temple in Jerusalem, we have noted that Josephus states: "They send [votive] offerings to the Temple, but perform their sacrifices using different customary purifications. For this reason, they keep away [or: are barred] from entering into the common enclosure, but offer sacrifice among themselves" (*Ant.* 18.19). This seems to indicate that the Essenes, like the sectarians reflected in the Qumran scrolls, had certain objections to the current re-

---

69. Contra S. Mason, who claims that they are a figment of Josephus's imagination (*Flavius Josephus: Translation and Commentary*, vol. 1B: *Judean War 2* [Leiden: Brill, 2008], 129–30).

70. C. Wassén observes that celibacy was not completely unknown in the Judaism of this period. Philo's Therapeutae practiced celibacy, and in the very early Christian community celibacy was an option ("Daily Life," in *T&T Clark Companion to the Dead Sea Scrolls*, ed. G. Brooke and C. Hempel [London: T&T Clark, 2018], 550). I would like to thank Professor Wassén for sharing this article with me prior to publication.

71. See also Stegemann, "Qumran Essenes," 114–22.

304

Who Owned the Scrolls? The Qumran-Essene Hypothesis Revisited

gime in the temple, and that the temple authorities also had difficulties with their purification practices. However, according to Josephus the Essenes continued to send offerings there. Josephus also locates Judah the Essene teaching in the temple (*J.W.* 1.78). All these references demonstrate that the Essenes, at least according to Josephus, did not entirely shun the temple precincts, but still visited them for prayer and teaching and to bring donations (votive offerings). This accords with the evidence of the sectarian scrolls, which, as we have seen, indicates that the sect thought the temple cult was corrupt but may have continued to participate in it in a limited way.

Thus far, then, the evidence favors an Essene identification. When we investigate the other classical sources that mention the Essenes, that identification becomes even stronger.

Both Pliny the Elder and Dio of Prusa (also known as Chrysostom) independently locate the Essenes in the region of the Dead Sea. To again quote Pliny's famous passage:

> To the west [of the Dead Sea] the Essenes have put the necessary distance between themselves and the insalubrious shore. They are a people unique of its kind and admirable beyond all others in the whole world, without women and renouncing love entirely, without money, and having for company only the palm trees. Owing to the throng of newcomers, this people is daily re-born in equal number; indeed, those whom, wearied by the fluctuations of fortune, life leads to adopt their customs, stream in in great numbers. Thus, unbelievable though this may seem, for thousands of centuries a race has existed which is eternal yet into which no one is born: so fruitful for them is the repentance which others feel for their past lives! Below [*infra hos*] the Essenes was the town of Engada [Engedi], which yielded only to Jerusalem [read: Jericho] in fertility and palm-groves but is today become another ash-heap. From there, one comes to the fortress of Masada, situated on a rock, and itself near the lake of Asphalt.

Again, when interpreting this passage we must consider both the author and the intended audience. Taylor characterizes Pliny's passage as "a caricature or a parody," meant to entertain and emphasizing the odd and fantastic rather than the staid and boring.[72] Pliny also used sources from which he

---

72. Taylor, *Essenes,* 133.

305

CONCLUSIONS

took his description of the Essenes. Therefore, the only new information to be found in Pliny concerning the Essenes is geographic. Reading *infra hos* as "below that," a progression from north to south, the Essene settlement is located south of Jericho (reading Jericho for Jerusalem, as most scholars agree) and north of 'Ein-Gedi.[73] After decades of excavations in the Dead Sea region, only the Qumran-'Ain Feshkha complex fits this description, and it is more than reasonable to identify it with Pliny's Essene settlement.

Dio's description is more general: "Also somewhere he praises the Essenes, who form an entire and prosperous city near the Dead Sea, in the centre of Palestine, not far from Sodom" (in Synesius of Cyrene, *Dio* 3.2). This description's importance lies in that it gives us a witness independent from Pliny who also locates the Essenes in the Dead Sea region.

Other, later classical sources mention the Essenes only briefly, and their evidence correlates with Josephus and Philo.[74] They include Julius Solinus, Hegesippus in Eusebius, Hippolytus, Epiphanius, and Porphyry. Hippolytus adds an apocalyptic note to his description missing from the other accounts: "for they affirm that there will be both a judgement and a conflagration of the universe, and that the wicked will be eternally punished" (*Haer.* 9.27).[75]

Taken together, then, the evidence of the sectarian scrolls, the archaeology of Qumran, and the classical sources overwhelmingly favor an identification of the Qumran sect as Essene, and Qumran itself as an Essene settlement. Some scholars have suggested, on the basis of the differences between the sectarian texts and the classical sources mentioned above, that the Qumran sect was an otherwise unknown group not mentioned in the classical sources.[76] However, this argument appears willful in its refusal to acknowledge how the various pieces of evidence fit together to form a coherent whole, what Edna Ullman-Margalit refers to as a "thick chain of evidence."[77] To suppose that a major group

---

73. There has been some disagreement about the meaning of *infra hos* in this context; some would take it to mean "above in elevation" and therefore indicating the cliffs above the Dead Sea to the west. See R. Kraft, "Pliny on Essenes, Pliny on Jews," *DSD* 8 (2001): 255–61; and Hirschfeld, *Qumran in Context*, 231–33. But see Taylor, *Essenes*, 135–39, for a strong defense of the meaning of *infra hos* as "south of," based on Pliny's use of the direction of water flow as a geographical locator.

74. Several of them undoubtedly used Josephus and/or Philo as a source.

75. See Cross, *Ancient Library of Qumran*, 80.

76. E.g., M. Goodman, "Constructing Ancient Judaism from the Scrolls," *OHDSS* 84.

77. E. Ullman-Margalit, *Out of the Cave: A Philosophical Inquiry into the Dead Sea Scrolls Research* (Cambridge: Harvard University Press, 2009), 41–60.

306

Who Owned the Scrolls? The Qumran-Essene Hypothesis Revisited

in Judaism, part of the learned, elite class of Jews (as indicated by their library), with an established settlement that existed for over one hundred years, went unnoticed in the classical sources, the NT, and the rabbinic works, strains credulity.[78] Therefore, given the state of our knowledge up to this point in time, the evidence strongly indicates that the Qumran sect should be identified with the Essene movement in the Second Temple period.

Finally, the objection concerning the absence of the name "Essene" in the Qumran scrolls or indeed the NT or the rabbinic literature should be addressed. The first point to make is that we should not be surprised by this; it was common in the Greco-Roman world for groups to have an internal name(s) for themselves, and to be called something else by outsiders.[79] The Pharisees did not call themselves Pharisees, nor did the Samaritans call themselves Samaritans. The name "Essene," then, is a descriptive sobriquet applied to the group to define them to outsiders.[80]

The name first appears in Philo, but did not originate with him, since he attempts to define it by tying it to the Greek word ὅσιοι, "holiness" (*Prob.* 12.75). This is not a perfect etymology and indicates that the origin of the name should be found in Hebrew or Aramaic, rather than Greek. The three most likely Semitic derivations are Aram. חסא, "pious," Aram. אסיא, "healers," or Heb. עושי, "doers," as in "doers of the Torah" (עושי התורה).[81] The last derivation is the most plausible, given the sect's emphasis on the correct interpretation and performance of the Torah.[82] This phrase עושי התורה occurs in 1QpHab 7 10–11 and 8 1, as well as 4QpPs[a] (4Q171 ii 15), referring to the sect.[83] In addition, the phrase עושי היחד appears in 4QCatena A 5–6, 16, indicating that עושי, "doers," may have been

78. Cross, *Ancient Library of Qumran*, 67–68n3, calls the idea "simply incredible." See also J. Taylor, "The Classical Sources on the Essenes," *OHDSS* 190: "Unless one insists on inventing a group attested nowhere else, the Essenes are an obvious choice."

79. Saldarini, *Pharisees, Scribes, and Sadducees*, 221.

80. See also G. Vermes, "The Etymology of 'Essenes,'" *RevQ* 2 (1960): 427–43.

81. Vermes, "Etymology of 'Essenes,'" 429–38; S. Goranson, "'Essenes': Etymology from עשה," *RevQ* 11 (1984): 483–98; and J. Collins, *Beyond the Qumran Community*, 156–60.

82. Amihay, *Theory and Practice*, 13, notes that the phonetic shift in the Greek makes this derivation problematic.

83. 1QpHab 7 10–11: פשרו על אנשי האמת עושי התורה, lit. "its interpretation concerns the men of truth, the doers of the Torah." 1QpHab 8 1: פשרו על כול עושי התורה בבית יהודה, lit. "its interpretation concerns all the doers of the Torah in the house of Judah." 4QpPs[a] ii 15: יזומו לכלות את עושי התורה אשר בעצת היחד, lit. "they will plot to destroy the doers of the Torah, who are in the council of the *Yaḥad*."

307

CONCLUSIONS

a common self-referent for the sect.[84] But ultimately the identification of the Qumran sect with the Essenes is independent of the name.

Conclusions

In this chapter we have presented decisive arguments in favor of identifying the sect that owned the library found in the Qumran caves and the inhabitants of the Qumran settlement with the Essenes. The arguments were based on the content of the sectarian scrolls and demonstrated the close parallels between the sectarian scrolls and the descriptions of the Essenes as given in Josephus, Philo, and Pliny. Further, we have shown that the archaeological evidence from the Qumran settlement is compatible with an Essene identification. The next task is to determine when and why an Essene settlement, with a contingent of scribes, was established at Qumran, and how and when their scrolls were deposited in the Qumran caves.

84. Schofield, *From Qumran to the Yahad*, 141 and 192.

CHAPTER 8

Scribes and Scrolls at Qumran: A New Synthesis

My thesis in this volume as I laid out in the introduction (ch. 1) is that the scrolls collection found in the caves near the site of Qumran in the northwest corner of the Dead Sea is one collection, a scribal library with a strong sectarian component, that belonged to the Essenes, a wing of Judaism in the late Second Temple period. The settlement at Qumran was established by the Essenes in the early first century BCE as their central library and scribal center, and it functioned as such until its destruction by the Romans in 68 CE. In the ensuing chapters I laid out the evidence in support of this thesis.

Chapters 2 and 3 set the stage by examining the textual and archaeological evidence for scribes and libraries in the ancient Near East and Mediterranean world, including ancient Israel and Judah. Chapters 4–6 presented the evidence that demonstrates that the Qumran scroll collection was indeed one collection that can be characterized as a sectarian library with a strong scribal component. In ch. 4 I demonstrated that the individual cave collections, although they have differences, are held together as one collection by overlapping contents, especially with the largest cave corpus, that of Cave 4Q, and by distinct scribal hands found across the caves. I also related the scroll caves to one another by their archaeological remains, demonstrating that all the caves in which scrolls were stored in antiquity (at present count Caves 1Q–11Q, GrQ29 [Timothy's Cave], and 53) were tied to each other by pottery types, in particular the hole-mouthed cylindrical "scroll" jars. In ch. 5 I laid out the archaeology of the settlement at Qumran, demonstrating that the best explanation for the anomalies of the site—the large number of stepped pools, the overall "poor" quality of the buildings and other material remains, the presence in quantity of the hole-mouthed cylindrical jars, the absence of family dwellings and lack of evidence for the presence of women and children, and the animal bone deposits—was that a sectarian community of male Jews lived

309

CONCLUSIONS

there throughout the site's Second Temple period existence. Further, I presented the archaeological evidence for a scribal presence at the site (e.g., inscriptions, inkwells, and scroll production and repair implements). I also argued that L1–2, 4, and 30 in the main building had suitable characteristics to be identified as a library complex and a scroll workshop. The same repertoire of pottery found in the caves and the settlement indicates that they are one archaeological complex; in addition, the settlement and the caves, even the most remote, are connected to each other by paths, allowing the inhabitants to reach the caves fairly quickly and easily. After this careful survey of the evidence there can be little doubt that the settlement at Qumran and the caves surrounding the site were used by one and the same sectarian Jewish community, and that that community utilized the caves for the deposit of their library.

In ch. 4 I also argued that the two geological types of caves, the natural caves found in the limestone cliffs at some distance from the settlement and the manmade marl terrace caves that are part of the "built" environment of the settlement, had different functions. The limestone cliff caves were used for long-term or permanent storage of some kind; most of the scrolls found in these caves would originally have been wrapped in linen covers and placed in cylindrical jars. The jars were placed in the caves, whose entrances were then sealed or at least concealed. The marl terrace caves, on the other hand, had different functions: Caves 7Q–9Q were used as workshops and/or temporary sleeping quarters, while Caves 4Q and 5Q (and perhaps 10Q) were used as an overflow storage space for manuscripts from the library complex in the buildings.

In ch. 6 I described the various components of the Qumran library. The largest single component of the overall collection are sectarian texts, closely followed by the classical texts of ancient Israel and Judah. The texts affiliated with the sectarian texts also made up a good percentage of the overall collection. Cave 4Q's scroll corpus was also shown to have a "local" component, since, while holding major scrolls from the classical, sectarian, and affiliated literatures, it also contained manuscripts meant for the use of or belonging to the inhabitants of Qumran itself, including the excerpted texts, scribal lists and exercises, and the only documentary texts found in the Qumran caves.

Finally, in ch. 7 I concluded that the best identification for those inhabitants, based on the internal evidence of the sectarian scrolls correlated with outside sources, was the Essenes, a particular wing of Judaism active in the late Second Temple period. The main inhabitants of Qumran were

310

Scribes and Scrolls at Qumran: A New Synthesis

Essene scribes and their support staff; the duties of the scribes were the collection, preservation, copying, and studying of the scrolls in the Qumran library.[1] The majority of these scrolls, according to their physical evidence, originated outside Qumran, although some may have been copied locally.

However, this summary, while it answers many questions about the purpose and function of the Essene settlement at Qumran, leaves some questions unanswered. Why was Qumran, a somewhat remote site in the Judean Desert, chosen as the site for the library of the greater Essene community? Why was it established during the reign of Alexander Jannaeus, and who established it? Why were some scrolls stored in jars in the limestone cliff caves, and how were they chosen? Can all of the information we have gathered be put together into a coherent narrative, the "story" of Qumran? I address these questions in the following pages.

The Essene Movement and the Establishment of Qumran

Josephus's earliest mention of the Sadducees, the Pharisees, and the Essenes comes in the context of the reign of Jonathan the Hasmonean in the mid-second century BCE (*Ant.* 3.171). This date indicates that the Essene movement already existed when Josephus discusses them in the context of the reign of Jonathan. Thus the origins of the movement must be placed no later than the first half of the second century BCE, approximately seventy-five years before Qumran was inhabited. Whatever the reasons for the rise of the Essene movement, which most likely included disputes with their fellow Jews concerning legal interpretation and practice, those reasons did not lead to the founding of Qumran. The difference in dates between the rise of the movement and the foundation of Qumran also implies that the Teacher of Righteousness, one of the putative founders of the sect, had nothing to do with the settlement at Qumran.[2] The attempt to tie the

---

1. Other activities were certainly pursued at Qumran according to the archaeological evidence. These activities included pottery making, in particular the hole-mouthed cylindrical jars used, among other things, for scroll storage, date cultivation and the manufacture of date honey, small-scale animal husbandry, and other undertakings of daily life. These activities supported the Qumran settlement, enabling the inhabitants to continue with their primary task, the work of the library and its scroll collection.

2. J. J. Collins, *Beyond the Qumran Community: The Sectarian Movement of the Dead Sea Scrolls* (Grand Rapids: Eerdmans, 2009), 91. Because of this discrepancy in dates,

CONCLUSIONS

establishment of Qumran with particular events in the life of the Essene movement has foundered on our lack of specific knowledge of the circumstances that gave rise to the movement or to the establishment of the Qumran settlement. Rather, we must rely on what we know generally about historical events during the period in which the settlement at Qumran was founded, the last years of the reign of Alexander Jannaeus.

Jannaeus, the son of John Hyrcanus I, was concerned to protect the territorial gains made by his father to the north, south, and east. He established a series of fortresses and other defensive installations along his eastern border, which included the Dead Sea region. The following fortified sites in the Dead Sea region were constructed by either John Hyrcanus or Alexander Jannaeus: Doq, Cypros, Hyrcania, 'Ein-Gedi, the harbor at Rujum el-Bajr, and Masada.[3] However, Qumran is not a fortified site;[4] its watchtower would have warned the inhabitants of an approaching enemy but would not have held off any kind of determined attack. Therefore, Qumran was not constructed under the auspices of Alexander Jannaeus to be part of the fortifications of his eastern frontier.

In addition, Qumran has none of the more luxurious features of royal or upper-class residences from the same period, such as frescoes, mosaic floors, or hot and cold baths, indicating that it is not a villa belonging to an upper-class family. The lack of fortified elements or luxury appointments makes it very unlikely that Qumran was part of any building program on the part of Alexander Jannaeus. Finally, Qumran was off the beaten track, connected to the outside world only by rough paths, which would have limited the number of visitors to the settlement.

---

attempts have been made to identify the Wicked Priest not with one of the early Hasmoneans but with Hyrcanus II, high priest under Alexandra Salome (76–67 BCE) and contender for the throne after her death with his brother Aristobulus II. See esp. M. O. Wise, "The Origins and History of the Teacher's Movement," *OHDSS* 92–122. If that identification were correct, then the Teacher of Righteousness would be the contemporary of Hyrcanus II in the mid-first century BCE. But all indications from the sectarian literature indicate that the sect existed prior to the first century BCE, and, at least according to the Damascus Document (CD 1:11), the Teacher of Righteousness was among the early leaders of the sect. Therefore the identification of the Wicked Priest with Hyrcanus II should be rejected.

3. Y. Hirschfeld, *Qumran in Context: Reassessing the Archaeological Evidence* (Peabody, MA: Hendrickson, 2004), 31, 213; J. Taylor, *The Essenes, the Scrolls, and the Dead Sea* (Oxford: Oxford University Press, 2012), 251.

4. J. Magness, "Was Qumran a Fort in the Hasmonean Period?," *JSJ* 64 (2013): 228–41, demonstrates decisively through comparative evidence that Qumran was not a fortress.

Scribes and Scrolls at Qumran: A New Synthesis

However, it is entirely possible that Qumran was built with the *permission* of Alexander Jannaeus; indeed, permission was probably necessary for a settlement so close to the frontier. To whom would Jannaeus have granted permission, and why?

Jannaeus, according to the testimony of Josephus, was an unpopular ruler, whose very appearance as high priest at the Feast of Sukkot caused a riot in Jerusalem (*Ant.* 13.372–374; *J.W.* 1.88). He faced internal rebellion, and the rebels went so far as to call in the Seleucid king Demetrius III Eukarios to support them against Jannaeus. Jannaeus retaliated by crucifying eight hundred of them (*Ant.* 13.379–383; *J.W.* 1.96–98). Among Jannaeus's enemies, as I have argued in ch. 7, were the Pharisees, also the enemies (the דורשי החלקות) of the Essene sect. Jannaeus's opinion of the Essenes is not recorded by Josephus, leading to the inference that his relations with them were, if not friendly, at least not hostile.[5] It is plausible, though in the realm of speculation, that the Essene leadership sought Jannaeus's permission to build their settlement at Qumran; and he, considering them a friendly or at least neutral party who would not be a threat to his border fortifications, granted it. The land itself may have been a grant from Jannaeus, or the property of a wealthy Essene who donated it to the movement. While we cannot be certain exactly why the site of Qumran was chosen as the location for the central library of the Essene movement, it would have been close enough to Jerusalem (where a major Essene community was evidently resident, since a city gate was known as the Essene Gate) to allow travel and transport back and forth between the two. On the other hand, Qumran was also remote enough to be removed from the politics and upheavals of life in the capital city, thus protecting its library and residents from falling victim to the conflicts that occurred in Judea in the first centuries BCE/CE. 'Ain Feshkha provided a spring, and the area was appropriate for date farming, which offered a source of economic support. All of these factors most likely went into the choice of Qumran for the Essene central library.

This scenario may also explain the presence in the Qumran library of the fragmentary manuscript 4Q448, which contains a prayer that mentions a "King Jonathan." This is most likely Alexander Jannaeus, since he was the first Hasmonean Jonathan (יונתן) to use the title "king." Its editors translate it as follows:

5. See also J. J. Collins, "Sectarian Communities in the Dead Sea Scrolls," *OHDSS* 167.

313

CONCLUSIONS

1. Guard (or: Rise up), O Holy One
2. over King Jonathan (or: for King Jonathan) [יונתן המלך]
3. and all the congregation of Your people
4. Israel
5. who are in the four
6. winds of heaven.
7. Let them all be (at) peace
8. and upon Your kingdom
9. may Your name be blessed.[6]

Scholars have puzzled over why the Qumran library contained a prayer that asks God to guard a Hasmonean king, since they did not approve of the temple cult under Hasmonean control; but if it was under Jannaeus's auspices that the settlement at Qumran was established, that anomaly is explained.

It is striking that the Qumran settlement continued on with no interruption from the time of its founding until its destruction at the hands of the Romans in 68 CE. The archaeological evidence from the site gives no indication that Qumran was involved in any way in the conflicts between the last Hasmonean rulers, the brothers Hyrcanus II and Aristobulus II. Pompey seems to have taken no notice of it when he conquered Judea in 63 BCE, and all was quiet when Herod put down rebellions and established his rule between 40 and 37 BCE.[7] Evidently the settlement at Qumran was not considered any kind of threat or important player in the conflicts of the first century BCE.[8] It was not until the Roman legion operating in the region of Jericho, which was charged with wiping out any trace of Jewish

6. E. Eshel et al., "448. 4QApocryphal Psalm and Prayer," in *Qumran Cave 4.VI: Poetical and Liturgical Texts, Part 1*, by E. Eshel et al., DJD 11 (Oxford: Clarendon, 1998), 421. The manuscript also contained two other compositions: a previously unknown psalm and Ps 154.

7. Indeed, Josephus claims that Herod favored the Essenes, on account of a prophecy made in his youth by an Essene named Menahem that he would become king (*Ant.* 15.371–379).

8. Magness originally claimed that the site suffered a violent destruction around 9/8 BCE and was subsequently abandoned for a short period before being reinhabited by the same group. She suggested that the destruction may have been part of "the revolts and turmoil which erupted upon Herod the Great's death." J. Magness, "The Chronology of the Settlement at Qumran in the Herodian Period," in *Debating Qumran: Collected Essays on Its Archaeology*, ISACR 4 (Leuven: Peeters, 2004), 46. However, she has abandoned that position. See D. Mizzi and J. Magness, "Was Qumran Abandoned at the End of the First Century BCE?," *JBL* 135 (2016): 303–4.

314

Scribes and Scrolls at Qumran: A New Synthesis

resistance, took notice of the small settlement that military action of any kind was taken against Qumran. This lack of involvement in the political conflicts of the day is further evidence for the nonmilitary nature of the Qumran settlement; its presence and activities were evidently considered completely nonthreatening to the political powers of the period.

Why did the Essenes establish this settlement with its library at this time? As we observed in ch. 2, the Greco-Roman period was characterized by a rise in book collecting, most famously by the establishment of the library at Alexandria by Ptolemy II Philadelphos in the mid-second century BCE. This Greek emphasis on literary culture had an effect in Judah as well; it is during the early Hellenistic period that "book culture" becomes more prominent in Jewish life. The fourth, third, and second centuries BCE were when much of the classical literature of ancient Israel was edited into their now familiar forms[9] and new works were being composed and/or redacted, including literature we have identified as affiliated with the Essene movement (e.g., the books of Enoch, the Aramaic Levi Document, Jubilees, and the Temple Scroll). In addition, by at least the mid-second century BCE the major sectarian works (e.g., the Damascus Document and the Serek Hayaḥad) had taken shape. Jewish book collections were growing in the Hellenistic period, and the Essenes had their own particular literature to collect and preserve.

Where was this collecting activity taking place? As we saw in ch. 3, the only library of any size in Judea for which we have any evidence was in the temple in Jerusalem. According to 2 Macc 2:13–14, Judas Maccabeus "refounded" the temple library originally begun by Nehemiah. Although

---

9. See D. Carr, *The Formation of the Hebrew Bible: A New Reconstruction* (Oxford: Oxford University Press, 2011), especially his chapters on the Persian and Hellenistic periods; and K. van der Toorn, *Scribal Culture and the Making of the Hebrew Bible* (Cambridge: Harvard University Press, 2007), 252–55. On the use of the term *form* see S. W. Crawford, "Interpreting the Pentateuch through Scribal Processes: The Evidence from the Qumran Manuscripts," in *Insights into Editing in the Hebrew Bible and the Ancient Near East*, ed. R. Müller and J. Pakkala, CBET 84 (Leuven: Peeters, 2017), 59–60. While most of the books of the classical literature had a stabilized form by the late Second Temple period, some, e.g., Psalms, did not. Further, some books, such as Jeremiah, circulated in two forms or editions. See E. Ulrich, *The Dead Sea Scrolls and the Developmental Composition of the Bible*, VTSup 169 (Leiden: Brill, 2015), 141–50, 194–98. While the form of most of the classical books had stabilized by the time Qumran was founded, the details of the texts of those books had not. That step would not occur before the late first century BCE. For surveys of the various classical books and their textual traditions, see A. Lange and E. Tov, eds., *The Hebrew Bible*, 3 vols., Textual History of the Bible (Leiden: Brill, 2016–2017).

315

CONCLUSIONS

this account is clearly legendary, it indicates some sort of library in the Jerusalem temple overseen by the Hasmonean priest-kings in the second half of the second century BCE. However, we have very little secure knowledge of what the temple library contained. According to Josephus, Torah scrolls from the temple were used in Vespasian's triumph in Rome (*J.W.* 7.150, 162). Josephus also claimed to have "sacred books" from Jerusalem as a gift from Titus (*Life* 25). In *Ag. Ap.* 1.38–41 Josephus notes that the Jews have twenty-two books that are "rightly trusted" (τὰ δικαίως πεπιστευμένα), which he essentially divides into Torah, Prophets, and hymns and ethical teachings. Regardless of whether this list represents a sacred canon of scripture,[10] Josephus's list may reflect books that were kept in the Jerusalem temple library. Beyond these few contemporary literary references nothing is known about what was kept there.

Whatever the details of its contents, the temple library was very unlikely to have contained copies of Essene texts, or even of its affiliated literature. David Carr has suggested that the Hasmonean priest-kings championed a limited corpus of authorized sacred scripture and that this move was opposed by the wing of Judaism that collected the Qumran library, which I have identified in this volume with the Essenes.[11] In this scenario, the Qumran library would have been established to ensure the survival of their literature. The makeup of the Qumran collection, with its pronounced sectarian/affiliated component, can support this reconstruction. Most of the sectarian and affiliated literature that has emerged from the Qumran caves was unknown prior to the discoveries; those few works that were previously known were preserved in Jewish circles that broke from emerging rabbinic Judaism and took their own paths. As examples, the Damascus Document was discovered in a Karaite synagogue in Cairo,[12] while 1 Enoch and Jubilees were passed down in Christian communities. Given these facts, it is improbable that sectarian or even affiliated literature was kept in the Jerusalem temple library.[13] Those works must have been

10. See T. Lim, *The Formation of the Jewish Canon*, AYBRL (New Haven: Yale University Press, 2013), 43–49, for a judicious discussion.

11. Carr, *Formation of the Hebrew Bible*, 158.

12. H. Stegemann, *The Library of Qumran: On the Essenes, Qumran, John the Baptist, and Jesus* (Grand Rapids: Eerdmans, 1998), 68–71, suggests that the early Karaites found Caves 2Q and 3Q in the eighth century, and it is from that discovery that they copied the Damascus Document. This scenario is, however, speculative.

13. The distribution of textual families in the books of Israel's classical literature as found in the Judean Desert caves may also support this hypothesis. E. Tov has demon-

316

Scribes and Scrolls at Qumran: A New Synthesis

preserved among the Essenes themselves, and thus the question arises of location.

According to both Josephus and Philo, the Essenes lived in scattered enclaves in Judea, and it is likely that the leadership, which had a strong priestly component,[14] lived in Jerusalem.[15] If each individual enclave had its own small library (necessary for the prayer and study mandated by the sect), as time went on and their numbers increased the need would have been felt for a central location to collect and preserve their literature, especially the literature unique to their movement. This need led to the establishment of the settlement at Qumran as the Essene central library, staffed by Essene scribes.

The initial scroll collection at Qumran may have come from the Essene leadership in Jerusalem who were establishing the center; this would account for the age of some of the scrolls in Cave 4Q (e.g., 4QExod[d], 4QExod-Lev[f], 4QDeut[a], 4QSam[b], and 4QJer[a]). This initial collection would have been augmented by minor collections brought in from the smaller Essene communities in Judea, as both John Collins and Alison Schofield have suggested.[16] This collecting activity from around Judea would account for the large size of the collection and the number of scribal hands found

---

strated that the classical texts found outside Qumran reflect without variation the consonantal text of the received MT, while the Qumran classical manuscripts contain much textual variation. He has suggested that these differing textual pictures indicate that by the first century CE the Jerusalem temple establishment was attempting to promulgate a uniform text, at least for the Torah. The Qumran collection may indicate an attempt to preserve variant forms of the text in the face of an attempt to impose uniformity. See ch. 6 n13 and the bibliography there. However, it is not entirely clear from the available evidence whether textual uniformity was an issue before the destruction of the Jerusalem temple.

14. For overviews and discussions with bibliography (which is vast) see R. Kugler, "Priests," *EDSS* 2:688–93; R. Kugler, "Priesthood at Qumran," in *The Dead Sea Scrolls after Fifty Years: A Comprehensive Assessment*, ed. P. Flint and J. VanderKam, 2 vols. (Leiden: Brill, 1999), 2:93–116; C. Hempel, *The Qumran Rule Texts in Context: Collected Studies*, TSAJ 154 (Tübingen: Mohr Siebeck, 2013), 195–227. I have noted in ch. 3 a strong overlap between priests and scribes in the Second Temple period. See M. Himmelfarb, *A Kingdom of Priests: Ancestry and Merit in Ancient Judaism*, Jewish Culture and Context (Philadelphia: University of Pennsylvania Press, 2006), 29, 45.

15. That Josephus places certain Essenes in Jerusalem, and knows of an Essene Gate in Jerusalem, corroborates this supposition.

16. J. Collins, *Beyond the Qumran Community*; J. Collins, "Sectarian Communities in the Dead Sea Scrolls," *OHDSS* 160; A. Schofield, *From Qumran to the Yaḥad: A New Paradigm of Textual Development for the Community Rule*, STDJ 77 (Leiden: Brill, 2009).

CONCLUSIONS

in it, as well as the fact that certain key sectarian and affiliated texts are preserved in multiple copies.

The resident scribes handled their growing collection in several ways. A portion was kept in the library complex in the main building; as the collection grew the "overflow" was stored in Caves 4Q and 5Q. Those scrolls were available for study and use in worship by the residents and visitors.[17] The scribes were also engaged in the correcting and copying of scrolls brought from the outside, in addition to creating and copying documents for their own use (e.g., the excerpted texts).[18] Further, they undertook the physical repair of scrolls, as the evidence for scroll repair implements from L30 and Cave 8Q demonstrates. Repaired scrolls as well as newly copied scrolls could have been sent back to Essene enclaves elsewhere, as Schofield suggests in her "radial-dialogic" model of the development of the S tradition.[19] Finally, some portion of the scrolls were prepared for permanent storage in the limestone cliff caves by being wrapped in linen and placed in scroll jars before being transported to the caves.

This picture can account for the differences noted among the individual limestone cliff cave collections. As we observed in ch. 4, the scrolls collection in Cave 1Q is statistically older than the collection as a whole, while that of Cave 11Q is statistically younger. Cave 2Q contained no sectarian texts. Cave 1Q contained a greater percentage of liturgical manuscripts than other caves (e.g., three copies of Psalms, two copies of the Hodayot, and at least nine other manuscripts of prayers or hymns).[20] The corpus in Cave 11Q is more "sectarian" and less "classical" than that of the other caves.[21] These differences (and others) can be explained if we assume that the scroll collections in the individual caves came from

17. As shown in ch. 4, Qumran was not closed off from the outside world, and our scenario of scrolls brought to Qumran from other Essene communities in Judea necessitates the presence of visitors. The idea of visitors may also account for the presence of female skeletons in the main cemetery, in what otherwise appears to have been an all-male community. See also J. Collins, *Beyond the Qumran Community*, 197–204.

18. Stegemann, *Library of Qumran*, 57, suggests a similar scenario.

19. Schofield, *From Qumran to the Yaḥad*, 47–51.

20. S. Pfann, "Reassessing the Judean Desert Caves: Libraries, Archives, Genizas and Hiding Places," *Bulletin of the Anglo-Israel Archaeological Society* 25 (2007): 158. Pfann argues for other differences among the cave collections, but he pushes his argument too far in the direction of difference, ignoring the commonalities.

21. E. Tov, "The Special Character of the Texts in Qumran Cave 11," in *Hebrew Bible, Greek Bible, and Qumran: Collected Essays*, TSAJ 121 (Tübingen: Mohr Siebeck, 2008), 421–27.

318

Scribes and Scrolls at Qumran: A New Synthesis

different local Essene communities before being processed for long-term storage at Qumran.

Envisioning Qumran as a scribal center and library for the wider Essene movement also accounts for the almost entire absence of archaeological evidence for the presence of women at the site. As we have seen in ch. 3, Jewish scribes in the Second Temple period were male, and many scribes were also priests or Levites. If they considered their scribal activities at Qumran a sacred duty analogous to the same scribal activities in the Jerusalem temple, they would have made every effort to avoid ritual impurity. This would have included avoiding sexual intercourse or contact with menstruating or parturient women. We know from the number of stepped pools at Qumran, which most likely functioned as mikvaoth, that the inhabitants were concerned with maintaining ritual purity. Thus Qumran, because of its special function as a scribal center for the Essene movement, may not have housed women and children, but only men. It is possible, but in the realm of speculation, that the scribes who resided at Qumran had families in Essene enclaves elsewhere, whom they would have visited from time to time. However, while in residence at Qumran they did not live in family units, but simply as one community of men.

Qumran continued as the Essene central library and scribal center throughout its history, its cadre of scribes and their support staff carrying on quietly throughout the upheavals of the first centuries BCE and CE. Whatever the involvement of individual Essenes in the historical events of the day,[22] the movement made sure that their central library remained functioning. Indeed, the need for it may have been felt more acutely as the political situation in Judea worsened.

The Essenes at Qumran would have been well aware of the events of the First Jewish Revolt beginning in 66 CE.[23] They would have known of the destruction at Jericho by the *Legio X Fretensis* and inferred that an attack on their settlement was imminent. No doubt their first instinct would have been to rescue their precious library from almost certain destruction. The caves, which were already being used for long- and short-term storage, were the most accessible hiding places, and the inhabitants

---

22. For example, Josephus names a John the Essene as one of the generals in the First Jewish Revolt (*J.W.* 2.567 and 3.11).

23. The latest coins from the Second Temple settlement at Qumran are from "Year 2" of the Jewish Revolt, indicating that Jews were at the site until that date; the absence of coins from the last years of the revolt shows that the site was destroyed by then.

319

CONCLUSIONS

of Qumran hoped that the Romans would be uninterested in book rolls in caves. They removed the scrolls from the library complex in the building and stacked them into the marl terrace caves, as well as the nearby Cave 6Q.[24] This scenario accounts for the unusual profile of some of these caves. Cave 6Q contained a high percentage of papyrus manuscripts, which may have come mainly from the "papyrus section" in the library complex. Only Greek papyri were recovered from Cave 7Q, which came from the "Greek section" of the library complex.[25] The final dump was made into Cave 4Q, which was already the main "overflow" storage cave; any written material that could be gathered in haste from the buildings was left there. This accounts for the presence of documentary texts, scribal exercises, and the other ephemera (lists, hastily scribbled notes, etc.) in Cave 4Q.[26] Because the manuscripts from Cave 4Q were brought to the Palestine Archaeological Museum in disarray (see ch. 4), we cannot distinguish between manuscripts that may already have been in the cave and manuscripts that may have been deposited there in the final days of the settlement.

We cannot know for certain if the Essene scribes of Qumran attempted to defend their home or simply fled before the Romans. We do know that the Romans shot flaming arrows into the buildings, setting off a conflagration that thoroughly destroyed all organic material at the site. It is thus to those panicked Essene scribes, rushing to save their book rolls from the Roman onslaught, that we owe the survival of the manuscripts that became known as the Qumran scrolls collection, the remnant of the Essene central library based at their scribal center at Qumran.

24. It is possible that at this time more manuscripts would have been placed in the more remote limestone cliff caves, but they would not have been carefully packed into scroll jars, but instead laid on the floors of the caves.

25. As discussed in ch. 2, Roman libraries divided their collections into Greek and Latin sections; it is not unreasonable to assume that Qumran's library had a separate section for Greek manuscripts.

26. Stegemann, *Library of Qumran*, 63–68, constructs a similar scene, but he believed that all the scrolls found in the caves, including the limestone cliff caves, came from the library at Qumran and were hidden in the caves all at once (the "quick-hiding" scenario) in anticipation of the Roman attack.

320

Bibliography

Abel, Félix M., and Jean Starcky. *Les Livres des Maccabées*. La Sainte Bible. 3rd ed. Paris: Cerf, 1961.

Adams, Samuel L. "The Social Location of the Scribe in the Second Temple Period." In *Sibyls, Scriptures, and Scrolls: John Collins at Seventy*, edited by Joel Baden, Hindy Najman, and Eibert J. C. Tigchelaar, 1:22–37. 2 vols. JSJSup 175. Leiden: Brill, 2017.

Adler, Yonatan. "The Distribution of Tefillin Finds among the Judean Desert Caves." In *The Caves of Qumran: Proceedings of the International Conference, Lugano 2014*, edited by Marcello Fidanzio, 161–73. STDJ 118. Leiden: Brill, 2017.

Ahituv, Shmuel. *Echoes from the Past: Hebrew and Cognate Inscriptions from the Biblical Period*. Jerusalem: Carta, 2008.

Albani, Matthias. "Horoscopes in the Dead Sea Scrolls." In *The Dead Sea Scrolls after Fifty Years: A Comprehensive Assessment*, edited by Peter W. Flint and James C. VanderKam, 2:279–332. 2 vols. Leiden: Brill, 1999.

―――, and Uwe Glessmer. "An Astronomical Measuring Instrument from Qumran." In *The Provo International Conference on the Dead Sea Scrolls: Technological Innovations, New Texts, and Reformulated Issues*, edited by Donald W. Parry and Eugene Ulrich, 407–42. STDJ 30. Leiden: Brill, 1998.

―――. "Un instrument de mesures astronomiques à Qumran." *RB* 104 (1997): 88–115.

Albani, Matthias, Jörg Frey, and Armin Lange, eds. *Studies in the Book of Jubilees*. TSAJ 65. Tübingen: Mohr Siebeck, 1997.

Alexander, Philip S. "Literacy among Jews in Second Temple Palestine: Reflections on the Evidence from Qumran." In *Hamlet on a Hill: Semitic and Greek Studies Presented to Professor T. Muraoka on the Occasion of His Sixty-Fifth Birthday*, edited by M. F. J. Baasten and W. Th. van Peursen, 3–24. OLA 118. Leuven: Peeters, 2003.

BIBLIOGRAPHY

————, and Geza Vermes. *Qumran Cave 4.XIX: Serekh ha-Yaḥad and Two Related Texts*. DJD 26. Oxford: Clarendon, 1998.

Allegro, John M. *Qumrân Cave 4.I (4Q158–4Q186)*. DJD 5. Oxford: Clarendon, 1968.

————. *The Treasure of the Copper Scroll*. London: Routledge, 1960.

Alster, Bendt. "Scribes and Wisdom in Ancient Mesopotamia." In *Scribes, Sages, and Seers: The Sage in the Eastern Mediterranean World*, edited by Leo G. Perdue, 47–63. Göttingen: Vandenhoeck & Ruprecht, 2008.

Amihay, Aryeh. *Theory and Practice in Essene Law*. New York: Oxford University Press, 2017.

Amitai, Janet, ed. *Biblical Archaeology Today: Proceedings of the International Congress on Biblical Archaeology, Jerusalem, April 1984*. Jerusalem: Israel Exploration Society, 1985.

Attridge, Harold, Torleif Elgvin, Jozef Milik, Saul Olyan, John Strugnell, Emanuel Tov, James C. VanderKam, and Sidnie White. *Qumran Cave 4.VIII: Parabiblical Texts, Part I*. DJD 13. Oxford: Clarendon, 1994.

Avigad, Nahman. *Bullae and Seals from a Post-Exilic Judean Archive*. Qedem Monographs of the Institute of Archaeology 4. Jerusalem: Hebrew University of Jerusalem, 1976.

Baasten, M. F. J., and W. Th. van Peursen, eds. *Hamlet on a Hill: Semitic and Greek Studies Presented to Professor T. Muraoka on the Occasion of His Sixty-Fifth Birthday*. OLA 118. Leuven: Peeters, 2003.

Baillet, M., J. T. Milik, and R. de Vaux. *Les "petites grottes" de Qumrân*. 2 vols. DJD 3. Oxford: Clarendon, 1962.

Barkay, Gabriel, Andrew G. Vaughn, Marilyn J. Lundberg, and Bruce Zuckerman. "The Amulets from Ketef Hinnom: A New Edition and Evaluation." *BASOR* 334 (2004): 41–71.

Bar-Nathan, Rachel. "Qumran and the Hasmonaean and Herodian Winter Palaces of Jericho: The Implication of the Pottery Finds for the Interpretation of the Settlement at Qumran." In *Qumran, the Site of the Dead Sea Scrolls: Archaeological Interpretations and Debates. Proceedings of a Conference Held at Brown University, November 17–19, 2002*, edited by Katharina Galor, Jean-Baptiste Humbert, and Jürgen Zangenberg, 263–80. STDJ 57. Leiden: Brill, 2006.

Barthélemy, D., and J. T. Milik. *Qumran Cave I*. DJD 1. Oxford: Clarendon, 1955.

Baumgarten, Albert I. *The Flourishing of Jewish Sects in the Maccabean Era: An Interpretation*. JSJSup 55. Leiden: Brill, 1997.

Baumgarten, Joseph M. "Miscellaneous Rules (4Q265)." In *The Dead Sea*

Scrolls: Hebrew, Aramaic, and Greek Texts with English Translations. Vol. 3: *Damascus Document II, Some Works of the Torah, and Related Documents,* edited by James H. Charlesworth and Henry W. M. Rietz, 253–70. PTSDSSP. Tübingen: Mohr Siebeck; Louisville: Westminster John Knox, 2006.

———. "The Pharisaic-Sadducean Controversies about Purity and the Qumran Texts." *JJS* 31 (1980): 157–70.

———. *Qumran Cave 4.XIII: The Damascus Document (4Q266–273).* DJD 18. Oxford: Clarendon, 1996.

———. *Studies in Qumran Law.* SJLA 24. Leiden: Brill, 1977.

———, Esther G. Chazon, and Avital Pinnick, eds. *The Damascus Document: A Centennial of Discovery.* STDJ 34. Leiden: Brill, 2000.

Baumgarten, Joseph, Torleif Elgvin, Esther Eshel, Erik Larson, Manfred R. Lehmann, Stephen Pfann, and Lawrence H. Schiffman. *Qumran Cave 4.XXV: Halakhic Texts.* DJD 35. Oxford: Clarendon, 1999.

Bélis, Mireille. "Révision commentée des différents systèmes de numérotation." In *Fouilles de Khirbet Qumrân et de ʿAïn Feshkha.* Vol. 2: *Études d'anthropologie, de physique et de chimie,* edited by Jean-Baptiste Humbert and Jan Gunneweg, 409–15. NTOA.SA 3. Göttingen: Vandenhoeck & Ruprecht, 2003.

———. "The Unpublished Textiles from the Qumran Caves." In *The Caves of Qumran: Proceedings of the International Conference, Lugano 2014,* edited by Marcello Fidanzio, 123–36. STDJ 118. Leiden: Brill, 2017.

Ben-Dov, Jonathan. *Head of All Years: Astronomy and Calendars at Qumran in Their Ancient Context.* STDJ 78. Leiden: Brill, 2008.

———, and Seth L. Sanders, eds. *Ancient Jewish Sciences and the History of Knowledge in Second Temple Literature.* New York: New York University and the Institute for the Study of the Ancient World, 2014.

Ben-Dov, Jonathan, Daniel Stökl Ben Ezra, and Asaf Gayer. "Reconstruction of a Single Copy of the Qumran Cave 4 Cryptic-Script Serekh haEdah." *RevQ* 29 (2017): 21–77.

Benoit, Pierre, J. T. Milik, and Roland de Vaux. *Les grottes de Murabbaʿât.* 2 vols. DJD 2. Oxford: Clarendon, 1961.

Bergren, Theodore A. "Nehemiah in 2 Maccabees 1:10–2:18." *JSJ* 28 (1997): 249–70.

Berlin, Andrea M. "Jewish Life before the Revolt: The Archaeological Evidence." *JSJ* 36 (2005): 417–70.

Bernstein, Moshe, Florentino García Martínez, and John Kampen, eds. *Legal Texts and Legal Issues: Proceedings of the Second Meeting of the Interna-*

BIBLIOGRAPHY

tional Organization for Qumran Studies Published in Honour of Joseph M. Baumgarten. STDJ 23. Leiden: Brill, 1997.

Berti, Monica. "Greek and Roman Libraries in the Hellenistic Age." In *The Dead Sea Scrolls and the Concept of a Library*, edited by Sidnie White Crawford and Cecilia Wassén, 33–54. STDJ 116. Leiden: Brill, 2016.

Bickerman, Elias J. "The Seleucid Charter for Jerusalem." In *Studies in Jewish and Christian History: A New Edition in English Including The God of the Maccabees*, edited by Amram Tropper, 1:315–56. 2 vols. AGJU 68. Leiden: Brill, 2007.

———. "A Seleucid Proclamation Concerning the Temple in Jerusalem." In *Studies in Jewish and Christian History: A New Edition in English Including The God of the Maccabees*, edited by Amram Tropper, 1:357–75. 2 vols. AGJU 68. Leiden: Brill, 2007.

Bigg, Robert D. "Ebla: Texts." *ABD* 2:263–70.

Black, Jeremy A., and William J. Tait. "Archives and Libraries in the Ancient Near East." *CANE* 4:2197–2210.

Blenkinsopp, Joseph. *Ezra-Nehemiah: A Commentary*. OTL. Philadelphia: Westminster, 1988.

———. "The Mission of Udjahorresnet and Those of Ezra and Nehemiah." *JBL* 106 (1987): 409–21.

Blum, Rudolph. *Kallimachos: The Alexandrian Library and the Origins of Bibliography*. Madison: University of Wisconsin Press, 1991.

Boccaccini, Gabriele. *Beyond the Essene Hypothesis: The Parting of the Ways between Qumran and Enochic Judaism*. Grand Rapids: Eerdmans, 1998.

———, ed. *Enoch and Qumran Origins: New Light on a Forgotten Connection*. Grand Rapids: Eerdmans, 2005.

———, and John J. Collins, eds. *The Early Enoch Literature*. JSJSup 121. Leiden: Brill, 2007.

Branham, Joan R. "Hedging the Holy at Qumran: Walls as Symbolic Devices." In *Qumran, the Site of the Dead Sea Scrolls: Archaeological Interpretations and Debates. Proceedings of a Conference Held at Brown University, November 17–19, 2002*, edited by Katharina Galor, Jean-Baptiste Humbert, and Jürgen Zangenberg, 117–32. STDJ 57. Leiden: Brill, 2006.

Briant, Pierre. *From Cyrus to Alexander: A History of the Persian Empire*. Translated by Peter T. Daniels. Winona Lake, IN: Eisenbrauns, 2002.

Brooke, George J. "Choosing between Papyrus and Skin: Cultural Complexity and Multiple Identities in the Qumran Library." In *Jewish Cultural Encounters in the Ancient Mediterranean and Near Eastern World*, edited by

Mladen Popović, Myles Schoonover, and Marijn Vandenberghe, 119–35. JSJSup 178. Leiden: Brill, 2017.

———. "Ezekiel in Some Qumran and New Testament Texts." In *The Madrid Qumran Congress: Proceedings of the International Congress on the Dead Sea Scrolls, Madrid 18–21 March 1991*, edited by J. Trebolle Barrera and L. Vegas Montaner, 317–38. STDJ 11, 1. Leiden: Brill; Madrid: Editorial Complutense, 1992.

———, John Collins, Torleif Elgvin, Peter Flint, Jonas Greenfield, Erik Larson, Carol Newsom, Émile Puech, Lawrence H. Schiffman, Michael Stone, and Julio Trebolle Barrera. *Qumran Cave 4.XVII: Parabiblical Texts, Part 3*. DJD 22. Oxford: Clarendon, 1996.

Brooke, George J., and Charlotte Hempel, eds. *T&T Clark Companion to the Dead Sea Scrolls*. London: T&T Clark, 2018.

Brooke, George J., and J. Høgenhaven, eds. *The Mermaid and the Partridge: Essays from the Copenhagen Conference on Revising Texts from Cave 4*. STDJ 96. Leiden: Brill, 2011.

Broshi, Magen. "Qumran: Archaeology." *EDSS* 2:735.

———, and Hanan Eshel. "How and Where Did the Qumranites Live?" In *The Provo International Conference on the Dead Sea Scrolls: Technological Innovations, New Texts, and Reformulated Issues*, edited by Donald W. Parry and Eugene Ulrich, 266–73. STDJ 30. Leiden: Brill, 1998.

———. "Residential Caves at Qumran." *DSD* 6 (1999): 328–48.

———. "Three Seasons of Excavations at Qumran." *JRA* 17 (2004): 321–32.

Broshi, Magen, and Ada Yardeni. "339. 4QList of False Prophets ar." In *Qumran Cave 4.XIV: Parabiblical Texts, Part 2*, by Magen Broshi, Esther Eshel, Joseph Fitzmyer, Erik Larson, Carol Newsom, Lawrence Schiffman, Mark Smith, Michael Stone, John Strugnell, and Ada Yardeni, in consultation with James C. VanderKam, 77–79. DJD 19. Oxford: Clarendon, 1995.

———. "340. 4QList of Netinim." In *Qumran Cave 4.XIV: Parabiblical Texts, Part 2*, edited by Magen Broshi, Esther Eshel, Joseph Fitzmyer, Erik Larson, Carol Newsom, Lawrence Schiffman, Mark Smith, Michael Stone, John Strugnell, and Ada Yardeni, in consultation with James C. VanderKam, 81–84. DJD 19. Oxford: Clarendon, 1996.

Broshi, Magen, Esther Eshel, Joseph Fitzmyer, Erik Larson, Carol Newsom, Lawrence Schiffman, Mark Smith, Michael Stone, John Strugnell, and Ada Yardeni, in consultation with James C. VanderKam. *Qumran Cave 4.XIV: Parabiblical Texts, Part 2*. DJD 19. Oxford: Clarendon, 1995.

Burdajewicz, Mariusz. "Typology of the Pottery from Khirbet Qumran (French Excavations 1953–1956)." *ASOR Newsletter* 51 (2001): 14.

BIBLIOGRAPHY

Carr, David. *The Formation of the Hebrew Bible: A New Reconstruction*. Oxford: Oxford University Press, 2011.

———. *Writing on the Tablet of the Heart: Origins of Scripture and Literature*. New York: Oxford University Press, 2005.

Carswell, J. "Appendix I: Fastenings on the Qumrân Manuscripts." In *Qumrân Grotte 4.II: Part I: Archéologie*, by R. de Vaux; *Part II: Tefillin, Mezuzot et Targums (4Q128–4Q157)*, by J. T. Milik, 23–28. DJD 6. Oxford: Clarendon, 1977.

Casson, Lionel. *Libraries in the Ancient World*. New Haven: Yale University Press, 2001.

Chalcraft, David J., ed. *Sectarianism in Early Judaism: Sociological Advances*. London: Equinox, 2007.

Charles, Robert H., and Arthur Cowley. "An Early Source of the Testaments of the Patriarchs." *JQR* 19 (1907): 566–83.

Charlesworth, James H., ed. *The Dead Sea Scrolls: Hebrew, Aramaic, and Greek Texts with English Translations*. Vol. 1: *Rule of the Community and Related Documents*. PTSDSSP. Tübingen: Mohr Siebeck; Louisville: Westminster John Knox, 1994.

———. Vol. 2: *Damascus Document, War Scroll, and Related Documents*. PTSDSSP. Tübingen: Mohr Siebeck; Louisville: Westminster John Knox, 1995.

———, and Henry W. M. Rietz, eds. *The Dead Sea Scrolls: Hebrew, Aramaic, and Greek Texts with English Translations*. Vol. 3: *Damascus Document II, Some Works of the Torah, and Related Documents*. PTSDSSP. Tübingen: Mohr Siebeck; Louisville: Westminster John Knox, 2006.

Charlesworth, James H., Nahum Cohen, Hannah Cotton, Esther Eshel, Hanan Eshel, Peter Flint, Haggai Misgav, Matthew Morgenstern, Catherine Murphy, Michael Segal, Ada Yardeni, and Boaz Zissu. *Miscellaneous Texts from the Judaean Desert*. DJD 38. Oxford: Clarendon, 2000.

Chazon, Esther G. "Is *Divrei Ha-me'orot* a Sectarian Prayer?" In *The Dead Sea Scrolls: Forty Years of Research*, edited by Devorah Dimant and Uriel Rappaport, 3–17. STDJ 10. Leiden: Brill, 1992.

———. "Psalms, Hymns, and Prayers." *EDSS* 2:710–15.

———. "Shifting Perspectives on Liturgy at Qumran and in Second Temple Judaism." In *The Dead Sea Scrolls in Context: Integrating the Dead Sea Scrolls in the Study of Ancient Texts, Languages, and Cultures*, edited by Armin Lange, Emanuel Tov, and Matthias Weigold, 2:513–31. 2 vols. VTSup 140. Leiden: Brill, 2011.

———, Ruth A. Clements, and Avital Pinnick, eds. *Liturgical Perspectives:*

Prayer and Poetry in Light of the Dead Sea Scrolls; Proceedings of the Fifth International Symposium of the Orion Center for the Study of the Dead Sea Scrolls and Associated Literature, 19–23 January, 2000. STDJ 48. Leiden: Brill, 2003.

Clamer, Christa. "Jewellery Finds from the Cemetery." In *Fouilles de Khirbet Qumrân et de ʿAin Feshkha*. Vol. 2: *Études d'anthropologie, de physique et de chimie*, edited by Jean-Baptiste Humbert and Jan Gunneweg, 171–83. NTOA.SA 3. Göttingen: Vandenhoeck & Ruprecht, 2003.

Clark, Kenneth Willis. "The Posture of the Ancient Scribe." *BA* 26 (1963): 63–72.

Clermont-Ganneau, Charles. *Archaeological Researches in Palestine in the Years 1873–1874.* 2 vols. London: Palestine Exploration Fund, 1898.

Cohen, Shaye J. D. "Hellenism in Unexpected Places." In *Hellenism in the Land of Israel*, edited by John J. Collins and Gregory E. Sterling, 216–43. CJAS 13. Notre Dame: University of Notre Dame Press, 2001.

Cohen, Yoram. *The Scribes and Scholars of the City of Emar in the Late Bronze Age.* HSS 59. Winona Lake, IN: Eisenbrauns, 2009.

Collins, John J. *Apocalypticism in the Dead Sea Scrolls.* Literature of the Dead Sea Scrolls. London: Routledge, 1997.

———. *Beyond the Qumran Community: The Sectarian Movement of the Dead Sea Scrolls.* Grand Rapids: Eerdmans, 2009.

———. *Daniel.* Hermeneia. Minneapolis: Fortress, 1993.

———. "Reading for History in the Scrolls." In *Scriptures and Sectarianism*, 133–49. WUNT 332. Tübingen: Mohr Siebeck, 2014.

———. "The Sage in the Apocalyptic and Pseudepigraphic Literature." In *The Sage in Israel and the Ancient Near East*, edited by John G. Gammie and Leo G. Perdue, 343–54. Winona Lake, IN: Eisenbrauns, 1990.

———. *Scriptures and Sectarianism.* WUNT 332. Tübingen: Mohr Siebeck, 2014.

———. "Sectarian Communities in the Dead Sea Scrolls." In *The Oxford Handbook of the Dead Sea Scrolls*, edited by Timothy H. Lim and John J. Collins, 151–72. Oxford: Oxford University Press, 2010.

———, and Deborah A. Green. "The Tales from the Persian Court (4Q550[a-c])." In *Antikes Judentum und Frühes Christentum: Festschrift für Hartmut Stegemann*, edited by Bernd Kollmann, Wolfgang Reinbold, and Annette Steudel, 39–50. BZNW 97. Berlin: de Gruyter, 1998.

Collins, John J., and Daniel C. Harlow, eds. *The Eerdmans Dictionary of Early Judaism.* Grand Rapids: Eerdmans, 2010.

Collins, John J., Tracy M. Lemos, and Saul M. Olyan. *Worship, Women and*

BIBLIOGRAPHY

War: Essays in Honor of Susan Niditch. Providence: Society of Biblical Literature, 2015.

Collins, John J., and Gregory E. Sterling, eds. *Hellenism in the Land of Israel*. CJAS 13. Notre Dame: University of Notre Dame Press, 2001.

Collins, Nina. *The Library in Alexandria and the Bible in Greek*. VTSup 82. Leiden: Brill, 2000.

Coqueugniot, Gaëlle. "Where Was the Royal Library of Pergamum? An Institution Found and Lost Again." In *Ancient Libraries*, edited by Jason König, Katerina Oikonomopoulou, and Greg Woolf, 109–23. Cambridge: Cambridge University Press, 2013.

Cotton, Hannah M. "Hever, Nahal: Written Material." *EDSS* 1:359–61.

———, and Erik Larson. "4Q460/4Q350 and Tampering with Qumran Texts in Antiquity," In *Emanuel: Studies in Hebrew Bible, Septuagint and Dead Sea Scrolls in Honor of Emanuel Tov*, edited by Shalom M. Paul, Robert A. Kraft, Lawrence H. Schiffman, and Weston W. Fields, 113–26. VTSup 94. Leiden: Brill, 2003.

Cotton, Hannah M., and Ada Yardeni. *Aramaic, Hebrew and Greek Documentary Texts from Nahal Hever and Other Sites*. DJD 27. Oxford: Clarendon, 1997.

Cowley, Arthur E. *Aramaic Papyri of the Fifth Century B.C.* Oxford: Clarendon, 1923.

Crawford, Sidnie White. "4QDeut^n." In *Qumran Cave 4.IX: Deuteronomy, Joshua, Judges, Kings*, by Eugene Ulrich, Frank Moore Cross, Sidnie White Crawford, Julie Ann Duncan, Patrick W. Skehan, Emanuel Tov, and Julio Trebolle Barrera, 117–28. DJD 14. Oxford: Clarendon, 1995.

———. "Has *Esther* Been Found at Qumran? *4QProto-Esther* and the *Esther* Corpus." *RevQ* 17 (1996): 307–25.

———. "The Identification and History of the Qumran Community in American Scholarship." In *The Dead Sea Scrolls in Scholarly Perspective: A History of Research*, edited by Devorah Dimant, 13–30. STDJ 99. Leiden: Brill, 2012.

———. "The Inscriptional Evidence from Qumran and Its Relationship to the Cave 4Q Documents." In *The Caves of Qumran: Proceedings of the International Conference, Lugano 2014*, edited by Marcello Fidanzio, 213–20. STDJ 118. Leiden: Brill, 2017.

———. "Interpreting the Pentateuch through Scribal Processes: The Evidence from the Qumran Manuscripts." In *Insights into Editing in the Hebrew Bible and the Ancient Near East*, edited by Reinhard Müller and Juha Pakkala, 59–80. CBET 84. Leuven: Peeters, 2017.

Bibliography

———. "Mothers, Sisters, and Elders: Titles for Women in Second Temple Jewish and Early Christian Communities." In *The Dead Sea Scrolls as Background to Postbiblical Judaism and Early Christianity*, edited by James Davila, 177–91. STDJ 46. Leiden: Brill, 2002.

———. "Not According to Rule: Women, the Dead Sea Scrolls and Qumran." In *Emanuel: Studies in Hebrew Bible, Septuagint and Dead Sea Scrolls in Honor of Emanuel Tov*, edited by Shalom M. Paul, Robert A. Kraft, Lawrence H. Schiffman, and Weston W. Fields, 127–50. VTSup 94. Leiden: Brill, 2003.

———. "Qumran Cave 4: Its Archaeology and Its Manuscript Collection." In *Is There a Text in This Cave? Studies in the Textuality of the Dead Sea Scrolls in Honour of George J. Brooke*, edited by Ariel Feldman, Maria Cioata, and Charlotte Hempel, 105–22. STDJ 119. Leiden: Brill, 2017.

———. "Qumran: Caves, Scrolls, and Buildings." In *A Teacher for All Generations: Essays in Honor of James C. VanderKam*, edited by Eric F. Mason, Samuel Thomas, Alison Schofield, and Eugene Ulrich, 1:253–74. 2 vols. JSJSup 153. Leiden: Brill, 2012.

———. "The Qumran Collection as a Scribal Library." In *The Dead Sea Scrolls and the Concept of a Library*, edited by Sidnie White Crawford and Cecilia Wassén, 109–31. STDJ 116. Leiden: Brill, 2016.

———. *Rewriting Scripture in Second Temple Times*. Studies in the Dead Sea Scrolls and Related Literature. Grand Rapids: Eerdmans, 2008.

———. "Samaritan Pentateuch." In *The Hebrew Bible*. Vol. 1A: *Overview Articles*, edited by Armin Lange and Emanuel Tov, 166–75. Textual History of the Bible. Leiden: Brill, 2016.

———. *The Temple Scroll and Related Texts*. Companion to the Qumran Scrolls 2. Sheffield: Sheffield Academic Press, 2000.

———, and Cecilia Wassén, eds. *Apocalyptic Thinking in Early Judaism: Engaging with John Collins' The Apocalyptic Imagination*. JSJSup 182. Leiden: Brill, 2018.

———, eds. *The Dead Sea Scrolls and the Concept of a Library*. STDJ 116. Leiden: Brill, 2016.

Crenshaw, James L. *Education in Ancient Israel: Across the Deadening Silence*. New York: Doubleday, 1998.

Cross, Frank Moore. *The Ancient Library of Qumran*. 3rd ed. BibSem 30. Sheffield: Sheffield Academic Press, 1995.

———. *Canaanite Myth and Hebrew Epic: Essays in the History of the Religion of Israel*. Cambridge: Harvard University Press, 1973.

———. "The Development of the Jewish Scripts." In *Leaves from an Epigra-

BIBLIOGRAPHY

pher's Notebook: Collected Papers in Hebrew and West Semitic Palaeography and Epigraphy, 3–43. HSS 51. Winona Lake, IN: Eisenbrauns, 2003.

———. "Paleography." *EDSS* 2:629–34.

———. "The Papyri and Their Historical Implications." In *Discoveries in the Wâdi ed-Dâliyeh*, edited by Paul W. Lapp and Nancy L. Lapp, 17–29. AASOR 41. Cambridge: American Schools of Oriental Research, 1974.

———. "Reminiscences of the Early Days in the Discovery and Study of the Dead Sea Scrolls." In *The Dead Sea Scrolls Fifty Years after Their Discovery: Proceedings of the Jerusalem Congress, July 20–25, 1997*, edited by Lawrence H. Schiffman, Emanuel Tov, and James C. VanderKam, 932–42. Jerusalem: Israel Exploration Society, 2000.

———. *Scrolls from Qumrân Cave I: The Great Isaiah Scroll, The Order of the Community, The Pesher to Habakkuk*. Jerusalem: Albright Institute of Archaeological Research and the Shrine of the Book, 1974.

———, and Esther Eshel. "Ostraca from Khirbet Qumrân." *IEJ* 47 (1997): 17–28.

———. "Ostraca from Khirbet Qumran." In *Qumran Cave 4.XXVI: Cryptic Texts*, by Stephen Pfann; and *Miscellanea, Part 1*, by Philip Alexander et al., 497–512. DJD 36. Oxford: Clarendon, 2000.

Cross, Frank Moore, Donald W. Parry, Richard J. Saley, and Eugene Ulrich. *Qumran Cave 4.XII: 1–2 Samuel*. DJD 17. Oxford: Clarendon, 2005.

Crowfoot, Grace M. "The Linen Textiles." In *Qumran Cave I*, by D. Barthélemy and J. T. Milik, 18–38. DJD 1. Oxford: Clarendon, 1955.

Curtis, A. "Ilimilku of Ugarit: Copyist or Creator?" In *Writing the Bible: Scribes, Scribalism and Script*, edited by Philip R. Davies and Thomas Römer, 10–22. Durham: Acumen, 2013.

Dávid, Nóra, and Armin Lange, eds. *Qumran and the Bible: Studying the Jewish and Christian Scriptures in Light of the Dead Sea Scrolls*. CBET 57. Leuven: Peeters, 2010.

Davies, Philip R. *The Damascus Covenant: An Interpretation of the "Damascus Document."* JSOTSup25. Sheffield: JSOT Press, 1983.

———. *Scribes and Schools: The Canonization of the Hebrew Scriptures*. Library of Ancient Israel. Louisville: Westminster John Knox, 1996.

———. *Sects and Scrolls: Essays on Qumran and Related Topics*. SFSHJ 134. Atlanta: Scholars Press, 1996.

———, and Thomas Römer, eds. *Writing the Bible: Scribes, Scribalism and Script*. London: Routledge, 2016.

Davila, James, ed. *The Dead Sea Scrolls as Background to Postbiblical Judaism and Early Christianity*. STDJ 46. Leiden: Brill, 2002.

330

Dearman, J. Andrew. "My Servants the Scribes: Composition and Context in Jeremiah 36." *JBL* 109 (1990): 403–21.

Delcor, Mathias, ed. *Qumrân: Sa piété, sa théologie, et son milieu*. BETL 46. Leuven: Leuven University Press, 1978.

Demsky, Aaron. "Scribe." *EncJud* 18:212–13.

Dimant, Devorah. "Apocrypha and Pseudepigrapha at Qumran." In *History, Ideology and Bible Interpretation in the Dead Sea Scrolls: Collected Studies*, 153–70. FAT 90. Tübingen: Mohr Siebeck, 2014.

———. "Between Sectarian and Nonsectarian: The Case of the *Apocryphon of Joshua*." In *History, Ideology and Bible Interpretation in the Dead Sea Scrolls: Collected Studies*, 113–33. FAT 90. Tübingen: Mohr Siebeck, 2014.

———. "The Composite Character of the Qumran Sectarian Literature as an Indication of Its Date and Provenance." *RevQ* 22 (2006): 615–30.

———, ed. *The Dead Sea Scrolls in Scholarly Perspective: A History of Research*. STDJ 99. Leiden: Brill, 2012.

———. *History, Ideology and Bible Interpretation in the Dead Sea Scrolls: Collected Studies*. FAT 90. Tübingen: Mohr Siebeck, 2014.

———. "Israeli Scholarship on the Qumran Community." In *The Dead Sea Scrolls in Scholarly Perspective: A History of Research*, edited by Devorah Dimant, 237–80. STDJ 99. Leiden: Brill, 2012.

———. "The Qumran Aramaic Texts and the Qumran Community." In *Flores Florentino: Dead Sea Scrolls and Other Early Jewish Studies in Honour of Florentino García Martínez*, edited by Anthony Hilhorst, Émile Puech, and Eibert J. C. Tigchelaar, 197–206. JSJSup 122. Leiden: Brill, 2007.

———. "The Qumran Manuscripts: Contents and Significance." In *History, Ideology and Bible Interpretation in the Dead Sea Scrolls: Collected Studies*, 27–56. FAT 90. Tübingen: Mohr Siebeck, 2014.

———. "Two 'Scientific' Fictions: The So-Called Book of Noah and the Alleged Quotation of Jubilees in CD 16:3–4." In *Studies in the Hebrew Bible, Qumran, and the Septuagint: Essays Presented to Eugene Ulrich on the Occasion of His Sixty-Fifth Birthday*, edited by Peter W. Flint, Emanuel Tov, and James C. VanderKam, 353–68. VTSup 101. Leiden: Brill, 2006.

———. "The Vocabulary of the Qumran Sectarian Texts." In *History, Ideology and Bible Interpretation in the Dead Sea Scrolls: Collected Studies*, 57–100. FAT 90. Tübingen: Mohr Siebeck, 2014.

———, and Lawrence H. Schiffman, eds. *Time to Prepare the Way in the Wilderness*. STDJ 16. Leiden: Brill, 1995.

Dommershausen, Werner. *1 Makkabäer, 2 Makkabäer*. Würzburg: Echter, 1985.

BIBLIOGRAPHY

Donceel, Robert. *Synthèse des observations faites en fouillant les tombes des nécropoles de Khirbet Qumrân et des environs / The Khirbet Qumran Cemeteries: A Synthesis of the Archaeological Data.* Cracow: Enigma, 2002.

——, and Pauline Donceel-Voûte. "The Archaeology of Khirbet Qumran." In *Methods of Investigation of the Dead Sea Scrolls and the Khirbet Qumran Site: Present Realities and Future Prospects,* edited by Michael O. Wise, Norman Golb, John J. Collins, and Dennis G. Pardee, 1–38. ANYAS 722. New York: New York Academy of Sciences, 1994.

Donceel-Voûte, Pauline. "'Coenaculum'—La salle à l'étage du *locus* 30 à Khirbet Qumran sur la Mer Morte." In *Banquets d'Orient,* edited by Rika Gyselen, 61–84. ResOr 4. Leuven: Peeters, 1992.

Doran, Robert. *Temple Propaganda: The Purpose and Character of 2 Maccabees.* CBQMS 12. Washington, DC: Catholic Biblical Association of America, 1981.

Drawnel, Henryk. *The Aramaic Astronomical Book (4Q208–4Q211) from Qumran: Text, Translation, and Commentary.* Oxford: Oxford University Press, 2011.

——. *An Aramaic Wisdom Text from Qumran: A New Interpretation of the Levi Document.* Leiden: Brill, 2004.

Driver, G. R. *The Judaean Scrolls: The Problem and a Solution.* Oxford: Blackwell, 1965.

Du Toit, Jaqueline S. *Textual Memory: Ancient Archives, Libraries and the Hebrew Bible.* Sheffield: Sheffield Phoenix Press, 2011.

Duke, Robert, with Daniel Holt and Skyler Russell. "Daniel 10:18–20." In *Dead Sea Scrolls Fragments in the Museum Collection,* edited by Emanuel Tov, Kipp Davis, and Robert Duke, 200–209. Publications of Museum of the Bible 1. Leiden: Brill, 2016.

Dupont-Sommer, André. *The Essene Writings from Qumran.* Translated by Geza Vermes. Oxford: Blackwell, 1961.

Dušek, Jan. *Aramaic and Hebrew Inscriptions from Mount Gerizim and Samaria between Antiochus III and Antiochus IV Epiphanes.* CHANE 54. Leiden: Brill, 2012.

Ekroth, Gunnel. "A View from the Greek Side: Interpretations of Animal Bones as Evidence for Sacrifice and Ritual Consumption." *JAJ* 7 (2016): 35–50.

Elgvin, Torleif. "Bronze Inkwells from Naḥal Ḥever(?) and Nabataea: MS 1655/2 and 1987/15." In *Gleanings from the Caves: Dead Sea Scrolls and Artefacts from the Schøyen Collection,* edited by Torleif Elgvin, Kipp Davis, and Michaël Langlois, 451–62. LSTS 71. London: Bloomsbury T&T Clark, 2016.

———. "The *Yaḥad* Is More Than Qumran." In *Enoch and Qumran Origins: New Light on a Forgotten Connection*, edited by Gabriele Boccaccini, 273–79. Grand Rapids: Eerdmans, 2005.

———, Kipp Davis, and Michaël Langlois, eds. *Gleanings from the Caves: Dead Sea Scrolls and Artefacts from the Schøyen Collection*. LSTS 71. London: Bloomsbury T&T Clark, 2016.

Elior, Rachel. *Memory and Oblivion: The Secret of the Dead Sea Scrolls*. [In Hebrew.] Jerusalem: Van Leer Institute and Kibbutz haMeuchad, 2009.

Emerton, J. A., ed. *Congress Volume: Jerusalem, 1986*. VTSup 40. Leiden: Brill, 1988.

Eshel, Esther. "477. 4QRebukes Reported by the Overseer." In *Qumran Cave 4.XXVI: Cryptic Texts,* by Stephen Pfann; and *Miscellanea, Part 1*, by Philip Alexander et al., 474–83. DJD 36. Oxford: Clarendon, 2000.

———. "Apotropaic Prayers in the Second Temple Period." In *Liturgical Perspectives: Prayer and Poetry in Light of the Dead Sea Scrolls; Proceedings of the Fifth International Symposium of the Orion Center for the Study of the Dead Sea Scrolls and Associated Literature, 19–23 January, 2000*, edited by Esther G. Chazon, Ruth Clements, and Avital Pinnick, 69–88. STDJ 48. Leiden: Brill, 2003.

———, Hanan Eshel, and Ada Yardeni. "448. 4QApocryphal Psalm and Prayer." In *Qumran Cave 4.XI: Poetical and Liturgical Texts, Part 1*, by Esther Eshel et al., 403–25. DJD 11. Oxford: Clarendon, 1998.

Eshel, Esther, Hanan Eshel, Carol Newsom, Bilhah Nitzan, Eileen Schuller, and Ada Yardeni, in consultation with James C. VanderKam and Monica Brady. *Qumran Cave 4.XI: Poetical and Liturgical Texts, Part 1*. DJD 11. Oxford: Clarendon, 1998.

Eshel, Hanan. "Excavations in the Judean Desert and at Qumran under Israeli Jurisdiction." In *The Dead Sea Scrolls in Scholarly Perspective: A History of Research*, edited by Devorah Dimant, 381–400. STDJ 99. Leiden: Brill, 2012.

———. *Masada: An Epic Story*. Jerusalem: Carta, 2009.

———. "Murabbaʿat, Wadi: Written Material." *EDSS* 1:583–86.

———, Magen Broshi, Richard Freund, and Brian Schultz. "New Data on the Cemetery East of Khirbet Qumran." *DSD* 9 (2002): 135–54.

Eshel, Hanan, Esther Eshel, Haggai Misgav, and Nahum Cohen. "Ketef Jericho 1–7." In *Miscellaneous Texts from the Judaean Desert*, by James Charlesworth, Nahum Cohen, Hannah M. Cotton, Esther Eshel, Hanan Eshel, Peter Flint,

BIBLIOGRAPHY

Haggai Misgav, Matthew Morgenstern, Catherine Murphy, Michael Segal, Ada Yardeni, and Boaz Zissu, 21–62. DJD 38. Oxford: Clarendon, 2000.

Eshel, Hanan, and Haggai Misgav. "A Fourth Century B.C.E. Document from Ketef Yeriho." *IEJ* 38 (1988): 158–76.

Falk, Daniel K. *Daily, Sabbath, and Festival Prayers in the Dead Sea Scrolls.* STDJ 27. Leiden: Brill, 1998.

Feldman, Ariel, Maria Cioata, and Charlotte Hempel, eds. *Is There a Text in This Cave? Studies in the Textuality of the Dead Sea Scrolls in Honour of George J. Brooke.* STDJ 119. Leiden: Brill, 2017.

Fidanzio, Marcello, ed. *The Caves of Qumran: Proceedings of the International Conference, Lugano 2014.* STDJ 118. Leiden: Brill, 2017.

———, and Jean-Baptiste Humbert. "Finds from the Qumran Caves: Roland de Vaux's Inventory of the Excavations (1949–1956)." In *The Caves of Qumran: Proceedings of the International Conference, Lugano 2014,* edited by Marcello Fidanzio, 263–332. STDJ 118. Leiden: Brill, 2017.

Fields, Weston. *Dead Sea Scrolls: A Full History.* Vol. 1: *1947–1960.* Leiden: Brill, 2009.

Fitzmyer, Joseph A. *The Gospel according to Luke (I–IX): Introduction, Translation, and Notes.* AB 28. Garden City, NY: Doubleday, 1981.

———. *The Gospel according to Luke (X–XXIV): Introduction, Translation, and Notes.* AB 28A. Garden City, NY: Doubleday, 1985.

Flint, Peter W. "Biblical Scrolls from Naḥal Ḥever and 'Wadi Seiyal': Introduction." In *Miscellaneous Texts from the Judaean Desert,* by James Charlesworth, Nahum Cohen, Hannah Cotton, Esther Eshel, Hanan Eshel, Peter Flint, Haggai Misgav, Mathew Morgenstern, Catherine Murphy, Michael Segal, Ada Yardeni, and Boaz Zissu, 133–36. DJD 38. Oxford: Clarendon, 2000.

———. *The Dead Sea Psalms Scrolls and the Book of Psalms.* STDJ 17. Leiden: Brill, 1997.

———. "The Greek Fragments of Enoch from Qumran Cave 7." In *Enoch and Qumran Origins: New Light on a Forgotten Connection,* edited by Gabriele Boccaccini, 224–33. Grand Rapids: Eerdmans, 2005.

———, and James C. VanderKam, eds. *The Dead Sea Scrolls after Fifty Years: A Comprehensive Assessment.* 2 vols. Leiden: Brill, 1999.

Flint, Peter W., Emanuel Tov, and James C. VanderKam, eds. *Studies in the Hebrew Bible, Qumran, and the Septuagint: Essays Presented to Eugene Ulrich on the Occasion of His Sixty-Fifth Birthday.* VTSup 101. Leiden: Brill, 2006.

Fox, Nili Sacher. *In the Service of the King: Officialdom in Ancient Israel and Judah.* Cincinnati: Hebrew Union College Press, 2000.

Fraade, Steven D. "To Whom It May Concern: 4QMMT and Its Addressee(s)." *RevQ* 19 (2000): 507–26.

Frey, Jörg, Carsten Claußen, Nadine Kessler, eds. *Qumran und die Archäologie: Texte und Kontexte.* WUNT 278. Tübingen: Mohr Siebeck, 2011.

Fröhlich, Ida. "Origins of Evil and the Apocalyptic Tradition in 1 Enoch." In *Apocalyptic Thinking in Early Judaism: Engaging with John Collins' The Apocalyptic Imagination,* edited by Sidnie White Crawford and Cecilia Wassén, 141–59. JSJSup 182. Leiden: Brill, 2018.

Galor, Katharina. "Plastered Pools: A New Perspective." In *Khirbet Qumrân et 'Aïn Feshkha.* Vol. 2: *Études d'anthropologie, de physique et de chimie,* edited by Jean-Baptiste Humbert and Jan Gunneweg, 291–320. NTOA. SA 3. Göttingen: Vandenhoeck & Ruprecht, 2003.

Gammie, John G. "The Sage in Sirach." In *The Sage in Israel and the Ancient Near East,* edited by John G. Gammie and Leo G. Perdue, 355–72. Winona Lake, IN: Eisenbrauns, 1990.

García Martínez, Florentino. "The Contents of the Manuscripts from the Caves of Qumran." In *The Caves of Qumran: Proceedings of the International Conference, Lugano 2014,* edited by Marcello Fidanzio, 67–79. STDJ 118. Leiden: Brill, 2017.

———. "The Groningen Hypothesis Revisited." In *The Dead Sea Scrolls and Contemporary Culture: Proceedings of the International Conference Held at the Israel Museum, Jerusalem (July 6–8, 2008),* edited by Adolfo D. Roitman, Lawrence H. Schiffman, and Shani Tzoref, 17–29. STDJ 93. Leiden: Brill, 2011.

———. "The Heavenly Tablets in the Book of Jubilees." In *Studies in the Book of Jubilees,* edited by Matthias Albani, Jörg Frey, and Armin Lange, 243–60. TSAJ 65. Tübingen: Mohr Siebeck, 1997.

———. "¿Sectario, no-sectario, o qué? Problemas de una taxonomía correcta de los textos qumránicos." *RevQ* 23 (2008): 383–94.

———, Annette Steudel, and Eibert Tigchelaar, eds. *From 4QMMT to Resurrection: Mélanges qumraniens en hommage à Émile Puech.* STDJ 61. Leiden: Brill, 2006.

García Martínez, Florentino, and Adam van der Woude. "A 'Groningen' Hypothesis of Qumran Origins and Early History." *RevQ* 14 (1990): 521–42.

———, Eibert J. C. Tigchelaar, and A. S. van der Woude. *Qumran Cave 11.II: 11Q2–18, 11Q20–31.* DJD 23. Oxford: Clarendon, 1998.

Gardiner, Alan H. "The House of Life." *JEA* 24 (1938): 157–79.

Gayer, Asaf, Daniel Stökl Ben Ezra, and Jonathan Ben-Dov. "A New Join of

BIBLIOGRAPHY

Two Fragments of 4QcryptA Serekh haEdah and Its Implications." *DSD* 23 (2016): 139–54.

Ginzberg, Louis. *An Unknown Jewish Sect.* New York: Jewish Theological Seminary, 1976.

Glessmer, Uwe. "Calendars in the Dead Sea Scrolls." In *The Dead Sea Scrolls after Fifty Years: A Comprehensive Assessment,* edited by Peter W. Flint and James C. VanderKam, 2:213–78. 2 vols. Leiden: Brill, 1999.

Goff, Matthew J. *Discerning Wisdom: The Sapiential Literature of the Dead Sea Scrolls.* VTSup 116. Leiden: Brill, 2007.

Golb, Norman. "Khirbet Qumran and the Manuscript Finds of the Judaean Wilderness." In *Methods of Investigation of the Dead Sea Scrolls and the Khirbet Qumran Site: Present Realities and Future Prospects,* edited by Michael O. Wise, Norman Golb, John J. Collins, and Dennis G. Pardee, 51–72. ANYAS 722. New York: New York Academy of Sciences, 1994.

———. *Who Wrote the Dead Sea Scrolls? The Search for the Secret of Qumran.* New York: Scribner, 1995.

Goldstein, Jonathan A. *1 Maccabees.* AB 41. Garden City, NY: Doubleday, 1976.

Goodman, Martin. "Constructing Ancient Judaism from the Scrolls." In *The Oxford Handbook of the Dead Sea Scrolls,* edited by Timothy H. Lim and John J. Collins, 81–91. Oxford: Oxford University Press, 2010.

Goranson, Stephen. "'Essenes': Etymology from עשׂה." *RevQ* 11 (1984): 483–98.

———. "Qumran—The Evidence of the Inkwells." *BAR* 19.6 (1993): 67.

Gorman, Robert, and Vanessa B. Gorman. *Corrupting Luxury in Ancient Greek Literature.* Ann Arbor: University of Michigan Press, 2014.

Grappe, Christian, ed. *The House of God.* Tübingen: Mohr Siebeck, forthcoming.

Grayson, A. Kirk. "Mesopotamia, History of: History and Culture of Assyria." *ABD* 4:732–55.

Greenfield, Jonas C., Michael E. Stone, and Esther Eshel. *The Aramaic Levi Document: Edition, Translation, Commentary.* SVTP 19. Leiden: Brill, 2004.

Gropp, Douglas M. *Wadi Daliyeh II: The Samaria Papyri from Wadi Daliyeh; and Qumran Cave 4.XXXVIII: Miscellanea, Part 2,* by Moshe Bernstein et al. DJD 28. Oxford: Clarendon, 2001.

Grossman, Maxine. *Reading for History in the Damascus Document: A Methodological Study.* STDJ 45. Leiden: Brill, 2002.

Gunneweg, Jan, and Marta Balla. "Neutron Activation Analysis: Scroll Jars and Common Ware." In *Khirbet Qumrân et ʿAïn Feshkha*. Vol. 2: *Études d'anthropologie, de physique et de chimie*, edited by Jean-Baptiste Humbert and Jan Gunneweg, 3–34. NTOA.SA 3. Göttingen: Vandenhoeck & Ruprecht, 2003.

———. "Possible Connection between the Inscriptions on Pottery, the Ostraca and Scrolls Found in the Caves." In *Khirbet Qumrân et ʿAïn Feshkha*. Vol. 2: *Études d'anthropologie, de physique et de chimie*, edited by Jean-Baptiste Humbert and Jan Gunneweg, 389–96. NTOA.SA 3. Göttingen: Vandenhoeck & Ruprecht, 2003.

Gutfeld, Oren, and Randall Price. "The Discovery of a New Dead Sea Scrolls Cave at Qumran." Paper presented at the Annual Meeting of the SBL. Boston, 19 November 2017.

Hachlili, Rachel. "The Qumran Cemetery Reassessed." In *The Oxford Handbook of the Dead Sea Scrolls*, edited by Timothy H. Lim and John J. Collins, 46–78. Oxford: Oxford University Press, 2010.

Haran, Menahem. "Archives, Libraries and the Order of the Biblical Books." *JANESCU* 22 (1993): 51–59.

———. "On the Diffusion of Literacy and Schools in Ancient Israel." In *Congress Volume: Jerusalem, 1986*, edited by J. A. Emerton, 81–95. VTSup 40. Leiden: Brill, 1988.

Harding, G. Lankester. "Introductory: The Discovery, the Excavation, Minor Finds." In *Qumran Cave I*, by D. Barthélemy and J. T. Milik, 3–7. DJD 1. Oxford: Clarendon, 1955.

———. "Khirbet Qumran and Wady Murabbaʿat: Fresh Light on the Dead Sea Scrolls and New Manuscript Discoveries in Jordan." *PEQ* 84 (1952): 104–9.

Harrington, Daniel J. "Wisdom Texts." *EDSS* 2:976–80.

Healey, John F., and Peter C. Craigie. "Languages: Ugaritic." *ABD* 4:227–29.

Hempel, Charlotte. "Close Encounters: The Community Rule and the Damascus Document." In *The Qumran Rule Texts in Context: Collected Studies*, 122–50. TSAJ 154. Tübingen: Mohr Siebeck, 2013.

———. "Community Structures and Organization." In *The Qumran Rule Texts in Context: Collected Studies*, 25–46. TSAJ 154. Tübingen: Mohr Siebeck, 2013.

———. *The Damascus Texts*. Companion to the Dead Sea Scrolls 1. Sheffield: Sheffield Academic Press, 2000.

———, ed. *The Dead Sea Scrolls: Texts and Context*. STDJ 90. Leiden: Brill, 2010.

———. "'Haskalah' at Qumran: The Eclectic Character of Qumran Cave 4."

BIBLIOGRAPHY

In *The Qumran Rule Texts in Context: Collected Studies*, 303–36. TSAJ 154. Tübingen: Mohr Siebeck, 2013.

———. "Part II: Beginnings." In *The Qumran Rule Texts in Context: Collected Studies*, 65–105. TSAJ 154. Tübingen: Mohr Siebeck, 2013.

———. *The Qumran Rule Texts in Context: Collected Studies.* TSAJ 154. Tübingen: Mohr Siebeck, 2013.

Hezser, Catherine. *Jewish Literacy in Roman Palestine.* TSAJ 81. Tübingen: Mohr Siebeck, 2001.

Himmelfarb, Martha. *A Kingdom of Priests: Ancestry and Merit in Ancient Judaism.* Jewish Culture and Context. Philadelphia: University of Pennsylvania Press, 2006.

———. "The Polemic against the *Ṭevul Yom*: A Reexamination." In *New Perspectives on Old Texts: Proceedings of the Tenth International Symposium of the Orion Center for the Study of the Dead Sea Scrolls and Associated Literature*, edited by Esther G. Chazon and Betsy Halpern-Amaru, 199–214. Leiden: Brill, 2010.

Hirschfeld, Yizhar. "The Library of King Herod in the Northern Palace of Masada." *Scripta classica Israelica* 23 (2004): 69–80.

———. *Qumran in Context: Reassessing the Archaeological Evidence.* Peabody, MA: Hendrickson, 2004.

———. "Qumran in the Second Temple Period." In *Qumran, the Site of the Dead Sea Scrolls: Archaeological Interpretations and Debates; Proceedings of a Conference Held at Brown University, November 17–19, 2002*, edited by Katherina Galor, Jean-Baptiste Humbert, and Jürgen Zangenberg, 223–40. STDJ 57. Leiden: Brill, 2006.

Hollenback, George M. "More on the Qumran Roundel as an Equatorial Sundial." *DSD* 11 (2004): 289–92.

———. "The Qumran Roundel: An Equatorial Sundial." *DSD* 7 (2000): 123–39.

Horsley, Richard A. "The Politics of Cultural Production in Second Temple Judea: Historical Context and Political-Religious Relations of the Scribes Who Produced 1 Enoch, Sirach, and Daniel." In *Conflicted Boundaries in Wisdom and Apocalypticism*, edited by Benjamin G. Wright III and Lawrence M. Wills, 123–45. SymS 35. Leiden: Brill, 2006.

———. *Scribes, Visionaries, and the Politics of Second Temple Judea.* Louisville: Westminster John Knox, 2007.

Houston, George W. *Inside Roman Libraries: Book Collections and Their Management in Antiquity.* Chapel Hill: University of North Carolina Press, 2014.

Bibliography

————. "The Non-Philodemus Book Collection in the Villa of the Papyri." In *Ancient Libraries*, edited by Jason König, Katerina Oikonomopoulou, and Greg Woolf, 183–208. Cambridge: Cambridge University Press, 2013.

————. "Papyrological Evidence for Book Collections and Libraries in the Roman Empire." In *Ancient Literacies: The Culture of Reading in Greece and Rome*, edited by William A. Johnson and Holt N. Parker, 233–67. Oxford: Oxford University Press, 2009.

Hultgren, Stephen. *From the Damascus Covenant to the Covenant of the Community: Literary, Historical, and Theological Studies in the Dead Sea Scrolls*. STDJ 66. Leiden: Brill, 2007.

Humbert, Jean-Baptiste. "Cacher et se cacher à Qumrân: Grottes et refuges. Morphologie, fonctions, anthropologie." In *The Caves of Qumran: Proceedings of the International Conference, Lugano 2014*, edited by Marcello Fidanzio, 34–66. STDJ 118. Leiden: Brill, 2017.

————. "Chronology during the First Century B.C., de Vaux and His Method: A Debate." In *Khirbet Qumrân et 'Aïn Feshkha*. Vol. 2: *Études d'anthropologie, de physique et de chimie*, edited by Jean-Baptiste Humbert and Jan Gunneweg, 425–38. NTOA.SA 3. Göttingen: Vandenhoeck & Ruprecht, 2003.

————. "L'espace sacré à Qumrân: Propositions pour l'archéologie." *RB* 101 (1994): 161–214.

————. "Les moyens de la chronographie." In *Khirbet Qumrân et Aïn Feshkha: Fouilles du P. Roland de Vaux*. Vol. 3A: *L'archéologie de Qumrân; Reconsidération de l'interprétation; Les installations périphériques de Khirbet Qumrân*, edited by Jean-Baptiste Humbert, Alain Chambon, and Jolanta Mlynarczyk, 115–25. NTOA.SA 5A. Göttingen: Vandenhoeck & Ruprecht, 2016.

————. "Qumran Period I Reconsidered: An Evaluation of Several Competing Theories." *DSD* 22 (2014): 1–42.

————. "Some Remarks on the Archaeology of Qumran." In *Qumran, the Site of the Dead Sea Scrolls: Archaeological Interpretations and Debates: Proceedings of a Conference Held at Brown University, November 17–19, 2002*, edited by Katherina Galor, Jean-Baptiste Humbert, and Jürgen Zangenberg, 19–40. STDJ 57. Leiden: Brill, 2006.

————, and Alain Chambon, eds. *The Excavations of Khirbet Qumran and Ain Feshkha*. Vol. 1B: *Synthesis of Roland de Vaux's Field Notes, English Edition*. Translated and revised by Stephen J. Pfann. NTOA.SA 1B. Göttingen: Vandenhoeck & Ruprecht, 2003.

————, eds. *Fouilles de Khirbet Qumrân et de Aïn Feshkha*. Vol. 1: *Album de*

BIBLIOGRAPHY

photographies; Répertoire du fonds photographique; Synthèse des notes de chantier du Père Roland de Vaux OP. NTOA.SA 1. Göttingen: Vandenhoeck & Ruprecht, 1994.

Humbert, Jean-Baptiste, Alain Chambon, and Jolanta Mlynarczyk, eds. *Khirbet Qumrân et Aïn Feshkha: Fouilles du P. Roland de Vaux.* Vol. 3A: *L'archéologie de Qumrân; Reconsidération de l'interprétation; Les installations périphériques de Khirbet Qumrân.* NTOA.SA 5A. Göttingen: Vandenhoeck & Ruprecht, 2016.

Humbert, Jean-Baptiste, and Jan Gunneweg, eds. *Khirbet Qumrân et 'Aïn Feshkha.* Vol. 2: *Études d'anthropologie, de physique et de chimie.* NTOA.SA 3. Göttingen: Vandenhoeck & Ruprecht, 2003.

Hurowitz, Victor Avigdor. "Tales of Two Sages—Towards an Image of the 'Wise Man' in Akkadian Writings." In *Scribes, Sages, and Seers: The Sage in the Eastern Mediterranean World,* edited by Leo G. Perdue, 64–94. Göttingen: Vandenhoeck & Ruprecht, 2008.

Ilan, Tal. "Women in Qumran and the Dead Sea Scrolls." In *The Oxford Handbook of the Dead Sea Scrolls,* edited by Timothy H. Lim and John J. Collins, 123–50. Oxford: Oxford University Press, 2010.

Jacob, Christian. "Fragments of a History of Ancient Libraries." In *Ancient Libraries,* edited by Jason König, Katerina Oikonomopoulou, and Greg Woolf, 57–84. Cambridge: Cambridge University Press, 2013.

Jacobus, Helen R. "Calendars in the Qumran Collection." In *The Dead Sea Scrolls and the Concept of a Library,* edited by Sidnie White Crawford and Cecilia Wassén, 217–43. STDJ 116. Leiden: Brill, 2016.

Jaillard, Dominique. "Memory, Writing and Authority." In *Writing the Bible: Scribes, Scribalism and Script,* edited by Philip R. Davies and Thomas Römer, 23–34. London: Routledge, 2016.

Jamieson-Drake, David W. *Scribes and Schools in Monarchic Judah: A Socio-Archeological Approach.* SWBA 9. Sheffield: JSOT Press, 1991.

Jastrow, Marcus. *A Dictionary of the Targumim, the Talmud Babli and Yerushalmi, and the Midrashic Literature.* 2 vols. Repr., New York: Shalom, 1967.

Johnson, Lora L. "The Hellenistic and Roman Library: Studies Pertaining to Their Architectural Form." PhD diss., Brown University, 1984.

Johnson, William A., and Holt N. Parker, eds. *Ancient Literacies: The Culture of Reading in Greece and Rome.* Oxford: Oxford University Press, 2009.

Jokiranta, Jutta. *Social Identity and Sectarianism in the Qumran Movement.* STDJ 105. Leiden: Brill, 2013.

———. "Sociological Approaches to Qumran Sectarianism." In *The Oxford*

340

Handbook of the Dead Sea Scrolls, edited by Timothy H. Lim and John J. Collins, 200–231. Oxford: Oxford University Press, 2010.

———. "What Is 'Serekh ha-Yahad (S)'? Thinking about Ancient Manuscripts as Information Processing." In *Sibyls, Scriptures, and Scrolls: John Collins at Seventy*, edited by Joel Baden, Hindy Najman, and Eibert J. C. Tigchelaar, 1:611–35. 2 vols. JSJSup 175. Leiden: Brill, 2017.

Josephus. Translated by Henry St. J. Thackeray et al. 10 vols. LCL. Cambridge: Harvard University Press, 1926–1965.

Kampen, John. *The Hasideans and the Origin of Pharisaism: A Study in 1 and 2 Maccabees*. SCS 24. Atlanta: Scholars Press, 1988.

———, and Moshe J. Bernstein, eds. *Reading 4QMMT: New Perspectives on Qumran Law and History*. SymS 2. Atlanta: Scholars Press, 1996.

Kartveit, Magnar. *The Origin of the Samaritans*. Leiden: Brill, 2009.

Keith, Chris. *Jesus against the Scribal Elite: The Origins of the Conflict*. Grand Rapids: Baker Academic, 2014.

Killebrew, Ann E., and Gabriele Faßbeck, eds. *Viewing Ancient Jewish Art and Archaeology: VeHinnei Rachel—Essays in Honor of Rachel Hachlili*. JSJSup 72. Leiden: Brill, 2015.

Klawans, Jonathan. *Impurity and Sin in Ancient Judaism*. New York: Oxford University Press, 2000.

Klein, Ralph W. *1 Chronicles: A Commentary*. Hermeneia. Minneapolis: Fortress, 2006.

Klijn, A. F. J. "A Library of Scriptures in Jerusalem?" TUGAL 124 (1977): 265–72.

Knoppers, Gary N. *1 Chronicles 1–9: A New Translation with Introduction and Commentary*. AB 12. New York: Doubleday, 2004.

———. *Jews and Samaritans: The Origins and History of Their Early Relations*. New York: Oxford University Press, 2013.

Kooij, Arie van der. "The Canonization of Ancient Books Kept in the Temple in Jerusalem." In *Canonization and Decanonization: Papers Presented to the International Conference of the Leiden Institute for the Study of Religions (LISOR), Held at Leiden 9–10 January 1997*, edited by Arie van der Kooij and Karel van der Toorn, 17–40. Leiden: Brill, 1998.

Kramer, Samuel N. "The Sage in Sumerian Literature: A Composite Portrait." In *The Sage in Israel and the Ancient Near East*, edited by John G. Gammie and Leo G. Perdue, 31–44. Winona Lake, IN: Eisenbrauns, 1990.

Kratz, Reinhard G. "Ezra—Priest and Scribe." In *Scribes, Sages, and Seers: The Sage in the Eastern Mediterranean World*, edited by Leo G. Perdue, 163–88. Göttingen: Vandenhoeck & Ruprecht, 2008.

BIBLIOGRAPHY

Kugel, James L. *A Walk through Jubilees: Studies in the Book of Jubilees and the World of Its Creation.* JSJSup 156. Leiden: Brill, 2012.

Kugler, Robert A. *From Patriarch to Priest: The Levi-Priestly Tradition from Aramaic Levi to Testament of Levi.* SBLEJL 9. Atlanta: Scholars Press, 1996.

―――. "Priesthood at Qumran." In *The Dead Sea Scrolls after Fifty Years: A Comprehensive Assessment*, edited by Peter W. Flint and James C. VanderKam, 2:93–116. 2 vols. Leiden: Brill, 1999.

―――. "Priests." *EDSS* 2:688–93.

Lange, Armin. *Handbuch der Textfunde vom Toten Meer.* Vol. 1: *Die Handschriften biblischer Bücher von Qumran und den anderen Fundorten.* Tübingen: Mohr Siebeck, 2009.

―――. "The Qumran Dead Sea Scrolls—Library or Manuscript Corpus?" In *From 4QMMT to Resurrection: Mélanges qumraniens en hommage à Émile Puech*, edited by Florentino García Martínez, Annette Steudel, and Eibert Tigchelaar, 177–93. STDJ 61. Leiden: Brill, 2006.

―――. Review of *Qumran Cave 4.X: The Prophets. DSD* 8 (2001): 100–104.

―――. "The Textual Plurality of Jewish Scriptures in the Second Temple Period in Light of the Dead Sea Scrolls." In *Qumran and the Bible: Studying the Jewish and Christian Scriptures in Light of the Dead Sea Scrolls*, edited by Nóra Dávid and Armin Lange, 43–96. CBET 57. Leuven: Peeters, 2010.

―――. "Wisdom Literature and Thought in the Dead Sea Scrolls." In *The Oxford Handbook of the Dead Sea Scrolls*, edited by Timothy H. Lim and John J. Collins, 455–78. Oxford: Oxford University Press, 2010.

―――, with U. Mittmann-Richert. "Annotated List of the Texts from the Judaean Desert Classified by Content and Genre: Masada." In *The Texts from the Judaean Desert: Indices and an Introduction to the Discoveries in the Judaean Desert Series*, edited by Emanuel Tov, 115–64. DJD 39. Oxford: Clarendon, 2002.

Lange, Armin, and Emanuel Tov, eds. *The Hebrew Bible.* 3 vols. Textual History of the Bible. Leiden: Brill, 2016–2017.

―――, eds. *The Hebrew Bible.* Vol. 1A: *Overview Articles.* Textual History of the Bible. Leiden: Brill, 2016.

―――, eds. *The Hebrew Bible.* Vol. 1B: *Pentateuch, Former and Latter Prophets.* Textual History of the Bible. Leiden: Brill, 2017.

―――, eds. *The Hebrew Bible.* Vol. 1C: *Writings.* Textual History of the Bible. Leiden: Brill, 2017.

Lapp, Paul W., and Nancy L. Lapp, eds. *Discoveries in the Wâdi ed-Dâliyeh.* AASOR 41. Cambridge: American Schools of Oriental Research, 1974.

Larson, Erik. "460. 4QNarrative Work and Prayer." In *Qumran Cave 4.XXVI:*

Cryptic Texts, by Stephen Pfann; and *Miscellanea, Part 1,* by Philip Alexander et al., 369–86. DJD 36. Oxford: Clarendon, 2000.

Lefkovits, Judah K. *The Copper Scroll—3Q15: A Reevaluation.* STDJ 25. Leiden: Brill, 1999.

Leiman, Sid Z. *The Canonization of Hebrew Scripture: The Talmudic and Midrashic Evidence.* Transactions of the Connecticut Academy of Arts and Sciences 47. Hamden, CT: Archon, 1976.

Leith, Mary Joan Winn. *Wadi Daliyeh I: The Wadi Daliyeh Seal Impressions.* DJD 24. Oxford: Clarendon, 1997.

Lemaire, André. "Administration in Fourth Century BCE Judah in Light of Epigraphy and Numismatics." In *Judah and the Judeans in the Fourth Century B.C.E.,* edited by Oded Lipschits, Gary N. Knoppers, and Rainer Albertz, 53–74. Winona Lake, IN: Eisenbrauns, 2007.

———. *Les écoles et la formation de la Bible dans l'ancien Israël.* OBO 39. Göttingen: Vandenhoeck & Ruprecht, 1981.

———. "Inscriptions du khirbeh, des grottes et de 'Ain Feshkha." In *Khirbet Qumrân et 'Aïn Feshkha.* Vol. 2: *Études d'anthropologie, de physique et de chimie,* edited by Jean-Baptiste Humbert and Jan Gunneweg, 341–88. NTOA.SA 3. Göttingen: Vandenhoeck & Ruprecht, 2003.

Lim, Timothy H., ed. *The Dead Sea Scrolls in Their Historical Context.* London: T&T Clark, 2000.

———. *The Formation of the Jewish Canon.* AYBRL. New Haven: Yale University Press, 2013.

———. "A Theory of the Majority Canon." *ExpTim* 124 (2013): 365–72.

———, and John J. Collins, eds. *The Oxford Handbook of the Dead Sea Scrolls.* Oxford: Oxford University Press, 2010.

Lipiński, E. "Royal and State Scribes in Ancient Jerusalem." In *Congress Volume: Jerusalem, 1986,* edited by J. A. Emerton, 157–64. VTSup 40. Leiden: Brill, 1988.

Lipschits, Oded. "Achaemenid Imperial Policy, Settlement Processes in Palestine, and the Status of Jerusalem in the Middle of the Fifth Century B.C.E." Pages 19–52 in *Judah and the Judeans in the Persian Period,* edited by Oded Lipschits and Manfred Oeming. Winona Lake, IN: Eisenbrauns, 2006.

———, Yuval Gadot, Benjamin Arubas, and Manfred Oeming. *What Are the Stones Whispering? Ramat Raḥel: 3000 Years of Forgotten History.* Winona Lake, IN: Eisenbrauns, 2017.

Lipschits, Oded, and Oren Tal. "The Settlement Archaeology of the Province of Judah: A Case Study." In *Judah and the Judeans in the Fourth Century*

B.C.E., edited by Oded Lipschits, Gary N. Knoppers, and Rainer Albertz, 33–52. Winona Lake, IN: Eisenbrauns, 2007.

Lipschits, Oded, and David Vanderhooft. "Yehud Stamp Impressions in the Fourth Century B.C.E.: A Time of Administrative Consolidation." In *Judah and the Judeans in the Fourth Century B.C.E.*, edited by Oded Lipschits, Gary N. Knoppers, and Rainer Albertz, 75–94. Winona Lake, IN: Eisenbrauns, 2007.

Loader, William. *The Dead Sea Scrolls on Sexuality: Attitudes towards Sexuality in Sectarian and Related Literature at Qumran.* Grand Rapids: Eerdmans, 2009.

Lönnqvist, Minna, and Kenneth Lönnqvist. "Parallels to Be Seen: Manuscripts in Jars from Qumran and Egypt." In *The Dead Sea Scrolls in Context: Integrating the Dead Sea Scrolls in the Study of Ancient Texts, Languages, and Cultures,* edited by Armin Lange, Emanuel Tov, and Matthias Weigold, 2:471–88. 2 vols. VTSup 140. Leiden: Brill, 2011.

Lubetski, Meir, ed. *New Seals and Inscriptions: Hebrew, Idumean, and Cuneiform.* Sheffield: Sheffield Phoenix Press, 2007.

Machiela, Daniel. "The Aramaic Dead Sea Scrolls: Coherence and Context in the Library of Qumran." In *The Dead Sea Scrolls and the Concept of a Library*, edited by Sidnie White Crawford and Cecilia Wassén, 244–60. STDJ 116. Leiden: Brill, 2016.

Machinist, Peter. "The First Coins of Judah and Samaria: Numismatics and History in the Achaemenid and Early Hellenistic Periods." In *Continuity and Change*, edited by Heleen Sancisi-Weerdenburg, Amélie Kuhrt, and Margaret Cool Root, 366–72. Achaemenid History 8. Leiden: Nederlands Instituut voor het Nabije Oosten, 1994.

Mack-Fisher, Loren R. "The Scribe (and Sage) in the Royal Court at Ugarit." In *The Sage in Israel and the Ancient Near East*, edited by John G. Gammie and Leo G. Perdue, 109–16. Winona Lake, IN: Eisenbrauns, 1990.

Magen, Yitzhak. *Mount Gerizim Excavations.* Vol. 2: *A Temple City.* Judea and Samaria Publications 8. Jerusalem: Israel Antiquities Authority, 2008.

———, Haggai Misgav, and Levana Tsfania. *Mount Gerizim Excavations.* Vol. 1: *The Aramaic, Hebrew and Samaritan Inscriptions.* Judea and Samaria Publications 2. Jerusalem: Israel Antiquities Authority, 2004.

Magen, Yitzhak, and Yuval Peleg. "Back to Qumran: Ten Years of Excavation and Research, 1993–2004." In *Qumran, the Site of the Dead Sea Scrolls: Archaeological Interpretations and Debates*, edited by Katherina Galor, Jean-Baptiste Humbert, and Jürgen Zangenberg, 55–113. STDJ 57. Leiden: Brill, 2006.

Bibliography

———. *The Qumran Excavation 1993–2004: Preliminary Report*. Judea and Samaria Publications 6. Jerusalem: Israel Antiquities Authority, 2007.

Magness, Jodi. *The Archaeology of Qumran and the Dead Sea Scrolls*. Grand Rapids: Eerdmans, 2002.

———. "The Community of Qumran in Light of Its Pottery." In *Debating Qumran: Collected Essays on Its Archaeology*, 1–15. ISACR 4. Leuven: Peeters, 2004.

———. "The Connection between the Site of Qumran and the Scroll Caves in Light of the Ceramic Evidence." In *The Caves of Qumran: Proceedings of the International Conference, Lugano 2014*, edited by Marcello Fidanzio, 184–93. STDJ 118. Leiden: Brill, 2017.

———. "Scrolls and Hand Impurity." In *The Dead Sea Scrolls: Texts and Contexts*, edited by Charlotte Hempel, 89–97. STDJ 90. Leiden: Brill, 2010.

———. *Stone and Dung, Oil and Spit: Jewish Daily Life in the Time of Jesus*. Grand Rapids: Eerdmans, 2011.

———. "Was Qumran a Fort in the Hasmonean Period?" *JSJ* 64 (2013): 228–41.

———. "Were Sacrifices Offered at Qumran? The Animal Bone Deposits Reconsidered." *JAJ* 7 (2016): 5–34.

———. "Why Scroll Jars?" In *Debating Qumran: Collected Essays on Its Archaeology*, 151–86. ISACR 4. Leuven: Peeters, 2004.

Marcus, Joel. *Mark 1–8: A New Translation with Introduction and Commentary*. AB 27. New York: Doubleday, 2000.

———. *Mark 8–16: A New Translation with Introduction and Commentary*. AB 27A. New Haven: Yale University Press, 2009.

Marcus, Ralph. *Josephus, Jewish Antiquities, Books XII–XIV*. LCL. Cambridge: Harvard University Press, 1961.

Mason, Steve. "Excursus 1: The Essenes of Josephus' *War*." In *Flavius Josephus: Translation and Commentary*. Vol. 1B: *Judean War 2*, 84–95. Leiden: Brill, 2008.

———. *Flavius Josephus: Translation and Commentary*. Vol. 9: *Life of Josephus*. Leiden: Brill, 2001.

McCane, Byron R. "Miqva'ot." *EDEJ* 954–56.

McDonald, Lee M., and James A. Sanders, eds. *The Canon Debate*. Peabody, MA: Hendrickson, 2002.

McKenzie, John L., ed. *The Bible in Current Catholic Thought*. New York: Herder & Herder, 1962.

Mébarki, Farah, and Claude Grenache. "Józef Tadeusz Milik: Memories of Fieldwork." *NEA* 63 (2000): 131–35.

BIBLIOGRAPHY

Medico, Henri E. del. *The Riddle of the Scrolls*. Translated by H. Garner. London: Burke, 1958.

Metso, Sarianna. "In Search of the *Sitz im Leben* of the *Community Rule*." In *The Provo International Conference on the Dead Sea Scrolls: Technological Innovations, New Texts, and Reformulated Issues*, edited by Donald W. Parry and Eugene Ulrich, 306–15. STDJ 30. Leiden: Brill, 1999.

————. "The Relationship between the Damascus Document and the Community Rule." In *The Damascus Document: A Centennial of Discovery*, edited by Joseph M. Baumgarten, Esther G. Chazon, and Avital Pinnick, 85–93. STDJ 34. Leiden: Brill, 2000.

————. *The Textual Development of the Qumran Community Rule*. STDJ 21. Leiden: Brill, 1997.

————, Hindy Najman, and Eileen Schuller, eds. *The Dead Sea Scrolls: Transmission of Traditions and Production of Texts*. STDJ 92. Leiden: Brill, 2010.

Metzger, Bruce M. "The Furniture of the Scriptorium at Qumran." *RevQ* 1 (1959): 509–15.

Meyers, Eric M. "Khirbet Qumran and Its Environs." In *The Oxford Handbook of the Dead Sea Scrolls*, edited by Timothy H. Lim and John J. Collins, 21–45. Oxford: Oxford University Press, 2010.

————, and Mark A. Chancey. *Archaeology of the Land of the Bible*. Vol. 3: *Alexander to Constantine*. New Haven: Yale University Press, 2012.

Michniewicz, Jacek, and Miroslaw Krzyško. "The Provenance of Scroll Jars in the Light of Archaeometric Investigations." In *Khirbet Qumrân et 'Aïn Feshkha*. Vol. 2: *Études d'anthropologie, de physique et de chimie*, edited by Jean-Baptiste Humbert and Jan Gunneweg, 59–99. NTOA.SA 3. Göttingen: Vandenhoeck & Ruprecht, 2003.

Milik, J. T. "Appendice: Deux jarres inscrites provenant d'une grotte de Qumrân." In *Les "petites grottes" de Qumrân*, by M. Baillet, J. T. Milik, and R. de Vaux, 1:37–41. 2 vols. DJD 3. Oxford: Clarendon, 1962.

————, ed. *The Books of Enoch: Aramaic Fragments of Qumrân Cave 4*. Oxford: Clarendon, 1976.

————. "Écrits préessénniens de Qumrân: d'Hènoch à Amram." In *Qumrân: Sa piété, sa théologie, et son milieu*, edited by M. Delcor, 91–106. BETL 46. Leuven: Leuven University Press, 1978.

————. "Milkî-ṣedeq et Milkî-reša' dans les anciens écrits juifs et chrétiens." *JJS* 23 (1972): 95–144.

————. "Les modèles araméens du livre d'Esther dans la grotte 4 de Qumrân." *RevQ* 15 (1992): 321–99.

Bibliography

———. "Le rouleau de cuivre provenant de la grotte 3Q (3Q15)." In *Les "petites grottes" de Qumrân*, by M. Baillet, J. T. Milik, and R. de Vaux, 1:201–302. 2 vols. DJD 3. Oxford: Clarendon, 1962.

———. *Ten Years of Discovery in the Wilderness of Judaea*. Translated by John Strugnell. SBT 1/26. Naperville, IL: Allenson, 1959.

Miller, Stuart S. *At the Intersection of Texts and Material Finds: Stepped Pools, Stone Vessels, and Ritual Purity among the Jews of Roman Galilee*. Göttingen: Vandenhoeck & Ruprecht, 2015.

Milstein, Sara J. "Reworking Ancient Texts: Revision through Introduction in Biblical and Mesopotamian Literature." PhD diss., New York University, 2010.

Mizzi, Dennis. "The Animal Bone Deposits at Qumran: An Unsolvable Riddle?" *JAJ* 7 (2016): 51–70.

———. "The Archaeology of Khirbet Qumran: A Comparative Approach." D.Phil. thesis, University of Oxford, 2009.

———. "The Glass from Khirbet Qumran: What Does It Tell Us about the Qumran Community?" In *The Dead Sea Scrolls: Texts and Context*, edited by Charlotte Hempel, 99–198. STDJ 90. Leiden: Brill, 2010.

———. "Miscellaneous Artefacts from the Qumran Caves: An Exploration of Their Significance." In *The Caves of Qumran: Proceedings of the International Conference, Lugano 2014*, edited by Marcello Fidanzio, 137–60. STDJ 118. Leiden: Brill, 2017.

———. "Qumran at Seventy: Reflections on Seventy Years of Scholarship on the Archaeology of Qumran and the Dead Sea Scrolls." *Strata: Bulletin of the Anglo-Israel Archaeological Society* 35 (2017): 9–46.

———. "'Rome' at Qumran?—What If? Some Remarks on the So-Called Roma Jar from Qumran Cave 7Q." In *The Lure of the Antique: Essays on Malta and Mediterranean Archaeology in Honour of Anthony Bonanno*, edited by Nicholas C. Vella, Anthony J. Frendo, and Horatio C. R. Vella, 351–74. ANESSup 54. Leuven: Peeters, 2018.

———, and Jodi Magness. "Was Qumran Abandoned at the End of the First Century BCE?" *JBL* 135 (2016): 301–20.

Mlynarczyk, Jolanta. "Qumran Terracotta Oil Lamps." In *Khirbet Qumrân et Aïn Feshkha: Fouilles du P. Roland de Vaux*. Vol. 3A: *L'archéologie de Qumrân; Reconsidération de l'interprétation; Les installations périphériques de Khirbet Qumrân*, edited by Jean-Baptiste Humbert, Alain Chambon, and Jolanta Mlynarczyk, 447–521. NTOA.SA 5A. Göttingen: Vandenhoeck & Ruprecht, 2016.

———. "Terracotta Oil Lamps." In *The Caves of Qumran: Proceedings of the In-*

ternational Conference, Lugano 2014, edited by Marcello Fidanzio, 109–22. STDJ 118. Leiden: Brill, 2017.

Mrozcek, Eva. "Testimonia." In *T&T Clark Companion to the Dead Sea Scrolls,* edited by George J. Brooke and Charlotte Hempel, 149–52. London: T&T Clark, 2018.

Murphy, Catherine M. *Wealth in the Dead Sea Scrolls and in the Qumran Community.* STDJ 40. Leiden: Brill, 2002.

Murphy-O'Connor, Jerome. "An Essene Missionary Document? CD II, 14–VI, 1." *RB* 77 (1970): 201–29.

———. "A Literary Analysis of Damascus Document VI, 2–VIII, 3." *RB* 78 (1971): 210–32.

———. "A Literary Analysis of Damascus Document XIX, 33–XX, 34." *RB* 79 (1972): 544–64.

Myers, Jacob M. *I and II Esdras: Introduction, Translation and Commentary.* AB 42. Garden City, NY: Doubleday, 1974.

Nagar, Yossi, Hanania Hizmi, and Yevgeny Aharonovich. "The People of Qumran —New Discoveries and Paleo-demographic Interpretations." Paper presented at the Annual Meeting of the ASOR. Boston, 16 November 2017.

Naveh, Joseph. "341. 4QExercitium Calami C." In *Qumran Cave 4.XXVI: Cryptic Texts,* by Stephen Pfann; and *Miscellanea, Part 1,* by Philip Alexander et al., 291–93. DJD 36. Oxford: Clarendon, 2000.

Neusner, Jacob, and Bruce Chilton, eds. *In Quest for the Historical Pharisees.* Waco, TX: Baylor University Press, 2007.

Newsom, Carol A. *Daniel.* OTL. Louisville: Westminster John Knox, 2014.

———. "'Sectually Explicit' Literature from Qumran." In *The Hebrew Bible and Its Interpreters,* edited by William Henry Propp, Baruch Halpern, and David Noel Freedman, 167–87. BJSUCSD 1. Winona Lake, IN: Eisenbrauns, 1990.

———. *The Self as Symbolic Space: Constructing Identity and Community at Qumran.* STDJ 52. Atlanta: Society of Biblical Literature, 2004.

Nickelsburg, George W. E. *1 Enoch 1: A Commentary on the Book of 1 Enoch, Chapters 1–36; 81–108.* Hermeneia. Minneapolis: Fortress, 2001.

———. "The Greek Fragments of *1 Enoch* from Qumran Cave 7: An Unproven Identification." *RevQ* 22 (2004): 631–34.

———, and James C. VanderKam. *1 Enoch 2: A Commentary on the Book of 1 Enoch, Chapters 37–82.* Hermeneia. Minneapolis: Fortress, 2012.

Niditch, Susan. *Oral World and Written Word: Ancient Israelite Literature.* Louisville: Westminster John Knox, 1996.

Bibliography

North, Robert. "The Qumran Reservoirs." In *The Bible in Current Catholic Thought*, edited by John L. McKenzie, 100–132. New York: Herder & Herder, 1962.

Norton, Jonathan. "Reassessment of Controversial Studies on the Cemetery." In *Khirbet Qumrân et 'Aïn Feshkha*. Vol. 2: *Études d'anthropologie, de physique et de chimie*, edited by Jean-Baptiste Humbert and Jan Gunneweg, 107–27. NTOA.SA 3. Göttingen: Vandenhoeck & Ruprecht, 2003.

Orton, David. *The Understanding Scribe: Matthew and the Apocalyptic Ideal*. JSNTSup 25. Sheffield: JSOT Press, 1989.

Pakkala, Juha, and Martti Nissinen, eds. *Houses Full of All Good Things: Essays in Memory of Timo Veijola*. Göttingen: Vandenhoeck & Ruprecht, 2008.

Pardee, Dennis, and Pierre Bordreuil. "Ugarit: Texts and Literature." *ABD* 6:706–21.

Parpola, Simo. "Assyrian Library Records." *JNES* 42 (1983): 1–29.

Pass, H. Leonard, and J. Arendzen. "Fragment of an Aramaic Text of the Testament of Levi." *JQR* 12 (1900): 651–61.

Patrich, Joseph. "Khirbet Qumran in Light of New Archaeological Explorations in the Qumran Caves." In *Methods of Investigation of the Dead Sea Scrolls and the Khirbet Qumran Site: Present Realities and Future Prospects*, edited by Michael O. Wise, Norman Golb, John J. Collins, and Dennis G. Pardee, 73–96. ANYAS 722. New York: New York Academy of Sciences, 1994.

———. "The Warehouse Complex and Governor's Palace (areas KK, CC, and NN, May 1993–December 1995)." In *Caesarea Papers 2: Herod's Temple, the Provincial Governor's Praetorium and Granaries, the Later Harbor, a Gold Coin Hoard, and Other Studies*, edited by Kenneth G. Holum, Avner Raban, and Joseph Patrich, 71–107. JRASup 35. Portsmouth, RI: Journal of Roman Archaeology, 1999.

Pearce, Laurie E. "The Scribes and Scholars of Ancient Mesopotamia." *CANE* 4:2265–78.

Peck, Dwight C. "The Qumran Library and Its Patrons." *Journal of Library History* 12 (1977): 5–16.

Pedersén, Olof. *Archives and Libraries in the Ancient Near East 1500–300 B.C.* Bethesda, MD: CDL, 1998.

Pedley, Katharine Greenleaf. *The Library at Qumran: A Librarian Looks at the Dead Sea Scrolls*. Biblio Series 1. Berkeley: Peacock, 1964.

Pestman, Pieter W. *A Guide to the Zenon Archive*. Leiden: Brill, 1981.

Pfann, Stephen J. "The Ancient 'Library' or 'Libraries' of Qumran: The Specter of Cave 1Q." In *The Dead Sea Scrolls and the Concept of a Library*,

BIBLIOGRAPHY

edited by Sidnie White Crawford and Cecilia Wassén, 168–216. STDJ 116. Leiden: Brill, 2016.

———. "Cryptic Texts." In *Qumran Cave 4.XXVI: Cryptic Texts*, by Stephen Pfann; and *Miscellanea, Part 1*, by Philip Alexander et al., 515–702. DJD 36. Oxford: Clarendon, 2000.

———. "The Mount Zion Inscribed Stone Cup: Preliminary Observations." *New Studies in the Archaeology of Jerusalem and Its Region* 4 (2010): *44–*53.

———. *Qumran Cave 4.XXVI: Cryptic Texts;* and *Miscellanea, Part 1,* by Philip Alexander et al., 515–701. DJD 36. Oxford: Clarendon, 2000.

———. "Reassessing the Judean Desert Caves: Libraries, Archives, Genizas and Hiding Places," *Bulletin of the Anglo-Israel Archaeological Society* 25 (2007): 147–70.

———. "Towards an English Edition of de Vaux's Notes: Progress Update from Stephen Pfann." *Center for the Study of Early Christianity.* http://www.csec.ac.uk/devaux.html.

———. "The Winepress (and Miqveh) at Khirbet Qumran (loc. 75 and 69)." *RB* 101 (1994): 212–14.

———. "The Writings in Esoteric Script from Qumran." In *The Dead Sea Scrolls Fifty Years after Their Discovery,* edited by Lawrence H. Schiffman, Emanuel Tov, and James C. VanderKam, 177–90. Jerusalem: Israel Exploration Society, 2000.

Pinto, Pasquale M. "Men and Books in Fourth-Century BC Athens." In *Ancient Libraries,* edited by Jason König, Katerina Oikonomopoulou, and Greg Woolf, 85–95. Cambridge: Cambridge University Press, 2013.

Poole, Henry. "Report of a Journey in Palestine." *Journal of the Royal Geographical Society* 26 (1856): 55–70.

Popović, Mladen. *Authoritative Scriptures in Ancient Judaism.* JSJSup 141. Leiden: Brill, 2010.

———. "Networks of Scholars: The Transmission of Astronomical and Astrological Learning between Babylonians, Greeks and Jews." In *Ancient Jewish Sciences and the History of Knowledge in Second Temple Literature,* edited by Jonathan Ben-Dov and Seth L. Sanders, 153–94. New York: New York University and the Institute for the Study of the Ancient World, 2014.

———. "Qumran as Scroll Storehouse in Times of Crisis? A Comparative Perspective on Judaean Desert Manuscript Collections." *JSJ* 43 (2012): 551–94.

———. "Reading the Human Body and Writing in Code: Physiognomic Divination and Astrology in the Dead Sea Scrolls." In *Flores Florentino: Dead*

Sea Scrolls and Other Early Jewish Studies in Honour of Florentino García Martínez, edited by Anthony Hilhorst, Émile Puech, and Eibert J. C. Tigchelaar, 271–85. JSJSup 122. Leiden: Brill, 2007.

———. *Reading the Human Body: Physiognomics and Astrology in the Dead Sea Scrolls and Hellenistic–Early Roman Period Judaism*. STDJ 67. Leiden: Brill, 2007.

———. "Roman Book Destruction in Qumran Cave 4 and the Roman Destruction of Khirbet Qumran Revisited." In *Qumran und die Archäologie: Texte und Kontexte*, edited by Jörg Frey, Carsten Claußen, and Nadine Kessler, 239–91. WUNT 278. Tübingen: Mohr Siebeck, 2011.

———, M. Schoonover, and M. Vandenberghe, eds. *Jewish Cultural Encounters in the Ancient Mediterranean and Near Eastern World*. Leiden: Brill, 2017.

Porten, Bezalel. *The Elephantine Papyri in English: Three Millennia of Cross-Cultural Continuity and Change*. DMOA 22. Leiden: Brill, 1996.

———, and Ada Yardeni. *Textbook of Aramaic Documents from Ancient Egypt*. 4 vols. Winona Lake, IN: Eisenbrauns, 1986–1993.

Posner, Ernst. *Archives in the Ancient World*. Cambridge: Harvard University Press, 1972.

Pritchard, James B., ed. *Ancient Near Eastern Texts Relating to the Old Testament*. 3rd ed. Princeton: Princeton University Press, 1969.

Puech, Émile. *The Copper Scroll Revisited*. Translated by David E. Orton. STDJ 112. Leiden: Brill, 2015.

———. "The Essenes and Qumran, the Teacher and the Wicked Priest, the Origins." In *Enoch and Qumran Origins: New Light on a Forgotten Connection*, edited by Gabriele Boccaccini, 298–302. Grand Rapids: Eerdmans, 2005.

———. "La paléographie des manuscrits de la Mer Morte." In *The Caves of Qumran: Proceedings of the International Conference, Lugano 2014*, edited by Marcello Fidanzio, 96–105. STDJ 118. Leiden: Brill, 2017.

———. *Qumrân Grotte 4.XXII: Textes araméens, première partie: 4Q529–549*. DJD 31. Oxford: Clarendon, 2001.

———. *Qumrân Cave 4.XXVII: Textes araméens, deuxième partie: 4Q550–4Q575a, 4Q580–4Q587*. DJD 37. Oxford: Clarendon, 2009.

———. "Sept Fragments de la Lettre d'Hénoch (1 Hén 100, 103 et 105) dans la grotte 7 de Qumrân (= 7QHén gr)." *RevQ* 19 (1997–1998): 313–23.

Qimron, Elisha, and John Strugnell. *Qumran Cave 4.V: Miqṣat Ma'aśe ha-Torah*. DJD 10. Oxford: Clarendon, 1994.

———. "An Unpublished Halakhic Letter from Qumran." In *Biblical Archae-*

BIBLIOGRAPHY

ology Today: Proceedings of the International Congress on Biblical Archae- ology, Jerusalem, April 1984, edited by Janet Amitai, 400–407. Jerusalem: Israel Exploration Society, 1985.

Rabin, Ira. "Archaeometry of the Dead Sea Scrolls." *DSD* 20 (2013): 124–42.

————, Oliver Hahn, Timo Wolff, Admir Masic, and Gisela Weinberg. "On the Origin of the Ink of the Thanksgiving Scroll (1QHodayot^a)." *DSD* 16 (2009): 97–106.

Radner, Karen, and Eleanor Robson, eds. *The Oxford Handbook of Cuneiform Culture*. Oxford: Oxford University Press, 2011.

Rainey, Anson F. "The Scribe at Ugarit: His Position and Influence." *Proceedings of the Israel Academy of Sciences and Humanities* 3 (1969): 126–47.

Rasmussen, Kaare L. "On the Provenance and Firing Temperature of Pottery." In *Khirbet Qumrân et 'Aïn Feshkha*. Vol. 2: *Études d'anthropologie, de physique et de chimie*, edited by Jean-Baptiste Humbert and Jan Gunneweg, 101–4. NTOA.SA 3. Göttingen: Vandenhoeck & Ruprecht, 2003.

Reed, Stephen A. "Find-Sites of the Dead Sea Scrolls." *DSD* 14 (2007): 199–221.

Reed, William L. "The Qumran Caves Expedition of March 1952." *BASOR* 135 (1954): 8–13.

Regev, Eyal. "Boethusians." In *The Encyclopedia of the Bible and Its Reception*, edited by Hans-Josef Klauck et al., 4:445–47. 30 vols. New York: de Gruyter, 2009–.

————. *Sectarianism in Qumran: A Cross-Cultural Perspective*. Berlin: de Gruyter, 2007.

Reich, Ronny. *Miqwa'ot (Jewish Ritual Baths) in the Second Temple, Mishnaic and Talmudic Periods*. [In Hebrew.] Jerusalem: Yad Yizhak Ben-Zvi and Israel Exploration Society, 2013.

————. "Miqwa'ot (Jewish Ritual Immersion Baths) in Eretz-Israel in the Second Temple and the Mishna and Talmud Periods." [In Hebrew.] PhD diss., Hebrew University of Jerusalem, 1990.

————. "A Note on the Function of Room 30 (the 'Scriptorium') at Khirbet Qumran." *JJS* 46 (1995): 157–60.

————. "Some Notes on the Miqva'ot and Cisterns at Qumran." In *Viewing Ancient Jewish Art and Archaeology: VeHinnei Rachel—Essays in Honor of Rachel Hachlili*, edited by Ann E. Killebrew and Gabriele Faßbeck, 414–24. JSJSup 72. Leiden: Brill, 2015.

Rengstorf, Karl Heinrich. *Hirbet Qumrân und die Bibliothek vom Toten Meer*. Stuttgart: Kohlhammer, 1960.

Reynolds, Bennie H. "A Dwelling Place of Demons: Demonology and Apocalypticism in the Dead Sea Scrolls." In *Apocalyptic Thinking in Early Ju-*

daism: Engaging with John Collins' The Apocalyptic Imagination, edited by Sidnie White Crawford and Cecilia Wassén, 23–54. JSJSup 182. Leiden: Brill, 2018.

Reynolds, L. D., and N. G. Wilson. *Scribes and Scholars: A Guide to the Transmission of Greek and Latin Literature*. 4th ed. Oxford: Oxford University Press, 2013.

Robson, Eleanor. "The Production and Dissemination of Scholarly Knowledge." In *The Oxford Handbook of Cuneiform Culture*, edited by Karen Radner and Eleanor Robson, 557–76. Oxford: Oxford University Press, 2011.

———. "Reading the Libraries of Assyria and Babylonia." In *Ancient Libraries*, edited by Jason König, Katerina Oikonomopoulou, and Greg Woolf, 38–56. Cambridge: Cambridge University Press, 2013.

Roche-Hawley, Carole. "Scribes, Houses and Neighborhoods at Ugarit." *UF* 44 (2013): 413–44.

Röhrer-Ertl, Olav, Ferdinand Rohrhirsch, and Dietbert Hahn. "Über die Graberfelder von Khirbet Qumran, insbesondere die Funde der Campagne 1956, I: Anthropologische Datenvorlage und Erstauswertung aufgrund der Collectio Kurth." *RevQ* 19 (1999): 3–46.

Roitman, Adolfo D., Lawrence H. Schiffman, and Shani Tzoref, eds. *The Dead Sea Scrolls and Contemporary Culture: Proceedings of the International Conference Held at the Israel Museum, Jerusalem (July 6–8, 2008)*. STDJ 93. Leiden: Brill, 2011.

Rollston, Christopher A. "Scribal Education in Ancient Israel: The Old Hebrew Epigraphic Evidence." *BASOR* 344 (2006): 47–74.

———. *Writing and Literacy in the World of Ancient Israel: Epigraphic Evidence from the Iron Age*. ABS 11. Atlanta: Society of Biblical Literature, 2010.

Rowe, Ignacio M. "Scribes, Sages, and Seers in Ugarit." In *Scribes, Sages, and Seers: The Sage in the Eastern Mediterranean World*, edited by Leo G. Perdue, 95–108. Göttingen: Vandenhoeck & Ruprecht, 2008.

Ruiten, J. T. A. G. M. van. *Primaeval History Interpreted: The Rewriting of Genesis 1–11 in the Book of Jubilees*. JSJSup 66. Leiden: Brill, 2000.

Ryholt, Kim. "Libraries in Ancient Egypt." In *Ancient Libraries*, ed. Jason König, Katerina Oikonomopoulou, and Greg Woolf, 23–37. Cambridge: Cambridge University Press, 2013.

Saldarini, Anthony J. *Pharisees, Scribes and Sadducees in Palestinian Society: A Sociological Approach*. Repr., Grand Rapids: Eerdmans, 2001.

Sancisi-Weerdenburg, Heleen, Amélie Kuhrt, and Margeret Cool Root, eds.

BIBLIOGRAPHY

Continuity and Change. Achaemenid History 8. Leiden: Nederlands Instituut voor het Nabije Oosten, 1994.

Sanders, Seth L. *From Adapa to Enoch: Scribal Culture and Religious Vision in Judea and Babylon*. TSAJ 167. Tübingen: Mohr Siebeck, 2017.

Sasson, Jack M., ed. *Civilizations of the Ancient Near East*. 4 vols. New York: Scribner, 1995.

Saukkonen, Juhana Markus. "A Few Inkwells, Many Hands: Were There Scribes at Qumran?" In *Houses Full of All Good Things: Essays in Memory of Timo Veijola*, edited by Juha Pakkala and Martti Nissinen, 538–53. Göttingen: Vandenhoeck & Ruprecht, 2008.

Schaeder, Hans Heinrich. *Esra der Schreiber*. Tübingen: Mohr, Nendeln, 1930.

Schams, Christine. *Jewish Scribes in the Second Temple Period*. LHBOTS 291. Sheffield: Sheffield Academic Press, 1998.

Schiffman, Lawrence H. *The Halakah at Qumran*. Leiden: Brill, 1975.

———. "The New Halakhic Letter (4QMMT) and the Origins of the Dead Sea Sect." *BA* 53 (1990): 64–73.

———. "Pharisaic and Sadducean Halakah in Light of the Dead Sea Scrolls: The Case of Tevul Yom." *DSD* 1 (1994): 285–99.

———. *Qumran and Jerusalem: Studies in the Dead Sea Scrolls and the History of Judaism*. Grand Rapids: Eerdmans, 2010.

———. *Reclaiming the Dead Sea Scrolls: The History of Judaism, the Background of Christianity, the Lost Library of Qumran*. Philadelphia: Jewish Publication Society, 1994.

———. "Sabbath." *EDSS* 2:805–7.

———, E. Tov, and James C. VanderKam, eds. *The Dead Sea Scrolls Fifty Years after Their Discovery: Proceedings of the Jerusalem Congress, July 20–25, 1997*. Jerusalem: Israel Exploration Society, 2000.

Schiffman, Lawrence H., and James C. VanderKam, eds. *The Encyclopedia of the Dead Sea Scrolls*. 2 vols. Oxford: Oxford University Press, 2000.

Schniedewind, William. *How the Bible Became a Book: The Textualization of Ancient Israel*. Cambridge: Cambridge University Press, 2004.

Schofield, Alison. *From Qumran to the Yaḥad: A New Paradigm of Textual Development for the Community Rule*. STDJ 77. Leiden: Brill, 2009.

Schuller, Eileen. "Women in the Dead Sea Scrolls." In *Methods of Investigation of the Dead Sea Scrolls and the Khirbet Qumran Site: Present Realities and Future Prospects*, edited by Michael O. Wise, Norman Golb, John J. Collins, and Dennis G. Pardee, 115–32. ANYAS 722. New York: New York Academy of Sciences, 1994.

———, and Cecilia Wassén. "Women." *EDSS* 2:981–84.

Schultz, Brian. "The Qumran Cemetery." *DSD* 13 (2006): 194–228.

Schwartz, Daniel R. *2 Maccabees.* CEJL. Berlin: de Gruyter, 2008.

Segal, Michael. *The Book of Jubilees: Rewritten Bible, Redaction, Ideology and Theology.* JSJSup 117. Leiden: Brill, 2007.

Shamir, Orit, and Naama Sukenik. "Qumran Textiles and the Garments of Qumran's Inhabitants." *DSD* 18 (2011): 206–25.

Shanks, Hershel. *The Copper Scroll and the Search for the Temple Treasure.* Washington, DC: Biblical Archaeology Society, 2007.

———. *Frank Moore Cross: Conversations with a Bible Scholar.* Washington, DC: Biblical Archaeology Society, 1994.

———, ed. *Understanding the Dead Sea Scrolls.* New York: Random House, 1992.

Shemesh, Aharon. "Halakhah between the Dead Sea Scrolls and Rabbinic Literature." In *The Oxford Handbook of the Dead Sea Scrolls*, edited by Timothy H. Lim and John J. Collins, 595–616. Oxford: Oxford University Press, 2010.

Sheridan, Susan Guise, Jamie Ullinger, and Jeremy Ramp. "Anthropological Analysis of the Human Remains: The French Collection." In *Fouilles de Khirbet Qumrân et de ʿAïn Feshkha.* Vol. 2: *Études d'anthropologie, de physique et de chimie*, edited by Jean-Baptiste Humbert and Jan Gunneweg, 129–69. NTOA.SA 3. Göttingen: Vandenhoeck & Ruprecht, 2003.

Shoham, Yair. "A Group of Hebrew Bullae from Yigal Shiloh's Excavations in the City of David." In *Ancient Jerusalem Revealed*, edited by Hillel Geva, 55–61. Jerusalem: Israel Exploration Society, 1994.

Skehan, Patrick W., and Alexander Di Lella. *The Wisdom of Ben Sira: A New Translation with Notes, Introduction, and Commentary.* AB 39. New York: Doubleday, 1987.

Smith, Jonathan Z. *Map Is Not Territory: Studies in the History of Religion.* Leiden: Brill, 1978.

Sokoloff, Michael. *A Dictionary of Jewish Babylonian Aramaic of the Talmudic and Geonic Periods.* Ramat-Gan: Bar Ilan University Press, 2002.

Soldt, Wilfred H. van. *Studies in the Akkadian of Ugarit: Dating and Grammar.* AOAT 40. Neukirchen-Vluyn: Neukirchener Verlag, 1991.

———. "Ugarit: A Second-Millennium Kingdom on the Mediterranean Coast." *CANE* 4:1255–66.

Stacey, David. "A Reassessment of the Stratigraphy of Qumran." In *Qumran Revisited: A Reassessment of the Archaeology of the Site and Its Texts*, edited by David Stacey and Gregory Doudna, 7–74. BARIS 2520. London: Archeopress, 2013.

BIBLIOGRAPHY

———. "Seasonal Industries at Qumran." *BAIAS* 26 (2008): 7–29.

Steckoll, Solomon H. "Marginal Notes on the Qumran Excavations." *RevQ* 7 (1969): 33–40.

———. "Preliminary Excavation Report in the Qumran Cemetery." *RevQ* 6 (1968): 323–36.

Stegemann, Hartmut. "Is the Temple Scroll a Sixth Book of the Torah—Lost for 2500 Years?" In *Understanding the Dead Sea Scrolls*, edited by Hershel Shanks, 126–36. New York: Random House, 1992.

———. *The Library of Qumran: On the Essenes, Qumran, John the Baptist, and Jesus*. Grand Rapids: Eerdmans, 1998.

———. "The Origins of the Temple Scroll." *VT* 40 (1988): 235–56.

———. "The Qumran Essenes—Local Members of the Main Jewish Union in Late Second Temple Times." In *The Madrid Qumran Congress: Proceedings of the International Congress on the Dead Sea Scrolls Madrid 18–21 March 1991*, edited by Julio Trebolle Barrera and Luis Vegas Montaner, 1:83–166. 2 vols. STDJ 11. Leiden: Brill, 1992.

———. "Weitere Stücke von 4QpPsalm 37, von 4Q Patriarchal Blessings und Hinweis auf eine unedierte Handschrift aus Höhle 4Q mit Exzerpten aus dem Deuteronomium." *RevQ* 6 (1967): 193–227.

Stemberger, Günter. "Sadducees." *EDEJ* 1179–81.

Stern, Sacha. "Qumran Calendars: Theory and Practice." In *The Dead Sea Scrolls in Their Historical Context*, edited by Timothy H. Lim, 170–86. London: T&T Clark, 2000.

Steudel, Annette. "אחרית הימים in the Texts from Qumran." *RevQ* 16 (1993): 225–46.

———. *Der Midrasch zur Eschatologie aus der Qumrangemeinde (4QMidr-Eschat^{a, b}): Materielle Rekonstruktion, Textbestand, Gattung, traditionsgeschichtliche Einordnung des durch 4Q174 ("Florilegium") und 4Q177 ("Catena A") repräsentierten Werkes aus den Qumran funden.* STDJ 13. Leiden: Brill, 1994.

Stökl Ben Ezra, Daniel. "Old Caves and Young Caves: A Statistical Reevaluation of a Qumran Consensus." *DSD* 14 (2007): 313–33.

Stone, Michael E. "Enoch, Aramaic Levi and Sectarian Origins." *JSJ* 19 (1987): 159–70.

———, and Jonas C. Greenfield. "Aramaic Levi Document." *In Qumran Cave 4.XVII: Parabiblical Texts, Part 3*, by George Brooke et al., 1–72. DJD 22. Oxford: Clarendon, 1996.

Strange, James F. "The 1996 Excavations at Qumran and the Context of the New Hebrew Ostracon." In *Qumran, the Site of the Dead Sea Scrolls: Archaeolog-*

ical Interpretations and Debates; Proceedings of a Conference Held at Brown University, November 17–19, 2002, edited by Katharina Galor, Jean-Baptiste Humbert, and Jürgen Zangenberg, 41–54. STDJ 57. Leiden: Brill, 2006.

Strocka, Volker Michael. "Römische Bibliotheken." In *Gymnasium Heidelberg: Zeitschrift für Kultur der Antike und humanistische Bildung* 88 (1981): 298–329.

Strugnell, John. "MMT: Second Thoughts on a Forthcoming Edition." In *The Community of the Renewed Covenant: The Notre Dame Symposium on the Dead Sea Scrolls*, edited by Eugene Ulrich and James C. VanderKam, 57–76. Notre Dame: University of Notre Dame Press, 1994.

Stuckenbruck, Loren T. *The Book of Giants from Qumran: Texts, Translation, and Commentary*. TSAJ 63. Tübingen: Mohr Siebeck, 1997.

———. "The Early Traditions Related to 1 Enoch from the Dead Sea Scrolls: An Overview and Assessment." In *The Early Enoch Literature*, edited by Gabriele Boccaccini and John J. Collins, 41–63. JSJSup 121. Leiden: Brill, 2007.

———. *1 Enoch 91–108*. CEJL. Berlin: de Gruyter, 2007.

Sukenik, Eleazar. *Hidden Scrolls from the Genizah Found in the Judaean Desert*, vol. 1. [In Hebrew.] Jerusalem: Bialik Institute, 1948–1949.

Sukenik, Naʿama. "The *Temple Scroll* Wrapper from Cave 11. MS 5095/2, MS 5095/4, MS 5095/1." In *Gleanings from the Caves: Dead Sea Scrolls and Artefacts from the Schøyen Collection*, edited by Torleif Elgvin, Kipp Davis, and Michaël Langlois, 339–49. LSTS 71. London: Bloomsbury T&T Clark, 2016.

Sweet, Ronald F. G. "The Sage in Mesopotamian Palaces and Royal Courts." In *The Sage in Israel and the Ancient Near East*, edited by John G. Gammie and Leo G. Perdue, 99–108. Winona Lake, IN: Eisenbrauns, 1990.

Talmon, Shemaryahu. "The Three Scrolls of the Law That Were Found in the Temple Court." *Textus* 2 (1962): 14–27.

———. "Was the Book of Esther Known at Qumran?" *ErIsr* 25 (1996): 377–82.

———. *The World of Qumran from Within: Collected Studies*. Jerusalem: Magnes, 1989.

———, Jonathan Ben-Dov, and Uwe Glessmer. *Qumran Cave 4.XVI: Calendrical Texts*. DJD 21. Oxford: Clarendon, 2001.

Tanret, Michel. "The Works and the Days? On Scribal Activity in Old Babylonian Sippar-Amnānum." *Revue d'Assyriologie* 98 (2004): 33–62.

Tappy, Ron E., P. Kyle McCarter, Marilyn J. Lundberg, and Bruce Zuckerman. "An Abecedary of the Mid-Tenth Century B.C.E. from the Judaean Shephelah." *BASOR* 344 (2006): 5–46.

BIBLIOGRAPHY

Taylor, Joan. "Buried Manuscripts and Empty Tombs: The Qumran *Genizah* Theory Revisited." In *"Go Out and Study the Land" (Judges 18:2): Archaeological, Historical and Textual Studies in Honor of Hanan Eshel*, edited by Aren M. Maeir, Jodi Magness, and Lawrence H. Schiffman, 269–315. JSJSup 148. Leiden: Brill, 2012.

———. "The Cemeteries of Khirbet Qumran and Women's Presence at the Site." *DSD* 6 (1999): 285–323.

———. "The Classical Sources on the Essenes." In *The Oxford Handbook of the Dead Sea Scrolls*, edited by Timothy H. Lim and John J. Collins, 173–99. Oxford: Oxford University Press, 2010.

———. *The Essenes, the Scrolls, and the Dead Sea*. Oxford: Oxford University Press, 2012.

———. "4Q341: A Writing Exercise Remembered." In *Is There a Text in This Cave? Studies in the Textuality of the Dead Sea Scrolls in Honour of George J. Brooke*, edited by Ariel Feldman, Maria Cioata, and Charlotte Hempel, 133–51. STDJ 119. Leiden: Brill, 2017.

———. "Khirbet Qumran in Period III." In *Qumran, the Site of the Dead Sea Scrolls: Archaeological Interpretations and Debates: Proceedings of a Conference Held at Brown University, November 17–19, 2002*, edited by Katharina Galor, Jean-Baptiste Humbert, and Jürgen Zangenberg, 133–46. STDJ 57. Leiden: Brill, 2006.

———. "The Qumran Caves in Their Regional Context: A Chronological Review with a Focus on Bar Kokhba Assemblages." In *The Caves of Qumran: Proceedings of the International Conference, Lugano 2014*, edited by Marcello Fidanzio, 7–33. STDJ 118. Leiden: Brill, 2017.

———, and Shimon Gibson. "Qumran Connected: The Qumran Pass and Paths of the North-Western Dead Sea." In *Qumran und die Archäologie: Texte und Kontexte*, edited by Jörg Frey, Carsten Claußen, and Nadine Kessler, 163–210. WUNT 278. Tübingen: Mohr Siebeck, 2011.

Taylor, Joan, Dennis Mizzi, and Marcello Fidanzio. "Revisiting Qumran Cave 1Q and Its Archaeological Assemblage." *PEQ* 149 (2017): 295–325.

Taylor, Joan, and Joan E. van der Plicht. "Radiocarbon Dating of the *Temple Scroll* Wrapper and Cave 11Q." In *Gleanings from the Caves: Dead Sea Scrolls and Artefacts from the Schøyen Collection*, edited by Torleif Elgvin, Kipp Davis, and Michaël Langlois, 351–56. LSTS 71. London: Bloomsbury T&T Clark, 2016.

Tcherikover, Victor. *Hellenistic Civilization and the Jews*. New York: Atheneum, 1970.

Teeter, D. Andrew. "Scribes and Scribalism." *EDEJ* 1201–4.

Thomas, Rosalind. *Literacy and Orality in Ancient Greece.* New York: Cambridge University Press, 1992.

———. "Writing, Reading, Public and Private 'Literacies.'" In *Ancient Libraries*, edited by Jason König, Katerina Oikonomopoulou, and Greg Woolf, 13–45. Cambridge: Cambridge University Press, 2013.

Tigay, Jeffrey H. *The Evolution of the Gilgamesh Epic.* Philadelphia: University of Pennsylvania Press, 1982.

Tigchelaar, Eibert J. C. "Aramaic Texts from Qumran and the Authoritativeness of Hebrew Scriptures: Preliminary Observations." In *Authoritative Scriptures in Ancient Judaism*, edited by Mladen Popović, 155–71. JSJSup 141. Leiden: Brill, 2010.

———. "Assessing Emanuel Tov's 'Qumran Scribal Practice.'" In *The Dead Sea Scrolls: Transmission of Traditions and Production of Texts*, edited by Sarianna Metso, Hindy Najman, and Eileen Schuller, 173–208. STDJ 92. Leiden: Brill, 2010.

———. "In Search of the Scribe of 1QS." In *Emanuel: Studies in Hebrew Bible, Septuagint and Dead Sea Scrolls in Honor of Emanuel Tov*, edited by Shalom M. Paul, Robert A. Kraft, Lawrence H. Schiffman, and Weston W. Fields, 439–52. VTSup 94. Leiden: Brill, 2003.

Tiller, Patrick. "The Sociological Settings of the Components of 1 Enoch." In *The Early Enoch Literature*, edited by Gabriele Boccaccini and John J. Collins, 237–55. JSJSup 121. Leiden: Brill, 2007.

Toorn, Karel van der. *Scribal Culture and the Making of the Hebrew Bible.* Cambridge: Harvard University Press, 2007.

Tov, Emanuel. "Categorized List of the 'Biblical Texts.'" In *The Texts from the Judaean Desert: Indices and an Introduction to the Discoveries in the Judaean Desert Series*, edited by Emanuel Tov, 165–83. DJD 39. Oxford: Clarendon, 2002.

———. "The *Discoveries in the Judaean Desert* Series: History and System of Presentation." In *The Texts from the Judaean Desert: Indices and an Introduction to the Discoveries in the Judaean Desert Series*, edited by Emanuel Tov, 1–26. DJD 39. Oxford: Clarendon, 2002.

———. "Excerpted and Abbreviated Biblical Texts from Qumran." In *Hebrew Bible, Greek Bible, and Qumran: Collected Essays*, 27–41. TSAJ 121. Tübingen: Mohr Siebeck, 2008.

———. "338. 4QGenealogical List?" In *Qumran Cave 4.XXVI: Cryptic Texts*, by Stephen Pfann; and *Miscellanea, Part 1*, by Philip Alexander et al., 290. DJD 36. Oxford: Clarendon, 2000.

———. "Further Evidence for the Existence of a Qumran Scribal School."

In *The Dead Sea Scrolls Fifty Years after Their Discovery*, edited by Lawrence H. Schiffman, Emanuel Tov, and James C. VanderKam, 199–216. Jerusalem: Israel Exploration Society, 2000.

———. *The Greek Minor Prophets Scrolls from Naḥal Ḥever (8ḤevXIIgr).* DJD 8. Oxford: Clarendon, 1990.

———. *Hebrew Bible, Greek Bible, and Qumran: Collected Essays.* TSAJ 121. Tübingen: Mohr Siebeck, 2008.

———. "The Orthography and Language of the Hebrew Scrolls Found at Qumran and the Origin of These Scrolls." *Textus* 13 (1986): 31–57.

———. "A Qumran Origin for the Masada Non-Biblical Texts?" *DSD* 7 (2000): 57–73.

———. *Revised Lists of the Texts from the Judaean Desert.* Leiden: Brill, 2010.

———. "The Sciences and the Reconstruction of the Ancient Scrolls: Possibilities and Impossibilities." In *The Dead Sea Scrolls in Context: Integrating the Dead Sea Scrolls in the Study of Ancient Texts, Languages, and Cultures,* edited by Armin Lange, Emanuel Tov, and Matthias Weigold, 1:3–26. 2 vols. VTSup 140. Leiden: Brill, 2011.

———. *Scribal Practices and Approaches Reflected in the Texts Found in the Judean Desert.* STDJ 54. Leiden: Brill, 2004.

———. "Septuagint." In *The Hebrew Bible.* Vol. 1A: *Overview Articles,* edited by Armin Lange and Emanuel Tov, 191–211. Textual History of the Bible. Leiden: Brill, 2016.

———. "The Special Character of the Texts in Qumran Cave 11." In *Hebrew Bible, Greek Bible, and Qumran: Collected Essays,* 421–27. TSAJ 121. Tübingen: Mohr Siebeck, 2008.

———, ed. *The Texts from the Judaean Desert: Indices and an Introduction to the Discoveries in the Judaean Desert Series.* DJD 39. Oxford: Clarendon, 2002.

———. *Textual Criticism of the Hebrew Bible.* 3rd ed. Minneapolis: Fortress, 2012.

———. "Textual History of the Pentateuch." In *The Hebrew Bible.* Vol. 1B: *Pentateuch and Former and Latter Prophets,* ed. Armin Lange and Emanuel Tov, 3–21. Textual History of the Bible. Leiden: Brill, 2017.

———, K. Davis, and R. Duke. *Dead Sea Scrolls Fragments in the Museum Collection.* Leiden: Brill, 2016.

Tov, Emanuel, and S. A. White. "4QReworked Pentateuch^d." In *Qumran Cave 4.VIII: Parabiblical Texts, Part I,* by Harold Attridge et al., 335–44. DJD 13. Oxford: Clarendon, 1994.

———. "4QReworked Pentateuch^e." In *Qumran Cave 4.VIII: Parabiblical*

Texts, Part I, by Harold Attridge et al., 345–52. DJD 13. Oxford: Clarendon, 1994.

Trever, John C. "Preliminary Observations on the Jerusalem Scrolls." *BASOR* 111 (1948): 3–16.

———. *The Untold Story of Qumran*. Westwood: Revell, 1965.

Tropper, Amram, ed. *Studies in Jewish and Christian History*. AJEC 68. Leiden: Brill, 2007.

Tucker, Gene M., and Douglas A. Knight, eds. *Humanizing America's Iconic Book: Society of Biblical Literature Centennial Addresses 1980*. Chico, CA: Scholars Press, 1982.

Tur-Sinai, Naphtali Herz [Harry Torczyner]. *The Lachish Ostraca*. Jerusalem: Bialik Institute, 1987.

Ulrich, Eugene. *The Dead Sea Scrolls and the Developmental Composition of the Bible*. VTSup 169. Leiden: Brill, 2015.

———. *The Dead Sea Scrolls and the Origins of the Bible*. Grand Rapids: Eerdmans, 1999.

———. "Identification of a Scribe Active at Qumran: 1QPs^b-4QIsa^c-11QM." In *Meghillot: Studies in the Dead Sea Scrolls* 5–6 (2007): *201–*10.

———. "The Notion and Definition of Canon." In *The Canon Debate*, edited by Lee M. McDonald and James A. Sanders, 21–35. Peabody, MA: Hendrickson, 2002.

———, Frank Moore Cross, Sidnie White Crawford, Julie Ann Duncan, Patrick W. Skehan, Emanuel Tov, and Julio Trebolle Barrera. *Qumran Cave 4.IX: Deuteronomy, Joshua, Judges, Kings*. DJD 14. Oxford: Clarendon, 1995.

Ulrich, Eugene, Frank Moore Cross, Joseph A. Fitzmyer, Peter W. Flint, Sarianna Metso, Catherine M. Murphy, Curt Niccum, Patrick W. Skehan, Emanuel Tov, and Julio Trebolle Barrera. *Qumran Cave 4:XI: Psalms to Chronicles*. DJD 16. Oxford: Clarendon, 2000.

Ulrich, Eugene, and Peter W. Flint. *Qumran Cave 1.II: The Isaiah Scrolls: Part 1: Plates and Transcriptions*. DJD 32. Oxford: Clarendon, 2010.

VanderKam, James C. *Calendars in the Dead Sea Scrolls: Measuring Time*. New York: Routledge, 1998.

———. *The Dead Sea Scrolls Today*. Grand Rapids: Eerdmans, 1994.

———. *Enoch: A Man for All Generations*. Studies on the Personalities of the Old Testament. Columbia, SC: University of South Carolina Press, 1995.

———. *Jubilees: A Commentary*. 2 vols. Hermeneia. Minneapolis: Fortress, 2018.

———. "The Pharisees and the Dead Sea Scrolls." In *In Quest for the Historical*

BIBLIOGRAPHY

Pharisees, edited by Jacob Neusner and Bruce Chilton, 225–36. Waco, TX: Baylor University Press, 2007.

——. "Those Who Look for Smooth Things, Pharisees, and Oral Law." In *Emanuel: Studies in Hebrew Bible, Septuagint and Dead Sea Scrolls in Honor of Emanuel Tov*, edited by Shalom M. Paul, Robert A. Kraft, Lawrence H. Schiffman, and Weston W. Fields, 465–77. VTSup 94. Leiden: Brill, 2003.

——, and J. T. Milik. "4Qpseudo-Jubilees^a-c." In *Qumran Cave 4.VIII: Parabiblical Texts, Part I*, by Harold Attridge et al., 141–76. DJD 13. Oxford: Clarendon, 1994.

——. "Jubilees." In *Qumran Cave 4.VIII: Parabiblical Texts, Part I*, by Harold Attridge et al., 1–140. DJD 13. Oxford: Clarendon, 1994.

Vaux, Roland de. *Archaeology and the Dead Sea Scrolls: The Schweich Lectures of the British Academy 1959*. Rev. ed. London: Oxford University Press, 1973.

——. "Archéologie." In *Les "petites grottes" de Qumrân*, by M. Baillet, J. T. Milik, and R. de Vaux, 1:3–44. 2 vols. DJD 3. Oxford: Clarendon, 1962.

——. "Fouilles au Khirbet Qumran: Rapport préliminaire." *RB* 60 (1953): 83–106.

——. "Fouilles de Khirbet Qumrân: Rapport préliminaire sur les 3e, 4e et 5e campagnes." *RB* 63 (1956): 533–77.

——. "La Poterie." In *Qumran Cave I*, by D. Barthélemy and J. T. Milik, 8–17. DJD 1. Oxford: Clarendon, 1955.

——, and J. T. Milik. *Qumrân Grotte 4.II: Part I: Archéologie*, by R. de Vaux; and *Part II: Tefillin, Mezuzot et Targums (4Q128–4Q157)*, by J. T. Milik. DJD 6. Oxford: Clarendon, 1977.

Veenhof, Klaas R. "Libraries and Archives." In *The Oxford Encyclopedia of Archaeology in the Near East*, edited by Eric M. Meyers, 3:351–57. 5 vols. New York: Oxford University Press, 1997.

Velde, Herman te. "Scribes and Literacy in Ancient Egypt." In *Scripta Signa Vocis: Studies about Scripts, Scriptures, Scribes and Languages in the Near East, Presented to J. H. Hospers by His Pupils, Colleagues, and Friends*, edited by Herman L. J. Vanstiphout, Karel Jongeling, Frederick Leemhuis, and G. Reinink, 253–64. Gröningen: Forsten, 1986.

Vermes, Geza. *The Dead Sea Scrolls: Qumran in Perspective*. London: Collins, 1977.

——. "The Etymology of 'Essenes.'" *RevQ* 2 (1960): 427–43.

——, and Martin Goodman. *The Essenes according to the Classical Sources*. Oxford Centre Textbooks 1. Sheffield: JSOT Press, 1989.

Vita, Juan-Pablo. "Les scribes des textes rituels d'Ougarit." *UF* 39 (2007): 643–64.

Wagemakers, Bart, and Joan E. Taylor. "New Photographs of the Qumran Excavations from 1954 and Interpretations of L. 77 and L. 86." *PEQ* 143 (2011): 134–56.

Wassén, Cecilia. "The Connection between Purity Practices and the Jerusalem Temple—the House of God—around the Turn of the Era." In *The House of God*, edited by Christian Grappe. Tübingen: Mohr Siebeck, forthcoming.

———. "Daily Life." In *T&T Clark Companion to the Dead Sea Scrolls*, edited by George J. Brooke and Charlotte Hempel, 547–58. London: T&T Clark, 2018.

———. *Women in the Damascus Document*. Academia Biblica 21. Atlanta: Society of Biblical Literature, 2005.

———, and Jutta Jokiranta. "Groups in Tension: Sectarianism in the *Damascus Document* and the *Community Rule*." In *Sectarianism in Early Judaism: Sociological Advances*, edited by David J. Chalcraft, 205–45. London: Equinox, 2007.

Webster, Brian. "Chronological Index of the Texts from the Judaean Desert." In *The Texts from the Judaean Desert: Indices and an Introduction to the Discoveries in the Judaean Desert Series*, edited by Emanuel Tov, 351–446. DJD 39. Oxford: Clarendon, 2002.

Weinfeld, Moshe. "Grace after Meals in Qumran." In *Normative and Sectarian Judaism in the Second Temple Period*, 112–21. LSTS 54. London: T&T Clark, 2005.

Wente, Edward F. "The Scribes of Ancient Egypt." *CANE* 4:2211–21.

Werman, Cana. *The Book of Jubilees: Introduction, Translation, and Interpretation*. [In Hebrew.] Between Bible and Mishnah. Jerusalem: Yad Izhak ben-Zvi, 2015.

Werrett, Ian. "Is Qumran a Library?" In *The Dead Sea Scrolls and the Concept of a Library*, edited by Sidnie White Crawford and Cecilia Wassén, 78–108. STDJ 116. Leiden: Brill, 2016.

Williams, Ronald J. "The Sage in Egyptian Literature." In *The Sage in Israel and the Ancient Near East*, edited by John G. Gammie and Leo G. Perdue, 19–30. Winona Lake, IN: Eisenbrauns, 1990.

———. "Scribal Training in Ancient Egypt." *JAOS* 92 (1972): 214–21.

Williamson, H. G. M. *Ezra, Nehemiah*. WBC 16. Waco, TX: Word, 1985.

———. *1 and 2 Chronicles*. NCBC. Grand Rapids: Eerdmans, 1982.

Wills, Lawrence M. *The Jew in the Court of the Foreign King: Ancient Jewish Court Legends*. Minneapolis: Fortress, 1990.

BIBLIOGRAPHY

Wilson, Andrew M., and Lawrence M. Wills. "Literary Sources of the Temple Scroll." *HTR* 75 (1982): 275–88.

Wilson, Edmund O. *The Scrolls from the Dead Sea.* New York: Oxford University Press, 1955.

Wilson, Robert R. "Orality and Writing in the Creation of Exilic Prophetic Literature." In *Worship, Women and War: Essays in Honor of Susan Niditch*, edited by John J. Collins, Tracy M. Lemos, and Saul M. Olyan, 83–96. Providence: Society of Biblical Literature, 2015.

Wise, Michael O. *A Critical Study of the Temple Scroll from Qumran Cave 11.* SAOC 49. Chicago: University of Chicago Press, 1990.

———. "The Origins and History of the Teacher's Movement." In *The Oxford Handbook of the Dead Sea Scrolls*, edited by Timothy H. Lim and John J. Collins, 92–122. Oxford: Oxford University Press, 2010.

———, Norman Golb, John J. Collins, and Dennis G. Pardee, eds. *Methods of Investigation of the Dead Sea Scrolls and the Khirbet Qumran Site: Present Realities and Future Prospects.* ANYAS 722. New York: New York Academy of Sciences, 1994.

Wolff, Timo, Ira Rabin, Ioanna Mantouvalou, Birgit Kanngießer, Wolfgang Malzer, Emanuel Kindzorra, and Oliver Hahn. "Provenance Studies on Dead Sea Scrolls Parchment by Means of Quantitative Micro-XRF." *Analytical and Bioanalytical Chemistry* 402 (2012): 1493–1503.

Wolters, Al. "Copper Scroll." *EDSS* 1:144–48.

Wood, Bryant G. "To Dip or to Sprinkle? The Qumran Cisterns in Perspective." *BASOR* 256 (1984): 45–60.

Wooden, R. Glenn. "1 Esdras." In *A New English Translation of the Septuagint*, edited by Albert Pietersma and Benjamin G. Wright III, 392–404. New York: Oxford University Press, 2007.

Wright, Benjamin G., III. "Ben Sira on the Sage as Exemplar." In *Praise Israel for Wisdom and Instruction: Essays on Ben Sira and Wisdom, the Letter of Aristeas and the Septuagint*, 165–82. JSJSup 131. Leiden: Brill, 2008.

———. "Conflicted Boundaries: Ben Sira, Sage and Seer." In *Praise Israel for Wisdom and Instruction: Essays on Ben Sira and Wisdom, the Letter of Aristeas and the Septuagint*, 229–53. JSJSup 131. Leiden: Brill, 2008.

———. *The Letter of Aristeas: "Aristeas to Philocrates" or "On the Translation of the Law of the Jews."* CEJL. Berlin: de Gruyter, 2015.

———. "The Master-Disciple Relationship in the Book of Ben Sira." Paper presented at Oxford University. Oxford, UK, 25 May 2016.

———. "Wisdom and Women at Qumran." *DSD* 11 (2004): 240–61.

364

————, and Lawrence M. Wills, eds. *Conflicted Boundaries in Wisdom and Apocalypticism.* SymS 35. Leiden: Brill, 2006.

Yadin, Yigael. "Is the Temple Scroll a Sectarian Document?" In *Humanizing America's Iconic Book: Society of Biblical Literature Centennial Addresses 1980*, edited by Gene M. Tucker and Douglas A. Knight, 153–69. Chico, CA: Scholars Press, 1982.

————. *The Temple Scroll.* 3 vols. and supplement. Rev. ed. Jerusalem: Israel Exploration Society, 1983.

Yardeni, Ada. "Appendix: Documentary Texts Alleged to Be from Qumran Cave 4." In *Aramaic, Hebrew and Greek Documentary Texts from Naḥal Ḥever and Other Sites*, by Hannah M. Cotton and Ada Yardeni, 283–317. DJD 27. Oxford: Clarendon, 1997.

————. *The Book of Hebrew Script: History, Palaeography, Script Styles, Calligraphy and Design.* 3rd English ed. Jerusalem: Carta, 2010.

————. "A Draft of a Deed on an Ostracon from Khirbet Qumran." *IEJ* 47 (1997): 233–37.

————. "234. 4QExercitium Calami A." In *Qumran Cave 4.XXVI: Cryptic Texts*, by Stephen Pfann; and *Miscellanea, Part 1*, by Philip Alexander et al., 185–86. DJD 36. Oxford: Clarendon, 2000.

————. "360. 4QExercitium Calami B." In *Qumran Cave 4.XXVI: Cryptic Texts*, by Stephen Pfann; and *Miscellanea, Part 1*, by Philip Alexander et al., 297. DJD 36. Oxford: Clarendon, 2000.

————. "A Note on a Qumran Scribe." In *New Seals and Inscriptions: Hebrew, Idumean, and Cuneiform*, edited by Meir Lubetski, 286–98. Sheffield: Sheffield Phoenix Press, 2007.

Yon, Marguerite. "Ugarit: History and Archaeology." *ABD* 4:695–706.

Zahn, Molly. "Building Textual Bridges: Towards an Understanding of 4Q158 (4QReworked Pentateuch A)." In *The Mermaid and the Partridge: Essays from the Copenhagen Conference on Revising Texts from Cave 4*, edited by George J. Brooke and Jesper Høgenhaven, 13–32. STDJ 96. Leiden: Brill, 2011.

Zeitlin, Solomon. "The Alleged Antiquity of the Scrolls." *JQR* 40 (1949): 57–78.

————. "A Commentary on the Book of Habakkuk: Important Discovery or Hoax?" *JQR* 39 (1949): 235–47.

————. "Scholarship and the Hoax of the Recent Discoveries." *JQR* 39 (1949): 337–63.

Zeuner, Frederick E. "Notes on Qumrân." *PEQ* 92 (1960): 27–36.

Zias, Joseph E. "The Cemeteries of Qumran and Celibacy: Confusion Laid to Rest?" *DSD* 7 (2000): 220–53.

Index of Authors

Abel, Félix M., 71
Adams, Samuel L., 9
Adler, Yonatan, 119, 205
Aharonovich, Yevgeny, 210
Ahituv, Shmuel, 50, 51
Albani, Matthias, 248, 249
Alexander, Philip S., 78, 159, 189, 221, 230, 249, 262, 274, 286, 289
Allegro, John M., 126, 195, 249
Alster, Bendt, 23
Amihay, Aryeh, 7, 280, 307
Amitai, Janet, 7
Arendzen, J., 90
Attridge, Harold, 85, 242
Avigad, Nahman, 64

Baasten, M. F. J., 221
Baden, Joel, 9, 224
Baillet, M., 85, 92, 121
Balla, Marta, 189, 191, 195, 198
Barkay, Gabriel, 53
Bar-Nathan, Rachel, 150–51
Barthélemy, D., 85, 91, 92, 119, 124
Baumgarten, Albert I., 10, 274
Baumgarten, Joseph M., 3, 7, 230, 260, 275, 282, 299
Bélis, Mireille, 116, 135, 152, 153
Ben-Dov, Jonathan, 83, 159, 245, 256
Benoit, Pierre, 102
Bergren, Theodore A., 98
Berlin, Andrea M., 197, 199, 211, 212, 216
Bernstein, Moshe, 7, 61
Berti, Monica, 42, 44
Bickerman, Elias J., 72

Bigg, Robert D., 32
Black, Jeremy A., 8, 31–32
Blenkinsopp, Joseph, 66, 67
Blum, Rudolph, 42
Boccaccini, Gabriele, 2, 4, 75, 78, 79, 271, 274
Bordreuil, Pierre, 29, 31
Branham, Joan R., 292
Briant, Pierre, 58
Brooke, George J., 91, 144, 240, 241, 304
Broshi, Magen, 122–23, 130, 136, 168, 171–72, 181, 182, 251
Burdajewicz, Mariusz, 199
Burrows, Millar, 166

Carr, David, 50, 56, 315, 316
Carswell, J., 195
Casson, Lionel, 33, 40, 43, 44, 45, 46
Chalcraft, David J., 10
Chambon, A., 117, 171, 183, 191
Chancey, M., 63, 64
Charles, Robert H., 78, 90
Charlesworth, James H., 7, 64, 102, 260, 275
Chazon, Esther G., 237
Chilton, B., 297
Clamer, Christa, 210
Clark, Kenneth Willis, 185, 186
Clements, R., 282
Clermont-Ganneau, Charles, 209–10
Cohen, Shaye J. D., 252
Cohen, Yoram, 23, 25, 26
Collins, John J., 2, 5, 58, 75, 79–80, 84,

INDEX OF AUTHORS

93, 94, 95, 228, 252, 275, 290, 293, 311, 313, 317–18

Collins, Nina, 42

Coqueugniot, Gaëlle, 45

Cotton, Hannah M., 102, 140, 145, 259–60

Cowley, Arthur E., 90

Craigie, P., 29

Crawford, Sidnie White, 3, 42, 43, 77, 95, 96, 121, 124, 132, 137, 138, 144, 221, 222, 231, 232, 241, 246, 252, 257, 273, 278, 283, 296, 315

Crenshaw, James L., 50

Cross, Frank Moore, 3, 4, 50, 51, 60, 61, 124, 131, 133, 139–40, 161, 167, 183, 187, 189, 203, 207, 222, 256, 269, 271, 274, 285–86, 306, 307

Crowfoot, Grace, 152

Curtis, A., 30

Dávid, Nóra, 221

Davies, Philip, 10, 21–22, 30, 40, 57

Davila, James, 278

Dearman, J. Andrew, 56

Delcor, Mathias, 95

Demsky, Aaron, 56

Di Lella, Alexander, 73, 75

Dimant, Devorah, 3, 6, 12, 13, 14, 15, 137, 156, 167, 217–19, 230, 233, 234, 237, 240, 253–54, 299

Dommershausen, Werner, 71

Donceel, Robert, 5, 169, 200, 210

Donceel-Voûte, Pauline, 5, 169, 187, 200

Doran, Robert, 98

Doudna, G., 6, 131, 169, 238

Drawnel, Henryk, 35, 78, 83, 87, 91, 92

Driver, G. R., 168

Du Toit, Jaqueline S., 8, 31

Duke, Robert, 92

Dupont-Sommer, André, 271

Dušek, Jan, 59, 60

Ekroth, Gunnel, 208

Elgvin, Torleif, 2, 92, 121, 152, 153, 195, 274

Elior, Rachel, 272

Elliott, M., 274

Emerton, J. A., 26, 52

Eshel, Esther, 91, 189, 191, 237, 251, 252, 285–86, 314

Eshel, Hanan, 64, 100, 122–23, 130, 136, 168, 171–72, 182, 209–11

Falk, Daniel K., 224, 237

Faßbeck, G., 179

Feldman, Ariel, 132, 143, 258

Fidanzio, Marcello, 116, 117, 118, 119, 126, 132, 134, 148, 150, 161, 164, 197

Fields, Weston, 1, 118, 122, 130, 133

Fitzmyer, Joseph A., 109, 110

Flint, Peter W., 78, 93, 102, 187, 233, 239, 244, 249, 317

Fox, Nili Sacher, 36, 54, 65

Fraade, Steven D., 226

Freedman, David Noel, 224

Freund, Richard, 171

Frey, Jörg, 176

Fröhlich, Ida, 77

Galor, Katharina, 6, 146, 150, 168, 169, 176, 181, 203, 205, 206, 286

Gammie, John G., 22, 23, 29, 75, 80

García Martínez, Florentino, 8, 13, 37, 81, 85, 126, 164, 274

Gardiner, Alan H., 27, 28

Gayer, Asaf, 159

Geva, H., 52

Gibson, S., 176

Ginzberg, Louis, 296, 297

Glessmer, Uwe, 244, 245, 248

Goff, Matthew J., 234, 235

Golb, Norman, 146, 169, 238, 293

Goldstein, Jonathan A., 71, 98

Goodman, Martin, 167, 273, 288, 294, 299, 306

Goranson, Stephen, 195, 307

Gordon, C., 30

Gorman, Robert, 300

Gorman, Vanessa, 300

Grabbe, L., 274

Grappe, Christian, 200

Index of Authors

Grayson, A. Kirk, 33
Green, D., 95
Greenfield, Jonas C., 91, 249
Grenache, G., 122, 139
Gropp, Douglas M., 61
Grossman, Maxine, 5
Gunneweg, Jan, 116, 135, 148, 172, 176–77, 185, 189, 191, 195, 196, 197, 198, 199, 209, 210, 257
Gutfeld, Oren, 116, 122–23
Guyat, A., 256
Gyselen, R., 187

Hachlili, Rachel, 209, 211
Hahn, Diebert, 212
Halpern, B., 224
Halpern-Amaru, B., 282
Haran, Menahem, 32, 52
Harding, G. Lankester, 117–18, 131, 153, 166, 171, 179
Harrington, Daniel J., 234
Healey, John F., 29
Hempel, Charlotte, 2, 13, 15, 137, 142, 144, 186, 200, 227, 241, 256–57, 260, 274–76, 277, 279, 304, 317
Hezser, Catherine, 144
Hilhorst, A., 249, 253
Himmelfarb, Martha, 282, 317
Hirschfeld, Yizhar, 5, 100–101, 169, 172, 181, 184, 201, 204, 293, 306, 312
Hizme, Hanania, 210
Høgenhaven, J., 240
Hollenback, George M., 248
Holum, K. G., 101
Horsley, Richard A., 76, 79, 81, 94
Houston, George W., 40, 41, 44, 45, 46–47
Hultgren, Stephen, 227–28
Humbert, Jean-Baptiste, 116, 117, 119–20, 121, 130, 131, 132, 134–36, 148, 149, 168, 171, 174, 176–78, 181, 183, 185, 189, 191, 195, 196, 197, 198, 199, 203, 207–9, 210, 211, 257, 292
Hurowitz, Victor Avigdor, 22, 23

Ilan, Tal, 231

Jacob, Christian, 43
Jacobus, Helen R., 246, 248
Jaillard, Dominique, 40
Jamieson-Drake, David W., 49–50
Johnson, Lora L., 46
Johnson, William A., 40
Jokiranta, Jutta, 10, 224

Kampen, John, 7, 71
Kartveit, Magnar, 58
Keith, Chris, 110
Killebrew, Ann E., 179
Klauck, H.-J., 295
Klawans, Jonathan, 282
Klein, Ralph W., 65, 66
Klijn, A. F. J., 99
Knight, D., 12
Knoppers, Gary N., 58, 59, 60, 65, 69
Kollmann, B., 95
König, J., 31, 36, 40, 41, 45
Kooij, Arie van der, 99
Kraft, R., 306
Kramer, Samuel N., 22, 23, 25
Kratz, Reinhard G., 67
Krzyško, Miroslaw, 198–99
Kugel, James L., 86, 88
Kugler, Robert A., 91, 92, 317

Lange, Armin, 8, 37, 103, 128, 156, 221, 222, 223, 234, 235, 237, 240, 258–59, 296, 315
Lapp, Nancy L., 61
Lapp, Paul W., 61
Larson, Erik, 140, 145, 259–60
Lefkovits, Judah K., 126
Leiman, Sid Z., 99, 186
Leith, Mary Joan Winn, 61
Lemaire, André, 50, 52, 64, 148, 177, 189, 194, 257
Lim, Timothy H., 99, 246, 274, 316
Lipiński, E., 26
Lipschits, Oded, 63, 64, 70, 202
Loader, William, 282, 283
Lönnqvist, Kenneth, 127–28, 151
Lönnqvist, Minna, 127–28, 151
Lubetski, Meir, 104, 162, 262

INDEX OF AUTHORS

Machiela, Daniel, 96, 252, 253–54
Machinist, Peter, 59
Mack-Fisher, Loren R., 29
Maeir, A. M., 122, 213, 220
Magen, Yitzhak, 6, 59, 60, 146, 169,
171–72, 176–79, 181–82, 189, 195, 200,
204, 207, 210–11, 213
Magness, Jodi, 5, 17, 100, 118, 119, 141,
150–51, 168, 173–76, 180, 185, 186,
196–98, 199, 200, 201–4, 207–9, 214,
301, 312, 314
Marcus, Joel, 106, 107, 108
Mason, E. F., 137
Mason, Steve, 294, 296, 298, 304
McCane, Byron R., 205
McDonald, Lee M., 11
Mébarki, Farah, 122, 139
Medico, Henri E. del, 5, 186–87
Metso, Sarianna, 2, 3, 6, 224, 262, 274,
276, 277, 289, 302
Metzger, Bruce M., 186
Meyers, Eric M., 32, 63, 64, 168
Michniewicz, Jacek, 198–99
Milik, J. T., 3, 52, 78, 79, 82, 85, 86, 91,
92, 94–96, 117, 119, 122, 124, 126, 130,
131, 133, 138–39, 147, 161–62, 165, 195,
251, 256–57, 271
Miller, Stuart S., 206
Milstein, Sara J., 25
Misgav, H., 64
Mittmann-Richert, U., 103, 258–59
Mizzi, Dennis, 6, 17, 118, 119, 122, 124,
134–37, 148, 151, 152, 154, 155, 168,
174–76, 185, 190, 195, 196, 200, 201,
208, 211, 214, 264, 314
Mlynarczyk, Jolanta, 132, 197
Moran, W., 36
Mrozcek, Eva, 241
Müller, H.-P., 84, 221, 315
Murphy, Catherine M., 177, 179–80,
200, 201, 285
Murphy-O'Connor, Jerome, 6
Myers, Jacob M., 70

Nagar, Yossi, 172, 210, 211, 292
Naveh, Joseph, 60, 143, 258

Nebe, G. W., 148
Neusner, Jacob, 297
Newsom, Carol A., 10, 13, 93, 161, 224
Nickelsburg, George W., 78–79, 81,
84, 85
Niditch, Susan, 50, 53, 57, 97
Nissinen, M., 191
North, Robert, 203
Norton, Jonathan, 209, 212

Oeming, M., 63
Ortiz, Steven, 121
Orton, David, 55, 80, 84, 88, 109, 110,
111, 126

Pakkala, Juha, 191, 221, 315
Pardee, Dennis, 29, 31
Parker, H., 40
Parpola, Simo, 33
Parry, D. W., 3, 137, 222, 248
Pass, H. Leonard, 90
Patrich, Joseph, 101, 120, 122, 181
Patton, P., 152, 184
Paul, S. M., 140, 161, 231, 260, 283,
297
Pearce, Laurie E., 22, 23, 25, 33
Peck, Dwight C., 2
Pedersén, Olof, 32, 34, 35, 64
Pedley, Katharine Greenleaf, 183, 184,
187
Peleg, Yuval, 6, 146, 169, 171–72,
176–79, 181–82, 189, 195, 200, 204,
207, 210–11, 213
Perdue, L., 22, 23, 29, 30, 67, 75, 80
Pestman, Pieter W., 41
Peursen, W. Th. van, 221
Pfann, Stephen J., 78, 124, 140, 159,
163–64, 171, 178, 230, 246, 248, 249,
255–57, 318
Pinto, Pasquale M., 41
Plicht, J. van der, 121, 153
Ploeg, J. P. M. van der, 162
Poole, Henry, 209–10, 213
Popović, Mladen, 83, 143, 144, 181, 242,
249, 250
Porten, Bezalel, 41, 62

Index of Authors

Posner, Ernst, 8, 31, 35, 42, 58
Price, Randall, 116, 122–23
Priest, J., 128
Pritchard, James B., 26
Propp, W. H., 10, 161, 224
Puech, Émile, 4, 78, 79, 93, 104, 126, 158, 161, 162, 191, 249, 250, 257, 271

Qimron, Elisha, 7, 226, 272, 282, 284

Rabin, Ira, 121, 157
Radner, Karen, 24, 34
Rainey, Anson F., 29, 30
Ramp, Jeremy, 212
Rappaport, U., 237
Rasmussen, Kaare L., 199
Reed, Stephen A., 140
Reed, William L., 122
Regev, Eyal, 10, 295
Reich, Ronny, 179, 185, 187, 203, 204, 205, 206
Rengstorf, Karl Heinrich, 5
Reynolds, Bennie H., 232, 251
Reynolds, L. D., 40
Robson, Eleanor, 24, 31, 34
Roche-Hawley, Carole, 38
Röhrer-Ertl, Olav, 212
Rohrhirsch, Ferdinand, 212
Rollston, Christopher A., 50, 51
Römer, T., 30, 40
Rowe, Ignacio M., 30
Ruiten, J. T. A. G. M. van, 88, 89, 90
Ryholt, Kim, 36, 37

Saldarini, Anthony J., 106, 108, 109, 111, 296, 298, 307
Saley, R. J., 222
Sancisi-Weerdenburg, Heleen, 59
Sanders, James A., 11
Sanders, Seth L., 24–25, 83–84, 96, 244, 254
Saukkonen, Juhana Markus, 191
Schaeder, Hans Heinrich, 67
Schams, Christine, 65, 70, 71, 109, 110, 111

Schiffman, Lawrence H., 7, 133, 140, 207, 248, 272, 273, 281, 282, 299
Schniedewind, William, 21, 55, 57
Schofield, Alison, 224, 275, 308, 317–18
Schuller, Eileen, 231–32
Schultz, Brian, 171, 212
Schwartz, Daniel R., 71, 98, 99
Segal, Michael, 81, 85, 88
Shamir, Orit, 152, 153, 303
Shanks, Herschel, 12, 126, 131
Shemesh, Aharon, 7
Sheridan, Susan Guise, 212
Shiloh, Yigal, 52
Shoham, Yair, 52, 57
Skehan, Patrick W., 73, 75
Smith, Jonathan Z., 9
Sokoloff, Michael, 148, 249
Soldt, Wilfred H. van, 29, 37, 39
Stacey, David, 6, 131, 146, 169–70, 187, 195–96, 204, 207, 214, 238
Starcky, J., 71
Steckoll, Solomon H., 171–72, 195, 210–11, 213
Stegemann, Hartmut, 3, 12, 183, 239, 270, 288, 295, 304, 316, 318, 320
Stemberger, Günter, 295
Sterling, G., 252
Stern, Sacha, 246
Steudel, Annette, 242, 290
Stökl Ben Ezra, Daniel, 133, 138, 157, 220, 256, 261
Stone, Michael E., 10, 83, 91, 92, 200
Strange, James F., 171–72, 189, 285–86
Strocka, Volker Michael, 100
Strugnell, John, 7, 131, 161, 226, 271, 272
Stuckenbruck, Loren T., 78, 79, 82
Sukenik, Eleazar, 166, 270
Sukenik, Na'ama, 121, 152, 153, 303
Sweet, Ronald F. G., 23

Tait, William J., 8, 31–32
Tal, O., 63, 70
Talmon, Shemaryahu, 99, 103, 219, 245, 247
Tanret, Michel, 23
Tappy, Ron E., 52, 53

371

INDEX OF AUTHORS

Taylor, Joan, 118, 119, 121, 122, 129, 134, 137, 141, 143, 153, 154, 155, 164, 166, 168–69, 175–76, 179, 180, 181, 182, 211, 213, 220, 258, 294–95, 299, 300, 301, 305–6, 312
Tcherikover, Victor, 71
Teeter, D. Andrew, 76, 108
Thomas, Rosalind, 40
Tigay, Jeffrey H., 25, 253–54
Tigchelaar, Eibert J. C., 140, 161, 262
Tiller, Patrick, 75
Toorn, Karel van der, 55, 57, 68, 99, 315
Tov, Emanuel, 4, 92, 102, 103, 104, 119, 125, 144, 145, 156, 157, 158, 161, 188, 219, 220, 221, 222, 239–44, 251, 255–57, 260, 262–63, 272, 296, 315, 316–17, 318
Trebolle Barrera, J., 3, 240, 271
Trever, John C., 124, 166, 188, 270
Tucker, Gene M., 12
Tur-Sinai, Naphtali Herz [Harry Torczyner], 51

Ullinger, Jamie, 212
Ullman-Margalit, Edna, 306–7
Ulrich, Eugene, 3, 11, 68, 92, 137, 162, 187, 221, 226, 241, 248, 315

Vanderhooft, D., 64
VanderKam, James C., 12, 78–79, 81, 84, 85, 86, 226, 244, 245, 246, 247, 249, 270, 297, 298, 317
Vanstiphout, H., 27
Vaux, Roland de, 3, 5, 116–22, 129, 130, 131–39, 148, 150, 154, 165, 166–96, 201–3, 206–7, 209–12, 257, 270
Veenhof, Klaas R., 32
Vegas Montaner, L., 3, 240, 271
Velde, Herman te, 27, 28
Vella, N. C., 148

Vermes, Geza, 3, 167, 230–31, 262, 271, 274, 289, 299, 307
Vita, Juan-Pablo, 30–31

Wassén, Cecilia, 10, 42, 43, 77, 96, 124, 138, 200, 205, 228, 231–32, 246, 252, 257, 273, 283, 304
Webster, Brian, 138, 141, 220, 230, 243, 261, 272
Weigold, M., 240
Weinfeld, Moshe, 242
Wente, Edward F., 27, 28
Werrett, Ian, 43, 45, 46
White, S. A., 242, 243
Williams, Ronald J., 26, 27, 28
Williamson, H. G. M., 65, 66
Wills, Lawrence M., 6, 76, 93
Wilson, Andrew M., 6
Wilson, Edmund, 3
Wilson, J. A., 26
Wilson, N. G., 40
Wilson, Robert R., 57
Wise, Michael O., 5, 6, 120, 169, 181, 200, 312
Wolff, Timo, 157, 272
Wolters, Al, 126
Wood, Bryant G., 181, 203, 206
Wooden, R. Glenn, 70
Woude, A. van der, 274
Wright, Benjamin G., III, 42, 73, 76, 234, 252, 274

Yadin, Yigael, 12, 33, 100
Yardeni, Ada, 51, 62, 102, 104, 143, 161–63, 251, 257, 258, 261–62, 285–86
Yon, Marguerite, 30, 37, 49

Zahn, Molly, 240
Zeitlin, Solomon, 168
Zeuner, Frederick E., 170, 207
Zias, Joseph E., 211

Index of Subjects

abecedaries: Iron Age Israel and Judah, 52–53; Qumran inscriptions, 191–92; Tel Zayit, 52–53

Acts of the Apostles, 303n67

Adapa, myth of, 36

Aeschylus, 44, 47

affiliated literature (Qumran scroll collection), 11–12, 17–18, 159–60, 218, 223, 232–36, 310, 316–17; Aramaic language, 223, 232–33; calendars and calendaric matters, 12, 232–33, 244–48; Cave 4Q scrolls, 140–41, 142, 159–60, 232–35; eschatological, apocalyptic worldview with angelology, 232, 233–35; legal interpretations, 232; New Jerusalem text, 159, 235, 253–54; revelations from mouths of remote ancestors (passed on in writing), 232, 233; shared traits of the compositions, 232; wisdom texts (Instruction and Mysteries), 234–35

Aharoni, Yohanan, 102

'Ain Feshkha complex, 170, 178, 306, 313

Akhenaten, 35–36

Alexander Jannaeus: coins of, 201; reign of, 5, 17, 311–15; treatment of Pharisees, 298

Alexander the Great, 60–61, 244

Alexandria, Museion library at, 40, 42–44, 315

Ammianus Marcellinus, 43

amulets of Iron Age Israel and Judah, 53

ancient Israel and Judah, scribes and libraries in, 16, 49–105; archaeological evidence, 97–101; epigraphic and literary evidence, 16, 49–96; Hellenistic and Roman period, 70–96; Iron Age, 49–58, 97, 104; non-Qumran Judean Desert text collections, 101–4; Persian period, 58–70, 104–5; postexilic period, 98–101

ancient Judaism. *See* classical literature of ancient Judaism (produced by Persian period scribes); classical literature of ancient Judaism (Qumran scroll collection)

ancient Near East, scribes and libraries in, 21–39, 47–48; archives and libraries, 31–39; clay tablets, 24–25, 29, 30, 32–33, 37–39; colophons, 24–25, 48; Egypt, 26–28, 35–37; elite priestly scholar-scribes, 23–26, 27–28, 47; languages, 21–22, 23, 27, 29, 36, 47–48, 96; literacy rates, 21, 40; Mesopotamia, 22–26, 32–35; private library collections, 32, 34–35, 36–37, 38–39, 48; royal court scribes, 29–30; scribal education/training, 22–23, 30, 38, 48; scribal families and apprenticeship system, 25–26, 29, 35; scribes and the scribal profession, 22–31, 47–48; scripts, 27, 29, 36, 38; Ugarit, 29–31, 37–39. *See also* Egypt, ancient; Mesopotamia; Ugarit

angelology, 232, 233–35

animal bone deposits at Khirbet Qumran, 206–9, 215, 288, 292

Antioch-on-the-Orontes, library at, 44

373

INDEX OF SUBJECTS

Antiochus III, 44, 59, 72–73, 108
Antiochus IV Epiphanes, 98, 246–47
Apocryphon of Jeremiah, 235n48, 236
Apocryphon of Moses, 236
Arad ostraca, 51, 97
Aramaic language texts, 18, 94–96, 163, 220–21, 223, 232–33, 237, 249–51, 252–55; Aramaic Levi Document (ALD), 90–92, 160, 233, 245; Aramaic magical book (4Q560), 249, 250–51; Elephantine papyri, 63; Enoch literature, 78–79, 83, 94–96; esoteric texts and lists (Cave 4Q), 249–51; inscriptions, 189, 191–94, 215; Jewish texts, 253–55; as language of scribal learning, 78–79, 83, 96; Persian period Israel and Judah, 58, 59–60, 61, 64; "scientific" and esoteric texts, 253; square script, 163, 220–21
Aramaic Levi Document (ALD), 12, 77, 90–92, 94–96, 159–60, 233, 235, 245, 253, 315
archaeology of Khirbet Qumran site and Qumran settlement, 17, 166–216, 309–10; absence of feminine-gendered objects and/or presence of women, 154, 155, 202, 214, 216, 292, 319; animal bone deposits, 206–9, 215, 288, 292; architecture, 176–81; cemeteries, 209–13, 215, 292; chronology of archaeological phases and revisions, 172–76; coins, 201–2; as community settlement of Jewish men, 215; conclusions based on archaeological evidence, 213–16; evidence that supports Essene identification and habitation, 170, 291–94; geographic location and linking paths, 149, 176, 310; glass vessels, 200; history of excavations, 118–23, 130–37, 138–40, 166–67, 171–76, 195, 201–13; inkwells, 195; inscriptions and other evidence for writing, 147–49, 189–94, 285; Iron II phase, 172, 176–77; library complex and possible scriptorium/scroll workshop, 17, 177,

182–88, 310; limestone cliff caves, 17, 117–29, 164, 310, 318–19; limestone vessels, 200; linen textiles and scroll wrappers, 152–53, 195–96, 292; main building, 177–78, 183–88; marl terrace caves, 17, 130–47, 164–65, 310, 320; metal implements, 200; mikvaoth and ritual purity concerns, 202–6, 215–16, 276, 292, 302–3, 319; miscellaneous artifacts and nonmanuscript remains, 150–54, 196–213; population estimates, 181–82; pottery corpus, 17, 134–35, 150–51, 196–99; Second Temple Period I, 172–73, 177–82; Second Temple Period II, 172–73, 177–82; as site of small-scale industrial and agricultural activities, 215; toilet facilities, 292–93; unusual features, 196–213; water installations and stepped pools, 178–79, 202–6, 215–16, 319. *See also* architecture of the Qumran settlement
architecture of the Qumran settlement, 176–81; changes, additions, and rebuilding, 180–81; destruction by fire, 181, 320; enclosure and additional buildings, 177–78; entrance to the complex, 177; Iron II site, 176–77; library complex and possible scriptorium or "scroll workshop," 177, 182–88, 310; main building, 177–78, 182–88; plain, undecorated, and utilitarian, 179–80, 197, 291; postdestruction phase (Roman military outpost), 182; Second Temple period site, 177–81; two-story watchtower, 177; as unfortified site (not a fortress), 214, 312–13
archives, distinction between ancient libraries and, 8, 31–32, 35–36
Aristophanes, 47
Aristotle, 42, 46–47
Asinius Pollio, 46
Assurbanipal, library of, 32, 33–34, 39, 48
astrology, 249–50

374

Index of Subjects

Astronomical Book, 78, 82–83, 232–33, 245, 246, 248
Atrahasis, myth of, 25, 34
Atticus, 45
Augustus, 46
Aulus Gellius, 43

Babylonian astronomical tradition, 244–45
Bar Kokhba revolt, 101, 102, 173, 182
bedouin shepherds: discovery of Cave 4Q and marl terrace caves, 130, 138–39; discovery of Qumran limestone cliff caves, 118–21
Behistun inscription of Darius I, 62–63
Ben Sira, as scribe, 73–77, 105
Boethusians, 295, 298
bullae: Iron Age Israel and Judah, 51–52, 97; Persian period Samaria, 61; Persian period Yehud, 64

Cairo Damascus Document (CD), 316, 224n19, 289
Cairo Geniza documents, 73, 90
calendar texts at Qumran, 12, 232–33, 244–48; and Babylonian astronomical tradition, 244–45; classical authors on Essene calendars, 304; and the Jerusalem temple cult, 287–88; texts embracing the 364-day calendar, 12, 232–33, 235, 244–48, 304
Callimachus, grammarian of the Museion, 44, 47, 48
Cambyses II, 32
Cave 1Q, 118–19, 124–25, 162–64; excavation, 119; location, 118; other material finds, 119, 152–53, 154; proportion of types of literature found, 125; scribal hand, 161–63; scroll jars, 118–19; sectarian literature, 124–25, 159–60, 229–30
Cave 2Q, 119–20, 125, 160–61, 163, 164
Cave 3Q, 117, 120, 125–26, 152, 164, 263
Cave 4Q, 4, 17, 129, 130–35, 137–46, 157–58, 165, 219–23, 240–44, 257–61,

320; affiliated literature, 140–41, 142, 159–60, 232–35; archaeology and excavation, 131–35, 138–40; calendar texts, 232–33, 245–46; Cave 4Qa and multiple chambers, 132–35; Cave 4Qb, 134–35; classical literature of ancient Israel, 138, 140–41, 158–60, 219–23, 238–44; discovery, 130, 138–39; diversity of manuscripts, 6, 138, 140–41, 158–60; esoteric texts and lists, 248–53; "excerpted" texts, 238–44; Hellenistic-Roman literature, 140–41, 142, 159–60; as hub of the collection, 137–38, 157–58; inscriptions found on vessels and sherds, 147–49; nonsectarian works composed in the Hellenistic-Roman period, 140–41, 142, 159–60, 236–37; oldest manuscripts in the Qumran collection, 141–42, 157–58, 220; opisthographs, 144–45, 260–61; overlaps in content with other caves, 17, 157–60, 320; palimpsests, 144–45, 260–61; papyrus texts, 144; pottery, 134–35; "scientific" texts, 253; scribal exercises and documentary texts, 143–44, 257–60; scribal hand, 161–63; scribal lists, 251–52; sectarian literature, 138, 140–41, 142–43, 159–60, 229–30; single-copy works, 142–43, 146, 160, 236–37; wall niches, 133, 165; "working" texts, 143–46, 257–61
Cave 5Q, 130, 135, 146, 165
Cave 6Q, 117, 120, 127, 129, 151, 163, 320
Cave 7Q, 130, 136, 146–49, 163, 165; Greek fragments on papyrus, 147, 163; inscriptions found on vessels and sherds, 147–49
Cave 8Q, 136, 146, 152, 165, 195–96
Cave 9Q, 130, 136, 146
Cave 10Q, 130, 135–36
Cave 11Q, 120–21, 127, 152–54, 162–64; material finds, 121, 152, 154; scribal hand, 162–63; Temple Scroll (11QT^a), 121, 127, 293

375

INDEX OF SUBJECTS

Cave 53 (limestone cliff cave), 116, 122–23, 164

celibacy and the Qumran sect, 230–32, 271, 299–304

cemeteries at Khirbet Qumran, 209–13, 215, 292; "classic form" graves and burials, 210–11; empty graves, 171, 213; gender identity of human remains, 212–13, 231, 292; history of excavations, 209–10; Main Cemetery and its extensions, 209–11; South Cemetery, 209, 211

children and the Qumran sect, 155, 212–13, 275, 292, 302; rules of entry for those born into the sect, 228–29, 231, 277–78

Chronicles, books of, 54n20, 65–66, 69, 71, 105; composition by scribes of Persian period, 65–66, 69; Levitical scribes, 66, 105; on scribal families at Jabez, 65–66

Cicero, 45, 46–47

classical literature of ancient Judaism (produced by Persian period scribes), 68–70; five books of the Torah, 68–69; Ketuvim, 69; non-canonical book of Tobit, 69; prophetic books (Nevi'im), 69

classical literature of ancient Judaism (Qumran scroll collection), 11, 17–18, 158–60, 218–23, 238–44; books of the Torah, 158, 219–21; Cave 4Q scrolls, 138, 140–41, 158–60, 219–23, 238–44; Cryptic A script texts, 256; different scripts, 220–21; "excerpted" texts, 238–44; languages, 220–21; variety demonstrating scribes' textual preoccupations, 221–23

clay tablets, ancient Near Eastern writing on, 24–25, 29–30, 31–34, 37–39

coins of Khirbet Qumran, 201–2

colophons, 24–25, 48

Community Rule (1Q28; also called Serekh Hayaḥad, Manual of Discipline, Order of the Community, S), 2, 3, 4, 6, 13, 118, 124, 139, 141, 142n96, 143n98, 159, 161, 162, 164n157, 187–88, 224–25, 224n18, 224n19, 226–28, 228n26, 229, 230, 231, 235, 243, 246, 260n133, 270, 271, 274–75, 274n15, 275n17, 276, 284, 285, 285n34, 291–92, 293, 294, 302, 303, 315

Copper Scroll, 8n19, 120, 126–27

covenant renewal ceremony and Qumran sect, 226–28, 276–78

cryptic script manuscripts in Qumran collection, 255–57; Cryptic A, 145, 163, 230, 250, 255–57; Cryptic B, 255–57; Cryptic C, 255–57

Damascus Document (D), 3, 7, 13–14, 224–26, 227–30, 231, 271, 274–75, 277–78, 280–85; concerning women and children in the sect, 228, 231, 271, 275–76, 277–78; and critiques of the Qumran-Essene hypothesis, 4–5; interrelationship with S (Serek Hayaḥad), 274–75; legal interpretations, 280–84; on sharing of property, 285

Daniel, book of, 92–94, 233–34; affiliated texts, 159, 233–34; on the *maskilim*, 94; pesher form of interpretation, 234; on scribal and esoteric skills, 93–94

Darius I, 62–63, 67

Day of Atonement, 247

Demetrius III Eukarios, 298, 313

Demetrius of Phalerum, 42, 43

Demosthenes, 47

Deuteronomy, book of, 53, 55n22, 102, 103, 103n177, 142, 158, 219, 220–21, 226n22, 240

de Vaux, Roland. *See* Vaux, Roland de

Diogenes Laertius, 42

Dio of Prusa (Dio Chrysostom), 294, 305, 306

Dream visions, of Enoch, 78, 233

Ebla corpus, 32–33

Ecclesiasticus, 11, 73–77, 103, 105, 111, 125, 160, 236

École Biblique et Archéologique

Index of Subjects

Française (EBAF) in Jerusalem, 5, 166

Egypt, ancient, 26–28, 35–37; archives and libraries, 35–37; elite priestly scholar-scribes, 27–28, 47; House of Books and storage of literary texts, 36, 48; House of Life scribal institution and workshop, 27–28, 36, 48; Middle Kingdom period, 26; New Kingdom period, 26; private libraries, 36–37; Pyramid Texts of the Old Kingdom period, 26; scribal education and apprenticeship, 26–27, 48; scribal languages and scripts, 27, 36; scribal specialties, 27; scribes/scribal profession, 26–28; state archive at Tell el-Amarna, 35–36; Tebtunis temple library, 36, 188; writing on ostraca and wooden tablets, 28; writing on papyrus, 28, 35–37

Elephantine papyri, 41, 62–63

elite scholar-scribes: ancient Egypt, 27–28, 47; in the ancient world, 23–26, 27–28, 47; Daniel on the *maskilim* (a wise circle of scholar-scribes), 94; defining, 9–10; and "excerpted" texts of classic literature of Qumran collections, 242–43; and leadership elite in the Synoptic Gospels, 107–8; Mesopotamia, 23–26

Enmeduranki, 80

Enoch, as scribe, 79–85, 87–88, 95, 105; "mantic wisdom" (esoteric wisdom), 84; as master scribe and visionary in Jubilees, 87–88; as priest in the garden of Eden, 87–88; priestly concerns, 84–85; prophetic tasks, 80, 82; role of the scribe, 79–85; specialized astronomical knowledge, 82–84

"Enochic" Judaism, 79, 274

Enoch literature, 77–85, 105, 232–34; Apocalypse of Weeks, 80, 84–85; Aramaic language, 78–79, 83, 94–96; Astronomical Book of Enoch, 78, 82–84, 232–33, 245, 248; Book of Giants,

79, 81–82, 232; Book of Parables (or Similitudes), 79; Book of the Watchers, 78–79, 84, 233; copies in Qumran cave collections, 78–79, 82–83, 85, 90–91, 92–93, 160; Dream Visions, 78, 233; Enoch and the role of scribe, 79–85, 87–88, 95, 105; Enoch as scribe, 79–85, 87–88, 95, 105; Epistle of Enoch, 78–79; heavenly tablets, 80–81, 86–87, 89–90

Enuma Anu Enlil, 25, 82–83

Enuma Elish, 34

Ephesus, library of Celsus at, 46, 182

Epic of Anzu, 25

Epicurus, 45

Epiphanius, 294, 306

eschatological, apocalyptic worldviews: affiliated texts on, 232, 233–35; classical sources on the Essenes and, 303, 304; sectarian texts on Qumran sect and, 290–91

esoteric texts at Qumran, 248–53; Aramaic magical book, 249, 250–51; horoscopy and astrology, 249–50; "scientific" esoteric texts, 253; Zodiacal Physiognomy, 249–50, 256

Essenes. *See* Qumran Essenes

Esther, book of, 58, 69, 95, 140, 219, 237

Eumenes II, 44–45

Euphorion of Chalcis, 44

Euripides, 44, 47

"excerpted" texts (classic literature of ancient Judaism), 238–44; evidence of work of a scholar-scribe, 242–43; no running text, 241; passages known for liturgical/religious use, 241–42; small dimensions, 241; as study guides, 244

Exodus, book of, 53, 68n68, 158, 208, 220, 239, 240

Ezekiel, book of, 69, 103, 158

Ezra, as scribe, 67–68, 70, 104–5

Ezra-Nehemiah, 66–68, 69, 70; Levitical scribes, 67–68; on role of the scribe Ezra and scribal activity at temple in Jerusalem, 67–68, 70

377

INDEX OF SUBJECTS

First Jewish Revolt against Rome
(66–73 CE): destruction of Qumran,
1, 4, 174, 181, 271, 314–15, 319–20; and
Jerusalem temple library, 46; and
refugee caves, 101, 154; and Vespasian's Temple of Peace and library,
46

Galen, 43–44
Ge'ez (language), 78
Genesis, book of, 68n68, 77n94, 102,
103, 125, 158, 220, 236, 240n61
Genesis Apocryphon (1QapGen),
118, 124–25, 144n104, 160, 235, 250,
253–54
Gezer Calendar, 51
Giants, Book of, 79, 79n103, 81–82, 125,
159, 232, 233, 253
Gilgamesh Epic, 25
glassware, Qumran, 200
Great Isaiah Scroll (1QIsaᵃ), 118, 129,
161, 222, 242, 256
Greek libraries, ancient, 41–45, 48,
315. *See also* Hellenistic and Roman
worlds, scribes and libraries in
Groningen Hypothesis, 274

Habakkuk, book of, 13, 288
Hegesippus, 294, 306
Hellenistic and Roman period Israel,
scribes and writing in, 70–96;
Aramaic as language of scribal
learning, 78–79, 83, 96; Aramaic Levi
Document (ALD), 90–92, 159–60,
233, 245; Ben Sira on the scribal
profession and ideal scribe, 73–77,
105; Daniel, 92–94, 233–34; Enoch
and role of the scribe, 79–85, 87–88,
95, 105; Enoch literature, 77–85,
105, 232–34; epigraphic and literary
evidence, 70–96; Ezra the scribe,
67–68, 70, 104–5; First Maccabees,
71; Jerusalem temple, 72–73, 98;
Jubilees, 85–90, 233; postexilic
period libraries and archives, 98–101;
Second Maccabees, 71–72, 98–99;

Seleucid Charter of Antiochus III,
72–73, 98; Wisdom of Jesus ben Sira,
73–77
Hellenistic and Roman worlds, scribes
and libraries in, 39–48, 70–96,
182–83, 315; anonymity of scribes,
41, 48; Antiochus III's library, 44;
Aristotle's private library, 42, 46–47;
Greek idea of authorship, 40; Greek
libraries, 41–45, 48, 315; Israel,
70–96; library at Pergamum, 44–45,
188; library classification systems, 44,
48; Museion library at Alexandria,
40, 42–44, 315; Oxyrhyncus papyri,
41, 47; Ptolemaic empire, 40–41;
public libraries, 46–47; Roman
libraries, 45–47, 48, 182–83; scribes
and scribal profession, 39–41, 48;
scribes' subordinate social position
(slaves), 39–40; Seleucid empire,
40–41; Villa of the Papyri at Herculaneum, 45, 188; writing materials, 41;
Zenon papyri, 41. *See also* Hellenistic
and Roman period Israel, scribes and
writing in
Hellenistic-Roman period texts in
Qumran collection. *See* nonsectarian
works composed in the Hellenistic-Roman period (Qumran scroll
collection)
Herculaneum, library in the so-called
Villa of the Papyri, 45, 188
Herodians, 295
Herodotus, 47
Herod the Great, 100, 173, 314
Hesiod, 47
Hippolytus, 294, 306
Homer, 40, 47
horoscopy and astrology, 249–50
House of Books (ancient Egypt), 36, 48
House of Life (ancient Egyptian scribal
institution), 27–28, 36, 48
House of Literary Texts (Ugarit tablet
collection), 38, 188
House of the High Priest (Ugarit tablet
collection), 38–39

Index of Subjects

House of the Hurrian (or the Magician) Priest (Ugarit tablet collection), 38

inkwells at Khirbet Qumran, 195
inscriptions and other evidence for writing at Qumran, 147–49, 189–94, 285; abecedaries and student exercises, 191–92; contents of inscriptions, 191–92; languages (Greek), 189, 191–94; languages (Hebrew/Aramaic), 189, 191–94, 215; loci of main building (L30, L34, L35, and L39), 190, 192; loci of southeastern annex (L61, L84, L143), 190–91, 193; loci of western industrial complex (L110, L111, L124, L129, L130), 191, 193–94
Iron Age kingdoms of Israel and Judah, scribes and writing in, 49–58, 97; abecedaries, 52–53; amulets and magical significance of writing, 53; archaeological evidence for libraries and archives, 97; biblical references to scribal activity, 53–57; bullae and seals, 51–52, 97; epigraphic and literary evidence, 49–58, 104; familial scribal profession, 52, 56–57, 66; locations for scribal activity, 56, 57; ostraca collections, 51, 97; papyrus palimpsest from Wadi Murabba'at, 52; scribal training, 50; script (Old Hebrew or Paleo-Hebrew), 50; Siloam Tunnel inscription, 51
Isaiah, book of, 2, 69, 102, 124, 158, 219
Ishtar's Descent to the Underworld, 25
Israel Antiquities Authority, 52, 116, 123, 172

Jabez, scribal families at, 65–66
Jeremiah, book of, 2, 69, 128–29, 158, 315n9
Jerusalem temple: evidence for a temple library, 98–100, 315–17; Ezra the scribe and scribal activity at, 67–68, 70; First Jewish Revolt and the temple library, 46; Josephus and, 72–73, 98, 99–100, 304–5, 316; Nehemiah and founding of library at, 98–99; rabbinic sources on temple housing of Torah scrolls, 99–100; Seleucid Charter of Antiochus III, 72–73, 98; temple cult and calendar texts, 287–88; temple cult and Qumran sect participation, 208–9, 287–89, 301, 304–5
Jewish movements of the late Second Temple period (classical sources on), 294–308; Boethusians, 295, 298; Essenes, 166–67, 269–70, 295, 299–308, 317; Herodians and Zealots, 295; Pharisees, 295, 296–98; Sadducees, 295, 298–99; Samaritans, 295–96. *See also* Qumran Essenes
Job, book of, 127, 158, 220, 221, 253, 254n107
John Hyrcanus, 59, 258, 295, 312
Jonathan the Hasmonean, 4, 311
Jordanian Department of Antiquities, 117, 118, 171
Josephus: descriptions of Essenes, 166–67, 270, 299–305, 317; and the Jerusalem temple library, 72–73, 98, 99–100, 304–5, 316; on Jewish movements of the late Second Temple period, 166–67, 270, 294, 295–98, 299–305; and Seleucid Charter of Antiochus III, 72–73, 98
Joshua Apocryphon, 240
Jubilees, 85–90, 233; Abram as scribe, 89; Enoch as first scribe and visionary, 87–88; Enoch as priest in the garden of Eden, 87–88; heavenly tablets, 80–81, 86–87, 89–90; Jacob as priest and scribe, 89–90; Kainan and abuse of scribal art (as sin), 88–89; Levi as scribe and priest, 90; Moses as scribe, 85–87; Noah as priest and scribe, 88; Qumran manuscripts, 85, 160
Judas Maccabeus, 98–99, 315–16
Judean Desert text collections from late Second Temple period (non-Qumran): archaeological evidence of

379

INDEX OF SUBJECTS

manuscript collections from, 101–4;
Jewish Masada scrolls, 103–4, 156,
160; manuscripts from Naḥal Ḥever
caves, 102–3, 104; manuscripts from
Wadi Murabba'at caves, 52, 101–2,
104

Judges, book of, 158

Julius Solinus, 306

Kando (Dead Sea Scrolls dealer), 33,
121, 195

Ketef Hinnom amulets, 53

Ketef Yericho, caves of, 64

Ketuvim, 69

Kings, books of, 56, 65, 69, 142, 158

Kuntillet 'Ajrud graffiti, 51

Lachish ostraca, 51

Lamentations, book of, 158

Legio X Fretensis (Tenth Roman Legion), 173, 174, 181, 319

Levitical scribes: Aramaic Levi Document (ALD), 91–92; book of Chronicles, 66, 105; book of Ezra-Nehemiah, 67–68; Jubilees, 90; Levi and
combined office of scribe and priest,
90, 91–92

Leviticus, book of, 103, 142, 158, 220–21,
253, 254n107, 256

libraries: ancient Egypt, 35–37; ancient
Greece, 41–45, 48, 315; ancient Israel
and Judah, 16, 49–105; ancient Near
East, 21–39, 47–48; ancient Rome,
45–47, 48, 182–83; of Aristotle, 42,
46–47; definitions of, 8; distinction
between ancient archives and, 8,
31–32, 35–36; evidence for a Jerusalem temple library, 98–100, 315–17;
Hellenistic and Roman worlds,
39–48, 70–96, 182–83, 315; Iron
Age Israel and Judah, 97; Masada,
100–101, 183; Mesopotamia, 32–35;
postexilic period, 98–101; Ugarit,
37–39. *See also* Qumran Essene
library and scribal center

limestone cliff caves (Qumran scroll

caves), 17, 117–29, 164, 310, 318–19;
archaeology, 117–24; Cave 1Q, 118–19,
124–25, 152–54, 162–64; Cave 2Q,
119–20, 125, 160–61, 163, 164; Cave
3Q, 117, 120, 125–26, 152, 164, 263;
Cave 6Q, 117, 120, 127, 129, 151, 163,
320; Cave 11Q, 120–21, 127, 152–54,
162–64; Cave 53, 116, 122–23, 164;
cylindrical "scroll jars" with bowl-
shaped lids, 16–17, 118–22, 128–29,
150–51, 164, 196, 199, 264, 309; de
Vaux's excavation, 118–22; de Vaux's
numbering system, 116, 172; discoveries by bedouin shepherds, 118–21;
functions and reasons for deposition
of scrolls, 127–29, 150–51, 164, 264,
318–19; later excavations, 122–23;
linen textiles, 152–53; long-term
scroll storage, 17, 128–29, 150–51, 164,
264, 318; ostraca inscriptions (south
of Cave 6Q), 147–49; other material
finds, 119, 121, 152–53, 154; "Timothy's
Cave" (GrQ29), 122, 123, 164, 309

limestone vessels at Khirbet Qumran,
200

linen textiles at Khirbet Qumran,
152–53, 195–96, 292

Lucullus the elder, 45

Lucullus the younger, 45, 46–47

Lugale, myth of, 34

Luke's Gospel, 105, 106n181; scribes in,
109–10

Maccabees, books of, 71, 94n149,
98–99, 238

Marcus Cato, 46–47

Mark's Gospel, 105; scribes in, 106–8

marl terrace caves (Qumran scroll
caves), 17, 130–47, 164–65, 310, 320;
archaeology, 130–40; Cave 4Q, 4, 17,
129, 130–35, 137–46, 157–58, 165, 219–
23, 240–44, 257–61, 320; Cave 5Q,
130, 135, 146, 165; Cave 7Q, 130, 136,
146–49, 163, 165; Cave 8Q, 136, 146,
152, 165, 195–96; Cave 9Q, 130, 136,
146; Cave 10Q, 130, 135–36; Cave A,

Index of Subjects

130; Cave F, 130; Cave H, 130; de Vaux's excavations, 131–37, 138–39; de Vaux's numbering system, 116, 172; discovery by bedouins, 130, 138–39; functions and reasons for deposition, 136–37, 150–51, 164–65, 264, 319–20; as habitation caves, 136–37; inscriptions, 147–49; man-made creation of, 130–31, 164–65; scroll storage, 137, 264, 319–20; as temporary resting places for burial of scrolls, 137, 220

marriage and the Qumran sect, 271, 282–83, 299–304

Masada: construction and architecture, 100–101; indications of Qumran inhabitants among refugees, 103–4; Jewish Masada scrolls, 103–4, 156, 160; wall niches and temple library at, 100–101, 183

maskilim (wise circle of scholar-scribes), 94

Masoretic recension and "proto-MT" recension manuscripts, 221–22

Matthew's Gospel, 105, 106n181; scribes in, 109–11

Melchizedek scroll, 160

Menander, 47

Mesopotamia, 22–26, 32–35; administrative texts, 32–33; archives and libraries, 32–35; colophons, 24–25, 48; Ebla corpus, 32–33; elite scholar-scribes and literary culture, 23–26; letters, diplomatic texts, and lexical lists, 33; library in the Shamash temple at Sippar, 32, 34, 188, 248; library of Assurbanipal at Nineveh, 32, 33–34, 39, 48; literary and documentary texts, 34–35; school texts, 34–35; scientific and religious lore, 34; scribal duties, 23; scribal education/training, 22–23, 48; scribal families and apprenticeship system, 25–26, 35; scribal languages, 23, 96; scribes/scribal profession, 22–26; *sepiru*, 22, 96; small, private collections, 32, 34–35; state-sponsored collections,

32; writing on cuneiform clay tablets, 24–25, 31–34

Metroon (central archive of Athens), 40

Miqṣat Maʿaśê ha-Torah (MMT), 7, 13–14, 224, 226, 230, 272, 280–84

mishmarot, 244–48. *See also* calendar texts at Qumran

Mount Gerizim inscriptions, 59–60

MUL.APIN (astronomical compendium), 82–83, 244, 245

Museion library at Alexandria, 40, 42–44, 315

Naḥal Ḥever caves: Cave of Horrors (Cave 8), 102–3, 155; Cave of Letters (Cave 5/6), 102–3, 155; manuscripts from, 102–3, 104, 128, 155; as refugee caves, 102, 155

Nahum, book of, 142, 288

Neleus, 42

Nergal and Ereshkigal, myth of, 36

Noah, birth of, in 1 Enoch, 78–79, 254

nonsectarian works composed in the Hellenistic-Roman period (Qumran scroll collection), 11, 17–18, 159–60, 218, 236–38; Cave 4Q scrolls, 140–41, 142, 159–60, 236–37; hymns, prayers, and liturgies (liturgical texts), 237; parabibilical works in Hebrew, 236; sapiential literature, 236–37; single-copy works, 236–37

Numbers, book of, 102, 158, 221, 240

opisthographs, 144–45, 260–61

ostraca collections: ancient Egypt, 28; Aramaic administrative ostraca in Persian period Yehud, 64; inscriptions found at Qumran, 147–49, 189–94, 285; Iron Age Israel and Judah, 51, 97

Oxyrhyncus papyri, 41, 47

"Paleo-Hebrew" script, 137, 141, 161, 163, 220–21, 250, 256, 262–63; inscriptions found on vessels and ostraca at Qumran, 189, 191–94, 215;

381

INDEX OF SUBJECTS

Iron Age Israel and Judah, 50; Mount Gerizim inscriptions, 59–60; Persian period Israel and Judah, 59–60, 61, 64; Wadi ed-Daliyeh papyri, 61

Palestine Archaeological Museum (PAM), 102, 131, 320

palimpsests: Cave 4Q, 144–45, 260–61; Wadi Murabba'at papyrus fragment, 52

Pantainos's library at Athens, 46

papyri: ancient Egypt, 28, 35–37; caves of Ketef Yericho, 64; Elephantine papyri, 41, 62–63; Oxyrhyncus, 41, 47; Persian period Israel and Judah, 41, 58, 60–61, 62–63, 64; Qumran Cave 4Q "working" texts, 144; Qumran Cave 6Q, 163, 320; Qumran Cave 7Q fragments, 147, 163; Villa of the Papyri at Herculaneum, 45, 188; Wadi ed-Daliyeh, 60–61; Wadi Murabba'at, 52; Zenon, 41

Parables or Similitudes, Book of, 79, 81

Pergamum, library at, 44–45, 188

Persian period kingdoms of Israel and Judah, scribes and writing in, 58–70, 104–5; Aramaic administrative ostraca, 64; Aramaic language and script, 58, 59–60, 61, 64; Aramaic stamp impressions, 64; book of Chronicles, 65–66; book of Ezra-Nehemiah, 66–68; clay bullae, 61, 64; coins, 64; Elephantine papyri, 41, 62–63; epigraphic evidence, 58–70, 104–5; fragile writing materials, 58; Levitical scribes, 66, 67–68, 105; Mount Gerizim inscriptions, 59–60; Paleo-Hebrew script, 59–60, 61, 64; papyrus documents from caves of Ketef Yericho, 64; Samaria province, 59–61; scribal families at Jabez, 65–66; scribes and classical literature of Jewish canon, 68–70; Wadi ed-Daliyeh papyri, 60–61; Yehud settlement, 63–68

pesharim, 3, 13–14, 15, 224, 226, 229–30, 290

Pesher Habakkuk (1QpHab), 13, 14, 15, 118, 124, 160, 161, 162, 221n9, 235, 287n35, 288n35, 290n38

Pharisees: Alexander Jannaeus's treatment of, 298; classical sources on, 295, 296–98; purity regulations, 282, 284; Synoptic Gospels on scribes and, 107–8, 109–10, 111

Philippi, forum library in, 46

Philodemus of Gadara, 45

Philo of Alexandria, 166, 294, 299–300, 303–4, 307, 317

physiognomy, 249–50

Pinakes of Callimachus, 44, 48

Pindar, 47

Plato, 47

Pliny the Elder, 167, 269–70, 294, 305–6

polygamy, 283

Porphyry, 294, 306

postexilic period Israel and Judah, libraries and archives of, 98–101

pottery corpus at Khirbet Qumran, 17, 134–35, 150–51, 196–99; absence of certain types of pottery, 197–99; plain, undecorated, and utilitarian, 197, 199, 291; samples subjected to Instrumental Neutron Activation Analysis (INAA), 197–99; samples subjected to petrographic analysis, 197–99; scroll jars, 16–17, 118–22, 128–29, 150–51, 164, 196, 199, 264, 309

Prayer of Nabonidus, 93n143, 142, 188, 233, 237, 254–55

property, communal: classical sources on Essenes and, 299, 300–301; Qumran sect and, 285–86, 299, 300–301; sectarian texts on, 285–86

prophetic books (Nevi'im), 69

Proverbs, book of, 69, 75, 82

Psalms, book of, 2, 69, 102, 103, 127, 158, 219, 230, 288, 315n9, 318

pseudo-Ezekiel texts, 236

Ptolemaic empire, 40–41

Ptolemy I Soter, 42–43

Index of Subjects

Ptolemy II Philadelphos, 42–44, 315

Ptolemy III Euergetes, 42–43

purity, ritual, 7, 281–84; classical sources on Essenes and, 302–3; food and drink, 7, 151, 283–84, 302–3; mikvaoth and, 202–6, 215–16, 276, 292, 302–3, 319; water installations and ritual immersion, 202–6, 276, 292, 319

Qumran-Essene hypothesis (classic), 3–7, 166–70, 269–73; anti–de Vaux camp, 168–70; basic hypothesis and historical overview, 270–73; critiques and objections, 4–7, 168–70, 269–73; a new synthesis, 18, 269–308; and nomenclature "Qumran Community," 273; revisions to, 5–7, 168, 272–73

Qumran Essene library and scribal center, 1, 18, 182–88, 263–65, 311–20; choice of site and reasons for establishment, 1, 315–17; last days and destruction of the settlement, 1, 4, 174, 181, 271, 314–15, 319–20; library complex and possible scriptorium or "scroll workshop," 17, 177, 182–88, 310; reign of Alexander Jannaeus, 5, 17, 311–15; scribes' collection of scrolls from around Judea, 161–63, 261–62, 272, 317–19; scroll storage, 17, 128–29, 150–51, 164, 264. *See also* archaeology of Khirbet Qumran site and Qumran settlement; Qumran scroll caves; Qumran scroll collections

Qumran Essenes, 18, 269–94, 299–308, 309–20; and absence of name "Essene" in the scrolls, 272, 307–8; apocalyptic eschatology and predeterminism, 290–91, 303, 304; archaeological evidence that supports Essene habitation, 170, 291–94; celibacy question, 230–32, 271, 299–304; characteristics, 273–91; classical sources on, 166–67, 269–70, 295, 299–308, 317; Dead Sea region location, 305–6;

foundation of settlement and library site, 311–17; and Jerusalem temple cult, 208–9, 287–89, 301, 304–5; as Jewish practitioners of Greco-Roman philosophical virtue, 299, 300; Josephus on, 166–67, 270, 299–305, 317; legal interpretations, 6–7, 229–30, 280–84; marriage question, 271, 282–83, 299–304; organization and leadership roles, 278–80; Philo on, 166, 294, 299–300, 303–4, 307, 317; Pliny on, 167, 269–70, 294, 305–6; population estimates, 181–82; prayer and worship, 286–89; procedures for admission into the sect, 226–28, 276–78, 302; procedures for expulsion from the sect, 227–29, 277; sectarian texts on, 273–91; separation from all Israel, 289–90; sharing of property, 285–86, 299, 300–301; women question, 155, 202, 212–13, 214, 216, 230–32, 292, 319

Qumran scroll caves, 16–17, 115–65; archaeology, 117–24, 130–40; cylindrical "scroll jars" with bowl-shaped lids, 16–17, 118–22, 128–29, 150–51, 164, 196, 199, 264, 309; discoveries by bedouin shepherds, 118–21, 130–38, 139; excavations, 118–23, 130–37, 138–39, 166–76; functions/reasons for deposition of scrolls, 127–29, 136–37, 149, 150–51, 164–65, 264, 318–19, 319–20; as habitation caves, 136–37; limestone cliff caves, 17, 117–29, 164, 310, 318–19; marl terrace caves, 17, 130–47, 164–65, 310, 320; scroll "burial," 129, 137, 164, 213, 220; scroll storage, 17, 128–29, 137, 150–51, 164, 264, 318–20. *See also* archaeology of Khirbet Qumran site and Qumran settlement; limestone cliff caves (Qumran scroll caves); marl terrace caves (Qumran scroll caves)

Qumran scroll collections, 17–18, 155–65, 217–65, 310; affiliated literature,

INDEX OF SUBJECTS

11–12, 17–18, 159–60, 218, 223, 232–36, 310, 316–17; Aramaic texts, 252–55; calendars and *mishmarot*, 12, 232–33, 244–48; classical literature of ancient Judaism, 11, 17–18, 158–60, 218–23, 238–44; composition of black inks, 156–57; conspicuously absent works, 238; content of manuscripts, 157–61, 163–65; cryptic script manuscripts, 255–57; esoteric texts of Cave 4Q, 18, 248–52; excerpted texts, 238–44; existence of a "Qumran scribal practice," 262–63; four categories, 11–16, 217–38; insights from paleography and orthography, 261–63; manuscripts, 155–65; nonsectarian works composed in the Hellenistic-Roman period, 11, 17–18, 159–60, 218, 236–38; places of manufacture, 156–57, 272, 317–19; scribal exercises and other documentary texts, 143–44, 257–60; scribal hands, 161–63, 261–62, 272; scribal lists (Cave 4Q), 251–52; scrolls gathered from around Judea, 161–63, 261–62, 272, 317–19; sectarian texts, 4–5, 12–16, 17–18, 159–60, 218, 223–32, 273–91, 310, 316–17; texts indicating scribal interests and activities, 18, 238–60

Ramat Raḥel, 64, 201
Ras Shamra site, 29
refugee caves: and Bar Kokhba revolt, 101, 102; feminine-gendered implements as evidence of, 154–55; First Jewish Revolt, 101, 154–55; Naḥal Ḥever, 102, 155; question of Qumran caves as, 154–55; Wadi ed-Daliyeh, 155; Wadi Murabba'at, 101, 154–55
Rogantinius's library at Timgad, 46
Roman libraries, 45–47, 48, 182–83. *See also* Hellenistic and Roman worlds, scribes and libraries in
Rule of Blessings (1Q28b; also called Sb), 13, 14, 161, 224, 276n18
Rule of the Congregation (1Q28a; also

called Serek Ha'edah, Sa), 13, 13n35, 14, 15, 124, 138, 159–60, 161, 164n157, 224–25, 228n26, 229, 230n33, 231, 271, 274n16, 276, 278n22, 291–92, 300, 302
Ruth, book of, 158

Sabbath observances of the Qumran sect, 281, 301
Sadducees, 272, 282, 295, 298–99
Samaria (Persian province), 59–61
Samaria ostraca, 51, 97
Samaritans, 295–96
Samuel, books of, 65, 69, 158
sapiential literature, 236–37
Schøyen collection, 121, 195
Scipio, 45
scribal lists (Cave 4Q), 251–52
scribes in the Synoptic Gospels, 105–11; Jesus on, 111; and leadership elite, 107–8; and the magi, 110; the so-called woe passages, 109–10, 111; teaching role, 106–7
"scroll jars" (cylindrical jars with bowl-shaped lids), 16–17, 118–22, 128–29, 150–51, 164, 196, 199, 264, 309
scroll wrappers at Khirbet Qumran, 152–53, 195–96, 292
"sect," as term, 10–11
"sectarian component," as phrase, 10–11
sectarian texts (Qumran scroll collection), 4–5, 12–16, 17–18, 159–60, 218, 223–32, 273–91, 310, 316–17; Cave 1Q, 124–25, 159–60, 229–30; Cave 4Q, 138, 140–41, 142–43, 159–60, 229–30; cryptic script texts, 256; definition and characteristics, 12–16, 224–30; differences among, 273–76; isolating characteristics of the Qumran sect through, 223–32, 273–91; legal interpretations, 6–7, 229–30, 280–84; procedures for admission and expulsion from the sect, 226–30, 276–78; purity regulations, 281–84; rules of entry for children born into the sect, 228–29, 231, 277–78;

384

Index of Subjects

sectarian emphasis on boundaries and group identity, 225–26; sectarian vocabulary peculiar to, 14–16, 229; and women in the sect, 228, 230–32, 271, 275–78

Seleucid Charter of Antiochus III, 72–73, 98

Seleucid empire: calendars, 246–47; scribes and scribal profession in, 40–41

Seneca, 43

sepiru, 22, 96

Serek Ha'edah (or Rule of the Congregation; Sa), 13–14, 124, 161, 224–25, 229, 231, 271; and issue of women and children in the sect, 229, 231, 271, 275–76

Serek Hayahad (S, Community Rule), 3, 13, 14, 118, 124, 223–27, 229, 232, 243–44, 274–77, 285, 286–89, 291; Doctrine of the Two Spirits and predestination, 291; on purity of food and drink, 284; recensions of, 274–75, 276; as rule text, 275–76; on sharing of property, 285

Shamash temple at Sippar, library of, 32, 34, 188, 248

Shaphan family of scribes, 52, 56–57, 66

Shimshai the scribe, 66, 70

Siloam Tunnel inscription, 51

Sirach / Ben Sira, Ecclesiasticus, 11, 73–77, 103, 105, 111, 125, 160, 236

Six-Day War (1967), 33, 171

Sobek, 36, 37

Song of Songs (Canticles), book of, 158

Songs of the Sabbath Sacrifice: Jewish Masada scrolls, 103–4, 160; at Qumran, 103–4, 160, 164, 224, 229

Sophocles, 44, 47

Stoicism, 46–47

Strabo, 42, 43

sundial, Qumran, 248

Tale of Ahiqar, 63

Tale of Sinuhe, 37

Tale of the Eloquent Peasant, 37

Teacher of Righteousness, 3–4, 226, 247, 288, 311–12

Tebtunis temple library, 36, 188

Tell el-Amarna, archive at, 35–36

Tel Zayit, abecedary of, 52–53

Temple of Peace, 46

Temple of Serapis (Alexandria), 43

Temple Scroll: as affiliated text, 12, 159, 160, 235; brought to Qumran from the outside, 157; Cave 11Q, 121, 127, 293; Kando family's possession, 33, 121; scroll wrapper, 153; on toilet facilities, 292–93

Thanksgiving Hymns (1QHᵃ; also called Hodayot), 3, 13, 14, 15, 118, 124, 157, 159, 221n9, 224, 229, 235, 286, 291, 318

Theophrastus, 42

Thucydides, 47

"Timothy's Cave" (GrQ29), 122, 123, 164, 309

Titus, 46, 99

Tobit, book of, 63n48, 69, 219n3, 221, 254

Torah: composition by Persian period scribes, 68–69; housing of Torah scrolls at Jerusalem temple, 99–100; and Qumran scroll collections, 158, 219–21; sectarian texts on the sect's legal interpretations, 6–7, 229–30, 280–84

Trajan, 46

Udjahorresnet (Egyptian scribe), 67

Ugarit, 29–31, 37–39; archives and libraries, 37–39; familial scribal profession, 29; House of Literary Texts, 38, 188; House of the High Priest, 38–39; House of the Hurrian (or the Magician) Priest, 38; private collections, 38–39; Royal Palace archives, 37–38; scribal function of record-keeping and ritual texts, 30–31; scribal languages, 29; scribal positions in royal court and temples, 29–30; scribal profession, 29–31; scribal training and schools, 30, 38;

385

INDEX OF SUBJECTS

scripts, 29, 38; writing on clay tablets, 29, 30, 37–39

Varro, 45

Vaux, Roland de: and animal bone deposits at Qumran, 206–7; and cemeteries at Qumran, 209–12; chronology of archaeological phases of Khirbet Qumran, 172–76; classic Qumran-Essene hypothesis, 5–7, 166–70; excavations, 122, 131–37, 138–39, 166–76, 201–13; labeling room L30 of main building a scriptorium/library, 177, 183–88; marl terrace cave excavations, 131–37, 138–39; numbering system, 116, 172; and pottery at Qumran, 150; and the stepped pools at Qumran, 203. *See also* Qumran-Essene hypothesis (classic)

Vespasian, 46, 99

Wadi ed-Daliyeh caves, 60–61, 128, 155

Wadi Murabba'at caves, 52, 101–2, 104, 128, 154–55, 257; Iron Age papyrus palimpsest, 52; manuscript collections from, 52, 101–2, 104; as refugee caves, 101, 154–55

War Scroll (1Q33; also called War Rules, M), 13, 14, 15, 118, 124, 159, 164n157, 224, 229n29, 230, 230n32, 290, 292, 293

Watchers, Book of the, 78, 78n96, 84, 84n118, 233

water installations at Khirbet Qumran, 178–79, 202–6, 215–16, 319; cisterns, 176, 178–79, 191, 202–3, 206; mikvaoth, 202–6, 215–16, 276, 292, 302–3, 319; and ritual immersion, 202–6, 276, 292, 302–3, 319; stepped pools, 178–79, 180, 202–6, 215–16, 309, 319

Wicked Priest, 4, 226, 247, 288, 312

Wisdom of Ben Sira, 73–77, 125, 236–37; on the scribal profession and qualities of the ideal scribe, 73–77, 105

Wisdom of Solomon, 238

women at Qumran: dearth of evidence for, 154–55, 202, 214, 216, 292, 319; gender identity of cemetery remains, 212–13, 231, 292; and the sectarian texts, 228, 230–32, 271, 275–78

Xenophon, 47

Yehud settlement, Persian period, 63–68

Zadok the scribe, 66

Zealots, 295

Zenodotus, librarian of the Museion, 44, 48

Zenon papyri, 41

Zephaniah, book of, 142

Zodiacal Physiognomy (4Q186), 249–50, 256

Index of Scripture and Other Ancient Texts

HEBREW BIBLE / OLD TESTAMENT

Genesis

1:27	283
5	80n106
5:21–24	77
5:23–24	80n106
5:24	87
5:25	84n118
7:9	283
11:1–9	89
11:27	254
27:19–21	143, 257

Exodus

5	56
12–13	241
15:17–18	289
18:21	278
18:25	278
19:9b	239n55
20:21	223, 241
21:35–22:5	242–43
22:2–4	243n70
28:2	107n187
29:21	107n187
30:7–8	88
31:10	107n187
34:10	239n55
34:27	86n125
35–40	68n68

Leviticus

10:10	281
11:47–13:1	243
15	204
15:2	204
15:5	204
15:12	204
15:13	204
15:14–15	243
15:19	204
15:22	204
15:25	204
15:27	204
18:13	282
19:1–4	243
19:9–15	243
19:26	84
20:13	243
24:20–22	241, 242, 243
25:38–43	242
25:39–43	241
26:25	297
27:30–34	243

Numbers

1–2	14, 278
6:24–26	53
19:1–10	281n28
24:15–17	223, 241
29:14–[25]	242, 243
29:32–30:1	241, 242, 243

INDEX OF SCRIPTURE AND OTHER ANCIENT TEXTS

Deuteronomy

1:15	56, 278
3	219n5
5	241
5:1–6:1	241
8	241
8:5–11	241, 241n64, 242
11	241
14:[13]–17	242
14:[13]–21	243
16:13–14	241, 242, 243
18:10–11	84
21:15–17	283
23:26–24:8	219n5
24:1–4	283
27:4–6	296n48
29:9	56
31:28	56
32	219n5, 241
33:8–11	223, 241

Joshua

1:10	56
1:16–17	128
3:2	56

2 Samuel

5:2	110
8:17	54
9	258
20:25	54, 65

1 Kings

4:3	54
14:19	97n158
14:29	97n158
15:7	97n158
15:23	97n158
15:31	97n158
16:5	97n158
16:14	97n158
16:20	97n158
16:27	97n158
22:39	97n158
22:45	97n158

2 Kings

1:18	97n158
8:23	97n158
10:34	97n158
12:10	65
12:11	54
12:19	97n158
13:8	97n158
13:12	97n158
14:15	97n158
14:18	97n158
14:28	97n158
15:6	97n158
15:11	97n158
15:15	97n158
15:21	97n158
15:26	97n158
15:31	97n158
15:36	97n158
16:19	97n158
18:13	51
18:18	54
18:26	54
18:37	54
19:2	54
20:20	97n158
21:17	97n158
21:25	97n158
22	57
22:3	54, 56
22:8	54
22:8–14	65
22:9	54
22:10	54
22:12	54, 56
23:28	97n158
24:5	97n158
25:19	54
25:22	56

1 Chronicles

2:55	65
18:16	65
24:6	66
24:7–19	245n76
27:32–34	66

388

Index of Scripture and Other Ancient Texts

2 Chronicles

24:11	65
26:11	66
32:30	51
34:13	66, 68
34:15–20	65

Ezra 93, 96, 255n110

4:8	66
4:9	66
4:17	66
4:23	66
7:1–6	67
7:11	67
7:12	67
7:21	67
7:25	67
10:10	67n66
10:16	67n66

Nehemiah

8:1	67
8:4	67
8:7	67
8:8	67
8:9	67
8:12	67
8:13	67
13:13	66

Esther

3:12	58n31
8:9	58n31

Job

12:24	297

Psalms

45:2(1)	54
90	239n57
91	251
91–118	239n57
94:21	297
103	239n57
104–111	239n57
107:40	297

112	239n57
119	241
151	222
154	314

Proverbs

3:35	91
25:1	55, 57

Song of Songs (Canticles) 158

Isaiah

33:18	55
36:1	51
36:3	54
36:11	54
36:22	54
37:2	54
40	240n58
45–49	239n58
52–54	239n58
58	239n58

Jeremiah

8:8	55, 57, 105
26:24	56
29:3	56
32:6–15	128
32:10–11	51
32:13–15	128
36:10	52, 55, 56
36:11	56, 57n27
36:12	55, 56
36:20	55
36:21	55
36:26	55
36:32	55
37:15	55
37:20	55
40:5	56
52:25	54

Lamentations 158

Ezekiel

10:6–11:1	240n59

389

INDEX OF SCRIPTURE AND OTHER ANCIENT TEXTS

23:14–15	240n59
23:17–18	240n59
23:44–47	240n59
40–44	84
41:3–6	240n59

Daniel

1	93n144
1–6	93n145
1–7	93n144
1:4	93, 234
2	93
2–7	93n144
4	93, 233, 237
5	93
7–12	93
7:1	93
7:10	94
7:25	246–47
8–12	93n144
9:2	93, 234
9:24–27	234
10:21	94
11:33	94
11:35	234
12:1	94
12:3	76, 94, 234
12:4	93
12:10	234

Micah

2:6	283
5:2	110

Nahum

3:17	55

Habakkuk | 13, 288

Zephaniah | 142

Malachi

1:10	288
3:23–24 MT	107
4:5–6	107

NEW TESTAMENT

Matthew

2:1–4	110
7:29	109
9:3	109
9:11	109
9:34	109
12:24	109
13:52	111
15:1	109
16:21	109
17:10	109
17:14	109
20:18	109
21:23	109
22:16	295n47
22:34–40	107n186
22:35	109
22:41–43	109
23:1–3	110
23:23–36	109–10
23:34	111
26:3–4	109
26:47	109
27:1	109

Mark

1:21–22	106
1:22	106
2:6	106
2:16	106, 107, 108
3:6	295n47
3:22	106, 108n189, 109
5:30	108
7:1	106, 107
7:5	106, 107, 108
8:31	106
9:11	106, 107, 109
9:14	106
10:33	106
11:18	106
11:27	106, 108
12:13	295n47
12:18–27	298
12:28	106, 107

390

Index of Scripture and Other Ancient Texts

12:32	106, 107		23:9	106n184, 108n191
12:32–33	107		24:5	270n1
12:35	106, 107, 109		24:14	270n1
12:38	106		26:5	270n1
12:38–40	107		28:22	270n1
14:1	106, 108			
14:43	106, 108		**1 Corinthians**	
14:53	106, 108		1:20	106n184
15:1	106, 108			
15:31	106			

APOCRYPHA AND PSEUDEPIGRAPHA

Luke				
4:32	109		**1 Enoch**	
5:17	109n194		1–36	78, 78n96, 84, 84n118, 233
5:21	109		10:20–22	84
5:30	108, 109		12:3–4	79
9:22	109		13:3–7	80, 82
9:37	109		13:4–6	84
10:25	109		14:1	80
10:25–28	107n186		14:4	80
11:37–38	109		14:7	80
11:42–44	110n196		15:1	80
11:42–54	109–10		37–71	79, 81
11:46–52	111n196		69:8–10	81
18:32	109		72–82	78, 78n97, 82–83,
19:47	109			232–33, 245, 246, 248
20:1	109		72:1	254
20:41	109		81:1	80n108, 82
20:46	109		81:1–2	82
22:2	109		81:2	80n108
22:47	109		82:1	82
22:66	109		82:1–3	82, 83–84
23:10	109		83–90	78, 233
23:35	109		83:2	82
			85–90	78n96
John			89:61	82
8:3	106n184		89:68	82
			89:73–74	84
Acts			89:76–77	82
4:5	106n184		91–107	79n96
5:17	270n1		91–108	79n100
5:34	109n194		91:1–4	82
6:12	106n184		92–105	78, 80–81, 233
15:5	270n1		92:1	80
19:35	106n184		93:2	80, 80n108, 82
23:8	298		98:11	78n96

391

INDEX OF SCRIPTURE AND OTHER ANCIENT TEXTS

98:15	81, 81n109	4:21	87
99:10	81	4:23	87–88
100:12	78n96	5:23–27	233
103:2	80n108	6:1–3	88
103:3–4	78n96	6:17	87n127
103:4	78n96	6:17–18	88
103:7–8	78n96	6:23–31	88
103:15	78n96	6:35	87n127
104:10	81	7:3–5	88
104:10–13	81	7:20–26	88
104:12	81	8:2	88
105:1	78n96	8:3–4	88
106–107	78–79, 254	8:10	88n131
106:1–2	250	8:11	88
106:19	80n108	10:10–13	88
		10:10–14	251
2 Enoch		11	89
23	84n118	11:8	88n132
		11:16	89
1 Esdras		12:16–18	88–89n132
2:15	70	12:25–27	89
2:16	70	13:4	89
2:21	70	13:9	89
2:25	70	13:16	89
8:3	70	14:11–12	89
8:8	70	14:19	89
8:9	70	15:2	89
9:39	70	15:25	87n127
9:40	67n62	16:20–24	89
9:42	70	16:30	87n127
9:49	67n62, 70	18:5–8	89
		18:12	89
2 Esdras / 4 Ezra		19:14	89
3–14	67n62	21:10	89
		23	81n108
Jubilees		24:33	87n127
1:5	85–86	31:3	90
1:7	86	31:14–17	90
1:25–38	85n121	31:26	90
1:26–27	86	32:1	90
1:27	86	32:3	90
1:29	86	32:4–6	90
3:10	86n127	32:21–26	89–90
3:27	88	32:27	90
4:5	86–87n127	32:30	90
4:17–19	87	44:1	90

Index of Scripture and Other Ancient Texts

45:15	90
47:9	85n124

Judith	238

Letter to Aristeas	
9	42n100, 43

1 Maccabees	
5:42	71
7:12	71
7:13	71

2 Maccabees	
2:13	98n161
2:13–14	315
2:13–15	98
2:14	98
2:23	71
6:18	71, 75

4 Maccabees	
5:4	71n78

Sirach / Ben Sira, *Ecclesiasticus*	
3:21–22	77
11:1	91
22:7	75n87
24:1–29	75
24:23	75
24:32–34	76
24:33	75n87
30:3	75n87
34:1–8	77
37:19	75n87
38	110
38:24	49
38:34–39:3	75, 76
38:34–39:11	74
39:4	75
39:5	75
39:6–8	75
39:7	76
49:11–13	67n62
49:13	98n161
50:1–3	73n81

50:1–21	73
50:27	73, 77
51	73n81

Testament of Abraham B	
11:3	88n129
11:3–10	84n118

Tobit	63n48, 69, 219n3, 221, 254

Wisdom of Solomon	238

DEAD SEA SCROLLS

Aramaic Levi Document (ALD)	
4:5–13	92
5:8	91
6–10	92
7:4	91
8:8	87n128
10:10	91
13:4	91
13:5	91
13:6	92

CD (Cairo Damascus Document)	
1:5–8	4–5
1:11	312n2
1:14–21	297
2:18–19	233
3:14–15	225, 246
4:14–18	288
4:15	233
4:17–18	209n168
4:19–5:1	283
5:7–11	235n47, 295–96, 282, 297
6:11–12	288
6:11–20	209n168
6:18–19	286
6:19	225
8:21	277
9:2–4	252
10:7–10	233
10:14–11:18	280–81
10:17–19	281

393

INDEX OF SCRIPTURE AND OTHER ANCIENT TEXTS

10:21	281
11:16–17	281
12:1–2	283
12:12	234
12:15–27	303
12:19–20	291
13:22	234
14:3–6	279
14:12–17	285
14:20–21	285
15:5–6	228, 277–78
15:7–9	228, 277
16:2–4	233, 246

1QIsaᵃ (Great Isaiah Scroll)

col. 12	187

1Q8 (Isaiahᵇ)   118, 222

1Q11 (Psᵇ⁾)   162

1Q14 (pMic)   287n35, 290n38

1QpHab (Pesher Habakkuk)

7 10–11	307, 307n83
8 1	307, 307n83
11:2–8	247

1Q17 (Jubᵃ)   85n122

1Q18 (Jubᵇ)   85n122

1Q19 (Noah)   236

1QapGen (Genesis Apocryphon)

19:25–26	84n118

1Q21 (Levi)   90

1Q23 (EnGiantsᵃ)   79n12

1Q26 (Instruction)   234

1Q27 (Mysteries)   234, 235, 246, 250n95

1Q28 (Serekh Hayaḥad, Manual of Discipline, Order of the Community, Community Rule, S)

cols. 3–4	291
1:6	231
1:7–9	225
1:9–11	225, 289–90
1:13–15	246
1:16–20	225
3:13	234
5:13	276n18
5:20–23	226–27, 276
5:23	14, 278
5:24–6:1	252
6:2–6	276
6:4-5	208n168
6:6–8	244, 287
6:7–8	217
6:8–9	279
6:13–23	227, 277, 302
6:22	208n168
6:27–7:2	227, 277
7:6–8	285
7:9–12	279
7:13	279, 303
7:16–17	227, 277
7:17	227, 277
7:22–24	277
7:22–25	227
9:3–5	288–89
9:12	234
9:21	234
9:26–10:4	286

1Q28a (Serek Ha‘edah, Rule of the Congregation, Sa)

1:5	225
1:6–9	229, 278n22
1:23–25	14
1:27–2:1	280
2:11–22	208n168
2:17–22	276, 287

1Q28b (Rule of Blessings, Sb)

1:1	234
3:22	234

394

Index of Scripture and Other Ancient Texts

5:20	234	4Q11 (paleoGen-Exod^{l})	222

1Q33 (War Scroll, War Rules, M)
7:6–7   293
9:1–5   290–91

1Q34 (Festival Prayers)   237

1QH^{a} (Hodayot, Thanksgiving Hymns)
5:12   234
7:20   234
7:21   234
10:23–27   290
10:31–38   297
12:5   297

1Q41–1Q70bis   125n38

1Q63–68   252n102

1Q70   145n107, 260n134

1Q71 (Dan^{a})   92n143

1Q72 (Dan^{b})   92n143

2Q3 (Exod^{b})   239n55

2Q18 (Sir)   73, 236

2Q19 (Jub^{a})   85n122

2Q20 (Jub^{b})   85n122

2Q26 (EnGiants)   79n12

3Q5 (Jub *olim* apProph)
3:1   85n122

3Q12–13   252n102

4Q1 (Gen–Exod^{a})   222

4Q2 (Gen^{b})   222

4Q7 (Gen^{g})   118, 188

4Q11 (paleoGen-Exod^{l})   222

4Q13 (Exod^{b})   222

4Q14 (Exod^{c})   222, 239, 241, 256

4Q15 (Exod^{d})   69, 75, 220, 239, 241, 241n65, 317

4Q16 (Exod^{e})   239, 241

4Q17 (Exod–Lev^{f})   69, 75, 138n82, 158, 220, 221–22, 317

4Q22 (paleoExod^{m})   221, 221n10

4Q27 (Num^{b})   162, 222

4Q28 (Deut^{a})   75, 219n5, 317

4Q30 (Deut^{c})   219n5

4Q34 (Deut^{g})   222

4Q35 (Deut^{h})   223

4Q37 (Deut^{j})   222, 239, 241, 243n72

4Q38 (Deut^{k1})   162, 239, 243n71, 243n72

4Q38a (Deut^{k2})   162

4Q41 (Deut^{n})   239, 239n55, 241, 241n64, 242, 243, 260

4Q44 (Deut^{q})   222, 239, 241, 243n72

4Q45 (paleoDeut^{s})   69, 75, 138n82, 220

4Q47 (Josh^{a})   222

4Q49 (Judg^{a})   222

4Q51–53 (Samuel fragments)   4n9

4Q51 (Sam^{a})   187, 187n87, 222

INDEX OF SCRIPTURE AND OTHER ANCIENT TEXTS

4Q52 (Sam^b)	138n82, 220, 222, 222n14, 317	4Q109 (Qoh^a)	220, 263
4Q53 (Sam^c)	161, 162	4Q111 (Lamentations)	142
4Q54 (Kings)	142	4Q112 (Dan^a)	92n143
4Q57 (Isa^c)	162, 297	4Q113 (Dan^b)	92n143, 162n152
4Q58 (Isa^d)	239, 239n58, 240	4Q114 (Dan^c)	92, 92n143
4Q69 (papIsa^p)	144n104	4Q115 (Dan^d)	92n143
4Q70 (Jer^a)	138n82, 222, 317	4Q116 (Dan^e)	92, 92n143
4Q71 (Jer^b)	69	4Q117 (Ezra)	142, 222
4Q72 (Jer^c)	188, 222	4Q118 (Chronicles)	142
4Q72a (Jer^d)	69	4Q122 (LXXDeut)	220
4Q73 (Ezek^a)	240, 240n59	4Q123 (4Qpaleo paraJosh)	221n9
4Q83(Ps^a)	221	4Q149 (Mez A)	140
ii 15	307	4Q156 (tgLev)	253
4Q84 (Ps^b)	239, 239n57, 240	4Q157 (tgJob)	142, 253
4Q85 (Ps^c)	239, 239n57	4Q158 (Reworked Pentateuch A)	142, 240n64, 243, 243n70
4Q86 (Ps^d)	222		
4Q89 (Ps^g)	239, 241, 243n72	4Q159 (Ordinances^a)	260, 280
4Q90 (Ps^h)	222, 239, 241, 243n72	4Q160 (Vision of Samuel)	142, 236
4Q92 (Ps^k)	118, 188	4Q161–165 (Pesher Isaiah)	15, 126, 164
4Q94 (Ps^m)	140	4Q161 (pIsa^a)	221n9
4Q101 (paleoJob^c)	220	4Q162 (pIsa^b)	262n142
4Q106 (Cant^a)	239n56, 240, 241n65	4Q163 (pap pIsa^c)	256, 297
4Q107 (Cant^b)	188, 239n56, 240, 241n65, 256	4Q168 (pMic)	14, 15, 142, 287n35, 290n38

Index of Scripture and Other Ancient Texts

4Q169 (pNah) — 15, 142, 262n142, 287n35, 290n38
3–4 i 2–3 — 298

4Q170 (pZeph) — 142

4Q171 (Pesher Psalms, pPs^a) — 14, 15
ii 15 — 307, 307n83

4Q174 (Florilegium) — 15, 142, 240n62, 260, 290
1–2 — 289
21 i 3–7 — 289

4Q175 (Testimonia) — 143, 161, 162, 223, 235n48, 240, 241, 242, 242n67, 243, 260

4Q176 (Tanḥumim) — 260
19–21 — 85n122

4Q177 (Catena A) — 15, 240n62, 290
5–6 — 307
9 4–5 — 297
16 — 307

4Q179 (apocrLam A) — 140

4Q181 (pPs^a) — 221n9

4Q182 (Catena B) — 240n62, 290

4Q184 (Wiles of the Wicked Woman) — 142, 236

4Q185 (Sapiential Work) — 236

4Q186 (Horoscope, Zodiacal Physiognomy) — 249, 250, 250n92, 250n93, 256
1 iii 2–5 — 250
2 i 1–5 — 250

4Q196 (papTob^a ar) — 256

4Q201 (En^a) — 78n96, 251n98

4Q202 (En^b) — 78n96

4Q203 (EnGiants^a) — 79n12
frag. 8 3–14 — 81–82

4Q204 (En^c) — 78n96

4Q205 (En^d) — 78n96

4Q206 (En^e) — 78n96

4Q206a (EnGiants^f) — 79n102

4Q207 (En^f) — 78n96, 162

4Q208 (Enastr^a) — 78n96, 82, 138n82, 236

4Q208–211 (EnAstr^a–d) — 82–83

4Q209 (Enastr^b) — 78n96, 82

4Q210 (Enastr^c) — 78n96, 82

4Q211 (Enastr^d) — 78n96, 82

4Q212 (En^g) — 78n96

4Q213 (Levi^a) — 90

4Q213a (Levi^b) — 90

4Q213b (Levi^c) — 90, 188

4Q214 (Levi^d) — 90, 162

4Q214a (Levi^e) — 91

4Q214b (Levi^f) — 91

4Q216 (Jub^a) — 85n122
iv 6 — 86n126

4Q217 (papJub^b) — 85n122

397

INDEX OF SCRIPTURE AND OTHER ANCIENT TEXTS

4Q218 (Jub[b])   85n122

4Q219 (Jub[d])   85n122

4Q220 (Jub[e])   85n122

4Q221 (Jub[f])   85n122

4Q222 (Jub[g])   85n122

4Q223–224 (papJub[h])   85n122

4Q225–227 (Pseudo-Jubilees)   85

4Q227 (Pseudo-Jub[c])
2 1–6   95

4Q234 (Exercitium
Calami A)   143, 257, 258
Gen 27:19–21   143

4Q242 (Prayer of Nabonidus)   93n143,
                                142, 188, 233,
                                237, 254–55
3:5   93n143

4Q243–245 (Pseudo-
Daniel[a–c])   94n148, 233, 254

4Q243 (psDan[a])   93n143, 233
5 2   93n143

4Q244 (4psDan[b])   93n143, 162n152, 233

4Q245 (4psDan[c])   93n143, 233
1   93n143

4Q246 (Aramaic
Apocalypse)   93n143, 233

4Q249 (Midrash
Sefer Moshe)   144, 230n33, 256

4Q249[a–i] (Serek Ha'edah
fragments)   230n33, 256, 256n115

4Q249[j–l]   256

4Q250   230n33

4Q251 (Halakha A)   229, 280
12   282

4Q252 (Commentary on
Genesis A)   15, 229n31, 230, 233, 246

4Q253 (Commentary on
Genesis B)   229n31

4Q254 (Commentary on
Genesis C)   229n31

4Q258 (S[d])   140, 289n37

4Q259 (S[e])   246

4Q261 (S[g])   140

4Q264a (Halakha B)   229

4Q265 (Miscellaneous
Rules)   13n35, 143, 226, 231, 260
6 6–8   281n26

4Q266 (Damascus
Document, D[a])   188, 275n16, 281
frag. 1a–b   225
frag. 2 i 4   225
8 i 4–6   228
10 ii 1–2   228, 277
11 5–8, 14   228, 277

4Q267 (Damascus
Document, D[b])   162, 275n16, 281
9 vi 4–5   278

4Q269 (Damascus
Document, D[d])   162

4Q270 (Damascus
Document, D[e])   2, 281
2 i 18–19   283

398

Index of Scripture and Other Ancient Texts

2 ii 15–16	283	4Q313^c	256
6 ii 6–7	228, 277		
7 i 7–8	228	4Q317	
7 i 11	228	(Phases of the Moon)	245n76, 256
7 i 12–13	228, 277		
7 i 13–14	277	4Q318 (Zodiology	
		and Brontology ar)	142, 220n8, 237, 249, 253

4Q271 (Damascus
Document, D^f) 2, 281
3 9–10 283

4Q319 (Otot) 244n73, 245, 245n76, 245n78, 246

4Q274 (Tohorot A) 229, 231, 280
3 i 6–8 284

4Q320 (Cal. Doc.
Mishmarot A) 244n73, 245n76

4Q276 (Tohorot B^a) 140, 229

4Q320–330 (Cal. Doc.
Mishmarot A–H) 245n76

4Q277 (Tohorot B^b) 229

4Q321 (Cal. Doc.
Mishmarot B) 244n73

4Q278 (Tohorot C) 229

4Q321a (Cal. Doc.
Mishmarot C) 244n73

4Q280 (Curses) 162, 237

4Q284
(Purification Liturgy) 142, 229n28

4Q324^{c-g} (Mishmarot E, cryptA Lit.
Cal^a, cryptA Lit. Cal^b, cryptA Lit.
Cal^c?, cryptA Cal. Doc. F?) 256

4Q286–290
(Berakhot texts) 224, 229n28, 230

4Q324/355 145, 145n108

4Q286 (Ber^a)
7a ii b–d 1–6 225n21

4Q334 (Ordo) 140, 245n76

4Q287 (Ber^b)
7 6 1–4 225n21

4Q337 (Cal. Doc. F) 245n76

4Q289 (Ber^d) 140

4Q338 (Genealogical List?) 251n98

4Q298 (Words of the Maskil
to All Sons of Dawn) 229n30, 256

4Q339 (List of
False Prophets) 144, 242n67, 251

4Q299–301
(Mysteries) 234, 235, 250n95

4Q340
(List of Netinim) 144, 242n67, 251

4Q301 (Myst^c) 256

4Q341 (Exercitium Calami C) 143, 143n100, 220n8, 257, 258

4Q313 (MMT) 256

4Q342–359 258

399

INDEX OF SCRIPTURE AND OTHER ANCIENT TEXTS

4Q342	145, 259, 259n130	frag. 3	242
		frag. 4i	241, 242
4Q343	145, 259, 259n130	frag. 5	242
4Q345	258n129, 259, 259n130	4Q367 (Reworked Pentateuch E)	240, 242, 243, 243n72
4Q346	258n129, 259, 259n130	frag. 1a–b	243
		frag. 2a–b	241n65, 243
4Q347	258	frag. 3	241n65, 243
4Q348	259, 259n130	4Q370 (Admonition on the Flood)	142, 236
4Q350	145, 145nn108–9, 258n129, 259n131	4Q379 (Joshua Apocryphon)	103–4, 104n179, 162, 235n48, 240, 240n60, 241, 261
4Q351	258n129		
4Q352	258n129	4Q380 (Non-Canonical Psalms)	237
4Q352a	258n129		
4Q353	258n129	4Q380–381 (Non-Canonical Psalms)	237
4Q354	258n129	4Q381 (Non-Canonical Psalms B)	140, 237
4Q355	258n129		
4Q356	258n129	4Q382 (Paraphrase of Kings)	236
4Q357	258n129	4Q385–386, 388, 391 (pseudo-Ezekiel)	236
4Q358	258n129	4Q387 (apocrJer C)	140, 235n48
4Q360 (Exercitium Calami B)	143, 257, 258	4Q392 (Works of God)	237
4Q364 (Reworked Pentateuch B)	222, 242–43	4Q394 (MMT^a)	
		i 7–8	284
		1–2	245n76, 246
4Q365 (Reworked Pentateuch C)	242	4Q395 (MMT^b)	
		13–16	281
4Q366 (Reworked Pentateuch D)	240, 242, 243, 243n70, 243n72	13–17	272
		21–23	282
		55–57	272
frag. 1	242	55–58	283
frag. 2	241, 242	77	283

Index of Scripture and Other Ancient Texts

80–82	283	4Q457b (Eschatological Hymn)		161

4Q396 (MMTᶜ)
7–8 — 226

4Q460
(Narrative Work and Prayer) — 259n131

4Q397 (MMTᵈ) — 162

PAM 40.978 — 140

4Q401 (ShirShabbᵇ) — 140

PAM 40.979 — 140
frag. 9 — 145, 145nn108–9

4Q414 (Purification Rituals) — 229n28

4Q362–363 (Cryptic B) — 255

4Q415–418
(Instructionᵃ⁻ᵈ) — 159, 234–35, 250n95

4Q363a (Cryptic C) — 255

4Q415 (Instructionᵃ)
2 ii — 234n42

4Q464
(Exposition on the Patriarchs) — 236

4Q417 (Instructionᶜ) — 76n90, 256
1 1:14–17 — 81n108

4Q468e (Historical Text F) — 144–45

4Q418c (Instructionᶠ?) — 140

4Q470
(Text Mentioning Zedekiah) — 236

4Q419
(Instruction-like Composition) — 140

4Q471b
(Self-Glorification Hymn) — 229n28

4Q422 (Paraphrase
of Genesis and Exodus) — 236

4Q473 (Two Ways) — 237

4Q423 (Instructionᵍ) — 140, 234

4Q474 (Rachel and Joseph) — 162, 236

4Q424 (Instruction-like
Composition) — 236–37

4Q475 (Renewed Earth) — 144

4Q432 (papHᶠ) — 140

4Q477 (Rebukes Reported
by the Overseer) — 144, 220n8,
251, 252, 276n19
frag. 2 i 1 — 252
frag. 2 i 3 — 252
frag. 2 ii 3 — 252, 252n101
2 ii 5–6 — 226
frag. 2 ii 6 — 252
frag. 2 ii 9 — 252n101

4Q441
(Individual Thanksgiving A) — 161

4Q443 (Personal Prayer) — 142, 161

4Q444 (Incantation) — 237, 251n97

4Q481a (Apocryphon of Elisha) — 236

4Q448 (Prayer for [or against]
King Jonathan) — 238, 313–14

4Q481b (Narrative G) — 161

4Q457a–b — 144

4Q483 (papGenᵒ) — 144n104

401

INDEX OF SCRIPTURE AND OTHER ANCIENT TEXTS

4Q488 (Apocryphon)   252n102

4Q489 (Apocalypse)   252n102

4Q502 (Ritual of Marriage)   231

4Q503 (Daily Prayers)   237n52

4Q504 (DibHam[a], Words of the Luminaries)   237, 256

4Q505 (Festival Prayers)   237

4Q506 (Words of the Luminaries)   237

4Q507 (Festival Prayers)   237

4Q508 (Festival Prayers)   237

4Q509 (Festival Prayers)   237

4Q510–511 (Songs of the Maskil)   229, 229n28, 251n97

4Q511 (4QShir[b])   256

4Q512 (Purification Rituals)   229n28

4Q513 (Ordinances[b])   280
13 4   303

4Q514 (Ordinances[c])   280

4Q521 (Messianic Apocalypse)   140

4Q524 (Temple Scroll)   235

4Q525 (Beatitudes)   237

4Q530 (EnGiants[b])   79n102
frag. 2 14   82

4Q531 (EnGiants[c])   79n102

4Q532 (EnGiants[d])   79n102

4Q533 (EnGiants[e])   79n102

4Q534 (The Elect of God)   235n48
1 i 1–3   250

4Q536–568   252n102

4Q540–541 (Levi Apocryphon)   233

4Q542 (Testament of Qahat)   94–95, 142, 161, 233, 253, 254
1 ii 9–13   95

4Q543–549 (Visions of Amram)   94–95, 233, 253, 254

4Q550 (proto-Esther Aramaic, Jews at the Persian Court)   95, 142, 237, 254, 255
frag. 2   96
frag. 5   96
frag. 6   96

4Q551 (Daniel–Susanna)   93n143

4Q552–553 (Four Kingdoms[a, b])   93n143, 235n48, 254

4Q560 (Magical Booklet ar)   249, 250–51, 253

4Q561 (Horoscope, Physiognomy ar)   142, 237, 249, 249n92, 253

4Q563   237

4Q570–575   252n102

4Q577 (Text Mentioning the Flood)   236

4Q580   252n102

4Q582   252n102

Index of Scripture and Other Ancient Texts

5Q1 (Deut)	220, 240
5Q5 (Ps)	240, 243n72
Ps 119	241
5Q11 (Serek Hayahad)	162
5Q13 (Rule)	162
5Q14 (Curses)	237
5Q24	252n102
6Q1 (paleoGen)	220
6Q3 (papDeut)	144n104
6Q4 (papKings)	144n104
6Q5 (papPsalms)	144n104
6Q7 (papDan)	92n143
6Q8 (papGiants)	79n12
6Q9 (Apocryphal Samuel–Kings)	236
6Q17	245, 245n76
6Q18 (Hymn frag.)	237, 251n97
6Q23	252n102
6Q26	127
7Q2 (Epistle of Jeremiah)	78n96, 160, 236, 238
7Q4	78n96
7Q8	78n96
7Q11	78n96
7Q12	78n96

7Q13	78n96
8Q5 (Hymn)	237, 251n97
11Q4 (Ezek)	222
11Q5 (Ps^a)	222, 246
21–22	73n83
27:2–11	251n97
11Q10 (tgJob)	253
11Q11 (Apocryphal Psalms^a)	237, 251n97
11Q12 (Jub)	85n122
11Q19 (Temple Scroll, T^a)	2n3, 6, 12, 33n67, 81n109, 121, 127, 129, 150n123, 153, 156, 157, 159, 160, 164n157, 235, 246, 274, 280, 292, 315
45:11–12	283
46:13–16	293
57:17–18	283
66:15–17	235n47, 282
11Q20 (Temple Scroll, T^b)	163, 235
11Q21 (Temple Scroll, T^c)	235
11Q23	255
11Q24–25	252n102

HELLENISTIC JEWISH LITERATURE

Josephus

Against Apion

1.28–29	99
1.30–35	99
1.38–41	316
1.370–380	173n24

Jewish Antiquities

2	72n79

INDEX OF SCRIPTURE AND OTHER ANCIENT TEXTS

2.164–165	298	2.428	99
3.171	311	2.567	319n22
5.51	99	3.11	319n22
10.57–58	99	4.486–490	174n30
11.165	98, 161	5.145	300
12.138–142	72	6.277	100
12.138–144	72–73	6.354	99
13	300	7.150	46, 99, 316
13.171–172	166	7.162	46, 99, 316
13.172	303	*Life*	300
13.372–374	313	10	270n1
13.376–380	298	25	316
13.379–383	313	75	99
13.401–402	298		
15.37	300	**Philo**	
15.121–147	173n24		
15.371–379	314n7	*Apologia pro Iudaeis*	299
15.373	303	*Hypothetica*	
18	300	1	272
18.18	303	8.6–7	299–300
18.19	301, 304	11.1	299
18.21	271n6, 301	14–17	271n6
18.22	300		
Jewish War		*In Flaccum*	
1.4	298	1.4	72n79
1.78	272, 303, 305	*Quod omnis probus liber sit*	
1.88	313	12.75	307
1.96–98	313	75	272
2	300	75–91	299
2.113	303	76	299
2.119	270n1	77–86	299
2.120	271n6, 301		
2.122	303		
2.123	303	**RABBINIC LITERATURE**	
2.129–131	302–3		
2.133	272	ʼAbot R. Nat.	
2.134	300n63	46	99
2.137–139	302		
2.143	302	**Assumption**	
2.147	279n23, 303	**(or Testament) of Moses**	128–29
2.148–149	301	1:16–17	128
2.154–158	303		
2.160–161	271n6, 301	Moʻed Qaṭ.	
		3:4	99

404

Index of Scripture and Other Ancient Texts

m. Ḥag.
2:4 — 298

m. Kelim
15:6 — 99

m. Menaḥ.
10:3 — 298

m. Parah
3:7 — 282n28

m. Ṭehar.
8:9 — 284n32

m. Yad.
4:7 — 284n32

Sipre Deut
356 — 99
Sop. 4.4 — 99

Targum Pseudo-Jonathan
Gen 5:25 — 84n118

y. Meg.
1:11 — 144n104
1:71 — 144n104

y. Sanh.
2:6 — 99

y. Šeqal.
4:2 — 99

y. Taʿan.
4:2 — 99

PAPYRI

Elephantine Papyri
TAD
A4.1 — 62n47

A4.7–8 — 62n47
A4.9 — 62n47
C1.1 (Tale of Ahiqar) — 63
C2.1 — 62–63

GREEK AND ROMAN LITERATURE

Ammianus Marcellinus

History
22.16.13 — 43

Athenaeus

Deipnosophistae
1.3a — 42n98

Aulus Gellius

Noctes atticae
7.17.3 — 43

Callimachus
Pinakes — 44, 48

Cicero

De finibus
3.2.7–10 — 46

Diogenes Laertius

Lives of the Philosophers
5.78 — 42n100

Galen

In Hippocratis librum iii epidemiarum commentarii
3.17a.605–606 — 43
3.17a.607–608 — 44

Hippolytus

Refutatio omnium haeresium
9.27 — 306

INDEX OF SCRIPTURE AND OTHER ANCIENT TEXTS

Pliny the Elder

Natural History
5.73   167, 270n3, 271n6, 272, 303n68, 305

Seneca

De tranquillitate animi
9.5   43

Strabo

Geographica
13.1.54   42, 42n99, 44
17.1.8   43

Synesius of Cyrene

Dio
3.2   306

CHRISTIAN LITERATURE

Eusebius

Praeparatio evangelica
8.6–7   299n59